The Suburb Reader

The Suburb Reader

Becky M. Nicolaides and Andrew Wiese
EDITORS

Foreword by Kenneth T. Jackson

Routledge
Taylor & Francis Group
New York   London

Routledge is an imprint of the
Taylor & Francis Group, an informa business

Routledge
Taylor & Francis Group
270 Madison Avenue
New York, NY 10016

Routledge
Taylor & Francis Group
2 Park Square
Milton Park, Abingdon
Oxon OX14 4RN

Printed in the United States of America on acid-free paper
10 9 8 7 6 5 4 3 2

International Standard Book Number-10: 0-415-94594-1 (Softcover) 0-415-94593-3 (Hardcover)
International Standard Book Number-13: 978-0-415-94594-3 (Softcover) 978-0-415-94593-6 (Hardcover)

Library of Congress Cataloging-in-Publication Data

The suburb reader / edited by Becky M. Nicolaides and Andrew Wiese.
    p. cm.
  Includes bibliographical references and index.
  ISBN-13: 978-0-415-94594-6 ISBN-10: 0-415-94593-3 (hbk.)
  ISBN-13: 978-0-415-94594-3 ISBN-10: 0-415-94594-1 (pbk.)
   1. Suburbs--United States--History. 2. Housing--United States--History. I. Nicolaides, Becky M. II. Wiese, Andrew.

HT352.U6S795 2006
307.76'0973--dc22   2005033521

Visit the Taylor & Francis Web site at
http://www.taylorandfrancis.com

and the Routledge Web site at
http://www.routledge-ny.com

For the children,
Lucas and Desmond

CONTENTS

PART II. POSTWAR SUBURBIA, 1940–1970

LIST OF FIGURES

ACKNOWLEDGMENTS

All academic projects rest on a web of mutual generosity. But this one especially has stretched tight the ties that bind us to a community of scholars. The process has been gratifying, a little surprising, and most of all humbling. Perhaps most gratifying of all has been the chance for us to share this enterprise as partners. Even as this book challenged us intellectually (and burned up our long distance minutes), it has enriched and deepened our friendship. And that has made everything else worthwhile.

We owe a debt of monumental gratitude to our many friends and colleagues who rummaged in old files for material, identified sources, shared ideas, criticism, and syllabi, and who encouraged us forward. First among the line of saints, however, are those colleagues who waived permission fees or interceded on our behalf to make their work more affordable, including John Archer, Edward Blakely, Dolores Hayden, Neil Jacoby, Ann Durkin Keating, Matt Lassiter, Robert Putnam, Adam Rome, William Schneider, Robert Self, Mary Corbin Sies, and Don Waldie. Their time and effort, as well as their belief in this project, have contributed immensely to the quality of this volume. We especially thank Dolores Hayden for allowing us to reprint two unpublished works; we deeply appreciate her willingness to work with us and to include her important voice in this collection. Lastly, we salute Kenneth Jackson, our mentor and friend, whose longstanding openhandedness is an example we only hope to emulate.

Many publishers and other organizations also extended us complimentary or deeply discounted use of their materials, and for this we are greatly appreciative. Several aided us in ways that deserve special appreciation, including the Congress for New Urbanism, Eco-City Cleveland, the Guildhall Library, Johns Hopkins University Press, *Redbook Magazine*, the Sagalyn Literary Agency, Sage Publications and the *Journal of Urban History*, the South Jersey *Courier-Post*, the University of Chicago Press, the Yale School of Law, and Yale University Press.

Special thanks belong to John Archer, who generously shared his gorgeous photographs of Madras and Llewellyn Park; to Richard Harris and Robert Lewis for sharing two maps, which appear in chapter 4; to Emil Pocock for the postcard of Kansas City's Country Club Plaza; to cartographer David Deis for incredibly fast—and charitable—eleventh-hour assistance with the map for chapter 5; to Wendy Plotkin for sharing the court transcripts in chapter 8; to Gregory Randall for the photos of Park Forest in chapter 9; to Lois Gelatt for permission to reprint the Claude Smith cartoon in chapter 10; to Duany, Plater-Zyberk, and Co. for sharing the images of Kentlands, Maryland in chapter 16; and to the Map and Imagery Library of University of California, Santa Barbara.

An award for going above and beyond goes to Ned Wiese, who found time on the eve of his wedding to fly over suburban Denver with his brother and a camera in tow. His boundless generosity, not to mention lifelong vehicular prowess, made possible the aerial photographs in chapter 16.

At Routledge, we found an early and enthusiastic supporter in David McBride. His acuity and dedication to this project were vital to its completion. Also at Routledge, Angela Chnapko proved an indispensable source of information, organization, and energy. We also especially appreciate the expert advice of three outside reviewers, Evan McKenzie, Carl Abbott, and Susan Fainstein, whose well-founded questions and suggestions immeasurably strengthened the volume. We are also grateful for a timely small grant from the University of California, San Diego Department of History.

Our long list of creditors also includes our students. Charles McKeown, Daniel Neidlinger, and Jared Feldman all volunteered their time and labor to assist us during various stages of this book. We are grateful for the important contributions they made. We also owe thanks to students in "The History of Suburbia" at San Diego State University and "History of American Suburbs" at the University of California, San Diego, who were this book's most critical reviewers, whose research projects brought to light fascinating primary materials (some of which appear in the pages that follow), and whose classroom comments (or lack thereof) helped us refine our table of contents.

Our deepest gratitude is reserved for our families. Despite swearing up and down after the last ones, we embarked once again on a lengthy book project, making ridiculous demands on time, patience, and assistance from our loved ones.

We owe a special debt to Barbara Weisenberg and Leonard Lipton, who basically took care of the Nicolaides-Weisenberg house for six weeks while Becky was recovering from surgery—and slipping in crucial work on the book. Your love, generosity, and frequent runs to Trader Joe's kept us going. Louie, Leslie, Anya, Alex, and Tina Nicolaides provided a bedrock of love and support that gave stamina for the day-to-day labor. Elizabeth Nicolaides once again deserves special acknowledgment for her total love and devotion, her many hours of babysitting, and her ongoing faith in our creative endeavors. She is a true inspiration on every level. David Weisenberg essentially made this book happen, with his endless patience, stamina, input, humor, and love. Thank you, David, for your sustained commitment to us and this book.

In the Wiese-Ibarra household, our thanks are dedicated to Maria Ibarra, whose devotion and labor provided the space in which this book took shape. A grant to pursue her research in Hawaii, when this project was in its early stages, afforded access to the excellent periodical collections of the University of Hawaii at Manoa—not to mention the restful influence of warm trade winds, afternoon rains, and green tropical sea. Back on the mainland, her abiding love helped keep this project on track and in perspective. Jim and Nancy Wiese also deserve our thanks. By creating a loving household in a suburb with every possible social advantage, they exemplified all that is rich and fine in the suburban dream. Their support, combined with that of Kate, John, Ned, Suzanne, Jonathan, and, yes, Uncle Paul, gave affectionate substance to the word *family*.

Desmond Weisenberg was two when this project started. He'll be six when the book finally appears on our kitchen tables. A very special "thank you" to Desmond for his patience while mama worked at the computer (interfering with his access to Internet checkers, as well as his mom's attention), and for devising the creative solution of working on his own books in the other room. His output is much larger than ours, and we're sure he'll be finding a publisher any minute. Desmond's sweet presence, his hugs, singing, and games of chess helped provide much needed perspective on it all.

For his part, Lucas Wiese-Ibarra came into the world amidst the piles of paper, computer discs, scanning equipment, and all-too-enticing library books that were the outward emblems of this work. The cycles of his sleep were the time-clock that governed its creation, and in wakeful hours, his tender grasping hands and cries of "papa! papa!" were the engine driving it to be finished. It is small surprise that "lapis," or pencil, was among his early and most cherished words. Here's wishing that "surfboard" is the next passionate addition to his vocabulary.

This book is dedicated to our children, in hopes that what we might learn from our suburban past will help us build more humane and equitable places for them in the future.

FOREWORD

In the fall of 1968, soon after moving from Dayton, Ohio to New York City, I became intrigued with the suburbs and especially with evidence of population deconcentration before 1850 in places like Manhattan, Boston, and Philadelphia. At the time, there was not much scholarship on the topic, and historians typically ignored the topic altogether. My model became Sam Bass Warner's pathbreaking *Streetcar Suburbs: The Process of Growth in Boston, 1870–1900* (Harvard, 1962), which looked at ordinary streets and houses, but in new and imaginative ways. Professor Warner asked logical questions, examined easily attainable but previously under-utilized public records, and reached sensible and persuasive conclusions. His book continues to inform and influence us almost half a century after its initial publication.

My book *Crabgrass Frontier: The Suburbanization of the United States*, which appeared in 1985, was about more than one city and more than one century, but it copied Professor Warner in many ways. It was about ordinary people and ordinary places, and it asked a simple question: why was the new world so obviously different from the old one? Europe offered dense urban environments even in small towns, efficient public transportation systems, and sharp divisions between rural and urban areas. The United States, by contrast, was a car culture that spread out in hodge-podge fashion along tens of thousands of miles of highways. Its cities were a mess, associated in the public mind with problems and outcasts. They were the refuge of last resort, the final destination of the destitute, the aged, and the infirm, not to mention the long-suffering and

long-oppressed African-American population. And with a few exceptions in weird places like New York and San Francisco, everyone with any sense or any resources seemed to be rushing headlong to escape from cities too dense, too dirty, too ugly, and too scary to call home. The 1960s riots hurried along a process that had been decades in the making, and by 1985, by almost any definition, the United States had become a suburban nation.

But of course that was the rub. What is a suburb? Hard to define in 1985, the term is even harder to define twenty years later. In 2005, for example, cities have become like suburbs, and suburbs have become like cities. Where is the central business district in our time that does not include some type of shopping mall? Or think of all the old downtowns where abandoned warehouses, industrial buildings, and office skyscrapers have been converted to upscale residential use. Or consider the back-to-the-city movement of empty-nesters and young urban professionals who prefer sidewalk restaurants and trendy galleries to the swimming pools, tennis courts, and free parking of outlying developments. Meanwhile, the suburbs have become racially and ethnically more diverse, and they now often make provision for "affordable" or higher density housing. While crime is down in big cities, it is flat or up in the suburbs. Along the way, street muggings have become less commonplace and frightening than suburban carjackings. Commuting itself has become problematic. In the twenty-first century, more people work at home, and more commuters travel from suburb to suburb than from suburb to city. Indeed, by

2005 the fastest growing segment of the population was that of the reverse commuters, those people who travel daily from homes in the central city to workplaces in the suburbs. In the New York area, for example, the Metro North Railroad began to charge peak fares to persons *leaving* the city at rush hour.

My intention in 1984 was to include three more chapters in *Crabgrass Frontier* than ultimately were included in the published book: one on planned suburbs, such as Tuxedo Park, New York; one on industrial suburbs, such as Paterson, New Jersey; and one on working-class suburbs, such as Harvey, Illinois. Each topic was and is obviously important to the study of the urban periphery. But the sudden death of my sixteen-year-old son in an automobile crash in 1984 drained me of inspiration, imagination, and energy, and so I just submitted what I had already finished to Sheldon Meyer and Oxford University Press, and we went with that. To this day, those unfinished chapters remain in thick file folders in my attic.

Fortunately, younger scholars have taken up the challenge, and they have collectively and individually done a far better job than I could have on a variety of topics. Indeed, the sheer amount of research on America's metropolitan fringe has been astounding over the past quarter century. And Becky Nicolaides and Andrew Wiese, both of whom I am proud to claim as former students, have gathered together much of the best and most impressive of the recent work in *The Suburb Reader*. To those articles and essays they have added primary sources and photographs to enhance the text. Taken together, this compendium corrects mistakes, fills in gaps, asks questions no one previously thought to ask, and moves us along, as the best books always do, toward places and topics we never previously imagined. The study of suburbs will never be finished because cities and metropolitan regions will continue to evolve in the decades and centuries to come.

KENNETH T. JACKSON

INTRODUCTION

"Turn back the clock to a simpler time and you'll find yourself at the highly acclaimed master planned community of RiverPark. Nestled in the small town of Oxnard [CA], RiverPark is everything that a community should be. It is neighbors you know. A Town Center you stroll to. Parks you relax and dream in. And 15 charming new home neighborhoods built around family and friends. At RiverPark, *home is a special place in the heart of it all*. And that place is like no other."

—Real Estate "Admail," latimes.com, June 22, 2005.

As the United States enters the twenty-first century, it does so as a suburban nation. The U.S. Census confirmed this fact in 2000 by reporting that 50 percent of Americans live in the suburbs. Suburbia is a landscape that is ubiquitous, a backdrop to life so commonplace that few take conscious notice of it. Freeways, shopping malls, commutes, lawns, detached homes, soccer games, mortgage payments, and home fix-it jobs define the texture of life for many of us, as we go through our daily routines shaped by a suburban framework of life.

Yet few of us stop to think critically about this backdrop, the spatial organization that shapes our everyday lives, how we spend our time, where we go, and even how we interact with—and think about—other people. Few of us ask questions like, why do I spend so much time in my car? Why can't I walk to places that I need to go? Why is my best option for housing a detached home set in the middle of a yard? Why is this house so expensive? If I have children, why does it seem like my best bet is to live in a suburb? Yet why do so many teenagers seem to hate the suburbs? Why do my neighbors seem so much like me, in terms of their skin color and their stuff? How did we make the choice, as a society, to become suburban?

This book introduces readers to the reasons why we have become a suburban nation. We might think of our metropolitan areas and their contemporary shape as the end product of a succession of choices that Americans have made over many, many years. These choices related to ideas about success, healthy family life, community and belonging, national strength, and what a civil society should look like. These choices were made by individuals as well as policymakers, profit-minded land developers as well as visionary planners. Not all choices were equal in this process nor were all Americans free to make them, but the cumulative result is the landscape that defines much of contemporary America.

While suburbia defines great swathes of our contemporary landscape, its impact has been much more than physical and geographic. Suburbanization is a process that has shaped crucial historical developments in America. The rise of suburbia was inextricably linked to ideas about class, race, and gender, changes in American political culture and the role of the state, the evolution of success ideologies, opportunities for social mobility, and the construction of American culture itself. The suburbanization process also represented a focal point for social conflict and competition, a spatial means through which people competed for the abundant resources of American society. Suburbia embodied the American Dream for many, a site of material plenty for building futures and moving up, a destination point for aspirations of wholesome family life, property ownership, and healthy community. Yet the perception of suburbia as the American Dream was often predicated on a restricted vision of belonging. Indeed, a major theme in this history has been the ongoing tension between inclusion and exclusion. For over a century, suburbia has acted as a potent arbiter of social distinctions. Yet at the same time, suburbia's history represents a rich, diverse story of many actors, some upholding these assumptions, others contesting them, others redefining them altogether.

This volume brings together some of the most important work published on the history of American suburbanization to introduce readers to this vibrant area of historical inquiry. This scholarship not only outlines the basic contours of suburban history, but it situates suburbanization in the larger context of American history—one strand that has contributed to the rich, complex story of the nation's past.

A THUMBNAIL SKETCH OF SUBURBIA'S PAST

Suburbs trace their origins back millennia, but their modern roots date to the mid-eighteenth century. In Great Britain and some of its colonial possessions, and later the United States and other nations, suburbs emerged as residential havens for an emergent upper and middle class, a place where the bourgeoisie could escape the ill effects of urbanization and capitalism: noise, crime, immorality, pollution, factories, poverty, and a mass working class. In the cool green rim of the city, they conceived suburbia as a site where they might nurture a separate class culture while still benefiting from the richness of city life. These early elite communities—dubbed Romantic suburbs for their aesthetic links to the nineteenth-century Romantic Movement—included places like Clapham outside London in the 1790s, and Llewellyn Park, New Jersey, and Riverside, Illinois, in the United States in the mid-1800s. They were designed to harmonize with nature, with curvilinear roads, spacious parks and preserves, and rambling properties without fences. The residents of these early communities were highly class-conscious, aware that their spatial surroundings bore directly on their self-image as a respectable bourgeoisie.

Although Romantic suburbs housed only a very small minority of urban residents, they were important for their articulation of an elite suburban ideal based on notions of healthy family life, piety, closeness to nature, well-defined gender roles, and class separation, all embodied in a distinctive design program (see Figure I-1). It is also important to recognize that in these early years, the suburban rim of cities was actually a place of striking diversity. Romantic suburbs did

Figure I-1 The Growth of Metropolitan and Suburban Areas in the United States, 1850–2000

Population in Thousands

Date	U.S. Population	Metropolitan Area Population (includes city and suburbs)	% of U.S. Population	Suburban Area Population	% of U.S. Population
1850	23,192[a]	2,228	9.6	731	3.2
1880	50,155	8,774	17.5	1,667	3.3
1910	91,972	30,236	32.9	6,359	6.9
1940	131,669	60,293	45.8	17,666	13.4
1970	203,302[b]	139,500	68.6	75,500	37.1
2000	281,422	225,982	80.3	140,604	50.0

Sources: U.S. Bureau of the Census, *Measuring America: The Decennial Census from 1790–2000* (Washington: Government Printing Office, 2002), Appendix A-l; U.S. Bureau of the Census, Census of Population: 1970, vol. I, *Characteristics of the Population*, pt. 1, *U.S. Summary*, section 1 (Washington: Government Printing Office, 1973), 258; Todd Gardner, "The Slow Wave: The Changing Residential Status of Cities and Suburbs in the United States, 1850-1940," *Journal of Urban History*, 27 (Mar., 2001), 297-298.

a. Metropolitan areas for 1850-1940 defined according to 1940 Census definition of metropolitan districts (incorporated places and townships with greater than 150 persons per square mile adjacent to a central city(ies) of 50,000 or more). See Gardner, "The Slow Wave," 297.

b. Metropolitan areas for 1970 and 2000 defined according to Census definitions for 1970 and 2000 (sufficiently urbanized counties adjacent to a central city(ies) of 50,000 or more). See U.S. Bureau of the Census, Census of Population and Housing: 2000, vol. I, *Summary of Population and Housing Characteristics*, pt. 1 (Washington: Government Printing Office, 2002), Appendix A-16.

not spring up in a wilderness, but alongside existing activities and people, such as urban-oriented agriculture, small rural industries, and their ethnically diverse workforces. The elite suburbs were hardly a dominant physical presence in this landscape. In fact, their appeal relied partly on their scarcity and the open, pastoral spaces that separated them. Their significance, rather, lay in the realm of ideology and material culture: the design and lifeways of early suburbia helped establish the basis of a suburban ideal and way of life that exerted influence for decades to come.

New means of transportation also played a role in shaping suburban growth. Around mid century, railroad companies began adding new commuter trains and stations along their lines radiating from the major cities, stimulating a new wave of suburban development for the upper classes. These "main line" railroad suburbs attracted businessmen and professionals, who could afford the cost of daily commuting, plus a cohort of shopkeepers, tradespeople, and others who provided goods and services for the commuters. Homes in elite sections were spacious, parks abundant, vistas picturesque, following the aesthetic conventions of the Romantic suburbs. Examples were places like Lake Forest (Chicago), Clayton (St. Louis), Villanova and Overbrook (Philadelphia), Brookline (Boston), and numerous towns and villages of Westchester County (New York City).

Streetcar suburbs followed after the Civil War. Horse-drawn streetcars quickly expanded the region of easily buildable land outlying American cities, and by the 1890s, new electric streetcars had become the dominant mode of urban transit, offering cheap 5-cent fares and fast, predictable service. A typical pattern of land development went like this: A streetcar company would buy land along a street radiating from the city, lay tracks along the property, and then reap tremendous profits reselling the land as suburban subdivisions. Turn-of-the-century transit moguls—such as F. M. "Borax" Smith in Oakland, Henry Huntington in Los Angeles, Francis Newlands in Washington, DC, and J. D. Spreckels of San Diego—made their biggest profits from land sales, not streetcar tickets. Small contractors and individual

homeowners bought up the properties and embarked on the process of land conversion to residential suburbs. The result was a new wave of streetcar suburbanization, aimed at an ever-broadening market of buyers, from the well-to-do Protestant businessman to the lace-curtain Irish Catholic worker. Distinct subdivisions were aimed at different classes of homebuyers; the suburbs had thus begun opening up to a broader cross-section of Americans while also sorting them along social class lines.

By the end of the nineteenth century, new suburbs had emerged that ran the gamut from the stylish to the humble. These communities were not only the products of middle-class family enterprise, but of profit-driven subdividers who laid out suburban building tracts, contractors who began building suburban homes "on spec," industrial firms seeking shelter for their workers, and individual families who built homes of their own. Thus, the suburban rim remained a landscape of diversity, containing an ever-widening variety of people and functions. Not only did the elite inhabit their exclusive suburban neighborhoods, but the periphery also contained modest streetcar suburbs, unplanned subdivisions of white and African-American workers, factories, and retail stores. What seemed new and different in 1900 was the character of this suburban diversity. Increasingly, the very things that elite suburbanites sought to escape—smokestacks, the poor, immigrants, people of color—were gaining footholds on the city's edge. Industrial suburbs, especially, proliferated. As Harlan Paul Douglass observed in 1925, some suburbs were "so full of factories that [they have] little room even for working people."[1] Most industrial suburbs, in fact, were also home to workers and their families. Some were planned communities, designed both to improve living conditions and enhance the productivity of the working class. Others were unplanned, modest communities, where native-born working-class Anglos, immigrants, and African Americans pursued economic security for their families. They did so by building their own homes, growing vegetables, and raising small livestock in backyards. In suburbs such as these, which reached their heyday in the early twentieth century, blue-collar families created family-oriented and self-determined communities—and formulated their own rendition of the suburban ideal.

While the suburban periphery diversified, elite and middle-class Americans sought to maintain the exclusivity of their own communities. Through statutory, ideological, and cultural means, they reinforced both the barriers and internal meaning of their own elite suburbs. Neighborhood associations and restrictive covenants became tools of segregation, operating at the local level. Domesticity as expressed through home design and family habits further inscribed middle-class respectability in the exclusive suburb. Political culture emphasized local control and political independence, as a means of controlling land use and population composition. Both through internal self-definition and local governance, the elite suburban ideal continued to thrive in the twentieth century. The result was a landscape of "segregated diversity" on the suburban rim.

The course of suburban history shifted profoundly in the 1930s, due particularly to the efforts of an expanding federal government. Initially enacted to stave off the collapse of the real estate market during the Depression, New Deal housing programs pumped federal money into the suburban housing market, enabling more Americans than ever to become homeowners through new, easy terms of home financing. This federal largesse laid the foundation for the suburban boom of the postwar era. In addition, state policy contributed to the construction of racial categories. By defining white suburbs as "good" and minority neighborhoods as "bad," the federal government helped codify the racial segmentation of metropolitan space. These federal standards not only reinforced existing patterns of segregation but extended them into the future. Access to federal assistance—increasingly the ticket to suburbia for Americans of moderate means—was denied to people of color and the poor, well into the 1960s. By thus linking race to suburban access, the state played a crucial role in racializing metropolitan space.

The post-World War II years saw a tremendous upsurge in suburban growth, setting off a wholesale demographic shift to the suburbs and influencing American life in whole new ways. Suburban communities took on new forms—mass-produced tract homes, baby-boom families, and more blue-collar households than ever. A new breed of large-scale developer-builders played a pivotal role in suburban land development, constructing acre after acre of tract housing around every major city. Suburbia also became invested with powerful social and cultural meaning. To many, it embodied the American good life, replete with the material goods of postwar economic abundance. After enduring years of hardship through the Great Depression and World War II, millions of Americans embraced suburbia as a welcome reward, a place where families could thrive in a tranquil, domestic setting. As millions attained these goals, suburbanization blurred older divisions along class and ethnic lines, while reinforcing distinctions on the basis of race and gender. Suburbia had become the spatial embodiment of the middle-class American Dream.

Yet beneath the Ozzie-and-Harriet exterior, the postwar suburb harbored deep tensions. A "cultural war" broke out between those who celebrated the suburbs and those who despised them. Boosters perceived suburbia as the fulfillment of middle-class ambitions, the place where clean-cut, young white families lived happy lives in sunny homes with tidy yards. The critics saw a darker side. To them, suburbia was a breeding ground for conformity, materialism, female loneliness, and even social pathologies like adultery and alcoholism. The debate played out on movie and television screens, popular novels and magazines, and indeed constituted a cultural preoccupation for several years.

Another source of tension centered on race. White suburbanites dug in their heels as new threats emerged to the racial purity of their suburban neighborhoods—particularly the civil rights movement and court decisions outlawing race restrictive covenants and de jure school segregation. White resistance manifested on many levels, from "crabgrass roots" political movements, to efforts at exclusive and expulsive zoning, to the formation of Common Interest Developments which encouraged new forms of privatism and separatism. In these ways, suburban life continued to construct and reinforce social distinctions within new historical contexts. Out of this milieu, distinct political sensibilities flourished, including antiliberalism among second-generation ethnics, right-wing conservatism among the new suburban middle class, and the emergence of a homeowner-taxpayer political culture. One repercussion of this continuing impulse to maintain white exclusivity was the ever-growing chasm between city and suburb, manifesting in stark inequality in opportunity, resources, and quality of life.

After the 1970s, suburbia became increasingly complex as it attracted an ever larger share of the nation's population. Suburbs witnessed increasing ethnic diversification, including the reemergence of large immigrant and multiethnic communities in the suburbs. The suburbs also experienced what many perceived as "urbanizing" tendencies—greater densities, aging infrastructure and housing, rising taxes and tenancy rates, and the decline of the nuclear family's dominance. At the same time, the environmental toll of suburban sprawl became more pronounced than ever. These trends, coupled with the relocation of jobs to the suburbs, the rise of so-called "edge cities," and a reorganization of social reproduction in American households, have sustained a lively debate over the meanings and definitions of suburbia. Some scholars argue that the suburbs represent a new frontier for economic and social opportunity, a new melting pot where old patterns of inequality and social distinction are becoming obsolete. Meanwhile, others point out that the suburbs remain profoundly riven by distinctions of class, race, gender, and ethnicity. Widespread black and Latino suburbanization is belied by segregation and fiscal inequality in suburbia. Suburban women's participation in the paid labor force has not substantially lessened their responsibilities for household work, and masses of immigrant suburbanites toil in subminimum wage service jobs, many of which directly support the landscape and lifestyle of middle-class and elite suburbia. The challenges posed by contemporary suburbs comprise important issues for planners, politicians, developers and residents alike.

TRENDS IN THE ACADEMY

Growing interest in the study of suburbia has coincided with exciting new developments in academic scholarship at large. Among the most significant of these has been renewed attention to race, gender, and class. Indeed, suburbia provided the context for several pathbreaking works in these areas.[2] Points of interpretation differ, but scholars today generally approach these categories as *social* distinctions, the ongoing result of history, ideology, and the exercise of power, rather than given facts of biology or nature. Such distinctions serve as a way to organize understanding, to connect individual and group experience, to distinguish among insiders and outsiders, and to produce, rationalize, and maintain inequality. Moving beyond past interpretations in which race or gender, for instance, figured as explanatory categories—a priori human gradations that shaped social interaction from outside of history—this body of scholarship asserts that such distinctions themselves require explaining. And they have sought to do it, exploring the formation of these identities as political processes in which state power, cultural representations, and routines of everyday life play key roles.

A growing number of writers, too, have begun to examine social distinction in a spatial context. Since the 1970s, a vital and multidisciplinary branch of scholarship has examined the social production of space: that is, the terrain of the world and the relationships among the things in it. Following the work of scholars such as David Harvey, Henri LeFebvre, and Manuel Castells, this work emphasizes that society is not merely reflected in space, but rather that society itself is a spatial phenomenon.[3] Thus, the social spaces in which we live—homes and yards, cities and suburbs, regions and bounded nations—the geographical relationships among them, and the meanings and memories they evoke are very much a product of history. For the first generation of scholars, working in a tradition of Marxian political economy, the history that mattered most in this connection was the formation of capitalism. Social space, they argued, was the direct outcome of this economic organization. More recently, however, scholars have attended to the ways that space is also connected to the making of social identities and categories of difference.

These insights have offered fertile ground for recent investigations of suburbia. Suburbs, after all, are intentional spaces, places in which people have sought variously to maximize profit, organize political power and public resources, and achieve deeply felt personal goals. These goals and the efforts devoted to them were inescapably linked to the production of space. In the transformation of farms into housing tracts, rural outskirts into tax generating municipalities, and houses into homes, suburbia emerged not only as a means of generating wealth and achieving social aspiration, but as a key means through which Americans organized both upward mobility and inequality over the past 150 years. Establishing social distinctions in metropolitan space—through such means as segregation in schools and housing, redlining and municipal neglect, restrictive land use policies, and environmental pollution, as well as domestic architecture and the gendered division of housework—served not only to reinforce and extend certain kinds of inequality, but to naturalize them, to make them an aspect of the landscape, the very world itself. Thus, spatial distinctions did not merely reify existing social hierarchies, but they helped shape ideas and understandings of them in ways that perpetuated them through time. In building suburbia, Americans built inequality to last.

By the same token, suburban space has served as the backdrop for efforts to undermine and erode racism, classism, and gender inequity. For example, mass suburbanization of the postwar period, while bolstering racial inequality, tended to undermine, often intentionally so, class, ethnic, and religious difference that had featured so largely in prewar life and politics. Likewise, minority efforts at suburbanization—planning for black suburban neighborhoods in the postwar South, pioneering in white suburbs, making productive and protective domestic landscapes, or

organizing to challenge white supremacy—hinged on a recognition of the empowering potential of metropolitan space. Suburban men and women, too, negotiated gender in the context of homes and neighborhoods. Suburbia, thus, has been a terrain of conflict as well as consensus, and its forms reflect as well as reinforce these influences. Unpacking the social production of suburban space, its economic, political, and cultural motives, the conflicts and agreements underlying it, is a necessary step to understanding the production of ideas, social divisions, and persisting inequality. It is, in short, a first stride toward completing the unfinished business of democracy.

These approaches to space and social distinctions have also drawn scholars to interrogate the politics of suburbia in new ways. In contrast to earlier traditions in the study of politics, which focused more narrowly on politicians, parties, and formal political processes, this new literature attends carefully to both grassroots politics and the broader political economy. Following Charles Tilly's dictum that scholars should integrate scales of analysis, exposing the links between daily life and the macroeconomic processes shaping our world at the broadest scale, these scholars have traced the process of community and city building to questions of profit and the needs of capital, to the production of real estate markets, and to contests over the allocation of resources in the context of global economic restructuring.[4] They have also reexamined the ties between local and national politics. In the second half of the twentieth century, historians emphasize, suburbanization was a crucible for the realignment of American political ideas and loyalties, a local basis for interests and assumptions that propelled the resurgence of conservatism and the decline of New Deal liberalism at every level of American politics. Thus, suburbia is no longer the quaint backwater of nonpartisan politics and volunteer officialdom, but a central crucible in the transformation of American political life in the twentieth century and beyond.

These debates inform many of the essays and documents that follow and help to define key themes in suburban history: the origins and development of suburban landscapes and ways of life, the evolution of suburban political culture, the ongoing relationship between cities and suburbs, the tension between diversity and exclusivity, the role of space in the production of social distinctions such as gender, class, and race, and finally, the history and social repercussions of suburban ideology.

DEFINITIONS AND HISTORIOGRAPHY

So, what is a suburb? Differing definitions abound, and consensus seems unlikely to emerge any time soon. Influenced by individual as well as disciplinary biases, scholars have classified suburbs on many bases: political status (independent municipalities outlying a larger urban center); economic and social function (dependence on a central city, especially dormitory communities of urban commuters); landscape and the built environment (the predominance of single-family homes with lawns, curvilinear streets, and other aesthetic symbols of harmony with nature); ideology and way of life (places shaped by elevated values for homeownership, secluded nuclear families, privacy, a distinctive, gendered division of labor, social exclusivity, semirural landscapes, dislike of cities, political home-rule, etc.); and process of development (the decentralization of population, jobs, and other urban functions from an older city core).

Of course, it doesn't take a PhD to know a thing or two about suburbia. All of us carry images in our heads that encapsulate ideas about "the suburbs." Say the word, and we may see Grosse Pointe or the Main Line, Levittown, Skokie, or "the Valley," Mount Laurel, Chula Vista, or Prince Georges County, the towns where we live, or came of age, or those to which we aspire. Just as likely, our images may spring from mass media: from *Father Knows Best* and *The Brady Bunch* to *South Park*, *The Boondocks*, and *American Beauty*.

As different as these images may be, most are likely to contain some common threads—a low-density, residential environment on the outskirts of larger cities, occupied primarily by families of similar class and race, with plenty of trees and grass. Historian Kenneth Jackson has perhaps best expressed this "common sense" definition of American suburbs. In 1985, he argued that the characteristic features of American suburbs could be summed up in a sentence: "affluent and middle-class Americans live in suburban areas that are far from their places of work, in homes that they own, and in the center of yards that by urban standards elsewhere are enormous."[5] Unspoken here and in many such images, however, is the assumption that suburbs are likely to be white communities. For most of their history, suburbs have been associated, by scholars and ordinary citizens alike, with the white middle class. This stereotype has never captured the totality of suburban life, and it is less and less a truthful representation today. But this perception of suburban space remains one legacy of a long history of exclusion and decades of imagineering in the mass media in which whites were the only suburbanites who mattered.

Despite the power and persistence of certain stereotypes about suburbia, the question of suburban definitions has emerged in recent years as a lively source of debate among historians and links closely with the evolution of the scholarly field itself. The most intensive argument has pivoted around the questions of class and race: Was a suburb only a suburb when it was white and middle or upper class? Pioneering scholars in the field, like Kenneth Jackson and Robert Fishman, implied that the answer was yes. In his sweeping synthesis of the U.S. history of suburbia, *Crabgrass Frontier*, Jackson defined suburbs as low-density residential areas, inhabited by middle and upper-class people who own their homes and commute to work some distance from their homes. Two years later, Robert Fishman's brilliant cultural history, *Bourgeois Utopias*, refined this view even further. Fishman defined suburbs as middle-class residential communities outside, yet economically dependent on, the city core, characterized by "a distinctive low density environment defined by the primacy of the single family house set in the greenery of an open, parklike setting." In a more emphatic linking of class to the suburban designation, he also defined suburbs by what they excluded—industry, commerce, and lower-class residents.[6]

By the 1990s, however, suburban "revisionists" had begun to challenge this "orthodox" version of suburbia for what it omitted: in particular, industry, multifamily housing, blue-collar workers, ethnic and racial minorities, and the poor. The revisionists proposed a more encompassing definition, emphasizing suburbanization as a process of development—the decentralization of jobs as well as housing from older urban cores. Suburbs comprised the range of communities and functions that this process produced. Focusing on the social and economic diversity of this wider suburbia, they argued that blue-collar workers and members of ethnic and racial minorities developed their own suburban ideals and practices.

Even as this debate has proceeded, the diversification of suburbia, especially in its more recent incarnations, has led some scholars to conclude that the era of suburbia has ended. More and more Americans may live in single-family homes on winding streets or cul-de-sacs, but by the criterion of orthodox definitions—functional dependence of suburb on city, widespread social exclusivity, and the seclusion of women and children in a green refuge from the world of commerce—the "true suburb" has gone the way of the slide rule and hula hoop.[7] By contrast, architectural historian Dolores Hayden has countered that the suburban residential ideal (of class-separated ownership of a detached single-family home with yards) is alive and kicking.[8] The admail that opens this Introduction is a testament to this view.

Meanwhile, other scholars have questioned the suburban moniker altogether. Geographers Richard Harris and Robert Lewis, whose work in the 1990s spearheaded the revisionist challenge, have argued that the manifest heterogeneity of places on either side of the city limits as early as 1900 renders the categories "city" and "suburb" inadequate descriptors of reality on the ground. Building on this insight, they and others have begun to emphasize the need for a new metropolitan scope of analysis, one that recognizes the inescapable connections across the totality of metropolitan areas as well as the implications of events in one part of the metropolis for conditions in the remainder.[9] It is our sense that the best works of suburban scholarship have always been metropolitan in character, attending to the sweep and consequences of urban development from the core to the periphery. One thing is clear: at the beginning of the twenty-first century, scholars are no closer to agreeing on what constitutes a true suburb, or, for that matter, whether such a thing even exists.

Rather than seeing the lack of scholarly consensus as a problem, we perceive it more as a virtue, a realistic way of approaching a contested and changing world. Furthermore, we find that this approach offers a praiseworthy model of scholarly investigation—not of defended territories and conclusive victory, but of an ongoing conversation that enriches our understanding with each turn.[10] As members of the revisionist cohort, our own scholarship has contributed to these debates. But we are partisans who have come back mellowed, more informed, and inspired by the generosity of colleagues with whom we have tussled. We have not relinquished our belief in the limitations of a suburbia defined by class, race, or appearance. And we still believe that it is most fruitful to approach suburbanization as a process of decentralization, with all the functional and social diversity it encompassed (and the resulting definitional confusion that this entails). Nonetheless, we also recognize, as the numerous illustrations in this volume demonstrate, that what a suburb is depends in large part on how and where one looks—and when. Many lives make a metropolis; only many views could begin to encompass them. Thus, we celebrate the rich and lively debate as a means to greater understanding and as evidence of the vitality and importance of the field.

In this volume, we present varying perspectives on American suburbia. Essays and documents advance a range of definitions, conveying a rich textual and visual portrait of suburbanization over the past two centuries. In doing so, we hope to offer readers entrée to this conversation so that they may join it. For battle-hardened enthusiasts, too, we hope that the abundant variety of essays and documentary evidence will offer fuel for renewed questions and debate. By predilection, we emphasize a broad definition of suburbia that encompasses a long sweep of time and a diverse collection of communities, landscapes, and functions. In practical terms, we treat as suburban the sprawling territory beyond the central city limits that lies within commuting distance and social orbit of the older core. In most metropolitan areas today, that includes almost every place within an hour's drive of the central business district. In the larger metro areas, it may include places as far as two hours away as job opportunities have leapfrogged outward and metropolitan commuting sheds have overlapped.

Because we emphasize suburbanization as a process of decentralization, we also pay attention to the historic suburbia that lies inside the boundaries of central cities, either because of annexation after the fact or because development at the urban fringe occurred within the city limits long before spilling into the surrounding countryside. In the Northeast and Midwest, for example, much of the nineteenth-century suburban landscape now lies well within the city limits. In the South and West, the same was true for much of the twentieth century. Key developments in the history of suburbia took place in areas that were or are part of a central city. A prime example is the Country Club District of Kansas City, Missouri, which was an influential planned, exclusive suburb in the early twentieth century. Its developer, J. C. Nichols was a national innovator in the real estate industry, who helped spread the idea of integrated "community building," restrictive covenants, municipal planning, and self-policing by homeowners associations, all of which feature prominently in the history of twentieth-century suburbs. When Nichols began work on his subdivision around 1905, the District lay just outside the city. By the time he completed work in the 1930s, annexation had brought the neighborhood within the city limits. Next door, Nichols' equally famous Country Club Plaza, a forerunner of the suburban shopping mall, was inside the city from the start. Thus, because suburbanization was a historical, cultural, and environmental phenomenon, as well as a political one, we attend to it where we find it. Political boundaries alone are insufficient to capture it.

We are aware of the pitfalls of these choices, not least the almost imponderable diversity of suburban places entailed by an expansive definition. But such is the metropolitan landscape as Americans have made and lived it for generations: complex, intriguing, alternately appealing and appalling, with borders that are shifting and permeable as well as sometimes rigidly defended.

ORGANIZATION OF THE BOOK

The Suburb Reader is divided into three chronological sections, Part I: The Emergence of Suburbia, 1750–1940; Part II: Postwar Suburbia, 1940–70; and Part III: Recent Suburbia, 1970–present. The chapters of Part I explore the themes of suburban origins, the making of gender and family ideals in suburbia, the role of technology and transportation, early diversity on the suburban fringe, political culture, planning visions, working-class, African-American, and ethnic suburbs, and tools of exclusion. Part II surveys the critical post-World War II years of suburban history, emphasizing the rise of mass-produced suburbs, the contentious national discourse about suburbia during the 1950s and 1960s, the role of race, and the shifting fortunes of city and suburb. Part III brings the story into the present, examining first the maturing of suburban politics across the whole postwar period, and then focusing on major trends since 1970: recent transformations in suburban communities, new mechanisms of inclusion and exclusion, and finally the present and future of suburbia. Each chapter contains several primary source documents and excerpts of published studies written by scholars from a number of disciplines. A short interpretive essay begins each chapter, setting it in context and introducing its contents. At the end of each introduction, we also present questions for consideration in the chapter, as a means of generating more careful reading and thinking, better discussion, more questions, and even further research.

NOTES

1. Harlan Paul Douglass, *The Suburban Trend* (1925; repr. New York: Johnson, 1970).

2. For example, see works in this volume by George Lipsitz, Betty Friedan, William H. Whyte, Bennett Berger, and Herbert Gans.

3. Henri LeFebvre, *The Production of Space*, trans. Donald Nicholson-Smith (1974; repr. Cambridge, MA: Blackwell, 1991); Manuel Castells, *The City and the Grassroots: A Cross-Cultural Theory of Urban Social Movements* (Berkeley: University of California Press, 1983); David Harvey, *The Condition of Postmodernity: An Enquiry into the Origins of Cultural Change* (Cambridge, MA: Blackwell, 1990).

4. Charles Tilly, "What Good Is Urban History?" *Journal of Urban History* 22 (September 1996): 702–19.

5. Kenneth T. Jackson, *Crabgrass Frontier: The Suburbanization of the United States* (New York: Oxford University Press, 1985), 6.

6. Robert Fishman, *Bourgeois Utopias: The Rise and Fall of Suburbia* (New York: Basic Books, 1987), 5.

7. Fishman, *Bourgeois Utopias*, chapter 7.

8. Dolores Hayden, *Building Suburbia: Green Fields and Urban Growth, 1820–2000* (New York: Pantheon Books, 2003). For a useful discussion of this debate, see William Sharpe and Leonard Wallock, "Bold New City or Built-Up 'Burb? Redefining Contemporary Suburbia," *American Quarterly* 46 (March 1994): 1-30.

9. Richard Harris and Robert Lewis, "North American Cities and Suburbs, 1900–1950: A New Synthesis," *Journal of Urban History* 27 (March 2001): 262–92; also Robert Self, *American Babylon: Race and the Struggle for Postwar Oakland* (Princeton, NJ: Princeton University Press, 2003); Thomas Sugrue and Kevin Kruse, eds., *The New Suburban History* (Chicago: University of Chicago Press, 2006).

10. See Mary Corbin Sies and Andrew Wiese, "Crossing the Tracks: Relationships between Black and White Suburbs, 1900–1950," Proceedings of the Annual Meeting of the International Planning History Society, Barcelona, Spain (June 2004).

PART I

The Emergence of Suburbia, 1750–1940

CHAPTER 1

The Transnational Origins of the Elite Suburb

INTRODUCTION

Although suburbs have existed since ancient times, only in the last 250 years did they emerge as a desirable place of residence. As the word implies, *suburb* initially represented a subordinate and inferior part of the city where odious activities and marginal people congregated. By the eighteenth century, the connotation began a radical transformation. Suburbs gradually came to represent a coveted, desirable place sought out by the wealthy and upwardly mobile as a place to live permanently, while still commuting to the city. Something profound had changed in public thought.

Why did perceptions of the city's edge shift from slum to Shangri-la? Since the 1980s, historians have debated this question and proposed different, sometimes conflicting answers. The first several chapters of this volume reflect on issues related to this change. In this chapter, historians offer differing interpretations about exactly when and where a new suburban ideology emerged. Despite these differences, certain factors recur. What can we generalize about this process? First, we know that the development of an elite suburban ideal was a transnational phenomenon. Whether via migration, imperialism, or the written word, ideas about suburbia alighted in parts of Europe, Asia, and the United States. This new, positive belief about the suburbs surfaced in different countries and continents, within roughly a one hundred year period. Second, a constellation of historical forces seemed to underlie the emergence of a "suburban ideal," playing roles of varying significance and meaning, depending on the setting. These forces included: the development of a new bourgeois class within expanding capitalist economies; the maturing of cities into large, diverse spaces marked by change and conflict; the emergence of a Romantic view of nature as a source of benign human enrichment; the redefinition of family and gender roles in the context of Protestant reformism and capitalist maturation; and new ideologies that emphasized the self, individuality, and independence. Looming large over all of this was an incipient Industrial Revolution, which reshaped so many aspects of life.

From the outset, the elite suburban ideal was deeply connected to issues of class. As early suburban ideologues and bourgeois suburbanites constructed this new conception of urban space, they were creating an important new badge of class identity. Only those who could afford it could buy into this new lifestyle. In the process, the bourgeoisie increasingly defined itself by where it lived. The value given to a particular space in the city, thus, was the product of careful human actions. The suburbs did not naturally emerge as desirable places. Rather, they gained value and meaning through conscious effort, planning, and design, in ways that allowed the middle and upper classes to define and differentiate themselves from the rest of society. It must be remembered, however, that the bourgeoisie did not have an exclusive claim on suburbia. Throughout its history, other classes and groups would define suburbia in ways that contrasted sharply with the elite suburban ideal, a theme that will emerge in later chapters.

Nevertheless, the ideal of suburbia as a place of quiet, beauty, wealth, and Arcadian delights became a powerful and influential new paradigm. It represented the spatial expression of a new value system that emerged out of broad changes in society, economy, religion, and culture. Rooted deeply in the history of the eighteenth and nineteenth centuries—across national boundaries—the elite suburb came to express a new bourgeois conception of the world.

DOCUMENTS

Document 1-1 expresses a distinctively Romantic view of nature, articulated by Ralph Waldo Emerson, who was the leading man of letters in the antebellum United States. The Romantic Movement, which originated in Europe and appeared in the United States in the nineteenth century, emphasized the value of nature as a vehicle for human perfection and a source of contact with the divine. Romantics believed that nature elevated the human spirit, far beyond the creations of men. By redefining nature as benign and virtuous—rather than dangerous or threatening—the Romantics set the ideological stage for an elite migration to the suburbs, a new kind of settlement that merged the advantages of urban life with the pleasures of the countryside. In **Document 1-2**, we see an illustrated example of this aesthetic developing in the suburban borderlands: a view of New York City from a suburban vantage point on the Jersey Palisades. According to landscape historian John Stilgoe, such depictions became popular in the antebellum period, suggesting the development of a new suburban point of view, a perspective that tried to balance the repose and natural beauty of the outskirts with the energy and attraction of the city beyond.[1] Together, **Documents 1-3** and **1-4** are early examples of a genre of suburban advice literature that blossomed in the mid-nineteenth century and would become the basis for the profusion of "home and garden" magazines of the twentieth century. **Document 1-3** is an early exhortation to the suburban way of life, set forth by John Claudius Loudon, an Englishman who wrote extensively on horticulture, architecture, and landscape design. In this excerpt from his 1838 book *The Suburban Gardener and Villa Companion*, he targets a "white collar" audience—persons whose daily work required little physical exertion and whose income provided the means to purchase properties in the new, emerging suburbs of Great Britain. Loudon's emphasis on gardening for exercise and relaxation in particular reflects the effects of industrialism in England and the rise of a new class of people sufficiently wealthy to pursue gardening as a hobby rather than a necessity. He also highlights the importance of class identity and class sorting in the suburbs.

In **Document 1-4**, the American horticulturalist Andrew Jackson Downing extols the virtues of building homes in the countryside as the means to improve American "civilization" and edify its people. While he borrowed liberally from British authors such as Loudon, Downing also distinguished himself by linking the American ideology of republicanism—which vaunted the independence of free-willed, hard-working citizens—with this emerging suburban ideal. He was careful to contrast this American system with old world aristocracy, whose spatial conventions it nonetheless invoked. Downing played an important role in disseminating a suburban aesthetic to a broad American audience. Under his tutelage and that of advocates like him, suburban architecture and landscaping would become important markers of taste and social prestige among the nation's growing professional and managerial classes.

Document 1-5 is the subdivision plan for Llewellyn Park, New Jersey, recognized as the first planned suburb in the United States to apply this new suburban paradigm. Designed by Alexander Jackson Davis in the 1850s at the behest of merchant Llewellyn Haskell, Llewellyn Park was nestled among the rocky outcrops, dense woods, and running streams of West Orange, New Jersey. Davis made a special effort to incorporate existing natural elements into his plan, a move that symbolized the blending of "nature" and residence as a defining element of suburban design. Among these devices were curvilinear roads and a fifty-acre wooded "ramble" at the center. Stately homes sat on three-acre lots, with lush landscaping that harmonized with the rustic character of the site. Llewellyn Park was just thirteen miles by train from Manhattan and attracted upper-class business-men, professionals, and their families. Davis's work also reveals that the "nature" that many Roman-tics idealized was often the product of careful design.

Document 1-6 presents two modern-day photographs of Llewellyn Park. The first shows the Nichols "cottage," designed by Davis in 1859, an evocative example of the picturesque gothic ar-chitecture that Downing and Davis advocated as a means of distinguishing "country" from city hous-ing. The second is a photo of The Glen, the rambling road that cut through the natural environment of the suburb. Notice the simple construction of the road—no curbs or sidewalks—which, more than a century after Llewellyn Park's planning, maximizes the feeling of closeness to nature.

Document 1-7 is a promotional pamphlet for a second important early suburb, Riverside, Illinois, which lay on the outskirts of Chicago. Riverside was planned by the renowned landscape architects Frederick Law Olmsted and Calvert Vaux, who had designed Central Park in New York City several years earlier. Like Llewellyn Park, Riverside's plan included generous lots, curved roadways, and designs that preserved the natural topography along a bend in the Des Plaines River; it also incor-porated large landscaped common areas, an artificial lake, and small pocket parks, which Olmsted and Vaux promoted as a means to enhance residents' connection with nature and each other.

What features characterized early elite suburbs? Who initiated the elite suburban ideal, and why? What were the most important elements of that ideal? What forces spawned this new vision of sub-urban life and landscape? How did suburbs in the eighteenth and nineteenth centuries differ from suburbs you are familiar with today? What features do they share?

1-1. RALPH WALDO EMERSON EXPRESSES A ROMANTIC VISION OF NATURE, 1836

Source: Ralph Waldo Emerson, *Nature Addresses and Other Lectures*, vol. 1 (New York: William H. Wise and Co., Current Opinion, 1923).

To speak truly, few adult persons can see nature. Most persons do not see the sun. At least they have a very superficial seeing. The sun illuminates only the eye of the man, but shines into the eye and the heart of the child. The lover of nature is he whose inward and outward senses are still truly adjusted to each other; who has retained the spirit of infancy even into the era of manhood. His intercourse with heaven and earth becomes part of his daily food. In the presence of na-ture, a wild delight runs through the man, in spite of real sorrows.... Nature is a setting that fits equally well a comic or a mourn-ing piece. In good health, the air is a cordial of incredible virtue. Crossing a bare com-mon, in snow puddles, at twilight, under a clouded sky, without having in my thoughts any occurrence of special good fortune, I have enjoyed a perfect exhilaration. Almost I fear to think how glad I am. In the woods too, a man casts off his years, as the snake his slough, and what period soever of life, is always a child. In the woods, is perpetual youth. Within these plantations of God, a decorum and sanctity reign, a perennial fes-tival is dressed, and the guest sees not how he should tire of them in a thousand years. In the woods, we return to reason and faith. There I feel that nothing can befal me in life,—no disgrace, no calamity, (leaving me my eyes,) which nature cannot repair. Stand-ing on the bare ground,—my head bathed by the blithe air, and uplifted into infinite space,—all mean egotism vanishes. I become a transparent eye ball. I am nothing. I see all. The currents of the Universal Being cir-culate through me; I am part or particle of God... I am the lover of uncontained and immortal beauty. In the wilderness, I find something more dear and connate than in streets or villages. In the tranquil landscape, and especially in the distant line of the hori-zon, man beholds somewhat as beautiful as his own nature....

The influence of the forms and actions in nature, is so needful to man, that, in its low-est functions, it seems to lie on the confines of commodity and beauty. To the body and mind which have been cramped by noxious work or company, nature is medicinal and restores their tone. The tradesman, the attorney comes out of the din and craft of the street, and sees the sky and the woods, and is a man again. In their eternal calm, he finds himself. The health of the eye seems to demand a horizon. We are never tired, so long as we can see far enough.

But in other hours, Nature satisfies the soul purely by its loveliness, and without any mixture of corporeal benefit. I have seen the spectacle of morning from the hill top over against my house, from day break to sun rise, with emotions which an angel might share. The long slender bars of cloud float like fishes in the sea of crimson light. From the earth, as a shore, I look out into that silent sea. I seem to partake its rapid transformations: the active enchantment reaches my dust, and I dilate and conspire with the morning wind. How does Nature deify us with a few and cheap elements!

1-2. A SUBURBAN PERSPECTIVE ON NEW YORK CITY, 1854

Figure 1-1 New York, from Weehawken, W. H. Bartlett, 1854. Popular city views such as this vista of New York from the Jersey Palisades signaled an emerging "suburban" point of view in the antebellum United States. T. Addison Richards, *American Scenery: Illustrated, with Thirty-two Engravings on Steel* (New York: Leavitt & Allen, 1854), 53.

1-3. BRITISH HORTICULTURALIST J. C. LOUDON LAYS THE FOUNDATION FOR A SUBURBAN IDEAL, 1838

Source: John Claudius Loudon, *The Suburban Gardener and Villa Companion* (London: The author, 1838).

The enjoyments to be derived from a suburban residence depend principally on a knowledge of the resources which a garden, however small, is capable of affording. The benefits experienced by breathing air unconfined by close streets of houses, and uncontaminated by the smoke of chimneys; the cheerful aspect of vegetation; the singing of birds in their season; and the enlivening effect of finding ourselves unpent-up by buildings, and in comparatively unlimited space; are felt by most people: but it requires some little knowledge of the progress or decline of vegetation throughout the year, and of rural nature generally, to be able to derive much enjoyment from the recurrence of the seasons, and their influence on plants; and much more knowledge of vegetation, botany, natural history, and the art of gardening, to derive the greatest amount of advantages which a country house and garden are calculated to afford....

Before proceeding to the garden itself, we shall endeavour to excite some interest in its favour, and to show the solid advantages which may be derived from a suburban residence....

Much of the enjoyment of a suburban residence depends on knowing what to expect from it.... [A]ll, in the way of house accommodation, that is essential to the enjoyment of life, may be obtained in a cottage of three or four rooms, as well as in a palace; and we shall prove, in this work, that a suburban residence, with a very small portion of land attached, will contain all that is essential to happiness, in the garden, park, and demesne of the most extensive country residence. Let us briefly make the comparison. The objects of the possessors of both are the same: health, which is the result of temperance and exercise; enjoyment, which is the possession of something which we can call our own, and on which we can set our heart and affections; and the respect of society, which is the result of their favourable opinion of our sentiments and moral conduct. No man in this world, however high may be his rank, great his wealth, powerful his genius, or extensive his acquirements, can ever attain more than health, enjoyment, and respect. The lord of an extensive demesne seeks after health by hunting, shooting, or other field sports, or by superintending the general management and cultivation of his estate; the lady seeks recreation in her pleasure-ground, or in airings in her carriage: and both find their enjoyment in their children, and in their house and garden, and other surrounding objects. Now, the master of a suburban villa finds health in the change it affords from his occupation as a citizen; or, if he has retired from business, in the personal cultivation of his garden. He also finds enjoyment, not only in his family, friends, and books, but in his garden,

and in the other rural objects which he can call his own, and which he can alter at pleasure, at a trifling expense, and often with his own hands. It is this which gives the charm of creation, and makes a thing essentially one's own....The master of a suburban residence, however small may be his demesne, may thus procure health and enjoyment at the same time, with more certainty than the possessor of a larger property; because his grounds lie more in his hands, and he can superintend every change himself. His wife's exercise consists in the personal management of her household affairs; and her enjoyments are the same as those of her husband. The respect, or the good opinion, of his friends and neighbours, or of the inhabitants of the parish in which he resides, are, to the citizen retired to the suburbs, of as great value as the respect of the inhabitants of a district, or of the whole nation, is to the wealthy landholder or the senator....

One immense advantage of a suburban residence over one isolated in the country consists in its proximity to neighbours, and the facilities it affords of participating in those sources of instruction and enjoyment which can only be obtained in towns: for example, public libraries and museums, theatrical representations, musical concerts, public and private assemblies, exhibitions of works of art, &c. The suburban resident, by his locality, has an opportunity of witnessing these spectacles with as much ease as the distant wealthy proprietor has by means of his establishment of horses and carriages. The small proprietor and the farmer in the interior of the country, on the other hand, are comparatively shut out from participating in the enjoyments which constant intercourse with society procures; as well as from receiving that refinement of mien and of manners which it produces.... The suburbs of towns are alone calculated to afford a maximum of comfort and enjoyment at a minimum of expense....

On the Choice of a Situation for a Suburban or Country House and Grounds...

The Kind of Neighbourhood is a consideration familiar to every one, and need not be enlarged on. Perhaps the best general principle to be followed in selecting a suburban residence, or a situation to build one, is to choose a neighbourhood where the houses and inhabitants are all, or chiefly, of the same description and class as the house we intend to inhabit, and as ourselves. To go into a neighbourhood where the prevailing character of the houses indicated a smaller income than that of the individual choosing a residence, would be to incur a risk of being marked out as the rich man of the locality; while to choose one where the majority of the houses was of a higher class, would be to incur the risk of either becoming unsocial on the one hand, or of being led into unsuitable expenses, by associating with persons of greater fortune, on the other. In the neighbourhood of large towns, many persons live in the midst of people with no one of whom, perhaps, they associate; but this arises from the inequality of education and morals which at present prevails, and is by no means a desirable state of things. Not only is social intercourse essential to the happiness of grown-up persons; but, as children must mix with the world sooner or later, it is better that they should do this with their neighbours, and under the eye of their parents, than that it should be deferred till they leave the paternal roof. To choose a neighbourhood where we can be neighbourly must, therefore, be far preferable to choosing one where we are likely to be isolated, either from an appearance of greater pretensions, or from actually having inferior means to those who are around us....

The Fortune of the individual, or the income which he derives from the exercise of his trade or profession, is by far the most important circumstance of a personal nature which requires to be considered in the choice of a suburban dwelling and garden....The most economical mode of having both a town and country residence is, to live a part of the year entirely at one house, and the other part of the year entirely at the other; as one set of servants will then be sufficient.

The Object which a person has in view in desiring a country residence will necessarily influence his choice. Health and recreation are the most universal objects; but joined to these, or independent of them, is the love of distinction; of retirement; of seclusion; of horses and dogs, which a country residence affords an excuse for maintaining; of astronomy, botany, gardening, and entomology; or of some other study which can be better carried on in the country, or in the suburbs of a town, than in the town itself.

The Connexions of an individual may influence his taste. A man in business is connected commercially with his employers or customers; by blood, with his relations; and by love and duty, with his immediate family. Under these circumstance, it will be for him to consider, whether proximity to either or all these connexions be desirable, or otherwise.

1-4. AMERICAN HORTICULTURALIST ANDREW JACKSON DOWNING DETAILS THE VIRTUES AND DESIGN OF COUNTRY LIVING, 1850

Source: Andrew Jackson Downing, *The Architecture of Country Houses* (New York: D. Appleton & Co., 1850).

There are three excellent reasons why my countrymen should have good houses.

The first, is because a good house (and by this I mean a fitting, tasteful, and significant dwelling) is a powerful means of civilization. A nation, whose rural population is content to live in mean huts and miserable hovels, is certain to be behind its neighbors in education, the arts, and all that makes up the external signs of progress. With the perception of proportion, symmetry, order and beauty, awakens the desire for possession, and with them comes that refinement of manners which distinguishes a civilized from a coarse and brutal people. So long as men are forced to dwell in log huts and follow a hunter's life, we must not be surprised at lynch law and the use of the bowie knife. But, when smiling lawns and tasteful cottages begin to embellish a country, we know that order and culture are established. And, as the first incentive towards this change is awakened in the minds of most men by the perception of beauty and superiority in external objects, it must follow that the interest manifested in the Rural Architecture of a country like this, has much to do with the progress of its civilization.

The second reason is, because the *individual home* has a great social value for a people. Whatever new systems may be needed for the regeneration of an old and enfeebled nation, we are persuaded that, in America, not only is the distinct family the best social form, but those elementary forces which give rise to the highest genius and the finest character may, for the most part, be traced back to the farm-house and the rural cottage. It is the solitude and freedom of the family home in the country which constantly preserves the purity of the nation, and invigorates its intellectual powers. The battle of life, carried on in cities, gives a sharper edge to the weapon of character, but its temper is, for the most part, fixed amid those communings with nature and the family, where individuality takes its most natural and strongest development.

The third reason is, because there is a moral influence in a country home—when, among an educated, truthful, and refined people, it is an echo of their character—which is more powerful than any mere oral teachings of virtue and morality....

The mere sentiment of home, with its thousand associations, has, like a strong anchor, saved many a man from shipwreck in the storms of life. How much the moral influence of that sentiment may be increased, by making the home all that it should be, and how much an attachment is strengthened by every external sign of beauty that awakens love in the young, are so well understood, that they need no demonstration here. All to which the heart can attach itself in youth, and the memory linger fondly over in riper years, contributes largely to our stock of happiness, and to the elevation of the moral character. For this reason, the condition of the family home—in this country where every man may have a home, should be raised, till it shall symbolize the best character and pursuits, and the dearest affections and enjoyments of social life....

What a Cottage Should Be

Nearly all the varieties of country houses in the United States may be considered as belonging to three classes—COTTAGES, FARM-HOUSES, and VILLAS....

What we mean by a cottage, in this country, is a dwelling of small size, intended for the occupation of a family, either wholly managing the household cares itself, or, at the most, with the assistance of one or two servants. The majority of such cottages in this country are occupied, not by tenants, dependants or serfs, as in many parts of Europe, but by industrious and intelligent mechanics and working men, the bone and sinew of the land, who own the ground upon which they stand, build them for their own use, and arrange them to satisfy their own peculiar wants and gratify their own tastes.

It is, therefore, as clear as noonday, that cottages of this class should be arranged with a different view, both as regards utility and beauty, from either farm-houses or villas. An industrious man, who earns his bread by daily exertions, and lives in a snug and economical little home in the suburbs of a town, has very different wants from the farmer, whose accommodation must be plain but more spacious, or the man of easy income, who builds a villa as much to gratify his taste, as to serve the useful purposes of a dwelling....

Something of a love for the beautiful, in the inmates, is always suggested by a vine-covered cottage, because mere utility would never lead any person to plant flowering vines; and much of positive beauty is always conferred upon simple cottage forms by the graceful growth of vines, through the rural and domestic expression they give to the cottage. We say domestic expression, because, as vines are never planted by architects, masons, carpenters, or those who build the cottage, but always by those who live in it, and make it truly a home, and generally by the mother or daughter, whose very planting of vines is a labor of love offered up on the domestic altar, it follows, by the most direct and natural associations, that vines on a rural cottage always express domesticity and the presence of heart....

DESIGN II. – *A small Bracketed Cottage*

Figure 1-2 Design II. Small Bracketed Cottage, 1850. Illustration in original, 78 facing plate.

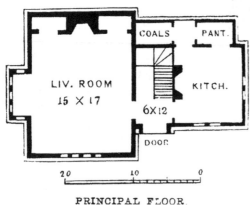

PRINCIPAL FLOOR.

What a Country House or Villa Should Be...

More strictly speaking, what we mean by a villa, in the United States, is the country-house of a person of competence or wealth sufficient to build and maintain it with some taste and elegance.... [A] villa is a country-house of larger accommodation, requiring the care of at least three or more servants....

The villa, or country-house proper, then, is the most refined home of America—the home of its most leisurely and educated class of citizens. Nature and art both lend it their happiest influence. Amid the serenity and peace of sylvan scenes, surrounded by the perennial freshness of nature, enriched without and within by objects of universal beauty and interest—objects that touch the heart and awaken the understanding, it is in such houses that we should look for the happiest social and moral development of our people....

In this most cultivated country life, everything lends its aid to awaken the finer sentiments of our nature. The occupations of the country are full of health for both soul and body, and for the most refined as well as the most rustic taste. The heart has there, always within its reach, something on which to bestow its affections. We beget a partiality for every copse that we have planted, every tree which has for years given us a welcome under its shady boughs. Every winding path throughout the woods, every secluded resting-place in the valley, every dell where the brook lives and sings, becomes part of our affections, friendship, joy and sorrows. Happy is he who lives this life of a cultivated mind in the country!...

The villa—the country house should, above all things, manifest individuality. It should say something of the character of the family within—as much as possible of their life and history, their tastes and associations, should mould and fashion themselves upon its walls....

[T]he true home still remains to us. Not, indeed, the feudal castle, not the baronial hall, but the home of the individual man—the home of that family of equal rights, which continually separates and continually reforms itself in the new world—the republican home, built by no robbery of the property of another class, maintained by no infringement of a brother's rights; the beautiful, rural, unostentatious, moderate home of the country gentleman, large enough to minister to all the wants, necessities, and luxuries of a republican, and not too large or too luxurious to warp the life or manners of his children.

The just pride of a true American is not in a great hereditary home, but in greater hereditary institutions. It is more to him that all his children will be born under wise, and just, and equal laws, than that one of them should come into the world with a great family estate. It is better, in his eyes, that it should be possible for the humblest laborer to look forward to the possession of a future country-house and home like his own, than to feel that a wide and impassable gulf of misery separates him, the lord of the soil, from a large class of his fellow beings born

beneath him. Yes, the love of home is one of the deepest feelings in our nature, and we believe the happiness and virtue of a vast rural population to be centred in it; but it must be a home built and loved, upon new world and not the old world ideas and principles; a home in which humanity and republicanism are stronger than family pride and aristocratic feeling; a home of the virtuous citizen, rather than of the mighty owner of houses and lands.

Designs for Villas or Country Houses

We have designed this villa to express the life of a family of refined and cultivated taste, full of home feeling, love for the country, and enjoyment of the rural and beautiful in nature—and withal, a truly American home, in which all is adapted to the wants and habits of life of a family in independent circumstances.

DESIGN XXVIII—
A Villa in the Rural Gothic Style

Figure 1-3 Design XXVIII. Rural Gothic Villa, 1850. Illustration in original, 322 facing plate.

[Fig. 149. Principal Floor.]

1-5. A. J. DAVIS PRESENTS A PROMOTIONAL PLAN FOR LLEWELLYN PARK, NEW JERSEY, 1857

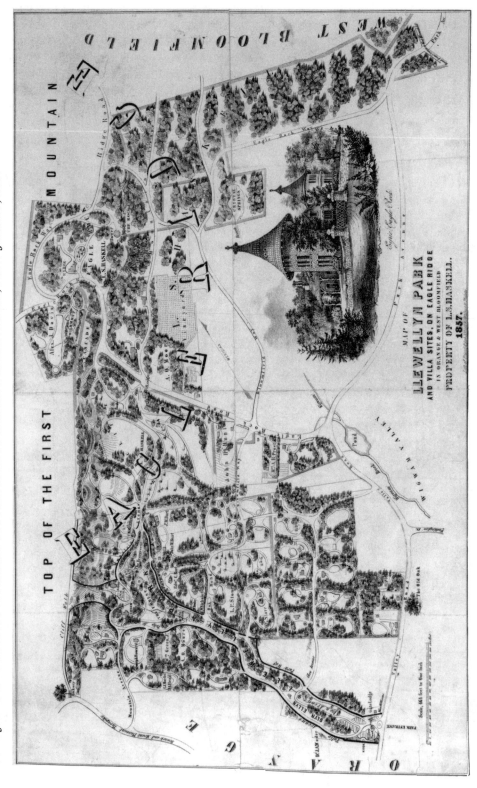

Figure 1-4 Map of Llewellyn Park and Villa Sites on Eagle Ridge in Orange and West Bloomfield, property of L.S. Haskell, Lithograph, 1857. Alexander Jackson Davis' 1857 plan for Llewellyn Park, New Jersey, marked the inception of suburban community planning in North America. The Metropolitan Museum of Art, Harris Brisbane Dick Fund, 1924 (24.66.1433) Photograph, all rights reserved, The Metropolitan Museum of Art.

1-6. PHOTO GALLERY: LLEWELLYN PARK, NEW JERSEY, 1978

Figure 1-5 Modest by comparison with many Llewellyn Park homes, A.J. Davis' Nichols Cottage (1859) highlights the informal, "country" architecture that early suburban designers favored. Courtesy of John Archer, 1978.

Figure 1-6 The private road through "the Glen" in Llewellyn Park illustrates the relationship with nature that many nineteenth century suburbanites sought, as well as the endurance of this landscape aesthetic over time. Courtesy of John Archer, 1978.

1-7. AN EARLY "ADVERTISEMENT" FOR RIVERSIDE, ILLINOIS, 1869

Source: Riverside Improvement Company, "Riverside, Progress Prospectus," 1869, reprinted from the collections of the Riverside Public Library in *Landscape Architecture* 21 (July 1931).

No modern city has long enjoyed much commercial prosperity without causing some beautiful rural neighborhoods to grow up near it, in which a large number of its most able and energetic citizens reside during a part if not the whole of each year. The aim of the Riverside Improvement Company has been to supply at once, and on a liberal scale, those deficiencies which at present cause Chicago to be an apparent exception to this rule.

Its first step has been to secure about two and a half square miles of land of inviting surface and suitable soil, adapted to perfect drainage, in the immediate vicinity of well-grown wood, permanent running water, and established railway stations, affording means of frequent, rapid and convenient communication with the city.

Having acquired by far the best ground near Chicago to operate upon, the Company next sought to engage professional services of the most unquestionable ability for its improvement.

Messrs. Olmsted, Vaux & Co., the designers and constructors of the Central Park of New York, Prospect Park, Brooklyn, and many of the finest Villa residences and private grounds on the Hudson, have accordingly been engaged, with a large staff of engineers and other assistants, during the last ten months, in the preparation designed to provide whatever, in their judgment, should be required, without restriction as to necessary expense, to make Riverside, in all respects, a

Model Suburban Neighborhood

The Company believe that when their plans are carried out, Riverside will combine the conveniences peculiar to the finest modern towns, with the domestic advantages of the most charming country, in a degree never before realized.

The attention of Business Men needing Country Seats, is especially called to the facts detailed under the following heads;

Accessibility, By Railway

Riverside is the first out-of-town station upon the double track of the Burlington & Quincy road, one of the best constructed and best managed railways in the country.

By Private Conveyance

Riverside Parkway—The Trustees of the town of Cicero have recently passed an Ordinance, providing for the construction, during the next four months, of a Park-like communication between Riverside and Chicago, having a width of from one hundred and fifty to two hundred feet....

The Riverside Park-way will include a bridle road and driving road, (the latter to be especially adapted, and to be restricted to the use of pleasure vehicles,) which will be constructed this year, and two side roads for heavy traffic, to be constructed next year. It will be lined with shade trees, and the wheel-ways will be of the best character. Riverside will thus be brought within an hour's drive or ride of the business parts of Chicago the distance by the line of the Park-way to the present western limits of the city being four miles; to its eastern border, on the lake, less than ten....

Climate

The climate of Riverside, influenced by its extensive groves, by the superior drainage of the soil and its distance from the lake, is found, even at present, less irritating to persons of delicate organization or weakened constitutions, than that of the more immediate neighborhood of Chicago. It will, undoubtedly, have a corresponding soothing and recuperating influence upon business and professional men, overtasked by duties in the City.

The really important difference to be found between the climate of Riverside and that of Chicago, is indicated by the fact that even the hardiest trees expand their foliage fully a week earlier in the Spring at Riverside than in the immediate environs of the City, only five miles further east. Many sorts of fruit trees, which are barren near the lake shore, produce fruit abundantly and of the finest quality at Riverside. During about two months of the year, evenings can be enjoyed out-of-doors at Riverside, when they cannot at Chicago. Residents at Riverside are much more exempt in hot weather from insect plagues than those of Chicago.

Purity of Air

The whole of the property will be intersected and divided at distances not exceeding four hundred feet, by groves of trees: each residence will stand at least 150 feet, on an average, apart from all others, and (except upon a narrow space near the railway,) no ground will be sold except upon condition that it shall be used solely for family residences, or for educational or other purposes consistent with purity of air, and aidful to refined and healthy domestic life. All the ordinary sources of malaria and noisome air, both of town and country, will be interdicted.

Drives, Walks and Recreations

The Company propose to construct about forty miles of carriage road, similar to the drives of the Central Park; all to be of easy grade, smooth surface, thoroughly drained, storm and frost proof, and equally serviceable and enjoyable, Winter, Spring and Summer....

Five miles of public walk will be laid out on the river banks; there will be numerous public ball and croquet grounds; the river affords pleasant opportunities for boating, and several bridges, balconies and pavilions will give special advantages for observing regattas and other aquatic sports.

The river, at present, abounds with fish and wild fowl, and will be stocked with Swans and other ornamental water-birds.

The river, also, presents in winter, a safe, sheltered and perfect skating-field, the ice forming on it being prized for its purity and solidity.

While all the property belonging to the Company will be laid out, ornamented, the roads constructed, and a considerable portion devoted to public use and pleasure grounds, so as to render the whole sixteen hundred acres one of the most charming Parks in the country, (although an inhabited one,) yet, the Company have determined to dedicate, for the use of the residents of Riverside, a tract of ground consisting of one hundred to one hundred and fifty acres, situated on both sides of the river, north of the railroad bridge, and have undertaken its formation into a

Public Park

agreeably to the advice of Messrs. Olmsted, Vaux & Co., given as follows:

"Next in order to the construction of the Park-way, we would advise you to begin the work of converting the woody district on both sides of the river, north of the railway bridge, into a Park, and of connecting it by a fine road and bridge with the Park-way."

Water

There are fine surface-springs of water: the river is sweet and seldom turbid, and the Company have already sunk an artesian well, to a depth of over seven hundred feet, from which a stream is now flowing, sufficient for the supply of a population of ten thousand.

The Company are now laying mains along each road way, and undertakes to send good water to the second story of every house. Gas works will also be established as soon as the population is sufficiently large to warrant their construction.

Progress...

Six Villas, a Refectory and Public Assembly Room are nearly completed, and contracts for the immediate construction of a very beautiful stone Church and fourteen handsome residences have been closed, and to maintain the high character of everything pertaining to Riverside, have been awarded to the well known and reliable master builders, Amos Grannis and Wm. E. Mortimer.

Plans for stores are nearly finished and will be immediately begun, while the construction of the Grand Park-way or Boulevard, is already commenced, to be completed to the city limits in eighty working days.

A limited number of Villa Sites can now be obtained, free from assessment for the improvements mentioned, and to parties purchasing with a view of residing at Riverside, upon the completion of the Drive, SPECIAL INDUCEMENTS will be offered.

We advise those who intend residing at Riverside next Spring to select their sites at once, and thus, while aiding the enterprise by their influence, secure to themselves advantages of selection at a comparatively low price.

ESSAYS

The first two essays come from two of the most important historical studies of suburbanization, both published in the 1980s. These works immediately launched a debate around our chapter's central questions: when, where, and why did a new elite suburban ideal emerge? In **Essay 1-1**, historian Kenneth Jackson emphasizes the American nature of the suburban trend, locating the causes in factors that sprang from American soil during the nineteenth century. He explores these forces, many of which grew out of the Industrial Revolution, yet also takes care to avoid "technological determinism," that is, attributing the suburban trend to technological developments—such as transportation—alone. Jackson's book stands as a classic on the history of American suburbanization. In **Essay 1-2**, historian Robert Fishman locates the roots of the suburban ideal in a different place and time. Reaching earlier in time and across the Atlantic, Fishman explores how an emerging British bourgeois class defined the new suburban ethos. As this class emerged, so did new ideas about proper comportment, culture, and values, which they came to see best expressed spatially in a tranquil suburban environment. **Essay 1-3**, by literary and architectural scholar John Archer, is a more recent work that casts the geographic net even wider. Uncovering evidence of suburban settlements in British colonial outposts in south Asia by the mid-1700s, Archer's work is a powerful reminder that ideas, like people, can travel along imperial and migratory tides. This essay shows similar elite suburban impulses manifesting in response to both local and imperial forces.

ESSAY 1-1. KENNETH T. JACKSON, *CRABGRASS FRONTIER: THE SUBURBANIZATION OF THE UNITED STATES* (1985)

Source: *Crabgrass Frontier: The Suburbanization of the United States* by Kenneth T. Jackson, copyright © 1985 by Oxford University Press, Inc. Used by permission of Oxford University Press, Inc.

The Transportation Revolution and the Erosion of the Walking City

Between 1815 and 1875, America's largest cities underwent a dramatic spatial change. The introduction of the steam ferry, the omnibus, the commuter railroad, the horsecar, the elevated railroad, and the cable car gave additional impetus to an exodus that would turn cities "inside out" and inaugurate a new pattern of suburban affluence and center despair. The result was hailed as the inevitable outcome of the desirable segregation of commercial from residential areas and of the disadvantaged from the more comfortable. Frederick Law Olmsted wrote that the city, no less than the private home, had to be divided into various segments that could perform specialized functions: "If a house to be used for many different purposes must have many rooms and passages of various dimensions variously lighted and furnished, not less must such a metropolis be specifically adapted at different points to different needs." Olmsted was writing soon after the Civil War when urban concentrations had generated enough people with enough wealth to provide the market demand for large numbers of private houses near major urban centers....

[E]normous growth to metropolitan size was accompanied by rapid population growth on the periphery, by a leveling of the density curve, by an absolute loss of population at the center, and by an increase in the average journey to work, as well as by a rise in the socioeconomic status of suburban residents. This shift was not sudden, but it was no less profound for its gradual character. Indeed, the phenomenon was one of the most important in the history of society, for it represented the most fundamental realignment of urban structure in the 4500-year past of cities on this planet.

In the most populous metropolitan areas, this shift in residential status between periphery and core began before the Civil War....

Outside of Boston, the most dramatic changes took place in the unannexed villages of Cambridge and Somerville. According to Henry Binford they developed three important suburban characteristics between 1800 and 1850: a set of clear municipal priorities, a preference for residential over commercial expansion, and a stubbornness to remain politically independent from Boston. As the metropolitan population swelled in the 1830s and 1840s, a handful of young, wealthy residents of old Cambridge and Cambridge Port pioneered local commuting. Called "transitional commuters" by Binford, these early suburban residents differed from later commuters because they did not use public transportation and because their original residences were located on the periphery, not in Boston.

In New York City, where extraordinary growth pushed the population of the city and adjacent Brooklyn well past the million mark by 1860, the "genteel" population moved northward from City Hall, especially to the high ground in the middle of the island a few blocks on either side of Fifth Avenue. Building substantial homes along King and Charlton streets or around small parks such as Washington, Gramercy, and St. John's, they brought their elite institutions—the Union Club, the First Presbyterian Church, Grace Church, and Columbia College—with them to the edge of the city....

As has usually been the case in the United States, the distribution of population was governed primarily by the desire of property owners and builders to enhance their investments by attracting the wealthy and by excluding the poor. Samuel Ruggles, an 1831 purchaser of the 22-acre Gramercy Farm between 19th Street on the south, 23rd Street on the north, the Bloomingdale Road (now Broadway) on the west, and Second Avenue on the east, was particularly adept at developing high-status real estate. Quickly subdividing the farm into 108 city lots, Ruggles then transformed the equivalent of 42 lots into a private park, 520 by 184 feet....

The value of the land was enhanced as the park—admission to which has traditionally been by a special key available only to the chosen—became the center of a wealthy neighborhood and gave an uptown push to the movement of the affluent away from lower Manhattan. By the time of the Mexican War, Gramercy Park had become a bastion of correct society....

The movement of the affluent toward Beacon Hill in Boston, Gramercy Park and Washington Square in New York, and Germantown near Philadelphia was duplicated in other metropolitan areas. In Cincinnati, travel writer Willard Glazer described the suburbs in 1883 as a "Paradise of grass, gardens, lawns, and tree-shaded roads." In San Francisco by 1860 the city's bankers, merchants, and doctors were moving away from downtown and putting up homes on the heights of Fern (Nob) Hill and Russian Hill. In Chicago most of the high-grade residential areas were still very near the center of the business district at the time of the Civil War, but a tendency for the fashionable to move toward the periphery was clearly apparent by 1873 and was widespread by 1899. In Nashville prominent citizens moved to Edgefield, lying east of the Cumberland River opposite the central business district, after the construction of a suspension bridge in the 1850s. And in Buffalo new elite residential areas were developed at the outer edges soon after 1860.

In smaller cities and towns, suburbs remained predominantly slums until well into the twentieth century. In Calgary, for example, clusters of cheap dwellings and "shack towns" were put up on the narrow flats below the ridge as late as World War I. And in country villages across North America, the best streets were often those toward the center as late as 1970. But by 1875 in the major urban centers, the merchant princes and millionaires were searching for hilltops, shore lands, and farms on which to build substantial estates; crowded cities offered fewer attractions with every passing year.

The First Commuter Suburb

Because land speculators have operated on the edges of cities for thousands of years and because many communities were labeled "suburban" before 1800, there is disagreement about the origins of the modern suburb. Robert A. M. Stern traces it to the booming expansion of London under King George III, when the newly prosperous merchants built small houses in remote villages in emulation of the gentry's country estates. Other possibilities include Clapham and John Nash's Park Village in London, Cambridge outside Boston, Greenwich Village north of New York, Spring Garden and the Northern Liberties near Philadelphia, and New Brighton on Staten Island. None of these communities offered the number of commuters, the easy access to a large city, and the bucolic atmosphere of Brooklyn Heights, which grew up across the harbor from lower Manhattan in the early decades of the nineteenth century....

Brooklyn remained essentially agricultural until 1800, and its economic ties to the metropolitan entrepôt were slight. As late as 1810, it was occupied mostly by farms, and its population was less than five thousand.

In the next four decades, however, the town of Brooklyn was transformed. Regular steam ferry service to New York City (then consisting only of Manhattan) began in 1814, and one year later the *Brooklyn Star* predicted that the town "must necessarily become a favorite residence for gentlemen of taste and fortune, for merchants and shopkeepers of every description, for artists, artisans, merchants, laborers, and persons of every trade in society." The accuracy of this prophecy soon became apparent. With its tree-shaded streets, pleasant homes, access to Manhattan, and general middle-class ambiance,

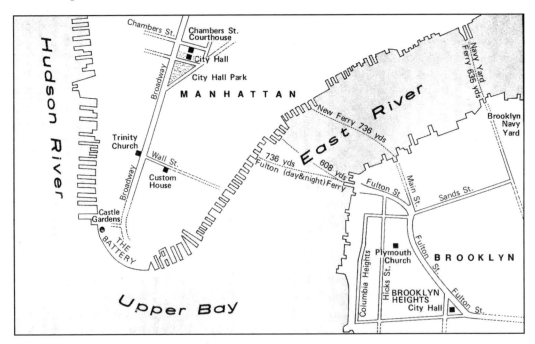

Figure 1-7 Map of Lower Manhattan and Brooklyn. Illustration in original, 26.

Brooklyn attracted those who sought respite from the extraordinary bustle and congestion of Gotham. Walt Whitman, whose office at the Brooklyn *Eagle* overlooked the Fulton Ferry slip, frequently commented on the suburb's phenomenal growth. "There," he said, "men of moderate means may find homes at a moderate rent, whereas in New York City there is no median between a palatial mansion and a dilapidated hovel." Writing often of the river, the fog and the ferries, Whitman captured the commuting character of the place he called "Brooklyn the Beautiful:"

> In the morning there is one incessant stream of people—employed in New York on business—tending toward the ferry. This rush commences soon after six o'clock....It is highly edifying to see the phrenzy exhibited by certain portions of the younger gentlemen, a few rods from the landing, when the bell strikes...they rush forward as if for dear life, and woe to the fat woman or unwieldy person of any kind, who stands in their way....

Whether the attraction was easy access, pleasant surroundings, cheap land, or low taxes, the suburb was growing at a faster rate than the city by 1800, and in almost every decade until the Civil War its population approximately doubled....By 1880... [n]ewspaper advertisements offered a home in the suburbs, no farther from the heart of Manhattan than many tenements, for 10 to 40 percent down and payments spread over three to five years. Developers were not only building elegant structures for the wealthy featuring "clean sea breezes and a glorious view of greater New York and its harbor," but inexpensive dwellings for the middle classes.

Far from seeing the growth of Brooklyn as an advantage, New York newspapers, politicians, and land developers by 1850 brooded over the intense competition and expressed concern over "the desertion of the city by its men of wealth."...

As a result of the continuing exodus and spillover from New York, Brooklyn was gradually transformed from a suburb into a major city in its own right, the fourth largest in the country in the latter part of the nineteenth century. By 1890 it counted more than 261,000 foreign-born residents, equal to its entire population only thirty years earlier. With this increase in size, the decay, noise, and fast lifestyle so many had fled Manhattan to avoid followed them across the river. Even though Brooklyn's initial budding was due to a quiet environment easily accessible to the central business district of the world's busiest seaport, its later growth was the result of the development of its own commerce and industry....

Transportation Innovation and Suburban Growth

Transportation change is not a sufficient explanation for the initial development of the suburban trend. If that were the case then every great city that shared the wealth of the Industrial Revolution and the technology of the horsecar and the railroad would have exhibited a similar residential pattern. To be sure, as Adna Ferrin Weber noted in his exhaustive *The Growth of Cities in the Nineteenth Century*, metropolitan growth on every continent was most rapid on the fringes. In London, a new environment was taking shape in Barnes, Hampstead, Putney, Hammersmith, and St. John's Wood by the end of the eighteenth century, and by the 1840s the vastness of these suburbs was filling visitors with wonder.... As in the United States, the upper classes were the first, and the working classes the last to move into the commuting suburbs....

This pattern was hardly inevitable. The privileged groups in large American and British cities could have retained their convenient domiciles in the core and left the shabby periphery to the poor. This is what happened in Europe, Asia, and South America, where new neighborhoods were typically densely settled and inhabited by the less fortunate, rather than the well-to-do....

For the underlying causes of the increasingly stratified and segregated social geography of great American cities, as well as their relatively low density as compared to Europe, we must look not just to transportation technology and the powerful mechanical forces unleashed by the Industrial Revolution but to the development of new cultural values.

Home, Sweet Home:
The House and the Yard

In 1840 suburbs had not yet developed into a recognizable entity, distinct from either the city or the farm. Peripheral towns were merely lesser versions of small cities. Outlying residents looked upon urban centers as agents of progress and culture....

By 1890, however, only half a century later, the suburban image was quite distinct from that of large cities. No longer mini-metropolises, peripheral communities, like Brookline outside of Boston, followed a different path. Moreover, the expectations about residential space shared by most Americans today had become firmly implanted in middle-class culture. This shift had many dimensions and sprang from many causes, but the suburban ideal of a detached dwelling in a semirural setting was related to an emerging distinction between *Gemeinschaft,* the primary, face-to-face relationships of home and family, and *Gesellschaft,* the impersonal and sometimes hostile outside society. In 1840 only New York and Philadelphia had as many as 125,000 residents, and the factory system was in its infancy. The typical urban worker toiled in an establishment employing fewer than a dozen persons. By 1890 when the Bureau of the Census announced that the Western frontier no longer existed, the United States had become the world's leading industrial nation. In that year the country was already one-third urban and the population of the Northeast was well over one-half urban (defined by the census as communities of 2,500 or more persons). New York was closing on London as the world's largest city, while Chicago and Philadelphia each contained about one million inhabitants. Minneapolis, Denver, Seattle, San Francisco, and Atlanta, which hardly existed in 1840, had become major regional metropolises. Perhaps more important was the rise of heavily layered government bureaucracies and of factories employing hundreds and sometimes thousands of workers. As more people crowded together in public spaces, families sought to protect home life by building private spaces. Conviviality and group interaction, despite the massive growth of fraternal societies in the late nineteenth century, gave

way to new ways of thinking about the family, the house, and the yard, and, ultimately, to new ways of building cities.

Family and Home

In both Christian and Jewish culture, the family has always occupied an exalted station. It represents the chosen instrument of God for the reproduction of the species, the nurturing of the young, and the propagation of moral principles. But as the French social historian Philippe Aries has noted, the family as a tightly knit group of parents and children is a development only of the last two hundred years. Prior to the eighteenth century, the community was more important in determining an individual's fate than was his family....In cities the population was arrayed around production rather than biological units. Each household was a business—a bakery, hotel, livery stable, countinghouse—and apprentices, journeymen, servants, and retainers lived there along with assorted spouses and children. Much of life was inescapably public; privacy hardly existed at all. In every case, the image of the home as the ideal domestic arrangement was missing. Even the word *home* referred to the town or region rather than to a particular dwelling.

In the eighteenth century, however, the zone of private life began to expand, and the family came to be a personal bastion against society, a place of refuge, free from outside control. Aries notes how the arrangement of the house and the development of individual rooms reflected this desire to keep the world at bay and made it possible, in theory at least, for people to eat, sleep, and relax in different spaces. The new social and psychological concept of privacy meant that both families and individuals increased their demand for personal rooms. In the United States, especially in the suburbs, intricate floor plans soon allowed for distinct zones for different activities, with formal social spaces and private sleeping areas.

Although this attitudinal and behavioral shift characterized much of European and Oriental culture, the emerging values of domesticity, privacy, and isolation reached fullest development in the United States, especially in the middle third of the nineteenth century. In part, this was a function of American wealth....

Aside from America's greater wealth, an important cultural dimension to the shift should be noted. In countless sermons and articles, ministers glorified the family even more than their predecessors had done, and they cited its importance as a safeguard against the moral slide of society as a whole into sinfulness and greed. They made extravagant claims about the virtues of domestic life, insisting that the individual could find a degree of fulfillment, serenity, and satisfaction in the house that was possible nowhere else....

Such injunctions took place as industrial and commercial capitalism changed the rhythm of daily life. Between 1820 and 1850, work and men left the home. The growth of manufacturing meant that married couples became more isolated from each other during the working day, with the husband employed away from home, and the wife responsible for everything connected with the residence. The family became isolated and feminized, and this "woman's sphere" came to be regarded as superior to the nondomestic institutions of the world. Young ladies especially were encouraged to nurse extravagant hopes for their personal environment and for the tendering of husband and children. For example, Horace Bushnell's *Christian Nurture,* first published in 1847, described how the home and family life could foster "virtuous habits" and thereby help assure the blessed eternal peace of "home comforts" in heaven....

The single-family dwelling became the paragon of middle-class housing, the most visible symbol of having arrived at a fixed place in society, the goal to which every decent family aspired. It was an investment that many people hoped would provide a ticket to higher status and wealth. "A man is not a whole and complete man," Walt Whitman wrote, "unless he owns a house and the ground it stands on." Or, as *The American Builder* commented in 1869: "It is strange how contentedly men can go on year after year, living like Arabs a tent life, paying exhorbitant rents, with no care or concern for a permanent house." The purchase of one's home became more than a proxy for success; it also conferred moral rectitude....

The Yard

Between 1825 and 1875, middle-class Americans adopted a less utilitarian expectation about residential space. They no longer needed herbs and vegetables from gardens, and, thanks to the mowing machine, a smooth lawn replaced the rough meadow cut by scythe or sheep. The suburban dream demanded an enlargement of open areas. In particular, the ideal house came to be viewed as resting in the middle of a manicured lawn or a picturesque garden. First, rural cemeteries, later parks, and then suburban cottages were advocated for the benefit of "aesthetic and moral nature," as well as physical health....

By 1840, as humankind was removed from the real troubles of nature, an idealized view of the outdoors was emerging. Historians have often focused attention on the new appreciation for grandeur and natural beauty that was fostered by the European romantic movement by the Napoleonic era and by American artists before the Civil War....

Epidemic disease was another powerful impetus for making one's escape from the crowded city. In Europe, from the thirteenth century onward, the dread of plague emptied inner precincts at every rumor of pestilence. In the United States, periodic outbreaks of smallpox, yellow fever, and cholera took a heavy toll in every community, particularly in the warm summer months. Sometimes it seemed as if the very survival of cities might be at stake.... As might be expected, scarcely a single suburban advertisement in the middle decades of the nineteenth century failed to contain the boast that residence among open spaces was more healthy than life in cities....

By 1870 separateness had become essential to the identity of the suburban house. The yard was expected to be large and private and designed for both active and passive recreation, in direct antithesis to the dense lifestyle from which many families had recently moved. The new ideal was no longer to be part of a close community, but to have a self-contained unit, a private wonderland walled off from the rest of the world. Although visually open to the street, the lawn was a barrier—a kind of verdant moat separating the household from the threats and temptations of the city. It served as a means of transition from the public street to the very private house, as a kind of space that, by the very fact of its having no clearly defined function, mediated between the activities of the outside and the activities of the inside. The sweeping lawn helped civilize the wild vista beyond and provided a carpet for new outdoor activities such as croquet (a lawn game imported from England in the 1860s), tennis, and social gatherings. More importantly, lawns provided a presumably ideal place to nurture children....

The Anti-Urban Tradition in American Thought...

Even before the Industrial Revolution transformed many English cities into gloomy slums, London inspired oppressive horror among such major authors as Daniel Defoe, Henry Fielding, Alexander Pope, and William Wordsworth. The very thought of re-creating Old World conditions filled Thomas Jefferson with dread. During an eighteenth-century epidemic of yellow fever, he derived consolation from the thought that it might discourage the growth of future urban centers. "I view large cities," Jefferson wrote in a famous passage, "as pestilential to the morals, the health, and the liberties of man. True, they nourish some of the elegant arts, but the useful ones can thrive elsewhere, and less perfection in the others, with more health, virtue, and freedom, would be my choice."...

In the United States many talented writers testified to the magnetic quality of the American metropolis, and they celebrated the economic growth and material progress that urbanization helped make possible. Pulp fiction, such as Horatio Alger's *Ragged Dick* (1868), depicted the city as the locus of nearly unlimited opportunity, while more talented writers, such as Walt Whitman, valued New York for the stimulation that could be derived from it....

On balance, however, the American metropolis was more a symbol of problems and of evil than of hope, love, or generosity. William Dean Howells, Henry George, Edward Bellamy, and Jacob Riis shocked their nineteenth-century readers with city tales of "hopeless-faced women deformed by hardship" and of "the festering mass of human wretchedness," while American politicians gloried in the frontier tradition and told their audiences that tillers of the soil represented the nation's best hope for the future....

The traditional American distrust of population concentrations was heightened in the nineteenth century, when every decennial census revealed that a larger proportion of the citizenry was rejecting agrarian life for the better opportunities of crowded settlements. Especially troublesome was the notion that size itself seemed to confound every temporary solution to periodic crises. As gains were made in public health, fire prevention, water supply, and sanitation, more severe emergencies rose to take their place....

Almost worse than pestilence was immoral behavior, which shifted from an earlier association with the frontier and the wild West to a clear urban emphasis. Irresolute, unsupervised, and alcoholic men and women too often gave in to wicked temptations....

The changing ethnic composition of the urban population also increased middle-class antipathy to the older neighborhoods, as Poles, Italians, Russians, and assorted eastern and southern Europeans, most of them Jews or Catholics, poured into the industrialized areas after 1880.... To this fear were added specific programs to tax property so as to create public improvements and jobs to benefit working-class voters. The observation of Lord Bryce that municipal government was "the one conspicuous failure of the United States" was often quoted. The import of such projections was not lost on middle-class families, who often took the opportunity that low price and good transportation afforded to move beyond city jurisdictions....

Although there were many critics of the isolated household, after the Civil War the detached house and the sizeable yard became the symbols of a very distinct type of community—the embodiment of the suburban ideal. The solid and spacious houses that lined the tree-arched avenues and fronted the winding lanes of dozens of suburbs exuded success and security. They seemed immune to the dislocations of an industrializing society and cut off from the toil and turbulence of emerging immigrant ghettoes. Pitched roofs, tended lawns, shuttered windows, and separate rooms all spoke of communities that valued the tradition of the family, to the pride of ownership, and the fondness for the rural life....

Such residences were attainable only by the middle and upper classes. For most Americans life consisted of unrelenting labor either on farms or in factories, and slight relaxation in decrepit lodgings. But the image had a growing attraction in a society in which urbanization's underside—the slums, the epidemics, the crime, the anomie—was so obvious and persistent a problem. The suburban ideal offered the promise of an environment visibly responsive to personal effort, an environment that would combine the best of both city and rural life and that would provide a permanent home for a restless people.

ESSAY 1-2. ROBERT FISHMAN, *BOURGEOIS UTOPIAS: THE RISE AND FALL OF SUBURBIA* (1987)

Source: *Bourgeois Utopias* by Robert Fishman. Copyright © 1987 by Basic Books, Inc. Reprinted by permission of Basic Books, a member of Perseus Books, L.L.C.

London: Birthplace of Suburbia

Like written constitutions, the novel, steam engines, and so many other innovations that have reshaped our lives, the middle-class residential suburb was a product of the eighteenth century. Its form and function reflect many of the most pervasive cultural elements in eighteenth century civilization, but the suburb also reflects the specific conditions of the city in which it was born. Perhaps inevitably, London was the site of this innovation in urban form: for London was the first of H. G. Wells's "whirlpool cities."

London had become the largest city in Europe by the end of the seventeenth century, and its predominance over its great continental rivals—Paris, Naples, and Amsterdam—increased markedly during the eighteenth century. While, for example, Paris reached 500,000 people by 1700 but hardly grew in the next hundred years, London went from 575,000 in 1700 to 675,000 in 1750 and reached 960,000 by 1800. Indeed, London's population exceeded 1.1 million in 1800, if one counts the whole metropolitan area now known to demographers as "greater London."

Perhaps even more impressive than these figures were the economic and political supremacies that made them possible. For London was the focus of a worldwide network of oceangoing trade routes, which made the city the international center of long-distance trade and banking. It was also the political capital of the British Empire and its center for the production and consumption of luxury goods. With this combination of functions (along with a prosperous hinterland that kept the city well supplied with food and fuel), London became the first modern city to overcome the barriers to growth that had kept the medieval and early modern cities in check.

The modern suburb was a direct result of this unprecedented urban growth. It grew out of a crisis in urban form that stemmed from the inability of the premodern city to cope with explosive modern urban expansion. It also reflected the unprecedented growth in the wealth and size of an upper-middle-class merchant elite. This London bourgeoisie had attained the critical mass in numbers, resources, and confidence to transform the cities of their time to suit their values....

The central principle of [London's] premodern ecology was that the wealthiest members of the community lived and worked closest to the historic core, while the poorest people were pushed to the periphery. Indeed, the word "suburb"...referred exclusively to these peripheral slums, which surrounded all large towns. These suburban poor lacked the means to expand their shantylike "suburbs" into the surrounding countryside. So London was like an increasingly overpacked container, continually bulging but never able to expand efficiently....

London thrived as a center of trade: in other words, as a center of information. Its leading merchants depended on rapid knowledge of markets throughout the world, a knowledge that was available to them only through a multitude of face-to-face contacts. The concentration of England's leading merchants in the few intensely crowded acres at the heart of the City (and just blocks from the port) was a highly efficient mechanism for promoting this exchange of information.

Thus, for the elite, crowding was productive. But it meant that not only their working lives but also their family lives were spent in the most congested part of the kingdom. As late as the middle of the eighteenth century, it was taken for granted that "home" and "work" were virtually inseparable. Even the wealthiest bankers conducted their business from their homes; great merchants lived, in effect, above the shop, with goods stored in their cellars and apprentices living in the attics. This identity of home and work was the basic building block of eighteenth century urban ecology....

I should emphasize here that even the relatively wealthy core areas were never upper-class neighborhoods in the modern sense. Just as the idea of a district devoted to a single function—a residential district or a business district—was foreign to the premodern city, so too was a single-class district....By the mid eighteenth century the city was clearly approaching an ecological crisis. The few examples of improvements—such as the filling in of the Fleet Ditch, a stream that had become a noisome sewer—could hardly keep pace with the difficulties. The streets, for example, were drained only by a "kennel" or ditch running down the middle, which was usually filled with rubbish and worse....

Thus the economics of the great city were attracting an increasingly wealthy elite to an urban core that was, at best, crowded, dirty, noisy, and unhealthy. In other centuries these conditions might have been tolerated even by the elite. The eighteenth century, however, was an "age of improvement" in which leaders were constantly seeking a better order for life, whether in government, manufactur-

ing, or cities. In retrospect we can see that there were two alternative models for this improvement. The first was for the elite to take possession of an area at or close to the core and rebuild it according to the most elegant eighteenth century models. The second was the far more radical decentralization of bourgeois residence that we have come to call suburbanization.

So deeply held were the traditional ideas of urban form—most notably, the identification of the elite with the urban core—that for most of the eighteenth century only the reconstruction of the core seemed possible and likely....

It is in this context that we can understand the true originality of the suburban idea: for the modern suburb involved discarding the old preference for center over periphery; radically disassociating home and work environments; creating neighborhoods based both on the idea of a single class and on that of a single (domestic) function; and, finally, creating a new kind of landscape in which the clear line...between city and country becomes thoroughly blurred in an environment that combines the two.

All these transformations were involved when, in the mid eighteenth century, the London merchant elite began to convert their combined homes and offices at the core into offices only; and then to move with their families not to adjacent urban squares but as much as five miles outside the city to spacious villas in the quiet agricultural settlements that ringed London. As we can now appreciate, this flight from the city was in fact a new and highly potent form of urban expansion.

The merchant elite leaped over the belt of poverty that had constrained the metropolis and used their wealth to establish a new kind of rapidly expanding urban periphery, which we now call suburbia. They realized that, with their private carriages and ample funds, they were no longer limited to the area traditionally considered the city. On the relatively inexpensive land still a surprisingly short commute to the core, they could build a world of privilege, leisure, and family life that reflected their values....

[T]his radical rethinking of the meaning of

the city and of domesticity was not the work of a single architect of genius, who proposed a new model and then convinced his clients of its worth. Rather, suburbia was a collective creation of the city's bourgeois elite, a gradual adoption of a new way of living by a class that had the wealth and confidence to remake the world to suit its values.

It was, indeed, this class that was transforming society in so many other ways as it reshaped the world to fulfill its needs. Suburbia was only one characteristic bourgeois invention, but one that has had a remarkable influence on the modern world. To understand suburbia—both in its earliest eighteenth century form and in its twentieth century incarnations—we must now look closely at the class that created it.

The London Bourgeoisie and Their City

Every true suburb is the outcome of two opposing forces, an attraction toward the opportunities of the great city and a simultaneous repulsion against urban life. This conflict, now deeply embedded in suburban design, first arose out of the tensions in the eighteenth century London bourgeoisie's feelings toward their metropolis. Every year made the city more important economically, yet, in the course of the eighteenth century, the very bourgeoisie who profited most from London's centralization came to hate and fear the social consequences of city life.

Suburbia can never be understood solely in its own terms. It must always be defined in relation to its rejected opposite: the metropolis. If the eighteenth century creators of suburbia bequeathed to their successors their positive ideal of a family life in union with nature, they also passed on their deepest fears of living in an inhumane and immoral metropolis. Buried deep within every subsequent suburban dream is a nightmare image of eighteenth century London.

But before elaborating this bourgeois critique of the city, we must first define the London "bourgeoisie" itself. I use the term to designate those most prosperous members of the middle class whose businesses and capital accumulation—at least £25,000 to more than £100,000—gave them an income comparable to the rural squirearchy and even to some of the aristocracy, yet who maintained the living and working habits of the urban middle class....

[A] member of the London bourgeoisie was characteristically a merchant engaged in overseas trade and the financial operations that accompanied it. Sugar from the West Indies, tea from China, spices from India, furs from North America, naval stores from Russia and the Baltic—these were among the immensely profitable items that filled bourgeois storehouses. A relatively small circle of entrepreneurs controlled the vast revenues that derived ultimately from Britain's naval and colonial supremacies....

If a seemingly inevitable logic drew merchants' premises as close as possible to the center, an equally compelling logic associated the family with the workplace. Even for the wealthy elite of merchants and bankers, the family was not simply (or perhaps even primarily) an emotional unit. It was at least equally an economic unit. The merchant's capital was essentially a family resource; his work force was his family—including his wife and older children—as well as apprentices who lived in the house and were treated like children. Virtually every aspect of family life was permeated by the requirements of the business.

This interpenetration is most clearly visible in the active role played by women in London commercial life. A wife's daily assistance in the shop was vital for smaller businesses, and even the most opulent merchants were careful to give their wives a role sufficiently prominent that they could participate in and understand the source of their income....

The typical merchant's townhouse, therefore, was surprisingly open to the city. Commercial life flowed in freely, so that virtually every room had some business as well as familial function. From the front parlor where customers were entertained and deals transacted, to the upper stories where the apprentices slept and the basement where goods were stored, there was little purely domestic space. As apprentices, teenage boys were inevitably drawn into this system, either within their own homes or as part of another family; at the same time, teenage girls were taught the necessary skills for playing their part in their future husband's business....

Nevertheless, the mid eighteenth century saw a crucial change in bourgeois attitudes toward the city that led directly to suburbanization. This growing repulsion was not, I think, the inexorable result of any drastic social change in the city itself. Despite the population growth and resulting overcrowding, London remained a city of commerce and small workshops. The Industrial Revolution, just beginning in the north of England, essentially bypassed London until the middle of the nineteenth century. Crime was serious, but there is no evidence that it was increasing dramatically; the lighting of streets at night had somewhat increased safety. Transportation within and outside the city remained restricted to stage coaches and private carriages traveling on still primitive roads....

The crucial changes occurred instead within bourgeois culture, within that complex of attitudes which defined the meaning of the city. The most important of them concerned the family; but I would also point to a subtle yet pervasive shift in the relation of the middle class to the rest of the city population. Anyone looking at eighteenth century life must be struck by what Ian Watt has called "the combination of physical proximity and vast social distance." English society was still something of a caste society in the sense that social distance was so marked that the privileged felt no need to protect themselves further from the poor by physical distance. That the richest bankers in London lived literally surrounded by poor families did not in the least diminish the bankers' status. One might even say that in a caste society the rich need the constant and close presence of the poor to remind them of their privileges.

In the course of the eighteenth century, this attitude slowly began to move closer to the nineteenth century idea that social distinctions require physical segregation. Part of the change was no doubt due to differing personal habits of the rich and poor, especially over personal cleanliness, that great divide of disgust which would culminate in the Victorian adage George Orwell reports hearing when he was young: "The lower classes smell."...

In any case, it is one of the paradoxes of urban history that the extremely unequal cities of the eighteenth century tolerated a great measure of close physical contact between rich and poor; whereas the more "equal" cities of the nineteenth and twentieth centuries were increasingly zoned to eliminate such contacts. For our purposes, the newly felt need for social segregation made the crowded, intensely mixed neighborhoods of the urban core appear all the more unpleasant and threatening to the bourgeoisie. Social segregation destroyed many of the most prized sites of eighteenth century urban social life: the pleasure gardens lost patronage largely because the respectable no longer wished to mix with "low" company. And the desire for segregation fueled that search for single-class neighborhoods securely protected from the poor which was to become a powerful motive in the spread of suburbia.

Even more fundamental was the profound change in the bourgeois family, which began as early as the last quarter of the seventeenth century and fully emerged in the mid eighteenth century. Lawrence Stone, in his important book *The Family, Sex and Marriage in England, 1500–1800*, has called this new bourgeois form "the closed domesticated nuclear family." He refers essentially to the emergence of the family as the primary and overwhelming emotional focus of its members' lives. For Stone, this "modern" family is not a natural biological unit that has remained constant through history but the product of a long historical evolution....

The importance of this new kind of family for this book is that the essential principles of the closed family contradicted the basic principles of the eighteenth century city. Just as the traditional urban ecology was unable to cope with the demands of modern growth, so the traditional urban form and domestic architecture were contrary to the needs of the new family. As we have seen, even the most opulent merchant's house was essentially open to the city; it provided little or no privacy for the emergence of a closed sphere of emotional intimacy. Further, the constant presence of urban amusements drew the family away from its domesticated attachments and into the older, wider networks of urban amusements.

This contradiction between the city and the new family was further sharpened by a religious movement that took hold with special strength among the upper middle class of London: the Evangelical movement. It first arose in the early eighteenth century as a response within the Anglican church to John Wesley's renewed emphasis on personal salvation. By the second half of the eighteenth century, however, the emphasis of its leaders had shifted to promoting a new ideal of conduct that emphasized the role of the family. One might call the Evangelicals the ideologists of the closed, domesticated nuclear family....

The Evangelicals were the most influential group in creating that complex of attitudes which we now call Victorianism, but which in fact originated in the late eighteenth century. Members of the Established church but uncertain of its efficacy, the Evangelicals taught that the most secure path to salvation was the beneficent influence of a truly Christian family. Anything that strengthened the emotional ties within the family was therefore holy; anything that weakened the family and its ability to foster true morality was anathema.

Chief among the enemies of the family was the city, with its social opportunities. Wilberforce's "reformation of manners" was essentially a broad attack on all forms of urban pleasures....The Evangelical movement went on to attack street fairs, taverns, ballrooms, pleasure gardens—the whole range of urban amusements, even the lottery. Whatever they could not close down entirely they attempted to prohibit on Sunday.

Perhaps the most significant aspect of Evangelical ideology was the attitude toward women. On the one hand, they gave to women the highest possible role in their system of values: the principal guardian of the Christian home. On the other, they fanatically opposed any role for women outside that sphere....

This contradiction between the city and the Evangelical ideal of the family provided the final impetus for the unprecedented separation of the citizen's home from the city that is the essence of the suburban idea. The city was not just crowded, dirty, and unhealthy; it was immoral. Salvation itself depended on separating the woman's sacred world of family and children from the profane metropolis. Yet this separation could not jeopardize a man's constant attendance at his business—for hard work and success were also Evangelical virtues—and business life required rapid personal access to that great beehive of information which was London. This was the problem, and suburbia was to be the ultimate solution.

Clapham, a Proper Paradise

In order to show more clearly the emergence of a true suburbia from the weekend houses of the London bourgeoisie, I will concentrate now on a single locale, the village of Clapham in Surrey, south of the Thames. Only five miles by a relatively good road to London Bridge and the City, it was nevertheless still open country in the mid eighteenth century, with one of the few commons left in the countryside near London and fine prospects of the Thames and the metropolis from nearby hills. It was near Clapham that Daniel Defoe stood in 1724 to get his sight of the metropolis, and even then he noted the presence of numerous opulent merchants' villas all around him.

If Clapham was typical of the former agricultural villages that became the favored sites of middle class estates in the eighteenth century, it also had one notable feature that recommends it to our attention. It became the favored home of the most prosperous and most prominent leaders of the Evangelical movement; not only William Wilberforce but so many of his closest colleagues made their home here that the movement was often known as the "Clapham Sect." In Clapham we can follow the influence of Evangelical domestic ideology on the new domestic suburban architecture as it was actually built and lived in by these bourgeois "saints" of the movement. Both in its design and in its ideology, this modest village was to have a profound influence on the Anglo-American middle class.

The connection between Clapham and the Evangelicals arose from a large estate that the Thornton family purchased overlooking Clapham Common in 1735. The Thorntons exemplified that "big bourgeoisie" which would champion both the Evangelical movement and suburbia. Bankers and merchants in the trade with Russia, with close family connections to the textile merchants of Yorkshire, they were also known for their philanthropy. John Thornton (1720–90) was not only a director of the Bank of England but the patron of the favorite Evangelical poet, William Cowper. John's son Henry Thornton (1760–1815), one of the wealthiest bankers in London, was also one of the most religious. When in the 1790s he settled into his own mansion, Battersea Rise, at Clapham, he built next door a substantial house for his close friend, colleague in Parliament, and fellow Evangelical, William Wilberforce....

The presence of these prominent leaders attracted lesser known but equally pious and prosperous London merchants to Clapham. A map of 1800 depicts seventy-two "gentlemen's seats" around the common, all with substantial houses on grounds of at least ten acres....

Because these merchants clearly retained their City townhouses (or similar premises) for business purposes after they had settled in Clapham, it is difficult to establish the exact moment they made their country residence their true abode on weekdays and weekends, and used the City establishment only as an office. Nevertheless, the evidence from letters, diaries, and other sources clearly indicates that as early as the 1790s Clapham had become a true suburb in my sense. Families settled there throughout the week, the men maintaining that all-important direct tie to London by commuting each working day by private carriage. A new style of life had been established.

As the Clapham Evangelicals such as Wilberforce, [Hannah] More, and their colleagues were the very moralists who were loudest in their condemnation of the city and its vices, there can be little doubt that this final break with the merchant's traditional residence in the urban core was motivated by their rejection of the urban social mores, especially as they applied to women. A location like Clapham gave them the ability to take the family out of London without taking leave of the family business. Equally importantly, it provided a whole community of people who shared their values. Unlike the City of London, this community did not have to be shared with the urban poor; neither was its design restricted by urban crowding or by the high price of urban land. Around

Figure 1-8 This anonymous watercolor in the Guildhall Library depicts Clapham Common circa 1800 with its suburban landscape of large detached villas on lawns sloping down to the Common. Courtesy of Guildhall Library, Corporation of London. Illustration in original.

Clapham Common the Evangelicals could create their serious-minded paradise.

The design of this prototypical suburban community might be described as the union of the country house, the villa, and the picturesque traditions, reinforced by the particular concerns of the Evangelical movement. The Evangelicals never tired of repeating that, if all urban social life must be rejected, the truly godly recreations were family life and direct contact with nature....

Contemporary drawings show wide tree shaded lawns sweeping up from the common to Palladian houses behind which large gardens and orchards were planted. Each house added its own well maintained greenery to the whole. What emerged was a collective environment extending not only to the common but to the villa grounds as well. The Evangelical village became an all encompassing park, an Edenic garden that surrounded the houses and made sweet the life of the families within them.

In the traditional country house or villa, the grounds related only to the centrally located house of the owner, who gazed out at his personal prospect. The true suburban landscape, as seen at Clapham, is a balance of the public and the private. Each property is private, but each contributes to the total landscape of *houses in a park*.

ESSAY 1-3. JOHN ARCHER, "COLONIAL SUBURBS IN SOUTH ASIA, 1700–1850, AND THE SPACES OF MODERNITY" (1997)

Source: *Visions of Suburbia*, ed. Roger Silverstone (London: Routledge, 1997).

Spaces and Practices

Suburbs and colonies, like other forms of human production, are instruments conceived to advance certain interests. Ordinarily the beneficiaries are the builders and people who may live or work there, though in many cases spaces are articulated just as intentionally to limit the interests of others. In any event, spaces of any sort that people occupy are more than mere containers or settings for human activity. The specific configuration of any space actually plays a crucial role in the formation and sustenance of the consciousness of all those who exist there. Likewise space is integral to the delineation and facilitation of the whole spectrum of relations among individuals, institutions, and social fractions (classes, castes, genders, races, etc.). Indeed the very terms and dimensions of human praxis—economic, political, moral, religious, artistic, etc.—are embedded in, and sustained by, the configuration of surrounding spaces.

In light of such considerations, the study of colonial spaces is particularly complex— and particularly rewarding—since colonial space simultaneously sustains not only two or more distinct cultures, but also the complex array of boundaries, relations, and negotiations among them. Embedded in this array are such processes as differentiation, amalgamation, segregation, domination, exploitation, and resistance. And of particular interest in the case of colonial suburbs, of new positionalities outside the canons of either culture—for example, the legitimation of practices outside the limits ordinarily imposed by caste or by class. The particular ways in which spaces are configured, then, are instrumental not only in the constitution, but also in the ongoing transformation of social structures and human practices.

Colonies and Suburbs

Colonies and suburbs (in the sense of a locale outside the settlement proper) have existed almost since the beginning of organized settlement. For much of this time colonies and suburbs were sites of exile and alienation. Both were politically and economically dependent on the metropole. And both served the same dual functions: they were places from which to import goods that could not be produced or finished within the settlement proper, and they were places to which the unwanted could be exported (criminals, heathens, pollution). Toward the end of the seventeenth century, however, the expansion of European mercantile economies and the corresponding expansion of European bourgeoisies occasioned the refinement both of colonial settlements and of suburbs into more sophisticated and purposeful instruments for the realization of specific societal practices and relations.

Suburbs in particular, instead of being unregulated sites for practices the cities found impermissible, slowly were transformed into highly desirable, detached, clearly circumscribed, exclusively residential (and generally bourgeois) enclaves. Central to this transformation was a fundamental change in the character of the relation between suburbs and cities from *hierarchical* to *contrapositional*. The positionalities of city and suburb no longer were tied to each other by simple relations of hierarchy (e.g. one locale being intrinsically superior to the other). Rather, those positionalities came to be predicated on an array of binary oppositions (e.g. commerce/domesticity, res publica/family) which gave to each locale an integrity in part defined by negation of—not subordination to—the other....

Throughout the eighteenth century and into the nineteenth, the further transformation of suburbs and colonial cities—and suburbs *of* colonial cities—served to articulate key dimensions in which European cultures were evolving: social differentiation, economic extraction and consumption, the political redefinition of property and of possessive individualism, and the aesthetic articulation of the self. All of these dimensions are evident in the suburban growth of three colonial cities to be discussed below, Batavia, Madras, and Calcutta. [Ed. note: Batavia would become Jakarta, Indonesia; Madras, now known as Chennai, and Calcutta are both located in India]....

Madras

A full history of modern Anglo-American suburbia has yet to be written, particularly with respect to its articulation of specific new modes of architectural and spatial organization that helped to define and advance emerging forms of bourgeois consciousness. The suburbanization of Madras constitutes a chapter in that history; but the story begins early in the eighteenth century with a concentration of houses in the Thames Valley, west of London in the general vicinity of Richmond. A good number were of diminutive size compared to other 'retreats' in the vicinity, a quality emphasized by introduction of the term 'villa' to describe them. But the most distinctive characteristic of these dwellings was that they were architecturally suited for little other than leisure pursuits. They were sited on parcels of land too small for the production of significant revenue through any form of husbandry, and in most cases the grounds were landscaped in a manifestly uneconomic manner according to the aesthetic conventions of the period. Located at a sufficient distance from London that the proprietors could feel wholly disconnected from the city—though necessarily they remained politically and economically quite connected—they were close enough to London that one could commute back and forth on a weekly, weekend, or even daily basis. The genesis of this and subsequent clusters of comparable dwellings cannot be explained simply as a matter of changing 'taste', or of geographic dispersion based on factors such as economics and transportation. Rather, it also is a matter of critical changes in English modes of consciousness at the beginning of the eighteenth century: consciousness that began to anchor identity primarily in the autonomous *self* rather than in a social hierarchy or collective. The suburban villa was instrumental in the construction of this consciousness: it did so, in part, by spatially differentiating private from public, by establishing the suburban plot as a site for cultivation of the self (e.g. through leisure pursuits) instead of commerce and politics.

Much the same predilection for enclaves of detached villas actually occurred simultaneously, or perhaps even earlier, in Madras. Occupied by the British since 1639, Madras quickly became the principal centre of East India Company activity in India. Though by no means the equal of Batavia, let alone London, it boasted a highly concentrated European trading centre at Fort St George, as well as adjacent quarters and villages in which indigenous populations lived and worked. And no less than in Batavia, the economic and political basis of Madras was narrowly mercantile: institutions, regulations, buildings, and personnel all were deployed for the purposes of trade and extraction. And yet the British mode of mercantile extraction differed from its Continental competitors: the British sought to be engaged as little as possible in designing or regulating the physical, financial, or political structure of their colonial settlements. Especially in the seventeenth and early eighteenth centuries they preferred, to the extent feasible, to adapt existing financial, mercantile, juridical, and physical structures to supply their needs.

These conditions help us understand the early appearance of suburban enclaves in the vicinity of Madras. A concentrated mercantile settlement such as the East India Company established within the limited confines of Fort St George did not provide very well for the differentiation of civic or social activities—let alone individual identities—from the narrow purposes of the Company. Certain locales for leisure activity did flourish adjacent to the Fort, within the city proper, and several are visible on the map prepared by Thomas Pitt about 1710. Most notable were the 'Company's Gardens' and an array of private 'gardens', many of which were laid out in formal avenues and parterres, and surrounded substantial residences....Still, as the basic character of the area was Indian, the few European gardens on the perimeter were hardly able to constitute a distinct, discrete suburban locale.

But another site, with precisely those qualities, was described by Captain Alexander Hamilton, who visited Madras as early as 1707. The place he visited, some eight miles south-west of the city at the foot of St Thomas's Mount, had become a popular site for erecting 'Summer-houses where Ladies and Gentlemen retire to in the Summer, to recreate themselves, when the Business of the Town is over, and to be out of the Noise of Spungers and impertinent Visitants, whom this City is often molested with'. This site, contemporary with comparable enclaves in the Thames Valley, was configured for much the same purposes: to afford people whose business was in the city proper the opportunity to 'retire' or escape from the city's 'Business' and 'Noise' for a week, a weekend, or possibly even an afternoon or an evening.

Here they could go about the business of 'recreating'—restoring, enlivening, gratifying—themselves in an explicitly antiurban, leisured setting.

By the 1740s European 'garden houses' had proliferated around Madras, but according to an increasingly dispersed pattern. Unlike the garden houses in Peddunaickenpetta and other parts of the city proper that were cheek by jowl with Indian properties, and unlike the isolated aggregation of garden houses at St Thomas's Mount, newer garden houses were scattered comparatively loosely within an arc of unsettled territory one to two miles south-west of the city, pointedly avoiding established Indian residential, commercial, and religious centres in the vicinity. Near Triplicane, about two miles south of the fort, a survey located some 67 garden houses as early as 1727. The Choultry Plain, about two miles west-south-west of the fort, soon became the most popular locale for country residences. Some of these are shown on a sketchy map of Madras made in 1746 by a French military officer, Captain Paradis (see Figure 1-9). Although the map is inaccurate in many respects, it renders very effectively the mapmaker's impression of a city ringed by partly inhabited terrain, substantial portions of which have been taken over by the enclosed garden-house tracts of private individuals—private domains closed off not only from the city beyond, but also from their neighbours, indigenous settlements, major roads, and their immediate surroundings (rendered here inaccurately, but tellingly, as empty land). Following the 1748 cessation of hostilities with France, which meant that Europeans could live outside the fort in comparative safety, maps show an explosion of garden houses across the Choultry Plain, along the road to St Thomas's Mount, and then even further inland in areas due west of the Fort.

Yet by 1759 it had become official policy to discourage residential building on the Choultry Plain: the stated rationale was couched in terms of personal morality: private garden estates served 'merely to gratify the Vanity and Folly of Merchants in having the Parade of Country Houses and Gardens'. But a more trenchant concern was the manner in which

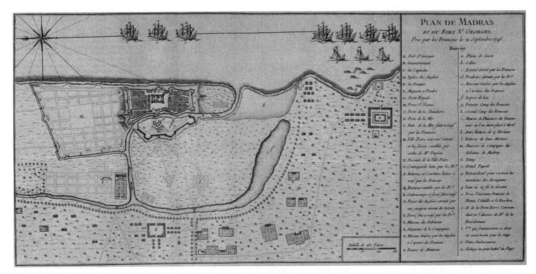

Figure 1-9 'Plan de Madras,' 1746, after Paradis. Henry Davidson Love, *Vestiges of Old Madras, 1640–1800* (London: John Murray, Ltd., 1913), 356 facing plate. Illustration in original, 43.

such a 'Parade' diminished the 'Distinctions which belong only to our Governour and the principal persons of Madras'. By 1769, official rhetoric had escalated: in summarily rejecting the application of a low-level 'Writer' on the Company's staff for a grant of land on which to build, the government based its decision on the grounds that privatization of space not only abetted moral corruption, but also diminished productivity and threatened the public order:

> the general Argument, which has been used very plausibly, Viz. That Cultivation and improvement tend to the publick Benefit, appears in the present Case to be liable to great exception....In the Grants made to Europeans, the Improvements are chiefly ornamental, such as Buildings and Gardens of Pleasure, which tend to the Encouragement of Idleness, Expence and Dissipation, the Consequences of which, in a Colony constituted as this is, are but too obvious.

In other words the uppermost rank of Company officials, for whom isolated country estates had long served as instruments of rank and distinction, sought to bracket and condemn as morally corrupt the class of bourgeois traders who now were locating here as well, because the proliferation of new houses cheapened and eroded that distinction.

And indeed some Company personnel may have construed this colonization of the city's peripheral space as an even more radical act. For the Choultry Plain and Mount Road areas, where large numbers of garden houses were concentrated, afforded the nouveaux riches more than the simple opportunity to emulate elite privilege. Rather, these were locales where their bourgeois, mercantile identity—both individually and as a class—could be realized. Distanced from the fort, adjacent to no commercial or administrative centre, and occupied by a homogeneous class of professional and mercantile residents who pursued much the same interests and activities as each other, these areas became prime locales for the articulation of personal identity as independent of the Company and its interests—precisely the sort of 'Vanity and Folly' the Company sought to condemn. This was more than a threat to the status of a few high-ranking Company officials. It amounted to the creation of an instrument by which Europeans (and, increasingly Indians) could anchor and legitimate their economic and political interests as private entrepreneurs *apart* and *distinct* from the interests of the Company, which remained confined to the Fort.

Less than two decades later the transformation of Madras into a suburban society was undeniable. Louis de Grandpré, visiting

Figure 1-10 J. D. White House (1810), Madras. Even in its modern decay, this early nineteenth-century garden house suggests the era's emerging spatial distinctions between individual pleasure grounds and the social hierarchy and commercial imperatives of colonial Fort St. George. Courtesy of John Archer, 1988.

in 1789, indicated that the White Town had been reduced to a business and administrative quarter, deserted at night by a commuting population that resided in the suburbs.

Estimates of the number of garden houses in the Choultry Plain ranged upwards of two hundred as early as 1780. By the early nineteenth century, over four hundred could be

Figure 1-11 Madras' nineteenth-century garden houses, such as this one, allowed colonial merchants to cultivate status and an autonomous sense of the self. Courtesy of John Archer, 1988.

counted in a broad swath south and west of the fort....

[I]n all of these enclaves, residents continued to emphasize the spatial construction of personal privacy. Visiting in 1804, Lord Valentia remarked on the consistency with which individuals screened out awareness of each other. Unlike Calcutta, he said, Madras has

> no European town, except a few houses, which are chiefly used as warehouses in the fort. The gentlemen of the settlement live entirely in their garden-houses, as they very properly call them; for these are all surrounded by gardens, so closely planted, that the neighbouring house is rarely visible. Choultry-plain...is now covered by these peaceful habitations, which have changed a barren sand into a beautiful scene of vegetation....

[G]arden compounds screened themselves from nearby settlements, and even were served by a largely separate road network. Thus suburbs and indigenous settlements existed in separate social and spatial systems. In part this can be understood on the basis of economics: purchasing uninhabited land is cheaper than taking over existing settlements. In part it can be understood as ethnic or even class prejudice. But also it needs to be understood in terms of the desire to configure space to sustain retreat, 'retirement', recreation, leisure, and other conditions necessary to the constitution of the private self. Thus the importance of screening out both indigenous settlements and European neighbours: creating a road system on which indigenous commerce would have little occasion to travel correspondingly sustains the apparent setting of private, Arcadian leisure.

NOTES

1. John Stilgoe, *Borderlands: Origins of the American Suburb, 1820-1939* (New Haven: Yale University Press, 1988).

CHAPTER 2

Family and Gender in the Making of Suburbia

INTRODUCTION

By the nineteenth century, new ideas about family life and gender provided a potent social context for the suburban trend. These ideas took hold especially among the white middle class, for whom the visible acceptance of these ideals became a badge of middle-class respectability and identity. Suburbia played an important part in this process, representing the spatial form of this evolving set of social relations. In essence, the emergent family ideal found its perfect location and spatial expression in the suburbs.

What was the new family ideal? Among the white middle and upper classes, families evolved from an outward institution that served community functions such as training apprentices and caring for the destitute, to a more inward focus on privacy, affection, and the nuclear family. As the workplace moved out of the household, families also shed their earlier function as an economic unit—a site of production in many cases—to become a more purely domestic entity. At the same time, gender roles took on wholly new meanings in ways that promoted this new family purpose. This transformation happened in two stages. First, women's and men's "spheres" separated. Men came to inhabit the world of work, while women became managers of the home. Some of the most important proponents of this separation were women, who endowed women's roles with deep moral and political significance. They would be the keepers of Christian and republican virtue, and it became their responsibility to instill these values in husbands and children. This new gender ideology became known as the "cult of domesticity." The detached single-family home in the suburbs came to be perceived as an optimal setting for women to nurture this virtuous family. Insulated from neighbors, purified by the "natural" environment, and separated from the supposed immorality of the city, suburban homes represented a sacred space in which morality and family privacy could flourish. While some middle-class suburban families continued to include elderly parents, grown children, and other extended family members, the trend toward nuclear family life was dominant. More important, suburban ideology and imagery promoted nuclear families as the normative household arrangement, the goal toward which everyone should strive.

By the turn of the century, a second transformation occurred among middle-class families, especially in suburban areas. Men reentered the domestic sphere, finding a new place in the workings of the home and family. The trend reflected the emergence of companionate marriage, which emphasized egalitarianism between husband and wife rather than patriarchal rule; family togetherness based on affection became the new paradigm. Among middle- and upper-class suburbanites, the notion of "separate spheres" thus began breaking down as men and women shared the sphere of the home. One sign was a new preoccupation with the house itself and with its smooth and efficient operation. Husbands and wives spent more and more leisure time on little fix-it jobs around the house, a kind of nineteenth-century precursor to the Home Depot mentality. On a broader level, this trend toward domesticity reflected a cultural shift from public to private life. Suburbia—as the ultimate locus of domesticity and privatism—was an integral part of this process. Indeed, the nation's move from city to suburb paralleled its move from a public to a private orientation.

Ironically, the maintenance of this idealized nuclear family and landscape often relied on the paid labor of domestic servants—most of whom were women of color or immigrants, often with children of their own. This fact reminds us that this particular suburban family ideal was highly class specific, aimed at middle- and upper-class Americans who possessed the means to afford this lifestyle. Yet it was not the sole model for suburban family life, as later chapters will show. Americans of different classes and cultural backgrounds would offer up their own suburban family ideals, at times in vivid contrast to this model. Still, the middle-class suburban family paradigm carried great weight into the twentieth century, and indeed became the standard by which many would define "the American dream" itself.

DOCUMENTS

In **Document 2-1**, Catharine Beecher offers a powerful justification for women's new roles as guardians and teachers of Christian virtue in the home. Beecher came from a famous family—including sister Harriet Beecher Stowe, author of *Uncle Tom's Cabin*, and father Lyman Beecher, an influential minister—that successfully spread the gospel of "the cult of domesticity." In this 1865 article, Beecher describes not only what women must do, but why they must do it, and more importantly, why they should be respected for it. The document also offers rich insights on mid-nineteenth century America: its keen consciousness about class and ethnic differences; its assertion that democratic and religious principles underlay the American republic; a respect for the work ethic; and the Civil War's devastating impact on families. The new family ideal, Beecher's article suggests, emerged out of a politically and ideologically charged period in American history. **Document 2-2** depicts how the ideal Christian home might look. This image appeared in *The American Woman's Home* (1869), by Catharine Beecher and Harriet Beecher Stowe, a classic work that spread the ideals of domesticity to a mass readership in nineteenth-century America. Although the Beecher sisters believed that such a home might be made in the city, they envisioned the ideal site in "the country or in such suburban vicinities as give space of ground for healthful outdoor occupation in the family service."

Document 2-3 shows another design for a suburban "cottage" in the Victorian style. Taken from *Palliser's New Cottage Homes*, a popular house pattern book of the 1880s, this design suggests the wealth and spaciousness of the upper-middle-class suburban home. Note, too, the planning for a "servant's room" and the architectural division between spaces of work and family life, both of which were common features in middle- and upper-class homes of the period. Despite the call for women to run their own homes—and to find fulfillment in doing so—many suburban families depended on domestic servants to help maintain the household.

Document 2-4 explains why the suburbs offered a superior setting for raising children. Typical of material published in the home and garden magazines of the day, the article, written in 1910 by Dr. William Sadler, repeats numerous urban and suburban stereotypes as a matter of "scientific" fact. **Document 2-5** reveals that, by 1909, women were already suffering from certain social repercussions of the suburban domestic ideal: loneliness, isolation, even boredom. Although this description foreshadowed feminist critiques of suburbia sixty years later, the writer fell back on a more conventional solution to the problem—women simply needed to adjust.

In **Document 2-6**, Harriet Beecher Stowe exhorts husbands to become "handy men," adept at fixing things around the house. This article captures the essence of an emerging ideal of "masculine domesticity," which would bring men back into the domestic sphere as active participants. All of these themes come together in **Document 2-7**, a 1925 story of a suburban husband and wife from *House Beautiful* magazine. As this loving couple grapples with a leaky roof, they reveal powerful attitudes about the virtue of suburban life, the gendered division of labor within a companionate marriage, and ultimately their embrace of the suburban ideal. **Document 2-8**, an illustration from a satirical essay on the "virtues" of suburban homeownership for working people, depicts the flip-side to the idea of home maintenance as an adventure in domestic bliss. Even so, it points to an ideal of companionate marriage and shared male responsibilities for a range of chores around the house. **Document 2-9** offers a pictorial rendition of the family ideal in suburbia. This painting, commissioned in 1893 by the U.S. League of Building and Loan Associations, a trade organization of home lenders, was meant to illustrate the League's slogan: "The American Home, The Safeguard of American Liberties." Like Beecher's essay, this painting implies a close connection between American democracy and a particular image of family, gender, and the domestic landscape. While the invocation of nation and freedom lent weight to the artist's view of family roles (not to mention the League's business efforts), it also tapped into a deeply held popular belief that the security of the American political system relied on a distinctive form of domestic life. For the middle class, that form was increasingly perceived in suburban terms.

According to the evolving ideals of family and gender, how were women and men expected to behave? What caused these new norms to emerge? What classes of people were included or excluded in this ideology? What were the costs and benefits to women? To men? How did the presence of servants complicate ideas about the cult of domesticity? Is there a necessary connection between political culture and a specific organization of families? How did suburbia promote and support this transformation? Is there a necessary connection between gender, family, and the physical spaces in which we live?

2-1. CATHARINE BEECHER OUTLINES THE PROPER ROLE FOR WOMEN, 1865

Source: Catharine Beecher, "How to Redeem Woman's Profession from Dishonor," *Harper's New Monthly Magazine* 31 (November 1865).

Woman, as well as man, was made to *work;* her Maker has adapted her body to its appropriate labor. The tending of children and doing house-work exercise those very muscles which are most important to womanhood; while neglecting to exercise the arms and trunk causes dangerous debility in most delicate organs.

Our early mothers worked and trained their daughters to work, and thus became healthy, energetic, and cheerful. But in these days, young girls, in the wealthy classes, do not use the muscles of their body and arms in domestic labor or in any other way. Instead of this, study and reading stimulate the brain and nerves to debility by excess, while the muscles grow weak for want of exercise. Thus the whole constitution is weakened.

In consequence of this there is a universal lamentation over the decay of the female constitution and the ruined health of both women and girls. At the same time vast numbers are without honorable compensating employment, so that in the wealthy circles unmarried women suffer from aimless vacuity, and in the poorer classes from unrequited toil and consequent degradation and vice.

It is believed that the remedy for all these evils is not in leading women into the professions and business of men, by which many philanthropists are now aiming to remedy their sufferings, but to train woman properly for her own proper business, and then to secure to her the honor and profit which men gain in their professions....

Each department of woman's profession is a science and art as much as law, medicine, or divinity. They are equal also in importance. Why should they not be equally honored by a liberal course of training and competent emolument?...

Queen Victoria set up schools for young women to be trained not only to read and write, but to perform all the work of woman in a thorough and proper manner. Her nobility followed her example, and with success.

American women can do the same, and in a way adapted to our democratic system.... In an aristocracy it is assumed that one class is to work for the benefit and enjoyment of an upper class. In a democracy it is assumed that every class is to work for their own welfare and enjoyment. In an aristocracy *work* is dishonored, in a democracy it is honored. In an aristocracy it is assumed as a distinctive mark of rank not to work, but to live to be waited on and worked for by a subordinate class. In a democracy it is assumed that both rich and poor are *to work,* and that to live a life of idle pleasure is disgraceful.

When, therefore, the attempt is made to

introduce industrial training into our schools, we are simply aiming to carry out practically the true democratic principle.

But there is a still higher aim. It will be found that the democratic principle is no other than the grand law of Christianity, which requires *work and self-sacrifice for the public good,* to which all private interests are to be subordinate. Children are to be trained to live not for themselves but for others; not to be waited on and taken care of, but to wait on and take care of others; to *work* for the good of others as the first thing, and amusement and self-enjoyment as necessary but subordinate to the highest public good. The family is the first commonwealth where this training is to be carried on, and only as a preparation for a more enlarged sphere of action.

Jesus Christ came to set the example of self-sacrificing labor for the good of our race; and family training and school training are democratic and Christian only when the great principle of *living for others more than for self* is fully recognized and carried out.

It is clear that great changes are to be made in all the customs and habits of our nation, especially among the wealthy, before the true democratic and Christian principle will triumph over the aristocratic and unchristian.

One of these changes will be in the style of *house building.*

When houses are built *on Christian principles* women of wealth and culture will *work themselves, and train their children to work,* instead of having ignorant foreigners to ruin their food in a filthy kitchen, and ruin their children in the nursery.

When houses are built to honor woman's profession, and to secure the beauty, order, and comfort of a perfected house, the kitchen, as it usually exists, will be banished. Instead of the dark and comfortless room for family work, there will be one provided with sunlight and pure air, and well supplied with utensils and comforts in tasteful and convenient forms....

Woman's work will be honorable and tasteful and agreeable when *cultivated* women undertake to make it so.

And when women of refinement and culture build houses on the Christian and democratic plan, work themselves, and train their children to work, they will never suffer for want of domestic helpers. Instead of coarse and vulgar servants, who live in the cellar and sleep in the garret, they will have refined and sympathizing friends to train their children, nurse their sick, and share in all their comforts, joys, and sorrows.

American women have abundant power to remedy all the wrongs and miseries of their sex, by simply *educating them properly for their proper business....*

[A] time will come when women will give... liberally to elevate the true profession of women as *the ministers of home,* as they have to elevate the professions of men.

The remainder of this article will give drawings and descriptions to illustrate one house constructed on democratic and Christian principles....

Every family, as the general rule, includes the parents as the educators, and the children to be trained to Christian life. To these are added aged parents or infirm and homeless relatives. These are preserved in life after their active usefulness ceases, and often when they would gladly depart, for the special benefit of the young, as the only mode in which, in early life, they can be trained to self-sacrificing benevolence, to reverence for the aged, and to tender sympathy for the sick and unfortunate. Instead of regarding such members of a family as a burden and annoyance, the wise and Christian parents will welcome them as suffering helpers aiding to develop the highest Christian virtues in their children.

This house is planned for a family of ten or twelve, which may be regarded as the average number in healthy families.

The *site* is a dry spot with a cellar well drained, in an open space, where the health-giving sun falls on every part, and the house so placed that the rooms in common use shall have the sun all day....

The *close packing of conveniences,* so as to save time and steps, and contrivances to avoid the multiplication of rooms to be furnished, cleaned, and kept in order, is indispensable to economy of time, labor, and expense. In many large kitchens, with various closets, half the time of a cook is employed in walking to collect her utensils and materials, which all might be placed together.

The plan given above is rather a hint to be farther wrought out than a completed effort.

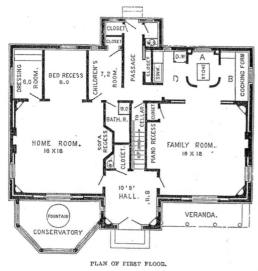

PLAN OF FIRST FLOOR.

Figure 2-1 Plan of first floor, 1865. Illustration in original, 713.

The house is fifty by thirty on the outside (excluding the projections of the back and front entrance). It faces south, giving to the two large rooms the sun all day....

A house on this plan will accommodate a family of ten, and afford also a guest-chamber, and it offers all the conveniences and comforts and most of the elegances of houses that cost four times the amount and require three or four servants.

If a new-married pair commence housekeeping in it, the young wife, aided by a girl of ten or twelve, could easily perform all the labor except the washing and ironing, which could be done by hired labor in the basement. The first months of housekeeping could be spent in perfecting herself and her assistant, whom she could train to do all kinds of family work, and also to be her intelligent and sympathizing helper when children come.

While it should be the aim to render woman's profession so honorable that persons of the highest position and culture will seek it, as men seek their most honored professions, there must still be the class of *servants,* to carry out a style of living and expenditure both lawful and useful, where large fortunes abound. For this class the aim should be to secure their thorough preparation and to increase their advantages. Should both aims be achieved, then a woman who prefers a style of living demanding servants, will be so trained herself as not to be dependent on hirelings at the sacrifice of self-respect. On

the other hand, a woman who chooses another style of living, so as to work herself and train her children to work, can do so without fear of losing any social advantages. Or, in case more helpers are needed, she can secure highly cultivated and refined *friends* to share all her family enjoyments, instead of depending on a class inferior in cultivation and less qualified to form the habits and tastes of her children.

But it is not the married alone who are privileged to become ministers in the *home church* of Jesus Christ. A woman without children, and with means of her own, could provide such a house as this, and take one child and a well-qualified governess to aid in training it. Then, after success inspires confidence, a second child might be adopted till the extent of her means and benevolence is reached.

There are multitudes of benevolent women, whose cultivated energies are now spent in a round of selfish indulgence, who would wake up to a new life if they thus met woman's highest calling as Heaven-appointed ministers of Christ, to train his neglected little ones for that kingdom of self-denying labor and love of which he is the model and head.

Thousands and thousands of orphans are now deprived of a father's home and support. Thousands of women, widowed in the dearest hopes of this life, are seeking for consolation in the only true avenues.

A great emergency in our nation has occurred, in which thousands of women are forever cut off from any homes of their own by marriage. Of these many are women of wealth and influence among Protestants, who in hospitals and battle-fields have been learning the highest lessons of self-sacrificing benevolence. Such will not return home to be idle, but will press toward those avenues that offer the most aid and sympathy; and if it is not provided by Protestants they will seek it in the Catholic fold....

When houses are built on Christian and democratic principles, and young girls in every condition of life are trained to a wise economy, thousands of young men, who can not afford to marry young ladies trained in the common boarding-school fashion, will find the chief impediment removed; and thus healthful and happy homes will multiply with our increasing wealth and culture.

2-2. CATHARINE BEECHER AND HARRIET BEECHER STOWE DEPICT "A CHRISTIAN HOUSE," 1869

Figure 2-2 Although the Beecher sisters held that women could create virtuous homes in city or country, they offered this illustration of "A Christian House," a suburban cottage set in a bucolic landscape. Catharine Beecher and Harriet Beecher Stowe, *The American Woman's Home, or Principles of Domestic Science* (Hartford, CT: The Stowe-Day Foundation, 1987; original copyright 1869), 23.

2-3. DESIGN AND FLOOR PLAN OF A SUBURBAN COTTAGE HOME, 1887

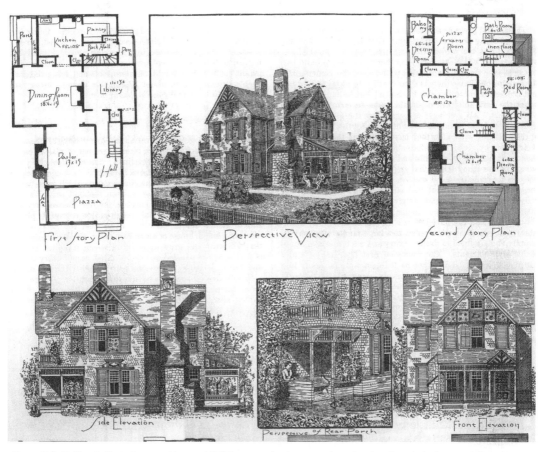

Designs 135 and 136.

Plate 45.

Figure 2-3 *Palliser's New Cottage Homes* (1887), a popular house pattern book, offered designs and floor plans to middle- and upper middle-class suburban homeseekers. Note the provisions for servants' quarters, library, and formal parlor. *Palliser's New Cottage Homes and Details* (New York: Palliser, Palliser & Co., 1887), Plate 45.

2-4. A DOCTOR EXPLAINS THE VIRTUES OF SUBURBIA FOR CHILDREN, 1910

Source: William S. Sadler, "The Suburban and the City Child," *Suburban Life* 10 (February 1910).

We must not expect to be able to raise healthy babies where trees and grass are stunted in their growth, as in some of the city parks, where they are subjected to the influence of smoke and coal-gas. It is almost impossible to get plants and trees to grow in some of these localities. It has also been found difficult to raise healthy and vigorous flowers in many of the tenement-house districts, due

not alone to lack of sunshine, but also to the fact that the atmosphere is poison-laden.

On the other hand, the green grass, the shrubbery, the plant life, and the trees of the suburbs, are a guarantee of atmospheric purity; as it is one of the functions of chlorophyl (the green substance of plants) to take the poisonous gases of animal respiration and transform them into starch and other useful foods for man and beast....

Next to pure air, there is probably no single influence so mightily influencing child growth and health as *sunlight*. Children are just as dependent upon sunlight for health and growth as are plants, and lack of sunshine unerringly produces both plants and babies which are pale, sickly and emaciated. It is the glorious sunshine that paints the bloom of health upon the cheeks of both the bud and the babe....

There is a great difference between the dead shade of the tall buildings and tenements of the city and the *living shade* of the green trees of the suburbs, which permit the soft light of the sun to sift down through their green leaves, to bathe with life-giving influences the little ones who find shelter under their spreading branches.

The outdoor life and physical freedom required for the healthy upgrowing of children is practically impossible in the city. However many and beautiful the playgrounds, they do not destroy or remove the health-destroying influences of city life, which fall with a peculiar force upon the infant and the growing child....

We have tried the city for children, and we have tried the country. We lost in the city, but we have won out in the country; and, therefore, I write this paper, not merely as a piece of professional advice, exhorting parents to flee into the suburbs for the sake of their children but I write it rather from a sense of duty, because of our personal experience.

At least from the standpoint of the health of children, the little boy was not far wrong when he wrote in his essay, "God made the country; man made the town; and the devil made the city."

In light of recent investigations, there can be little doubt that the incessant noise of the city has a tendency to somewhat dull certain special nervous sensibilities, as in the case of hearing; and it may yet develop that, in some measure at least, the stupidity characteristic of some of the children of the slums and other sections of the city subject to unusual noise is due to these unnatural conditions.

The sleep of the suburban child is found to be much more even, normal, and refreshing, as compared with the rest of city children.

In case of children who are growing up, city life tends to breed childish discontent and unnatural love for change and excitement; while the suburb, from its every influence,— the clear sky, the singing birds, the majestic trees, the peaceful and serene atmosphere of the community, in fact, everything,—tends to produce the spirit of joy and contentment without in the least quenching the natural desire for exploration and childish adventure; all of which finds its full satisfaction in instructive tramps through the woods, along the brooks, through the meadows, and over the hills.

The cities must be reckoned as the strongholds of vice; the suburbs and rural communities as the hope of virtue. Of the 800,000 young men who reach ages of maturity every year in this country, one-half million plunge themselves into the vice and iniquity of the social plague spots of our great cities, and of this number 400,000 annually are smitten with the unmentionable diseases of social transgression....

Last, but not least, children are welcome in the suburbs. The people of the suburbs, as a rule, love children. Their childish exuberance and even their gleeful noise are welcome; while the landlord of the city closes his flats against the little ones; and, from the standpoint of health and hygiene, this is scarcely to be regretted. It would be a blessing to coming generations if all the flats of all the cities were forever closed against all parents and their babies. This might result in driving more families to the "land of promise"—the suburban community—where they with their children rightly belong.

2-5. AN EXPERIENCED SUBURBANITE COUNSELS YOUNG WOMEN ABOUT THE PROBLEMS OF SUBURBIA, 1909

Source: Grace Duffield Goodwin, "The Commuter's Wife, A Sisterly Talk by One Who Knows Her Problems," *Good Housekeeping* 49 (October 1909).

The advantages of suburban life have all been set forth by the real estate dealer, by the artistic pamphlet, and by dear human nature's imperishable, if somewhat shamefaced, belief in "love in a cottage." It is a tribute to unspoilable manhood and womanhood that there is today in all these suburban towns so implicit a confidence in this individual home, where the family may sacredly guard its right to live and sleep and eat and develop and love and quarrel and repent—*alone*, albeit there are noted women who, never having known the joy of these things, deny their right to exist....

The Young Wife in Lonelyville

But you, my dear commuter's wife... It has been hard for you, and you are in no mood to be laughed at. The pretty house is all in order; your husband is away all day; you know nobody; there is nothing to do, nowhere to go; there are no little people to occupy heart and hands, for you are at the beginning of all things, and everything is flat, stale and unprofitable. The great flood of genuine emotion that has indeed "borne you far," is running out as flood tides ever must, and it is always muddy on the ebb.

The days are long in these suburban towns. The busy men, an hour or more from the city, leave on early trains, and are at once plunged in the rush of their accustomed life among their usual associates. The little wife, left standing behind the struggling young vines of her brand new piazza, turns back into the house, to face a day devoid of interest and companionship. She may read a little—she who has been brought up on lectures; she may practice a little—she who has been educated on concerts; she may sew or cook, neither of which interests her in the least, and both of which she does badly as yet. She may walk until she finds that the cab habit has been so long indulged that she wearies easily, and all her walking is through endless streets of houses like her own, pretty, with well-kept lawns and drives, and apparently, like her own, tenanted by one lonely young woman and perhaps a maid or two.

The most hopeful thing is the frequent perambulator with its tiny occupant. The lovely children of these suburban towns make city dwellers open their eyes in amaze, and I well remember a beautiful suburban church that had such an attractive and charming primary class that it was one of the sources of pride for the whole town. But as she walks about, the commuter's wife, for whom all this is in the future, wonders a little dismally why she was ever induced to leave New York, or Boston or Chicago. Torn from all her natural environment, her problem is how not to droop too discouragingly in the process of transplanting. Her present task is the watering of these disturbed roots, the putting out of timid new leaves....

The Church a Social Center

How, then, shall a young wife, going as an entire stranger into such a place secure a foothold and become a part of such life as the place may boast? An experience of eighteen years as a resident of suburban towns bids me say without hesitation that the safest and best way is through the church. So much has been said in derision of those who use the church to foster social ambition that the real good which the church can do just here, in these towns which are full of strangers, is being overlooked. Every suburban town of any pretensions has a church and a schoolhouse and probably a clubhouse. The church one may be sure of finding, and the chances are that the minister and his wife are either young enough to sympathize, or old enough to give counsel. Ministers, as a rule, know their towns. It is their business to call upon newcomers, to find out about people and to make the Father's House a home, indeed, for all these stranger children.

Go, then, to church; return the call which the minister's wife and other women of the congregation will surely make upon you after you have been to church for a few Sundays, and do not disdain to make use of this gladly proffered aid in finding friends and a place for yourself in your new home....

A Thorn in the Flesh

One serious thorn in the flesh of the suburban woman is her husband's love of a quiet evening. He is tired and wants to rest. She is feeling perfectly fresh, after a dull day, and wants social life. On this small rock of disagreement some very estimable young people have all but come to grief. And when once the habit of disagreement is formed (it is only a habit), anything will serve as a peg to hang a quarrel on. The commuter and his wife, loving each other dearly, are, through their enforced separation, their different environment, their diverse interests, in great danger of falling after a while into a nagging, fretting, dual existence, which springs from the fact that they fail to realize that they, more than other people, have need of forbearance.

Tom is fagged when he reaches his late dinner; he wants to rest and be comfortable. He returns late from the city, too tired almost to eat, and his wife meets him, charmingly dressed, with hurry in voice and air:

"Make haste, Tom, dear—we're going to dine at the Smiths; your clothes are all laid out. I'm sorry you are so awfully late. They'll just have to wait, that's all, but *do* hurry!"

Tom had gone in on the 7.45 that morning; he rushed all day; he ate a cold, hasty, pay-when-it's-over luncheon—lunch is the proper word for what Tom ate; he was jammed and elbowed by the hot and weary crowd of men surging down Barclay street; he stopped to buy fruit and had to run for his boat. It was the train boat and he stood up all the way home, with a long, uphill walk from the station. It is to his credit that he went to his dressing room without a word, but his wife cried because he neglected to kiss her. He was so tired that he forgot absolutely that she had been lonely and bored all day, and, thinking each of his or her own hardships, they spent a strained and uncomfortable evening.

These were real people, who loved each other sincerely, and they talked their problem out, so that each saw and understood the other's point of view; each made concessions, and the outside engagements were arranged to suit Tom's work.

The Servant Problem

The servant problem is one of the difficulties of suburban life. Many a man comes from town escorting and placating a belligerent and suspicious woman who, having worked in the fields at home, is now superciliously contemptuous of the country and all that in it is. The sources of domestic help are running dry; there are fewer girls and women willing to "live out," as they phrase it and near a city the difficulty of getting good servants is well-nigh insurmountable....

There is no way out of it for the commuter's wife. She *must* herself know how to handle all the affairs of her own home if she expects to be happy or to make her husband contented. In the city it matters less; one can always dine well somewhere. In the country one must dine, either well or badly, at home. This stimulates a woman's pride in accomplishment, and that is why one may find more real homes in suburban towns than in some other places. American women do not easily reach that uncomfortable mental state known as "wits' end." They can always do something, and usually do it well.

When the Children Come

When the children come into these homes, many of these early trials are things of the past, and all but forgotten, but the commuter's wife is still a woman apart, and even with her children finds that her problems continue to be unique. They will not classify. You may generalize about women and homes and children, but all the woman contributes is the "footnote to history." Her conditions are explanatory and parenthetical. Child culture specialists may descant upon the joint influence of father and mother over the developing lives of children. How much influence does the man have who leaves before his children are awake in the morning, and sees at night only the sweet, rosy faces and curly heads of his sleeping boys and girls? Therefore, the mother has a double problem. She must train the children unhelped, and must form for them a mental image of the father from whom they may not be separated in thought for love's sake. She must decide alone all minor matters of conduct and life, not an easy task....

Taken at its best, suburban life is sane and wholesome and conducive to the best sort of happiness. It has its trials and difficulties; it has great compensating advantages. It calls for independence, courage, cheerfulness, resource, and it produces by its demands those eminently attractive and capable young women, each one of whom at heart is proud of her home and her children, proud of the little town she lives in, proud of one especial man on the 8.17—proud, in fact, of being a commuter's wife.

2-6. HARRIET BEECHER STOWE EXHORTS MEN TO BE "HANDY," 1869

Source: Harriet Beecher Stowe, "The Handy Man," *Saturday Evening Post,* October 30, 1869.

A handy man is so practiced in the regulation of the little utilities of the house he inhabits, that by a slight touch here and there—a screw turned here and a screw loosened there, and a nail driven in time—he keeps all working smoothly, and averts those domestic catastrophes and break-downs of which Punch makes so much capital in his pictures.

The handy man knows how to use every sort of tool that keeps his house in order. They are all neatly arranged, in his own private drawer, sacred from the meddling of children and the borrowing of the careless. Is a pane of glass shivered on a cold day, the unhandy man first stuffs it with a bundle, or pastes it over with a newspaper, and then rushes to a glazier's, who of course is not at home, or who says he will come and mend it immediately, and doesn't come—meanwhile the wind blowing in gives the baby the croup, and the mother a severe cold.

The handy man, on the contrary has his diamond, his measuring rule, his putty, all in readiness at a moments notice, and the replacing of the pane of glass is an affair of a quarter of an hour, before he goes to his office or store.

The handy man has no small bills to pay to any kind of mechanic, for he stops every leak in its commencement, and replaces every screw the moment it is loose....

In like manner there is a leak somewhere in the roof of the house, and every time that it rains through this leak, the water drops down through the ceiling of the room. The unhandy man is exhorted by his wife that this ought to be attended to. He promises to attend to it and forgets it; he never thinks of it until it begins to rain, and the water begins to drop, and pails and tubs are requisite to catch the superfluous moisture. Then, agonized and penitent, he flies to the house of the carpenter, who promises to come, and forgets it likewise; and so on through successive showers and floodings, till finally there comes an avalanche of plastering, which

ruins the carpet and furniture underneath, and makes the question of mending the roof no longer doubtful. Repairs of some two hundred dollars have now to be done, on account of a leak which the handy man would have stopped in two hours.

The handy man not only can do all these things which properly belong to men's department, but in cases of sickness or other causes that disable the female part of his household, he can distinguish them in their peculiar department. He can cook nicely, he can make bread, and bake it so as thereafter to be enabled to instruct the cook in many points which have escaped Hibernian observation. He can set a table and cut bread with a deft nicety that has been supposed peculiar to female hands alone.

But in the same manner that it is desirable that a man should understand and be able to occasionally do the work of a woman, and as he can do it without becoming unmanly, so woman can learn to understand and do many things which pertain to the work of men, without becoming unwomanly.

A woman who lives in the country, for example, may sometimes be able to save a life by knowing how to harness or drive a horse. It is, of course, not a proper feminine employment, but it is a thing quite easily learned, and the knowledge of which may come in play in exigencies.

We think it would be an advantage for women to learn to use the more ordinary tools of a carpenter—the plane, the gimlet, the screw, and the screwdriver—in which case they might stop many of the little domestic leaks we have indicated.

2-7. A SUBURBAN COUPLE FINDS DELIGHT IN THE CHALLENGE OF A LEAKY ROOF, 1925

Source: "Twenty Miles Out: Indiscretions of a Commuter's Wife," *House Beautiful,* January and February 1925.

The space that we have an option on is almost entirely outside the house, two acres bounded with a brook. Inside the house you think there is no space at all....

We took the option on it, with the understanding that we might lease it for a year, and then decide whether we wanted to apply the rent we had paid to the purchase of the house, on what the owner cheerfully called "Terms."

"I wish," said Gregory to me before we moved in, "that you would keep a sort of weekly Ledger of your opinions about the house. At the end of the year when we have to make the decision, we can consult that record, and guard ourselves against deciding rashly on the strength of some emotion that may be uppermost at the time."…

One evening I was jotting down enthusiastically as follows:

"*November 2.* Rain all the week. House behaving its best. Every night rain pattering on roof. To-night extra cozy. Fire in the fireplace, drops of rain ticking down the chimney, slanting gusts across window-panes. Dinner ready, waiting for Gregory. Hard on him driving out from town. Perfect for me, and for him when he gets here. Item to remember: A country cottage out in a storm is more actively comfortable than an apartment in town. Sense of comfort vivid, completely sheltered, yet surrounded by rain. One seems so near the rain, like a woodland creature snug and warm in a hollow tree. Gives sense of intimacy, tranquility, privacy, the reality of the earth. Very—"

Just then I heard the splash of our vehicle, which is of a make so well known and so broadly smiled upon that Gregory delicately calls it our "quadrucycle." I heard the whish of the wheels through the water that had collected at the entrance of our drive. I stepped out through the kitchen to wave, and as I unlocked the back door I noticed something queer about the wall paper on the ceiling of the tiny pantry in the ell. While waiting for Gregory to come in, I investigated. The ceiling paper was undoubtedly sagging in the middle. Could it always have curved down that way without my noticing it? Or had the roof leaked and unstuck the paper to that extent? I scrutinized it from all angles, and sure enough there were tiny drops standing on the surface of the paper where it drooped downward at the deepest curve. Was the plastering under the paper also coming down? I seized my broom, and with the handle cautiously poked the baggy area above my head. It was not stiff like plaster. It was pliable like a jelly-bag, and I could push it up in little hollows with the handle of my broom. I decided not to bother Gregory with this discovery until after he was warm and dry and fed. So, closing the door to the ell, I met him at the threshold and captured his wet things.

"Now, if this isn't perfect, never mind," remarked Gregory after dinner, as he stretched out in the big wing-chair before the fire. "You can't imagine it, being here all day, but it's like all the dreams in the world to get out here after that drive in the rain. Think of having this little house to ourselves, tight as a drum.

Figure 2-4 In the home and garden press of the early twentieth century, even roof repair could be an adventure in domestic bliss. Illustration in original, 158.

All day in the laboratory it seemed perfectly natural to be under cover, no miracle at all. But out here you appreciate the simple fact of being so safe and snug and *dry*."

"Yes, dear," said I, selecting a fresh tea-towel from the linen-drawer and vanishing to the kitchen. How could I spoil that mood, I thought, as I whisked the piles of dishes to their shelves. Still, if I had discovered a crack in our roof-tree, I supposed it was my duty to tell. I tried to spin out my work as long as I could, but the moment came at last. I took my trusty broom firmly in my hand, and presented myself at the study door....

"Computing?" said I.

"Not now," said he affably, poising pencil at parade rest.

"Well," said I politely, "could you possibly spare a minute to come and compute the liquid contents of the ceiling-paper in the ell?"

"Does it leak?" asked Gregory, springing up.

"Not now," said I, "but it's hanging down in the middle. You see," I went on as I led the way into the ell, "how the paper curves downward?..."

I raised the handle of my broom. "You notice," I went on, "how it gives when I poke it?" I poked it, and it "gave" indeed. The handle of the broom went neatly through.

"Hi!" roared Gregory, snatching at me, but too late.

When Niagara suddenly drops and hits you in the eye, you do not pause to reason out your acts. Ducking instinctively, I tried to push back the torrent with my broom. But the handle of a broom, though admirable in its way, is inadequate as a dike. I felt like the Maid of the Mist. Gregory, bent almost double with his prudent efforts to choke back unseasonable guffaws, was swiftly fetching pails. Meanwhile the rent in the paper, tearing lengthwise, was letting down a longitudinal shower.

"To catch it all," observed Gregory, diligently arranging a single file of pans and pails, "I wish we had a narrow tub about the length of the Cape Cod Canal."

"What shall we do about the leak?" I inquired later when I was drying my hair before the fire.

"If we lived on the top floor of a city apartment and this happened at all," mused Gregory, "we'd telephone to the Real Estate Company who held our lease, and they'd have a man on the roof next day."

"We could write to the owner," I suggested.

"Yes, and while we waited for a man to get out here, the whole ceiling would come down and the pantry would be a pond. Luckily I know a seam where that leak must be, and you noticed that the ceiling under the torn paper had one good firm crack that will act as a safe drain for to-night. But as soon as it's daylight, if you'll set the alarm-clock, I'll get out on the roof myself."

Late in the evening we went out into the ell again, and emptied all the pails and basins, and set them back in a row once more, like a military drill of refrigerator pans. The dripping of the rain on aluminum and tin played quite a little tune.

"Gregory," said I, as we stood gazing up at the tattered banners of the ceiling-paper above our heads, "you know Emerson says there is a crack in everything that God has made. Does this leak in the roof make you wish we had a flat in town?"

"Oh no," said Gregory, "not at all! You little know what pleasure you gave me when you showed me just how that ceiling-paper *gave*."

The last thing that night I went to my desk to jot down one more brief item in my ledger for that day:

"*November 2*. P S. A country house in a storm does indeed convey a sense of 'reality,' just as I said this afternoon. But why should reality be so much more charming when perceived at one remove? For instance, why is the patter of a raindrop on the roof so much more soothing than the patter of a raindrop in a pail?"

And then I closed the ledger, and put it away, and trudged up the stairs, and set the alarm-clock carefully at half-past-five.

"Gregory," said I, as we stood peering out of the hall window at quarter of six on the morning after we discovered the leak in our roof, "Don't you want me to go with you when you climb out to mend the roof?"

"Oh, no," said Gregory easily, "You get breakfast and keep dry."

In the half-darkness we could just see the glistening slant of the ell. The rain had held up, but everything in the world was dripping after our week of storm....

Gregory with a lantern, looking like a burglar in a raincoat, was assembling his tools.

"It seems to me," said I, gazing out, "as if one of those electric wires has sagged in the storm. Be careful not to touch it, won't you?" I implored. "Everything is so wet, you might get a shock."

"Trust *me*," promised Gregory, "you just run along and get breakfast and don't worry about wires."

Obediently I ran along. But as I stepped about making the fires and starting breakfast, I could not help listening attentively to the sounds of tramping and hammering on the roof. Half an hour of thunderous tinkering went by. Then suddenly, all sounds ceased.

I strained my ears. Dead silence. Had he finished? If so, why did he not come in? This profound hush was unnatural. I stopped stirring the cereal and set it back a little in the double boiler. Still blank silence. I could hear the cereal bubbling intermittently to itself, and my own heart beating. Not another sound.

Then all at once I heard a tremendous shout from Gregory. He was calling my name.

"That wire!" thought I, and darted across the kitchen to the back stairway door. It was locked. Feverishly I wrenched back the bolt. Another shout from Gregory. He must have touched the wire, and was unable to let go. How should I pull him off? As I went leaping up the narrow stair, I saw halfway up, on a shadowy hook, a great pair of hip-rubber-boots that Gregory keeps for fishing excursions. Even in the headlong haste of the moment I wondered whether he would ever go fishing again. Tearing them off their hook as I flew past, I thrust my hands into them, and fitted them up my arms to the shoulder, like evening gloves. Insulated with these, I thought, I could pull him off the wire. A third roar from Gregory. At least he was still able to speak my name. He was just setting up another shout when I burst out through the window.

"Why didn't you *answer*?" inquired Gregory as I appeared. "Why, *Puss*-in-Boots!" he exclaimed in amazement after a good look at me. "Why the rubber mitts?"

But I was too breathless for wordy repartee. I clambered out beside him on the roof, shook the heavy boots from my arms, arranged them side by side on the roof for a cushion, and sat down.

"I thought maybe you were shocked," I explained briefly.

"Oh, no," Gregory assured me politely, "just surprised."

"What were you yelling for?" I inquired severely.

"Oh yes," said Gregory briskly. "I wanted to ask you a question. I find that the actual leak is only a six-inch crack, and I can make a very passable repair-job with this old license-plate of ours. Now what I want to ask is, shall I nail it on with the lettered side up, or with the lettered side down?"

I gazed at the old license-plate thoughtfully. It was the dark-blue and white one that had been on the car when we became engaged: Massachusetts 86,349.

"Oh," I decided promptly. "Massachusetts side up, of course."

"I thought so," agreed Gregory, hammering industriously. "I only wanted to be sure you didn't mind if the airplanes got our number."

"No," said I dreamily.

Daybreak was gleaming on the wet shingles, and a crow flapped over slowly toward the hills. I blew out the lantern and watched Gregory as he neatly lapped the good shingles over the upper edge of the license-plate to make a perfect rain-shed against the next storm....

"Don't go in yet," begged Gregory as I rose and gathered up my top-boots in shivering hands. "Just take a look at that sky in the east. It's going to clear off cold."

"It has already," said I through chattering teeth, but I turned to take a final bird's-eye-view. The level gray bars of cloud were parting in the east, and a freezing wind came piping over the November fields. A nervous little chipmunk ran along the branch of our apple tree, leaped to the far corner of our eaves, and stood regarding us, jerking his bushy tail. One feels on an equal footing with a chipmunk on a roof. We accepted his greeting as a good omen for the day, and Gregory departed in high feather, after breakfast, to catch his train.

2-8. ANOTHER TAKE ON THE JOYS OF HOME IMPROVEMENT, 1910

Figure 2-5 "Something that you can work at summer evenings after supper," Horace Taylor, 1910. Even suburbia's early critics often depicted its marriages in companionate terms. For suburbanites such as these, the new garden was a shared headache. Eugene Wood, "Why Pay Rent?" *Everybody's Magazine* 22 (June 1910), 769.

2-9. "THE AMERICAN HOME, SAFEGUARD OF AMERICAN LIBERTIES," 1893

Figure 2-6 The American Home, Safeguard of American Liberties, 1893. Artists' renderings of suburbia often combined gendered notions of home and family with symbols of class, race, nation, and religious morality, creating a suburban landscape replete with social meaning. H. Morton Bodfish, *History of Building and Loan in the United States* (Chicago: United States Building and Loan League, 1931), 183.

ESSAYS

The approaches taken in the following essays mirror important trends in women's history scholarship. The field emerged in earnest in the 1970s, as feminist scholars sought to raise women out of historical obscurity. The earliest studies focused on the twin themes of female contributions and oppression. By the 1980s, the field expanded to include the broader study of gender. **Essay 2-1**, from a 1988 book by architectural historian Gwendolyn Wright, examines the "cult of domesticity" and its impact on the built landscape. Wright explores the critical connections of this gender ideology to the nineteenth-century suburb, and shows how architectural styles supported the tenets of these ideals. In the next development in the field, scholars turned their attention to the history of masculinity, acknowledging that gender roles could be constructed for men as well as women. In **Essay 2-2**, historian Margaret Marsh explores a potent moment in the history of male gender ideology: the turn of the twentieth century. Detecting a trend toward what she terms "masculine domesticity," Marsh reminds us that men's roles, too, underwent a transformation in the nineteenth century in ways that did not always conform neatly to "separate sphere" ideology. Marsh also pays particular attention to the ways that space—particularly the suburban form—contributed to the construction of this new masculine ideal.

ESSAY 2-1. GWENDOLYN WRIGHT, *BUILDING THE DREAM: A SOCIAL HISTORY OF HOUSING IN AMERICA* (1988)

Source: *Building the Dream* by Gwendolyn Wright, copyright © 1981 by Gwendolyn Wright. Used by permission of Pantheon Books, a division of Random House, Inc.

When post-Civil War suburban builders advertised through brochures and newspapers, they promised potential buyers more than comfortable surroundings and well-built houses. Those who moved to the new suburbs were assured of an escape from the problems of poor health, social unrest, and vice associated with urban life. The private dwelling in a safe residential neighborhood would protect the wife and children from the dangers of the wicked city. The theme of redemption for one's own family—less often now for the nation as a whole—occurred again and again. Picturesque site planning and natural building materials evoked a return to nature, to a lost innocence and an earlier stability. Individuality was attainable here, too. The diversity of floor plans and ornament for façades proclaimed unequivocally the unique qualities of each family. And finally, as the note of progress in this idyllic reverie, each

house, street, and depot would be equipped with "A. M. I.—All Modern Improvements."

It was an appealing package. Several million American households put their savings and dreams into a new suburban home. The great migration began in the 1870s and gathered momentum as the century wore on. Builders' guides and construction journals, books on political economy and magazines of domestic tips, unleashed a deluge of advice, encouragement, and images about the model home. The authors all reiterated the same themes of suburban salvation and security. This chorus, extolling the personalized, arcadian dwelling, marked the opening up of the American suburbs to Victorian middle-class and working-class families....

In the decades after the Civil War, suburbs took on a new meaning and social organization. Promoters tried to identify their projects with the more exclusive, picturesque retreats for the wealthy, but they were aiming for a different market. Subdivisions of small or moderate-sized lots, near transit lines, were intended to attract the families of salesmen, schoolteachers, clerks, and carpenters. Those who could afford to own a suburban house can be labeled "middle class," comprising, in income, the upper half of the population in an average city. Even among this group there were restrictions, for most of the new communities were implicitly segregated by income and ethnic group. By no means were all suburbanites able to buy their houses. In fact, statistics for Boston, like those for many other cities, show that only a quarter of the suburban households owned their homes in 1890 and half of these homesteads were actually held by mortgage-financing institutions. Yet the move itself was considered crucial, whether the household had a lease or a mortgage, whatever size lot or caliber of suburb could be afforded. The suburban home, how it was furnished, and the family life the housewife oversaw, contributed to the definition of "middle class," at least as much as did the husband's income....

Victorian ideology perceived women and children as especially close to nature, much more so than men, who could withstand the harsh demands of supposedly unnatural city life—provided they had their retreats in the suburbs. During the last decades of the nineteenth century, the cult of home and motherhood, which had emerged in the 1830s, reached its pinnacle. Novels, poems, lithographs, children's books, and domestic guides extolled the virtues of domesticity so much that the good family and their suburban home became almost interchangeable concepts. George Palliser, a New York builder, could open his pattern book of house designs with the sentimental exclamation: "Home, what tender associations and infinite meanings cluster around that blessed word!" Authors of guides for women likewise insisted that the best domestic architecture, which was not necessarily the most expensive, would evoke the most lofty associations.

The very qualities that made the home so meaningful also made it precarious. Victorian Americans worried about the rising divorce rate and the declining number of births among white women of the educated classes, a trend they called race suicide. They recognized the restlessness of many homebound women, and a child's desire for excitement that could lead that son or daughter astray. The potential influence of the home over family behavior, for good or for evil, therefore loomed dramatically large....

Since women and children were considered the most susceptible to the dangerous influences associated with the city, they had to be sheltered from urban life. The search for isolated, purified protection in the suburbs was obviously a middle-class ideal, for many women had labored long hours in factories or stores before their marriages, and then took in boarders or did laundry or piecework in an urban tenement to make ends meet. At the other end of the spectrum, it was fashionable for women to spend afternoons going about town enjoying theaters, museums, shopping, or calling on one's friends, perhaps undertaking philanthropic work among the poor, all pastimes available in the city. Nor was the ideology of the domestic retreat binding on the middle-class woman. The streetcars that took husbands to work also carried their wives and daughters to the downtown corner, where department stores offered the latest items for their homes and wardrobes, and even special restaurants and reading rooms, exclusively for ladies, where they could relax from the demands of shopping. Against this backdrop, the sentiments celebrating the pure suburban home, isolated from contact with market values and factory conditions, took on a heightened intensity. With the expansion of the suburbs, concepts of the home as a private refuge, a place of peace and inspiration, a reward for diligence and thrift, became something more than abstract images.

What did this ideal expect of the middle-class home and the women who saw over it? First, home would be as unlike the world of business and industry as possible. The spheres of men and women, city and suburbs, were cast as fiercely antagonistic to one another in every way. The widely held expectation that the impersonal market was grueling and cutthroat, harshly competitive and draining, posed the home as compensation. "[T]his stirring career away from home," wrote one contented husband, "renders home to him so necessary as a place of repose, where he may take off his armor, relax his strained attention, and surrender himself to perfect rest." Home was to be a setting of luxury and comfort, softness and frivolity, at once a place of refinement and exotica. It was to be private, contrasting with the frenzied activity of the skyscraper, which now symbolized the business environment.

Home should never be simply a sensuous indulgence, though, for it was the source of spiritual education; a mother's guiding values and the indelible images of home were supposed to carry her son or daughter safely through the difficulties of adult life. In the late nineteenth century, middle-class children spent much of their time at home. Despite compulsory school attendance laws in many states, the average American received four years of formal schooling in 1880, and only five years a decade later. The mother was responsible for education, as well as character training and social skills; and the home was the principal place for every aspect of this training. One text for children's moral education captures the spirit, if not the actual procedure, for domestic influence: "From such homes the children go out into the world only when necessity calls them; they return to its hallowed precincts with delight, and the remembrance of its pleasant associations is ever a silent monitor standing guard over them." The suburban home was part of a strategy to keep children far from the world of the city streets, to ensure their entry into the proper, disciplined class of present and future suburbanites.

In the parlor, the housewife would show off the family's best possessions, striving to impress guests and to teach her children about universal principles of beauty and refinement. One popular symbol of domesticity was the fireplace....Elaborately carved mantels, some in marble but most in inexpensive painted and incised wood, provided the suburban home with its ritual center; it did not matter if some hearths were fitted with imitation logs, fired by gas, or hid a furnace register. Here too were the "artistic" pieces the wife had purchased: sculpture, vases, chinoiserie, and all manner of bric-a-brac. These objects she skillfully juxtaposed with her own handmade creations, or "household elegancies," which might include crocheted lambrequins, hand-painted cabinets, rustic furniture, shadow boxes and Easter eggs, screens and easels bedecked with ribbons and flowers. The balance, however, was shifting toward items purchased from a store or catalogue, which captured the refinement and culture that the home was supposed to encourage....Since the mother sought to teach her children values in and through the home, she had spared no expense in acquiring beautiful works of art that were both "interesting and instructive."...

In order to make the home an alternative to the commercial world, the housewife had to become a diligent consumer. Ironically, the home as haven from the world was actually filled with worldly goods, industrial products, and fashionable details.

The intricate floor plans of middle-class Victorian houses, especially those in the suburbs, created distinct zones for different activities. The formal social spaces, the kitchen/work area, the private rooms upstairs, each had its particular aesthetic. The Victorian home was, in this way, a splendid setting for family life, providing places for children to hide and for friends to visit, places for disarray and for formality under the same roof.

The kitchen was almost always isolated in the back of the house. This was a commodious work space, often shared by several women. In most urban and suburban areas in 1880, only 20–25 percent of all households employed a servant, and this ratio was noticeably higher than the national average. Even with a daily servant, who was both housemaid and cook, and perhaps a weekly laundress as well, the average housewife and her daughters had a great deal to do in the kitchen. Washing entailed boiling water on the stove, mixing up one's own soap and starch, rubbing the clothes fiercely up and down on a washboard, then hanging them up to dry. Most meals, even breakfasts, consisted of many courses, and each dish underwent an elaborate ritual of presentation. Fanny Farmer's cookbook explained how to make a green aspic for a ham, how to wrap a meatloaf in crackers so that it resembled a box, how to cut radishes and celery into decorative floral shapes. Consequently, given this approach to food preparation, special storage space was required. One usually found a rear pantry, which contained bins for flour and sugar, which had been bought in bulk, next to open shelves for the food put up by the household—preserved fruits and vegetables, jellies and pickles—and for recently available canned foods like tomatoes, corn, milk, corned beef, and sardines. A cooler, either in a window or in the cellar, protected from insects by a screen, kept such perishables as homemade pies and cakes, dairy products, and oleomargarine. The large amount of space allocated to the kitchen and pantry reflected the quantity of work that women still did in the suburban home.

Places for privacy within the home were carefully defined. Guides to home decoration passed over the sleeping areas with a slight blush, but general guidelines emerged. Bedrooms were usually large enough to serve as sitting rooms, where a mother might spend the afternoon with her child, or a young woman with her girlfriend. Mementos and handmade objects would be proudly displayed in an artistic, stylized arrangement. It was primarily in well-to-do families that the husband and wife would keep separate rooms. Most married couples shared a double bed, and their children usually shared rooms with siblings of the same sex. Often the servant woman was allocated a room on the same floor with the family bedrooms, off a common hallway, instead of being assigned to the attic. But it was increasingly likely that she was married and "lived out."

As family size decreased, so did the pressure on domestic space. The average American family had slightly more than five children in 1870 and only four in 1890. Despite the smaller size, separate rooms for each individual were not considered necessary. Privacy for the Victorian family was still associated with short periods of time alone, in a special place in the house: a window seat, a cubbyhole under the stairs, a man's library, or "growlery." Within the home, there was always somewhere to retreat from the intensity of family life.

The irregular outline of Victorian houses revealed the occupants' search for individuality and their interest in functional design. Each bay window, porch, and other protrusion was considered evidence of some particular activity taking place within; it made the space exactly right for playing the piano, sewing, reading, or tending a hot stove. As the number of rooms in a moderate-cost suburban house increased, floor plans burst into extraordinary shapes. Closets and storage rooms provided for a larger number of possessions; a special music room or nursery or library could be found in quite unpretentious houses. The names of these many rooms were a further statement about family life. Debates about sitting rooms, family rooms, parlors, living rooms, and living halls filled builders' guides as well as many novels. The characters in William Dean Howells's *The Rise of Silas Lapham* (1885), H. C. Bunner's *The Suburban Sage* (1896), or Henry Blake Fuller's *With the Procession* (1895) wanted houses that fit their needs and announced their social aspirations....

Middle-class Victorians wanted to believe that their houses were impressively unique. At the same time, certain patterns were necessary so that other people could clearly read the symbolism of social status and contented family life in the details. Many suburban Americans connected their highly ornate dwellings with their own individualism, just as they connected the separateness of each suburban household with the self-sufficiency and autonomy of the family. In fact, the majority of moderate-cost suburban houses were built on speculation, not for a particular family; yet the ideal of personalized expression was a principal selling point. Ignoring the evidence of standardization, people identified themselves with their homes. The legacy of that rhetoric of domestic bliss, so closely associated with detached houses and elaborate architectural ornament, still resides, to a great extent, in the suburbs today.

ESSAY 2-2. MARGARET MARSH, "SUBURBAN MEN AND MASCULINE DOMESTICITY, 1870–1915" (1988)

Source: *American Quarterly* 40:2 (1988), 165-171, 174-181. © The American Studies Association. Reprinted with permission of The Johns Hopkins University Press.

When historians think about American men at the turn of the twentieth century, among the images they usually conjure up are these: a bored clerk or middle-manager in some impersonal office of a faceless corporation, pushing papers or counting the company's money, longing nostalgically for a time when a man could find adventure and get rich at the same time—by becoming a robber baron, or conquering new frontiers; or Theodore Roosevelt, the delicate child who grew up to relish big-game hunting and war, and whose open disdain for softness and "effeminacy" made him the symbol of rugged masculinity in his own time.

We owe the association of the corporate drone with the flamboyant Rough Rider to an influential essay by John Higham, who argued that one of the most significant American cultural constructs at the turn of the century was a growing cult of masculinity, attended by the insecurities of middle-class men about their own virility and "manliness." Beginning in the 1890s, Higham argued, the country witnessed a national "urge to be young, masculine, and adventurous," when Americans rebelled against "the frustrations, the routine, and the sheer dullness of an urban-industrial culture." He cited the growing popularity of boxing and football, a disaffection from genteel fiction, and not least, the rise in the level of national bellicosity, as important indicators of a new public mood.

Higham's article, published in 1970, triggered an interest in the historical meaning of masculinity. His insights, and those of others who have followed his interpretive lead, have been of undeniable value. Nevertheless, his work defined an entire generation of middle-class men— young and middle-aged, married and single, urban, suburban, and rural—in terms of anxieties about manliness. Those anxieties, and the men who faced them, undoubtedly existed, but in the course of my research on suburban families, I have discovered a different manner of middle-class man. The evidence to date is scattered, but there is enough to suggest that historians supplement the image of the dissatisfied clerk with an additional picture of a contented suburban father, who enjoyed the security of a regular salary, a predictable rise through the company hierarchy, and greater leisure. This last prerequisite was facilitated by shorter commuting times—often thirty minutes or less—to and from the suburbs of most cities. (With the exception of some New York lines, men could expect to spend less time going to

and from work than had their fathers, who had to rely on horse-drawn streetcars and omnibuses.)

Alongside the idea of the cult of masculinity, which offered an explanation for some elements of middle-class male culture, we should consider the model of masculine domesticity. Masculine domesticity is difficult to define; in some ways, it is easier to say what it was not than what it was. It was not equivalent to feminism. It was not an equal sharing of all household duties. Nor did it extend to the belief that men and women ought to have identical opportunities in the larger society. It was, however, a model of behavior in which fathers would agree to take on increased responsibility for some of the day-to-day tasks of bringing up children and spending their time away from work in playing with their sons and daughters, teaching them, taking them on trips. A domestic man would also make his wife, rather than his male cronies, his regular companion on evenings out. And while he might not dust the mantel or make the bed except in special circumstances, he would take a significantly greater interest in the details of running the household and caring for the children that his father was expected to do.

The evidence for the growth of masculine domesticity comes from a variety of places. Prescriptive literature is one important source. Tantalizing clues from domestic architecture, records of community groups in the suburbs themselves, letters, and diaries provide others....[S]uggestions of changing male roles also appeared in the reconfiguration of interior space in suburban houses, in the rise of suburban institutions which included both husbands and wives, and in the daily lives of suburban families....

Masculine domesticity required three conditions for its emergence: an ideal of marriage that emphasized companionship instead of either patriarchal rule or the ideology of domesticity, both of which encouraged gender separation; an economic system that provided sufficient job security for middle-class men so that husbands could devote more attention to their families; and a physical location in which the new attitudes toward family could find their appropriate spatial expressions. It was not until the power relations within middle-class marriage underwent subtle shifts, until the rise of the corporation provided relatively secure jobs with predictable patterns of mobility, and until suburbs began to be viewed as the appropriate space within which to create the companionate family, that the development of masculine domesticity was possible. By the early twentieth century, all three of the conditions had been met.

During the second third of the nineteenth century the patriarchal family, softened by love and mutual obligation, had served as the principal model for middle-class families. This ideal of family life had depended on what twentieth-century historians have come to call the ideology of domesticity, a social theory articulated most persuasively by Catharine Beecher in the 1840s....The success of the ideology of domesticity required, in the words of Beecher's biographer, "the isolation of women in the home away from full participation in the society." To compensate them for their voluntary abdication of the right to a position in the world of men, women held sway within the home, thereby (at least theoretically) stabilizing society as a whole....

The doctrine of separate spheres began to break down after the Civil War. During the past two decades, historians have extensively chronicled the incursions of women into the masculine sphere. But changing roles for women also meant changes in male roles. As women entered the masculine world, men began to enter the sphere assigned to women.

We can begin to understand this phenomenon—which ended in the masculine domesticity of the Progressive Era—by looking first at changes in the kinds of advice given to young men about the organization of their lives. In the middle of the nineteenth century, male advice-writers...rarely concerned themselves with the role of husband or father. Instead, they emphasized economic and social mobility, urging young men to develop the qualities of sobriety, honesty, and a capacity for hard work because these qualities were essential to economic success, not because they would help a man become a better husband or father. Neither did these male

writers offer suggestions on choosing a suitable wife, or on appropriate behavior toward one's children. Although the moral young man understood from these advice manuals what to avoid—prostitutes, gambling dens, and the questionable pleasures of urban life—they offered him no positive assistance in settling his personal life....

In fact, it was women writers who began first to refuse to pay even lip service to the patriarchal ideal. Harriet Beecher Stowe, one of the nineteenth century's most popular writers, ridiculed patriarchal pretensions and praised domestic men in her last two novels....

By the 1890s, women advice-givers were arguing that men should help out around the house and stop expecting their wives to wait on them. As one of Margaret Sangster's friends complained, she was tired of picking up after her husband, who every day "manages to give my drawing room, sitting room, and library an appearance of having been swept by a cyclone. One traces him all over the house by the things he has heedlessly dropped...." Sangster urged her friend to tell her husband to pick up after himself, since a good husband would surely make an effort to reform, at least "to some extent." Such advice, and the relationship that it implied, was far removed from a world in which a father's convenience was of principal importance....

The domestic lives of middle-class families reflected the changes in the attitudes toward marriage....The golden age of male fraternal organizations had passed by the turn of the century, according to historian Mark Carnes. Male clubdom would rise again later in the century, but for the moment suburban men sought their leisure closer to home, in tennis and country clubs that welcomed the whole family, and in social groups that included their wives. In one New Jersey suburb, for example, during the first decade of the twentieth century, the Men's Civic Club had difficulty in attracting members, and the Women's Sewing Society was forced to disband completely in 1903; but the Penn Literary Society, the Debating group, and the Natural Science Club, all of which included both men and women and numbered many married couples in their ranks, flourished.

So, too, did the new family-oriented tennis club, founded in the same period....

Advice to men had also changed. While male advice-givers rarely insisted that men take on the administrative or physical duties of running a household, they did urge them to trade the burdens of patriarchal authority and work-induced separation from family life for emotional closeness to their wives and the pleasures of spending time with their children as companions. Of course, not all men were in agreement with such advice. However, even criticism could inadvertently highlight the new domesticity of suburban men. Richard Harding Davis, writing for *Harper's* in 1894, found his married suburban friends boring because they had no interests beyond each other, their house, and their suburban pleasures. Davis found their contentment incomprehensible....

As middle-class men gained respite from the economic pressures that had plagued the previous generation, they had the time to give their families greater attention. This change, along with the prodding of feminists, triggered the recognition of the importance of male domestic responsibility....

Women, however, wanted men to do more than share in the process of making decisions about household furnishings. They also wanted them to be nurturing fathers. Some of them pinned their hopes on the next generation. Kate Wiggin, who before she wrote *Rebecca of Sunnybrook Farm* had been a kindergarten teacher, attempted to develop "the father spirit" in little boys. At school, her charges played a bird game, in which "we had always had a mother bird in the nest with the birdlings...." Wiggin then introduced a "father bird" and similarly reorganized other games. Finally, she incorporated the boys into "doll's day," previously a girls' game only. Wiggin asked one of the boys to play "father" and rock a doll to sleep. To her delight, all the other little boys then wanted to play.

Wiggin published her kindergarten techniques and they enjoyed wide circulation. Perhaps it was the imagined sight of thousands of little boys rocking dolls to sleep that encouraged men to start getting involved in rearing their children, in order to save their sons from such influences. In fact, some of the motivation for greater fatherly involvement with their children was surely to balance the preponderant female presence in the lives of young children. But the word is *balance,* not *overshadow.* Masculine domesticity, as it had evolved by the early twentieth century, was incorporated into the concept of manliness, as men became convinced that in order to have their sons grow up to be "manly" they should involve themselves more substantially in their children's upbringing.

Senator Albert Beveridge was one of a growing number of men who applauded masculine domesticity in the early twentieth century. These men encouraged fathers to form direct and immediate bonds with their children, by playing games with them, taking them on camping trips, and simply spending time with them. Of course, before the entrenchment of the ideology of domesticity in the second third of the nineteenth century, fathers had maintained a large role in family government, but in the earlier period the emphasis was on obedience, discipline, and the importance of the father's role as head of the household. In the early twentieth century the stress was on friendship: fathers were encouraged to be "chums" with their children, especially, but by no means exclusively, with their sons. Male writers on parenthood differed from their female counterparts in that they placed greater importance on independence, approving of boys having, from about the age of seven on, a sort of freewheeling companionship with other boys—a "gang" or "bunch," to use the terms of the period. They argued that fathers could encourage such freedom because the new closeness of father and son would prevent the boy from falling into evil ways. His father would play baseball with him, take him and his friends camping and swimming, and in general play the role of a caring older companion rather than a stern patriarch....

The final condition for the development of masculine domesticity was spatial. The suburbs were assumed to be the natural habitat of domestic man. [Bernarr] Macfadden claimed that the purchase of a "modest little home" would give the young married man a sense of stability, as well as the necessary physical distance from urban temptations. Having come to New York City from the midwest to make his fortune, Macfadden himself moved to the suburbs at the first opportunity, and held resolutely anti-urban sentiments. Albert Beveridge had expressed similar views. Devoting an entire chapter of his advice book for young men to "The New Home," he informed his readers that "'Apartments' cannot by any magic be converted into a home.... Better a separate dwelling with [a] dry goods box for a table and camp-stools for chairs than tapestried walls, mosaic floors, and all luxuriousness...." Furthermore, once the young man had got himself a wife, a nice suburban house, and some children (because "a purposely childless marriage is no marriage at all"), he "will spend all of [his] extra time at home," listening to his wife play the piano, reading, and not least, playing with the children.

Two things are important about the domestic advice of Macfadden and Beveridge. First, successful men advised their juniors to cultivate domestic habits. Second, they advised them to do so in the suburbs. Macfadden and Beveridge were among a growing number of Americans in the early twentieth century who viewed urban life as a direct threat to family happiness. As late as the 1880s, the city had still seemed redeemable to urban residents and social critics alike. When people moved to the urban fringe they were often waiting for the city to catch up to them, not trying to escape it. But by the turn of the century the suburban flow had an escapist quality to it; one symbol of that escapism, as Kenneth Jackson points out, was the decline of annexation as a means of holding suburbs and city together. And a number of sociologists who specialized in the study of the city during the first decade of the twentieth century contended that urban life and stable family life seemed incompatible....

The advice-givers and academics hoped that middle-class fathers, with more secure careers and houses in the suburbs, would spend their time with their wives and children rather than male friends. The great popularity of family-oriented recreational activities around the turn of the century and afterward suggests that suburban families wanted to play together. According to the most comprehensive study of American leisure, in this period croquet and roller skating were more popular than baseball (and many families, including the girls, apparently tried to play baseball on the lawn). Bicycling did not become a craze until it became a sport for women and girls as well as boys and men. Suburbs institutionalized the relationships that marked the companionate family by creating various kinds of clubs, such as "wheel clubs," athletic fields used by both sexes, and tennis and golf clubs. (If early twentieth-century photographs and real estate advertisements are reliable, men played golf with their wives, not business associates.)...

The most striking thing about the middle-class domestic architecture produced in the second and third quarters of the nineteenth century, as Gwendolyn Wright has pointed out, was its design for separation. The most striking thing about suburban houses in the early twentieth century was their design for family togetherness. In middle- to upper-middle-class homes, the living room replaced the separate parlor, study (commonly considered a male refuge), and sitting room that had characterized Victorian upper-middle-class houses. Both modest and fairly expensive new houses had more open floor plans. Architects in the early twentieth century, ranging from the iconoclastic Frank Lloyd Wright to the very conservative Joy Wheeler Dow, explicitly designed houses for family togetherness. And architectural writers made the same statement in home magazines....

The redefinition of manliness to include some traditional female functions, one suspects, represented a collective masculine response to feminists like Charlotte Perkins Gilman, who insisted that the traditional family was anachronistic in an urban society, and who demanded that women seek for themselves the sense of individual achievement and separate identity that had been reserved for men. Urban feminists endorsed Gilman's ideas. Her writings and lectures received considerable attention in the periodical press of the day, although it is unlikely that all middle-class men knew her by name. Whether they could identify her, however, is not the point; no one who read the newspapers could have been ignorant of the views she espoused. On the whole, men responded to those views by moving their families to the suburbs. There, fathers would draw themselves into the domestic circle, where individual needs could take second place to the needs of the family.

Masculine domesticity, in that sense, served as a male reply to the feminists' insistence that women had as much right to seek individual achievement as did men. It offered an alternative to feminism: men would acknowledge the importance of the domestic sphere, not only rhetorically, but also by assuming specific responsibilities within it. Women, however, shared only partially in the world of men. Reform activities, mothers' clubs, even voting became acceptable, but taking on roles in the larger society identical to those of men did not. Men who espoused masculine domesticity, it seems logical to speculate, deflected feminist objectives. Suburbanism was neither incidental nor accidental to this process. Suburban advocates in the early twentieth century preached that removal from the city would both encourage family unity and discourage excessive attention to one's individual wants. The suburb served as the spatial context for what its advocates hoped would be a new form of marriage. Husbands and wives would be companions, not rivals, and the specter of individualist demands would retreat in the face of family togetherness.

CHAPTER 3

Technology and Decentralization

INTRODUCTION

The nineteenth century is aptly remembered as an age of invention. New machines, transportation and communication technologies, sources of energy, and household gadgets evolved in concert with the most profound social changes of the era. The railroad and telegraph accelerated the transit of goods, people, and information. Electric lighting transformed day and night. Industrial machines replaced craft manufacturing, and domestic appliances altered work, leisure, and social relations while raising the standard of living and cleanliness of households in line with a Progressive penchant for scientific hygiene.

New technologies also facilitated a revolution in urban space. For millennia, walking had been the primary means of urban transportation. As a result, cities everywhere were compact, congested, and heterogeneous. New means of transportation—steam ferries and railroads, horse drawn omnibuses and streetcars, and finally electric and gasoline powered vehicles—accelerated movement within and between cities, facilitating a radical restructuring of urban settlement patterns. New transportation brought large parts of the urban hinterland within daily commuting distance of urban workers. Districts of new housing, stores, and factories soon traced the railroad and streetcar lines that radiated from the core. Each new mode of transportation left its own impression on the landscape: compact "railroad suburbs" clustered about evenly spaced suburban train stations, like pearls on a necklace; linear "streetcar suburbs" flanked the trolley lines; and, later, sprawling "auto suburbs" covered the spaces in between. Across metropolitan areas, too, distinct districts began to coalesce around singular functions—residence, offices, retail, and industry—connected by new forms of transit and communication.

Technological innovations supported decentralization indirectly as well. The application of new machines to old work processes drove ever greater industrial production. Manufacturers, seeking to maximize economies of scale, began building new factories on the urban fringe as early as the 1860s and 1870s, drawing workers, small businesses, and social institutions in their wake. Equally important, innovations in the building materials industries reduced the cost of comfortable, up-to-date housing, and advancements in urban infrastructure, such as water, sewers, and, later, gas and electric services, made it feasible and affordable for a growing number of American families to move to new neighborhoods on the city's doorstep.

As might be expected, technologies were not adopted evenly across the metropolis. Indeed, differences in technology came to signify class status: higher class suburbs tended to have good transportation, an array of infrastructure and utilities, and homes with the latest appliances, while lower class suburbs often did without. In some ways, technology served to sort suburbanites by class.

Despite the obvious and far-reaching effects of new technologies, the relationship between technological and social change is complicated and historically varied. One thing on which historians agree is that technologies do not act by themselves (a view known as technological determinism); rather, they are tools that people create, use, and adapt to accomplish specific purposes. As historian Steven Lubar writes, "technologies can shape and suggest, but they rarely demand."[1] As such, most historians recognize that advances in transportation, utilities, and household technology did not *cause* suburbanization per se, but rather made it feasible for a greater number of urban dwellers than before.

Thus, the study of technology and suburbanization compels us to ask: Why were some technologies widely adopted while others were ignored? What role did politics and public policy play in these choices? How did cultural values, consumer choices, the organization of business enterprises, and the quest for profit shape the development and use of new technologies? What did new machines mean to the people who used them, and how did these meanings change over time? If new technologies did not, in and of themselves, cause suburbanization, exactly what role *did* they play?

DOCUMENTS

Among the earliest advancements in suburban transportation was the steam-powered ferry. Following the introduction of steam service between New York and Brooklyn in 1815 by entrepreneur and inventor Robert Fulton, ferries began plying urban waters on the East Coast and inland rivers. By the 1840s, when the engraving in **Document 3-1** was made, ferries crossing the East River from Brooklyn to Lower Manhattan transported thousands of daily commuters, in addition to agricultural produce from the city's rural hinterlands, and suburban women lavishly dressed for a day in the city.

Land-based urban transit was decidedly less romantic than the sweeping passage of ferry boats across open water. **Document 3-2** is a sardonic look at the shortcomings of travel by "omnibus," a horse-drawn urban stagecoach that served a fixed route. Introduced to the United States from Europe in the 1830s, by mid-century omnibuses moved thousands of daily passengers in urban America. Despite the access they gave to settlement in outlying areas and to short cross-town trips, omnibuses were widely satirized for their cramped cabins and spine-jarring ride. Others criticized the conditions under which horses and drivers labored, traversing sundry urban pavements in all kinds of weather. As this cartoon points out, progress in urban transportation was not free of human, environmental, and ethical costs.

One of the most significant innovations in urban transportation in the nineteenth century was the streetcar, which appeared in East Coast cities in the early 1850s. A marriage of the omnibus and the railroad, streetcars, such as the one pictured in **Document 3-3**, featured a horse-drawn coach that ran on grooved rails in the street. Streetcars were larger, faster, more comfortable, and more capital intensive than omnibus coaches. Because streetcars operated in traffic, their speed was limited to the flow of other vehicles. In open areas, however, they reached speeds of three to five miles per hour, coming to a full stop only for female passengers. Even before the arrival of electric power in the 1890s, streetcars symbolized "progress" in cities of the United States and across the world. A handwritten inscription across this photograph from the frontier town of Grand Junction, Colorado, proudly announces the city's "1st streetcar." This same booster spirit is apparent in **Document 3-4**, an 1876 newspaper article from Oakland, California, which celebrates the influence of new street railways on city growth. The car lines were opening up Oakland's outlying reaches for the construction of "villa residences," raising property values as they went. The article also highlights the aim of many traction firms to speculate on real estate along their routes—for some, transit was merely a sidelight to their primary business, which was selling suburban property. By contrast, in other industrializing countries, transit companies were prohibited by law from dealing in real estate adjacent to their lines. In the United States, this new technology did not reshape residential patterns by itself, but was promoted by private enterprises with the support of the law to turn a profit.

Electrification marked a milestone in metropolitan transportation. Following its introduction to transit in the late 1880s, streetcar firms quickly shifted from animal to electric power on their urban lines. Another important innovation was the electric trolley, which sped between stops on its own right-of-way, extending the speed and reach of public transportation dozens of miles into the metropolitan hinterland. The photograph of a trolley between Denver and Boulder, Colorado in **Document**

3-5 illustrates the great distances opened up by electric power, as well as the penchant of traction companies to extend service beyond the limits of current development, giving impetus and direction to future development.

Document 3-6 offers subtle commentary on the superiority of public over private transportation in inclement weather. Nonetheless, as auto registrations surged in the 1910s and 1920s, street-car companies struggled for financial survival. Political decisions hastened this shift as public dollars flowed to road construction for the automobile, while municipal authorities prevented privately owned transit firms from setting rates that might have maintained profitability. Political and economic support given the automobile over mass transit indicates that the social adoption of one technology over another is not simply a matter of efficiency or quality, but also politics.

The next three documents highlight the impact of new technologies on the suburban home. **Document 3-7** contains excerpts from an architectural pattern book published in the 1880s by the New York architectural firm of Palliser and Palliser. This popular guide pictured dozens of model home designs set against suburban or semirural backdrops. Each plate included exterior views, floor plans, and architectural details, plus accompanying text describing daily activities appropriate to each model. These passages also educated readers about advances in building and sanitary technology—such as indoor water closets and properly ventilated hearths—promoting a new standard of living that suburbanites could come to expect. Detailed views of ornamental woodwork, standard to each plate, also signaled the proliferation of industrial wood-working machines, which made such fancies affordable to a mass market. **Document 3-8,** an illustration from H. C. Bunner's popular 1896 short story collection, *The Suburban Sage*, spoofs suburbanites' fascination with (and dependence upon) the domestic technologies that made their comfortable lives possible. In this view, a suburbanite shows off his basement furnace to a group of admiring male guests. The image suggests some of the many emotions that new technologies evoked among those who gave up the comforts of city life for the suburbs in the late nineteenth century. **Document 3-9** likewise illustrates the close connection that many Americans perceived between technology and suburbia. By the early twentieth century, advertisers, such as the creators of this 1923 washing machine ad, reinforced familiar suburban ideals about landscape, leisure, technology, and female domesticity in an effort to sell their wares. Documents 3-8 and 3-9 indicate further that many technologies were given gendered meanings from the very outset.

Document 3-10 provides a startlingly prescient description of the emerging megalopolis along the eastern seaboard of the United States. Writing in 1905, journalist Frederick Coburn illustrates that metropolitan dispersal was well advanced even before widespread use of the automobile—the technology most associated with urban sprawl. His explanation? Electrified rail transportation and the telephone. **Document 3-11** reinforces this same tendency to ascribe agency—even extraworldy "mission"—to new machines. It also reveals the enthusiasm with which millions of Americans welcomed the automobile. The author, automotive writer Herbert Towle, enumerates the myriad ways that cheap cars had altered urban life, especially emphasizing their impact on suburbanization.

What were the major ways that new technologies affected suburban life? Compare and contrast the impact of different means of transportation on settlement patterns, ways of life, and perceptions of the suburbs. Why did emotional responses to these new means of transit differ in the ways that they did? Of the varied reactions of nineteenth- and early twentieth-century Americans to technological change, which was most surprising to you? Why? Why were commentators so apt to attribute agency to machines?

3-1. A STEAM FERRY IN NEW YORK HARBOR, 1840

Figure 3-1 Steam Ferry in New York Harbor, engraving 1840. For more than half a century, steam ferries were the principle link between Manhattan and growing suburbs in Brooklyn. This image, published in a volume of grandiose natural views, suggests something of the emotions with which Americans met this technological advance. Nathaniel Parker Willis, *American Scenery* (London: George Virtue, 1840), 91.

3-2. *HARPER'S MAGAZINE* RECOUNTS "THE DOLEFUL HISTORY OF THE OMNIBUS HORSE," 1860

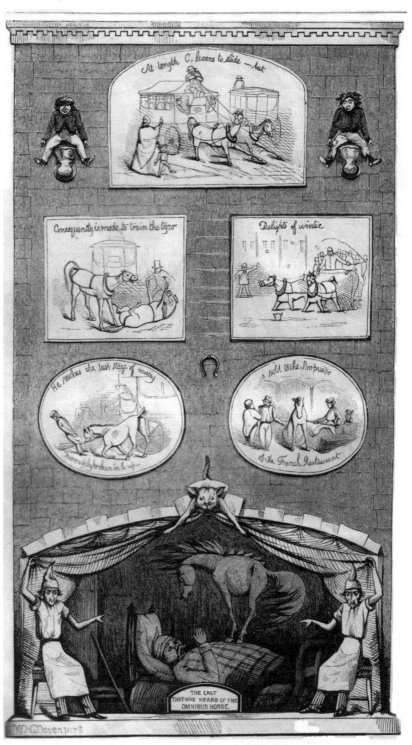

Figure 3-2 The Doleful History of the Omnibus Horse, 1860. Horsedrawn transportation predominated in urban America throughout the nineteenth century. To the chagrin of many observers, sick and broken horses were a common sight. In this view, the maltreated draft animal takes its revenge by haunting its driver in a nightmare. *Harper's New Monthly Magazine* 21 (August 1860), 430.

3-3. HORSE-DRAWN STREETCAR, GRAND JUNCTION, COLORADO, 1887

Figure 3-3 First Streetcar, Grand Junction, Colorado, 1887. Through the late nineteenth century, streetcars were a symbol of urban progress and civic pride. The traveling billboards on this horsecar also indicate that entrepreneurs were quick to recognize the cars' many commercial possibilities. Denver Public Library, Western History Collections, X-8687.

3-4. *OAKLAND DAILY EVENING TRIBUNE* CELEBRATES THE WORK OF "OUR STREET RAILROADS," 1876

Source: "Our Street Railroads," *Oakland Daily Evening Tribune*, December 12, 1876.

[T]he fact is acknowledged by all intelligent and observing people that

Railroad Enterprises

Have done more towards attracting desirable immigration, populating the State and increasing the value of real estate than any or all other artificial influences combined.... What is true in this respect of our long lines of railroad is equally true on a small scale of street railroads—a fact which

Sagacious Property-Owners

Recognize and act upon, to their own benefit as well as to the advantage of the community generally. Oakland is now increasing rapidly and steadily in population, and dwellings are going up in every direction with a rapidity that indicates general confidence in a prosperous future. Of course this rapid growth must be attributed mainly to the topographical beauty, and the healthfulness of the locality and its contiguity to the commercial center of the State.... Yet with all these natural advantages, dealers in real estate find it necessary to improve property, and construct avenues and streets, and use every means their ingenuity can suggest to increase the value and attraction of their lots in order to secure purchasers. Among the

Artificial Means

Thus employed, probably none has proved more successful, or paid a better return on the capital invested, than street-railroad enterprises. The very first experiment of the kind in Oakland was a grand success, and has led to new enterprises of like character. The first street railroad projected in Oakland was the Oakland, Brooklyn and Fruit Vale Railroad, put in operation less than three years ago.... The length of the road is a little less than two miles, passing through the

Business Centre of the City

For a few blocks, the continuation of the line east being flanked on either side by some of the most elegant dwellings, a[nd] tastefully cultivated grounds on the coast.... While the object in view in the construction of this line was to increase the value of property contiguous to the route, and it was not expected to "dividend" largely, the result has proved it to be a wise outlay of capital. The road has been a

Paying Investment

From the start, and property along the line, and on the streets intersecting it, has been greatly enhanced in value. Hundreds of fine dwellings have been erected in East Oakland that would not have put in an appearance for years to come but for this judicious enterprise. Another example of the value of street railroads as an investment to improve or open up real estate may be seen in the Broadway and Piedmont Railroad, which was completed last Spring.... This was a private enterprise...solely to give access to their landed property and enhance the value of property along the line.

At Piedmont

And elsewhere along the line of the road are some of the finest sites for villa residences to be found in the State. The cost of construction of the road was $25,000. Tickets are sold at the rate of four for 25 cents. Children's tickets five for 25 cents, or twenty for 75 cents. It has paid expenses from the start, and during last summer paid dividends. The increase in the value of property along the line, besides considerable sales of the property which the road was especially designed to open up, have proved the wisdom of the enterprise, and the line has proved a great

Convenience to the Public

The Oakland and Alameda Railroad, the Brooklyn and Fruit Vale Railroad, and the East Oakland, Fruit Vale and Mills' Seminary Railroads—in fact every line in this city—may be cited as enterprises which have proved paying investments for their enterprising projectors, and institutions of very great convenience to the public and prominent among the artificial influences which are accelerating the growth of our city.

3-5. ELECTRIC TROLLEY NORTH OF DENVER, CIRCA 1910s

Figure 3-4 Electric Trolley of the Denver and Interurban Railway, L. C. McClure, ca. 1908–1926. In addition to providing rapid and relatively cheap transportation across far flung metropolitan areas, interurban trolleys offered a fleet, quiet ride that was unlike anything riders had previously experienced. Denver Public Library, Western History Collection, MCC-966.

3-6. AUTOMOBILE AND MAN IN DEEP SNOW AS TROLLEY CAR PASSES, CHICAGO, 1929

Figure 3-5 Automobile and Man in Deep Snow as Trolley Car Passes, *Chicago Daily News,* 1929. Through the 1920s, proponents of streetcars and automobiles fought a running public relations battle. Here the *Chicago Daily News* weighs in. The Chicago Historical Society, DN-0090258.

3-7. ARCHITECTURAL PATTERN BOOK INTRODUCES THE LATEST DOMESTIC TECHNOLOGIES, 1887

Source: *Palliser's New Cottage Homes and Details* (New York: Palliser and Palliser and Co., 1887).

Plate 14.

Design 38 gives us a most excellent plan admirably adapted to a lot about fifty feet wide and is a good design for a suburban home. This plan is well adapted to a large class of house-owners who need a cosey and comfortable home for their own use, and who take a pride in seeing their families comfortably housed and provided for....

The arrangement of plan is clearly shown by the drawings, and it requires very little study to see and take in the good features illustrated. The hall and staircase are very nicely arranged, the fireplace being on opposite side of stairs, is well lighted, and the general perspective effect upon entering at the front doors could not fail but please the most exacting, for the first impressions obtained upon entering a house are always valuable and tend to help the mind of a visitor to a solution of what they may expect to find in the other part of the house, and also as giving some characteristics of the lives spent under the roof. A hall of this kind will generally be furnished and trimmed with as much skill and taste as most any part of the house.

The toilet-room under stairs will be found a very useful arrangement both for toilet and general closet purposes and, although not quite so privately situated as is the case generally, it is only used by the family itself, who can appreciate the convenience thus afforded by its location enough to excuse any little unpleasantness arising from the same; and since the improvements that are now in use in water-closets, and the excellent system and means of ventilation they afford, there is no excuse for bad smells any more from bathrooms and water-closets; but such places can be kept as sweet and as clean and free from anything objectionable as any other part of the house, and we know of bath-rooms that have had these vent pipe arrangements applied where the room could be filled with smoke and it would all pass out through the water-closet in less than five minutes. It is needless to add that with such facilities for ventilation as this no smell can emanate from a water-closet at any time.

The time has surely come when everybody having to put in water closets and using them will make this their first care, and certainly it is the duty of all architects who have the welfare of their clients at heart to be diligent in their efforts to give them of the best appliances and to see that the same are properly set and put in place....

To those requiring a home at a cost of from $5,000 to $6,000, this design will have special interest and will, we trust, assist many in making up their minds on a plan and serve as a guide to the practical solution of what, to many, is a very knotty problem—the planning of a home....

Plate 51....

Balloon framing is technically as well as sarcastically applied to a system of putting together frame buildings, that had its origin in the early settlement of our prairies, where it was impossible to obtain heavy timbers and skillful mechanics, and its simple, effective and economical manner of construction has been of great benefit in building up of new territory and sections of this country, and being stronger than any other method of framing has led to its universal adoption for buildings of every class throughout the United States. In olden times, before the portable saw mill, or easy transportation by railroad of timber and lumber usurped the functions of the broad-axe, the skillful framing of a building required no inconsiderable talent and practice....

Now, in these days of cheap things, substantial frames are, as it were, knocked together, and men who appear to indifferently wield hammer and saw, are employed in the carpentering.

The balloon frame is a characteristic American invention, and like all successful improvements, has thrived on its own merits, the balloon frame has passed through and survived the theory, ridicule and abuse of all who have seen fit to attack it, and may be reckoned among the prominent inventions of the present generation, an invention neither fostered nor developed by any hope of great rewards, but which plainly acknowledges its origin in necessity....

Plate 56....

Every cellar under a dwelling-house should be sweet and clean at all times, and no excuse allowed for its being foul. Ventilate and purify it always. Decaying vegetation should not be tolerated in it. The floor should be well grouted in cement, walls and ceilings should be whitewashed, and ceiling, if possible, plastered; and one flue of the chimney should start from and open into the cellar for ventilation.

In fact, pure air and enough of it is the cheapest blessing one can enjoy, and to deny ones self so necessary an element of good health is the sheerest folly, if not criminal. Yet thousands who build at much expense to protect their health and that of their families, as they allege and sometimes suppose, by neglecting the simplest of all contrivances in the work of ventilation, invite disease and infirmity from the very pains they so unwittingly take to ward off such afflictions. Their memory carries them back to their boyhood days, perhaps, and the old homestead with its fire-places, scarcely throwing off sufficient heat to warm one side of a person at a time, with plenty of good air coming in at ill-fitting doors, windows, etc., which they did not regard as much of a luxury, but which, however, made them healthy and vigorous, and they say to themselves that their children shall be made comfortable, so that in their house building they take extra pains and expense to

make a tight, warm house. They discard the open fire-place, perhaps, entirely, and put in an air-tight furnace or air-tight stoves in the various rooms, and provide no means of carrying off the bad air, and the rooms, as a rule, become overheated; windows and doors are sometimes opened to cool a room, and as a result all sorts of bodily afflictions follow in the family, and they wonder what is the matter, but never dream that day after day they are breathing decomposed air, which cannot escape, because there is no means for it to do so, and go where you may into houses that are without fire-places, and you will invariably find the subject of ventilation entirely overlooked.

Health and comfort depend on proper ventilation, which ought always to be considered carefully. In connection with the heating, the air in the room must be kept in constant circulation, and there is no better ventilator than an open fire-place with a fire; this will carry off the chilled, foul air as it falls to the floor, and keep the purer air circulating, and the fire-place even without a fire will aid in this way to equalize the temperature.

In all rooms that have no fire-places there should be a vent opening with register in the inner wall near the floor. Another vent opening and register near the ceiling is also desirable, that the room may be cooled when too hot and avoid draughts and also for the purpose of summer ventilation. These openings should be connected with tin pipe carried up to attic and to a hot, tight flue in chimney. Closets, pantries and bath-rooms are seldom ventilated even in houses of considerable pretention, yet it can be done at a very small cost by a tin pipe with an area of four inches square with an opening near the ceiling carried up to the ventilating flue.

Figure 3-6 Like other aspects of late nineteenth century suburban housing, the profusion of decorative ornaments reflected the industrialization of building materials production—in this case, the development of complex power wood-working machines. Illustration in original, plate 45.

3-8. SUBURBAN MEN AND FURNACE, 1896

Figure 3-7 The shift from shared urban heating and plumbing systems to private household systems evoked pride, trepidation, and endless conversation among turn-of-the-century suburbanites. H. C. Bunner, *The Suburban Sage: Stray Notes and Comments on His Simple Life* (New York: Keppler and Schwartzman, 1896), 85. Illustration by H. J. Taylor.

3-9. ADVERTISEMENT FOR EDEN WASHING MACHINE, 1923

Figure 3-8 Advertisements for domestic appliances promised women freedom from the drudgeries of household labor even as they reinforced existing gendered expectations about work. "On the Line at Nine," *House Beautiful* 53 (April 1923), 415.

3-10. FREDERICK COBURN FORESEES A "FIVE-HUNDRED-MILE CITY," 1906

Source: Frederick W. Coburn, "The Five-Hundred-Mile City," *The World Today* 11 (December 1906).

A city five hundred miles long and one hundred miles wide, extending over a strip of the Atlantic coast from Portland, Maine, to Washington, D.C., is actually in the making. This unified metropolis of the East—the greatest New York, if one may so call it—was proclaimed some years ago by John Brisben Walker as a dream of the distant future, and others have forecasted such a growth of the larger municipalities that overlapping must eventually take place. The present disposition of civic populations to spread out gives renewed force to such predictions. People are unwilling to spend more than two hours a day, that is, one hour each way, in getting to and from the business center. Such a prescription in the pedestrian days circumscribed a radius of less than four miles as the outer limit of a town's expansion. With the introduction of omnibuses the radius was doubled. Afterward came the railway with its local and express services, making it possible for the homeseeker to live twenty-five or thirty miles from the business center and still be within reasonable distance of his daily work.

But transportation facilities are in process of constant development: It has been demonstrated experimentally in Germany that train speeds of 125 miles an hour are feasible. When these have been rendered commercially practicable, a man living in Hartford [CT] or Springfield [MA] will be only an hour from his business office in Wall Street or State Street [in Boston]. The resident of Chester [PA] or Wilmington [DE] may be either a government employee in one of the departments of the federal ward on the Potomac or may be engaged in private enterprise on Manhattan Island.

The overflowing of big towns toward each other must strike forcibly whoever travels observantly by automobile or, better still, by trolley from New York either northward or southward. The now familiar route of the electric cars from the metropolis to the New England capital lies through a land of disappearing provincialism. The rusticity of ancient villages in Yankeeland is passing. The changed characteristics one may like or may dislike; the change at all events is everywhere evident. Between New York and New Haven [CT], though revolutionary and colonial relics described in guidebooks and cherished for the delectation of trolley-trippers still abound, and though elm-shaded streets preserve a little of pristine tranquility, yet the omni-present suburban villas, improved residential parks, beach properties, trolley car stations and clanging trolleys, telephone pay stations, newsboys hawking late editions of the metropolitan "yellows"—these assure the traveler that he has not left the city universal behind....

[E]verywhere are the evidences of a wide distribution of an urban and polyglot population—Jews, Poles, Italians, Germans and Finns, who are replacing the unprolific Yankee throughout the Connecticut valley. Every few miles is encountered the convergence of several of the trolley lines that have enmeshed the entire map of southern New England. Everywhere the suburban outposts of one manufacturing town stand within hailing distance of the outposts of the next. Suburbia is still crude, too often a hodge-podge of jerrybuilt atrocities. But it is the city of the future....

Now that betterments are being effected in trolley and train services..., and that real estate companies are carrying on extensive advertising campaigns to boom suburban property, the expansion has become cumulative in character. Commutation books are sold in surprising numbers to Greenport [Long Island], ninety-five miles from New York. Both sides of Long Island Sound are being lined with series of well-built suburbs of the metropolis....

On the other side of New York similar conditions of diffusion are present. Those counties of New Jersey which are on the route between Gotham and the big city between the Delaware and the Schuylkill are growing most rapidly....

Obviously if the municipalities of this strip of the Atlantic seaboard continue to throw out suburbs farther and farther from their business centers, and if improved means of transportation bring the cities nearer each other, then the entire district will ultimately present the phenomenon of a single city.

The agencies which, above others, are furthering this consummation are unquestionably electric transportation and the telephone, the one offering cheap and regular communication between centers of population, and the other, with the extension of long-distance facilities, bringing virtually every citizen within speaking distance of every other. Each of these classes of public service will be immensely improved within the next few years, and will be even more powerful than now in transforming the whole section. Rapid transit plans, involving the electrification of steam roads, are being worked out. The telephonic art, meantime, is undergoing equally important modifications, and the engineers confidently expect a time when long-distance talking will be far more generally practiced than at present.

Facilities for communication are even now eradicating distinctions between city and country. New York cockneyism disappears in proportion as people of the metropolis form the habit of occasionally getting away from Manhattan Island. Boston provincialism and Philadelphia self-satisfaction likewise tend to vanish. Rusticity of speech and manners is being outgrown in the most isolated communities. A voice expert asserted not long ago that the now prevalent use of the long-distance telephone is eliminating differences of accent among the sections.

Telephonically connected, often by special wires, a Connecticut factory may have its selling office on Manhattan Island, and the two departments seem hardly further apart than in the case of a manufactory with offices downtown and plant in Harlem. The farming districts between cities, which through an enlightened policy have been plentifully supplied with cheap telephonic facilities, have usually been annexed as suburbs. Across New Jersey the lines of the New York and New Jersey Telephone Company have gone everywhere, bringing that state of prosperous suburbs into closest business and social communication with the metropolis. Philadelphia and Baltimore…have likewise witnessed a great expansion of their circuit of influence through the energetic solicitation of village and farm line business which, for several years past, has been practiced by the Bell companies.

If the telephone, relieving people from the necessity of travel, brings them together even while it keeps them apart, the extension, on the other hand, of the trolley service, while it enables them to meet readily at the same time encourages them to live separately. Every electric car is a moving argument against gregariousness.

All classes of people are listening to its rattling argument. As rapid transit companies are consolidated, sometimes with steam railroads, and as greater and greater distances can be traversed for a moderate fare, suburban estates will continue to supplant rustic farmsteads, while the overcrowding of tenement districts in large cities will be effectually checked. The physical fact of consolidation and unification of services, together with the high speeds that are in prospect, will make for a very wide distribution of population, just as the virtually complete unification of telephone lines under a single comprehensive system is imparting maximum usefulness to that utility....

The five-hundred-mile city, it may be argued from present indications, will be, mainly, one of residences of the suburban type situated reasonably near together and grouped about centers where municipal buildings, schoolhouses, stores, churches, and other institutions offer urban advantages. A large unity will prevail, for all the subordinate groups will be thoroughly interconnected by such facilities for communication that it will be hard to say just where one community leaves off and another begins. Every here and there a reservation of some particularly beautiful tract about a river bank or a lake or a chain of hills will have been made. For the rest, all the coast land from Portland [ME], certainly through the city of Washington, and perhaps far into the neighboring State of Virginia, will have been filled with a practically homogeneous population whose interests, whatever their occupation, will be urban and suburban rather than rural.

How governed? That, of course, can not

be predicted. One may, at least, believe that a new group will have been formed transcending the limitations and obliterating the prejudices of the component communities as they now exist. In that day Mr. [William Dean] Howells, if he is still alive, will have to obey the advice of fellow literary men and stop hating New York. There won't be any New York.

3-11. AUTOMOTIVE WRITER HERBERT TOWLE EXPLAINS THE SUCCESS OF THE AUTOMOBILE, 1913

Source: Herbert Ladd Towle, "The Automobile and Its Mission," *Scribner's Magazine* 53 (1913).

Fifteen years ago the automobile was only a traveller's tale and the hobby of a few crack-brained experimenters. Five years ago the automobile factories of the United States produced about 100,000 cars. This year about 500,000 cars will be built, whose total value will exceed $600,000,000. One city alone will produce 300,000 cars—one factory, 200,000. In 1908 the lowest practical price for an automobile was $900; to-day a better one costs but $600.…

Five years ago the automobile was a transcendent plaything—thrilling, seductive, desperately expensive. Its oldest devotees could view with patience neither abstention from its charms nor the bills which followed surrender. To-day the harrowing alternative is mitigated at both ends. The bills are less and some of the excitement has worn off. Neighbor Brown, who sensibly refused to mortgage his house to buy a car in 1908, is now piling his family into a smart little black-and-red car, and is starting out on a four-day run to the [Delaware] Water Gap and return.…

You yourself have seen the Water Gap, have explored every sunny road and leafy byway within a hundred miles of your home, have seen the speedometer needle hang at 50 or 60, and have come unscathed through adventures which, when you think of them in cold blood, bring a creepy stirring to your spine. Your present car is good, but not showy; you keep it in a little garage behind your house and use it soberly—you and your family—nearly every day; and your motoring costs about half what it did five years ago. You seldom drive now for the mere pleasure of driving; yet your car is as much a part of your daily life as your walk to the office.

What does it all signify? This tremendous industry that has grown up almost overnight, and has made itself so necessary that a million owners of cars are giving food and roofs and clothing to another million—wage-earners and their families—for supplying them with the new means of locomotion—what does this new industry portend? How many more people are going to buy cars? Are automobiles a permanent development or a temporary fad? If permanent, how do they justify themselves—in mere pleasure, which a few can afford but more cannot, or in genuine service? Are they at bottom a liability or an asset?…

How is it with you, the seasoned motorist? If you had no car, in what respect would your life and your family's be changed?

You and I—all of us—used to choose our homes for their nearness to train or trolley. A mile from the station, half a mile from the trolley, was our immutable limit. The gates of Paradise would not have tempted us further. Rents soared; the lucky first owners of land near a new transportation line retired from business and lived in luxury on the fruits of their fortune; still we cheerfully paid tribute, and dotted the map with little disks and bands of high-priced real estate. Horses were expensive and a nuisance, and we did not know that we might become each his own motor-man.

But to-day your home is in a suburb, handy for the motorist but otherwise dependent on trolley service. Were it not for the automobile, your wife's need of companionship would compel removal either to the city or to a more central part of your village. Part, at least, of what you saved on the car would go out in higher rent. Then you would need some other forms of exercise and recreation—golf, weekends at the shore, or the theatre. More money! When you visit friends in the next town, you take your maid to visit *her* friends. Without the car she would have to shift for herself. And the children—you can already hear the lamentations when they learn that they have seen the last of Green Pond, and that these Saturday picnics by the babbling Wanaque River will be no more! You moved to your country home after you began motoring. Dare you say that that change was for the worse?

Perchance you have no car—as yet. But you have friends living five miles away by road. To visit them by rail, you must go half a mile to the station, ride ten miles to a junction, wait an hour, and travel a dozen miles more to a station half a mile from their home. How often do you see your friends?

Or you are a nature-lover and a busy man. The city stifles you and the daily ordeal of strap-hanging is a horror. Yet your wife declares that she will be "buried alive" if she goes where houses are more than a hundred feet apart. She has a right to her view, too. How shall yours and hers be reconciled?

Or you have children. Shall they be reduced to "tag" on the streets and in a bric-a-brac-filled apartment, or shall they have green grass, a sand-pile, trees, and a swing? ...

For hundreds of thousands of families the automobile is at last supplying the happiest of answers. Bridging as it does the gap between rail travel and the horse, at a possible cost less than that of the latter, it has added threefold or more to the habitable areas outside of our cities. Double a certain radius and you quadruple the enclosed area. Make three miles your limit and the area becomes nine. Think what this will lead to in the course of a generation or two, and you will realize the transformation which the low-cost automobile is working....

The logic of the situation points to the growth of motor colonies. It is the exceptional city family that removes outright to the farming hinterland, and in most cases distance from transportation has hitherto produced an inferior neighborhood. That latter condition is visibly giving way to the new order; already the cities have many automobile "commuters," and in every large suburb the morning and evening trains are met by scores of motor-cars. In a few years there will be hundreds....

Has not the automobile proved its mission? Greater liberty, greater fruitfulness of time and effort, brighter glimpses of the wide and beautiful world, more health and happiness—these are the lasting benefits of the modern motor-car. Its extravagance is passing with the novelty of speed; the rational balance of service and expense will ere long be struck, and cars built in conformity thereto. And then we shall thank God that we live in the Motor-Car Era!

ESSAYS

The starting point for scholarship on technology and suburbanization was Sam Bass Warner, Jr.'s 1962 book, *Streetcar Suburbs: The Process of Growth in Boston, 1870–1900*, which unveiled the deep and varied connections between transportation, home building, ideology, and the creation of a class-separated suburban metropolis.[2] The two essays selected for this section build implicitly and explicitly on Warner's foundation. In **Essay 3-1**, historian Henry Binford examines the adoption of mass transit in Boston's suburban fringe during the early the nineteenth century. Rather than viewing the shift from walking to riding as the logical or inevitable outcome of advances in transportation technology, Binford illustrates that residents of the urban periphery put new means of transportation to old uses, organizing and lobbying for improvements that suited their needs, and eventually laying the groundwork for the adoption of commuting by later suburbanites. In his view, the "mobility revolution" was a gradual process, interweaving older habits and expectations on the urban fringe with expanding economic opportunities, changing technologies of transportation, and changes in the city itself. The essay also reveals a process of suburban development in which picturesque, planned suburbs like Llewellyn Park or Riverside played as yet little role.

In **Essay 3-2**, architectural historian Gwendolyn Wright explores the economic and technological changes that underlay the growth of residential suburbs after the Civil War. In contrast with middle-class domestic ideology, which emphasized "home" as a refuge from the world of industry,

Wright illustrates that suburban housing depended implicitly on industrial technology and production. These changes involved not only innovations in transportation, but the intensive application of new machines and manufacturing processes in the building industry. Wright reveals not only the complex relationship between the nation's burgeoning industrial economy and urban decentralization, but she shows that the meanings attributed to cultural artifacts, such as housing, may bear little relation to the process that created them.

ESSAY 3-1. HENRY C. BINFORD, *THE FIRST SUBURBS: RESIDENTIAL COMMUNITIES ON THE BOSTON PERIPHERY, 1815–1860* (1985)

Source: University of Chicago Press. Copyright © 1985 by The University of Chicago.

Among fundamental changes in nineteenth-century urban life, the shift from walking to public transportation was at least as important as the spread of work in factories, and the two kinds of change were in many ways similar. The revolution in mobility, like the one in industrialization, did not begin with complex technology, did not occur all at once, and affected some places and some people far more quickly than others. Like industrialization, the mobility revolution accelerated and changed character in the late 1840s and 1850s, when urban mobility came to involve corporate organization, sophisticated equipment, and large numbers. Although relatively few people worked in factories before 1860, and relatively few rode omnibuses, trains, or horsecars, the organized activity of these few gradually changed the habits and expectations of the whole society.

Between the 1820s and the 1850s, the revolution in mobility changed the pattern of community building in the suburbs from one based on small, road-centered villages and irregular contact with the city to one based on continuous, predominantly residential settlement and routine daily movement through the metropolis. For residents of Jacksonian cities and towns, the significance of this change stretched far beyond the innovations in transport technology which have fascinated many historians. The overall change took place in every mode of travel from walking to commuter trains. It involved new possibilities as much as new devices: a lowering of barriers and costs to moving about; an increase in the variety and reliability of carriers; a new set of expectations about possible journeys; and ultimately a new vision of how the city would grow, how its parts would fit together.

Suburban residents...played a crucial role in beginning the change. Given their long experience as brokers, processors, and gateway entrepreneurs, suburbanites had a strong and continuous interest in better access to the city. By the 1830s they also had clout: fringe expansion gave them capital, talented leaders, and votes. Moreover, suburban residents saw a possibility that Bostonians were slow to recognize: the systematic development of land for commuter residence through a combination of public and private means. Until the mid-forties, peripheral residents, not Bostonians, led the way in promoting local transportation, changing their careers and habits to take advantage of it, and adapting local government to a new set of assumptions about future growth....

The Walking and Riding City

The walking city of the early nineteenth century was actually several cities—with different boundaries for different purposes. Long before mass transportation appeared, many individuals were accustomed to occasional long trips, and a few were involved in routine travel. The shift from walking to riding was revolutionary because it *combined* distance and regularity. The exceptional trip became ordinary; the range of ordinary trips expanded. The initial pressure for removing these various limits of walking mobility arose from the fringe, and arose naturally from its economic and social interests.

When the errand was important and the time ample, walking could take early suburban residents over extensive territory. Farmers, shoemakers, and tanners from the far distant suburbs customarily brought their wares to Boston on foot. Country storekeepers acquired stock the same way. Down to the 1840s, churchgoers and women marketing or visiting commonly walked from Cambridge and Charlestown to the city. Special occasions produced uncommon efforts. Two young men of Woburn, attending a lecture series at Harvard, spent a term walking sixteen miles daily for the purpose....

Extension of the city's economic reach also involved some people in regular trips. Suburban innkeepers of the 1820s and 1830s geared their business to the needs of professional teamsters and crack stage lines. Long-distance teaming brought huge vehicles, traveling in groups at announced intervals, taking goods on commission, and keeping to set timetables. The last stop on these trips was usually at some tavern in the suburbs where the drivers could rest and arrange their wares, and from which they might journey into Boston, complete their sales and return within a day. Along with the teamsters came the long-distance stagemen employed by highly competitive companies and straining to outdo their rivals in speed and regularity. In the inner suburbs, transportation of farm produce, milk, bricks, sand, lumber, and eventually ice made work for short-haul teamsters, some of whom employed extra drivers and ran wagons in and out of Boston several times daily.

Ordinary people, through energetic walking or for purposes of business, might thus expand the city when time and resources allowed. For a few members of the elite, who always had time and money, energetic walking and driving might expand it further and more consistently. Until the 1830s, stamina and a flexible schedule were as important as money. Ill-kept and unlighted roads were often impassable and sometimes unfindable, especially in darkness or bad weather. In the words of a contemporary, "people walked at night by faith."...

By the early 1830s, it was possible for a few people to pursue schedules that might daunt a modern commuter—but only a few, and only those who did not need much sleep.

Josiah Quincy, leaving office as mayor of Boston in 1829, became president of Harvard. Living in Old Cambridge, he retained an office in Boston and went there almost every day. In order to do both Harvard's business and his own, Quincy rose at 4:00 A.M., finished off college affairs in the morning, drove his own chaise to the city about noon, and returned for dinner....

Occasional exertions by the majority, business trips by a few, uncommon regimes for the elite marked out the boundaries of the pre-mass transportation city. All of these interests fed the process of change from the 1820s on....

The Suburbs Discover Mass Transportation

[One] group of suburbanites reduced the barriers of time and energy, through the introduction of scheduled public vehicles—coaches, omnibuses, and commuter railroads. Each of these early mass carriers appeared because fringe residents bent long-distance transportation to serve their particular needs....

Taverners, stablers, and teamsters of the suburbs had long been acquainted with the overland stages. During an explosive growth of staging between 1800 and 1830, men of the suburban towns served the passengers, built the vehicles, repaired them, and sometimes owned shares in the stage companies. The larger suburbs had their own daily stage connections with Boston before 1820. The Old Cambridge line, a typical example, operated in a manner identical to that found in the longer runs: the driver stopped in front of a designated tavern at each end of the line and sounded a horn to summon passengers. A traveler might also book passage in advance, just as he could for overland runs, leaving his name at the local tavern, being picked up at its door in the morning and taken directly to any address in central Boston.

In the mid-1820s, citizens of Roxbury, Charlestown, and Cambridge took the radical step of instituting coaches every other hour....

[T]hese lines quickly found a pool of demand, bought more vehicles, hired extra drivers, and attracted rivals. By the early 1830s an assortment of vehicles ran into Boston from the three Cambridge villages and from Neck Village in Charlestown. That decade saw the introduction of omnibuses, the first vehicles designed specifically for local service. Early versions resembled elongated stage coaches, but featured a door at the rear and seats placed along the sides instead of crosswise. For the courageous, more seats were provided on the roof, bringing total capacity to about twenty. The first true omnibus in the United States was built from French plans and began service in New York in 1831. The first omnibus in New England appeared on the Old Cambridge–Boston run, making its maiden trip on Harvard's commencement day in 1834.

From the mid-1830s until the coming of the streetcar in 1856, through good times and bad, coach and omnibus proprietors continuously expanded their operations. In 1840 the Charlestown omnibuses ran every 15 minutes, and 8 vehicles provided half-hour service to Old Cambridge and Cambridgeport. Equipment and routes changed hands rapidly among the semitransient proprietors, while competition and consolidation produced ever larger partnerships that carved up the suburban territory....

Competition also reduced the cost of the ride. During the late 1830s and early 1840s all the omnibus proprietors offered fare reductions through the sale of tickets in package lots. In this "commutation" of fares they borrowed a device from the turnpikes and steamboats. Within a few years, railroad and streetcar companies carried the procedure to higher levels of refinement and introduced the word "commuter" to the language. But the omnibus firms laid the basis. With package tickets, the cost of a round trip dropped below 25 cents on all the routes in Charlestown and Cambridge....

By itself, the coach-omnibus network did not work a revolution in travel. Yet it did provide a regular means of mass access to Boston, and it demonstrated a substantial demand for the service. This pool of demand, so quickly seen and exploited by suburban opportunists, eventually became visible to the lofty Bostonians who backed the first railroads, but not until suburban residents forced them to look at it.

Railroads Discover the Suburbs

Trains, as first conceived, had little to do with the suburbs. Like the bridge and canal projects of the preceding generation, the first railroads were meant to be links to distant markets and resources. They were gigantic ventures, backed by the wealthiest and most powerful men of Boston, who devoted years to their vision of hinterland connections.

Four railroad lines, all aimed at remote goals, traversed the inner Middlesex suburbs. Only two of these actually passed through Cambridge and mainland Charlestown, but these communities were affected by the route choices and policies of all four. The Boston and Lowell, opened in 1835 as the first passenger railway in the state, joined Boston to the Merrimack Valley textile mills. It was, in E. C. Kirkland's words, "an adjunct to an existing industrial development." The Boston and Worcester, opened in stages from 1834 onward, aimed first at the Connecticut River Valley and then at Albany and the West. After a delay during the nationwide depression, competing lines entered the fray. To the west, Fitchburg businessmen launched a rival to the Worcester, a railroad that would give their city its own "access to deep water." The Fitchburg Railroad opened on a route through Cambridge and mainland Charlestown between 1843 and 1845. To the north, the Boston and Maine entered competition with the Lowell and finally obtained its own access to Boston in 1845.

In the ten years between the opening of the Lowell and the arrival of the Maine, managers of all four railroads experienced a wholesale change in their thinking about local passengers. The men who built these lines had dreams of Vermont produce, Lowell fabrics, and New York wheat. They had no initial interest in local travelers. Yet between 1839 and 1845 they rebuilt their facilities to encourage suburban travelers, introduced specially designed and scheduled commuter trains, developed an array of commutation tickets, and plunged heavily into advertising and selling suburban house lots.

This change occurred for two reasons: first, the railroads immediately found an unexpected demand for passenger accommodation, especially in the suburbs. Second, the economic depression of 1837–42, which caught some companies with their lines half-built, gave peculiar importance to a nearby and obvious source of revenue. With their visions of distance temporarily clouded, railroad men had more reason to examine the experience of omnibuses and to bend to appeals from suburban customers....

[A]fter 1837 demand appeared in ways that even [railroad director, Nathan] Hale could not resist. In that year the Lowell established its first intermediate station, opening a makeshift office in a Woburn shoe store. Within two more years the manager had permanently altered the schedule to include regular stops for "way passengers." In 1839 the Eastern Railroad became the first Boston company to adopt season tickets. The first trains over the route of the Fitchburg, intended to carry ice from Fresh Pond in Cambridge, provoked calls for passenger service all along the line. Within a year the managers instituted all-passenger trains and began to make intermediate stops at the north Cambridge cattle market and the bleachery in Somerville. And by the beginning of 1844 they frankly admitted changing their policy:

> The passenger business was deemed of little moment when our road was chartered, and no suitable provision has ever been made for it. But such numbers have desired and patronised regular trains, that the same have been adopted with success; and when proper depots and arrangements shall be made therefore, there is every reason to anticipate a very considerable gain from this source....

Once they recognized a pool of demand, railroad men moved quickly to enlarge it. The Fitchburg promoters found new riders with every station they opened, and ticket sales outstripped their predictions even in the dead of winter. The lesson was not lost. In building the rest of their line they completely reversed the original railroad policy. Delaying their construction schedule, they deviated from the initially surveyed route in order to bring "facilities to important towns of business and travel." Their guide, as they expressed it in January 1845, was "a policy of running for dense population and business villages."

Abandoning their resistance to "separate contracts," the railroad companies now borrowed and improved the device of commutation from the turnpikes, steamboats, and omnibus lines. When the Maine pushed through its extension to Boston in 1844–45, it adopted the entire panoply: suburban depots, special trains, and package and season tickets. Reading their reports, one would think they had invented local travel....

The City of Occasional Riders

The omnibus and the railroad, shaped by suburban pressures, in turn shaped suburban habits and expectations. By themselves, the new facilities made only small changes in metropolitan society. They were too expensive and served too limited an area. At this period, too, before Irish immigration compounded Boston's land shortage, there was little incentive for many city residents to move outward. But these first public carriers opened the way for a revolution later, by changing travel habits, stimulating the sale of residential lots, and enlarging the small but powerful Boston-employed group in the suburban population.

Very quickly, coach and omnibus stretched the realm of occasional journeys. Package tickets, usable at any time, were suited to the needs of shoppers and men on business errands. In the early 1830s, observers spoke of the omnibus as a tool of such intermittent travel, not as a commuter vehicle. It was "the businessman's convenience and the man of pleasure's luxury." Wealthy Bostonians used public transportation to extend their visits and vacations. The train, especially, became a new kind of pleasure carriage. Coach and railroad proprietors tried to spread this practice, encouraging middle-class summer outings to suburban hotels and cemeteries....

Nevertheless, the riding habit spread. A woman who grew up in Cambridge later recalled rides on the omnibus in 1842. Her fellow passengers—Harvard faculty and Cambridge businessmen—had already adopted the commuter custom of reading newspapers while they rode. Throughout the 1830s and 1840s, suburban residents viewed the increase in riding with fascination and distaste.

Charlestown and even Old Cambridge were now increasingly visited by all kinds of city intruders—coaches, chaises, people on horse-back—even on the Sabbath.

In this changing environment of travel, a few suburban landowners began to divide old farms and estates into large house lots. These sales began in the mid-1830s, flagged during the depression years, and revived in the early 1840s. By the middle of that decade, residential subdivision had produced two clusters of new settlement near the omnibus and railroad lines....

In addition to these systematic subdivisions, a number of small operators in Cambridgeport stepped up dealings in house lots. In peculiar alliances, Boston merchants, local tradesmen, and young opportunists began a kind of residential promotion that would shape suburban growth for decades to come. They built side streets off the main arteries, and petitioned the town for public maintenance. They pooled resources to buy land for long-term speculation. They persuaded town authorities to change the name of the old Concord turnpike to the more seductive "Broadway."...

True "commuting"—daily journeys from suburban residence to city work using public carriers—arose gradually out of irregular travel and suburban lot promotion. Before the mid-1840s there was no massive out-migration of transit-riding Bostonians. Throughout the early nineteenth century the mercantile elite was notoriously citybound, venturing into the suburbs mainly for entertainment, retirement, or burial in Mount Auburn Cemetery (opened in 1831). Improved roads encouraged summer rentals of suburban farmhouses, and the very rich had their estates, but many Bostonians continued to think of peripheral residence as a kind of rustication—a cheaper expedient when one could not find or afford suitable housing in the city. Newly arrived or financially embarrassed people might live in the environs, but the city was the place for active and successful men....

Instead of true commuters, the suburbs gained what might be called "transitional" commuters—who could afford omnibus or railroads but were not transportation-dependent. Many owned vehicles; many walked in

good weather. This expansion of the Boston-employed group of suburbanites drew in two kinds of men: previous suburban residents whose work arose from the fringe economy's city linkages and Bostonians who were well-to-do but not wealthy—wholesalers and other specialized merchants rather than ship-owners or textile magnates.

In the 1830s, there was nothing dramatic about this change, either for society or for the individuals concerned. They were a tiny fraction of both the suburban population and the Boston work force. Moreover, for both kinds of Boston employees, entrance to "commuting" involved an extension of old practices. For previous suburban residents, going to work in the city was a part of fringe expansion, when those who processed farm goods opened outlets for selling them. For Bostonians, moving to nearby Cambridgeport continued a separation of home and workplace that had already begun within the city. The West End of Boston, at the city end of the bridge to Cambridge, had become fashionable in the 1820s. Observers noted that merchants were moving there, "not for the sake of business, but to get out of the way of it." In the 1830s, this movement spilled over the bridge into Cambridge.

Yet the transitional commuters soon became a revolutionary force in the suburbs. They joined the interests and leadership patterns of fringe and city, mobilizing the resources of each in a way that would never quite be repeated. They worked in the city and carried city institutions to the suburbs. They were unusually active in suburban society. They owned enough land to allow speculation, and their holdings were geographically concentrated....

With energy, property, and talents, the new wave of Boston employees slipped easily into suburban leadership. In Cambridge, the 80-odd commuters [in 1841] furnished 22 long-term stewards: selectmen, deacons, bank directors. Ten more of the commuter group would eventually serve on the school committee or the city council. [Ed. note: author's data reflect analysis of "all 1,527 white male suburban householders" in four suburban towns, 1841.]

In all of these respects—youth, stability,

concentrated property, and active leadership—the transitional commuters differed from the majority of the suburban population *and* from a later generation of true commuters. They also shared two strong interests: a desire for better access to Boston and a taste for city amenities. Along with the land speculators and suburban tradesmen, and building on the achievements of the young opportunists, they worked to strengthen the city-suburban connection....

Commutation

All of the changes discussed so far—the evolution of the fringe, the first alterations in habits and institutions of travel, and the planting of new, residentially oriented communities in the fringe environment—occurred when the suburbs were still very sparsely populated and rather loosely connected to the city. Only after these developments did the great migration of commuters begin. Mass commuting climaxed and completed the shift from walking to riding communities. Yet unlike the earlier stages of the mobility revolution, the commuter explosion was largely unexpected. Suburban residents opened the way for what they presumed would be a modest number of well-heeled rail and omnibus riders, but the growth of commuting far surpassed their expectations. Between 1845 and 1860 the number of Boston workers living outside the city rose from a few hundred to more than ten thousand. In Cambridge and Somerville the hundred-odd transitional commuters of 1840 became six hundred by 1850, and at least fifteen hundred by the late fifties....

The Migration: Promotional Dream and Economic Reality

Starting in the mid-forties, the commuter migration drew notice as an unprecedented phenomenon. In the absence of either experience or hard data, residents throughout the region were free to indulge in speculation. A few interested parties—first the suburban entrepreneurs, then the Boston railroad men and realtors—encouraged a vision of suburban change that ran well in advance of reality. Reading contemporary accounts, one might well imagine that the whole business community was flocking to suburban homes.

Boston writers, having ignored the suburbs for decades, suddenly became conscious of the number of "Bostonians" who lived beyond the city limits. This outlook extended the views of the merchant elite, who for years had considered anything connected with their commerce to be properly part of Boston. Since they built the railroads to link their wharves to the interior, they tended to think of all riders on public carriers as men of the city. The mobility revolution, in this view, emanated from and centered on Boston. The editor of the *Boston Directory* for 1846 estimated that "2,000 persons daily arrive and depart by Rail Roads, and all other conveyances." Noting the dramatic rise in suburban population, he asserted that "this increase is made up chiefly of men doing business in Boston and who, with their families, reside in these towns."

Boston and suburban speculators fed this dramatic but vague notion of the change. When the railroads finally committed themselves to the commuter trade, they did their best to promote a migration. They cut fares, sold lots themselves, and ran free special trains to carry prospective buyers to new subdivisions....

The land developers responded by stressing the excellence of transportation. Ads for suburban lots summarized the appropriate schedules for trains or omnibuses. By 1850 such literature portrayed a land where every lot was a country paradise, yet all were "within a few minutes' walk of the station."...

From the Boston viewpoint, the growth of commuting involved a spread to some new occupation groups, but not all. Wholesale merchants, the core of the transitional commuter population in the 1840s, were joined by bank workers and lawyers. Bankers, with short hours and relatively high incomes, were among the first to migrate. In 1846, roughly 30 percent of the 128 major staff members of the large Boston banks lived in the suburbs and 65 percent in the city....By 1851, bank personnel numbered 186, of whom 44 percent commuted and 50 percent were Boston residents.

Even among bank workers, the expansion of commuting was a selective process. The presidents and cashiers had prestigious homes on Boston's crescents and squares. Few of them moved in this period. Neither did low-ranking messengers and porters, who could not afford high fares. Instead, commuting spread among the middle-ranking staff of Boston's banks—tellers, bookkeepers, and clerks. These men enjoyed stable, moderately high incomes, but could not pay for a fashionable address. In a period when available middle-class housing in Boston was shrinking, they sought suburban residence....

On the other hand, many kinds of workers did *not* enter the commuting pattern before the late 1850s. The process evident within the banks—a sifting of workers by rank—reflected changes in the whole labor force. The financial-mercantile elite stayed in the city. So did those whose work involved long, strict hours and/or low wages. Physicians, for example, remained close to their patients and facilities in Boston, despite incomes that might allow commuting.... Henry Ingersoll Bowditch, a staff member of Massachusetts General Hospital, exemplified the doctors' dilemma. He made a brief entry into commuting about 1850, buying a house in Weston near the Worcester Railroad. But the journey became a strain on his finances and his schedule, and he sold the house in 1856.

Most shopkeepers and artisans also remained city-bound. Among those listed in the Boston business directory as bakers, apothecaries, and mechanics, only a small percentage had suburban residences before the Civil War. The proportion was a bit higher for carpenters, masons, and painters.... In this period of widespread construction, they could find work in both city and suburbs. High wages and plentiful job openings allowed a few to move outside Boston—but not far outside; in 1855 almost all of the suburban-resident building tradesmen lived in the contiguous suburbs. They could be walking rather than riding "commuters." Furthermore, at least 80 percent of the workers in these trades still lived in Boston....

Thus the commuter migration recruited people selectively from the Boston labor force and inserted them selectively into some areas and occupational levels in the suburbs. Commuting to work was still a practice open only to those with high income and flexible schedules, but there were now large blocs of such people in the inner suburbs. Moreover, the impact of commutation went far beyond the journey to work. The commuter migration went hand-in-hand with a still more intensified use of public transportation for other purposes....

Contemporary accounts by suburbanites—not Bostonians—hinted at the varied pattern of public transportation usage. A description of Malden in 1846 noted the impact of the railroad on town society. Fifty years earlier, said the author,

> a Malden lady wishing to visit Boston by land, had to rise early, and travel by wagon, side-saddle, or pillion..., and when arrived, was so fatigued by her day's journey, that she had to rest a day or two before she was able to make her "calls." But now, how changed! Those cruel turnpike killers, and despisers of horse-flesh, the legislators of Massachusetts, have granted permission to a number of men to set up a long, narrow building on trundles, a sort of travelling-meetinghouse, with a bell to it, and a row of pews on each side of the aisle....By this mode of travelling, a lady or gentleman at Malden may leave home at almost any hour, go down south to Boston, a distance of five miles, see their friends, do their errands, and return, in one short sunny hour.

The railway worked this sort of revolution in many suburban towns, bringing them suddenly from the hinterland to within a few minutes' reach of the city. Many residents of these towns shared the reaction of their contemporary Thoreau: the train whistle of the 1840s remained a lifelong symbol of their shattered solitude.

By the mid-1850s the shift from walking to riding was far advanced. More commuters, and more use of public carriers for trips once accomplished on foot, had firmly established a pattern of travel that was to characterize suburban life for decades to come....

ESSAY 3-2. GWENDOLYN WRIGHT, *MORALISM AND THE MODEL HOME: DOMESTIC ARCHITECTURE AND CULTURAL CONFLICT IN CHICAGO, 1873–1913* (1980)

Source: University of Chicago Press. Copyright © 1980 by The University of Chicago.

The rapid growth of American industrial capitalism in the late nineteenth century generated not only more products but also a larger urban middle class with enough money and stability to invest in houses and in goods for homes. In fact, home ownership was, by and large, taken as a central part of a family's definition as "middle class"—a word just coming into the national vocabulary. Most of the members of this group could not afford the services of an architect to custom design their homes. Yet they were extremely susceptible to current ideas about house design.

This widespread interest in residential architecture was one aspect of a more general focus on the home itself in the late nineteenth century. As [writer] Abba Gould Woolson sought to emphasize, the home was supposed to be a haven apart from the industrial and commercial world. Home was idealized as a retreat for men and a refuge for women. The late Victorian sentimentalization of womanhood—that is, middle-class womanhood—was intimately bound up with the highly expressive, supposedly organic architectural motifs which had come to be so popular for American homes. Moreover, as we shall see, the opening of the suburbs to middle-class families, a development made possible by the dramatic breakthroughs in public transportation of the 1880s and 1890s, would further intensify this cult of difference between men and women, work and home. But it was a tenuous distinction. Obviously, it relied upon advances in industrial technology—quite directly in fact. And it would not last.

The Industrialization of Home-Making

The ideology celebrating the ornamented, personalized home was facilitated by the increased availability of descriptions and images of model homes. Advances in printing technology, reproduction techniques for illustrations, and transportation services refined and disseminated ideas for the home.... The illustrations of houses in builders' guides and in professional architectural journals could now, as never before, emphasize details of texture and ornament as well as mood. Although the popular media certainly did not create the cult of the romantic home, these technological advances allowed that ideal to be intimately connected to specific symbolic details of architecture.

As these images crossed the country, becoming available in every town and city, other dramatic advances were also reshaping the production of homes. House-building itself was central to the American economy throughout most of the nineteenth century. In every city, private expenditures for construction, both residential and commercial, and developers' or communities' outlays for public services—including roads, sewer systems, water works and fire departments—constituted the single most important contribution to the nation's economy. Although the proportion of national and family income that went into housing began to decline by the end of the century (and dropped even more at the beginning of the next), production of housing units remained high, and was crucial to the growth of American industry. There were jobs not only in construction but also in affiliated fields, from the production of building materials and furniture to plumbing equipment and kitchen utensils. Although the depression of 1873 slowed housing starts in most cities, these other industries continued to expand.

As the nation's population rose—increasing almost threefold between 1860 and 1900, with the urban population increasing fourfold—new housing stock was urgently required. Growth in the Midwest was especially rapid. Chicago's population rose from 300,000 in 1870 to 500,000 ten years later, and to twice that by 1890. In large part, this remarkable boom occurred because the city was emerging as a national center for almost every aspect of the flourishing housing industry.... Chicago became the country's principal source for raw materials for housing—especially lumber, but also brick and stone; it produced great quantities of plumbing fixtures and window glass; it was the nation's largest manufacturer of furniture. Chicago was also the distribution center for all of these goods....

In Chicago, as elsewhere in the country, the number of people who could be considered middle-class was on the rise. Clerical workers, salespeople, government employees, technicians, and salaried professionals increased in the census figures more rapidly than the old middle class of business entrepreneurs and independent professionals; more rapidly, in fact, than the population of the nation as a whole. National income was, consequently, increasing too, from $237 per capita in 1870 to $309 in 1880 to $492 by 1900. While families were insecure about their social status and financial future in many ways—since the major earners were generally in someone else's employ—they could rely on steady incomes at these salaried jobs. A clerk in an insurance firm in Chicago earned about $1,500 a year in 1880, and $1,800 by 1890. A lawyer in a small firm might be earning $4,000 by 1890. (In contrast, many skilled workers brought home only $500 to $800 in a year, and most working-class families lived on less than that.) These income levels and occupational groups defined the middle classes.

But so did home ownership. By American standards, as expressed in the popular builders' texts, women's domestic guides, and other literature of the late nineteenth century, the "middle-class family" was recognized by home ownership, and by the quality of that home, as well as by the man's employment. Certainly the range of middle-class families I have just cited were able to buy their own homes, often in the outlying suburbs by the end of the century, and to furnish them fairly stylishly—although probably only the young lawyer could consider a professional architect's services in designing his home. Most of the families who, by their own definition, were middle-class would either work with a local carpenter (who asked only a flat fee to interpret a pattern-book design) or purchase a speculatively built house from a builder or from a previous owner who was moving.

However, home ownership was not as widespread as many Americans wanted to believe. A survey which was first made part of the census in 1890 showed that, nationwide, only 48 percent of American families owned their own homes; in cities of over 100,000, that figure dropped to 23 percent....Thus, when builders like S. E. Gross began to offer "easy payment" systems of financing for houses that cost between $1,000 and $5,000 (plus financing charges and land), they indeed seemed to offer an opportunity to expand the ranks of the American middle class by making inexpensive suburban homes more widely available....

The availability and the very appearance of these homes were made possible by recent industrial advances. A new range of machinery allowed builders to apply the architectural complexities of the Eastlake or the Queen Anne or the Moorish styles to relatively inexpensive dwellings. It was not, however, industrial production itself that was new. Since the 1850s, American mills had produced machine-cut moldings and kept them in stock for builders, but the moldings had been fairly plain and coarse. The advent of steam power permitted the use of equipment that made such ornament faster and in greater variety. By 1870, 70 percent of the lumber-milling firms in this country that made stock blinds, window sashes, doors, and ornament relied on fast, heavy steam-powered equipment rather than on foot-velocipedes for each machine. After 1871 there was a flood of inventions for even faster, cheaper machines....

By the late 1870s, much of the decoration for the stylish middle-class dwelling was already being produced in a factory, shipped across the country by railroad, and then simply tacked onto the dwelling. Strips of detailing were produced in an increasingly wide assortment of shapes, sizes, and grades. They were mostly in wood, although there was also factory-produced ornamental work in metal, plaster, and terra-cotta. A great variety of more delicate shapes replaced the old jigsawn, straight-edged ornament of the pre-Civil War "gingerbread age," crafted by the carpenter on the site. Carpenters' pattern books continued to show how to carve imaginative ornament, but in the back of the same books were advertisements for the latest woodworking machinery.

Shingles, cut to resemble fish scales or snowflakes, or left rough-edged and "natural," could be produced cheaper and faster by a factory. Moldings were available in elegant beading or floral designs, always regular and precise. Spindles in delicate cylindrical shapes, Venetian blinds with beveled slats, capitals in every order and disorder came from architectural supply companies. The pieces had only to be bradded and glued into place. Most doors, frames, window sash, and wainscotting panels were produced in the mill. Entire porches and stairs could be ordered from catalogues….These economies…were essential in any house costing less than $4,000—that is, any moderately priced middle-class home.

The major difference during the 1870s and 1880s was not mechanization per se, but the greatly increased output and variety. Mechanization of house-building and decorating did not arrive all of a sudden, spurred by a particular fashion or even an ingenious inventor. Devices like lathes and templates had been used in woodworking for generations. But now productivity improved dramatically with new precision equipment. Higher-grade steel blades allowed the steam-powered machines to be used at full speed, without cease, with no danger of metal fatigue….

New machinery also speeded up and systematized the production of other building materials. A factory worker could cut recessed panels in stone, embellishing the blocks with flat arabesque ornament modeled from templates. Since brick had become more expensive (doubling in price just two weeks after Chicago's 1871 fire, then rising more gradually), brickworks soon shifted from handmade to machine-made product…. New processes for grinding tints and mixing mineral paints or oil stains expanded the range of colors that could be used to adorn any house. Paint and sand combinations were also used to simulate other materials, for instance, giving galvanized sheet metal the rough texture of sandstone.

The new techniques encouraged extravagant display, while making ornament more accessible to American builders and homeowners. In fact, by the late 1880s, architects and builders were demanding some restraint. John Root protested the "disastrous effects" of the fast-expanding range of colors and textures available in manufactured bricks, terra-cotta, and paint, condemning the metallic sheens, the glaring clashes of colors, the artificiality of the products. The carpenter Fred Hodgson was encouraged by the spread of Richardsonian motifs, with their simple, unadorned lines. Most people were still delighted with the spectacle of complex shapes and varied materials, however.

Industrial processes were transforming the inside of the house too. There were large assortments of wooden latticework screens, stairway balustrades, and plaster rosettes. During the 1880s, as the use of steam power and new machinery revolutionized the plaster industry, it was also easier to have a smooth, plain surface for a wall. Hand-applied plaster, like brick mortar, had required time and skill. After being mixed, on the site, the combination of lime, sand, and animal hair had to wait "in stack" before it could be "wet up" and readied for use. With patented chemical plasters made in a factory, quality could be controlled and time saved on the site, since the materials could be transported wet and ready to apply. By 1896, when it was said that 99 percent of the homes in the United States had plastered walls, ceilings, and partitions, workers relied almost solely on factory-produced plaster, wire-lathe, and mortar….

Perhaps the most conspicuous and most discussed improvement in domestic building technology was in heating and plumbing fixtures. Basement hot-air or hot-water furnaces, connected to a maze of flues and registers, were still fairly expensive in 1880; but they were being introduced into some middle-class homes (although stoves were still the norm and fireplaces were a highly symbolic additional source of heat). Furnaces had to be frequently stoked with coal, and the register in each room adjusted by hand, until automatic controls became available in the early twentieth century. These systems were thus troublesome as well as expensive. Nonetheless, room stoves, registers, and even furnaces were displayed as proud possessions and works of art. Whether in the parlor, the kitchen, or the basement, heating appliances were encrusted with ornament to make them artistic....

Plumbing was an even more complicated matter. Although drainage systems were still primitive (pipes usually emptied into cesspools or pigpens rather than municipal sewage lines) and hot water was a luxury, more careful planning for sanitation was taking place. Manufacturers of plumbing equipment reported soaring sales in the 1880s. Changing public attitudes about home sanitation, directly related to fears about germs and "sewer gas," stimulated the technological advances....The year 1880 had been epochal, according to the *Architectural Record*; after this date, "true sanitary plumbing" began, with porcelain fixtures, exposed pipes in galvanized wrought iron, and careful specifications issued by architects and builders. The outdoor privy and indoor earth-closet seemed primitive now; the modern flush toilet, developed about 1778, came into general use a hundred years later. The practice of installing washstands in every bedroom, with porcelain or tile "splashers" on the wall behind them, was often discarded in new homes. By the end of the century, the bathroom would no longer be looked upon as an effeminate luxury. Toilets would no longer be isolated outside the house's walls. Taking a bath would not be considered potentially dangerous. Of necessity, the new plumbing systems for fresh water and for waste were now connected to municipal sewage and water supplies in the major cities and well-to-do suburbs. The older systems periodically overflowed with the vast amounts of waste water emptied into them.

Both the municipal services and the more refined home-fixtures greatly increased the homeowner's average expenditures. The cost for plumbing an average (that is, $3,000) American house in 1860 had been estimated at about $250; by 1890 similar estimates ranged between $500 and $1,000, often reaching a fifth of the total cost of the house. Americans were willing to pay. They had come to trust the manufacturers of their plumbing equipment and the sanitary engineers with their health.

The impact of technology on the late-nineteenth-century dwelling also extended to public transportation and the construction process itself. The expansion of American cities in the 1870s, while remarkable, had been contained by the still primitive public transportation networks of slow horsecars and infrequent, expensive railroads. In Chicago, in the aftermath of the fire of 1871, which had destroyed three and a half square miles of the city center, residential settlement began to move outward. But the process was gradual and the new neighborhoods were often congested. Investment proved, however, quite profitable. In Hyde Park and Englewood, to the south of the city, but still fairly close to the downtown, investors reaped benefits of 1,000 to 15,000 percent in five or six years. A belt of frame workingmen's cottages, erected by development companies or building and loan associations and owned by their inhabitants, formed a semicircle around the outskirts of Chicago to the south and west, although the ring was a narrow one. Strict municipal legislation preventing the use of wood construction within designated fire limits prompted much of the new building. Since stone and brick were so expensive, many builders who specialized in moderate-cost dwellings concentrated on the nearby suburban towns or undeveloped areas rather than increase their construction costs....

The difficulties of existing transportation did contain Chicago's expansion of the 1870s to a mere half-mile beyond the existing limits. But there were experiments going on which would change this pattern, in hundreds of cities, within a decade. The introduction of the cable car in 1882 was followed by the electric trolley in 1888 and the first elevated railroad in 1892. Chicago quickly installed each of these services, but the major commitment was in electrifying the municipal streetcar lines in 1889. This made commuting on the streetcar from the suburbs easy and much faster. Speeds were twice those of the old horsecars, even if conditions were crowded. In 1890, at the insistence of commuters, the legal rate of speed for the suburban streetcars was increased from ten to twenty miles per hour in the city, and up to thirty miles per hour outside the city limits, cutting the time even more. Railroad service was soon extended to match the new competition. The Blue Island Land and Building Company, in operation since 1869, developed Morgan Park on the suburban branch of their Rock Island Railroad. By 1905, there were fourteen daily trains each way from Morgan Park to downtown Chicago, thirteen miles away; it was a daily round trip of from thirty-five to fifty minutes, with a monthly ticket costing only $2.25, about the price of a new pair of men's pants and within a middle-class family's budget.

The proliferation of these services, together with the relatively inexpensive fares and faster speeds, allowed formerly urban middle-class families to commute to work or shopping from the suburbs. The streetcar lines brought thousands of Chicagoans to the small, ornamented, romantic houses going up outside the city. In making suburban life available to so many families, the streetcar service brought about an extraordinary increase in the size—both population and area—of many cities. The city limits of Chicago swelled outward after the improved transportation facilities were installed. To provide for necessary services, new territory was annexed, increasing the municipal tax base. In 1870, the outer limits of Chicago were five miles beyond the main downtown corner; by 1890, the combination of new transportation networks, record construction figures, a fourfold increase in the city's population, and a massive annexation of land to the west the year before, had pushed the limits to twelve miles.

The expansion was controlled and manipulated by a few private investors. Yet because of the enthusiastic public support for the suburban services, city councils made great concessions to those businessmen who provided the services. Charles Yerkes centralized the transportation lines in Chicago, for instance, and thus became one of the most powerful of a new breed of American streetcar magnates. Together with a group of aldermen known as the "Gray Wolves," he made a fortune by investing in transportation companies and real estate. By 1893, after eight years of dealing, Yerkes owned not only most of the five hundred miles of streetcar tracks in and around Chicago, but he had been able to sell the land along the routes he had planned. The situation was similar in many other American cities—Omaha, Denver, Oakland, Minneapolis—where unprecedented population increases and the almost desperate demand for transportation services gave such entrepreneurs a free hand, at least for a time. The progressive reform campaign at the end of the century would later turn against the traction trusts, and in Chicago's case, force Yerkes to leave the city. During the 1880s and early 1890s, however, he seemed to promise much the same package as most popular builders: the rediscovery of nature, the escape from the city's problems, the preservation of the family. He assured Chicago of health, individuality, and freedom in the suburbs, made possible with streetcar commuting....

The Home as Retreat from Industry

This rapidly expanding world of industrial production supported a rich, complex imagery for American residential architecture. The popular styles of the 1870s and 1880s held the public's fancy in large part because the forms supposedly represented and reinforced an ideal of the home and family. The celebration of home, family, and womanhood—now known as the cult of domesticity—took shape in the early nineteenth century. And it flourished. Later, toward the end of the century, with the opening of the suburbs to many middle-class families and the dramatically increased production of ornament for facades and furnishings for interiors, it was easier to celebrate the individual distinctions between families and the more general distinction between homes and the tall buildings going up in downtown areas. What had been a rhetoric proclaiming "the home" and "the world" as separate realms now became much more of an actual physical reality....

In fact, it was the industrial production of goods and the commercialism of their presentation to the public that allowed the very ideal of the home as a separate world to flower as it did. Yet, the two worlds of Victorian men and women did have their own distinct aesthetics now, representing symbolically their opposite, symbiotic systems: the skyscraper and the Queen Anne cottage; one soaring high, of stone, plain and functional; the other low to the ground, of wood, and ornately decorated. Each kind of architecture relied upon advances in American industry, and each, in its turn, was a reaction to the pressures of the industrial, capitalist city.

NOTES

1. Steven Lubar, Syllabus to HSSC003, "Technology and Society," University of Pennsylvania, http://ccat.sas.upenn.edu/slubar/handout.html (accessed, September, 2005).

2. Sam Bass Warner, Jr., *Streetcar Suburbs: The Process of Growth in Boston, 1870-1900* (Cambridge, MA: Harvard University Press, 1962).

CHAPTER 4

Economic and Class Diversity on the Early Suburban Fringe

INTRODUCTION

The notion of suburbia as a uniformly affluent space—the "cool green rim" of the city turned over to wealthy commuters and their well-appointed homes—was an illusion from the start.[1] While the suburban ideal juxtaposed the smokestacks, poverty, and social diversity of the city against the natural landscapes and social refinement of the suburbs, in reality suburbia encompassed a variegated environment of people and land uses linked to expanding urban centers. Moreover, as the nineteenth century progressed, those very emblems of the industrial city—smokestacks and the people who toiled beneath them—were moving to suburbia in growing numbers. The city's edge, it turns out, was a region of striking economic and class diversity.

Recognition of this trend has been a point of some controversy. Early elite suburbanites themselves were well aware of the variety of people and landscapes that surrounded them. And some early social scientists, such as Graham Taylor and Harlan Paul Douglass, pointed out the growing diversity of suburbia in the 1910s and 1920s, but their work went largely unnoticed by subsequent scholars and historians. Why? One reason was the almost single-minded focus of the popular media on elite and middle-class suburbia, and the narrow definition of "suburb" that it helped promote. National magazine articles, product advertisements, and house plans depicted affluent suburbia as the ideal for all Americans. If there was another reality on the ground, the volume and reach of these suburban images obscured it. Another reason was academic. In the 1920s, scholars working at the University of Chicago developed a model of urban space—known as the concentric zone model—which, among other things, juxtaposed a poor inner city with an affluent suburban periphery. Scholars then and later used the concept as a handy framework for critically assessing North American cities. Eventually, the public accepted it as conventional wisdom. Especially in the post-World War II era, scholars preoccupied with inner city decline and middle-class suburban conformity found the Chicago School theories a useful context for their own arguments. In the process, they down-played the model's inherent complexities and they ignored older evidence—like the work of Taylor and Douglass—which complicated the picture. As geographers Richard Harris and Robert Lewis caution, "we would do well to remember that places and patterns are always more complex than is implied by the way we label them."[2] This chapter offers evidence that suburbs were indeed places of significant economic and class diversity by the late nineteenth century, a trend that would continue to the present day. Factories, retailers, and offices were all migrating to the periphery, as were white workers, immigrants, and African Americans. Often settling in their own enclaves, separate from affluent suburbs, they created a pattern of "segregated diversity" on the suburban edge.

This exodus offers another way of thinking about the decentralizing trend. Thus far we have seen how an emerging affluent suburban ideal, facilitated by technological advances and the profit-motive of real estate promoters, represented a driving force for suburbanization. Another set of forces revolved around the needs of manufacturers, retailers, and working people. Factory owners saw certain advantages in suburban locales: cheaper land, minimal traffic congestion, lower taxes, and a more malleable labor force. Working people sought homes close to these workplaces, as well as communities of kin and friends, open space, and affordable land. And retailers followed their customers to the city's edge.

The result was a suburban landscape of striking diversity: exclusive elite communities of rambling homes set in park-like environs, industrial sites of vigorous production, towns of modest working-class homes, streetcar suburbs with vast tracts of speculative housing, shopping areas large and small. In its complexity, this suburban portrait complicates certain stereotypes and assumptions. For one, it challenges the notion of a singular affluent suburban ideal and invites exploration of alternative ideals. It also challenges a clear-cut dichotomy that pits poor city versus affluent suburb.

The mélange of people and activities in suburbia did not spell the end of the suburban ideal. To the contrary, affluent suburbanites would seek to protect their ideal in the face of this variety, devising new methods to ensure community exclusivity. At the same time, suburbanites of more modest means would fashion suburban ideals of their own. Diversity in suburbia existed, thus, on many levels: in how land was used, in who lived there, and finally in what people believed about the places where they lived.

DOCUMENTS

In the 1920s, a group of sociologists and urban scholars at the University of Chicago coalesced around the study of the modern city, forming what became known as the Chicago School. A central part of their urban theory was the notion that every city shared the same general social geography: a congested downtown of mixed activity surrounded by rings of increasingly spacious and affluent residential neighborhoods. The seminal statement of this "concentric zone theory" is presented in **Document 4-1**, by sociologist Ernest Burgess. Although Burgess acknowledged variation within cities and suburbs, later scholars would oversimplify his model, creating an urban framework that juxtaposed inner-city poverty and suburban prosperity.

Document 4-2 provides a poetic counterpoint to the Chicago model. In it, William Dean Howells, one of the leading men of letters in nineteenth-century America, describes "a pedestrian tour" through the environs surrounding his home in Charlesbridge, Massachusetts, just north of Boston (the same landscape that Henry Binford examines in chapter 3). Howells exposes class, cultural, and religious conflicts set against a suburban landscape undergoing rapid, almost dizzying change. In **Document 4-3**, the social diversity Howells describes is presented pictorially. Two images from Howells's *Suburban Sketches* (1882) depict an Italian organ grinder, and two Irish women in the Dublin neighborhood (described in Document 4-2), just three of the many working-class and immigrant characters who peopled the author's neighborhood in the developing suburbs of Boston. The third image from a popular collection of short stories by the humorist H.C. Bunner depicts a suburban couple and their Irish landscaper, "Pat Brannigan." While these illustrations purposely emphasize the impression of social difference and inequality among their subjects, they nonetheless indicate that social heterogeneity was a familiar feature of late nineteenth century suburbia.

Working in the early part of the twentieth century at about the same time as the Chicago School, a group of lesser-known urban scholars produced research that mirrored the insights of early suburbanites like Howells, and challenged the city/suburb dichotomy of their Chicago colleagues. **Document 4-4** and **Document 4-5** present examples from this work. **Document 4-4** is an excerpt from reformer Graham Taylor's 1915 book, which surveys industrial suburbs across the United States. His work offers vivid details about the scope and conditions of these communities. In true Progressive fashion, he aims to present a factual profile of these suburbs as a first step to reforming them, particularly through more active, enlightened planning. **Document 4-5** is an excerpt from Harlan Douglass's, *The Suburban Trend* (1925), the first comprehensive survey of American suburbs. In this important work, Douglass documents a remarkable variety of suburban types, from rich to poor, planned to unplanned, as well as variations characterized by race, ethnicity, even age of residents. While Douglass identified two main categories of suburbs, residential and industrial (the latter more numerous), he recognized that these labels did not capture the full extent of suburban variation.

Document 4-6 includes pictures from upper-crust enclaves, middling streetcar suburbs, and industrial suburbs. Two images depict the presence of industry in the suburban periphery: a bird's eye view of South Chicago showing the scale of industrial decentralization as early as 1874, while the 1939 photo of a Birmingham, Alabama area steel plant and worker housing offers a more human-scale perspective on industrial suburbanization. Photos of spacious estate homes in elite suburban areas of Birmingham, Alabama, Brookline, Massachusetts, and Madison, New Jersey, suggest the wealth and expansiveness that continued to define upper-class suburbia in the late nineteenth and early twentieth centuries. Of note, the Schlesinger estate in Brookline shown here was landscaped by Frederick Law Olmsted. Photos of early streetcar suburbs suggest a middling range of suburban residence.

Document 4-7 and **Document 4-8** chronicle another aspect of the decentralizing trend, the movement of retail stores to suburbia. Although the *Business Week* writer in **Document 4-7** emphasizes the factors pushing stores out of downtown, the pull of expanding suburban markets was also at work. In **Document 4-8,** we see two early examples of planned suburban shopping centers designed to accommodate shoppers who arrived by automobile—early precursors to the postwar suburban shopping mall. The first is a postcard of Kansas City's Country Club Plaza, renown as the first automobile-oriented shopping center in America. The brainchild of developer J. C. Nichols, it brought together retail on the first floor and professional offices (doctors, dentists, and attorneys) on the second, with plenty of parking for customers. The Plaza was designed in Spanish-Moorish style, with waterfalls, fountains, and lavish landscaping designed to appeal to upscale patrons who lived in adjacent suburbs. Country Club Plaza was completed in 1925. The second image shows an early example of an auto strip shopping center—what we today call a "minimall"—the aptly named Park and Shop center. Constructed in 1930 in an affluent residential area of northwest Washington D.C., it was designed to appeal to local shoppers and passing auto commuters on their way home.

How is "suburb" defined in this chapter? How do these definitions contrast with the elite suburban ideal outlined in earlier chapters? What, in your opinion, constitutes a suburb, and why does the definition matter? What are the differing explanations for the causes of industrial suburbanization, and which do you agree with? Why?

4-1. ERNEST BURGESS OUTLINES THE CHICAGO SCHOOL'S "CONCENTRIC ZONE THEORY," 1929

Source: Ernest Burgess, "Urban Areas," in *Chicago: An Experiment in Social Science Research*, eds. T.V. Smith and Leonard D. White (Chicago: University of Chicago Press, 1929).

A human community, like a biological organism, grows by the process of subdivision. As a city grows, its structure becomes more complex and its areas more specialized. Increasing differentiation, however, involves more rather than less co-operation and interdependence. The specialized areas of the city, as the central retail business district, the industrial community, the residential neighborhood, and suburban towns and villages are all organic parts of the city, because of rather than in spite of their differentiated functions....

Accordingly, an analysis of the factors and forces in the growth of the city was first made in order to understand the general pattern of the formation of urban areas.

Out of the many factors affecting the pattern of city formation, three may be selected as, perhaps, decisive:

1. The radial character of city growth, or the tendency of a community to outward expansion from its center.
2. Natural or artificial variations in the topographical features of the city, including elevation, site on coast, lake, or river, barriers like river, elevated railroad lines, and parks.
3. The general features of the street plan of the city, including the structure of the local transportation system.

Of these factors in city growth, that of radial expansion seems to leave its deepest impress upon the structure of the city. The various studies of urban areas in Chicago have traced out the factors in city growth, movement of population, and community organization.

Radial Expansion and the Five Urban Zones

As any community increases in numbers of inhabitants, expansion naturally takes place by movement of residents beyond the out-skirts of the already settled territory. The expansion of the urban business district may be in the air, via the skyscraper; but it also presses outward into the surrounding residential district. This outward expansion in all directions from the center toward the peripheries of the community may be called the force of radial extension. In the absence of counteracting factors, the assumption is advanced that the modern American city would take the form of five concentric urban zones as represented in the figure 4.1.

Zone I: The Central Business District.—At the center of the city as the focus of its commercial, social, and civic life is situated the Central Business District. The heart of this district is the downtown retail district with its department stores, its smart shops, its office buildings, its clubs, its banks, its hotels, its theaters, its museums, and its headquarters of economic, social, civic, and political

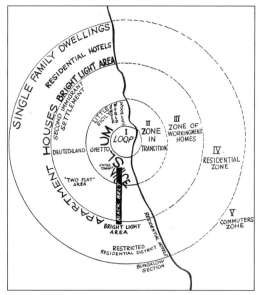

Figure 4-1 Urban Zones and Areas, 1929. Illustration in original, 115.

life. Encircling this area of work and play is the less well-known Wholesale Business District with its "market," its warehouses, and storage buildings.

Zone II: The Zone in Transition.—Surrounding the Central Business District are areas of residential deterioration caused by the encroaching of business and industry from Zone I. This may therefore be called a Zone in Transition, with a factory district for its inner belt and an outer ring of retrogressing neighborhoods, of first-settlement immigrant colonies, of rooming-house districts, of homeless-men areas, of resorts of gambling, bootlegging, sexual vice, and of breeding-places of crime. In this area of physical deterioration and social disorganization our studies show the greatest concentration of cases of poverty, bad housing, juvenile delinquency, family disintegration, physical and mental disease. As families and individuals prosper, they escape from this area into Zone III beyond, leaving behind as marooned a residuum of the defeated, leaderless, and helpless.

Zone III: The Zone of Independent Workingmen's Homes.—This third broad urban ring is in Chicago, as well as in other northern industrial cities, largely constituted by neighborhoods of second immigrant settlement. Its residents are those who desire to live near but not too close to their work. In Chicago it is a housing area neither of tenements, apartments, nor of single dwellings; its boundaries have been roughly determined by the plotting of the two-flat dwelling, generally of frame construction with the owner living on the lower floor with a tenant on the other. While the father works in the factory the son and daughter typically have jobs in the Loop, attend dance halls and motion pictures in the bright-light areas, and plan upon marriage to set up homes in Zone IV.

Zone IV: The Zone of Better Residences.—Extending beyond the neighborhoods of second immigrant settlements, we come to the Zone of Better Residences in which the great middle-classes of native-born Americans live, small business men, professional people, clerks, and salesmen. Once communities of single homes, these are becoming in Chicago apartment-house and residential-hotel areas. Within these areas at strategic points are found local business centers of such growing importance that they have been called "satellite Loops." The typical constellation of business and recreational units includes a bank, one or more United Cigar Stores, a drug store, a high class restaurant, an automobile display row, and a so-called "wonder" motion-picture theater. With the addition of a dancing palace, a cabaret, and a smart hotel, the satellite Loop also becomes a "bright-light area" attracting a city-wide attendance. In this zone men are outnumbered by women, independence in voting is frequent, newspapers and books have wide circulation, and women are elected to the state legislature.

Zone V: The Commuters' Zone.—Out beyond the areas of better residence is a ring of encircling small cities, towns, and hamlets, which, taken together, constitute the Commuters' Zone. These are also, in the main, dormitory suburbs, because the majority of men residing there spend the day at work in the Loop (Central Business District), returning only for the night. Thus the mother and the wife become the center of family life. If the Central Business District is predominately a homeless-men's region; the rooming-house district, the habitat of the emancipated family; the area of first-immigrant settlement, the natural soil of the patriarchal family transplanted from Europe; the Zone of Better Residences with its apartment houses and residential hotels, the favorable environment for the equalitarian family; then the Commuters' Zone is without question the domain of the matricentric family. The communities in this Commuters' Zone are probably the most highly segregated of any in the entire metropolitan region, including in their range the entire gamut from an incorporated village run in the interests of crime and vice, such as Burnham, to Lake Forest, with its wealth, culture, and public spirit.

The pattern of concentric zones may be carried even beyond the Commuters' Zone, whose outer boundary is ordinarily understood to be coterminous with that of the metropolitan region. But beyond the metropolitan region of Chicago, with a radius of sixty miles and including sixteen counties in three states, lies the great hinterland which looks to the metropolis as its market and its jobbing center. This larger Chicagoland includes all or practically all of the five states of Illinois, Michigan, Indiana, Iowa, and Wisconsin. Its leadership in certain activities extends over all the North Central States.

If the principle of radial extension outward from the center of the city were the only factor operating to determine urban growth, then we might expect Chicago and every other rapidly growing American city to exhibit perfect examples of the five-zone pattern. Even with the complications caused by lake front location and the Chicago River with its north and south branch, the studies made by the Local Community Research Committee, the Institute of Juvenile Research, and the Department of Survey of the Chicago Church Federation, and the Congregational City Missionary Society show how phenomena of poverty, delinquency, crime, boys' gangs, home ownership, increase or decrease in population, increase or decrease in church membership rise or fall as the case may be, with only slight irregularities from zone to zone as one proceeds from the center of the city to the Commuters' Zone. This distribution of these phenomena would seem to indicate the predominance of this factor of urban extension in city growth over counteracting forces.

4-2. WILLIAM DEAN HOWELLS DESCRIBES A WALK ABOUT HIS SUBURBAN NEIGHBORHOOD, 1872

Source: William Dean Howells, *Suburban Sketches* (Boston: Houghton, Mifflin and Co., 1882, original copyright 1872).

[I]t is certain that some sort of recreation is necessary after a day spent within doors; and one is really obliged nowadays to take a little walk instead of medicine; for one's doctor is sure to have a mania on the subject, and there is no more getting pills or powders out of him for a slight indigestion than if they had all been shot away at the rebels during the war. For this reason I sometimes go upon a pedestrian tour, which is of no great extent in itself, and which I moreover modify by keeping always within sound of the horse-car bells, or easy reach of some steam-car station....

As I sally forth upon Benicia Street, the whole suburb of Charlesbridge stretches about me,—a vast space upon which I can embroider any fancy I like as I saunter along. I have no associations with it, or memories of it, and, at some seasons, I might wander for days in the most frequented parts of it, and meet hardly any one I know. It is not, however, to these parts that I commonly turn, but northward, up a street upon which a flight of French-roof houses suddenly settled a year or two since, with families in them, and many outward signs of permanence, though their precipitate arrival might cast some doubt upon this....[F]or all my admiration of the houses, I find variety that is pleasanter in the landscape, when I reach, beyond them, a little bridge which appears to span a small stream. It unites banks lined with a growth of trees and briers nodding their heads above the neighboring levels, and suggesting a quiet water-course, though in fact it is the Fitchburg Railroad that purls between them, with rippling freight and passenger trains and ever-gurgling locomotives....If I descend...and follow the railroad westward half a mile, I come to vast brick-yards, which are not in themselves exciting to the imagination, and which yet, from an irresistible association of ideas, remind me of Egypt, and are forever newly forsaken of those who made bricks without straw....A little farther on I come to the boarding-house built at the railroad side for the French Canadians who have by this time succeeded the Hebrews in the toil of the brick-yards, and who, as they loiter in windy-voiced, good-humored groups about the doors of their lodgings, insist upon bringing before me the town of St. Michel at the mouth of the great Mont Cenis tunnel, where so many peasant folk like them are always amiably quarreling before the cabarets....Well, it takes as little to make one happy as miserable, thank Heaven! and I derive a cheerfulness from this scene....With repaired spirits I take my way up through the brick-yards towards the Irish settlement on the north, passing under the long sheds that shelter the kilns....

It is perhaps in a pious recognition of our mortality that Dublin [Ed. note: the name of the neighborhood] is built around the Irish grave-yard. Most of its windows look out upon the sepulchral monuments and the pretty constant arrival of the funeral trains with their long lines of carriages bringing to the celebration of the sad ultimate rites those gay companies of Irish mourners. I suppose that the spectacle...is not at all depressing to the inhabitants of Dublin; but that, on the contrary, it must beget in them a feeling which, if not resignation to death, is, at least, a sort of subacute cheerfulness in his presence. None but a Dubliner, however, would have been greatly animated by a scene which I witnessed during a stroll through this cemetery one afternoon of early spring....Whilst I stood revolving this thought in my mind, and reading the Irish names upon the stones and the black head-boards,—the tatter adorned with pictures of angels, once-gilt, but now weather-worn down to the yellow paint,—a wail of intolerable pathos filled the air: "O my darling, O my darling! O – O – O!" with sobs and groans and sighs; and, looking about, I saw two women, one standing upright beside another that had cast herself upon a grave, and lay, clasping it with her comfortless arms, uttering these cries. The grave was a year old at least, but the grief seemed of yesterday or of that morning. At times the friend that stood beside the prostrate woman stooped and spoke a soothing word to her, while she wailed out her woe; and in the midst some little ribald Irish boys came scuffling and quarreling up the pathway, singing snatches of an obscene song; and when both the wailing and the singing had died away, an old woman, decently clad, and with her many-wrinkled face softened by the old-fashioned frill running round the inside of her cap, dropped down upon her knees beside a very old grave, and clasped her hands in a silent prayer above it....

In yet earlier spring walks through Dublin, I found a depth of mud appalling even to one who had lived three years in Charlesbridge. The streets were passable only to pedestrians skilled in shifting themselves along the sides of fences and alert to take advantage of every projecting doorstep. There were no dry places, except in front of the groceries, where the ground was beaten hard by the broad feet of loafing geese and the coming and going of admirably small children making purchases there. The number of the little ones was quite as remarkable as their size, and ought to have been even more interesting, if, as sometimes appears probable, such increase shall—together with the well-known ambition of Dubliners to rule the land—one day make an end of us poor Yankees as a dominant plurality....

[T]hough the streets of Dublin were not at all cared for, and though every house on the main thoroughfare stood upon the brink of a slough, without yard, or any attempt at garden or shrubbery, there were many cottages in the less aristocratic quarters inclosed in palings, and embowered in the usual suburban peartrees and currant-bushes. These, indeed, were dwellings of an elder sort, and had clearly been inherited from a population now as extinct in that region as the Pequots, and they were not always carefully cherished....

It is amusing to find Dublin fearful of the encroachment of the French, as we, in our turn, dread the advance of the Irish. We must make a jest of our own alarms, and even smile—since we cannot help ourselves—at the spiritual desolation occasioned by the settlement of an Irish family in one of our suburban neighborhoods. The householders view with fear and jealousy the erection of any dwelling of less than a stated cost, as portending a possible advent of Irish; and when the calamitous race actually appears, a mortal pang strikes to the bottom of every pocket. Values tremble throughout that neighborhood....In my walk from Dublin to North Charlesbridge, I saw more than one token of the encroachment of the Celtic army, which had here and there invested a Yankee house with besieging shanties on every side, and thus given to its essential and otherwise quite hopeless ugliness a touch of the poetry that attends failing fortunes....The fortunes of such a house are, of course, not to be retrieved. Where the Celt sets his foot, there the Yankee (and it is perhaps wholesome if not agreeable to know that the Irish citizen whom we do not always honor as our equal in civilization loves to speak of us scornfully as Yankees) rarely, if ever, returns. The place

remains to the intruder and his heirs forever....

As I leave Dublin, the houses grow larger and handsomer; and as I draw near the Avenue, the Mansard-roofs look down upon me with their dormer-windows, and welcome me back to the American community. There are fences about all the houses, inclosing ampler and ampler dooryards; the children, which had swarmed in the thriftless and unenlightened purlieus of Dublin, diminish in number and finally disappear; the chickens have vanished; and I hear the pensive music of the horsecar bells....

Most of our people come from Boston on the horse-cars, and it is only the dwellers on the Avenue and the neighboring streets whom hurrying homeward I follow away from the steam-car station. The Avenue is our handsomest street; and if it were in the cosmopolitan citizen of Charlesbridge to feel any local interest, I should be proud of it. As matters are, I perceive its beauty, and I often reflect, with a pardonable satisfaction that it is not only handsome, but probably the very dullest street in the world. It is magnificently long and broad, and is flanked nearly the whole way from the station to the colleges by pine palaces rising from spacious lawns, or from the green of trees or the brightness of gardens. The splendor is all very new; but newness is not a fault that much affects architectural beauty, while it is the only one that time is certain to repair: and I find an honest and unceasing pleasure in the graceful lines of those palaces, which is not surpassed even by my appreciation of the vast quiet and monotony of the street itself. Commonly, when I emerge upon it from the grassy-bordered, succory-blossomed walks of Benicia Street, I behold, looking northward, a monumental horse-car standing—it appears for ages, if I wish to take it for Boston—at the head of Pliny Street; and looking southward I see that other emblem of suburban life, an express-wagon fading rapidly in the distance. Haply the top of a buggy nods round the bend under the elms near the station; and, if fortune is so lavish, a lady appears from a side street, and, while tarrying for the car, thrusts the point of her sun-umbrella into the sandy sidewalk. This is the mid-afternoon effect of the Avenue....On market-days its superb breadth is taken up by flocks of bleating sheep, and a pastoral tone is thus given to its tranquillity; anon a herd of beef-cattle appears under the elms; or a drove of pigs, many-pausing, inquisitive of the gutters, and quarrelsome as if they were the heirs of prosperity instead of doom, is slowly urged on toward the shambles....

The summer is waning with the day as I turn from the Avenue into Benicia Street. This is the hour when the fly cedes to the mosquito, as the Tuscan poet says, and, as one may add, the frying grasshopper yields to the shrilly cricket in noisiness. The embrowning air rings with the sad music made by these innumerable little violinists, hid in all the gardens round, and the pedestrian feels a sinking of the spirits.... This is in fact the hour of supreme trial everywhere, and doubtless no one but a newly-accepted lover can be happy at twilight. In the city, even, it is oppressive; in the country it is desolate; in the suburbs it is a miracle that it is ever lived through....

In town your fancy would turn to the theatres; in the country you would occupy yourself with cares of poultry or of stock; in the suburbs you can but sit upon your threshold, and fight the predatory mosquito.

4-3. PHOTO GALLERY: SOCIAL DIVERSITY IN NINETEENTH-CENTURY SUBURBIA

Figure 4-2 "But I Suppose This Wine is Not Made of Grapes, Signor?" Augustus Hoppin, 1872. Social diversity in suburbia was no secret to nineteenth-century observers. From his perch in suburban Boston, William Dean Howells catalogued a parade of working-class "doorstep acquaintances," peddlers, craftsmen, musicians, and this Italian organ grinder, who passed by his door. William Dean Howells, *Suburban Sketches* (Boston: Houghton, Mifflin and Co., 1882, original copyright, 1872), 42.

Figure 4-2 "Looking About I Saw Two Women," Augustus Hoppin, 1872. William Dean Howells encounters two Irish women while strolling about his Boston suburb (see Document 4-2). Illustrations such as this one emphasized a social distance separating affluent and working-class suburbanites even as they revealed the physical proximity between them. William Dean Howells, *Suburban Sketches* (Boston: Houghton, Mifflin and Co., 1882, original copyright 1872), 64.

Figure 4-4 "And you send for Pat Brannigan, and order a garden made," A.B. Frost, 1896. The presence of working-class "ethnics" and people of color in suburban service jobs was a social reality that popular media transformed into a lasting stereotype. The challenge for critical observers is to understand how these suburbanites saw their world. H.C. Bunner, *Jersey Street and Jersey Lane: Urban and Suburban Sketches* (New York: Charles Scribner's and Sons, 1896), 192.

4-4. REFORMER GRAHAM TAYLOR DOCUMENTS EARLY INDUSTRIAL SUBURBS, 1915

Source: Graham Taylor, *Satellite Cities: A Study of Industrial Suburbs* (New York & London: D. Appleton & Co., 1915).

The Outer Rings of Industry

"Back to the land" has come to mean more than the migration of a few tenement dwellers to farms. The big opportunity for the escape from crowded cities is through the wholesale removal of the work which city people do. Huge industrial plants are uprooting themselves bodily from the cities. With households, small stores, saloons, lodges, churches, schools clinging to them like living tendrils, they set themselves down ten miles away in the open....

From the middle of Philadelphia, several departments of the Baldwin Locomotive Works have been shunted out into a small suburb. Flint, Michigan, two hours from Detroit, has been seized as the place for huge automobile factories. While the population was trebling in the first three years, several hundred operatives had to be housed in tents throughout one summer. A big corn-products plant moved from the middle of Chicago to the near-by prairies and a "glucose city," Argo, started up. It occupies part of a tract of ten square miles, which one promoting company is developing as an "industrial district" and into which Chicago has already emptied more than two dozen establishments. Just outside Cincinnati a residential suburb, Norwood, is now the home of a score of manufacturing concerns. Impelled partly by the arbitrary tolls charged on coal carried across the Mississippi River, industrial plants have moved over the bridges from St. Louis and founded a group of new towns in Illinois. The Standard Oil Company, a few years ago, poured out $3,500,000 on the bank of the Missouri a few miles from Kansas City, and the town of Sugar Creek sprang up....

Many reasons are readily apparent for the location of these new industrial communities. The impulse toward cheap land, low taxes and elbow-room throws them out from the large centers of population. These are the centrifugal forces. The centripetal forces are equally powerful and bind them as satellites beyond the outer rings of the mother city. Even the towns which, like Gary [IN], have attained a considerable measure of self-sufficiency and lie perhaps across state boundaries are bound by strong economic ties. Through switchyards and belt-lines, practically all the railroad facilities developed during years of growth, which are at the disposal of a downtown establishment, are at the service of the industry in the suburb. It means much to be within easy reach of at least one large market for finished product. Proximity to a big labor market is a more important factor....

The industrial exodus, in which Pullman [IL] early played the role now taken by Gary, is, in its individual parts, a consciously directed movement. It therefore presents repeated opportunities for shaping the civic and social conditions under which large groups of working people are to live for decades to come. It raises in new and searching ways questions as to the obligations which go with economic control, as to the future of local self-government in relation to that control, and as to the organization and large-scale civic development of our industrial districts.

Like the foundlings which were dropped in the turn-cradles of the old-time orphanages, these young communities which industry is leaving at the doorsteps of our cities are no longer things apart and by themselves. For better or worse, they come to share in the common lot....

Industry's Escape from Congestion

The suburbanite who leaves business behind at nightfall for the cool green rim of the city would think the world had gone topsy-turvy if at five-thirty he rushed out of a factory set in a landscape of open fields and wooded hillsides, scrambled for a seat in a street car or grimy train and clattered back to the region of brick and pavement, of soot and noise and jostle. Yet this is daily routine for many thousands of factory workers.

When industry moves out from the city center it is seeking economic advantage. It may provide also a made-to-order "model" town, or merely build rows of "company houses," or leave housing to haphazard real-estate enterprise, or depend on traction to bring workers to the suburban shops. But its own purpose is always paramount—to escape from the handicaps of congestion and secure elbow-room, to establish an efficient modern plant where conditions are easy and land is cheap.

The "model town" is not the typical result of the movement of industry to the suburbs. Much more usual, if not so conspicuous, is the shifting of factories one by one to the edge of the city. The environs of Cincinnati present unusual examples of this shift to escape congestion with industrial advantage the impelling motive, the workers continuing mainly to live in the crowded sections of Cincinnati.

The most widely known industrial plant on Cincinnati's outskirts is the soap factory of the Procter and Gamble Company. But Ivorydale, as the plant with its neighborhood is called, is chiefly noted for its profit-sharing schemes rather than the development of the community around it. Our interest is attracted by the recent and rapid industrial development of Norwood and Oakley which adjoin each other on the city's northeastern edge.

Starting as residential suburbs of the usual type, their shaded streets have been outflanked by a cordon of big factories stretching along the line of the Baltimore and Ohio Railroad. Most of these plants have emigrated from Cincinnati's center....

Less than one-third of the operatives in Norwood and Oakley factories live within easy walking distance of their work. The great majority of those who must depend on traction facilities ride out from more or less congested parts of central Cincinnati. Some others even live in Kentucky, and thus, after journeying to and across the Ohio River, have then to traverse the city itself from boundary to boundary in order to reach their place of employment....

The situation has thus created other social problems for managers and work-people than the simple one of human freightage. The willingness of employees to make the long trip twice a day was problematical. Yet so far from discouraging employees, the remov-

al to the outskirts has been followed, most managers declare, by a longer average job tenure than was the case in Cincinnati. One manager said that although the well-lighted, ventilated, clean and roomy workshops are an appreciated advantage, an important factor is that workers have less opportunity to learn of new jobs offering real or fancied betterment. Their contact with workers in other factories, with whom they might compare work conditions and wages, is much less frequent. At noon hours and on the way to and from work they are now thrown only with those employed in the same factory, or else those employed in near-by factories requiring a different kind of work.

In this connection it would be interesting to know whether the evident success of employers in keeping trade unionism weak in most of the Norwood and Oakley factories is due in part to this isolation of the workers from fellow-workers and trade-union representatives in the same industry. It is possible to discover not a little discontent among work-people in various plants. The employment by one plant of some negroes and "hunkies" is cited by other employees as an effort to cut under the wage standards demanded by "white men."...

The exodus of industry from the congested center of Cincinnati has shown us no comprehensive and intelligent civic policy on the part of the big city to promote and guide community development. Equally in their smaller spheres, Norwood and Oakley have failed.

If the same degree of forethought, skill, intelligence and enterprise, which was applied to the planning of the "factory colony," had also been applied to the scheming of the community life of Oakley and Norwood, the environs of Cincinnati might now have developed the most interesting and significant industrial suburbs in America, might even have shown us our nearest approach to the garden suburbs of England in point of cooperative land ownership and building as well as in physical arrangement. With broad fields, trees, gentle hillsides, and a ravine with a water course, nature has done her part to provide beauty. But, except in the efforts of Mr. [J. G.] Schmidlapp [a Cincinnati developer], not the slightest attempt has been made to solve the problem of the workers' household in these surroundings near his work. The recreation of the working girl seems to have received scarcely a thought. The removal of the factory to the rim of the big city is not an adequate solution of our civic-industrial problem if it leaves the workers' home behind in a congested area, or even if it transplants it to a region where the whole system of community life is left to remain undeveloped.

The intelligence which is so skillfully applied to the planning of industrial expansion should be directed to the great opportunity for guiding civic and social development in the outer belts of growth.

4-5. HARLAN PAUL DOUGLASS SURVEYS MULTIPLE SUBURBAN TYPES, 1925

Source: Harlan Paul Douglass, *The Suburban Trend* (New York & London: Century Co., 1925).

Cities and Their Suburbs

Out toward the fringes and margins of cities comes a region where they begin to be less themselves than they are at the center, a place where the city looks countryward. No sharp boundary line defines it; there is rather a gradual tapering off from the urban type of civilization toward the rural type. It is the city thinned out.

Confronted with the expanding cities the adjacent country also begins to look cityward. The result is not, however, a compromise of equals. The original movement was, and the major movement is the city's. The suburb is a footnote to urban civilization affecting the near-by country-side. It is not a true mediating type…. It is a part of urban civilization. Even though it is a town in form, the brand of the city is stamped upon it. It straddles the arbitrary line which statistics draw between the urban and rural spheres; but in reality it is the push of the city outward. It makes physical compromises with country ways but few compromises of spirit. It is the city trying to escape the consequences of being a city while still remaining a city. It is urban society trying to eat its cake and keep it, too.

The View from Eagle Rock Park

What does an actual sample of suburbs look like? Probably the world's greatest panorama of a metropolitan area is that of New York and its suburbs seen from New Jersey from a vantage-point on the "First Mountain" [Ed. note: Eagle Rock Park is in West Orange].

In the foreground, glimpsed at intervals through the green of trees, winds a historic thoroughfare skirting the base of the mountain. Mansions and villas creep up its lower slopes. On the middle horizon are silhouetted the city's towers, accenting the most marvelous sky-line ever made by man. To the right lies the faintly gleaming bay with ships moving across the background of Staten Island. Between the two opens the unseen gateway to the Atlantic and to all the world. To the left the back slopes of the Palisades stretch in long unbroken line.

Between the mountain and the city a spacious suburban area is spread out. The dominant impression it makes is that of roominess. Its spaces seem more open than occupied. Its habitations, half buried in foliage, are uncrowded….

The lesser suburbs, too numerous to count, spot the picture. Ranging the open spaces, the eye passes from the white-walled college to the red-roofed country-club house and smooth golf-links; then over peach-orchards, market-gardens, forest-patches, to the gray-green marshes which the sea here interposes between the city and suburb.

The mountain ridge on which one stands separates the first line of suburbs from the second. It was George Washington's first line of defense during the Revolutionary War. The later suburbs lie more thinly scattered, less connected with the city, maintaining more of the old rural traditions. They thin out in turn into a region of great country estates encroaching upon old-time farms. In the valleys are factory villages adjoining which immigrant workers are buying the old farms and cutting them up into peasant holdings. Beyond, in the farthest zone immediately touched by the city, are forested watersheds, Alpine lakes, the playground and the scenic background of the Colossus of urban civilization.

Ribbons of gleaming rails, often obscured by trails of smoke, and highways filled with processions of motorcars, turn the panorama into a living picture and tie its parts together.

A First Approach to the Suburban Problem

Such is the rich and bewildering reality which the environs of a great city present. Seeking to reduce it to terms which the mind can grasp and discuss, the common device is to conceive of a metropolitan or complete urban area as consisting of three zones: (1) The urban zone in the narrow sense; that is to say, the city itself or the closely related cluster of cities. (2) The suburban zone proper. (3) The rural zone....

In the most general sense the suburbs are thus a belt of near-by but less crowded communities which have "close connections" with the city, made possible by physical arrangements for the rapid transfer of people and goods between the two. It is the area within which many people go to the city to work and come back at night, the area within which numerous shoppers flock to city stores which make daily deliveries of purchases....

The Major Suburban Types

Suburbs so manifestly differ from one another that even the most generalized account of their character...could not ignore the fact....

Even though only a part of the city can be decentralized, and all the suburbs combined are not as varied as the city, nevertheless the suburban fragments represent a wide range of interesting variations....

The Decentralization of Consumption

The basic distinction of economic science is that between production and consumption; that is to say, between the creation of wealth and its expenditure. The residential suburb represents the decentralization of consumption. Man creates wealth in the central city and spends it in the suburbs. He makes his living in town but lives at home in an intentionally contrasting environment. He leaves his work in the city but takes wife and children and moves out to the country, going back and forth daily in order to keep both aspects of life going.

Part of the pay which he receives for his work in the city he immediately pays out there in return for services or goods, but the goods which he buys are chiefly consumed at home, and in the suburb are his major expenditures—for rent and taxes, for most of his food, for doctor and dentist, for automobile, church and club, for charity, self-improvement and self-indulgence. There could hardly be a greater error than to think of the residential suburbs as mere dormitories. They are rather the realms of consumption as over against production, of play in contrast with work, of leisure in exchange for business. Only incidentally are they places to sleep.

Of course some work is done in the residential suburbs, but it is primarily in the service of rest, recreation, and refreshment for others. The gainfully employed breadwinner goes to the city, but the work of the homemaker...is decentralized along with the home; and round it gather the types of business immediately related to consumption....

The Decentralization of Production...

Urban congestion as experienced by populations is largely due to the reception, transportation, handling and processing, storage and reshipment of material things. The sidewalks are blocked by barrels of produce and bales of goods, and the streets are crowded with trucks.

In the industrial suburb these things are decentralized, together with the manufacturing plants and facilities which go with them. The factory becomes suburban as well as the home. Production moves out as consumption has already done. Both halves of the city reestablish themselves in the country in a roomier environment. The industrial suburb is more independent of the parent city than is the residential one because the workers work near home as well as live there. Nevertheless, marked relations to the city continue, and subordination is definitely a fact although taking different forms. The city constitutes the major center where the brains, credit facilities, the docks and railroad terminals which are the ultimate factors of transportation, and the primary labor markets all remain.

Industrial suburbs and residential suburbs thus constitute the major suburban types. For both the city continues the economic center as well as the focus of ideals and imagination....

Demographic and Economic Variations: Rich Suburbs and Poor Suburbs

Within the boundaries of the city the social complexion of its more prosperous districts is in most glaring contrast with that of its poverty-stricken ones. The same contrasts occur along the margins of the city and out into the suburbs. Rich and poor suburbs constitute for practical purposes different kinds.

It follows from the ordinary distribution of human fortunes that the residential suburbs are richer than the industrial ones. Extreme cases occur in which their average wealth as measured in real property is two or even three times that of the parent city and much more beyond the average place of the same size. Housing costs in the better residential suburbs catering to the upper middle class are so high as to exclude all but about ten per cent. of the population of the urban area. Nevertheless, both major types of suburbs occur on all economic levels. Somewhat rarely an industrial suburb gathering skilled laborers in selected industries, develops a surprisingly high average of community wealth. Plainfield, New Jersey, is such a community.... All the others standing toward the top of the list are residential suburbs.

Most suburbs, either residential or industrial, are inhabited by people of the middle class on the economic scale. This is because there are relatively few rich people and because...the suburb is not generally available for the very poor. There are, however, many residential suburbs of the better-paid industrial classes, but they are usually closer to cities, especially to minor cities within the suburban zone. The industrial worker cannot ordinarily commute so far as the salaried man. Consequently his residential suburb must lie nearer his work....

Besides the very poor industrial suburbs where foreign immigrants in industry live on a characteristically low level in the shadow of the factory, many purely residential suburbs exist on exceedingly unsatisfactory economic planes. Thus the projection of the Delaware River Bridge between Philadelphia and Camden started hordes of poorly paid workers to building mushroom suburbs in the country beyond. Many of them were cheap, planless, vulgar, and inconvenient to the last degree. Some indeed started in temporary summer bungalow communities and adapted their style of architecture and standards to year-round living. Without civic coherence or community consciousness, suburbs of this sort present many of the aspects of the frontier mining-camp. Scores of them exist along the edges of the Los Angeles oil-fields, their sordidness redeemed only by the outdoor climate and the somewhat esthetic tradition of the California bungalow. Nearly every great city since the war shows similar phenomena. There has been a veritable suburban hegira of the very poor in an effort to escape high rents....Genuinely frontier life along the margins of cities is thus a grim reality, subject to many shortcomings in spite of the undoubted relief which it affords from central congestion.

There are also numerous examples of downright suburban slums typified by the squatter community of shanty-boatmen in St. Louis, the "tin-can colony" hidden away in the pine thickets in the outskirts of Springfield, Massachusetts. Similar pauper or degenerate suburban types survive here along the margins of most great cities.

The rich suburb, the middle-class suburb, and the poor suburb, with their minor variants, furnish then a set of typical distinctions of genuine importance for social analysis....

Foreign and Negro Suburbs

Considering first racial composition, one comes upon the striking discovery that the heaviest concentrations of foreign-born populations in the United States are not urban but suburban. Also that no Northern city has massed so large a proportion of negro population as some of the Northern suburbs.

The relation between industry and the presence of these alien groups of population is well understood. It is in the industrial suburb, therefore, that we must look for these extreme concentrations of alien population.

A limited sampling of the industrial suburbs seems to show that as a group they have about the same percentage of foreign-born as have the parent cities. No great city, however, has so high a number of foreigners as East Chicago, Indiana, or Passaic, Garfield, and Perth Amboy, New Jersey. No Northern city has relatively so many negroes as the residential suburbs of Englewood, East Orange, and Montclair, New Jersey, and Evanston, Illinois, where the negro colonies represent primarily domestic service groups.

On the other hand, there are distinctly industrial suburbs actually with fewer foreigners than the average residential suburbs of the cities have. Examples are Hammond, Indiana, and Plainfield, New Jersey. These strikingly American suburbs may, as already noted, stand on a high economic level.

The foreign industrial suburb, the residential suburb with a subsidiary alien colony, and the exclusively American industrial suburb are important variants having the value of subtypes....

Popular Categories

Our study accordingly must confess its inability to furnish a satisfying list of the types of suburbs which surround American cities. The rough categories, "poor industrial suburbs," "decentralized residential suburb," "well-marked suburban residential community," and "mixed suburb," will have to serve until very much more intimate and comparative social studies of individual cases enable us to do better. The resort suburb, the school suburb, the exclusive suburb of the very rich, the suburban mill-town, also furnish self-defining characteristics sufficient for practical use. But our analysis at least satisfies the major purpose of this chapter, which is to awaken a realization of the wide variations which lie beneath the necessary shorthand of generalization. If, therefore, we continue to talk about the suburbs as a group we shall also continue to remember the wealth of concrete variety which the term embraces.

4-6. PHOTO GALLERY: VARIED SUBURBAN LANDSCAPES

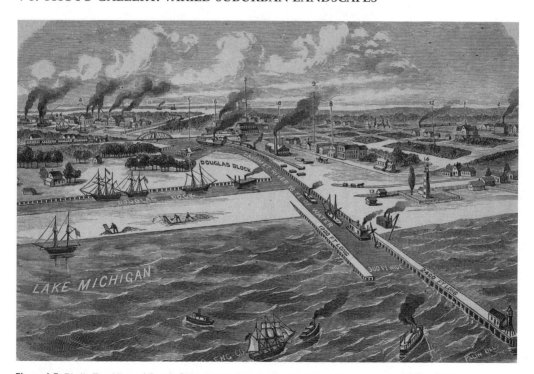

Figure 4-5 Bird's Eye View of South Chicago Harbor, 1874. Published in a volume promoting Chicago real estate after the 1871 fire, this view of Chicago's suburban fringe portrays a landscape of economic progress with small homes, farmsteads, and woodlots overshadowed by smoke-spewing trains, boats, and factories. Everett Chamberlin, *Chicago and its Suburbs* (Chicago: T.A. Hungerford & Co., 1874), 360.

Figure 4-6 Steel Plant and Workers' Houses, Birmingham, Alabama, photographed by Marion Post Wolcott, 1939. Depression-era photographers documented the rough-edged outskirts of metropolitan America, where decentralized industry anchored working-class suburban communities such as this one near Birmingham. Courtesy of Library of Congress, Prints and Photographs Division, FSA/OWI Collection, LC-USF 34-051864-D DLC.

Figure 4-7 Red Mountain Suburbs, Crest of Red Mountain, Birmingham, Jefferson County, Alabama, photographed by Jet Lowe, 1993. The vicinity of Red Mountain and Mountain Brook on Birmingham, Alabama's southern limits marked the pinnacle of verdant suburban privilege crafted by the city's white elite in the early twentieth century. Courtesy of Library of Congress, Prints and Photographs Division, Historic American Buildings Survey, HABS, ALA, 37-Birm, 22-2.

Figure 4-8 Schlesinger Estate, Brookline, Massachusetts, 1904. Estate properties in suburbs like Brookline, Massachusetts, set the standard for suburban aesthetics in turn-of-the-century America. The Schlesinger Estate was the handiwork of designer Frederick Law Olmsted, whose plans for central city parks and early suburbs pioneered the field of American landscape architecture. Courtesy of the Frances Loeb Library, Harvard Design School, # 119278.

Figure 4-9 A Country Place of Seven Acres, with Pond, in the Midst of Open Country, Madison, New Jersey, 1893. In addition to landscaped estates in well-populated municipalities, early suburbia also encompassed outlying "country" homes dispersed among farms and rural towns. Samuel Parsons Jr., "Small Country Places," in *Homes in City and Country*, ed. Russell Sturgis et al. (New York: Charles Scribner and Sons, 1893), 149.

Figure 4-10 Streetcar Suburb, Pittsburgh, Pennsylvania, ca. 1910. Well-built frame homes, narrow lots, up-to-date urban amenities, and a pedestrian-oriented layout near a car line characterized "streetcar suburbs" across the United States. Blocks such as this one near Pittsburgh reflected suburbanization by an expanding middle class. Pittsburgh Survey (presumed) / source unknown.

Figure 4-11 "Dezendorf's delightful dwellings," Queens, New York, Joseph Smith, ca. 1920s. In New York City's outlying boroughs, elevated railways (extensions of the city's subway system) coupled with experiments in mass home building to produce a boom in housing construction and home ownership after 1910. Courtesy of Library of Congress, Prints and Photographs Division, FSA-OWI Collection, LC-USF344-000877-ZB DLC (b&w film neg.).

4-7. *BUSINESS WEEK* REPORTS ON THE PROLIFERATION OF SUBURBAN DEPARTMENT STORES, 1930

Source: "Department Store Branches in Suburbs Succeed, Multiply," *Business Week*, October 1, 1930.

Traffic and parking congestion increase migration to suburbs, [and] cause substantial diversion of business from "downtown" shops to neighborhood stores.

Unsatisfactory and slow transportation in crowded trains and trolleys, congested streets, inadequate parking facilities in shopping districts have combined to make shopping in the large department stores a hardship. So they are finding it necessary to open branch stores in outlying districts which until recently accounted for a substantial slice of the total sales volume.

In most instances no attempt is made to make suburban branches a small but complete edition of the big store. But the stocks commonly carried at branches include excellent assortments of a wide range of lines, selected to cover the particular demands of the territory as revealed through a study of sales records and charge accounts.

Personnel is selected to suit the needs of the neighborhood, routine procedures and type of service to customers being identical with those maintained at the main establishment.

Contrary to expectation, branch stores have not perceptibly reduced sales volume of the parent house; have proved self-sustaining from the start; in many instances contribute satisfactorily to net profit.

Marshall Field & Co., Chicago, first experimented with a branch opened at Lake Forest in 1928; found performance satisfactory; since then has opened 5-story branch stores at Evanston and Oak Park, both suburbs; reports these branches necessary to convenience of customers....

In New York City the branch store plan is gaining steadily and may eventually reach its highest point of development....

James A. Hearn & Son, 102-year-old department store, on 14th Street, New York, has just opened a complete branch in Stamford, Conn. carrying a full line of merchandise, expects to extend all benefits of main store buying to the new branch but will develop it as a community enterprise serving like a small town merchant....

Best & Co. appear to follow a definite and comprehensive plan for branch store development, having selected locations for permanent as well as resort service, two of the former at Garden City, L.I. [Long Island] and Mamaroneck, N.Y. A third community branch is now being built at East Orange, N.J.; it is said that other locations are under consideration....

Practice of establishing branches as a means of self-preservation is spreading rapidly to other large cities.

4-8. PHOTO GALLERY: EARLY SUBURBAN SHOPPING CENTERS

Figure 4-12 Country Club Plaza, Kansas City, postcard, ca. 1920s. Built to increase the appeal of his nearby subdivisions, J.C. Nichols' Country Club Plaza is considered the nation's first planned shopping center designed for auto passengers. Courtesy of Emil Pocock.

Figure 4-13 Park and Shop. View of Park and Shop from high point across Connecticut Ave, Theodor Horydczak, ca. 1930s. The decentralization of people and businesses in the early 20th century triggered innovations in the design of retailing. Suburban shopping plazas and auto strip malls, such as this one in Washington D.C., both had their roots in the suburban boom of the 1920s. Courtesy of Library of Congress, Prints and Photographs Division, Theodor Horydczak Collection, LC-H814-T01-1049 DLC (b&w film dup. neg.).

ESSAYS

Essay 4-1 offers a Marxian perspective on the suburban trend. In this sweeping and provocative analysis of the historical evolution of American urban form, geographer David Gordon rejects explanations that hinge on technological innovation or consumer preference, emphasizing instead the imperatives of political economy. He argues that to fully understand the making of city and suburban spaces, one must consider the role of class struggle. Gordon's work is a good example of Marxist scholarship that emerged in the 1970s, which sought new solutions to the perceived urban crisis of the 1960s and 1970s. These scholars challenged neoclassical economic geographers—who embraced a Weberian framework of rational choice—as well as liberal analysts who stopped short of questioning the systemic problems of capitalist economies. Significantly, Gordon not only recognizes the presence of manufacturers on the suburban periphery by 1900, but he emphasizes their role in the suburbanization process itself. **Essay 4-2** provides an overview of economic and social diversity on the suburban periphery from 1900 to 1950. The authors, geographers Richard Harris and Robert Lewis, have been at the forefront of recent challenges to orthodox views of suburban history. As revisionists, they dispute the conception of early suburbia as a haven of the affluent alone, emphasizing instead the diverse land uses and peoples that characterized suburbia. Their arguments open the door for analysis of alternative experiences, motives, and histories of the suburbs.

ESSAY 4-1. DAVID M. GORDON, "CAPITALIST DEVELOPMENT AND THE HISTORY OF AMERICAN CITIES" (1978)

Source: "Capitalist Development and the History of American Cities" by David Gordon, from *Marxism and the Metropolis*, Second Edition, edited by William Tabb and Larry Sawers, copyright © 1978, 1984 by Oxford University Press, Inc. Used by permission of Oxford University Press, Inc.

More and more people live in cities as capitalism develops. And it appears that more and more people dislike many aspects of urban life. Many complain about urban chaos and irrationality, about urban inequality and poverty, about urban impersonality and physical confinement.

More important, most people apparently regard these urban problems as inevitable. People seem to believe that the modern urban form is inexorably required by advanced industrialism. We may not like our lives in cities, but we seem to think that cities must continue to develop as they have if we are to maintain our present standards of living. How can we forget the need for coordina-tion, for economies of scale, for urban agglomerations, for urban amenities?

This fatalism about our cities resembles an analogous fatalism about technology. That view is often called *technological determinism*. It suggests that our dominant technologies are the *only* kinds of machines which will permit our current standard of living. We may not like the alienated, specialized, hierarchical jobs associated with those machines, but we have to accept them as requisites of our current affluence.

Analogously, our views of cities are suffused with a sense of (what I call) *spatial determinism*. This view suggests that there is only one way of organizing economic life across space, generating only one set of community relationships, which is consistent with advanced industrial standards of living. We may not like those urban relationships, but we have to accept them in order to enjoy what we have. Let them eat concrete!

Recent political struggles and social analyses have begun to challenge the technological-determinist position....

We must also begin to reconsider the spatial-determinist view. The new view of technology has led us to the conclusion that capitalist machines develop at least partly in order to control us as workers. So may we also conclude, if we look closely enough, that capitalist spatial forms also develop at least partly to reproduce capitalist control, helping maintain the class relationships prevalent in capitalist societies.

This reconsideration clearly requires direct historical investigation. If we hypothesize…that "capitalism, as a mode of production," has "created our kinds of city," then we must be able to trace the historical mechanisms through which these spatial consequences have gradually evolved. We must explicitly examine, in short, *the historical links between capitalism and urban development*. This essay explores those ties through a case study of American history.

Orthodox and Marxian Perspectives

In turning toward that history, we quickly confront a conventional wisdom in the orthodox social sciences. Most urban histories treat the growth of cities as a gradual, evolutionary, and ineluctable process. The outcomes seem destined. In any developing society, as Kingsley Davis writes with assurance, "urbanization is a finite process, a cycle through which nations go in their transition from agrarian to industrial society." Cities become continuously larger, more complicated, more specialized, and more interdependent. Hans Blumenfeld describes the determinants of this historical process:

> The division of labor and increased productivity made concentration in cities possible, and the required cooperation of labor made it necessary, because the new system called for bringing together workers of many skills and diverse establishments that had to interchange goods and services. The process fed on itself, growth inducing further growth.

Because the United States has become the prototypical advanced industrial society, orthodox historians view American urban development as the consummate reflection of this universal process of urbanization.

In the Marxian view, that history must be seen in a different light. The Marxian analysis of the spatial division of labor suggests that no particular pattern of urban development is inevitably "destined," somehow deterministically cast in a general spatial mold. Spatial forms are conditioned, rather, by the particular mode of production dominating the society under study; they are shaped by *endogenous* political-economic forces, not by *exogenous* mechanisms. Marxians also argue that urban history, like the history of other social institutions, does not advance incrementally, marching step by gradual step along some frictionless path. Urban history advances *discontinuously*, instead of *continuously*, periodically experiencing qualitative transformations of basic form and structure. During the capitalist epoch, in particular, the instability of the accumulation process itself is bound to lead to periodic institutional change. The current economic crisis and its attendant urban crisis, from this perspective, are just another in a long series of these kinds of transformations.

This essay applies the Marxian perspective. According to that view, we have witnessed three main stages of capital accumulation in the advanced capitalist countries: the stages of *commercial* accumulation, *industrial* (or competitive) accumulation, and advanced *corporate* (or monopoly) accumulation. I argue that urban development in the United States has passed through *three corresponding stages*— each conditioned by the dynamics of capital accumulation that characterize that stage. I argue that the process of capital accumulation has been the most important factor structuring the growth of cities; city growth has not flowed from hidden exogenous forces but has been shaped instead by the logic of the underlying economic system. Finally, I argue that the transitions *between* stages of urban development have been predominantly influenced by problems of *class control in production,* problems erupting at the very center of the accumulation process….

The Contradictions of the Industrial City

Although the Industrial Cities grew rapidly, their growth did not proceed smoothly for long. As the end of the century approached, certain characteristic contradictions began to erupt. Accumulating friction began to threaten the speed of the industrial machine. These frictions assumed both quantitative and qualitative dimensions.

Quantitatively, some diseconomies of scale began to plague the increasingly crowded central cities. Before the second wave of immigration flooded the Industrial Cities after 1890, demand for labor was piling up more quickly than supply could meet it, and wages were beginning to rise. (The index of money wages rose from 66 in 1880 to 74 in 1890, despite falling prices.) Transportation was getting increasingly clogged in some factory districts, and some manufacturers were beginning to complain about congestion. Increasing concentration was creating some pressure on land prices. And, to the degree that political machines were beginning to take advantage of the political isolation of the working classes, governmental corruption was beginning to affect business-property taxes.

None of these sources of friction, for the time at least, seemed decisive. The flood of immigrants after 1890 reduced wage pressure. The rapid extension of electric trolleys during the 1890s helped relieve some downtown traffic congestion, easing the strain on intermediate goods supply. The urban construction boom of the 1890s increased building supply and eased land prices. And businesses began to handle the tax problem themselves, helping spur the "good government" movement after the turn of the century to gain increasing control from corrupt bosses.

The qualitative contradictions were much more decisive. The latent explosiveness of the concentration of workers became more and more manifest. At first, the impersonality and isolation of the factory and working-class districts had helped subdue the industrial proletariat. Gradually, through the 1880s, the dense concentrations of workers began to have the opposite effects. As spreading mechanization and speedup drove industrial workers to increasing resistance during the 1880s, individual strikes and struggles began to spread, infecting neighboring workers. Isolated moments of resistance took increasingly "political" forms. Strikes bred demonstrations not only at the plants but throughout the downtown districts. As the Wisconsin

Commissioner of Labor and Industrial Statistics observed about the growing movement for the eight-hour day in Milwaukee in 1886, "the agitation permeated our entire social atmosphere."

The evidence for this relatively sudden intensification of labor unrest in the largest cities, spilling from one sector to another within the working class, seems reasonably persuasive....The data reveal a sharp increase in the numbers of workers engaged in strike activity during the 1880s and a steady quantitative increase after the first five years of the period covered. Data on character and location of the strikers are also suggestive. A rising percentage of strikes focused on disputes over "recognition" and "sympathy." The percentage of strikes "ordered by labor organizations" also rose. Most important, workers seemed to be gaining increasing strength; comparing the period between 1886 and 1890 with the years from 1897 to 1899—two junctures of relatively comparable prosperity—we find that the percentage of strike resolutions which were "unfavorable to workers" fell dramatically from 41.1 percent in the former years to 19.6 percent ten years later. It appears, finally, that many of these spreading and more militant strikes were taking place in the largest industrial cities....

As these contradictions began to erupt, in short, it appeared likely that the form of the Industrial City would have to change. Its original structure had been premised on its sustenance of capitalist control over production. The increasing centralization of the industrial proletariat that it promoted, however, was beginning to backfire. Labor control was threatening to dissolve. Something clearly had to give.

Corporate Accumulation and the Corporate City

We now know that the Industrial City was itself short-lived. For about half a century, at least, our cities have been pushed in different directions. A new kind of city form has framed American urban development. Corporate skyscrapers have come to dominate the downtown districts of many cities.

Factories have moved away from the central cities. Cities have become politically fragmented.

Once again, our application of the Marxian perspective leads us to begin our analysis of these changes with an examination of the pace and pattern of capital accumulation. Around the turn of the century—between 1898 and 1920—the United States experienced a transition from the stage of industrial accumulation to advanced corporate accumulation. The accumulation process, still grounded in the production and realization of surplus value, was being guided by the decisions of many fewer, much larger economic units. Those economic units—the giant corporations—now had sufficient size to permit a qualitatively new level of rationalization of production and distribution. Their size and scope led them increasingly to search for stability, predictability, and security. That search, I argue, played a central role in shaping the Corporate City.

The Decentralization of Manufacturing

Through the 1890s, as we saw, manufacturing had been concentrating in the largest central cities. Factories had been piling more and more densely into downtown districts. Workers were crowding nearby. And some contradictions of that geographic concentration were beginning to erupt.

Suddenly, around 1898 or 1899, manufacturing started moving out of the central city. In twelve of the thirteen largest industrial districts in the country, a special Census study showed that manufacturing employment began to increase more than twice as fast in the "rings" of the industrial districts as in the central cities. Between 1899 and 1909, central-city manufacturing employment increased by 40.8 percent while ring employment rose by 97.7 percent.

These numbers refer to a real and visible phenomenon noted by contemporary authors—in Graham Taylor's words, to "the sudden investment of large sums of capital in establishing suburban plants." Between 1899 and around 1915, corporations began to establish factory districts just beyond the city limits. New suburban manufacturing towns were being built in open space like movie sets. Gary, Indiana, constructed from 1905 to 1908, is the best-known example. Other new industrial satellite suburbs included Chicago Heights, Hammond, East Chicago, and Argo outside Chicago; Lackawanna outside of Buffalo; East St. Louis and Wellston [sic] across the river from St. Louis; Norwood and Oakley beyond the Cincinnati limits; and Chester and Norristown near Philadelphia.

Orthodox economic historians have conventionally explained the decentralization of manufacturing in the twentieth century as the product of technological change. Somebody invented the truck, and the truck made it more efficient to locate manufacturing outside the central city. Somebody else invented land-intensive automated processing machinery, they add, which placed a premium on employers finding cheap land outside dense central-city manufacturing districts.

But these conventional explanations cannot explain this sudden explosion of satellite suburbs at the turn of the century. The truck certainly had nothing to do with the development, since the truck was not an effective commercial substitute for freight transport until the late 1920s. There is no obvious evidence that there was a sudden rash of new inventions prompting a shift to land-intensive technologies; indeed, there is some evidence that the sudden decentralization took place *despite* shifts to less land-intensive technology in some industries.

Other "factor price" explanations also provide little help. I can find no evidence either that land-cost increases had accelerated at the turn of the century or that these increases were directly linked to the sudden decentralization. And one can hardly argue that the factories began to move out to the suburbs because the working class had already begun to leave the central cities for "dormitory suburbs." Workers were still tightly locked in central-city tenement districts, they had not been moving out to the suburbs, and many continued to live in the central city even after they had begun to work in the satellite factories.

It appears that conventional economic historians have overlooked the major reason for the sudden dispersal of central-city factories.

Throughout the late 1880s and 1890s..., labor conflict had begun to intensify in the downtown central-city districts. Employers quickly perceived one obvious solution. Move!

In testimony presented before the U.S. Industrial Commission from 1900 to 1902, employer after employer explained the crystallizing calculus. Some examples:

The President of Fraser and Chalmers Co. in Chicago: "Chicago today is the hotbed of trades unionism....If it were not for the high investment [manufacturers] have in their machines and plants, many of them would leave Chicago at once, because of the labor trouble that exists here....In fact, in Chicago, within the last two months we have lost some of the very largest corporations that operated here."

Chairman of the New York State Board of Mediation and Arbitration: "Q: Do you find that isolated plants, away from the great centers of population, are more apt to have non-union shops than in a city? A: Yes. Q: Do you know of cases in the State where they do isolate plants to be free...from unionism? A: They have been located with that end in view."...

Graham Taylor, in his study of the satellite-city movement written in 1915, confirms that employers were particularly concerned about the contagiousness of central-city labor unrest....When factories did move to the industrial suburbs, Taylor notes, workers were automatically more isolated than they had been downtown....In general, Taylor concludes the decentralization served its purpose and the unions were much less successful than they had been in the central-city districts.

If labor trouble had been burgeoning since the 1880s, why did this movement wait so long and begin so suddenly? I would propose that the abrupt inauguration of industrial dispersal could not have begun until the great merger wave of 1898 to 1903. Movement to the suburbs required huge funds for new capital investment. The small entrepreneurial firms of the nineteenth century could scarcely afford plant expansion, much less wholesale reconstruction. Falling profits and prices in the late 1880s intensified the squeeze on their capital. The depression of 1893–1897 further delayed what was beginning to seem inevitable. Finally, as corporations rapidly centralized capital after 1898, they acquired enough extra investment cash to be able to finance the new satellite-plant construction.

I do not mean to imply that the sudden construction of the satellite cities represented some massively engineered, carefully calibrated classwide conspiracy steered by the new corporate giants. Individual corporations understood the reasons for and the implications of their actions, to be sure.... But individual corporations were largely acting on their own, without central coordination or suggestion, perceiving and protecting their own individual interests. There were some examples of collective planning, Taylor notes, but "much more usual, if not so conspicuous, is the shifting of factories one by one to the edge of the city." The individual corporations did not need to be directed in their flight from the central-city labor turmoil. They had little choice.

The great twentieth-century reversal of factory location, in short, began because corporations could no longer control their labor forces in the central cities. As with the transition to the Industrial City, problems of labor control had decisive effects. U.S. Steel's creation of Gary metaphorically expressed the importance of this spatial effect. "The Steel Corporation's triumphs in the economics of production," Taylor concluded, "are only less impressive than its complete command over the army of workers it employs."...

Suburban Fragmentation

The third major change in urban form during the twentieth century involved its political fragmentation [Ed. note: the second big change, Gordon argues, was the rise of the central business district]. Conventional analysts emphasize the importance of residential decentralization as a source of this political suburbanization. People began to prefer suburban autonomy, in this view, over central-city domination.

Once again, we must be very careful about the timing of events. Up to the end of the nineteenth century, central cities habitually annexed outlying residential districts as people moved beyond the traditional city boundaries. Central cities continued to unify their political jurisdictions as they spread outward. This process of annexation continued steadily until the end of the century.

Then the continuing spread of the Industrial City suddenly slowed. Chicago completed its last major annexation in 1889. New York City did not physically grow after the great incorporation of Brooklyn in 1898. Philadelphia and Boston had discontinued annexation even earlier. Of the twenty largest cities in 1900, thirteen enjoyed their last geographic expansion by 1910.

This rapid deceleration of central-city annexation cannot be explained by some exogenous shift in people's preferences about suburban autonomy. People had been fleeing the central city since the 1860s. From the beginning, the refugees typically preferred autonomy and opposed annexation. Despite their opposition, extending suburban populations were simply reclaimed for the central-city government by legislative *fiat*. They were continually subjected, in Kenneth Jackson's words, to "the local or downtown brand of urban imperialism."

What changed at the end of the century? Residential suburbanization did not accelerate. There was not yet a widespread use of the car. The electric streetcar developed rapidly through the 1890s, permitting somewhat more distant intra-urban travel, but it represented a simple improvement on a long succession of carriages and horse cars dating from the 1840s rather than a qualitative transformation of urban transit.

What changed most dramatically, it appears, was that manufacturers themselves began to move out of the central cities. Obviously they wanted to avoid paying central-city taxes. It was now in their interest to oppose further annexation. Given their influence over state legislatures, they easily satisfied their desires. Earlier residential opposition to annexation had not been strong enough to resist central-city aggrandizement. Now, with manufacturers switching sides, the scales dramatically tilted. After industrialists joined the movement against central-city extension, political fragmentation was the natural consequence.

The Form of the Corporate City

Once this transitional period had culminated in a stable pattern of urban reproduction, American cities had acquired a qualitatively new structure. It is reasonably easy to review the central political-economic features of the Corporate City.

If a city had reached maturity as an Industrial City during the stage of industrial accumulation, its character changed rapidly during the corporate period although its physical structure remained embedded in concrete. Its downtown shopping districts were transformed into downtown central business districts, dominated by skyscrapers....Surrounding the central business district were emptying manufacturing areas, depressed from the desertion of large plants, barely surviving on the light and competitive industries left behind. Next to those districts were the old working-class districts, often transformed into "ghettos," locked into the cycle of central-city manufacturing decline. Outside the central city there were suburban belts of industrial development, linked together by circumferential highways. Scattered around those industrial developments were fragmented working-class and middle-class suburban communities. The wealthy lived farther out. Political fragmentation prevailed beyond the central-city boundaries.

Many other, newer cities—particularly those in the South, Southwest, and West—reached maturity during the stage of corporate accumulation. These became the exemplary Corporate Cities. They shared one thundering advantage over the older Industrial Cities: they had never acquired the fixed physical capital of an earlier era. They could be constructed from scratch to fit the needs of a new period of accumulation in which factory plant and equipment were themselves increasingly predicated upon a decentralized model....There was consequently no identifiable downtown factory district; manufacturing was scattered throughout the city plane. There were no centralized working-class housing districts (for that was indeed what capitalists had learned to avoid); working-class housing was scattered all over the city around the factories. Automobiles and trucks provided the connecting links, threading together the separate pieces. The Corporate City became, in Robert Fogelson's term, the Fragmented Metropolis. No centers anywhere. Diffuse economic activity everywhere.

These two models help underscore the significance of the *reversals* reflected in the Corporate City form. Manufacturing had been clustering toward the center of the Industrial City; now it was moving anywhere across the urban space. Working-class housing had been packed into dense central zones; now it was scattered around the metropolitan area and increasingly segmented. Central business districts had been dominated by shopping centers; now, in at least some cities, they were dominated by corporate headquarters. (The shopping centers, at least in the newer cities, were scattered everywhere.) The middle and upper classes had been fleeing but were continually reabsorbed; now, in the older cities, they fled more successfully into separate suburbs. Before, the city had crammed around its center; now, the Corporate City sprawled.

Once this new urban form crystallized, of course, many additional influences affected urban growth. Patterns of defense spending, federal housing policies, the power of the auto-energy-construction block, the shifting dynamics of urban-land speculation—these and many other factors contributed to the content of urban America after World War II. All of these factors had secondary effects, however, in the sense that they tended to reproduce the structure of the Corporate City rather than to change or undermine it. The foundations of that urban form were so strong that simple political influences could not change its basic shape.

ESSAY 4-2. RICHARD HARRIS AND ROBERT LEWIS, "THE GEOGRAPHY OF NORTH AMERICAN CITIES AND SUBURBS, 1900–1950: A NEW SYNTHESIS" (2001)

Source: Richard Harris and Robert Lewis, "The Geography of North American Cities and Suburbs." *Journal of Urban History* 27 (2001), 262–272, 274–278, 280–284. Copyright © 2001 by Sage Publications, Inc. Reprinted by permission of Sage Publications, Inc.

It is time to rethink the geography of American cities and suburbs in the first half of the twentieth century. Theoretical argument and substantive research have both challenged the received wisdom, which continues to rely heavily on the ideas of the Chicago school of sociology and especially those of Ernest Burgess. In theoretical terms, writers have challenged the view that geographical patterns merely reflect society, suggesting instead that space is integral to economic and social processes. A company does not make its production and location decisions separately: each implies the other. Similarly, a household chooses to live where it can afford, and what it can afford depends on the mix of work strategies that a certain location allows. Such theoretical insights imply that even if the geography of urban areas conformed to the models of the Chicago school, it must be conceptualized anew.

In fact, historical research is challenging the substantive accounts offered by Burgess and by many later writers. The enduring model assumes that jobs were concentrated near the city center, except for a few large factories at the fringe. It supposes that jobs and low wages kept immigrant workers in central cities, sometimes in sectors along radial rail lines. Supposedly, only affluent families could afford new suburban homes, while the exclusivity of the suburbs was ensured by suburban self-rule. This view stresses inner-city poverty and suburban affluence. It has inspired many studies of central immigrant ghettoes and slums and, following [Sam Bass] Warner, the suburban experiences of the middle class. Recently, however, some writers have provided disconfirming evidence of industrial decentralization and of fringe settlement by workers and immigrants, facts of which contemporaries were well aware. Arguably, prewar suburbs were as socially diverse as the cities that they surrounded, and it is doubtful whether the city-suburban dichotomy was very significant. Theory and evidence suggest that we need to rethink the nature and significance of urban patterns in the first half of the twentieth century, and together they constitute the basis for a new synthesis.

This article outlines a new interpretation of the changing geography of North American cities and suburbs from about 1900 to 1950. By *North American*, we refer to Canada and the United States because…the processes and patterns of urban development in these two countries were broadly similar.… We note that decentralization of employment was well under way by 1900, typically in polycentric clusters. It involved offices and stores, as well as factories, and encouraged the large-scale suburbanization of workers and immigrants. As a result, although individually homogeneous, suburbs in the aggregate were socially diverse, as were most central cities. We believe that it is inaccurate to think of cities in this period as poor and suburbs as affluent. Perhaps the most original and controversial element to our argument is the one that we present last. Contradicting the idea that suburban self-rule guaranteed the social exclusivity of the suburbs, we argue that the fragmentation of municipal government allowed all sorts of people to settle at the fringe. It blurred rather than sharpened the line between city and suburb, rendering such a distinction moot.…

The Urban Economy

Nothing matters more to a city than jobs, but we know less about the urban economy than about any other important aspect of metropolitan development. Contemporaries documented the growth of manufacturing at the suburban fringe from the late nineteenth century. This research was soon forgotten.…[W]e argue that the decentralization of manufacturing employment began very early and that patterns have long been polynuclear. We also suggest that much office (and even retail) employment had developed outside the CBD [Central Business District] before World War II, blurring their supposed contrasts with manufacturing.

Manufacturing
The fringes of North American cities have always contained some manufacturing, but a trend toward decentralization gained mo-

mentum in the third quarter of the nineteenth century. Case studies of Baltimore and Montreal have shown that in this period, companies were creating diverse and substantial industrial districts at the edge of the built-up area. These were more typical than not. By 1900, 32 percent of all manufacturing jobs in U.S. metropolitan centers were located beyond city limits. In absolute and relative terms, suburban employment continued to grow, reaching 41 percent of the metropolitan total by 1947. Moreover, many of the city's jobs lay close to its limits. Chicago is a case in point. In 1929, Chicago still contained 74 percent of manufacturing jobs in the metropolitan area, but many of the most important clusters, such as portions of the Clearing and the Central Manufacturing Districts to the west and the mills of the Calumet basin on the South Side, lay near city limits (see Figure 4-14).

Such geographies of manufacturing have been described in various ways. Drawing on the work of Burgess and Hoyt, many writers speak of zones and sectors. Burgess implied that manufacturing was concentrated in a zone that encircled the CBD. Contemporaries knew this to be an inaccurate simplification, and some noted that jobs were concentrated in sectors along radial railroads. In our view, however, the most flexible and accurate label for the geography of manufacturing is *polynuclear*, a term that owes much to ideas first advanced by [Chauncy] Harris and [Edward] Ullman half a century ago. Visual inspection of the maps of manufacturing districts in Chicago, Los Angeles, Toronto, and Montreal demonstrates the inadequacy of *zone* as a label. Sectoral patterns, while present, are discontinuous and often appear in clustered segments. Polynuclear acknowledges the typical existence of concentrations both near the center and elsewhere and of varying shapes and sizes.

Los Angeles is often taken to be the exemplar of polynuclearity (see Figure 4-15). Viehe has argued that from the late nineteenth century, the geography of Los Angeles was shaped by manufacturing and dispersed oil production in places such as El Segundo, Fullerton, and Vernon, with associated residential suburbs such as Torrance, Hawthorne, and Hun-

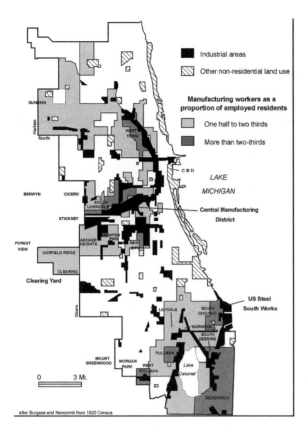

Figure 4-14 Manufacturing and Blue-Collar Districts, Chicago, 1920. Prepared from data reported in E.W. Burgess and John Newcomb, Census Data of the City of Chicago (Chicago: University of Chicago Press, 1931). Illustration in original, 266.

tington Park. After Goodyear established a large tire factory in 1919, glass, steel, auto, and chemical plants encouraged the growth of new centers of suburban manufacturing, including San Pedro and Long Beach. The late 1930s and World War II saw a new phase of industrial investment, led by aircraft, ship-

building, and Kaiser's steel plant in Fontana. Supporting this polynuclear pattern was an extensive transportation network, suburban services, and the concerted actions of real estate developers. Early polynuclear clusters were not unique to Los Angeles. By 1940, Chicago had as many "employing" suburbs

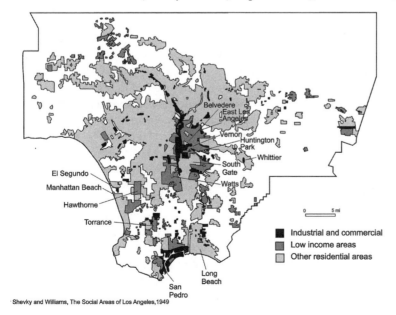

Figure 4-15 Manufacturing and Low-Income Areas, Los Angeles County, 1940. Redrawn from census information reported in E. Shevky and M. Williams, *The Social Areas of Los Angeles* (Los Angeles: University of California Press, 1949). Illustration in original, 267.

as did Los Angeles. The Pittsburgh area, with its numerous suburban industrial districts, was more decentralized still. By 1900, a large industrial district had developed on the eastern banks of the Mississippi in East St. Louis across from St. Louis. Smaller centers were also fragmented. During the interwar years, Peoria, Illinois, was challenged by an industrial satellite across the Peoria River. In terms of employment patterns, Los Angeles was more typical than it was extraordinary.

To make sense of this polynuclear pattern of manufacturing, we need to reconceptualize the process by which companies make location decisions. Traditionally, manufacturing location has been interpreted within a Weberian framework, which states that a firm's location decision is the result of a rational appraisal of transportation costs, land prices, taxes, labor, and proximity to other firms. This approach informed most research on the geography of manufacturing in the 1950s and 1960s....Working within this framework, researchers came to favor a polarized interpretation. At one extreme, they recognized "heavy," capital-intensive industries (steel and later auto and aircraft assembly) that were drawn to fringe locations to take advantage of more convenient rail (and later truck) transportation. At the other extreme were "light," labor-intensive industries, such as garment manufacture, that could thrive in expensive, central locations by using multistory buildings. The Weberian approach came under a series of attacks....In the 1970s, Marxist writers argued that firms make production and location decisions jointly. In the aggregate, patterns of employment not only reflect economic forces but also help to constitute them. By attracting suppliers, buyers, or a labor force, a company can create the conditions for its continued existence.

From our point of view, the organization of production can involve different combinations of work processes, scales of operation, and methods of distribution, or what one of the present authors has termed *manufacturing pathways*. This approach recognizes that investment occurs in waves, that locational inertia ensures that such investments endure

for decades, and that at any moment the industrial geography of an urban area is composed of several layers of history. Using this framework, it is possible to make sense of the polynucleated patterns of employment. Polynucleation reflects both historic legacy and current conditions....In an urban context, the typical result is a series of employment nodes, each originally established at the urban fringe and later enveloped by the expanding urban field. Chicago provides a clear case (see Figure 4-14). The construction of a steel mill in South Chicago in 1880 set into motion the rapid expansion of steel and ancillary production in the southern portion of the city. By 1900, this area had been enveloped by the expanding metropolis, and new metalworking nodes had developed farther south in the Calumet district....

If polynucleation is a result of successive waves of development, it also reflects the diverse needs of industries and specific companies. Individual companies may combine capital, technology, land, and labor in different ways....Moreover, in any period, different industries have typically been characterized by very different pathways. In the 1920s, for example, auto assemblers never conformed to any stereotype of mass production....[G]iven that cities differ in their industrial structure, it is impossible to make generalizations that can usefully be applied everywhere. The only certain generalization is that polynucleation took varied forms because cities and industries had different histories and that these translated into an elaborate urban spatial division of manufacturing....

This formulation may seem loose, but it is precisely this quality that makes it helpful. Rather than trying to make the geography of manufacturing conform to models that are spuriously precise, we should acknowledge that scattered polynucleation reflected histories and processes that were correspondingly complex. As a result, urban manufacturing space was spread throughout the metropolitan area, with employment zones differentiated by industrial mix, production organization, age and type of buildings, location of markets, type of labor force, and transportation facilities.

Offices and Retailing

Much of what we have suggested about manufacturing probably applies equally to office employment and, in a different way, to retailing. Each company's location decision was part of its business strategy while, for both functional and historic reasons, aggregate patterns were complex. Here, however, there is a particular difficulty in making useful generalizations: if the geography of manufacturing has been neglected, the pattern of office and retail activity outside the CBD has been almost wholly ignored.

We suspect that in the first half of the twentieth century, there was a good deal more office employment outside the CBD than is generally supposed. In early twentieth-century Toronto, for example, banks shifted archival, stationary, and printing services to distant industrial districts while retaining high-order activities downtown. Office decentralization was most common in the manufacturing sector. Especially in small- and medium-sized companies, there were a number of advantages in keeping factory and office together. With limited management specialization, many companies found it easier to direct office and factory operations at one site. When they moved their production facilities to the suburbs, many manufacturers took their office staff with them.... The largest companies found more advantages in separating factory and office, but this did not always mean that the latter stayed downtown. [Joel] Garreau has interpreted the relocation of GM's Detroit headquarters to a suburban site in the 1920s as America's first "edge city" office node....

Our knowledge of early twentieth-century retailing is similarly meager. Although almost all writers have concentrated on the CBD, as Richard Longstreth has observed, "Ordinary commercial landscapes lying beyond the city center rank among the least studied and most readily forgotten urban environments." In fact, important clusters of retail activity emerged outside of the center city by the end of the nineteenth century, Milwaukee being a case in point. In Los Angeles, by the 1930s, the downtown "was only one, and by no means the most stylish, of its business districts." In 1930s, Chicago "the central business district [was] duplicated on a smaller scale at many places in the city by large commercial nucleations," and by 1935, three-quarters of all retail sales were outside the city core....

[R]etail as well as office and manufacturing employment was moving steadily into fringe and suburban nodes in the first half of the twentieth century.

Social Geographic Patterns

Residential Patterns

If the geography of employment did not conform to a simple model, neither did patterns of residence. Certainly, no general contrast can be made between city and suburb in terms of social class. Contemporaries knew this well enough. They agreed that central cities contained low-income families, including racial and ethnic minorities.... At the same time, however, some writers noted the persistence of older, prosperous enclaves....

Segregated diversity was also apparent beyond city limits....[By 1940] Rents in industrial suburbs were rarely high but in half of all cases were near the metropolitan average, belying the notion that industrial suburbs were poor. Most significant, many residential suburbs were not affluent: one-third had rents well above the metropolitan average, while one-quarter were well below. Overall, low-rent suburbs accounted for a third of the total, of which a substantial minority, again about a third, contained few jobs. By 1940, many low-income families lived in the suburbs and not necessarily in the shadow of the mills. By mid-century, as informed observers recognized, suburbs, like cities, had long contained all classes of people....

There was a tendency for immigrants and racialized minorities to concentrate in the cities, but this can easily be overstated. Innumerable studies have documented the settlement of diverse groups in central immigrant ghettoes. In fact, the ethnic and racial composition of the suburbs was almost equally complex. Prosperous suburbs were populated by native-born Americans and Canadians, while lower-income districts often contained immigrants. Some of this fringe settlement occurred within city limits: the migration of Jews to the Bronx and Brooklyn between 1900 and the 1920s was essentially suburban even though it occurred within New York City.... The extent of immigrant settlement beyond the central districts was often striking. In Philadelphia, "decentralized but highly clustered patterns of urban settlement were characteristic...of all the newer immigrant peoples...between 1880–1920."...

Just because immigrants settled away from the center did not necessarily mean that they were socially or residentially integrated. In Philadelphia, for example, segregation took the form of clusters around fringe manufacturing plants. Commonly, the ethnic composition of working-class fringe areas varied a good deal. Immigrants concentrated in industrial as opposed to residential suburbs. Micro-scale segregation developed within such communities, good examples being Steelton and Vandergrift [PA] as well as Fall River [MA] and Gary [IN].... To complicate the picture, ethnic segregation sometimes occurred within rather than between suburbs. For example, most of Cleveland's Lakewood was white and middle class, but in the 1890s, the establishment of a national carbon plant created an adjacent Slovak enclave.

Much more than immigrants, African Americans were confined to the central city, in part because of discriminatory lending practices. Although by 1950, immigrants made up almost as high a proportion of the population of suburbs (9 percent) as of cities (11 percent), the respective percentages for blacks (4.5 and 12.6 percent) were quite different. Even so, African Americans moved into fringe districts, albeit in segregated settings. This pattern was once common around southern cities such as Birmingham, Atlanta, Richmond, and Memphis. Elsewhere, black suburbs developed outside Cincinnati, Chicago, Cleveland, and Washington, D.C., as well as in satellite towns such as Gary, Indiana, and Harvey, Illinois. Sometimes, later annexation obscured the suburban character of original settlement. Chicago's Morgan Park and the Watts area of Los Angeles are notable examples (see Figures 4-14 and 4-15). Then again, a few blacks settled in small enclaves in predominantly white suburbs. In the Detroit area, Ecorse and River Rouge were good

examples of this, as was Evanston, north of Chicago. The black urban experience in the first half of the twentieth century was one of marked segregation usually but not necessarily within the central city....

Overall, then, we believe that the social geography of urban areas did not conform even approximately to the stereotype of urban ghetto slums and affluent suburban enclaves.

Jobs, Transportation, and the Journey to Work

What can explain the social diversity of cities and suburbs? In particular, since so many writers have assumed that only middle-class families could afford to commute from new suburban homes, how can we explain the growth of immigrant working-class settlement at the fringe?...

The location of jobs was of fundamental importance. Factories and freight yards repelled the affluent and drew workers. It is true that few people enjoyed living in the shadow of the mills, and from the 1890s, streetcars allowed many to commute several miles. By the 1920s, to a greater extent in the United States than in Canada, automobiles extended commutes and loosened the urban fabric. But most workers could not spare much time or money and so had little choice but to live close to work....

It was the early decentralization of jobs that allowed many immigrant workers to settle beyond city limits, most obviously in industrial suburbs.... Workers were at least as eager as the middle classes to own suburban property and readily followed jobs into the suburbs.... There are many examples of industrial satellites and suburbs where residential settlement clearly depended heavily on local industry. Examples include the mill towns around Pittsburgh, the oil-based settlements around Los Angeles, planned suburbs such as Montreal's Maisonneuve, and unplanned suburbs such as Toronto's Junction....

But job location was not everything. Especially in larger centers, the settlement of residential areas depended on improvements in transportation technology. It is conventional to argue that mass transit allowed better paid workers to commute further. New York, with its cheap and extensive subway network, is the extreme case. In smaller places, however, transit was not always critical. After 1900, immigrant workers settled Toronto's suburbs even though those areas were without transit. Commuters walked a mile or two to the end of the streetcar line and, in some cases, all the way downtown....By the 1930s, automobiles allowed some workers to scatter into the rural-urban fringe. Proportionately, this was most common around small- and medium-sized industrial centers such as Eugene (Oregon), Flint (Michigan), Rochester (New York), and Norwich (Connecticut). The same process occurred around larger urban centers....By 1950, suburbanization was encouraged by but by no means dependent on the decentralization of manufacturing. The automobile had come to play an important role....

The Home as a Place-Dependent Work Site
Changes in the location of jobs and in methods of transportation do not provide a wholly adequate explanation of residential patterns. In particular, they do not explain how low-income families could afford to acquire and maintain new suburban homes. To understand how this was possible, we need to expand our notion of the household economy. Most urban historians have viewed households as consumers of housing and transportation, with levels of consumption being dependent on wage income. In fact, as feminists have emphasized, homes were also sites of unpaid labor. Much of this work, especially cooking, cleaning, and child rearing, was undertaken by women. Some, however, including home construction, repair, and maintenance, was generally men's work. Such unpaid labor and sweat equity added much to the household economy.

Of particular importance for the present argument, unpaid labor varied with residential location. Cooking and cleaning took longer in areas, usually suburban, that lacked piped water. Owner building was easier and sometimes only possible in areas where building regulations were permissive. Again, these were typically suburban. The unserviced and unregulated suburb offered households the best opportunity to supplement monetary income with unpaid labor. This opportunity appealed to the families of immigrant workers, who were willing to make exceptional sacrifices to acquire a home. In one sense, it was a willingness to undertake extensive unpaid labor that created this type of residential workers' suburb. At the same time, such a work strategy was necessary for those who wished to move there: it was a "price" of entry. With households, as with companies, location and work strategy were a package deal.

Given the gender division of labor, the choice of the suburban work package had different implications for men and women. Most discussions of gender and suburbia in this period have been framed in terms of the middle-class experience. They have pointed to the isolation of suburban life, the difficulties of obtaining "help," and the slow rise of male domesticity. It was among workers, however, that the choice of suburban residence at first carried the greatest implications. A case study of Toronto has shown that in the city, many women took in boarders and quite a few worked for pay. At the urban fringe, the great majority did neither, devoting themselves to homemaking. The lack of services meant that basic tasks took longer. This fact, combined with physical isolation, made it impossible to combine homemaking with paid employment. For such women, the city and suburban ways of life were different indeed. The social diversity of early twentieth-century suburbs was bound up with class—and doubtless ethnic—differences in the gender division of labor and in ways that we have as yet only begun to understand....

Political Fragmentation

Varied patterns of house building and land development, as well as the emergence of social diversity at the urban fringe, depended on the fragmentation of government within the metropolitan area. This assertion might seem strange. Scholars have argued that political fragmentation enabled rich suburbs to exclude the poor, along with racial and ethnic minorities, thereby confining them to the city. These powers were reinforced by the

Euclid [*v. Ambler*] decision of 1926, which in effect gave local governments the power to zone as they wished. This interpretation has been strengthened by those who have shown how, early in the twentieth century, private deed restrictions served the same sort of function as publicly enforced zoning and building regulations. Indeed, it is probably true that for much the first half of the twentieth century, deed restrictions had a greater impact than municipal zoning.

There was a good reason why many suburban areas did not develop under such exclusive regulations. From a fiscal point of view, the most desirable land uses were commercial and industrial. Depending on how local property taxes were structured, these users typically demanded the fewest services for each tax dollar paid. This argument was unpersuasive to residents of affluent suburbs because industry brought undesirable side effects, notably pollution and noise. However, it spoke eloquently to almost everyone else. Workers' suburbs welcomed factories, not just because they paid for municipal services but because they offered jobs to residents who could ill afford to commute elsewhere.

The clout of industrial capital guaranteed that its need for factory sites toward the urban fringe would be accommodated by suburban and city governments. One result was the organized factory district. Usually located in suburbs, these were planned privately by railway and real estate companies and supported by local government. Of small account before World War I, there were 122 such districts in 84 cities by mid-century. Places such as New York's Bush Terminal offered manufacturers cheap land, low taxes, direct freight car service, building design, financial assistance, and other external economies....

Although planned industrial districts became more common, new factories usually moved to the suburbs in a more ad hoc fashion. Individual companies bargained with suburbs for tax breaks, playing off one against the other. In the 1880s, for example, the new industrial suburb of West Toronto felt compelled to offer substantial tax holidays to attract employers. The same happened in East St. Louis. Alternatively, corporations ac-

quired unincorporated land and fashioned a government to suit their needs....In various ways, then, companies levered their way into the suburbs on favorable terms and ensured that many fringe areas became industrial and not residentially exclusive.

Partly for this reason, the political fragmentation of metropolitan areas favored the suburban settlement of low-income families. Industrial suburbs such as West Allis [WI] or the Toronto Junction could subsidize the settlement of workers, assuming that workers would in turn attract more industry....

If industrial suburbs sought workers, unincorporated districts accepted all comers through benign neglect. Although often overlooked, unincorporated areas played a vital role in shaping suburban development. In 1950, more than one-third of the urban population that lived outside central cities resided in unincorporated territory. Because most scholars have focused on larger metropolitan centers, they have missed this fact. The unincorporated share was barely 20 percent for the largest metropolitan areas but more than 60 percent in the smallest centers....

In one sense, the political fragmentation of metropolitan suburbs reflected the needs of manufacturers and the social diversity of those who wished to settle there. Supply responded to demand. At the same time, fragmentation made suburban diversity possible. Different governments catered to different needs, and some needs were met by governmental neglect. The evolving geography of the metropolitan area did not merely reflect but helped to constitute the political, economic, and social processes of urban development.

Conclusion...

Americans have persuaded themselves that the distinction between central cities and surrounding suburbs is basic to our understanding of the character of urban growth. In the first half of the twentieth century, this was not true. In terms of employment and social composition, we have argued that differences between cities and the suburbs as a whole were quite minor and were dwarfed by variations within the city and among the suburbs.

To assume otherwise is to risk making egregious errors. Those who are interested in the immigrant experience, for example, may not conveniently confine their attention to the city. Those who wish to understand the lives of middle-class families should not look only to the suburbs. For many purposes, we must learn to ignore political boundaries and think simply of metropolitan, urbanized areas. Of course, in some contexts, political boundaries mattered a good deal, but the city's limits were only one of those that deserve attention. The jostling and striving that went on within and among the suburbs were at least as important, increasingly so by mid-century. We need to know much more about this suburban jostling, particularly about the development of those industrial and low-income suburbs that do not fit the suburban myth.

In emphasizing these sorts of unfashionable suburbs, we imply another sort of geographical agenda. Low-income suburbs—and persistently high-status inner districts—were probably most typical of the urban experience in the southern states, in Canada, and in smaller urban centers everywhere. These are regions and the sorts of places that have always lain outside of the mainstream of North American urban history, which to this day has focused on the larger industrial cities of the northeastern and midwestern states. We need to know more about these other centers, not only because they contained a large number of people but also because they embodied processes that were at work everywhere....

Our agenda places more emphasis on economic processes and constraints than has been usual in North American urban research. There is a strong tradition, especially in the United States, of viewing urban history through a political filter, while many interpretations of suburban development have emphasized how individuals have expressed a cultural preference for privacy and property ownership. We do not wish to suggest that the political and cultural dimensions of urban life were unimportant. We have argued that political fragmentation was very important in defining the shape of urban development, while our explanation of the growth of lower-income suburbs acknowledges that immigrant workers brought with them a strong desire to own suburban property. But we do believe that the urban economy, interpreted broadly to include both paid and unpaid work, defined the limits of the possible in the first half of the twentieth century, as indeed it does to this day.

NOTES

1. Graham Taylor penned the phrase "cool green rim." See Document 4-3.
2. Richard Harris and Robert Lewis, "Constructing a Fault(y) Zone: Misrepresentations of American Cities and Suburbs, 1900–1950," *Annals of the Association of American Geographers* 88, no. 4 (1998), 636.

CHAPTER 5

The Politics of Early Suburbia

INTRODUCTION

As suburbanization continued apace in fin-de-siècle America, the suburbs spawned a new style of politics and governance that would have long-lived repercussions. Suburbanites exerted their political will on several levels: from the local to the metropolitan. In later years, the "suburban vote" would resonate even in national politics as a bastion of low tax, limited state, and pro-middle-class policy. The early period, however, was formative for suburban politics: the structure of suburban governance was established, a political culture in suburbia took shape, and suburban citizens worked to establish and protect their political autonomy vis-á-vis the city.

The early history of suburban politics raised a fundamental question about the proper scale of political units—large, comprehensive areas vs. small, local ones—that remains very much an issue of debate today. This tension first surfaced in conflicts between cities and suburbs over municipal autonomy during the late nineteenth century. The proliferation of suburban developments raised numerous questions: Who would govern these new communities? Would they fall within the political boundaries of the greater city? If outside those boundaries, would they remain the responsibility of county and township governments? Or would they operate independently? What would the role and responsibilities of these new governments be? As more and more suburban communities were built, cities and suburbs alike struggled to find effective solutions to these questions. Because population was a matter of urban prestige and a measure of influence in state and national politics, cities were reluctant to lose the growing number of people moving to suburbia. At first, cities employed the tool of "annexation"—the absorption of outlying areas into existing city boundaries—to politically contain them. In the nineteenth century, some suburban residents welcomed annexation because it meant access to much-needed services that big cities could afford. The annexation trend peaked in the Northeast and Midwest around 1900, but thereafter, suburbanites resisted annexation with growing fervor, as they came to see greater value in political autonomy. Annexation remained popular a bit longer in the rapidly growing metropolitan areas of the South and Southwest, but by 1960, the wave of annexation had receded. The suburbs' success in resisting annexation testified to their growing political clout, which would only increase as the century wore on.

One method suburbanites used to resist annexation was municipal incorporation. When a suburban area incorporated, it gained political autonomy and the advantage of local control over the physical and social environment. But incorporation also meant that a suburb was on its own when it came to providing services, such as police and fire protection, paved streets, clean water, sewers, libraries, parks, and sometimes schools. Many residents of middle- and upper-class suburbs had come to *expect* these amenities. They wanted the best of both worlds: local control over local affairs, with the most up-to-date conveniences of modern urban living at low cost. The political challenge for suburbs was how to deliver all of these promises. When it came to services, which were both complex and costly, cities benefited from economies of scale and centralized coordination. How could a tiny suburb hope to promise comparable services at an affordable price? And how would multiple, small suburban governments avoid the chaos of uncoordinated development—discontinuous streets, mismatched sewer and water systems, gaps in police and fire service? As the essays and documents below suggest, suburbanites devised solutions to these problems in ways that revolutionized structures of metropolitan governance, but also exacerbated metropolitan inequalities. Political independence meant that suburbs shared limited responsibility for the metropolitan commonweal. Suburbanites found ways to "have their urban amenities without the urban problems," as historian Kenneth Jackson put it.[1]

The issues shaping early suburban political life—the drive for local control and concerns about services—played out differently among suburbs of different classes. In well-to-do communities, the powers conferred by political autonomy were often deployed to protect the town's class and racial exclusivity. For example, the municipal tool of zoning could be used to exclude apartments (with their lower-income tenants) and industries (with their odious by-products). Residents in such suburbs also had high expectations for good services. In affluent suburbs, thus, citizens harnessed politics to ensure a suburban ideal of homogeneous, high-class neighborhoods in picturesque settings, with the very best standard of living. In working-class suburbs, the story could contrast sharply. There, political autonomy was also valued but was often used in ways that served very different local needs. Local land use laws might welcome industry (and the jobs and tax base they provided), productive land use, and cheap housing. And residents often opposed the installation of costly services out of concerns about property taxes. They were willing to live in a rough-hewn physical environment, if it meant keeping tax rates low. The quality of services, in fact, emerged as a kind of social "sieve," sorting out the suburbs by class, as Ann Durkin Keating suggests in her essay. The common denominator among suburbs of all classes, however, was a desire among residents for local control, for the power to shape their communities according to their particular ideals and aspirations.

In this period, a distinctive political culture emerged in suburbia as well, characterized by nonpartisanship, volunteerism, parsimony, and a tendency toward conservatism. In many areas, suburbanites harnessed politics to protect and defend their particular vision of the suburban ideal. The result was a parochial, inward orientation that put the needs of the local community above the welfare of the greater metropolitan commonweal.

The effects of these developments reverberated deeply. The new political structure granted formidable power to suburbanites over the future of metropolitan growth, created novel approaches to power sharing in metropolitan areas, exacerbated inequality between cities and suburbs, and promoted political fragmentation that undermined a sense of shared responsibility for problems at the metropolitan level. These trends would only intensify during the twentieth century, creating some of the greatest challenges facing metropolitan areas in our own time.

DOCUMENTS

Document 5-1, by the noted social scientist Adna F. Weber, is a sweeping description of the annexation trend among cities in Europe and the United States, written at the turn of the twentieth century. In this article, Weber celebrates the potentials of both annexation and suburbanization, reflecting the optimism of many urbanites at the time. After peaking in 1900, annexation efforts began to wane in Northeastern and Midwestern cities, in the face of growing resistance by suburban communities. **Document 5-2** offers the perspective of one such suburb, Highland Park, outside Detroit. The site of Ford Motor Company's first auto assembly line, Highland Park was also home to thousands of white-collar and skilled blue-collar householders, who enjoyed not only the proximity of high paying employment but the infusion of industrial property taxes to local coffers. The case of Highland Park illustrates how crucial the twin issues of taxes and services were to the question of political autonomy. Once suburban areas devised ways to deliver services efficiently and cheaply (in Highland Park's case, the role of big industrial taxpayers was key), this freed them to resist annexation by the big city.

By the 1930s, suburban resistance to annexation deepened, especially in older and larger cities. The result was a patchwork of politically independent suburbs scattered across metropolitan areas, creating a balkanized political landscape. **Document 5-3** explores the implications of this trend. Written by political scientist Thomas Reed, the essay highlights the inefficiencies and inequalities created by this fragmentation, and it suggests a solution in a new "federated" type of metropolitan governance. Reed's critique was prescient in identifying problems that would mount as the century wore on, even if his prediction of metropolitan governance was not. In subsequent years, urban experts would echo his call for a metropolitan approach to problem solving; indeed, this is the cornerstone of many present-day proposals to reform the suburban metropolis, as detailed in chapter 16.

The final documents profile political life in the suburbs of Los Angeles. In **Document 5-4,** newspaper reports from Glendale and South Pasadena convey the political tranquility characteristic of many middle-class suburbs. As these articles on local elections illustrate, suburban politics reflected a spirit of consensus and even inconsequentiality. Both communities were predominantly white and middle class; Glendale was incorporated in 1906, South Pasadena was incorporated in 1888. In **Document 5-5**, a different political culture emerges. These articles come from South Gate, a working-class suburb south of downtown Los Angeles. A conflict had been brewing in this community over services, pitting working-class homeowners against local merchants. Many homeowners, barely making ends meet, opposed taxes to finance service improvements, while the businessmen—who dominated city hall—favored improvements in the name of South Gate's progress. The result was raucous political turmoil. Note that in both South Pasadena and South Gate, a "Board of Trustees" served the same function as a city council. **Document 5-6,** a map of Los Angeles County in 1940, illustrates the geographic results of political balkanization. By this time, the Los Angeles area was home to forty-four independent political jurisdictions. This figure actually paled in comparison to some eastern cities, such as Pittsburgh (113 municipalities), Philadelphia (91 municipalities), and Chicago (116 municipalities).

What were the benefits and drawbacks for cities of large-scale annexations? Similarly, what were the benefits and drawbacks of suburban political independence? Why did Highland Park oppose annexation by Detroit? What was Reed's solution to the problem of metropolitan government? What problems would this approach solve, or leave unsolved? What were the future implications of political balkanization in metropolitan areas? Can we generalize about the political culture of early suburbia? Why or why not?

5-1. SOCIAL SCIENTIST ADNA WEBER DOCUMENTS THE TREND OF SUBURBAN ANNEXATIONS, 1898

Source: Adna F. Weber, "Suburban Annexations," *North American Review* 166 (May 1898).

The latest forecast of American life in the twentieth century predicts the downfall of the "boss," the abolition of political corruption and class legislation, equality of opportunity, the triumph of international arbitration, the cessation of sectional discords, and a universal reign of peace—until the cities of New York and Chicago go to war to decide which shall annex Texas! Chicago was the target of every journalistic joke-maker in New York

up to two years ago, when the "Greater New York" idea came to the front. But Chicago with all her annexations has only 189 square miles of territory, while New York now covers 360 square miles of land. This gives New York the first place among the cities of the world, so far as mere extent of territory goes. For London (administrative county) has an area of only 118 square miles, Paris 30, Berlin 24, Philadelphia 129. What, then, is the justification of this immense annexation, or is it only a land-grabbing scheme to gratify local vanity and a false municipal pride?

A brief survey of the population statistics of Europe and America suffices to show that the great cities have ceased to grow as rapidly as the smaller cities and large towns. Thus the recent German census (1895) showed a gain for Berlin in the census period 1890–95 of only 6.2 per cent., as compared with 11 per cent. for the province of Brandenburg, in which Berlin is situated....

Liverpool [England] actually had a smaller population in 1891 than in 1881....

One now begins to understand why the great cities of the world are apparently falling behind smaller places in the rapidity of their growth. On the one hand is the process of "city building," the tearing down of dwellings to make room for business blocks; on the other hand are the improvements in transportation, which enable an increasing proportion of the city's population to reside at a distance from their places of business. The double movement is relieving the congested districts and filling up the suburbs....

The larger American cities have also reached the "point of saturation," where the first settled districts have been losing their population. "Down town" New York was more populous in 1860 than in 1890. In fact, the only wards that gained in population in the last census period, 1880–90, were the wards above Forty-second Street, with the exception of that part of the tenement district lying south of Fourteenth Street and east of the Bowery....

The decentralizing movement has also extended to the suburbs, especially in those cities like Boston where the electric trolley has been so highly exploited. Even in the case of New York, whose suburban railway system is very poor, there has been a growth of the suburban towns and cities far in advance of New York's growth....

It thus appears that the Borough of Manhattan comprises really less than one-half of the true metropolis. And the increase in the population of the environs far exceeded that of the city itself, the respective percentages for 1880–90 being 42.66 and 25.62.

The conclusion to be drawn from the statistics here presented is that the movement toward suburban annexation is not an artificial one, but is simply the legal recognition of new economic conditions. It is a movement confined to no one country, least of all to the United States. In Europe there have

been large suburban annexations in recent years. Vienna in 1891 incorporated suburbs with a population of 464,110 (as compared with 798,719 in the old city), and is already looking forward to the necessity of making further annexations to provide room for her citizens. Leipzig incorporated many suburbs in 1891 and again in 1892. Munich, Dresden, Hanover have also annexed outlying territory, and there are few of the German "great cities" that are not obliged to face the problem.

The "rise of the suburbs" is by far the most cheering movement of modern times. It means an essential modification of the process of concentration of population that has been taking place during the last hundred years and brought with it many of the most difficult political and social problems of our day. To the Anglo-Saxon race life in the great cities cannot be made to seem a healthy and natural mode of existence. The fresh air and clear sunlight, the green foliage and God's blue sky are dear to the heart of this people, who cannot become reconciled to the idea of bringing up their children in hot, dusty, smoky, germ-producing city tenements and streets. But a solution of the problem is now in sight; the suburb unites the advantages of city and country. The country's natural surroundings, the city's social surroundings—these are both the possession of the suburb.

5-2. A DETROIT SUBURB RESISTS ANNEXATION, 1922

Source: "Highland Park, Very Well Satisfied, Is Deaf to Annexation," *Detroit Saturday Night*, November 25, 1922.

Will Highland Park annex itself to Detroit's tax rate? That is the question, a question which is as futile as it is perennial, because the answer is "No."

It was brought forward this time by Mayor Couzens of the larger city in a speech before the new Highland Park Progressive Voters' Association, child of the ill-starred Taxpayer's League of a year ago.

Mayor Couzens didn't invade the suburb

to start annexation propaganda, nor did he demand anything of the kind. He went there on invitation and in the course of his talk admitted that he believed in home rule, which made it Highland Park's own problem. But he did tell why he thought the merger should be effected, and gave more time to that than to the proposed metropolitan area which it had been announced he would discuss....

He began, as they all do, with the statement that Highland Parkers use Belle Island and Palmer Park without paying for them, which will brook no denial. He followed with a statement about the suburbanites using the Detroit streets for their automobiles and riding in the street cars. He did not mention that those who ride the street cars pay their nickels and help the D[etroit].S[treet].R[ailway]. to pile up the "profits" which it has been advertising the first of each month. Nor did he mention that more traffic passes Woodward and Manchester Avenues [in Highland Park], carrying suburbanites to and from their business in Detroit, than passes State Street on Woodward Avenue [in Detroit], which about balances that account.

He told how Detroit, for years, had fought all of the public utility rate battles in the courts and before the legislature without the assistance of the suburbs, although they all benefited by the reduction in rates. He probably said this in good faith, but the facts are that many a time Highland Park has hired lobbyists to work with the Detroit lobby at Lansing, and that Claude H. Stevens, city attorney, has "sat in" with Detroit's corporation counsel in the preparation of many of the court cases and has volunteered his services in all of them.

Which brings us to the real reasons why Highland Park will not annex. Some of them are logical, others have their origin in prejudice and some, of course, are purely political. Of the logical ones it might be well to start with the fact that Highland Park's tax rate is lower than Detroit's and still coming down. This year, to be specific, it is $5.179 cents less per thousand of assessed valuation. This despite the fact that the entire city has been developed in a period of 10 years.

The streets are 95 per cent paved, the al-leys 60 per cent paved and most potent argument of all, there is a seat in school for every child all day. Last year there were 250 seats left over, which Detroit used and for which it paid.

The people are supplied with plenty of water from their own system and it is filtered.

There is a policeman past every home in the city every hour of the night and every school crossing is protected by a uniformed policeman.

There are more policemen per thousand population, more firemen per thousand population and more fire stations per square mile than in Detroit, and let us add parenthetically that when a new fire station is constructed in the southwest section, bonds for which have been approved, Highland Park will be the only class 1 fire insurance city in the state.

This, if you mind, with a tax rate lower than the bigger city's and all done in 10 years. What's the answer? Bonds, you say. Guess again. For all purposes, including schools, the bonded indebtedness is only $6,000,000 and the physical properties which these bonds have bought have already increased in value, particularly the real estate, to such an extent that they are worth more than they cost by several millions.

If the answer isn't in bonds it is in something else. For one thing, it is generally admitted a small city can be better governed than a large one. There isn't the overhead expense in the first place and in the second place, the administration is nearer to the people, both personally and geographically. Everyone lives within a mile of the city hall and everyone with a grievance is good for a dozen or two votes at the next election. It is also true that men have been elected with majorities of only two or three votes. And then too, the ever present fear of annexation has a tendency to keep the officeholders on their good behavior.

So much for the logical reasons.

Now for the prejudices. Highland Park—let us be frank about it—distrusts Detroit. It can work with it and does, but it is afraid to accept too literally its promises. It has had sad experiences in the past. Detroit sold it sewer connections and water connections and then tried to abrogate the contracts in order to force annexation. That resulted in Highland Park building its own water works and pumping its supply 11 miles from Grosse Pointe and a supreme court decision giving it "adequate sewer outlets forever." The latter cost some $680,000, which the suburb, then a village, paid in cash, and dinged if they didn't have to go to courts a second time to get Detroit to give the service that had been paid for.

Four years ago, a rider attached to a bill before the legislature provided for annexation without so much as the consent of Highland Park. It was taken for granted that the dumbbells (who become such immediately they move across the alley between Webb and Tuxedo Avenues) wouldn't get wise, but they did, showed the upstate members of the legislature what was being attempted and the rider was killed....As for the political reasons, they have two phases. In the first place, this is the first time the question has come up after election. It has almost universally been proposed just before election by some candidate for office in Detroit. In Mr. Couzens' case, it has all the earmarks of being sincere....

[Highland Park residents] have been told their taxes were higher "per capita" than in Detroit. 'Tis true, but they know that Ford and the Maxwell and the D.S.R. together are paying half of them. They may read that they haven't any libraries, but since most of them use one or the other of the city's two public libraries, they aren't deceived. And finally, they haven't forgotten that only a year ago the Detroiters who live north of them were seeking to de-annex because they couldn't get service from the city, which brings home pointedly that they can't annex on trial. Once in Detroit they would be in forever and forever, amen.

Let us close with an anecdote, none the less pointed for being true. Major Martin B. Hansz was acting mayor when the annexation question was last broached. Approached for an interview, he said:

"Tell them that half of the people of Highland Park came here because it wasn't Detroit. They'll stay here for the same reason."

5-3. POLITICAL SCIENTIST THOMAS REED CALLS FOR CONSOLIDATED METROPOLITAN GOVERNMENT, 1933

Source: Thomas H. Reed, "Metropolitan Government," in Roderick D. McKenzie, *The Metropolitan Community* (New York: McGraw-Hill Book Company, Inc., 1933).

The rapid centrifugal movement of urban population and the relatively slow progress of annexation have produced a general dislocation between population and units of local government which is characteristic of all metropolitan areas. This phenomenon is no novelty. London had an acute problem of the sort in the latter part of the eighteenth century, Philadelphia in the second quarter, and Boston in the third quarter of the nineteenth century. Annexation has habitually lagged behind the spread of population, but it is only in the twentieth century that the situation has become universal and of great quantitative importance. Every great city now has around it a metropolitan area, one with it economically and socially but without political unity.

Problems

The consequences in many instances have been little short of disastrous. The problems that face a metropolitan area do not differ in kind from those of any great city, but they assume a special character from the fact that the area is split into dozens or even hundreds of independent governments without means of common action. Metropolitan Boston, for example, includes 80 cities and towns and portions of at least six counties. Metropolitan New York covers parts of three states, all or part of 19 counties, and almost 300 cities, villages, and other minor units. Allegheny County, Pennsylvania, almost identical with the metropolitan area of Pittsburgh, contains more than 130 cities, boroughs and townships. Under these circumstances it is exceedingly difficult to provide for the preparation and execution of plans of growth. There has been a great deal of talk about regional plans, but very few of them have gone much beyond the stage of maps and reports which are promptly filed away and forgotten. In order to have effective regional planning there should be some unit of government commensurate with the task—with power to establish the plan and with the financial and legal ability to execute it.

Similarly, the problems of water supply and sewerage, which depend essentially upon topography, need to be dealt with either for the whole metropolis or for large sections of it without reference to the arbitrary boundaries of the existing units of government. The protection of public health in an area within which there is a daily movement of a large portion of the population can be secured only by means of a unit of government embracing the whole area; one or two units in which health laws are slackly enforced can menace the safety of all the rest. Police administration can scarcely be made effective in a metropolitan area if certain of the metropolitan units are cities of refuge for gangsters and bandits.

Other difficulties arise out of inequality of financial ability on the part of the various divisions of the metropolis. The central city, with its high-valued business district, usually occupies a position of financial advantage midway between the wealthy residential suburb with few governmental problems and high property values on the one hand, and the working-class community with large population and low values on the other. Under such circumstances education, for example, is very unevenly provided throughout the metropolis. The broad well-kept thoroughfares of one unit debouch into the ill-paved, unkept streets of another. The very communities which need them most are quite unable to provide themselves with parks and playgrounds or even with essential sanitary services. This does not by any means exhaust the list of metropolitan problems: it simply suggests their extent and importance.

Methods

Such a situation has naturally led to attempts at solution. The most obvious method of meeting a metropolitan problem affecting several units of government is the establishment of a special or *ad hoc* district for the purpose of dealing with that problem.... When a metropolitan problem has become acute, it is fairly easy to secure the creation of a special district to take care of it. This is at least partly due to the fact that its creation does not mean the disruption of any existing unit or the displacement of any political power or influence.

It is obvious, however, that while individual problems of the metropolis may be solved in this way, the metropolitan problem as a whole remains unsolved. It is possible to create one, two, three districts covering much the same area, but the establishment of each one of them may serve only to complicate the governmental situation and help to make the citizen's task more difficult than ever. Where several functions are joined in the same commission, as in the Massachusetts Metropolitan Commission for the Boston area, the result is something closely approximating a general unit of local government for the metropolis. The consequence is an increasing tendency to strive for some more complete solution than that offered by the special district.

Annexation.—In the old days the problems created by the spread of urban population over the area surrounding a city were taken care of by annexation, but annexation is no longer practicable as a means of coordinating with the central city the vast areas into which the automobile and the paved highway have poured urban population; and while great cities continue to grow by annexation, it is safe to say that the tendency of today is toward less annexation....In general, the process of annexation has been so far retarded that it cannot be said in the least to keep pace with the spread of population. This results in part from a growing spirit of resistance to annexation on the part of outlying communities and in part from a growing disposition to respect the right to local autonomy of such communities. The resistance is especially strong in well-established municipalities with a distinct independent history and a reasonable degree of financial ability. Los Angeles achieved her vast proportions largely by taking in rather sparsely settled unincorporated territory; it is significant that she could not bring Pasadena into her fold. The last great forcible annexation was that of Allegheny to Pittsburgh in 1907, and it caused such a reaction throughout the country that few politicians have even dared to suggest a repetition of that performance.

Alternatives.—On the assumption that there will be no tendency toward more extensive annexation, there are but two alternatives left. One of these is the performance directly by the state of functions that concern several local units. There is a tendency for the state to take a larger and larger share in the matter of highway construction and maintenance. For a long time the state highway authorities refused to spend money inside the boundaries of municipalities, but this policy is now being generally abandoned....The trend toward state centralization, however, falls outside the scope of this chapter. It is enough to say that there is such a tendency but that it will doubtless stop far short of a complete solution of the metropolitan problem.

The second alternative is the creation of units of metropolitan scope possessing sufficient powers to deal with those matters which affect the metropolis as a whole but leaving other matters to be dealt with either by the existing units or by new units to be created for the purpose. This is no more than saying that we need a new unit of government to replace the county, sometimes larger in area, and always endowed with broader powers and more effective organization than characterize counties today. The trend in this direction cannot be proved by any concrete changes in the structure of local government. So far none of the projects for the creation of this type of metropolitan government have been put into practice in the United States. The only examples to which we can turn are the Administrative County of London, set up in 1888, and the City of Greater Berlin, established in 1920. But there is no doubt of the movement of many minds in the direction of this solution....In St. Louis, Cleveland, Portland (Oregon), Los Angeles, and Chicago, there are well-defined movements for metropolitan consolidation, while in Buffalo, Detroit, St. Paul-Minneapolis, Dallas-Fort Worth, and other centers there is evidence of the serious consideration which men of affairs are giving to the so-called federated plan of metropolitan union....

Summary

It may safely be assumed that the metropolitan problem discussed here will continue to grow. The spread of city population over larger and larger areas is steadily taking place, even though the general movement of population from country to city has been somewhat checked by the depression. Even unprosperous cities are continuing to spread out; as time goes on, the maladjustment of areas of government to areas of population will become more and more serious. All the metropolitan problems will become more intense until readjustments are essential. The fact that the weight of local taxation is now so bitterly felt may open the way to the solution of the metropolitan problem, which cannot be divorced from the larger problem of the maladjustment of political units to population. Townships are passing away, dying of financial anemia. The old one-room school district is apparently about to slip into the limbo of forgotten things. Many counties are proving too small to meet their financial obligations, and in some parts of the country pressure for their consolidation is becoming vigorous. There is a real reason for readjusting our notions of the areas of government—town, township, city, county—which exist largely because of tradition and setting up units which conform to the social and economic facts of our national life.

Among these units will be the metropolitan area. We may call that area a city of a county or a city and a county. It may possess a unified or a federated type of government. But it will correspond to the facts of modern urban existence. We shall have larger and probably more powerful counties, with independent cities and villages functioning within them, but there will be within the county no subordinate units of rural local government—only cities and villages; and this will be true of the metropolitan area as of the agricultural county.

5-4. POLITICAL CONSENSUS: ELECTION REPORTS FROM TWO LOS ANGELES SUBURBS, 1910

"The Election," *The Glendale News*, April 8, 1910

Before this paper goes to press again, the municipal election in Glendale will have passed and the city's officials be named for the next two years. Whatever the result may be we congratulate the people upon their sane conduct of the campaign. Probably there have been statements made in a more or less private manner reflecting upon some of the candidates, but of these the general public knows nothing, and does not need to be informed. As we have said before there is no issue dividing the people; all of the candidates possess ability and have good records in their private life. There is always more or less risk in trying new officials, but in Glendale there are no conditions implying that the risk is great and always there is the possibility that a public officer from whom not much is expected will give the best service, while the reverse is equally true. The NEWS has no advice to give the people as to whom they should support, and will be perfectly satisfied with the result. We take this stand not through any fear of giving offense, but because we candidly can conceive of no good reason why any one of the men in nomination should not make a good officer. We do, however, advise every voter to exercise his prerogative as a citizen and to turn out on Monday to cast a vote.

"Political Announcements," *South Pasadena Record*, March 17, 1910

Citizens Party Platform

"The Citizens' Party of South Pasadena announces the following as its declaration of principles:

"We favor a progressive policy in the administration of city affairs to the end that South Pasadena may be kept abreast of the foremost cities in Southern California in the matter of public improvements.

"We pledge ourselves to the support of any efforts on the part of the Board of Trustees which shall have for their object the obtaining of better streets, an increased water supply, increased fire protection, an extension and improvement of the lighting system, and sewer facilities.

"We commend the movement to secure a bridge across the Arroyo Seco, and urge upon the members of the Board of Trustees that they do all in their power to further this important and greatly needed public improvement.

"We indorse the actions of previous city administrations in prohibiting the operation of pool rooms in South Pasadena, and strongly urge upon the incoming Trustees the necessity for continuing this policy in force without the slightest deviation or compromise.

"We favor such measures against the liquor traffic as will afford ample protection to the homes of South Pasadena against an invasion of this evil, and which will encourage the better class of people to come here and make their homes in this city."

Independent Party Platform

"We, the Independent party of the city of South Pasadena, being opposed to ring rule in our city, and who did not participate in the secret meeting held Wednesday evening, March 3, 1910, that organized the Citizens' party, and nominated candidates for the Board of Trustees, do adopt the following as our platform:

"1. We are firm believers of law and order, good government, purity in politics, and an economical administration of the city's affairs.

"2. We are heartily in favor of the proposition to construct the Arroyo bridge at the westerly boundary of the city at once.

"3. We endorse the following improvements, as fast as the same can be acquired consistent with an economical administration: (a) Better fire protection. (b) A sewer system. (c) A City Hall and park. (d) The paving of a thoroughfare from the proposed bridge at the westerly boundary of the city, easterly through the city, a portion of the expense to be paid by the city at large.

"4. We pledge our candidates to office to carry out the pledges of this platform as speedily as is consistent with an economical administration of the city's affairs."

5-5. POLITICAL ACRIMONY: THE CASE OF SOUTH GATE, A SUBURB OF LOS ANGELES, 1925

"Letter to the Editor," *South Gate Tribune*, July 3, 1925

The following open letter to the mayor and trustees of the city of South Gate was received this week by the South Gate Tribune from L.C. Baier of 8174 San Antonio avenue. [Ed. note: Baier's occupation as listed in the city directory was carpenter]

Mr. Baier's letter follows:

"The citizens of South Gate appreciate your efforts in endeavoring to make this a desirable community in which to live and own our homes. But there is a limit to all things.

"Before adding more financial burdens upon us such as the proposed street lighting improvements, wouldn't it be well to stop and consider these various improvement questions from several angles?

"Of course all progressive citizens are in favor of value-increasing improvements, but, however much these may be desired, for a great many it would mean deprivations and hardships over a long period.

"I think I am safe in stating that the majority of South Gate home-owners are in the wage-earning class and are buying their homes on the monthly payment plan.

"With the every-increasing taxes and the business depression and lack of employment during the past year, the average wage-earner has about all he can pay for now.

"The water and the city hall bonds are necessities for the good of the city, but wouldn't it be possible for South Gate citizens to perambulate our side streets of evenings with the present lighting, for a short time to come?

"Of course we want the world to know of South Gate and South Gate IS becoming TOO well-known in some respects.

"In many instances people were ready to buy or trade for South Gate property, when, upon learning of its being an incorporated city and of the many planned improvements, the deals were called off and the invariable statement was made: 'South Gate is only an infant in municipal affairs, It is trying to do too much and too rapidly in the way of improvements.'

"It is financially burdening its property owners too fast. 'No, we don't want to buy in South Gate.'

"Nice drawing card that.

"No disrespect is intended, but may it be suggested that if the weeds and grass were removed from the street and the parkway along Liberty blvd., and the other streets it would improve the appearance of our city just about as much as the proposed new lights.

"Have mercy upon the laboring man and woman who is struggling to make and pay for a home within your borders.

L. C. BAIER,
8174 San Antonio Ave."

"Trustees Pass Light Bill," *South Gate Tribune*, July 17, 1925

At the most largely attended and stormiest session of the city council ever held in the city of South Gate, members of the board on Thursday evening of last week unanimously voted to overrule the protests and to proceed with the work of installing a complete ornamental lighting system throughout the city of South Gate.

The session was an adjourned regular meeting from the preceding Tuesday night, when the regular meeting was held, which, too, was quite turbulent, due to discussions on the lights....

The largest crowd that ever congregated in the city hall was present at the meeting.

Interest, of course, centered around the lights, and it was this question which drew out such a large gathering.

There were several hundred objectors present, but, unlike the meeting which was held on Tuesday night, there were also a large number of persons present who favored the lights....

Several hot fights featured the meeting, and one man narrowly missed being thrown out by an officer when he openly insulted Mayor A.J. Schoby by addressing him in very uncomplimentary terms, calling him a "pussyfoot" and other names, which were resented not only by Mayor Schoby but by other members of the board and by a large number of persons in the audience as well....

[T]here are undoubtedly a large number who are against lights because they have been misinformed and have been led to believe things which are absolutely untrue.

Representatives of this losing concern are said to have been instrumental in circulating petitions against the lights throughout the city and to have made erroneous statements concerning the cost and quality of the Union Metal standards.

They have been present at every civic meeting and at every session of the city council, and have spent hours knocking their competitions and their product. They have engaged in mudslinging speech-making and have hurled dirty tirades at...our city officials.

They have been ungentlemanly, abusive and underhanded at every stage of the proceedings....

[T]his is a direct insult to the people of South Gate and should not be tolerated under any consideration. It is an insult to the people, because Mayor Schoby and all of the board of trustees are direct representatives of the people, elected by them to transact their business.

Mayor Schoby is a splendid man, and all of the citizens of South Gate are proud of him. His character is absolutely above reproach, and the people of this city resent any attacks upon him, especially when such attacks are launched by outsiders who are here at the behest of "foreign" interests for the express purposes of making trouble among our people....

At the council meeting last Thursday night, it was unanimously voted to overrule the protests and to proceed with the work on the city's new lighting system, using Union Metal standards.

That does not necessarily mean that everything will be smooth sailing from now on, however. The people of South Gate should be on their guard and be prepared for further attacks from the rear, because that is the enemy's favorite method of warfare.

5-6. THE MUNICIPALITIES OF LOS ANGELES COUNTY, 1940

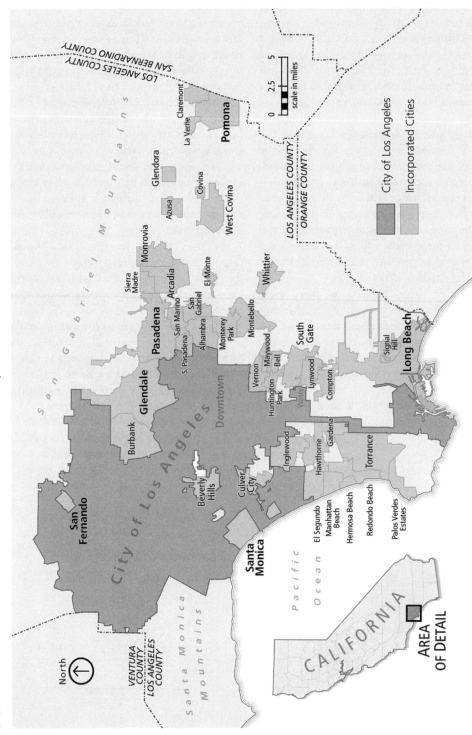

Figure 5-1 Los Angeles County Municipalities, 1940. Suburban incorporation caused small, independent communities to proliferate, contributing to the political balkanization of metropolitan areas. Map by David Deis.

ESSAYS

Historians exploring the origins of suburban politics have emphasized its hybrid nature—a melding of city and village approaches. They note too that suburban political structures have had certain negative consequences for broader metropolitan life. In **Essay 5-1**, historian Ann Durkin Keating uses a case study of nineteenth-century Chicago to explore the early roots of suburban politics. Her account highlights the experimental nature of the process, as new suburbs groped to find the most suitable form of governance. Some stayed within city limits and tried to use city politics to their advantage, others sought to adapt rural-oriented county government to their needs, while others started from scratch by forming their own municipalities. In some cases, the initiative came from real estate developers, in others from suburban residents. Suburbs followed multiple paths, but through it all, Keating emphasizes, services and taxation were the twin issues driving early suburban political formation and ultimately carving the earliest divisions among suburbs. Her work helps explain the origins of political balkanization in metropolitan areas.

In **Essay 5-2**, historian Jon Teaford picks up the story in the twentieth century to provide an overview of both the political culture and political structure of suburbia to 1940. His work is based on an analysis of six "postsuburban" counties—Suffolk and Nassau Counties in New York; Oakland County, Michigan; DuPage County, Illinois; Saint Louis County, Missouri; and Orange County, California—counties that developed as suburban but eventually grew into important centers in their own right, occasionally eclipsing the nearby central city. In this essay, Teaford describes the political roots of these areas, tracing the emergence of a suburban political culture that valued both political and social homogeneity and was particularly responsive to white middle- and upper-class residents. When political fragmentation resulted, reformers sought remedies like political consolidation at the county level, but they found themselves limited by an entrenched suburban proclivity for local control.

ESSAY 5-1. ANN DURKIN KEATING, *BUILDING CHICAGO: SUBURBAN DEVELOPERS AND THE CREATION OF A DIVIDED METROPOLIS* (1988)

Local Government Responds to Suburbanization

Until the mid-nineteenth century, there was no such thing as "suburban government": there were only urban or rural governments. Suburban government evolved from these older forms as a hybrid....

Incorporated governments became the exclusive domain of urban, and then suburban, governments in Illinois. The first incorporation in Cook County was Chicago's, in 1833. In contrast to counties and townships [which were established directly by the state], local communities petitioned the state legislature for charters for incorporated government. These incorporated governments, then, were initiated within the community, not imposed by the state legislature. If the state legislature granted the petition, and this generally appears to have been the case, the community became an incorporated town, village, or city. The area remained under the jurisdiction of counties and townships for some purposes, while new functions and representation were afforded by the incorporated government. Among the functions possible only with incorporation were: increased taxing powers, higher debt limits, and the ability to provide many urban infrastructure improvements....

One further form of incorporated government found in nineteenth-century Cook County was the incorporated township, which took the imposed rural township designation and grafted incorporated government upon it. Unlike an incorporated village or city, which could consist of only a piece of one or several townships, the incorporated township encompassed the whole of the designated rural township. Once a township was incorporated, no sub-area of it could incorporate separately as a village or city.

Suburban government emerged from this set of imposed/community-generated and incorporated/unincorporated governments. This chapter will build on these available forms to show how residents of outlying Cook County took the options available to them and created the first suburban governments in Illinois. To do this, the story must return to outlying settlers and their demands.

Suburban Growth

The discreteness of urban and rural settlement in Cook County eroded following the Civil War. Commuter railroad stations, streetcar lines, parks and boulevards, institutions, and industries drew settlement outward from the city in an irregular fashion, resulting for a time in geographically isolated suburban communities surrounded by farmland and empty tracts. The development of suburban areas in Cook County was the result of both a transition of older settlements, made for resort or agricultural purposes, and new subdivisions aimed specifically at prospective suburban dwellers....

Outlying residents looked for urban services such as water, sewers, gas, and electricity. Former residence in the serviced city shaped these expectations.

Local governments did not initially make improvements in these outlying districts, for they were far beyond the scope designated to traditional rural governments. Instead, real-estate developers, who understood that "at the root of all urban growth is the land development process—the conversion of rural or vacant land to some sort of urban use," initiated improvements. Speculators provided these services to outlying areas as a means of drawing purchasers to their properties....

These developers acted as brokers for the varied demands of residents concerning residential growth in much the same way as urban government did. In contrast to local government, however, the developers were directors rather than reactors in the city building process. Of course, developers did not operate in a governmentless vacuum. Nor did they make all of their improvements independently of government. On the contrary, many successfully manipulated the functions and power of local government to their own advantage. Within the city, this could mean making political donations to key aldermen who made locational decisions for services or simply working through regular channels of government.

For instance, some real-estate developers in Chicago worked quite closely with the Department of Public Works when arranging improvements for their outlying tracts. Ogden, Sheldon, & Co., which had substantial holdings on the west and north sides of the city, developed its property near Wicker Park on the northwest side in the mid-1870s. This area was inside the city's boundaries but was only lightly settled and lacked urban services. The firm paid to extend the city water system to the tract rather than create an independent water supply. The cost to the company was nearly seven thousand dollars, but the city agreed to refund that "as soon as the extension would pay 15% interest on the investment." This was the point at which the city normally would extend water mains. The move was so successful that within the year the firm had its money refunded and the city was working directly with other property owners in the area about extending water service even farther.

Outlying Government and Service Demands

Outside of the city boundaries, the story was a bit different. Although Chicago was first incorporated in 1833, it was decades before other areas in Cook County followed suit. The rural population outside Chicago made few demands on local government, in contrast to city residents. Before the Civil War, only Chicago's chartered government had the power to provide municipal services and collect taxes or special assessments for them. It was the only settlement where local government was actively involved in the provision of water and sewerage. Settlements outside of the city either did without these services or provided them privately. The county served as the only government for these outlying areas, collecting taxes, supervising elections, operating courts and schools, and maintaining roads and bridges. After 1850, the twenty-seven townships took over many of the county's functions by serving a growing rural population.

Although these new townships improved representation for outlying communities, their basic functions remained rural. In contrast, their populations became more and more urban-oriented as the century came to a close. Both the number of people living in outlying areas and the population densities on the city's outskirts increased dramatically in the closing decades of the nineteenth century. The location of this outward expansion of population was influenced by a variety of factors, foremost among them innovations in transportation. These changes affected the settlement of the county by making time rather than distance to the city center a decisive factor. The introduction of new railroad lines, the continued expansion of horsecar and cable car routes, and, after 1890, electric streetcar routes, as well as the creation of the area's first elevated railroads in the late 1890s, dramatically changed the relation of many outlying areas to the city center, bringing them into much closer orbit.

Of course, this outward expansion did not simply encompass undeveloped tracts of prairie awaiting the growth of Chicago. Subdivisions like Ravenswood, Austin, and Hyde Park Center had originally been developed under older transportation and economic constraints and were forced to adapt to changing conditions. Although a relatively new population center, Cook County by the 1880s was engaged, not only in a settlement process along its fringes, but a filling-in process, as new technologies and conditions made different lands attractive for settlement and development. A straightforward method of dealing with increasing densities was simply to increase the number of townships in heavily settled areas. Six new townships emerged by 1880. They provided better representation and a smaller area to negotiate but did not expand on the rural functions designated township government by the state....

Neither the county nor the townships had the power to provide the sorts of services available through the incorporated urban government at Chicago. Because of this, many developers, especially the early ones, made whatever improvements they considered useful for the marketability of the land without the help of local government. Some developers provided more substantial service improvements, including water and sewer connections. A few continued to provide these services without the aid of local government. A local improvement association, organized by Joseph Sears, made major improvements in Kenilworth without any initial help from local government. At Pullman:

> The car company assumed many of the functions usually held by a city corporation. It furnished the residences with water, gas and electric light....

Most developers, however, did not have the resources available to Pullman and Sears to provide a full range of services outside of government. They turned to local government for aid in providing services that would make their subdivisions attractive as suburban settlements. The immediate problem with petitioning local governments outside of the city for these services, however, was that they did not possess the powers to provide them either. And even if the townships could have supplied the services, their many rural residents were opposed to tax increases to offer better services to suburban communities within their midst.

Incorporated Villages

One answer to this quandary was to adapt urban government to suburban needs—that is, to create incorporated villages in outlying areas which would have much the same powers as incorporated urban government, but on a much smaller scale. This was a new concept in incorporated government, which up until the mid-nineteenth century remained primarily the province of cities. By the mid-nineteenth century, state legislatures across the country, especially those strongly influenced by precedents in New York, granted village charters to virtually any community that requested them, encouraging this new application of what had once been a rarely granted privilege. Tremendous geographic and population expansion left western legislatures with little time to consider each case carefully. At first, boosters in western towns used incorporations to further their civic pretensions. Would-be metropolises, not suburbs, first took advantage of legislatures' loosened grip on charters. Suburbs followed their lead.

The first six outlying settlements in Cook County that incorporated did so between 1865 and 1870: Evanston, Barrington, Palatine, DesPlaines, Glencoe, and Winnetka....Each, located miles from downtown but adjacent to a railroad depot, accommodated hundreds of new residents in the years around the Civil War. Residents sought incorporation as a means of responding to this growth. When settlement remained largely rural, as in Barrington, Palatine, and DesPlaines, incorporation helped residents to improve roads and regulate animals and nascent agricultural industry. In contrast, the settlers of Evanston, Glencoe, and Winnetka used their new powers to initiate improvements like those being made in Chicago....

In addition, sixteen new communities incorporated as villages between 1870 and 1880. New suburbs, founded after the Civil War, were numerous among this group of newly incorporated communities....Among the group of suburbs incorporated were several that owed their origins to development companies and real-estate speculators. Washington Heights, South Evanston, Rogers Park, Wilmette, Riverside, and Norwood Park were all part of this group.

The incorporated village form became even more popular as the decades progressed. Eleven new communities were founded and incorporated in Cook County between 1881 and 1900....Over half—Chicago Heights, Grossdale, Harvey, Kenilworth, Riverview, and Edison Park—were founded by a developer planning on commuter or industrial settlement. Three of these—Grossdale, Harvey, and Kenilworth—had improvements made before or soon after being founded. The incorporation of many of these communities came in response to the demands of property owners for urban services such as water, street improvement, gas lights, and sewers. Residents expressed these demands through public meetings, newspaper articles, and other more informal channels. Considerable discussion concerning incorporation generally accompanied these proposals, and residents held numerous meetings to debate the move.

The powers granted to local areas under both the special incorporations and the general incorporations after 1870 were similar. They included: actions protecting the health of the communities, police and fire protection, the establishment of hospitals, the construction and maintenance of streets, sidewalks, sewers, bridges, streetlights, and parks. Perhaps most important, the incorporated city or village had the power to make special assessments to pay for these improvements. This was a power never granted in Illinois to the rural-based county or township, so that "if part of a township or county wanted a special service, and this part was not within the jurisdiction of a governmental form that had the power of special assessment, the service could not be provided."

Turlington Harvey and Samuel Gross were among the most successful real-estate men to foster the incorporation of an outlying subdivision to aid them in its development. They saw incorporation as a means of legitimizing claims about their subdivisions, in a way not unlike the boosters of Chicago who had backed its original incorporation. As in Chicago, public works and improvements ultimately convinced investors and future residents that potential growth was legitimate....

Developers, like Gross and Harvey, who worked early with incorporated government received help in financing improvements for their subdivisions, but their interests were quickly subsumed by resident demands.

Of course, outlying areas did not incorporate simply at the instigation of developers. For instance, in communities where the original developers provided few services, later residents organized local government to do so. Rogers Park is an example of a settlement that incorporated after much of its land had been sold by the Rogers Park Land Company. The Land Company, organized in 1872, opened and graded streets, sold lots, and "induced the purchasers to build on them." The company did not attempt major improvements, nor did it actively seek incorporation....By 1874, at least fifty homes had been constructed costing between twelve hundred and eighteen thousand dollars. This was clearly not a settlement with a homogeneity of homes. The fact that the Land Company initially made few improvements left open the possibility for settlement by a wide range of economic classes. Still, within a matter of years, these residents were able to reach agreement on the need for further improvements....In 1878, they decided to incorporate as a village "in order to improve the streets, take care of storm water, install sanitary sewerage, and consider means of getting a supply of water for household use."

In this case, the dearth of improvements made by the original improvement company caused residents to band together early in their history to form a village government that could administer the public works projects. As one later source explained, "the people felt that they must organize to secure these improvements." Incorporation was one clear way of making improvements demanded by commuters but not originally provided by development companies....

By 1880, the incorporated village was an established fixture in the Cook County governmental landscape. Born of the demands of outlying residents and real-estate developers for government provision of services previously only available in urban areas, the incorporated village serviced a growing suburban population. It was used by developers intent on servicing their outlying subdivisions, by residents who demanded services not originally provided by developers, and by residents intent not so much on obtaining services as exerting local prerogatives on issues like temperance.

Suburban subdivisions were clearly set apart from adjoining rural areas and served as centers for many newly incorporated villages. The subdivisions and improvements made by original development companies determined the nucleus of the community and the base from which future work would be done. The early work of developers fostered homogeneity. Of course, it was not a strict

homogeneity such as that found since World War II in suburbs like Levittown. It was just that roughly equal land prices and improvements attracted similar residents. This homogeneity was crucial to the governments that emerged after incorporation....

These governmental forms were closely tied, of course, to the growth of outlying suburban settlement. Underlying that suburban growth were changing demands for urban services, transportation advantages, and the work of real-estate developers. These factors radically changed the rules regarding government in areas outside core urban settlements. For the first time, outlying residents were demanding services and improvements previously only found in cities. Because of these new demands of suburban residents, older urban and rural forms changed. Truly suburban forms did not emerge overnight. They evolved slowly from older ones until the best match was achieved....

The Suburb Arrived

The emergence of the improved subdivision on the outskirts of cities like Chicago over the second half of the nineteenth century signaled the arrival of the modern suburb. Because these improvements were new to most nineteenth-century residents, only slowly did a consensus concerning what constituted a core of basic services in outlying areas emerge. Improvements provided a means of sorting urbanites as they moved outward from city centers. A variety of improvement packages provided a crude method of class segregation that would be refined, but not substantially altered, in the twentieth century.

Suburban government in Cook County evolved in both form and function in response to these increasingly homogeneous subdivisions. Real-estate interests, along with outlying residents, fostered suburban government as a means of satisfying service demands. At the same time, the ability of local government to respond to changing settlement patterns fostered further suburban growth, for suburban government provided a stability that institutionalized developers' patterns.

The entrenchment of suburban governments was perhaps most strongly exhibited in the increasing failure of annexation attempts. Annexation decelerated in Chicago, as contiguous residential growth hit the ring of incorporated villages and cities beyond the annexed incorporated townships after 1890, and came to a halt by 1930....

Critical Social Scientists

The arrival of suburbs and their governments by the turn of the century did not go unnoticed by social scientists. They, too, provide a record of the institutionalization of forms. One of the first to describe the modern suburb was Adna Ferrin Weber, in his 1899 study of city growth. According to Weber, a suburb combined "at once the open air and spaciousness of the country with the sanitary improvements, comforts and associated life of the city." Weber's suburb was an area with a lower population density than the city, and was distinguished from the surrounding countryside by the existence of city improvements, comforts, and society.

Suburbs were seen by many early social scientists and reformers as a means to humanizing the city. Ebenezer Howard's garden city idea was essentially a plan for moving individuals, as well as industry, out from the city center in order to provide a more healthful environment. Like Weber, Howard called for further suburbanization (deconcentration), in order that more metropolitan residents could take advantage of the benefits of suburban living.

In contrast to this positive reaction of suburbs themselves, few heralded the arrival of suburban government as a stunning achievement for modern American society. Instead, critics such as Roderick D. McKenzie viewed it as "little short of disastrous," because "every great city now has around it a metropolitan area, one with it economically and socially, but without political unity." Critics blamed political fragmentation both for the inadequate provision of basic services to protect the health and safety across entire metropolitan regions, and for widely varying tax rates. Contemporary and historical commentators argued against the exclusivity of suburban government and wanted services

and their costs distributed equally across a metropolitan area.

Underlying all of these criticisms was an indictment of the segregation institutionalized by suburban government. This situation placed a considerable strain on the competing tensions between local control and equal opportunity. These tensions had grown considerably since the founding of the United States. The local community in preindustrial society necessarily contained a wide range of people and economic functions. The separation of work and home made possible through new industrial techniques and transportation advances fostered the separation of residential from industrial and commercial areas, as well as the creation of class-segregated neighborhoods. It was suddenly feasible for local governments to serve these class-segregated residential areas exclusively, thereby linking segregation by class, race, and ethnicity to questions of local control.

Suburban government to many of its critics was (and is) local control run amok. Suburbanites exploited the concept of local autonomy, gaining charters from state governments. Local control of this sort is argued to hinder equal opportunity. It remains a pressing conflict even today. Perhaps no issue illustrates the strength of the tensions as much as the school desegregation plans enacted since the 1954 Brown decisions underscoring the importance of class and race to the discussion. At the root of the debate lies the fact that, for better or worse, metropolitan residents find their housing (and choose it) segregated on the basis of class, race, and ethnicity. Because of this segregation, differential access to services can be argued as a legitimate product of local prerogative, or as a hindrance to equal access to services and programs within a metropolitan area.

Getting away from this indictment of suburban government in order to understand it is a difficult task. But suburban governments, as I have shown in this study, are not in themselves the problem. To say they are would be somewhat on the order of blaming the messenger for the bad news. Local government, more than any other facet of our public life, closely reflects forms of settlement and community demands. Suburban governments emerged in response to suburban settlement, which in turn was based quite clearly on the emergence of the homogeneous residential subdivision as the preferred form of real-estate development.

The problem is, then, *not* simply suburban governance, but the segregated settlement patterns fostered by nineteenth-century real-estate developers, and ultimately preferred by their customers. If suburban areas were microcosms of a city's heterogeneity, there would be little problem with suburban governments (at least in principle), especially regarding the issue of equal opportunity. Instead, the emergence of suburban governance is closely tied to the development of the homogeneous residential subdivision, which was based on differences from, not similarities to, other areas across a metropolitan area. A real-estate developer sought ways of making his subdivision especially marketable to a homogeneous group of purchasers, who made similar demands for improvements and amenities and had the means to provide them. This homogeneity of settlement did not disappear when the original developer faded from the scene. Rather, it became the basis for the future....

In this context, the real criticism of suburban government becomes the fact that it was responsive to newly emerging, homogeneous subdivisions, allowing the institutionalization of segregation. Suburban governments did not *create* segregation, they responded to and then fostered it.

ESSAY 5-2. JON C. TEAFORD, *POST-SUBURBIA: GOVERNMENT AND POLITICS IN THE EDGE CITIES* (1997)

Source: Jon Teaford, *Post-Suburbia*. Copyright © 1997 The Johns Hopkins University Press. Reprinted with permission of The Johns Hopkins University Press.

The Age of the Suburban Haven

"Nestled among the estates of rolling hills, beautiful trees and natural beauty unmarred by city invasion, there is afforded every home owner the restful and healthful license of a country atmosphere." With these words from a 1928 advertisement, one Oakland County [Michigan] developer expressed the suburban dream of the 1920s and 1930s. Suburbia was a haven, a retreat, where one could escape the evils and annoyances of the city and find rest and health nestled among the beauties of nature and the estates of the wealthy. A Saint Louis County [Missouri] promoter promised prospective homeowners they would "awake with the song of birds, and feel the warmth of a clear sun shining through pure air."...A Nassau County [New York] developer emphasized not clear air but socially desirable neighbors. "The people that you want for neighbors are here," promised the backer of Great Neck Gardens. These ideal neighbors were people who could "appreciate" and "afford to enjoy" the beauty of the supposedly ideal suburban subdivision.

In one advertisement after another the message was the same. Suburbia was a residential environment where nature and the best people mingled to the benefit of anyone fortunate enough to purchase a homesite. It was advertised as an upscale reincarnation of the village of the past with its spreading elms, good neighbors, and socially homogeneous community life....The suburbs of the 1920s and 1930s were not intended to be extensions of the city, identical to urban neighborhoods except farther from the center. What developers were selling, and urban refugees were buying, was an alternative vision of life that specifically rejected the city and embraced the village.

Yet amid the sylvan prose were reminders that America's suburban havens were not actually quaint country villages. They were integral parts of expanding metropolises and they would not attract any residents unless they offered urban conveniences and transportation links to the urban core....

During the 1920s and 1930s emerging governmental institutions reflected this mix of the practical and the ideal. Through their municipal and county governments, suburbanites sought to realize the ideal of the suburban village yet enjoy the best public services possible. Thus they created scores of new municipalities armed with zoning powers to protect and preserve the social homogeneity and low density of their villages. The village governments were guardians of the suburban ideal embodied in the real estate advertisements. They were small-scale governments aimed at keeping the big city and its way of life at bay. The neocolonial village halls built in one community after another announced to visitors and residents alike that these suburban municipalities intended to protect the values of a supposedly simpler and purer past. City halls in the great metropolitan centers were stone-sheathed and monumental with massive facades proclaiming the material success and magnitude of the metropolis. The village halls were designed to be quaint and charming, advertising to all the ideals of suburbia.

Yet at the same time suburbanites were increasingly recognizing the need for a broader overarching authority to supplement the village. To handle the problems of the increasingly populous periphery, suburbanites began to adapt traditional units, especially county governments, to the new reality....

The Suburban Polity

During the first two decades of the twentieth century, Suffolk, Nassau [NY], Oakland [MI], DuPage [IL], Saint Louis [MO], and Orange [CA] Counties remained largely rural. Yet these fringe areas were already experiencing the first wave of contact with urban dwellers as both the very wealthy and vacationers of more modest means sought a summer retreat in the country. In the late nineteenth century the beaches and breathing space of Nassau and Suffolk Counties lured thousands of New York City residents, and the army of summer visitors increased in the early twentieth century. America's most wealthy citizens fashioned opulent estates from the meadows and woodlands of Long Island, and by 1920 more than six hundred of these manorial domains sprawled along the north shore of the island....

During the 1920s, however, full-scale suburbanization transformed these fringe areas. Members of the middle class joined the wealthy along the metropolitan outskirts, and three-bedroom homes on quarter-acre lots encroached on hunt clubs and polo fields....The rate of population growth slowed during the depression-ridden 1930s as fewer Americans could afford to purchase suburban homes. But the rate of increase still considerably outpaced that of the nation as a whole and of the nation's central cities....

The influx of newcomers...changed the social complexion of the suburbanizing counties. An increasing number of middle- and upper-middle class commuters invaded the domain of plutocratic estate owners along the metropolitan fringe. This was most evident along the south shore of Long Island in Nassau and Suffolk Counties. As early as 1928 the *New York Times* wrote of the "large country estates" in this area as "pretty well decimated." One manor after another was sold to developers and subdivided into lots....

Suburbanization was the wave of the future...and all of the outlying counties, except for Orange, were already acquiring a suburban identity. Moreover, the suburban ideal of home and garden nestled in a quiet village was becoming a more significant factor in the life and politics of the fringe areas....

To better realize this vision, the migrants to the periphery opted for a suburban form of government. They did not dream of creating big-city government with impersonal bureaucracies or irresponsible partisan political machines such as they had known in New York, Chicago, or Saint Louis. Instead, they founded scores of small municipalities that were the governmental antithesis of the nation's urban giants. They sought to fashion an idealized village form of government, a small-scale, nonpartisan polity characterized by volunteerism, cooperation, and consensus. Essential elements of the suburban ideal were neighborliness and homogeneity. The village governments of suburbia were expected to nurture these traits. Disinterested civic service to one's neighbors was the goal of the ideal village official in the new suburban world of the 1920s and 1930s.

As the suburban population soared, the number of small, supposedly neighborly municipalities likewise rose....[T]he number of municipalities increased especially sharply in rapidly suburbanizing Nassau County, but in the other counties as well new village governments were forming to realize the governmental goals of suburbanites. By 1940 Nassau County could boast sixty-five municipalities, the number having more than tripled in the previous two decades....[T]he trend was toward governmental fragmentation, and any new wave of massive migration seemed to promise the creation of scores of additional governmental units.

Though some of the new municipalities were created to provide necessary public services, a more common motive for incorporation was to protect and preserve the small-scale, homogeneous community life style of the villages. Suburbanites did not opt for incorporation as a means of fashioning the public infrastructure for a future great city. They chose municipal status to protect the existing suburban environment and to ensure a way of life different from that of a city. Municipal incorporation was, then, a wall designed to preserve and protect and not an avenue to facilitate change and urbanization.

This was evident in the scores of municipalities that sprouted up in Nassau County. Many of those in the northern half of the county were estate communities that incorporated so that the local lords of the manor would have the legal authority to keep out unwanted persons or influences that might disrupt their aristocratic seclusion....

Nearby upper-middle-class communities as well turned to incorporation to protect themselves from taxes and incompatible land uses. Fearful of unregulated development that could lower property values, residents of Munsey Park were just as eager to adopt zoning ordinances to protect their half-acre plots as the estate owners of Lake Success or Centre Island were to preserve their one-hundred-acre manors....

In the suburbanizing areas of Oakland, DuPage, and Saint Louis Counties incorporation also was, in many instances, a defensive measure to preserve small-scale, homogeneous communities compatible with the village ideal. In 1926 Oakland County's Huntington Woods incorporated in part to avoid annexation to, and taxation by, the adjacent municipalities of Royal Oak and Ferndale. Planned as a community of single-family residences, Huntington Woods soon employed its municipal powers to keep out commercial development and multiple-family structures. The enforcement of single-family zoning, in fact, was to become the predominant theme in the history of the community. In 1924 DuPage County's Clarendon Hills, likewise, opted to preserve its separate identity and ward off annexation to Hinsdale by incorporating as a village....

Not all of the suburban municipalities remained tightly knit villages running only a few blocks in each direction. By 1940 nine of Nassau County's municipalities had more than 10,000 inhabitants, yet even in these communities residents attempted to preserve the village image....The term *city* had a negative connotation in suburbia, where the village was the ideal. Hempstead and Freeport were larger than 40 percent of the cities in New York, but they continued to accept village status and embrace the image of intimacy and homogeneity it implied.

The proliferating villages of suburbia not only rejected the legal structure of the city but eschewed the political practices associated with the nation's largest municipalities. Almost invariably, village elections in suburbia did not involve national political parties, with neither the Republicans nor the Democrats offering a slate of candidates. Such party politics smacked of the city with its legendary political machines and bosses. Suburbanites were dedicated to sparing their ideal villages this corrupting influence. Moreover, party leaders generally agreed to stay out of village politics....Local parties did exist, but they usually presented themselves as good-government organizations dedicated to finding the best person for public office regardless of his or her national party affiliation. They adopted party labels that advertised their high-minded devotion to the village's welfare. Thus in one community after another, such groups as the "Citizens Party," the "Village Party," the "Independent Party," and the "Taxpayers Party" vied for office....

In scores of suburban villages...competition was rare or nonexistent. Year after year candidates ran unopposed and no one seemed concerned that elections were mere formalities, deciding nothing. For example, in March 1927 thirty Nassau County villages elected officials but there were contests in only seven of them, and one year later thirteen of the thirty-four villages had contested elections. Likewise, in Saint Louis County single-slate elections were commonplace. Candidates in many of the smaller villages seemingly never faced opponents.... In suburban municipalities, the much-vaunted nonpartisan elections were, then, often no elections at all. If there were no vital issues facing the villagers and few ambitious individuals seeking what little glory or power village office conferred, then there was no contest.

In a nation that had long lauded two-party politics as a necessary ingredient to healthy democracy, the uncontested elections might have been seen as a perversion of the political process. But in suburbia the lack of competition was no disgrace and was often praised as a virtue. The suburban village was supposed to be a haven of consensus and neighborliness in contrast to the abrasive heterogeneity and cold-hearted exploitiveness of the big city. In the minds of some suburbanites, one-party rule by a coterie of high-minded citizens was actually one of the crowning achievements of their community....

Volunteerism was another foundation stone in the ideology of the suburban village. Participation in village government was not an occupation; it was a civic duty. The model suburban villager was, then, expected to volunteer his or her services to the community. Paid party ward heelers and professional politics were big-city phenomena. Government by volunteers was the goal of village idealists in Glen Ellyn and Garden City.

In many communities village officers were not even paid, for salaries were deemed to corrupt the political process....

Harnessing this volunteer spirit were the community or civic associations that played a significant role in the government of many suburban areas. These associations often were founded before the incorporation of their communities and were instrumental in the effort to achieve municipal status. Once incorporation was attained, the civic associations acted as watchdogs of the municipal governments, ensuring that mayors and councils adhered to the basic principles on which the community was founded. They prodded village officers to provide needed services and to protect property values and the suburban way of life....

Reality may have deviated from the ideal, and there were certainly many apathetic suburbanites who did not flock to civic association meetings and possibly did not know civic associations existed. Moreover, entrenched community leaders dominating community caucuses or associations might well have proved a greater hindrance to meaningful participation in the political process than any big-city boss or bureaucrat. In some communities one-party politics might have produced a suburban oligarchy rather than participatory democracy. And even when there was competition in village elections, the voter turnout was often low. Many suburbanites simply did not fit the concerned-citizen, dedicated-volunteer mold. But the suburban dream exercised a powerful influence on those who migrated to the metropolitan fringe. Suburban villages valued homogeneity, both political and social, and miniature government of the type unknown in New York City or Chicago. Even those who voted irregularly and did not know who was village mayor probably would have bridled at the thought of substituting a government similar to that of the big city. The suburban ideal sounded good even to those who did not live up to it.

Villages, however, were not the only pieces in the puzzle of suburban government. Suburbia was served as well by an increasing array of special districts, governmental units created to provide only a single service. Thus there were sewer districts dealing with the drainage of outlying areas, refuse districts to handle the garbage, mosquito abatement districts to eliminate pesky insects, and fire districts to battle blazes. Many reasons justified creating these districts. Often they were the only means for providing services to a populated but unincorporated area....In some cases drainage districts were desirable because the natural drainage pattern of an area did not conform to the existing political boundaries.

The facts of nature recommended that neighboring municipalities and unincorporated areas join in a single district. State-imposed debt and taxation limits on municipalities also encouraged creation of special districts. If a municipality was approaching such limits, citizens might have to resort to the creation of a special district to handle any additional costly governmental functions. For a number of reasons, then, special districts proved either convenient or necessary.

The result was a proliferation of such units. In heavily suburbanized Nassau County, the number of special districts almost doubled, from 87 in 1920 to 173 in 1933. By the latter date there were 53 lighting districts to provide street lighting, 52 fire districts, and 38 water districts to supply water to suburban homes and businesses. DuPage County was not quite as prolific in the creation of special districts, but a state report from 1934 discovered 120 separate taxing units, including municipalities, high school and grade school districts, park districts, and sanitary districts. By the mid 1940s Saint Louis County had 42 special districts offering sewer, water, drainage, and fire protection services as well as an additional 89 school districts....

By the 1930s this abundance of governmental units was the subject of increasing criticism and complaint. According to a survey of Nassau County's government, "There are so many local jurisdictions that it was not possible to prepare a map of the county or even of one town[ship] showing local unit boundaries." This investigation found that within a single area of 120 acres, 24 governmental units exercised authority, "or one for every five acres of ground."...Having escaped from the governmental giantism of the big city, suburbanites seem to have gone to the other extreme, opting for miniature polities with overlapping jurisdictions that confused many taxpayers and angered some.

Encompassing a broader expanse of territory than most special districts or municipalities were the townships. Suffolk, Nassau, Oakland, and DuPage Counties were divided into townships with governmental service functions, whereas in Saint Louis and Orange Counties townships were not governing units. In the Missouri county they were simply voting districts, comparable to city precincts, and in Orange they were merely judicial districts, each with a justice of the peace....Their exact duties differed according to state law, but the construction and maintenance of roads and the administration of relief for the needy were two of the most common and significant responsibilities.

Much criticized by experts in public administration and good-government reformers as unnecessary relics of the horse-and-buggy era, townships were on the defensive by the 1930s and seemed an endangered governmental species. Yet like the multitude of village governments, the townships touched a chord deep in the ideological heart of America. In the popular imagination they represented a simpler rural existence and Jeffersonian grass-roots rule. Though they were remnants of the rural past, they thus fit into the suburban ideal of small-scale neighborly government. Attempts to eliminate them could arouse the same fears of centralized, impersonal government that stirred the souls of suburban villagers. Despite repeated discourses on the obsolescence of the township, it was, then, not as vulnerable as some believed. It had a secure niche in the emerging suburban ideology, and as long as small and simple were deemed good, the township would survive.

Townships were significant not only as providers of services but also as units of representation for county government. The principal governing body of Nassau, Suffolk, Oakland and DuPage Counties was the board of supervisors, composed of the supervisors from each township. The supervisor was the township executive, responsible for administering that governmental unit, but he or she was, in addition, the township's spokesperson on the county board. In some counties cities enjoyed representation on the county board as well....

The counties that these supervisors governed were far different from the villages of the suburban ideal. Whereas the village was a haven from the world and its government was dedicated to preserving and protecting its special status, the county was part of the larger world, an arm of the state and a link between the locality and the state capital.

From the founding of the nation, the county had been deemed an agent of the state, created to impose the will of the state on localities. Its sheriff enforced the laws made in Albany and Springfield, its courts applied state legislative dictates, and its assessors and collectors were responsible for raising the state's revenues. Throughout American history it had been more of an administrative tool of the central government than a local policymaking body. Though it exercised some welfare functions and maintained some rural roads, the county traditionally had not engaged in the expansive provision of services characteristic of America's largest municipalities.

Moreover, the county was the principal unit of representation in state legislatures. Legislative districts generally conformed to county boundaries and each county usually had at least one representative in the state legislature. In the legislative proceedings, that representative was identified as the member from his or her county and he or she was regarded as the spokesperson for the county in the state capital. Thus the county was the instrument whereby the state imposed its will on the locality and whereby the locality expressed its concerns to the state....

Whereas village politics was nonpartisan, at the county level Republicans openly battled with Democrats. County officials ran on partisan tickets and party conflict was often sharp and bitter. The only exception was in Orange County, the nonpartisan tradition being particularly strong and pervasive in California. Elsewhere suburban villagers who abhorred partisan politics at the municipal level lined up loyally behind national party candidates in county elections....

Powerful political organizations with armies of loyal party workers underscored the deep partisanship at county levels. Suffolk's Republican organization was long regarded as having a secure stranglehold on the county, and in the mid-twentieth century DuPage County's Republican Party was a GOP counterpart to Chicago's powerful Democratic machine. On election day DuPage County leaders could produce reliable Republican majorities as effectively as Chicago's organization piled up votes in the Democratic column.

The most successful and durable political organization, however, was Nassau County's Republican Party. Before World War I the township of Hempstead had been loyally Republican, but in the townships of North Hempstead and Oyster Bay Democrats were able to win some victories. In 1915 G. Wilbur Doughty secured control of the Nassau Republican organization and put an end to any Democratic chances for electoral success. Until his death in 1930 Doughty efficiently produced the votes on election day and made Nassau a seemingly insuperable GOP stronghold. Following a struggle for power in the early 1930s, Doughty's nephew J. Russel Sprague secured unchallenged control of the organization and proved an even more effective leader than had his uncle....

Doughty and Sprague built their political empire, in part, by consciously placing the GOP in the role of great suburban defender. Nassau's Republicans constantly characterized themselves as the chief bulwark against the forays of New York City's notorious Tammany Democratic machine....Republicans were the party of the suburbs and the GOP would man the barricades to fight any attempt to make Nassau the sixth borough of New York City. In the end, though, the Sprague organization was as much a machine as the hated Tammany. Actually, Sprague had an even tighter grip on his domain than did the big-city bosses. As one observer noted, "Tammany is sometimes defeated in New York; Sprague is never beaten in Nassau."

Along the suburban fringe, there was, then, a dual political culture. At the village level partisanship along Republican and Democratic lines was unacceptable. The party boss was anathema and the political machine was deemed one of the horrors of the big city....Yet the county was an open battlefield for the two national parties. Sprague himself proved that suburbia could nurture powerful party organizations that could deliver the votes and wield clout in Albany and Washington.

During the coming decades this schizoid view of politics would continue to prevail, and any reform of the governments of suburbanizing counties would have to take it into account. The suburban ideal of the village haven would have to be respected; voters who had migrated to suburbia to invest and live in such havens would not permit structural reforms in government to destroy their dream. Already in the 1930s, academics, journalists, and political leaders were complaining about the multiplicity of governmental units, the overlapping jurisdictions, the lack of coordination in the delivery of services, and the general inefficiency and confusion of suburban government. Something had to be done. But whatever changes were made could not violate the political realities of the bifurcated suburban world.

Reforming Suburban Government

Responding to the proliferation of both people and governments in emerging suburbia, some policymakers during the 1920s and 1930s began to work for change. As populations doubled and more municipalities and special districts cluttered the map, many leaders believed the structure of government had to adapt. There had to be greater coordination and cooperation among government units and some overarching authority to deal efficiently and effectively with problems common to the entire suburban region. While recognizing the devotion to grass-roots rule in the small municipality, a number of reform-minded individuals suggested the creation or strengthening of broader units of government that could unite the governmentally fragmented fringe....

[T]he first signs of a new centralization of authority arose that could bring some unity to fragmented suburbia. For example, Du-Page County was assuming some new and unusual powers that seemed to promise a strengthened role for the county in suburban government. As early as 1917 the Forest Preserve District of DuPage County was organized to acquire and maintain a county park system. DuPage was only the second county in Illinois, and the fifth in the nation, to assume responsibility for the creation of a network of parks. Then in 1933 DuPage became the first county in Illinois to adopt a zoning resolution. Two years later DuPage was instrumental in securing a county zoning act from the state legislature. With this state authorization, the county was able to dictate land uses in unincorporated areas and influence the pattern of suburban development in northeastern Illinois....

Meanwhile, Californians were pioneering in the expansion of county powers. In 1921 Orange County initiated free library service to residents in unincorporated areas; three years later it began providing public health services throughout the county in both incorporated and unincorporated territory; in 1927 the board of supervisors took charge of the newly created Orange County Flood Control District; and in 1933 a county building department was organized to regulate building practices in unincorporated areas....Though municipalities within the counties retained their authority to provide these same services, the larger unit of the county was expanding its responsibilities and becoming a possible future competitor of the smaller units.

The most marked changes in county government and the pattern of suburban rule, however, took place in Nassau County. Labeled America's fastest growing county during the 1920s, rapidly suburbanizing Nassau seemed most in need of an overhaul in government. Throughout the 1920s and the first half of the 1930s, the county's leaders and residents struggled with the problem of adapting the governmental framework to the soaring population growth. In the end, they fashioned a new structure that balanced demands for centralization and the deep-seated desire for small-scale, grass-roots rule. Moreover, this new structure would be a model for other suburbanizing counties....

In January 1934, the Republican-controlled board of supervisors hired Professor Thomas Reed to survey Nassau County government....Reed found "the number of villages and districts...excessive" and urged efforts "to regulate the formation of new villages and districts and to reduce as far as possible the number...existing."...Yet in the end he accepted practical realities and recognized "the necessity for the continued existence" of the townships and villages. In fact, his list of recommendations for change were not radical but instead were familiar to Nassau political leaders. Like past charter committees, Reed favored a county executive and the transfer of all authority over welfare, health, and tax assessment to the county.

Having received the report, in late 1934 the board of supervisors then appointed another charter commission. As chairman of the county board as well as Republican party chieftain, Russel Sprague was the leading figure pushing the GOP into the camp of governmental reform....If there was going to be reform, Sprague was dedicated to making sure that it was reform advantageous to the Republicans.

In January 1936 the new charter commission presented its proposed charter to the public....As had often been suggested, the county would assume full charge of welfare, health, and assessment functions. This meant a shift of some authority from the municipalities and townships....In addition, the proposed charter would abolish township justices of the peace and create a new system of inferior county judges. And the charter authorized the formation of a county planning commission charged with adopting a master plan to guide the physical development of the county. Townships and municipalities retained planning authority, but the county could veto any changes in the zoning of property within three hundred feet of a municipal or township boundary. In other words, the county had authority to regulate boundary areas so that municipalities would not zone their fringes in a manner incompatible with the land use pattern of neighboring cities or villages. One municipality would not be able to locate factories adjacent to another municipality's expensive residences.

Equally significant were the omissions from the proposed charter. It did not include any mention of "village districts" or other novel local units that might be deemed a threat to existing municipalities....

The commission proposed, then, reform, but not radical reform. It did not assault the local bastions of the Republican party nor did it seriously bruise the suburban ideal of small-scale, grass-roots government. It reflected Russel Sprague's realistic assessment of the problem. According to Sprague, the charter was based on "the theory of the 'two layers' of government." "In the lower layers," Sprague explained, "there were to be retained or preserved to the several communities such as the special districts, villages, two cities and three towns, complete control and power over those functions of government which were closest to them, which they knew the most about and which they genuinely desired to have continued under the authority of their respective inhabitants." This ensured "the preservation of 'home rule' to the separate communities." County government was to constitute the upper layer. "This county governmental layer was to be brought up to date," according to Sprague. "It was to be made businesslike in full sense, designed to meet the needs and demands of a continuously fast-growing population." Whereas the charter preserved the lower layer, it reformed this upper layer so as "to give the greatest number of governmental improvements and services possible for each tax dollar."

Thus the villages and towns, which represented tradition and the antithesis of the big city, were perpetuated at the same time the county was transformed into a governmental dynamo suitable for an up-to-date, rapidly urbanizing area. The charter offered both old and new, small scale and big scale. Moreover, it built upon the traditional roles of the village and county. The villages could remain inward-turning, defensive, and quaint, with village greens reminiscent of the past and exclusionary zoning to guard against an unwanted future. The county, however, was given new strength to confront the harsh realities of growth and dense population....

New York's state legislature approved this carefully balanced document, and a local referendum on the proposal was held in November 1936....On election day Nassau's voters endorsed the Republican compromise by a substantial margin, with 57,000 in favor and 37,000 opposed....

Thus even though the government of Nassau appeared fragmented, authority was actually highly concentrated in the hands of the dominant party chieftain. During his long tenure as county executive, Sprague personally centralized the government of Nassau. He made a career of warning about the depredations of Democratic bosses in New York

City, but he wielded a power that any Tammany politico would have envied.

Sprague, in part, owed his strength to an acute understanding of the political facts of life in suburbia, upon which he fashioned his governmental framework. Suburbanites clung to the village ideal and would fend off any attacks on small, neighborly, homogeneous communities. Yet they wanted the best services at the cheapest prices, so they would compromise for the sake of economy and efficiency. With his two-layer theory, Sprague negotiated the acceptable compromise, and throughout his years in politics he was careful to adhere to the terms of this compromise....Sprague knew the dreams and fears of his suburban domain, and he fashioned a governmental system to satisfy his constituents and thereby perpetuate the power of his GOP organization.

Moreover, Sprague's creation was to serve as a model for American suburbia. His compromise between centralization and decentralization was to be repeated in fringe areas throughout the nation. Like Sprague, reformers in Oakland, DuPage and elsewhere would seek to balance the suburban village ideal against the need for strengthening the overarching authority of the county. This balance was the key to Sprague's successful formula, and it would remain the preeminent feature of government in suburban and post-suburban areas of the future.

NOTE

1. Kenneth T. Jackson, *Crabgrass Frontier: The Suburbanization of the United States* (New York: Oxford University Press, 1985), 153.

CHAPTER 6

Imagining Suburbia

Visions and Plans from the Turn of the Century

INTRODUCTION

Responding to unsettling changes wrought by the Industrial Revolution, North American and European cities gave rise to a host of efforts to reform urban life. These efforts ranged widely from utopian novels such as Edward Bellamy's *Looking Backward* (1888) and the dark futurism of H.G. Wells; to the rise of urban socialism; feminist designs for cooperative housing; the journalistic muckraking of Jacob Riis; and the outpouring of middle-class activism known as the Progressive Movement. The growing popularity of suburbs was another manifestation of this impulse. As the modern city grew in size, density, and diversity, many Americans pictured suburbia as its antithesis. This vision drew on an increasingly well-defined suburban ideal—a century in the making—that melded pastoral landscapes, efficient services, responsive government, and secluded family life. These qualities seemed more than ever to meet the needs of the day. Progressive reformers, too, endorsed decentralization as a solution to urban ills, and they proposed model suburbs that reflected their hopes for the future. By the turn of the twentieth century, the undeveloped spaces of suburbia had become a canvas for the imagination, luring Americans to dream, to plan, and to take steps to build a better society.

If suburban proponents agreed that decentralization was the answer to urban woes, they differed over the form these new suburbs should take. On the one hand, housing reformers, settlement workers, and city planners viewed the decentralization of population and jobs as an urgent step toward improving living conditions for the urban poor. They advocated the suburbanization of industry, model town planning, and the construction of affordable "workingmen's homes" in the suburbs. Their designs emphasized diversity—of people, housing, and land use. To keep housing affordable, they often sought to limit speculation and profit, which they blamed for the deplorable condition of urban slums. On the other hand, many affluent and middle-class Americans saw suburbs as private havens insulated from the urban masses. Like Progressivism's most ardent supporters, most were white, Protestant, and native born, and they shared many of the movement's social and political commitments. They, too, perceived suburbs as instruments of reform, but theirs was a more restricted vision: their suburbs would be model communities designed to enhance and promote their own way of life. Indeed they saw themselves as cultural and moral tastemakers, exemplars for all of society to follow. Their plans stressed exclusivity, uniformity, social separation, and the restriction of land use to private residence. By 1900, suburbanization had become firmly linked with the idea of social reform, but suburbs themselves would embody the conflicting hopes and ambitions that underlay the reformist impulse.

Despite their differences, the advocates of suburbanization shared important values that left a lasting imprint on the landscape of twentieth-century suburbs. Like many urban reformers of that era, most evinced a faith in environmental reform—the idea that by improving physical surroundings one could enhance social behavior. They invested suburban space with a revolutionary power to change society, to produce better families, mold better citizens, and heal the social, political, and economic ills of their day. They emphasized landscape, architecture, and other aesthetic details as a source of moral influence on everyday life. Collectively, they promoted consistent images of the ideal suburb, replete with curvilinear streets, picturesque views, parks and open space, lawns and gardens, and detached homes in the company of similar neighbors. These design precepts applied to suburbs for the lowliest worker and for the richest socialite. Through the relentless dissemination of this image in the popular media, by builders, product advertisers, and ultimately by government, they exerted a powerful influence on American expectations about suburbs for decades to come.

Many suburban proponents advocated city and regional planning to ensure the success of these physical reforms. Like other Progressives, they expressed confidence that professional and technical expertise could be consciously applied to improve society. They were also mindful that unrestrained real estate speculation had produced many unwanted consequences. Rather than leaving metropolitan growth to the happenstance of the market, they supported comprehensive community planning by private developers and local governments, reflecting the Progressive faith in activist government and empowered experts. Many suburban advocates proposed prescriptive plans of their own, translating their imagined ideals into actual designs.

Reading these plans almost a century later reveals volumes about this vision. Not only do they include a host of mundane physical specifications (like ideal lot sizes and setbacks), but many devote careful attention to the kind of social life that these designs were meant to promote. Here, then, is vivid evidence of the faith in environmental reform, imbued with an expansive optimism for a better society. But like many Progressive projects of this era, this one had its limits. As chapter 8 will explore in greater detail, many of these plans were exclusionary, shutting out "undesirable" people, and intended to keep the city at bay.

By the early twentieth century, a broad consensus existed in the United States in favor of urban decentralization. Although a few observers, including Lewis Mumford and other members of the Regional Planning Association, warned about the pitfalls of suburban sprawl, it was not until the 1950s that these suburban critiques reached a wide audience. By then, the die had been cast. Decentralization had become the common sense of the age, and its logic would dominate policy, planning, and popular thought for the remainder of the twentieth century. Whether suburbia would be the salvation for all or just some of the urban population, however, remained an open question.

DOCUMENTS

Among the most influential designs for suburban reform was the work of a British bureaucrat, Ebenezer Howard. Inspired by the idea that the human condition might be improved through rational planning, Howard devised a city plan that tackled the problems of late nineteenth-century urbanization. His solution was the "garden city." In **Document 6-1**, Howard outlines the problem and sets forth the guiding principles for a "marriage of town and country." Even though Howard's work called for a true mixture of urban and rural elements, suburban planners latched onto the aspects of Howard's approach that emphasized the city–country hybrid. His 1902 book *Garden Cities of To-morrow* inspired the construction of several faithful-to-the-text garden cities in England—for example, Letchworth (1903) and Welwyn (1920)—and it influenced generations of suburban planners in Europe and the United States. It is considered a classic text in the evolution of suburban thought and planning.

In **Document 6-2**, housing reformer Carol Aronovici underscores the Progressive faith in suburbanization as an antidote to urban ills. Following Howard and other garden city designers, he extols the virtues of suburbanization for workers and industry and advocates careful town planning to ensure that the woeful living conditions caused by urban industrialism were not reproduced in the suburbs. **Document 6-3** is an example of the type of suburban planning that Aronovici advanced. Firestone Heights was a planned subdivision for white industrial workers established by the Firestone Rubber Company at the edge of the booming city of Akron, Ohio in 1916. Its designer, Alling DeForest, had been a pupil of Frederick Law Olmsted and earned his living planning suburban gardens and estates for wealthy clients. This promotional publication also exposes the varied motives that underlay such reforms. While housing reformers looked to town planning as a means to improve living conditions and inculcate middle-class residential values among working families, manufacturers like Firestone hoped to generate a stable, efficient, and compliant workforce through good community design. The Southern Pine Association, publisher of the pamphlet, was a trade association formed to promote lumber sales.

Document 6-4 reflects on suburban planning of a very different kind. Exemplifying a genre of didactic suburban literature, this essay profiles the privately planned, exclusive suburb of Kenilworth, Illinois, north of Chicago. The writer not only depicts the charms of this community, but also seeks to educate readers to "all the advantages" that a model suburb should have. Nowhere among these are business enterprises or industrial workers. By the early twentieth century, essays of this kind found a wide audience through popular magazines such as *House Beautiful, House and Garden, The Craftsman,* and *Suburban Life.* Supported by advertisements from building material and appliance manufacturers, and devoured by a growing suburban clientele, this suburban life literature became one of the most important conduits for promoting an upper-middle-class image of suburban living.

Among the business interests that promoted suburbanization in these years, perhaps none was as important as Sears and Roebuck. The Chicago retail giant offered prefabricated homes to its customers from 1916 to 1933. As **Document 6-5** illustrates, the Sears 1926 Honor Bilt Modern Homes catalogue included a well-developed pitch for suburban home ownership. Sears sold houses fitting a range of incomes, but it took special pains to attract urban working families with a suburban vision that melded middle-class imagery with working-class economic concerns.

The concluding documents present two iconic suburban models designed on American soil. **Document 6-6** is a description of Radburn, New Jersey, one of the most important attempts to translate "garden city" ideas to an American setting. Clarence Stein, its author, helped plan this community in the late 1920s. This "town for the motor age" aimed especially to separate autos from pedestrians in its physical design, while its social planning sought to create an active community life, including voluntary self-governance and abundant recreation in its large interior parks. Radburn served as a model for the subsequent Greenbelt Town program of the New Deal, as well as for new town building internationally. Elements of Radburn's plan, such as cul-de-sac streets and neighborhood unit planning became mainstays of postwar suburban design, while its self-governing community association influenced future trends in private common interest developments.

The ideology of decentralization found its most radical expression in the imagination of architect Frank Lloyd Wright. The image in **Document 6-7** depicts the "civic center" of "Broadacre City," Wright's vision of the future American metropolis. Thoroughly decentralized, with each household occupying plots of an acre or more, Broadacre City relied on private autos and helicopter taxis to move residents from point to point without need for a congested center. In contrast to Radburn, where designers sought to insulate residents from the automobile, Wright embraced the vehicle as a tool for liberation from the traditional city. "Broadacre City" represented the gospel of decentralization taken to its extreme: the centerless city.

Compare and contrast the varied plans for suburbia advanced at this time. What values most influenced these visions? What was similar or different about plans for different classes of Americans? Who designed them? In what ways did they shape or predict future metropolitan realities? What assumptions did Progressives make about the efficacy of public planning versus private community building? Were they right? Where did their visions of suburbia converge and diverge from those of free market real estate developers?

6-1. EBENEZER HOWARD'S *GARDEN CITIES OF TO-MORROW*, 1902

It is wellnigh universally agreed by men of all parties, not only in England, but all over Europe and America and our colonies, that it is deeply to be deplored that the people should continue to stream into the already over-crowded cities, and should thus further deplete the country districts....

All, then, are agreed on the pressing nature of this problem, all are bent on its solution, and though it would doubtless be quite Utopian to expect a similar agreement as to the value of any remedy that may be proposed, it is at least of immense importance that, on a subject thus universally regarded as of supreme importance, we have such a consensus of opinion at the outset....Yes, the key to the problem how to restore the people to the land—that beautiful land of ours, with its canopy of sky, the air that blows upon it, the sun that warms it, the rain and dew that moisten it—the very embodiment of Divine love for man—is indeed a *Master Key,* for it is the key to a portal through which, even when scarce ajar, will be seen to pour a flood of light on the problems of intemperance, of excessive toil, of restless anxiety, of grinding poverty—the true limits of Governmental interference, ay, and even the relations of man to the Supreme Power....

Whatever may have been the causes which have operated in the past, and are operating now, to draw the people into the cities, those causes may all be summed up as 'attractions'; and it is obvious, therefore, that no remedy can possibly be effective which will not present to the people, or at least to considerable portions of them, greater 'attractions' than our cities now possess, so that the force of the old 'attractions' shall be overcome by the force of new 'attractions' which are to be created. Each city may be regarded as a magnet, each person as a needle; and, so viewed, it is at once seen that nothing short of the discovery of a method for constructing magnets of yet greater power than our cities possess can be effective for redistributing the population in a spontaneous and healthy manner....

'What,' some may be disposed to ask, 'can possibly be done to make the country more attractive to a workaday people than the town—to make wages, or at least the standard of physical comfort, higher in the country than in the town; to secure in the country equal possibilities of social intercourse, and to make the prospects of advancement for the average man or woman equal, not to say superior, to those enjoyed in our large cities?'...The question is universally considered as though it were now, and for ever must remain, quite impossible for working people to live in the country and yet be engaged in pursuits other than agricultural; as though crowded, unhealthy cities were the last word of economic science; and as if our present form of industry, in which sharp lines divide agricultural from industrial pursuits, were necessarily an enduring one. This fallacy is the very common one of ignoring altogether the possibility of alternatives other than those presented to the mind. There are in reality not only...two alternatives—town life and country life—but a third alternative, in which all the advantages of the most energetic and active town life, with all the beauty and delight of the country, may be secured in perfect combination; and the certainty of being able to live this life will be the magnet which will produce the effect for which we are all striving—the spontaneous movement of the people from our crowded cities to the bosom of our kindly mother earth, at once the source of life, of happiness, of wealth, and of power. The town and the country may, therefore, be regarded as two magnets, each striving to draw the people to itself....

But neither the Town magnet nor the Country magnet represents the full plan and purpose of nature. Human society and the beauty of nature are meant to be enjoyed together. The two magnets must be made one. As man and woman by their varied gifts and faculties supplement each other, so should town and country. The town is the symbol of society—of mutual help and friendly co-operation, of fatherhood, motherhood, brotherhood, sisterhood, of wide relations between man and man—of broad, expanding sympathies—of science, art, culture, religion. And the country! The country is the symbol of God's love and care for man. All that we are and all that we have comes from it. Our bodies are formed of it; to it they return. We are fed by it, clothed by it, and by it are we warmed and sheltered. On its bosom we rest. Its beauty is the inspiration of art, of music, of poetry. Its forces propel all the wheels of industry. It is the source of all health, all wealth, all knowledge. But its fullness of joy and wisdom has not revealed itself to man. Nor can it ever, so long as this unholy, unnatural separation of society and nature endures. Town and country *must be married,* and out of this joyous union will spring a new hope, a new life, a new civilization. It is the purpose of this work to show how a first step can be taken in this direction by the construction of a Town-country magnet; and I hope to convince the reader that this is practicable, here and now....

The Town-Country Magnet....

The reader is asked to imagine an estate embracing an area of 6,000 acres, which is at present purely agricultural, and has been obtained by purchase in the open market at a cost of £40 an acre, or £240,000. The purchase money is supposed to have been raised on mortgage debentures, bearing interest at an average rate not exceeding £4 per cent. The estate is legally vested in the names of four gentlemen of responsible position and of undoubted probity and honour, who hold it in trust, first, as a security for the debenture-holders, and, secondly, in trust for the people of Garden City, the Town-country magnet, which it is intended to build thereon. One essential feature of the plan is that all ground rents, which are to be based upon the annual value of the land, shall be paid to the trustees, who, after providing for interest and sinking fund, will hand the balance to the Central Council of the new municipality, to be employed by such Council in the creation and maintenance of all necessary public works—roads, schools, parks, etc.

The objects of this land purchase may be stated...in short, to raise the standard of health and comfort of all true workers of whatever grade—the means by which these objects are to be achieved being a healthy, natural, and economic combination of town and country life, and this on land owned by the municipality.

Garden City, which is to be built near the centre of the 6,000 acres, covers an area of 1,000 acres, or a sixth part of the 6,000 acres, and might be of circular form, 1,240 yards (or nearly three-quarters of a mile) from centre to circumference. ([Figure 6-1] is a ground plan of the whole municipal area, showing the town in the centre....)

Six magnificent boulevards—each 120 feet wide—traverse the city from centre to circumference, dividing it into six equal parts or wards. In the centre is a circular space containing about five and a half acres, laid out as a beautiful and well-watered garden; and, surrounding this garden, each standing in its own ample grounds, are the larger public buildings—town hall, principal concert and lecture hall, theatre, library, museum, picture-gallery, and hospital.

The rest of the large space encircled by the 'Crystal Palace' is a public park, containing 145 acres, which includes ample recreation grounds within very easy access of all the people.

Running all round the Central Park (except where it is intersected by the boulevards) is a wide glass arcade called the 'Crystal Palace', opening on to the park. This building is in wet weather one of the favourite resorts of the people, whilst the knowledge that its bright shelter is ever close at hand tempts people into Central Park, even in the most doubtful of weathers. Here manufactured goods are exposed for sale, and here most of that class of shopping which requires the joy of deliberation and selection is done. The space enclosed by the Crystal Palace is, however, a good deal larger than is required for these purposes, and a considerable part of it is used as a Winter Garden—the whole forming a permanent exhibition of a most attractive character, whilst its circular form brings it near to every dweller in the town—the furthest removed inhabitant being within 600 yards.

Passing out of the Crystal Palace on our way to the outer ring of the town...we find a ring of very excellently built houses, each standing in its own ample grounds; and, as

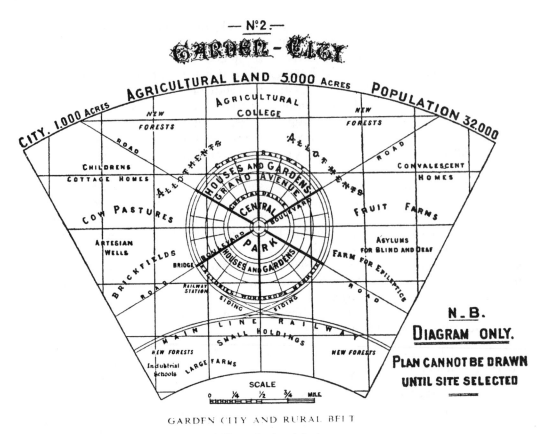

Figure 6-1 Garden City and Rural Belt, 1902. Illustration in original.

we continue our walk, we observe that the houses are for the most part built either in concentric rings, facing the various avenues (as the circular roads are termed), or fronting the boulevards and roads which all converge to the centre of the town. Asking the friend who accompanies us on our journey what the population of this little city may be, we are told about 30,000 in the city itself, and about 2,000 in the agricultural estate, and that there are in the town 5,500 building lots of an *average* size of 20 feet x 130 feet—the minimum space allotted for the purpose being 20 x 100. Noticing the very varied architecture and design which the houses and groups of houses display—some having common gardens and co-operative kitchens—we learn that general observance of street line or harmonious departure from it are the chief points as to house building, over which the municipal authorities exercise control, for, though proper sanitary arrangements are strictly enforced, the fullest measure of individual taste and preference is encouraged....

On the outer ring of the town are factories, warehouses, dairies, markets, coal yards, timber yards, etc., all fronting on the circle railway, which encompasses the whole town, and which has sidings connecting it with a main line of railway which passes through the estate. This arrangement enables goods to be loaded direct into trucks from the warehouses and workshops, and so sent by railway to distant markets, or to be taken direct from the trucks into the warehouses or factories; thus not only effecting a very great saving in regard to packing and cartage, and reducing to a minimum loss from breakage, but also, by reducing the traffic on the roads of the town, lessening to a very marked extent the cost of their maintenance. The smoke fiend is kept well within bounds in Garden City; for all machinery is driven by electric energy, with the result that the cost of electricity for lighting and other purposes is greatly reduced....

[I]t is easily conceivable that it may prove advantageous to grow wheat in very large fields, involving united action under a capitalist farmer, or by a body of co-operators: while the cultivation of vegetables, fruits, and flowers, which requires closer and more personal care, and more of the artistic and inventive faculty, may possibly be best dealt with by individuals, or by small groups of individuals having a common belief in the efficacy and value of certain dressings, methods of culture, or artificial and natural surroundings....

Dotted about the estate are seen various charitable and philanthropic institutions. These are not under the control of the municipality, but are supported and managed by various public-spirited people who have been invited by the municipality to establish these institutions in an open healthy district, and on land let to them at a pepper-corn rent, it occurring to the authorities that they can the better afford to be thus generous, as the spending power of these institutions greatly benefits the whole community. Besides, as those persons who migrate to the town are among its most energetic and resourceful members, it is but just and right that their more helpless brethren should be able to enjoy the benefits of an experiment which is designed for humanity at large.

6-2. HOUSING REFORMER CAROL ARONOVICI CALLS FOR SUBURBAN PLANNING, 1914

Source: Carol Aronovici, "Suburban Development," *Annals of the American Academy of Political and Social Science* 51 (January 1914).

The astounding growth of urban communities in the United States and throughout the civilized world that has taken place within the life of the generation just past is at last facing a hopeful reaction. The city has, humanly speaking, proven to be a failure.

Congestion of population and concentration of industrial activity have been overcapitalized and no contingent means have been provided to meet the needs for a normal human development and efficient industrial growth of our cities. These two important factors are now pointing the way toward a

hopeful solution of ultra-urbanization of all human activities. The decentralization of human habitation first found expression in the splendid development of our metropolitan suburbs, and now the growing need for industrial expansion, the over-capitalization of city land values and a demand for more healthful industrial conditions are fostering an industrial exodus countryward that presents one of the most hopeful tendencies in modern society.

It is through this exodus that we hope to solve a considerable share of our housing problem, improve living conditions and create a closer cooperation and deeper sympathy between the worker and his work. Pullman [IL], Gary [IN], and Fairfield [AL], in this country; the many flourishing garden cities of England and Germany, the rapid growth of suburbs in the vicinity of metropolitan cities and the numerous industrial satellite cities are convincing evidence of the decentralization of human habitation and industrial activity....

These are hopeful signs that should be seriously considered as one means of decentralizing our business and residential life and reducing congestion, if its complete abolition is impossible. The protection of these outlying districts against the repetition of the evils of the metropolitan cities can be secured only through proper suburban planning....

The facts just stated [Ed. note: statistics showing growth in suburban population] point the way toward the solution of one of our most serious problems, "congestion," but the hope for the solution of this momentous problem is not in the mere shifting of population, but in the far-sighted control of this growth in the direction of constructive community planning. The small communities are quick to imitate the cities in both their good and bad features and while they realize the importance of the growth of population, they are often ill prepared for or entirely ignorant of the responsibilities involved in the educational, physical and moral care of the increasing numbers of human beings.

Health conditions in the smaller cities and towns which have been affected by industrialism are generally as bad or worse than those of the larger cities. The city slum is being transferred into the open country and the barrack-like tenement often stands out in bold defiance to nature's beautiful surroundings. Industries seeking the smaller communities are permitted to locate anywhere, without regard to human or community needs. Doctor [Werner] Hegemann characterized the congestion in the business and financial district of our cities as "the slumification of business centers." The suburban development of recent years may, in many instances, be justly described as "the slumification of the countryside."…

As all evils must sooner or later find their remedy, so our abhorrent methods of city building are finding their remedy in the development of the town-planning idea.

Parks, playgrounds, proper homes, transportation, water supply, amusement centers, art galleries, schools, museums, etc., are essentials of civilized community life and constitute the field of town and city planning. The town and city planner must coordinate these essentials and so humanize them as to embrace the highest ideals of present community development backed by a community patriotism that will stand the test of the highest standard of social well-being.

The cost of community planning may be measured in dollars and cents, but a more accurate measurement is to be found in the rate of infant mortality and the daily deaths and the amount of ill health and crime that we must suffer and pay for. The well-planned garden cities of England and Germany are teaching us the lesson that health, morals and industrial efficiency are possible of control by proper community planning. Statistics show us that density of population goes hand in hand with frequency of deaths, sickness and crime. On every side we find overwhelming evidence of the value of proper community planning and development and the growing desire for better living conditions among the people. The diagnosis is made, the remedy—town planning—is known and we shall pay a well deserved penalty if we do not apply it.

The suburbanizing of the wage-earner is a great social and economic opportunity. The increase in the population of our smaller cities and towns as well as the growing countryward industrial exodus that is taking place in this country hold out a golden opportunity, and it is for us to say whether this growth will result in a contamination of the open country by the city slums or whether garden communities will look upon the bleak horrors of our urbanized existence and give men, women, and children a new lease on life and industry and chance to serve men rather than to enslave them.

The large cities present a possibility for reconstruction, for palliative town planning, while the younger cities and towns have the open country before them, little to rebuild and readjust, and a great advantage over the congested city slums which they have now the opportunity to condemn to everlasting death by their superior living advantages and their advantage for shaping their future growth to meet future as well as present needs.

The Utopian city of yesterday can be realized in the growing suburbs of our own times and the future will praise us or blame us as we realize or fail to realize the practical ideals that science and art and a living democracy make possible this day.

6-3. A PLANNED INDUSTRIAL SUBURB: FIRESTONE PARK, OHIO, 1919

Source: H.S. Firestone, "Firestone Park, Akron, Ohio: A Splendidly Conceived Housing Development of the Firestone Tire and Rubber Company," in *Homes for Workmen: A Presentation of Leading Examples of Industrial Community Development* (New Orleans: Southern Pine Association, 1919).

Introduction

The purpose of this publication is to present certain general and specific facts concerning industrial housing which may be of value in directing those interested in arriving at correct conclusions as to how best to solve this problem in their own communities.

A difficult though insistent problem confronting industry today is that of providing proper living conditions for workmen and their families, to insure the adequacy, stability and efficiency of labor. At hundreds of places there is need for more houses and better houses. In some centers where abnormal development has taken place the housing shortage is so acute that factory output cannot be brought up to the required volume. Community housing enterprises, undertaken along proper lines, will avoid the methods of speculative builders, and will not find their incentive in the earning of large dividends and profits to investors. While industrial housing projects should, and will if properly managed, yield a return on the investment, those financing housing companies will derive their principal gain indirectly through general community betterment, which has a distinct and tangible value. The manufacturer will, of course, be the principal beneficiary, and will accordingly bear the greater

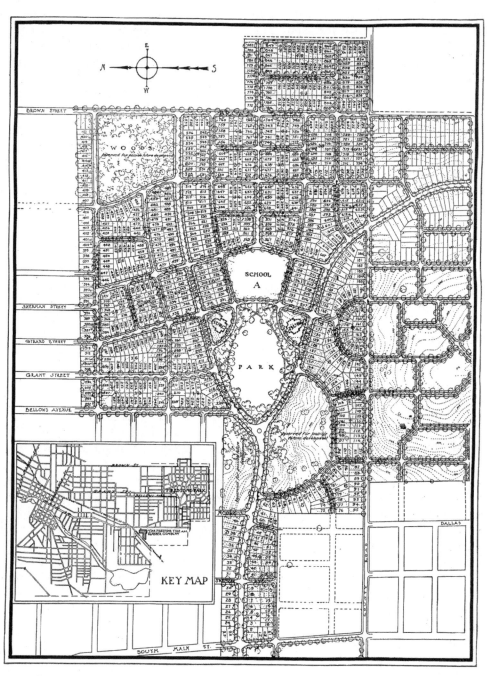

Figure 6-2 Plot Plan, Firestone Park, 1919. Illustration in original, 200.

part of the housing burden, if there must be a burden. While the benefits to the manufacturer are quite generally recognized, the community benefits derived from a well-housed and, therefore, contented and self-respecting labor element, have rarely been given proper consideration in this country. An established industrial community can have no better asset than an adequate supply of well-built, attractive homes, for the reason that it is to that town or city in which the labor supply is stable, and its standards of morality and industry in consequence high, that the manufacturer seeking industrial location instinctively turns. Everywhere that a properly conceived housing program has been put into effect in a manufacturing community it has been attended by an increase in the prosperity of all the mercantile and financial, as well as the manufacturing elements of the community, and also an advance in educational and moral standards....

SOUTHERN PINE ASSOCIATION...

Firestone Park, Akron, Ohio

A Splendidly Conceived Housing Development of the Firestone Tire and Rubber Company

By H. S. Firestone

President of the Firestone Tire and Rubber Company

It was the Firestone idea from the beginning to build here a community with all the delights of small town life, yet with all the advantages of proximity to a large city.

Mr. Alling DeForrest, one of the foremost landscape architects of the United States, was brought to Akron to lay out Firestone Park. Many plans were considered before the final plan was accepted. The improvements and the amount of money already invested in Firestone Park are great, but the results speak for themselves. We have developed over 300 acres of land. There are 300 more acres which will be developed soon. We have nine miles of sanitary sewer, five miles of storm drain, one-half mile of which is 6 feet in diameter. We have seven and one-half miles of water main, three and one-half miles of street paving completed, and we expect to complete another five and one-half miles

this season. We have six miles of cement sidewalk completed, and expect to complete six more miles this summer. The main Firestone Boulevard is 110 feet wide for a distance of 1,500 feet, branching off into two boulevards each 80 feet in width. There is a community park of sixteen acres in the center, and at the head of this park stands the largest and best equipped school in the State of Ohio. It will be complete and in operation in the fall. We already have a thriving church which is attracting "standing room only" crowds every Sunday. Two churches have announced that they desire to come to Firestone Park. One is a Methodist church, which has offered to put up a $30,000 building, and the other is a Lutheran church.

Firestone Park is a church-going community and we are proud of the fact.

The new Y.W.C.A. building has forty-four rooms and will house seventy-five girls. The restaurant seats 125.

We are going to make Firestone Park the best part of Akron to live in and to bring up a family. Every one has heard of the Firestone Club House. In the great auditorium activities are constantly going on. The restaurant we think has done much to reduce the high cost of living in Firestone Park. The whole structure has paid its own way and Akron can be proud of the fact that it has been a model for other industries in other cities.

6-4. *SUBURBAN LIFE* PROFILES KENILWORTH, AN EXCLUSIVE SUBURB OF CHICAGO, 1907

Source: F.E.M. Cole, "Chicago's Most Unique Suburb," *Suburban Life* 5 (November 1907).

About fifteen miles from Chicago along the North Shore, lying directly on the banks of Lake Michigan, is the beautiful little suburban town of Kenilworth, Illinois. It has excellent train service by railroad and interurban. Sheridan Road, which extends from Chicago to Fort Sheridan and beyond, passes through Kenilworth near the lake and links a dozen or more towns of various sizes, but, of all the towns along this North Shore, Kenilworth is conceded to be the most attractive.

Stepping from the train, after a thirty minutes' ride from Chicago, one is impressed with the beauties of the low-lying stone depot half hidden in vines and shrubbery and gay with flowering plants. Passing through the stone archway, the beauty of Kenilworth makes itself manifest, for this is really Kenilworth's front door.

Here, at the head of Kenilworth avenue, which extends from the depot to Lake Michigan, a distance of about half a mile, we are greeted by a fountain in full play. On either side stone abutments are built, and in them are low, broad seats, where the children congregate and wait for the in-coming trains, or the visitor may rest and enjoy the quiet of the summer day. The abutments are surmounted at either end by huge urns filled with gay-colored flowers and vines, and at the opposite corners are large bronze lamps which shed a mellow light at night....

Kenilworth is strictly a residential spot, and, because of its easy access to a great city, its ideal location and its many charms, natural and otherwise, it is admirably suited to the wants of the business and professional man who has a family and wishes to make his home in an attractive suburb. It is a good deal to say of a village that it has no unat-

tractive features, but this is literally true of Kenilworth. There are no manufacturing plants, no unsightly buildings, only one store, and no livery-stables, power-houses or greenhouses, to mar its natural beauty,—nothing, in fact, which would in any way lessen the value of property in any portion of the village. This condition has been made possible by a rigid enforcement of building restrictions incorporated in every deed. These restrictions require that no houses shall be constructed below a stipulated price, and that all buildings must be set at least forty feet back from the street. As all lots are of one hundred feet or more frontage, there is a uniformity which is very pleasing....

No effort has been spared to make the village as beautiful as possible, and those who make their homes here strive to preserve the natural beauties which everywhere abound. In some sections of the village the streets are winding, and large trees have been allowed to remain in the middle of them where they do not interfere with traffic. The vacant spots are kept free from refuse, while wild flowers and vines grow in tangles.

There are some portions of the village still unimproved, and a few steps away from a stone sidewalk bring one into a miniature

Figure 6-3 One of the Attractive Homes Showing the Appreciation of Foliage and Flowers Which is Characteristic of the Town, 1907. Illustration in original, 283.

wilderness. Great trees of oak, elm and ash, many of them covered with Virginia creeper, wild grape and bittersweet, form a thicket well nigh impassible. The wild rabbit finds a home here and occasionally one hears the Bob-White call of the quail, and oft, when the shades of night are falling, the soft note of the whip-poor-will is heard. To sit on one's porch and listen to the various night sounds in a community like this gives a new lease of life and helps prepare the mind and body for the world's business battles....

As Lake Michigan is so accessible, there is an excellent beach for bathing, and a bath-house with an attendant in charge is open during the season. Nearly all the children and a great many of the older people make the best of the bathing season. The children, particularly, are to be found here nearly every warm day. The younger people, home from school and college, find Kenilworth an ideal spot to spend vacation time, and a large majority of the residents do not go away for the hot season.

The homes of Kenilworth are not of the pretentious kind. There are no marble palaces, although there are many charming effects in architecture, and one feels the influence of these little gems of homes in their setting of tree and flower. Thirty thousand dollars would probably buy the most elaborate home in the suburb, and ten to fifteen thousand would probably be the price placed upon many, were they for sale. Hedges form pretty dividing lines between the homes and, until very recently, a fence was an unknown quantity....

As the improvement association seems to be the order of the day in towns as well as certain sections of large cities, Kenilworth also has one which was brought into being several years ago; and, by working in conjunction with the town officials, the village has been greatly benefited, and many of the features which make the town so attractive would be impossible were it not for this association, for all the money which is derived from taxation is needed for more practical purposes.

Considering that there are only about one hundred and twenty-five families in the suburb, four to five hundred dollars in the way of voluntary contributions for the improvement association is liberal—and this is about the amount given each year. The largest single item of expense is for the flowers necessary to fill the beds, urns and boxes. The geranium and salvia have been found most satisfactory for this particular purpose, as either will grow and flourish if there is not too much shade. After the first hard frost these are taken out and the beds are prepared and filled with tulips for the early spring display.

During the summer the streets are kept well sprinkled, and in winter the snow-shovel makes its rounds long before the average citizen is ready to take his accustomed train. Lake Michigan furnishes the village with its water, which is filtered, thereby insuring not only pure water but an inexhaustible supply. Gas comes from a neighboring town, as well as electricity, which is installed underground. It took several years to convince the electric light company that the unsightly poles and objectionable overhead wires were not wanted in this ideal town. Now that the town has won, we regret that the telephone wires are not out of sight also, but we live in hope. The end is not yet.

The social features of the town are not lacking. There are several clubs, the largest being known as the Kenilworth Club, membership in which entitles one to the use of the golf-links, the lawn-tennis courts and the bath-house, and, in winter, various entertainments are held at the assembly hall without any additional cost. The woman's club of the town is The Neighbors, at whose semi-monthly meetings some well-known personage always speaks on some subject of interest to the majority of womankind.

There are two churches, the Episcopal and the Union, a graded school, a building accommodating about three hundred, and, within sight, is the New Trier high school, considered one of the finest in the state. The excellent train service to Chicago makes it very convenient for those who wish to attend the theater or other form of entertainment in the city. One can even stay for a late supper and get home in time for a good night's rest.

The visitor to Kenilworth has the feeling that he has come upon a spot blessed with all the advantages which a suburban town should offer. If he is a flat-renter in the city, he realizes the manifold advantages offered his family and has a desire to own a home in a suburban town where life is well worth living.

6-5. SEARS, ROEBUCK AND CO. ADVERTISES SUBURBAN HOME OWNERSHIP, 1926

Figure 6-4 Retailers of all kinds employed suburban imagery as a way to sell their products. In this Sears ad for prefabricated homes, home ownership and escape from "the renter's class" are linked to a landscape of middle-class suburbia. Sears, Roebuck and Company, *Honor Bilt Modern Homes* (Chicago: Sears, Roebuck and Co., 1926), 1.

6-6. ARCHITECT CLARENCE STEIN ASSESSES THE PLANNING FOR RADBURN, NEW JERSEY, 1957

Source: Clarence S. Stein, *Toward New Towns for America* (New York: Reinhold Publishing, 1957).

THE NEED FOR RADBURN.—American cities were certainly not places of security in the twenties. The automobile was a disrupting menace to city life in the U.S.A.—long before it was in Europe. In 1928 there were 21,308,159 automobiles registered (as compared with 5 in 1895). The flood of motors had already made the gridiron street pattern, which had formed the framework for urban real estate for over a century, as obsolete as a fortified town wall. Pedestrians risked a dangerous motor street crossing 20 times a mile. The roadbed was the children's main play space. Every year there were more Americans killed or injured in automobile accidents than the total of American war casualties in any year. The checkerboard pattern made all streets equally inviting to through traffic. Quiet and peaceful repose disappeared along with safety. Porches faced bedlams of motor throughways with blocked traffic, honking horns, noxious gases. Parked cars, hard grey roads and garages replaced gardens.

It was in answer to such conditions that the Radburn plan was evolved. For America it was a revolution in planning: a revolution, I regret to say, which is far from completed.

Elements of the Radburn Plan

"The Radburn Idea," to answer the enigma "How to live with the auto," or, if you will, "How to live in spite of it," met these difficulties with a radical revision of relation of houses, roads, paths, gardens, parks, blocks, and local neighborhoods. For this purpose it used the following elements:

1. The SUPERBLOCK in place of the characteristic narrow, rectangular block.
2. SPECIALIZED ROADS PLANNED AND BUILT FOR ONE USE INSTEAD OF FOR ALL USES: service lanes for direct access to buildings; secondary collector roads around superblocks; main through roads, linking the traffic of various sections, neighborhoods and districts; express highways or parkways for connection with outside communities. (Thus differentiating between movement, collection, service, parking, and visiting.)
3. COMPLETE SEPARATION OF PEDESTRIAN AND AUTOMOBILE, or as complete separation as possible. Walks and paths routed at different places from roads and at different levels when they cross. For this purpose overpasses and underpasses were used.
4. HOUSES TURNED AROUND. Living and sleeping rooms facing toward gardens and parks; service rooms toward access roads.
5. PARK AS BACKBONE of the neighborhood. Large open areas in the center of superblocks, joined together as a continuous park....

Precedents

None of the elements of the plan was completely new. The distinctive innovations of Radburn were the integrating superblocks, specialized and separated means of circulation, the park backbone, and the house with two fronts. Radburn interwove these to form a new unity, as a practical and attractive setting for the realities of today's living....

How the Radburn Plan Worked

Those who live in Radburn and have lived there for any great length of time find that it has served its objective of making home and community life more reposeful, pleasant and safe—and particularly safe for children. The physical plan of central parks, superblocks without through traffic, safe walks, houses facing on gardens and parks along with the convenience of service have, they find, given them a quality of living that, as medium-income folks, they could not find elsewhere. My associates and I have observed the actions and reactions of the people. We have talked it over with a good many of them, and we have studied the investigations of others.

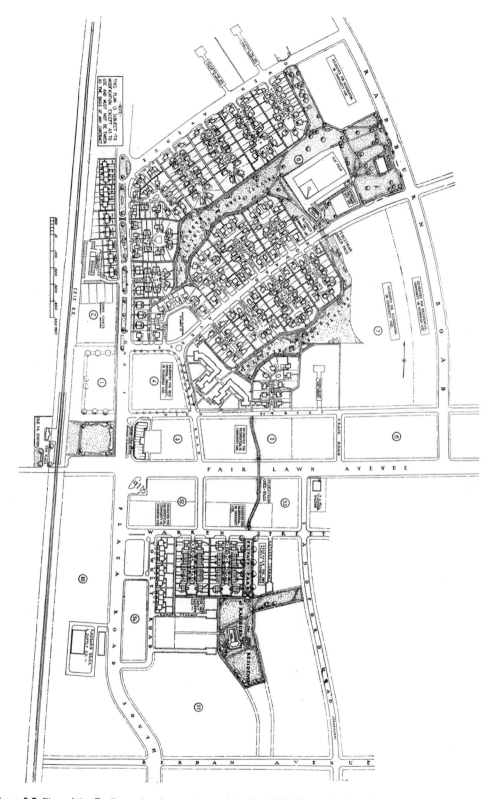

Figure 6-5 Plan of the Radburn development completed by 1930. Illustration in original, 49.

We find that the general feeling, after twenty years of trial, is enthusiastic approval....

SAFETY FOR CHILDREN.—Radburn is above all a town for children. The safety features, the free safe life in the open, is what drew young parents to it in the beginning. The first forty families who moved into the town were young folks in their thirties with children of early or pre-school age. Although Radburn was affected by the national shifting of population during 1939–1945, stability has returned to the town. Old residents are re-appearing. Former Radburn children have married and have come back to bring up their own youngsters. Seventy-five per cent of the present Radburn men are veterans of the recent war. They are starting their married life in Radburn apparently because they want their families, and particularly their children, to have the same background for free living which they knew as youngsters.

In regard to safety, let us look at the figures. In Radburn's 20 years there have been only two road deaths. Both were on main highways, not in lanes. There has been only one serious accident on any lane, which resulted in a little girl's arm being broken....

GOVERNMENTAL COMMUNITY ORGANIZATION....The City Housing Corporation devised a plan for maintaining property and for a shared responsibility.... At Radburn restrictions to protect architectural harmony were made part of the purchase deed. These restrictive covenants provided for public services required in an urban community, but not yet adequately provided in the local semi-rural Borough of Fairlawn. These included sewage disposal, garbage collection, street lighting, policing and operation of the large park areas, playgrounds and recreation facilities.

As the local tax rate of Fairlawn would not cover the cost of these extra services, the Radburn Association was empowered to impose an additional annual charge which could never exceed one-half the current Borough taxes.

RADBURN ASSOCIATION.—The Radburn Association was incorporated as a non-profit, non-stock corporation to fix, collect, and disburse the annual charges, to maintain the necessary community services, parks and recreation facilities, and to interpret and apply the protective restrictions.

The Association was governed by a self-perpetuating Board of Trustees. The first nine trustees were civic leaders of New Jersey or officers of the City Housing Corporation....

In short, the Radburn Association was to have the power and functions of a municipal government, including taxation. An American government without public representation! Luckily it was well administered for the good of the Radburn people by one of the ablest town managers in America...chosen by the Trustees....

RADBURN REVISITED.—The impressive feature of Radburn superblocks are the inner parks. You enter from the highway by a path between hedges. These are of varied height. Some partially hide, others disclose, the gardens beyond: well-cared-for, very personal gardens, many of them gay with early flowers and shaded by varied trees—a quarter of a century old or more. They partly conceal the two-story houses of brick and wood.

It is late spring: people are burning off old paint and putting on a new white coat, or trimming hedges or spading gardens.

Then at the path's end the park opens up to you. An apparently endless grassy lawn, with groups of trees. Around the edges are the paths, alive with children on bicycles and velocipedes. Beyond the hedge's border are the private gardens of the end houses of the lanes....[A]bove all it is the natural green that dominates and controls the picture. Your architecture cannot look bad when time makes it part of the bigger composition of landscape. Radburn has come of age architecturally because time has mellowed it into a oneness. Harsh lines are subdued and enveloped by the verdure....

The picture constantly goes through kaleidoscopic changes of planting and distant structures as one walks up the center of the broad lawn. It is so spaciously open that one thinks of a lordly estate, but it is filled with democratic life. Little girls playing tag; boys playing baseball or on their backs looking up through the leaves at the blue, their bicycles at their sides; and here comes a whole family in dripping bathing suits.

The outdoor swimming pool is the real

center of Radburn's summer life. During the long hours after work it is gay with youthful color and movement. Next to it is the wading pool for the little ones. Beyond is the large field for baseball or other big games, and enclosed nearby is the playground for the younger ones, with slides and other apparatus. On our way we have passed sandboxes for the tots at the end of each block, each enclosed by a little fence and hidden by bushes. Beyond the pool and playground is the elementary school.

We go through an underpass to the next superblock. If we look up we may see an automobile against the sky. We had forgotten that our civilization is dominated by motors. Nowhere within the peaceful superblocks are you reminded of their existence. In early June the rosebushes dominate the landscape in the passage between the two superblocks.

The second inner park is different in form, in topography, in planting. There is a small unobtrusive natural theater, and on the higher ground a rustic pavilion. The lawns again are spacious and broad. The trees and bushes are massed so as to leave large open spaces, easy for machine mowing.

At the end of the park are two low but massive apartment buildings....

The function of the auto side of the houses is the reverse of that facing parks and gardens. The two sides are as different as night and day. The dead-end lanes are some 400 feet in depth. On most of them houses stand out, perhaps too strongly, for lack of green foreground and hiding foliage. Some of the earlier buildings seem crowded: we architects had planned for short rows intermingled with single units. We were finally restricted to free-standing units. Our sense of economy in paving and utilities led to some tightness. It creates annoyance where there are semi-public paths connecting lanes and walks, and people pass close to windows. Later, with houses attached in twos or threes...we achieved a greater sense of spaciousness.

On the service side the washing is festooned—and I recollect that in the days when houses were first opened to public inspection the dominant problem was where to hang the laundry. Mr. [Alexander] Bing [the developer] and his associates had gone

with us in our American planning revolution: street and walk divorced, house faced round, superblocks. But here the salesmen rebelled. They could not sell houses to good Americans if the week's washing was to be displayed on the public side. So, on the days when the houses were first shown, we tried the drying lines on different sides of various houses. The public decided that laundry naturally belonged with other services, and not in the park or garden. And there it has remained....

Radburn: Success or Failure?

Radburn was never completed. Only a small portion of the new town was built before the operation was engulfed by the depression. On the surface Radburn may appear a failure. But essentially it was a great success.... The two superblocks that were built, and in which people have lived happily and safely for twenty years, have demonstrated the essentials of the new form of city that is increasingly accepted as the basis of planning urban residential areas in Europe and America. With this in mind let us examine and evaluate its apparent shortcomings.

Radburn did not become a Garden City. It lacked in complete greenbelt. It did not succeed in securing industry. Its underlying land, excepting the inner block parks, was not retained in single ownership for or by the community. All this is true—but the fact remains that in spite of the avowed intention of the Corporation to create a Garden City, eventually the pressing need of demonstrating the Radburn Idea overshadowed the Garden City idea. In large part it superseded it. For instance, our thoughts, as planners, were concentrated on the value of the living green close to homes in the midst of the superblocks: it seemed more essential than greenbelts. The retention of the ownership of the underlying land was not part of the program of Mr. Bing and his associates.... They considered this impractical in the New York region at that time.... As to industry: we planned for it physically, but our timing was bad. This was probably due less to bad judgment than to the unforeseen breakdown of the national economy....

Figure 6-6 Air view of Radburn. Photo taken in 1929. Illustration in original, 46.

That was twenty years ago. The Radburn idea is now accepted as a fundamental basis of urban residential planning in many lands. I visited Sweden this summer. In Stockholm, I found that the basic form for the remainder of that beautiful city—which is to be completed in about ten years for an additional 100,000 people—will be derived in large part from the Radburn plan. It will consist of green communities, made up of superblocks with central parks, and the separation of walks and roads. Gothenburg's growth will follow a similar general pattern. Other countries are planning variations on the Radburn Idea. Warsaw intends to reconstruct on that basis. Radburn is influencing the plans for New Towns in England. Back in America, the Greenbelt Towns and wartime housing developments are direct or indirect descendants.... And so, though the seeds that Alexander Bing and his associates planted in the Borough of Fairlawn had a limited growth at Radburn, they are germinating, developing and flowering in varied forms throughout the world.

6-7. FRANK LLOYD WRIGHT IMAGINES "BROADACRE CITY," 1935

Figure 6-7 View of Civic Center, Broadacre City. Frank Lloyd Wright's 1935 plan for "Broadacre City" imagined a form reflecting human freedom as he saw it. Key elements were the decentralization of population, government, and economic life, and the redistribution of land for small homesteads. For Wright, Broadacres represented the antithesis of the bureaucratic, industrial city. Drawings of Frank Lloyd Wright are Copyright © 1958 The Frank Lloyd Wright Foundation, Taliesin West, Scottsdale, AZ.

ESSAYS

In **Essay 6-1**, planning historian Margaret Crawford explores the trend toward industrial town planning in the early twentieth century. As chapter 4 demonstrates, many large American manufacturers opened suburban factories during this period. While many left the question of housing for their workers to the unpredictable market, many others strove for greater control over their workforces, especially as urban labor militancy intensified during these years. Facing the twin challenges of labor unrest and a poor public image, many industrialists sought professional help to design new towns where, they hoped, model conditions would create model workers. In a nod to the growing strength of a Progressive Movement that was mistrustful of unregulated industry, corporate leaders recognized that hiring well-known planners and architects would burnish their image as benevolent employers. These designers envisioned communities that mimicked features of affluent suburbia despite their cost limits and proximity to the mills.

In **Essay 6-2**, American studies scholar Mary Corbin Sies expands the definition of suburban planning and its practitioners to include suburbanites themselves. By the early twentieth century, she argues, members of a growing "professional-managerial class" espoused an increasingly coherent residential ideal. Using local evidence from four "planned, exclusive suburbs," Sies illustrates that affluent suburbanites shaped suburban planning and design—even in suburbs where planner-developers and architects were very active. Both essays in this chapter reveal the importance of class concerns to the rise of suburban planning, and they highlight the role of an assertive American upper middle class in promoting a class-specific suburban ideal as the solution to urban ills.

ESSAY 6-1. MARGARET CRAWFORD, *BUILDING THE WORKINGMAN'S PARADISE: THE DESIGN OF AMERICAN COMPANY TOWNS* (1995)

Source: London: Verso, 1995.

Labor and the "New" Company Town

By 1910,...[f]acing major labor problems, industrial clients began, for the first time, to value professional [town planning] expertise. If many industrial employers had remained equivocal about making substantial and permanent investments in company towns, the changing labor climate convinced them of the need to rethink their position on welfare, housing, and town planning. The situation had begun to change after 1905, when a seven-year "honeymoon" between labor and capital ended with a new series of strikes. Beginning in 1909, each year brought at least one major outbreak; the garment workers strike of 1909, the Philadelphia general strike of 1910, the Harriman railroad strike the next year, the 1912 textile strikes in Lawrence and Paterson, followed by miners' uprisings in West Virginia, Colorado, and the Upper Michigan copper fields. Unionism grew rapidly, not only among conservative AFL craft unions, but also with the appearance of more militantly radical labor organizations such as the Western Federation of Miners and the Industrial Workers of the World. The IWW brought new groups into the labor movement, organizing women, immigrants, unskilled workers, and even the unemployed into "one big union."

On the defensive, capitalists fought back with increasingly violent means. In isolated company towns, the tension between capital and labor escalated. Old-style paternalism proved to be a weak defense against newly militant labor....

Colorado Fuel and Iron also operated its mining camps with absolutist control; according to one miner, the absentee owner, John D. Rockefeller, Jr, was "invested with what is virtually the power of life and death over twelve thousand men and their families." When the miners finally struck against poor working and living conditions, the mine owners demonstrated their power by bringing in a private army made up of company guards, private detectives, and the state militia. Armed with machine guns, detectives roamed the countryside in a special armored car with a Gatling gun mounted on top, known as the "Death Special." On 20 April 1914, the company forces attacked a tent colony inhabited by strikers at Ludlow, Colorado. Raking the miners and their families with machine guns and high-powered rifles for an entire day, the troops completely destroyed the colony, finally burning it to the ground. Thirty-two people were either shot or burned to death. The "Ludlow Massacre" and similar incidents of employers' violence increased public sympathy for labor and focused national attention on living and working conditions in isolated company towns....

The crisis in industrial relations worked to the advantage of the design professions. Under attack, capitalists began to seek new methods of improving their relations with their workers and upgrading their public image. Already involved in industrial betterment, they began to look to the "new" company town as a possible solution to their labor problems. For the first time, many employers were willing to listen to and accept direction from professional designers. As historian Burton Bledstein observed, the culture of professionalism flourished in an "atmosphere of constant crisis—emergency—in which practitioners both created work for themselves and reinforced their authority by intimidating their clients." At the same time, however, the employers' priorities did not necessarily coincide with the views of housing and urban reformers. Industrial employers continued to make a distinction between unskilled, usually immigrant, workers and skilled, English-speaking workers. Concerned with attracting skilled workers and avoiding unionization, employers hoped that professionally designed communities would build loyalty and stability and thus head off more strikes. Seeking new and more effective ways of addressing these persistent problems, manufacturers accepted the design profession's claims to have mastered the industrial environment and relinquished physical control of the company town to them.

The outlines of the "new" company town emerged with three very similar towns built between 1909 and 1913: Fairfield, Alabama; Torrance, California; and Goodyear Heights, Ohio. Although none of these towns was completely successful as a design, as a group they established the social and aesthetic criteria for a new generation of company towns. These commissions validated the claims of architects, landscape designers, and planners to the same systematic rationality that characterized industrial and urban reform. In all three towns, the clients selected well-known practitioners, rather than local designers. This reinforced professional aspirations to establish nationally accepted norms of good design. Arriving with standardized and generalizable solutions, these professionals rarely addressed local traditions or conditions in their designs. Similarly, the sponsor's willingness to incur the additional expense of hiring both architects and landscape designers acknowledged the importance of professional specialization and demonstrated a commitment to comprehensively designed environments. Encouraged by the degree of authority these firms gave them, company town designers began to assert their autonomy.

Hiring professional designers also served the clients' interests. In spite of the aesthetic freedom they allowed the designers, the clients' instructions reflected their current preoccupations. The sponsors of all three towns were responding to severe labor problems that plagued many large industrial employers. The struggle was taking place on a national scale, with unions conducting well-publicized campaigns to organize entire industries and regions. Large corporations, under increasing public scrutiny, exploited the experts they imported to demonstrate their good intentions and lack of paternalism. They incorporated the designers and their designs into corporate publicity, focusing national attention on the company's efforts to improve their employees' living conditions. At the same time, concerned about protecting their investments, employers refused to take risks, preferring to follow existing precedents rather than experimenting with new ideas or methods. Attempting to attract stable families and skilled workers by offering them homes to buy, employers had to address their workers as consumers as well as employees. As a result, they took great pains to give workers the type of housing they preferred, instructing their architects to design model houses with prices and styles that would appeal to them. This gave the workers a significant role in evaluating the company town. With the company's large investments at stake, the workers became the final arbiters of a town's success....

Consensus: Goodyear Heights, Ohio

Goodyear Heights, Ohio used the lessons of Fairfield and Torrance to consolidate a new image for the company town. Like Fairfield and Torrance, Goodyear Heights owed its existence to Akron's labor problems. In August 1912, Frank Sieberling, president of Goodyear Tire and Rubber, concerned about a growing housing shortage, bought a tract of land intending to build housing for his workers sometime in the future. The next month, Industrial Workers of the World organizer Elizabeth Gurley Flynn arrived in town. Fresh from victory in Lawrence, she exhorted the rubber workers, "The IWW will lead the war...what was done in Lawrence textile mills may be done in Akron rubber shops." Rubber workers in Akron, an open shop town, were ready to be organized. The rubber plants had recently introduced Taylorism, imposing new piecework wages set according to the pace of the fastest worker. To maintain their wages, the other workers had to speed up their pace and work long hours. On 10 February, Firestone tire makers walked out, joined the next day by Goodyear workers. A week later twenty thousand workers were on strike and six thousand had joined the IWW. Sieberling, like other owners, refused to meet with workers, and instead organized local vigilante groups to oppose the strikers. Martial law and vigilante violence finally broke the strike, although a state senate investigation into the causes of the strike acknowledged that the strikers' grievances were justified. Even though the strike was defeated, Sieberling, anticipating future labor problems, decided to start building a new town immediately: this would be Goodyear Heights.

Goodyear Heights followed the pattern that Fairfield and Torrance had established. Looking for an experienced company town planner, Goodyear brought in Boston landscape architect Warren Manning, widely known as an advocate of company-sponsored communities. They also hired the New York architectural firm of Mann and MacNeille, specialists in low-cost housing design. Like Torrance and Fairfield, Goodyear Heights targeted skilled workers who could afford to purchase houses or lots. Manning...zoned the town according to the price of the houses and provided restrictive deeds that established minimum house prices, controlled future architectural and landscape development, and prohibited unsightly additions such as fences and garages. Limiting commercial development and prohibiting the sale of alcohol further guaranteed Goodyear Heights' appeal to upwardly mobile workers and their families.

However, unlike the developers of Fairfield and Torrance, Goodyear was not interested in selling houses and lots to make a profit. This gave Manning the freedom to plan Goodyear Heights as a harmonious garden village. He emphasized the community's physical and symbolic distance from the Goodyear plant, a quarter mile away, by building a concrete bridge over the railroad tracks that passed in front of the town. The main street, Goodyear Avenue, on axis with the bridge, led from this dramatic entrance to a town square surrounded by shops, apartments, churches, and a dormitory for women workers. An alternative to Fairfield and Torrance's gridded downtowns, the square provided a physical and social focus for the town, invoking the symbolism of the American town square. The rest of the town was planned informally, following garden city precedents. The street pattern, adapted to the sloping site, combined long straight blocks along the lower boundary with gently curving roads that sloped up the hillside to a reservoir park overlooking Akron's city center, two miles away. Small irregular parks and large stands of existing trees broke up the loose grid of streets. Planting reinforced the image of the garden. Each street was lined with a different shade tree with smaller trees planted in between and each lot came with fruit trees, a grape-arbor, and ornamental plants.

Goodyear Heights offered workers a choice of housing styles. In order to determine which house types the employees preferred, the architects Mann and MacNeille designed ten different styles of five- and six-room houses, priced between 2,000 and 3,000 dollars. The most popular were simple but spacious two-story frame houses. Rather than proposing any new design ideas, the houses resembled contemporary middle-class dwellings. Goodyear sold these houses at cost. Still unwilling to relinquish control completely, they tried to protect their investment by imposing complex financing arrangements designed to eliminate speculation. Mortgage payments for the first five years were based on market values; if the buyer was still employed after five years, the company would reduce payments by 25 percent. Workers could also buy life insurance that would pay off the mortgage in the event of their death.

Comprehensively planned, with housing tailored to the tastes of its working-class residents, Goodyear Heights established a new standard for company town design. Although still largely dependent on English garden city design techniques, the town square at the center of the settlement suggested the possibilities of historic American forms as a source of new imagery. In an article published in *American City*, "A Step Towards Solving the Industrial Housing Problem," Manning described Goodyear Heights' achievements while acknowledging its limitations. As the title suggests, he saw Goodyear Heights as only the first step in solving a much larger problem. Towns such as Fairfield and Tor-

Figure 6-8 The Plan of Goodyear Heights by Warren Manning, 1913. A clear and coherent plan in which the town is entered across a bridge at the lower left. A broad avenue leads to a public square of shops and churches. Illustration in original, 97.

rance revealed that high costs limited professional planning and design to the highest paid workers; architects were still not able to design houses that unskilled workers could afford. Dissatisfied with the conventional nature of the housing offered to workers, Manning…wanted to investigate new methods of construction, new forms of housing, and new ways of life. Inspired by the social and design experimentation taking place in English garden cities, he called on the sponsors of industrial housing to break away from established precedents and expand the possibilities of the company town.

Graham Taylor's important book, *Satellite Cities*, published in 1914, echoed Manning's conclusions, but placed them in a broader economic and political context. Taylor, an economist and editor of *The Survey*, was in touch with both Progressive reformers and the growing number of architects and planners interested in industrial communities. Evaluating the evolution of "satellite cities" from Pullman to Torrance, Fairfield, and Goodyear Heights, Taylor concluded that industrial decentralization was irreversible, but that, without proper management, uncontrolled suburban development would inevita-

bly recreate the political, social, and physical problems of the cities it was replacing. Praising the skills of "scientific" city planners, who "have the problem in hand," Taylor called on housing reformers, industrialists, and Progressive public officials to sponsor new satellite cities that would "combine living and livelihood" in innovative ways.

In the final chapter of his book, Taylor surveyed well-known architects, city planners, housing reformers, and Progressive businessmen, asking them how to bring new industrial satellite cities into being. Although all agreed on the necessity of new settlements, two distinct positions on their ownership emerged. Many, like Taylor himself, argued that new industrial settlements should be based on "co-partnership," the cooperative form of ownership used in the English garden cities, with land and houses held in common by a cooperative organization. In addition to encouraging comprehensive planning, Taylor felt that co-partnership would give workers a sense of ownership without tying them down. This would finally resolve the contradiction between democracy and improved living conditions that had always plagued company towns. Another group felt that the employers' involvement was still necessary. Their spokesman, Flavell Shurtleff, secretary of the National Conference on City Planning, asserted that to create new towns, "we must continue to depend on the enthusiastic cooperation of industrial managers."

Shurtleff's assessment proved to be correct, but, once again, changes in the labor market provided the impetus for the cooperation of industrial employers. In 1914, the outbreak of war in Europe exacerbated the labor shortage. The increase in demand for American products stimulated an economic boom that promised unprecedented profits for American industries. Expanding productive capacity, however, depended on the availability of workers, and the war in Europe simultaneously cut off the supply of immigrant labor. The result was a serious labor shortage. The situation gave already militant workers an even greater sense of power, and they joined unions in ever larger numbers. Hoping to divert workers from unionization, employers expanded welfare programs even further. The booming economy provided profits for increasingly elaborate programs. As factories grew, serious housing shortages developed. Wages increased, but the cost of living spiraled out of control. Providing adequate housing became an even more important means of attracting scarce labor. Now firmly in the hands of professionals, the "new" company town promised to solve these problems.

ESSAY 6-2. MARY CORBIN SIES, "'GOD'S VERY KINGDOM ON THE EARTH': THE DESIGN PROGRAM FOR THE AMERICAN SUBURBAN HOME, 1877–1917" (1991)

Source: *Modern Architecture in America: Visions and Revisions*, eds. Richard G. Wilson and Sidney K. Robinson (Ames, Iowa: Iowa State University Press, 1991).

When in his introduction to *Examples of American Domestic Architecture* [1889] Albert Winslow Cobb characterized the American home as "God's very kingdom on the earth," he merely stated what clients and architects alike believed to be true as they commissioned or designed the new suburban homes of the late nineteenth and early twentieth centuries. They believed that the American home was the repository of moral purpose, the register of the character of the American people, the expression of America's most righteous democratic ideals. More than aesthetic and professional considerations influenced the shape of the new suburban house type. The architect-designed suburban home of the period 1877 to 1917 can only be fully appreciated when we understand the social and cultural aims that influenced those persons who decided in each instance upon its form. It was both a repository of the social ambitions, anxieties, and cultural ideals of those who designed and consumed it and a model, a vehicle of reform, expected to benefit the urban populace as a whole…

We need, in other words, to study the design of the suburban home in its many-faceted historic context. In the next few pages, I shall discuss the design consensus embodied in the new architect-designed suburban houses that emerged around the turn of the century in a unique set of communities: the planned, exclusive suburbs of major American metropolises. In communities like these across the nation, architects and clients belonging to a new social stratum in urban America gave the suburban house its characteristic twentieth-century form. My argument is based upon an analysis of *all* the houses constructed between 1877 and 1917 in four such communities: Short Hills, N.J.; St. Martin's in Philadelphia, Pa.; Kenilworth, Ill.; and Lake of the Isles in Minneapolis, Minn.…

From this research I discovered that in planned, exclusive suburbs across the nation, communities consisting of the architects, developers, upper middle-class residents, and others interested in the housing question vigorously debated and experimented with the design of the new American suburban home. By 1917, when construction virtually ceased for the duration of the war, members of these communities had worked out a firm consensus regarding the program for the ideal American home. In defining that program, they evinced a dual aim that was both personal and reform-oriented. They sought (1) to accommodate and formalize their own lifestyle and social position in a suitable setting and (2) to devise a model environment that would address the worst housing and social conditions of the cities. To accomplish their purposes, they created a domestic design program of at least seven principles—efficiency, technology, nature, family, individuality, community, and beauty—which they incorporated into their own houses and, in turn, disseminated as a general formula for ordering the residential environment of the city. Their program of scientifically appointed and artistically designed one-family suburban houses with plenty of outdoor space remains the most prominent American residential ideal of the twentieth century.

Studying the domestic design process as it occurred in actual suburbs brings fresh insight to our understanding of the logic of the design of the new suburban home. We find, for example, that the design program that emerged during the period was more concerned with content than with style. It did not advocate a unified style of expression.... Instead, it called for designs that embodied a unified set of assumptions concerning the purpose of the American home and promoted a unified set of principles for achieving that purpose. The most consistent influences on the design program were not aesthetic, professional, or regional issues...but a set of cultural and prescriptive assumptions about the home that were truly national in their scope. Regardless of whether the new houses were built in suburban New York or Chicago, whether they were conservative or progressive in ornamentation and executed in the colonial revival or the Prairie style, they embodied the same essential design principles and rationale....

It may help to clarify the domestic design process if we think of those persons who participated in it in a given suburb as constituting a "community of discourse." This was a set of persons engaged in a continuous discussion concerning, in this instance, the proper design of the ideal home environment. Whether in Short Hills, Kenilworth, or any similar planned, exclusive suburb, the community of discourse included many

persons besides the architects who designed the residents' homes. It is important to remember, as Dell Upton pointed out recently, that "throughout American history, clients have always been unwilling to grant architects control over such an important aspect of everyday life as the design and furnishing of their houses." But there were other participants besides clients and their architects in each suburb's debate: developers, housing reformers and other civic leaders, domestic scientists and clubwomen, neighbors and social critics. Although each community's ideas took shape in the form of new suburban houses—and they remain our most articulate evidence about the content of the debate—its members were also listening and contributing to a larger discussion nationwide on the meaning of the American home. That debate took place on the pages of popular magazines and domestic design manuals, in architectural journals, in lectures sponsored by women's clubs, and in thousands of architect-client transactions occurring in such suburbs across America.

In Short Hills, St. Martin's, Kenilworth, and Lake of the Isles, the overwhelming majority of participants in the design process belonged...to...a group I will call the professional-managerial stratum of the urban upper middle class. This distinctive population cohort emerged in major cities after the Civil War as a result of the coalescence of three historic trends: the administrative restructuring of business enterprise, the new respect accorded professional and technical expertise, and the organization of a national mass market for consumer goods. These factors created the three categories of occupation that defined members of the stratum: they were either businessmen, professionals, or the producers or transmitters of culture. Besides similarities in occupation and in professional or technical training, these individuals shared similar social origins and affiliations, and pursued similar life-styles, social practices, and consumption patterns. The vast majority were native-born Americans of northern European descent who possessed high school and often college educations and hailed from privileged, Protestant backgrounds. Keenly ambitious, they were eager to create a market for their services and opportunities for social and economic advancement. As the first non-wealthy group of citizens in American history anxious and able to afford to have an architect design the family home, they were the dominant sponsors of suburban residential building prior to World War I.

The shared experiences and mutual interests of those belonging to the professional-managerial stratum fostered a common belief system among them, a common way of defining the world and their place in it. That belief system, the product of a group emerging during a period of profound change, was bifurcated—split between the old mid-century, middle-class values of family, domesticity, and republicanism and the new values of cost efficiency, career ambition, and the urban marketplace. These individuals, in other words, characteristically embraced both traditional and modern values without acknowledging that they perceived any inherent contradictions between them. For example, they continued to view home and family as a moral haven and the Christian values learned there a guarantor of social stability. At the same time, they recognized that home and family must also supply children with the aptitudes that would bring them success in the occupational realm. While parents reinforced beliefs in the spiritual rewards of hard work, frugality, virtue, and dedication, they also emphasized the financial rewards of efficiency, aggressive self-confidence, opportunism, and cunning. Although most members of the professional-managerial stratum genuinely believed in democratic idealism and equality of opportunity, they simultaneously promoted their own families' social exclusivity.

The new suburban clientele endowed the novel act of commissioning the family home with tremendous personal and social meaning. They brought an ambitious program of domestic assumptions to the task, but they did so with confidence that their architects, themselves members of the professional-managerial stratum, shared their most precious values. Architects and clients alike hoped to create an environment that would embody all of the values from their belief system and bring order and cleanliness to their everyday lives and the lives of those around them.

Most contemporary urban observers recognized the difficulty of accomplishing these goals within the existing residential sections of cities. The residents who founded these planned, exclusive suburbs had experienced at firsthand the toll that periodic epidemics, soot, foul odors, neighborhood saloons, noise, and crime could exact on the quality of urban dwellers' daily lives. The most reasonable solution to their own housing needs, it seemed to them, was one that would simultaneously address these pressing urban residential problems, problems that threatened the well-being of all who, like themselves, were tied by occupation and inclination to the city. They would create a home environment that, since it was designed to accommodate their own wholesome family life-style, could serve as a model for housing reform for all the members of the urban community.

Thus, the professional-managerial stratum's ardent participation in the debate concerning the design of the ideal home environment was driven by their desire to satisfy their own residential needs while devising a strategy for positive environmental reform. Both aims were based on a fundamental belief in the power of the environment to influence human behavior and stimulate social change. By transforming that most basic social unit, the family home, professional-managerial stewards would engineer an environment that would subtly but effectively evoke in the urban populace character traits of morally upstanding and socially responsible citizens. As one well-known writer of domestic design manuals put it, "A well-ordered home…is a tremendous missionary society. The light streaming from its windows is an ever-burning beacon of safety to our most cherished social institutions."…

Several anxieties and deeply held convictions focused the debate on the American home and influenced the design program that emerged by consensus from that nationwide discussion. Whether offering one's professional design services, campaigning for housing reform, or simply contemplating the commissioning of one's own home, participants in the debate agreed, first of all, on the gravity of the domestic design problem. Between 1877 and 1917, no other reform strategy seemed so promising, so capable of promoting public health, of stimulating virtue and industry in the urban populace, and fulfilling America's democratic goal "of the lodging of all citizens in good, wholesome habitations." Architect George Maher spoke for many of his colleagues when he declared that "it is in the home that the heart of the nation is most responsive and therefore naturally subject to the most advancement." Stewart Hartshorn, the founder of Short Hills, intended that the careful and original design of suburban houses there would bring about "a moral, social, and intellectual, as well as aesthetic betterment of condition" for residents. In 1904, sociologist Samuel Warren Hue argued that the creation of a better home life offered "the greatest single aid to the relief of society from the burdens of crime." Eugene Gardner, a well-known author of domestic design manuals, was more blunt on this point....."Homebuilding," he said, with all the drama and fervor typical of his social stratum's attitude of the time, "is not the mere spending of money,...it is the shaping of human destiny."

The promotion of home ownership, particularly among the urban lower classes, was an important component of the professional-managerial stratum's positive environmental reform campaign. Widespread suburban home ownership, or as historian Adna Weber phrased it in 1898—the goal of "every man residing in a cottage of his own"—symbolized the essence of the American egalitarian dream. But many individuals also advocated home ownership as a practical means of quelling social unrest and labor agitation in the cities. It could be harnessed, as one Progressive sociologist put it, using the jargon of the day, as "a force in promoting personal and social efficiency." In his 1912 domestic design manual, architect Charles E. White, Jr., summarized several factors that made home ownership a "worthy ambition" and a "lofty ideal": "The houseowner is a broader-minded individual than the tenant. His credit is better.....The houseowner makes a better citizen for he abides more strictly by the law; he is temperate in all things because of his added responsibility. He is more frugal, more thrifty, more likely to seize an opportunity

when it comes his way, because he knows from experience the value and power of money."

The strong advocacy of social change through home design and home ownership placed several crucial constraints upon the design program for the suburban home. For example, the ideal home environment had to be articulated in the form of a model—a general formula adaptable to a variety of domestic and local circumstances. It also had to be economical to build so that it would be suitable for families with limited financial resources. The location of the model home was important as well. If professional-managerial stewards were to create an environment capable of transforming human character, then they had to select a location that allowed them to control all of the factors that they had considered detrimental to family life in the city. Thus, the ideal home environment was conceived as *suburban*, combining "the culture and conveniences of the city with the domestic advantages and natural scenery of the country." Only in such a "middle landscape" could design professionals command both "the primal art of nature and the latest interpretations of science" and technology—the two forces with which they expected to effect a real behavioral transformation.

Most members of the new suburban communities believed that technology, in the hands of experts, possessed nearly limitless potential for bringing continued social and material progress. They viewed the engineering of the ideal home environment, in fact, as a broadly technological process that they promoted, essentially uncritically, as a social panacea. Their infatuation with technology was also revealed in their inclusion of all the latest modern conveniences in the specifications for the model suburban home.

At the same time, these individuals retained the conviction that nature's beauty and goodness could inspire the spiritual and moral regeneration that they hoped would take place in the urban populace. By designing a home so as to place its occupants in daily contact with "fresh air, sunlight, green foliage, and God's blue sky," one might rescue urban commuters from the physically and morally debilitating effects of their contact with the city. The new suburbanites considered the civilizing influence of nature an especially important ingredient in the upbringing of children. In Kenilworth, for example, the Kenilworth Company urged prospective residents to think of the impact of the home environment on the child's character and physical constitution: "Almost imperative becomes the necessity of such a home to parents, where their children, freed from the confinements and frequently undesirable influences of city life, can revel and thrive physically as well as morally in pure air." But many adults also experienced dramatic improvements in health after moving to suburban homes and engaging in the kinds of domestic activities that forged a kinship with nature, such as gardening, strolling, porch-sitting, and the more active forms of outdoor recreation. Their assumption "that the healthiest and happiest life is that which maintains the closest relationship with out-of-doors" remained one of the strongest influences on the design program for the new suburban home.

The model behavior that those belonging to the professional-managerial stratum wished through a carefully engineered home environment to educe in others was based, of course, on their own mode of living. Thus, they tailored the new design program to accommodate and demonstrate their own suburban life-style, which was, first and foremost, family-centered. The new suburbanites, much like conservative civic leaders today, worried that the traditional home and family were falling victim to rampant individualism and the moral decay characteristic of contemporary urban life. Their insistence on the building of "one-family house[s] with private garden and plenty of open space" was premised on their belief that those conditions would best provide parents with the resources for reestablishing moral authority and nourishing familial bonds. Especially important was an environment that in every detail would contribute to the proper upbringing of children, upon which the social future of the stratum's families depended. Fathers and mothers were cautioned that "in constructing their houses they [were] educating their children, teaching them the most lasting lessons in honesty or deceit, as well as in true artistic taste."

The safeguarding of family members' health—"the first essential of good homemaking"—was perhaps the most acute necessity of the family-centered suburban life-style. A home designed to secure a clean water supply, proper drainage, and fresh air offered obvious advantages over residential alternatives in the city. Many individuals were persuaded that a clean and hygienic home environment offered moral benefits, too. As Albert Winslow Cobb put it, "Noisome, corrupt surroundings stupef[ied] human beings and ke[pt] them powerless to break away to something better."…

Parents also hoped to create a repository of those values, so threatened by urban culture, that inspired each person's noblest instincts. Thus, the cultivation of beauty in the design of the home was, to them, a domestic imperative. As far back as 1869, Catharine Beecher and Harriet Beecher Stowe called for the artistic furnishing of the home: "While the aesthetic element must be subordinate to the requirements of physical existence,…it yet holds a place of great significance among the influences which make home happy and attractive, which give it a constant and wholesome power over the young, and contribute much to the education of the entire household in refinement, intellectual development, and moral sensibility."

Although they practiced a family-centered life-style, the new suburbanites did not turn their backs on membership in the larger community. Nor did they relinquish a sense of responsibility for addressing the social problems of the nearby city. We can characterize their life-style most accurately as one that sought to balance family, individuality, and community to include both privacy and social stewardship. To compensate for the loss of individual expression that seemed endemic to urban mass society, members of suburban design communities believed that the home environment ought to strengthen the character and individuality of each household member. Although they occasionally decried the selfish individualism that drove commerce and industry, they recognized that strong personal qualities correlated positively with occupational and social success.

Placing the family in a friendly community of homogeneous, like-minded neighbors was an equally important goal. The loss of community that members of the professional-managerial stratum had experienced in the city— their inability to trust their neighbors or to control their social contacts—was remedied with their removal to planned, exclusive suburbs where community spirit and social interaction prevailed. In Short Hills, St. Martin's, Kenilworth, and Lake of the Isles, residents reported keeping busy with a strenuous round of musical entertainments, card parties, lectures, amateur theatricals, club meetings, and informal dining in each others' homes. They needed dwellings that were hospitable, designed to accommodate the frequent informal gatherings of suburban social life.

Beyond the home and local community, the new suburbanites directed their attention to the alleviation of some of the more challenging social problems in the city. Many of their social reform activities were the special purview of women whose leisure to engage in them depended upon their efficient management of household responsibilities. A majority of the female residents of the four communities devoted considerable time to educational reform, charity, social settlements, public health reform, and other "social housekeeping" and public policy concerns. Although most could count upon at least part-time domestic assistance, they demanded efficiently designed homes equipped with rationally planned service and storage spaces, labor-saving appliances, and easily cleaned and maintained surfaces that minimized the housekeeper's daily workload.

Over the period 1877 to 1917, the debate on the proper design of the home reached a climax and a consensus emerged regarding the program for the model suburban home. The new design program was an ingenious if difficult creation; it reconciled most of the special concerns of those participating in the debate—balanced their potentially conflicting values, accommodated the new suburban life-style, and assuaged their uneasiness about urban social problems. Contributors

to the consensus in communities like Short Hills, St. Martin's, and Kenilworth thought of the home in a fundamentally different way than had their mid-century predecessors. To them, a dwelling was no longer just a private family retreat; it was also a powerful agent of social progress, one that would induce prescribed patterns of behavior in the inhabitants. They believed that only a professionally trained architect could be entrusted with the challenge of applying the new design program to the actual construction of suburban homes. It required the "technical and artistic knowledge" of the architect to "prepar[e] a proper and correct background for family life."…

Those who contributed to the design of houses in suburbs like Short Hills, St. Martin's, Kenilworth, and Lake of the Isles fashioned a domestic environment that precisely represented how they wished to structure their daily lives. During the initial design process, each community also seemed intent upon creating a model—an ideal home environment that might inspire moral and physical improvement in other urban residential communities. Numerous testimonials suggest that the residents of planned, exclusive suburbs did, indeed, liken life in their new suburban houses to "God's very kingdom on the earth." And although their model houses failed to transform the rest of the urban populace, they did inspire the postwar housing that raised the quality of living for thousands of new suburban home owners from the middle reaches of society. The distinctive qualities of the new suburban house type—and, no doubt, of many suburban tract houses modeled on them—did not issue simply from aesthetic considerations, from the architect's desire to make an original or traditional stylistic statement. They were the result of a design community's effort to give real form to the suburban ideal of living in the most straightforward, economical, and artistic manner possible. Despite the constraints imposed on the local design process, the new suburban houses embodied many progressive principles and practices. As Kenilworth's resident architect, George Maher, understood, "originality in design arises from obvious local reasons."

CHAPTER 7

The Other Suburbanites

Class, Racial, and Ethnic Diversity in Early Suburbia

INTRODUCTION

Since suburbs first emerged in North America, working people have claimed a place within them. From the earliest presence of artisans and outcasts in the suburbs of colonial walking cities to a diversity of laborers in twentieth-century suburbia, the working class has occupied an important—if not always recognized—place in American suburban history. For working people, decisions about where to live hinged on multiple factors: cost of living, location of kin and friends, proximity to transportation, availability of affordable housing, ideals about a desirable living environment, and finally, the location of jobs. The last factor had greater influence among these suburbanites than the well-to-do, since most laborers could not always afford the expense of a regular commute. Because the laboring class historically has been dominated by immigrants and people of color, this meant too that suburbia housed a racially and ethnically diverse populace. Their presence suggests a multiplicity of suburban histories, experiences, and meanings. Not only did these "other suburbanites" embrace suburban opportunity with great enthusiasm, but they fashioned their own suburban ideals and ways of life in the process. Their stories bring great richness and complexity to the history of American suburbanization, while provoking controversial questions about the social and cultural meanings of suburban life. At the heart of that controversy lies the question: Who controls and defines the suburban ideal?

Suburbs for working people have assumed many forms. In the era of the walking city, when primitive transportation and communication technologies made proximity to the city center desirable, the outskirts became the place where odious businesses congregated. Meat slaughterers, leather dressers, ragpickers, brewers, junkmen, even prostitutes plied their trades on the city's edge, as did artisans and maritime workers. By the mid-1800s, as the first elite romantic suburbs were emerging, a parallel outward movement of industry and workers occurred. The residential suburbs that developed to house these workers took on various forms. Planned suburbs, such as the model company towns described in chapter 6, reflected the visions and needs of factory owners who hoped to create a pliant labor force. Whether operating from profit motive, paternalistic benevolence, a reform impulse, or a combination of these drives, suburban planners exerted considerable control over the shape and uses of property. While laboring class residents might exert their will within this context, as illustrated vividly in the bloody strike at Pullman, Illinois, in 1894, they faced real constraints to their command of residential space. A second type of suburb, the unplanned, working-class suburb, offered greater freedom and control to residents. The abundance of affordable land around cities before World War II allowed these bare-bones communities to flourish. In unplanned suburbs, residents could build their own homes, raise food on their property, and shape the suburban environment to meet economic need. Geographer Richard Harris, who first characterized these suburbs in historical terms, recognized them as vivid counterpoints to both planned and elite suburbs.[1] In between these two poles was a broad range of working-class suburban neighborhoods in which speculators built rental housing, hoping to profit from workers' demand for space. Housing and living conditions in these suburbs varied from crowded barracks by the mills to commodious streets of owner-occupied homes with yards and gardens. Working-class suburbs can also be classified by their relationship to employment patterns. Industrial suburbs housed factory workers, while many affluent commuter suburbs housed large numbers of domestic workers—often African Americans and immigrants—who serviced the homes of nearby wealthy suburbanites.

Working-class suburbs were remarkably widespread in North America. As Harris found, by 1940 suburbs had proportionately more working-class residents than the inner-city core in three of the six largest cities in the United States.[2] Similarly, political scientist Todd Gardener concluded that, among all but the largest metropolitan areas, "the suburbs were generally of lower status than central cities."[3] Even in a city like Chicago, where blue-collar suburbs were in the minority, the families of steelworkers, tool makers, railroad laborers, and domestic servants lived in modest suburbs like Chicago Heights, Blue Island, Maywood, and parts of Evanston and Glencoe. Ethnic suburbanites, in turn, were numerous: Poles in Cicero and Posen, Czechs in Berwyn, Italians in Stone Park, Jews in Skokie, and African Americans in Robbins, Phoenix, and East Chicago Heights. The story was similar in city after city.

Recent scholarship on African-American, immigrant, and working-class suburbia has touched off debates among urban scholars, particularly around the contested meanings of home ownership and the suburban ideal. As in most historical debates, point of view is critical. Home ownership is a case in point. From the perspective of industrialists like Harvey Firestone or Henry Ford, home ownership was a way to make workers loyal, tractable, and invested in the status quo. More broadly, they saw it as a means to promote social and cultural assimilation, to "Americanize" immigrant and ethnic families. Some scholars took off from this assumption, arguing that home ownership became a tool in the hands of industrialists to create dependency among the working class—the "lawns for pawns" thesis.[4] From the perspective of laboring families, however, home ownership could mean something radically different—independence, freedom, and security against unpredictable employment. Historians have waged arguments in all of these directions.

Similarly, debate has swirled around the meaning of the suburban ideal. Recent studies contend that these "other suburbanites" embraced a distinctive suburban ideal, sometimes starkly dissimilar from the elite ideal. These contrasts raise questions about who controls cultural understanding—in this case, the meaning of suburbs and suburban life. To what extent did social distinctions such as class and race produce different ideologies and ways of life? We have seen that the rise of a pastoral suburban ideal was closely related to the formation of a middle class in the nineteenth century. But did this elite ideal trickle down to the lower classes? Or did working people ascribe their own meanings to suburban life, independent of middle- or upper-class mores? How powerful—or hegemonic—were upper-class ideas? In what ways did these ideals intersect, overlap, and influence one another?

This chapter offers documents and essays that engage these questions, suggesting diverse perspectives on working-class suburbanites and their communities. The selections reinforce the point that suburbia was not only a physical fact, but also a cultural idea that was often contested. The debate over how to define suburbia and its social meaning is more than a matter of mere semantics. As the twentieth century wore on, the concept of suburbs as a place apart, a haven for a restricted class of Americans, became a spatial basis for social power, privilege, and wealth. By laying exclusive claim to the suburban moniker, this privileged class sought to inscribe suburban space with potent meanings about who belonged and who didn't, meanings that reinforced hierarchies of race and class in America. "Suburb," in this view, meant *only* white and well off. The presence of workers, people of color, and immigrants in suburbia challenges these assertions on multiple levels and invites a nuanced, contested perspective on meanings of space in the modern metropolis.

DOCUMENTS

Document 7-1 is an interview with Samuel Eberly Gross, a Chicago subdivider and builder who styled himself "the World's Greatest Real Estate Promoter." Gross developed affordable suburbs for both the middle and working classes, involving himself at multiple levels of the land development process: subdivision, home building, even financing. In this sense, he was a forerunner to twentieth-century "community builders" like J.C. Nichols and William Levitt. These for-profit developers played a fundamental role in the suburbanization process. In this 1890 interview, Gross not only places American workingmen's homes in international perspective, but inevitably advertises the superiority of American models—such as the ones he built and sold. **Document 7-2** is an advertisement for one of Gross's Chicago subdivisions aimed at working people. Noted for their theatricality, his ads were published in handbills distributed outside of factories and in a variety of newspapers, including the labor and foreign language press. This leaflet also evokes an ideology of home ownership meant to appeal to working-class buyers. In **Document 7-3**, Progressive reformers Sophonisba Breckenridge and Edith Abbott depict working-class home ownership in a wholly different light. As advocates for child welfare reform associated with the famous Hull House, they wrote this study of truant and nonattending schoolchildren in Chicago in hopes of bringing about greater enforcement of compulsory school attendance laws. In this excerpt, they identify the great sacrifices that immigrant families made to achieve home ownership, in ways that clashed with middle-class mores. As a result, the authors reach a somewhat surprising conclusion about working-class home ownership.

Document 7-4 is an excerpt from Margaret Byington's book *Homestead: The Households of a Mill Town*, published in 1910 as part of the Pittsburgh Survey, a path-breaking study of urban social conditions. Byington and her colleagues on the Survey were Progressives, intent on improving living conditions in the industrial metropolis by conducting empirical studies and then agitating for reform. *Homestead* is a remarkable document for its close, detailed descriptions of everyday life in an industrial suburb outside of Pittsburgh. In this excerpt, Byington perceptively points out the contradictions in working-class home ownership—its capacity to foster both independence and dependency. She conveys, too, the multiple meanings that homes held for the steel workers of Homestead. **Document 7-5**, a publicity booklet published by the Los Angeles Chamber of Commerce in 1927, offers an argument for working-class home ownership from the perspective of manufacturers. Since the 1910s, LA had been aggressively "open shop," discouraging labor unions and nurturing a "probusiness" climate. Central in this effort was the creation of an image of LA as a suburban metropolis inhabited by contented laborers who owned homes, which sealed their commitment to the capitalist status quo.

Document 7-6 offers a view of working-class suburbia from the inside out. It comes from the memoir of Mary Helen Ponce, who grew up during the 1940s in Pacoima, a suburb of working-class Mexicans and Mexican Americans northeast of Los Angeles. Ponce's description evokes a distinctive suburban ideal among these residents—an intermingling of nature, gardens, pride in one's home, family, even picket fences. Economic and cultural imperatives also shaped this suburban ideal, affording space for extended family, productive gardens, and the freedom to build without restriction. In **Document 7-7**, baseball legend Hank Aaron recalls his childhood in Toulminville, a suburb of Mobile, Alabama. His rich description conveys not only the look and feel of the homes and community, but also their meaning to his family. **Document 7-8** is a gallery of photographs of working-class suburbs, taken by photographers working for the federal government during the 1930s and 1940s. These photographers revealed widespread evidence of informal building and domestic production in rough hewn suburbs. Two photographs taken by John Vachon near Detroit capture the operation of a cheap real estate market and owner-building by families drawn to the area for wartime jobs. Similar subdivisions were common in the Motor City in the early twentieth century. A third photograph captures the outcome of similar efforts near New Brunswick, New Jersey. Advertisements for low-cost building lots in this area appeared in African-American newspapers of the Northeast during the 1920s. Many of the resulting homes were makeshift, but they sheltered close-knit families whose members used the surrounding landscape in economically productive ways.

How did working-class suburbs differ from those of the middle class? What was different or similar? Was there a working-class, African-American or Mexican-American suburban ideal? What were its elements? What were the multiple meanings of home ownership — to the working class, to industrialists, to Progressive reformers? Were these meanings contradictory or compatible?

7-1. DEVELOPER S. E. GROSS COMPARES EUROPEAN AND AMERICAN HOMES, 1890

Source: "European versus American Homes," *Chicago Tribune*, January 19, 1890.

S. E. Gross, the well-known home builder and subdivider, saw much on his recent European trip that escapes the ordinary tourist's eye. The following remarks by him on real estate methods abroad contain interesting points which cannot be found in any guidebook nor in the note-books of the foreign newspaper correspondents:

"I first visited the principal cities of Ireland. In none of them did I find a system such as we have in Chicago for furnishing lots and houses to the industrial classes. Upon inquiry I found that this condition arose not from any lack of desire to acquire property and homes, but from an inherited and otherwise established policy among the large landed proprietors and nobility who own vacant tracts and country seats around the cities not to parcel it out to small owners, the result being that the larger part of the population of the cities is congregated in crowded tenement quarters. In Scotland this condition did not exist to the same extent, and in the City of Glasgow, which contains a vast industrial population, I found considerable attention being paid to extending suburban growth by building and selling houses to the industrial class.

"The City of London, among all those visited, stands at the head in suburban growth and the ownership in fee by small proprietors. However, the method of granting the use of property to house-owners on ninety-nine year leases of ground is very extensively adopted by land-owners, and much more so than it should be for the interests of the people....

"I was several months in Paris, and attended the World's Exposition in all its departments, besides doing some work for the interests of Chicago for the World's Fair in 1892. I found there a department for the exhibit of houses for workingmen, a number of which were erected on the grounds. Had I known of this in time I should certainly have put up a model Chicago cottage, and I have no doubt that it would have received most favorable mention and probably the highest award, for the Chicago cottage contains the maximum of artistic taste and comfort in homes of this class. The exposition exhibit was interesting to me as showing the idea in regard to building for workingmen as developed abroad. I found that the grace and sentiment which usually surround the American home, however humble, were here in a great measure, sacrificed to the expediency of simple shelter and plainness of construction. A cottage in America for a workingman does not usually or necessarily bear upon it a badge of class inferiority and can be inhabited with comfort and due regard to appearances equally by a capitalist in independent circumstances or by a workingman receiving ordinary wages; but the home of the workingman, as developed abroad, seems to have placed upon it in the method of construction a badge which conveys to the observer an idea of poverty and a servile condition of the owner, and has not the stamp of individuality and independence of character found usually in American homes, even of the most ordinary workingman. That is to say, the home sentiment does not seem to have been cultivated, or to have the same importance either to the builder or the owner of a home as that in America.

"In Paris, Rome, Naples, and other large cities I found the prevalent tendency to be that of crowding the population into large structures near the centers of cities rather than in extending it to the circumference in more diversified and healthful homes....

"After investigating the condition and resources of the industrial classes of Europe my conclusions are that the comparative lack of ownership of homes among them may be attributed to many centuries of oppressive laws and class hostility, to the uncertainty of employment and scantiness of wages, and to devastating wars which place both homes and lives in jeopardy; but in America all these adverse environments are changed, and the same classes of people under our institutions become the most earnest and appreciative owners of what, in fact, is the noblest result of the civilization of the nineteenth century, the American home."

7-2. S.E. GROSS ADVERTISES "THE WORKING MAN'S REWARD," 1891

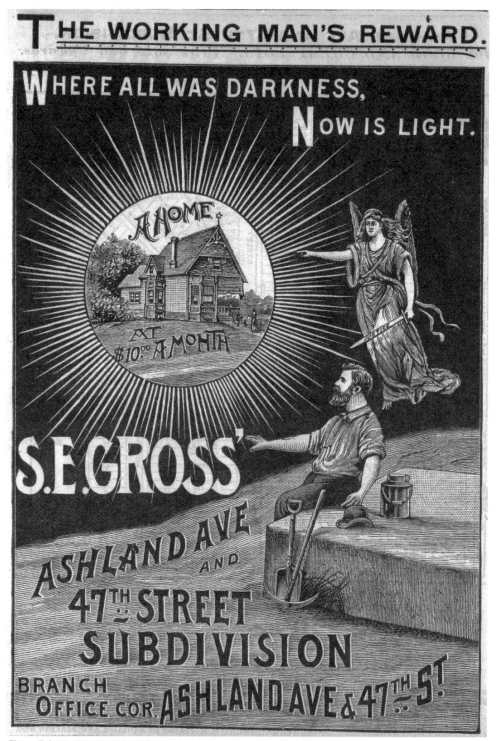

Figure 7-1 The Working Man's Reward, ca. 1891. Advertisement for a Chicago subdivision developed by S.E. Gross, targeting working-class families. The Chicago Historical Society, ICHi-03656.

7-3. TWO PROGRESSIVE REFORMERS CRITIQUE WORKING-CLASS HOME OWNERSHIP, 1912

Source: Sophonisba P. Breckenridge and Edith Abbott, *The Delinquent Child and the Home* (New York: Charities Publication Committee, 1912).

Perhaps the most striking single effect of poverty that seems to have a direct connection with delinquency is the heavy burden of pecuniary responsibility which the child helps to bear. It is the normal thing [in two case study groups of the poor]…for children to leave school and go to work at fourteen. But many of them begin to work much earlier.…

This question of the control of the mother over what the child earns is often a source of much ill feeling between them.…

It must not be overlooked that in many instances it is not simple poverty, but undue frugality, or even avarice, that is responsible for the attitude of the parents to the child's wages. One very common form of saving which frequently works a hardship upon the children is the purchase of a home, a practice peculiarly common to the foreign groups. Among the families of the delinquent boys whose homes were visited, it was found that 148 out of 584, one-fourth of the whole number, claimed to own the houses in which they lived. In many cases, of course, the property was heavily mortgaged, or they were making the purchase by the instalment plan and all the family savings went to meet the necessary payments. This "land-hunger" of the European peasant, as it is sometimes called, reacts upon the children in many ways. Not only does it mean that they go to work early, giving all their small earnings over to their parents, with no allowance for recreation or small personal expenditures so dear to the heart of the young girl or boy, but often it means that the mother goes out to work and leaves the house and the children uncared for, that the home is overcrowded, and that the children are encouraged to pick up wood and coal—a practice which so often leads to petty depredations. One German family, after a struggle of years, succeeded in paying for the home, but the family history shows how much the mother had sacrificed to obtain this satisfaction. She was said to "encourage the children to bring stolen things home, such as coal, chickens, food, etc." One of the little boys was brought into court when he was nine years old, charged with stealing all these things, but it was the mother, of course, who really needed to be put on probation.…

In another case, where the family economized in a small way by always getting grain from empty freight cars for their chickens, they had paid for their home in spite of the fact that the father was only a poor lumber yard laborer, earning $3.00 a week through a large part of the winter. The family were extremely frugal, never spent any money except for absolute necessities, and had no amusements or recreation of any sort.

The cases of young girls who are exploited by parents who want to buy a home or who are avaricious and miserly, are almost too pitiful to record. A German girl was taken out of school and put in a tailor shop when she was very small. Her father was dead, her grandfather was miserly, and her mother cared too much about buying her house. She had always made the girl work very hard, took all she earned, and was cruel and exacting. When the girl was fifteen she ran away, worked in the office of a cheap hotel, became immoral, and was sent to Geneva. The mother is interested in her now only because she hopes to get the girl back so that she can have her wages again.

7-4. MARGARET BYINGTON PROFILES THE INDUSTRIAL SUBURB OF HOMESTEAD, PENNSYLVANIA, 1910

Source: Margaret F. Byington, *Homestead: The Households of a Mill Town* (New York: Charities Publication Committee, 1910).

Homestead gives at the first a sense of the stress of industry rather than of the old time household cheer which its name suggests. The banks of the brown Monongahela are preempted on one side by the railroad, on the other by unsightly stretches of mill yards. Gray plumes of smoke hang heavily from the stacks of the long, low mill buildings, and noise and effort dominate what once were quiet pasture lands.

On the slope which rises steeply behind the mill are the Carnegie Library and the "mansion" of the mill superintendent, with the larger and more attractive dwellings of the town grouped about two small parks. Here and there the towers of a church rise in relief. The green of the parks modifies the first impression of dreariness by one of prosperity such as is not infrequent in American industrial towns. Turn up a side street, however, and you pass uniform frame houses, closely built and dulled by the smoke; and below, on the flats behind the mill, are cluttered alleys, unsightly and unsanitary, the dwelling place of the Slavic laborers. The trees are dwarfed and the foliage withered by the fumes; the air is gray, and only from the top of the hill above the smoke is the sky clear blue.

There is more to tell, however, than can be gained by first impressions. The Homestead I would interpret in detail is neither the mill nor the town, but is made up of the households of working people, the sturdy Scotch and Welsh and German of the early immigration, the sons of Yankee "buckwheats," and the daughters of Pennsylvania Dutch farmers....

Homestead is a community of approximately 25,000 people, chiefly mill workers and their families....

In 1871, the Homestead Bank and Life Insurance Company, which had bought the farms, cut them up into building lots and put them on the market, intending that Homestead should be a residential suburb....

In 1881, when [Andrew] Klomans built a steel mill on the banks of the river, the step definitely determining the future of Homestead was taken. The Klomans mill was absorbed by the Carnegie Steel Company in 1886, and became in turn one of the most important plants of the United States Steel Corporation on its organization in 1901. The site of Homestead made its part in this industrial development almost inevitable....

Rent in the Household Budget

As in most American towns of the last century's building, the original lay-out of Home-

stead had little to commend it....It is the customary checker-board plan, ill adapted to the gullied hill slopes and triangular flats of a river bend....The lots in Homestead are usually narrow, not more than 20 or 25 feet in width. Originally, there was ample room between the streets for each house to have a good garden in the rear, with plenty of air and freedom, and in the more open parts of the town these gardens are still a source of pleasure. But in other sections they are being built upon and rear houses are multiplying along the alleys which were cut between parallel streets to give access to back doors. In the district nearest the mill, the alleys are paved and are built up almost solid. The houses here, though still only two stories high, cover so large a proportion of the land as to limit the amount of air and light within doors, as well as the space left for the children to play outside. The region is occupied by the Slavs....

There are in scattered sections attractive residences belonging to business and professional men; but in those parts of Homestead where the working people live, few evidences are to be found of attempts to make dwellings attractive architecturally. They are of that dreary type of small, closely-set frame structure so characteristic of a rapidly growing industrial community. The real estate companies, in their desire for economy, naturally plan their houses on an inexpensive and, as far as possible, uniform scale, and rising land values lead to the use of narrow lots. The common type of house has four rooms, two on a floor, the front door opening directly on the streets....The monotony of street after street is broken only by bits of lawn and flowers in front. Where there are yards in the rear, they serve as play places for the children, and offer rest and refreshment to the grownups. As the men are usually too tired to enjoy working in them, the women often assume the task of keeping the flowers and grass in order and find it a welcome change from the hot kitchen....

On the hill the gardens have a substantial aspect. One family utilized an empty lot, and the beans, squashes, and other vegetables raised there so decreased the family's cost of living that they declined to keep an account since they said it would not fairly represent

Figure 7-2 Backyard possibilities in Homestead, I and II, 1910. Photos by Hine. Illustration in original, 48 facing plate.

their table expenses. An item of sixty cents for garden seeds in the early spring in another family's budget gave promise of both pleasure and profit. Many of the families also save a good deal by keeping hens. On one visit, hearing a curious noise beneath my chair, I looked down to find a friendly chicken which had come for a feast of crumbs. One woman kept a few hens to provide fresh eggs for her husband's bucket. After his death she found that by selling them she could add a little to a slender income. The gardens too develop neighborliness of spirit, since the women often discuss over the fences their horticultural ambitions....

[O]vercrowding is ordinarily a result of financial necessity, rather than of either hoarding or spendthrift habits. I am speaking here of the families who rent small houses or let out their rooms...When income permits, most families secure room enough to make a genuine home life possible. How long people would maintain this standard in the face of prolonged hard times it is difficult to say....A couple who had considered a $25 five-room house none too spacious, sublet two rooms for $8.00 to another couple who had formerly occupied a three-room $12 tenement. This process, which was going on throughout the town during the months of the depression, shows that rent is an item that is cut down when economy becomes necessary....

Throughout the part of the town occupied by the English-speaking workmen, we find these evidences of a very real interest in the home. More substantial proof of the instinct of homemaking is shown in the often heroic

efforts to buy the house. In view of the number of families who could not pay sufficient rent to secure either rooms enough for comfortable living or sanitary conveniences, it is a striking fact that according to the census figures of 1900, 586 families in Homestead borough, 25.7 per cent of the total number, held title to their homes; and 47.4 per cent of these were free from encumbrance. Personal interviews have corroborated this evidence that mill-town workingmen wish to own their dwellings....

Some of the other means adopted to secure a home are illustrated in the story of a delightful Englishman, once a silk weaver but now an engineer in the mill, who lives in Munhall Hollow. The meaning of the word Homestead is all but forgotten by its people, but the story of this man's house building shows much of the spirit of the old settlers. When he wished to build, he had very little money. Mr. Munhall, who was then living, gave him a note to a lumber firm, who sold him $200 worth of lumber on credit. He paid down $24 for the lease of a lot. Since he did part of the work, the labor cost on his three-room house was only about $40. As soon as these debts were paid, he incurred another for $200 in order to enlarge the kitchen and build a second bedroom over it; then he added a front porch and later a shed in the rear for a storehouse, with a chicken coop beside it. All this was done while there were three children at home, and on the income of an engineer, not over $3.00 a day. Now he and his wife, despite the disadvantage of not having a freehold in the land, take in their

Figure 7-3 1. Frame Houses, 1910. Five rooms and bath. 2. Brick Houses. Four rooms and bath; cemented cellars; yard 40 x 400. $2700 to $2800. Built by Homestead Realty Co. 3. Residence Street. Tenanted largely by business and professional men. The first and third houses are owned by mill men not superintendents. Illustration in original, 60 facing plate.

comfortable though simple home the pride of the creator as well as of the owner—a feeling rare in these days of huge tenements and "company houses," when men accept whatever can be had for the renting and when long shifts make it difficult for them to put the work of their hands into their homes if they would....

Since work in Homestead is steady, loss of income due to lack of employment has not been so serious a menace to house buying as in many communities....If a man has shown any disposition to honesty,—and in Homestead it is possible to know people intimately,—the real estate company will allow him,

when in a hard place, to suspend all payments except interest on the mortgage....

The house-buyer, nevertheless, has his hazards, and they are very real ones. The greatest difficulty arises from periodical cuts in wages. In 1908 for example, in mid-winter, I was told that the rate of wages of tonnage men was reduced in some cases 16 2/3 per cent. A family which by careful economy out of the wages current in the fall, could make the extra expenditure toward buying a house, might after such a cut find itself in a serious predicament. To keep on with payments would mean cutting down everywhere margins that are already small. As these wage cuts can never be foreseen, they introduce so serious an element of uncertainty that many doubt the wisdom of embarking their entire capital, though small, in such a venture....When a family has put all its savings into a house, death, discharge, or displacement of the man by a machine, may compel a forced sale; a strike or season of hard times, or the removal of a plant from a given town, may leave him in a worse predicament.

Home owning, moreover, lessens the mobility of labor, since when one is partly paid for a man will pull up stakes and seek work elsewhere only under extreme pressure. From the point of view of the company, this is an ever present advantage. For the employe it is a potential disadvantage, especially in a town like Homestead where, since the strike of 1892, the men have had no voice in the matter of wages and no security as to length of employment. Hitherto the disadvantages to the employe house-owners have not been extreme because with the lack of sufficient houses in Homestead it has been easy to realize upon them. In the average mill town, however, house ownership may prove an encumbrance to the workingman who wants to sell his labor in the highest market....

Homestead has its ideals,—ideals of a genuine home life for the family, if possible in a home of its own, where there shall be sufficient leisure and attractive enough surroundings to make it the center for happy lives; ideals of such security as in time of sickness or misfortune shall enable the home to care for its own. With the wages offered by the industry many of the workers can attain these ideals, if at all, only by unremitting work and inexorable compromises. We find housekeepers facing cheerfully the problem of providing wholesome and attractive food, that shall at the same time be economical, three times a day; giving up even five-cent treats at the nickelodeon to save for a house. We find them failing often, failing through ignorance or indifference, but also succeeding against heavy odds. To the onlooker it is a brave fight, the braver that it is so full of deadly monotony, a fight the weapons of which are pots and pans and bargain sales. In its outcome, however, is bound up the happiness and efficiency of the next generation.

7-5. THE LOS ANGELES CHAMBER OF COMMERCE SELLS SUBURBIA TO INDUSTRIALISTS, 1927

Source: Los Angeles Chamber of Commerce, Industrial Department, *Facts About Industrial Los Angeles: Nature's Workshop* (Los Angeles: Los Angeles Chamber of Commerce, 1927).

Los Angeles does not boast of cheap labor. It boasts of efficient labor, and efficient labor is what the manufacturer today is looking for.

The real secret of the efficiency of the workers of Southern California may be found in their home life....A tenement is unknown here and the workers live in their own little bungalows, surrounded by plenty of land for fruits, vegetables and flowers, and where children romp and play throughout the entire year under climatic conditions that are as nearly ideal as exist anywhere on the face of the earth. This spells contentment and contentment spells efficiency.

But there is another angle to the climatic conditions and that is, throughout the year, the nights are cool and humidity is unknown. Consequently, the worker finds rest and refreshment for his daily tasks....

There is no need for the manufacturer in Southern California to think of expenditures for recreational purposes. Nature provides such for him free of expense. There are few families here who do not own some kind of an automobile or conveyance, and in their spare time, within an hour they can go from the mountains to the sea and play under those same conditions and in those same surroundings that attract our tourists and visitors by the hundreds of thousands.

There is pride of ownership and industrial productiveness in the breast of the Los Angeles worker, for here he finds the mecca of his hopes and ambitions, contentment for his family and living conditions incomparably better than he could secure anywhere else.

For a little effort on his part he can have the fruits and vegetables known in the East, at much less cost, his living expenses can be sharply reduced and his family supplied with luxuries from his own backyard.

To the less favored manufacturer who has and is concerned with labor difficulties, inefficient workers and a constantly rising labor cost, Los Angeles and Southern California offer a real opportunity for him to operate WHERE NATURE HELPS INDUSTRY MOST.

7-6. MARY HELEN PONCE RECOLLECTS LIFE IN A MEXICAN-AMERICAN SUBURB, 1993

Source: Mary Helen Ponce, *Hoyt Street: An Autobiography* (Albuquerque: University of New Mexico Press, 1993).

The town of Pacoima lay to the northeast of Los Angeles, about three miles south of the city of San Fernando. The blue-grey San Gabriel Mountains rose toward the east; toward the west other small towns dotted the area. Farther west lay the blue Pacific and the rest of the world. The barrio, as I knew it, extended from San Fernando Road to Glenoaks Boulevard on the east and from Filmore and Pierce streets on the north. We lived in the shadow of Los Angeles, twenty odd miles to the south.

Most of the townspeople were Mexican immigrants, as were my parents, who had moved to Pacoima in the 1920s. Across the tracks lived the white folks, many of them Okies. There were few blacks in the area up until the early fifties, when the Joe Louis housing tract near Glenoaks Boulevard allowed black ex-GIs to buy there.

Many men in the barrio worked in agriculture, en el fil, weeding, pruning, or watering various crops. Others worked as troqueros, as did Rocky, my father's compadre, who each fall drove workers in his truck to the walnut orchards of Camarillo. Men who owned their own trucks worked for themselves. They lugged fertilizer from poultry farms to nearby ranches or trucked produce into Los Angeles. Still others took the bus to the union hall in San Fernando, where they hired out as "casual laborers" or found work in the packinghouse in that same town. A neighbor, el Señor Flores, owned a flower nursery; Don Jesús, a kind, rotund man, had his own grocery store. For the most part men either hired out as unskilled laborers or worked for themselves, as did my father, who sold used wood from our backyard.

Pacoima streets were unpaved, full of holes and rocks. During a rain the rich, brown mud clung to our shoes. Van Nuys Boulevard, the main street, was paved and lit with lamps that burned till late at night; that was where most stores and businesses were located. The boulevard cut through the middle of the barrio, then continued west to Van Nuys, North Hollywood, and other towns....

Homes in Pacas, as we called Pacoima, were modest, ranging from a one-room shack where people slept in the "front room," to the more elegant homes such as Rocky's, which boasted an ample living room, a bathroom with tile and chrome faucets, and a separate bedroom for each child. On our street, and in the immediate neighborhood, houses were one story high except for that of the Torres family; theirs had upstairs bedrooms with tall windows. In the next block was the quasi-Victorian structure belonging to Doña Mercedes. It sat back from the street, as if ashamed to be seen next to older, shabbier homes.

On Hoyt Street the houses were neither fancy nor ugly, but like the houses of poor folks everywhere. While some were constructed of stucco, the majority were of wood, madera. Wood was plentiful and cheaper than cement, so wood it was. The houses, while not uniform, had some similarities: a window on each side and a door smack in the middle. Others appeared lopsided because of the many additions tacked on as a family grew. Still others were of different types of wood bought for price and not appearance. From afar it was easy to spot the short boards nailed next to the smooth planks of polished wood bought at the lumberyard. People were innovative, too, and sometimes built houses of rock and cement....

Not all homes had electricity or indoor plumbing. Many casitas on Hoyt Street still had an outhouse somewhere in the back, hidden behind a nopalera or standing blatantly in the middle of the yard. Once the electrical lines reached Van Nuys Boulevard, and local residents were allowed to connect, my father was among the first to do so. After he wired our house, he did that of Doña Luisa, our adopted grandmother, who lived next door. She, like others in our town, continued to use la lámpara de petroleo, which had a long wick and gave only a faint light. She felt that electricity was terribly expensive, and insisted that every time el foco was turned on, it cost a penny! Each time I yanked the string hanging from the light bulb on the ceiling, Doña Luisa pursed her thin lips and reminded me I was wasting electricity—and pennies. She then lit the kerosene lamp and set it next to the trunk alongside her bed.

Mejicanos in our town took pride in their homes and, when money allowed, repaired a dilapidated roof or painted their casitas a bright color. They took special pride in having a yard full of plants and flowers, and these grew well in the rich California soil. La familia Santos had a pretty front yard with bright red geraniums growing in old cans and fruit trees along the side. Like other women in our street, each morning Mrs. Santos raked the front yard, sprinkled water on it to keep the dust down, then trimmed her geraniums....Still other casitas sported a porch swing where, on warm summer evenings, adults gossiped or told stories of la llorona to pesky children, the soft Spanish words drifting down Hoyt Street and dissolving into the night. While the homes on our street were different in color, shape, and size, they had one thing in common: each had a junk pile somewhere in the back yard.

El yonque was important for folks who were short on money but full of ingenuity. The junk pile held the necessary parts to wire a car together or replace rusted pipes, and it helped keep folks from spending hard-earned cash at the hardware store in town. The Morenos had not one but several junk piles in their huge yard. On one side la Señora Moreno grew flowers and vegetables. On the other were two piles of junk that included automobile parts: engines, carburetors, dented fenders, old batteries, and flat tires. Except for la familia Soto, whose backyard held only a crude table and benches and a row of apricot trees, the junk pile was an accepted part of a Mexican household.

My father, too, clung to junk, a thing that bothered my mother, who functioned best in a clean and orderly household. The yonque, or clutter as I thought of it, was of value to my father as it was to other pobres. Pipes, rusty tin tubs, old tires, wood, wire, and car radios lay scattered here and there. My father was certain that at some point, good use could be made of the stuff. Neighbors and friends would come by for a piece of pipe, a strip of tar paper, or some two-by-fours, all from the junk pile and all freely given to someone in need.

People in Pacoima, I often thought, needed more space than did those in upwardly mobile San Fernando, where homes had sidewalks and paved streets, but sat close together, as if afraid to breathe too much of their neighbor's air. On Hoyt Street most residents had once lived in Mexican ranchitos and had a greater need for land. In the large double lots, they planted fruit trees, vegetable and flower gardens, and assorted hierbas that also grew in Mexico. The Garcias had a nopalera, a wall of prickly pear cactus in the back that served two purposes: it was a fence that kept out errant dogs and kids, and it also provided food. The succulent cactus, nopalitos, were popular during Lent along with deep-fried camarones, shrimp; the prickly pear fruits, or tunas, fell off when ripe and were quickly gobbled up....

Our house was built by my father when he and my mother and their three older children moved from Ventura to the San Fernando Valley, sometime in the 1920s. Originally our house had three rooms: a kitchen and two bedrooms. The large kitchen extended the length of the house. Later, as his family grew, my father added on to the house, with some interesting results—our kitchen had a window that opened into the living room!...

As we grew older, my father built los cuartitos. The men's rooms, as we called them, were separate from the main house, with windows that looked out on the front and back yards, and had room for several beds. My two older brothers slept there. Later, when my mother had her own bedroom, my father too slept there. Josey, the youngest, slept in my mother's room. From the age of three, I slept with Doña Luisa. Later my uncles, who emigrated as braceros, also slept in the men's rooms. As was the custom, they first stayed with a close relative, in this case my father. Much later their sons laid claim to the beds used earlier by their fathers....

Facing the street was a garden with rambling roses and yellow and white daisies. In spring and summer, Shasta daisies, called margaritas, bloomed next to healthy weeds. In the middle of the lawn, toward the right, grew an orange tree with glossy green leaves; in the summer the intoxicating, sweet smell of orange blossoms attracted hordes of bees, but it never gave oranges. Near the front porch was una rosa de castilla, a bush of roses with velvet petals and huge thorns. A wisteria vine grew alongside my mother's bedroom window; its branches, like tentacles, reached to the corner, where they met the rambling roses growing on the opposite wall....

In the back, near the alley, was the outhouse made of old, old wood with a rickety door and two seats, or holes. I hated to use it, scared stiff of falling into the bigger hole. I refused to use Doña Luisa's outhouse, as it was too close to the alley, and was relieved when my father, who wanted the best for his family, built our first bathroom. He left the outhouse for emergencies. Although I had to wait my turn for the bathroom, I refused to use el excuzado after that.

My father had a thing about fences. We had many different ones! One year I counted eight different fences on our property. A picket fence on cement faced Hoyt Street. The wall facing the Montalvos' was made of chicken wire, and cement slabs on a cement foundation. Alongside the men's rooms was

Figure 7-4 Hoyt Street, Pacoima, California, 2005. The construction of in-fill housing and modern infrastructure has transformed the landscape of Mary Helen Ponce's home town, but residents' affinity for single family homes and individuated fencing appears to have endured through time. Photograph by Becky Nicolaides.

a wooden fence that connected with the garage. The back fence next to the alley was made of wood overgrown with cactus. The side fence behind which the goats and chickens were kept was part of the cactus wall. No fence was to be found between Doña Luisa's house and ours, only my mother's flowers and my father's chiles and tomatoes. Doña Luisa, though not a blood relative, was considered family; *entre familia* there was no need for fences.

My father's pride and joy was the white picket fence. It faced Hoyt Street and was his original design, or so he liked to think. The wooden spikes were set in cement; the bottom half was of wood and cement slabs set in concrete. Each picket was exactly the same size; each was nailed to a thin cross-piece. When finished it was sanded and then painted white. We were not allowed to hang onto this fence, which was the only one of its kind on our street. I hated el cerco that faced the Montalvos; it looked like a huge cement wall and was out of place next to the pretty picket fence. But this too was my father's original design.

On the summer day on which he poured the concrete for this wall, my father allowed Josey and me to scratch our names on the still wet cement. Josey, acting like the brat he was, insisted on putting his handprint on the cement too! When I tried to do the same he pushed me; I fell on the cement, and left two knee holes on the smooth finish! My father became angry, but just for a minute. After that he no longer let Josey and me help him but told us to go play on the tree swing. For years I could still make out the names on the wall. Josey. Mary Helen. June, 1945.

While studying the many fences I often thought that perhaps my father's family had not owned property in Mexico. It was important for him to fence, to secure the right of ownership. Or perhaps, unknown to us, my father was an artist who liked to express himself in works of cement, wire, and wood. Probably he liked to keep busy. Like most men of his generation, my father hated to be de oquis, with nothing to do.

Josey and I were always alert for the sound of cement being mixed in the big wheelbarrow. This meant a new wall would soon go up at 13011 Hoyt Street, where we might record our names for posterity.

7-7. HANK AARON RECALLS A CHILDHOOD IN TOULMINVILLE, ALABAMA, 1991

Source: Hank Aaron and Lonnie Wheeler, *I Had a Hammer.* Copyright © 1991 by Henry Aaron and Lonnie Wheeler. Reprinted by permission of HarperCollins Publishers.

I was eight when we moved to Toulminville in 1942. They were tearing down an old house close to where we lived in Down The Bay [a neighborhood in Mobile], so we grabbed up the lumber and Mama spent her days pulling out nails. Daddy bought two overgrown lots at $55 apiece and paid a couple of carpenters $100 to build us six rooms, which was twice as many as we were accustomed to. When the walls and roof were up, we moved in, and that was it—no rent or mortgage, it was ours. We were a proud family, because the way we saw it, the only people who owned their own homes were rich folks and Aarons. After the house was built, we just kept patching it up and putting on new layers—shingles, felt, brick, whatever we could get. When I made some money in baseball, we added a back room, and my parents still live there. I've told Mama I would buy her a big house in a new neighborhood, but she says she's not looking for any big house, she's just looking for Jesus.

There were only two or three houses on Edwards Street when we moved there. It was wide open, with a dairy on the corner and country things on every side of us—cows, chickens, hogs, cornfields, sugarcane, watermelon patches, pecan groves, and blackberry thickets. The streets were just mudholes that cars were always getting stuck in. We took out water from a well, and for heating and cooking we brought in whatever wood we could find. Sometimes we'd strip it off an old abandoned farmhouse. There were no lights in our house—not even windows. A kerosene lamp was all we needed. The bathroom was an outhouse in the backyard. It was a good outhouse—we built it ourselves—but Mama was always scared to death that one of us would fall down that hole.

Mama stayed at home and looked after the kids during the day. Now and then she would clean somebody's house for two dollars, but she likes to brag that she never hired a baby sitter in her life—which is something to brag about, considering that there were eight of us. I often wonder how Mama and Daddy managed with all those kids. Nobody knew anything back then about family planning; they just kept having kids whether there was room and food for them or not. None of us ever had a bed to himself. And we almost never ate anything that was store-bought. I've gone many, many weeks with just corn bread, butter beans, and collard greens. Maybe we'd have a piece of pork to season the greens but we were practically vegetarians before we ever heard of the word. We tried to keep a hog in the backyard to kill every year, and everything else came from the garden. You can believe the Aaron kids didn't have any fat on them. My sister Gloria was so skinny that I called her Neck Bone. My brother Tommie's nickname was Pork Chop, because he always wanted one. We all described ourselves as six o'clock—straight up and down. But we didn't know to feel sorry for ourselves, because everybody else was in the same boat. Nobody made fun of me for wearing my sister's hand-me-down clothes, because they were probably wearing their sister's clothes, too.

My father was a boilermaker's assistant at the dry docks, which meant that he had to hold up sixty-pound steel plates while somebody else riveted them to the ships. But it seemed like he was laid off almost as much as he was working. To make some extra money, he ran a little tavern next to the house, called the Black Cat Inn. It was the only tavern for black people in Toulminville, and it was a pretty lively place—music and dancing and people coming in and out all night. After a while, Daddy had to shut it down because the neighbors complained about the ruckus. But he always had something going on the side. He sold a little moonshine—white shinny, they called it....

My sister Sarah, the oldest child, ran the tavern for my father. Herbert Junior was next in line, and he always had some job or another. For a long time, he worked for a lady named Miss Higgins in a grocery store on St. Stephens Road, which is the main road running past Toulminville. Miss

Higgins would give Herbert Junior clothes and groceries. She helped raise him. I had a few jobs, too, but I wasn't a worker like Herbert Junior. I mowed some yards and picked some potatoes. The potato truck would come by at about seven in the morning; we'd hop on, and they'd take us out to the country, then bring us back around suppertime with eight or nine dollars in our pocket.... The best job I had, though, was delivering ice. It would come in twenty-five-pound blocks, and we had tongs to carry it into the houses. Later on, I used to tell sportswriters that I built up my wrists by hauling ice up flights of stairs, but I doubt if that had anything to do with it. The truth is, I didn't have the job for very long. My mistake was that I told them I'd drive the truck, although I was only fourteen and didn't quite know how to drive yet. I was doing all right until I pulled away from a stop when I was on a hill and all the ice went sliding off the back of the truck.

After that, I pretty much just helped my mother around the house, tending the garden and cutting wood. Herbert Junior and I both had to cut wood for the stove, and I usually tried to sneak a few of my sticks onto Herbert Junior's pile so I could get out of there and play ball. It wasn't easy to get away, because Mama always had work for us to do. If we didn't feel like doing it, she'd let us cut a little switch off a tree. Then she'd braid it together like girls' hair and whale on us for a while. It got to where doing the chores didn't seem so bad, except that it wasn't baseball....

[I]t was in Toulminville that I became a ballplayer. There were open spaces in Toulminville, and before long, enough kids had moved in that we could generally get up a game. After we had been there a few years, they cleared the pecan grove that was on the other side of a vacant lot across the street from my house, and we carved out our own ball diamond. Then the city (Toulminville had been annexed to Mobile in 1945) built its own diamonds on that very spot—Carver Park, the first recreational area for blacks in all of Mobile. It was like having Ebbets Field in my backyard.

7-8. PHOTO GALLERY: WORKING-CLASS SUBURBIA

Figure 7-5 Real Estate Office. Outskirts of Detroit, Michigan, John Vachon, 1941. Hand-lettered signboards for cheap building allotments were a signature of blue-collar suburbia into the mid-twentieth century. During World War II, informal housing markets flourished at the edges of many cities, fueled by migration to booming defense industries. Courtesy of Library of Congress, Prints and Photographs Division, FSA-OWI Collection, LC-USF34-063658-D DLC (b&w film neg.).

Figure 7-6 Family living in tent beside foundation of house which they are building themselves. Outskirts of Detroit, Michigan, where much cheap housing is going up, John Vachon, 1941. Owner building was a common practice among working-class Americans in the early twentieth century. Building "sweat equity" opened the door for families such as these to own a suburban home. Courtesy of Library of Congress, Prints and Photographs Division, FSA-OWI Collection, LC-USF34-063665-D DLC (b&w film neg.).

Figure 7-7 Untitled, Bound Brook, New Jersey, Carl Mydans, 1936. This family's makeshift home in an unplanned subdivision near New Brunswick, New Jersey, stretches common perceptions of the term "suburban." During the 1910s and 1920s, advertisements for lots in this area appeared in New York's black press, promising home ownership, urban employment, and a semi-rural atmosphere. Courtesy of Library of Congress, Prints and Photographs Division, FSA-OWI Collection, LC-USF33-000433-M4.

ESSAYS

The following essays are examples of revisionist work in the suburban historiography. The authors, both former students of Kenneth Jackson, challenge the assumption that suburbia was the exclusive preserve of the white middle and upper classes. In **Essay 7-1**, Becky Nicolaides uses a case study of South Gate, California, a suburb of Los Angeles, to explore the meaning of suburban life and home ownership to its blue-collar residents. In the years before 1940, this town exhibited traits of unplanned suburbia, such as owner building of homes, productive gardens, few building regulations, and sparse services. Nicolaides emphasizes the importance of home ownership in the lives of residents, especially for affording them a degree of economic security in the years before state-based social welfare provided a safety net. In **Essay 7-2**, historian Andrew Wiese outlines a working-class African-American suburban ideal. A part of a larger work documenting the history of African-American suburbs in the twentieth century, Wiese shows that blacks drew on a combination of Southern cultural roots and urban survival strategies to seek out a better life on the suburban fringe. Wiese makes a case for the existence of a distinctive suburban ideal, one that both resembled and diverged from the white, middle-class model. His work raises important questions about how society defines space, and ultimately how space contributes to constructions of race and class.

ESSAY 7-1. BECKY NICOLAIDES, *MY BLUE HEAVEN: LIFE AND POLITICS IN THE WORKING-CLASS SUBURBS OF LOS ANGELES, 1920–1965* (2002)

Source: University of Chicago Press. Copyright © 2002 by The University of Chicago.

Building Independence in Suburbia

Nestled in the borderland between rural and urban life, working-class suburbs fused elements from both to fulfill the particular needs of their inhabitants. In contrast to upper-class suburbs that melded rural and urban elements to create an aesthetic of romantic pastoralism, the working-class suburb combined these milieus for the more prosaic purpose of economic survival in the modern industrial metropolis. These suburbs enabled families to secure the basic necessities of shelter and food cheaply and efficiently. Especially in Los Angeles of the early twentieth century, where land was cheap, abundant, and often vacant, such suburbs fulfilled these functions effectively and often.

South Gate was one of these suburbs. Located about seven miles south of downtown Los Angeles in the heart of the metropolitan industrial hub, South Gate shared many of the characteristics typical of the blue-collar suburbs that proliferated across North America before World War II. The story of its early development richly conveys the tenor of life in working-class suburbia. In the community building process, both developers *and* residents shaped the suburb. The early developers made pivotal choices that determined the demographic, economic, and housing profile of the community. Local realtors, the occupational descendants of the developers, continued to exert these influences in subsequent years. Even more important, however, were the residents. Particularly in Home Gardens, the poorer part of town, minimal planning and provisioning threw the initiative for development into the hands of residents. Far from a planned, garden community of ready-built homes and shady streets, South Gate offered its citizens only the bare bones of suburbia. From the barren raw materials of vacant lots and dirt roads, residents had to build the rest. South Gate was a product of the sweat, labor, and vision of its inhabitants. If the developers laid a scaffolding, it was up to residents to build—often literally—the structure. In the process, they became critical agents in the process of suburbanization....

Inventing the "Detroit of the Coast"

The SEC [Southern Extension Company] originally pictured South Gate Gardens as a self-sufficient community of wage-earning residents, small shopkeepers, and factories....

More striking was the developers' vision of industry in South Gate. Belying any pretense of rural romanticism, South Gate's boosters embraced manufacturing as an integral part of the suburb by the 1920s. They opened wide the door to industry, encouraging factories to sink roots in and around the community. Indeed, they envisioned South Gate at the heart of brisk industrial growth in southern Los Angeles. By the 1920s, they had jettisoned any concern for maintaining a rural ideal far from the industrial smokestacks—they were luring those very smokestacks into their own backyard.

As early as 1924, city promoters spoke enthusiastically of a $4 million "industrial program" of plant construction for South Gate, destined to make it "one of the most important [communities] in Southern California."...

Industries quickly responded to the call. In 1922, Bell Foundry became the first plant to locate in South Gate, followed two years later by the A.R. Maas Chemical Company, which produced chemicals for the film industry. In 1928, South Gate scored a major coupe with the arrival of Firestone Tire and Rubber, which employed about fifteen hundred people by 1940. By the late 1920s, fifteen major industries had established plants in and adjacent to South Gate; the value of manufactured products in South Gate topped $24 million in 1928, with $4.7 million paid in wages. Remarkably, twenty-two more major industries arrived during the Depression decade, including a large GM auto assembly plant in 1936. The majority of South Gate's factories produced durable goods, such as iron products, concrete pipe, machinery, automobiles, tires, and products used in manufacturing. As the underbelly of glamorous Hollywood, South Gate supplied 70 percent of the chemicals used by motion picture processing plants. About half of the suburb's plants were local start-ups, while the others had relocated from other parts of Los Angeles or were national branch plants. Local industrial expansion was so impressive that by the late 1930s, South Gate had earned the appellation "Detroit of the Coast." Indeed, the suburb sat squarely within Los Angeles's industrial heartland: by 1940, there were nine hundred factories within a two-mile radius of South Gate.

By the late 1920s, South Gate had solidified its identity as a community of white working-class families. As boosters vigorously targeted industries and their workforces, they squarely identified the suburb as a prime destination for working-class homeseekers. Home Gardens, which annexed to South Gate in 1927, did this most strikingly. From the days of its earliest subdivision in 1922, Home Gardens touted itself as "the workingman's ideal home town" that was "situated conveniently to scores of factories in different industrial centers, and with property values and terms within the reach of every honest workingman."...

Homeseekers and Owner-Builders: Shaping the Suburb

If the developers erected a scaffolding for the suburb, the residents built the structure themselves—often literally. In the process, they imprinted their own vision of suburbia upon South Gate. Theirs was an image shaped by class needs, motivated by the desire for family security, and driven by an intensive need to economize. As relatively poor people, many living on the brink of ruin, they turned to the suburb to fulfill their class-specific needs. Molded by these concerns and pressures, South Gate became a rough-hewn suburb where homes were humble, yards were productive, streets were dusty, and families made do. The "quiet of the country" extolled so romantically by South Gate's poet-boosters gave way to the squawks of chickens, the shaky wails of goats, and the sharp crack of hammers driving nails into solid wood.

It is no coincidence that migrants to California in the early twentieth century were labeled "homeseekers." The quest for homes reflected several important impulses, motivations that extended beyond the ideology and controlling influences of the developers and builders. It is true that land developers controlled the housing options of many, yet we need to look beyond these forces "from above" to understand how and why these Americans embraced homeownership so fervently. Their perspective is critical for understanding not only the development of working-class suburbia specifically, but also the phenomenal growth of homeownership nationally in the twentieth century. To workers in 1920s Los Angeles, a home represented independence, a goal highly valued in both American and immigrant traditions.

For workers living on the edge of poverty, particularly in the period before the New Deal ushered in the welfare state, family security and autonomy were the pressing goals. They pursued these goals in many ways: some through workplace actions like unionization and demands for job security, others in realms outside of work such as neighborhoods, popular culture, and public space. As workplace autonomy became more elusive for the laboring class with the maturing of industrial capitalism in the late nineteenth century, life beyond the factory gates took on greater significance....

Housing represented a crucial aspect of this quest for independence. To working-class residents of suburbs like South Gate, individual housing production and ownership were perceived as a viable route to family security. A solid piece of land and shelter became tangible forms of stability within the context of an unpredictable job market, where sources of cash income were often fleeting. Longtime South Gate resident John Sheehy explained that homeownership "meant nobody could evict you. Security for your family, when you're raising five kids you pretty much think you need to own a place....It was tragic if you couldn't buy a house. You really were at the bottom...floundering around, trying to survive. There was no such thing in those years as real stability in employment that we came to have later." Economic stability, via homeownership, was the key aspiration of South Gate's citizenry. With homeownership such a central goal, it followed that their status as "homeowner" would profoundly shape their identity.

The meaning of homeownership for working-class suburbanites takes on added significance if seen in light of the movement toward welfare capitalism during the 1920s. In the wake of Progressivism, it was widely acknowledged that industrial capitalism required a safety net for working Americans

Figure 7-8 Bill Zeigler stands in front of a Home Gardens, California, house, ca. 1920s. Home ownership —often achieved through owner building—became the basis of economic security for many residents of blue-collar suburbs. Courtesy Glenn T. and Helen L. Seaborg.

living on the edge, those most vulnerable to unpredictable swings of the economy. In the era before state-based welfare, sickness, old age, or simply bad luck could spell doom and poverty for an otherwise hardworking family. Large industrialists proposed one solution in the form of welfare capitalism. By offering new forms of security to labor, business hoped both to chill simmering radical tendencies spreading during that era and to circumvent new state intrusions into corporate autonomy. Yet welfare capitalism received a lukewarm reception from many working Americans, who embraced the concept yet resented the failure of business to deliver on its promises.

Another solution was suburbanization and single-family homeownership, for the middle and working classes alike. Both capital and labor supported this approach. Some scholars have stressed the manipulative role of capital in supporting homeownership, claiming it was a means of co-opting worker interests by tying them down to property and making them "slaves to the bungalow." This, ultimately, worked against labor militancy and autonomy since the working-class homeowner had a stake in the status quo. To Marxist scholars, this "lawns for pawns" scenario enervated an assertive working class. Yet this perspective does not tell the whole story, because it leaves out the voice of workers themselves. To many working Americans, homeownership promised family autonomy and a palpable sense of security in the soil they could call their own. The historically higher rates of working-class homeownership—compared to the middle class—attests to this belief. Moreover, they considered homeownership far superior to welfare capitalism, under which workers paid the price of flagrant dependency on their employers in exchange for "security." As suburban dwellers and homeowners, they perceived themselves as more independent and insulated from an unpredictable marketplace. This was a more viable solution to the problems of industrial capitalism, and it acted as a surrogate to Los Angeles workers who lacked an alternative in a strong labor movement because of the city's rabidly open-shop climate....

The critical functions of homeownership were evident in South Gate during the early years, particularly in the processes of settlement, home production, and domestic property use. These processes reflected not only how workers used suburbia but also how they shaped it. The first requirement for entrance into South Gate was the resources to move there, particularly since many residents migrated from other states. Having the means or connections to come west set them slightly apart from the truly down-and-out worker. Some families...relied on kin for assistance. Such networks were common among newcomers to the suburb.

Once they arrived, the initial settlement process could be an arduous ordeal.... [M]any families purchased a vacant lot then immediately erected temporary shelter to house the family during the self-building process. This could be a tent, a shack made of old boxes or tar paper, a trailer, or a garage. In 1920, thirty-six South Gate families were living in garages while building their homes. Later in the decade, the South Gate City Council passed several rulings that allowed residents to live in tents and garages on their property while their homes were under construction. Other families opted for auto camps, such as the Parker Auto Camp on the suburb's outskirts, which rented one-room cottages with car shelters for five dollars per week. These camps, often shoddy and run down, were waystations on the road to homeownership.

The next step was to build the home. Self-builders needed at least some cash to purchase building materials such as lumber and nails. Some families like the Smiths arrived with modest cash reserves, raised by selling off property back home or by borrowing from generous relatives. Some families managed the expenses by extending the building process over a long period of time or by purchasing secondhand lumber. As a self-builder in nearby Bell Gardens remarked, "You can almost always scrape together ten dollars a month as long as you can have a place to live. We've built our house a little at a time as we could pay for it." By the late 1920s, seven lumber supply houses were operating in South Gate, catering to these homebuilders.

While the precise frequency of owner-building is difficult to determine, several sources indicate the practice was fairly widespread in South Gate. Sanborn Fire Insurance Maps are one clue. Especially for Home Gardens, they suggest frequent self-building by revealing an erratic pattern of dwelling placement on the lots: some at the front, some in the middle, some at the back. By contrast, homes constructed by the same builder tended to have uniform setbacks. Oral histories and building permits also disclose the prevalence of owner-building during the 1920s. Similarly suggestive is a sociological study conducted in the early 1930s of neighboring Bell Gardens, close to South Gate in terms of class and physical appearance. It revealed that 73 percent of the homes there were self-built; 5 percent were purchased partially completed, meaning the buyer had to finish the job; and 17 percent were purchased as finished homes.

The task of self-building—and the conditions it created—were wrought with dif-

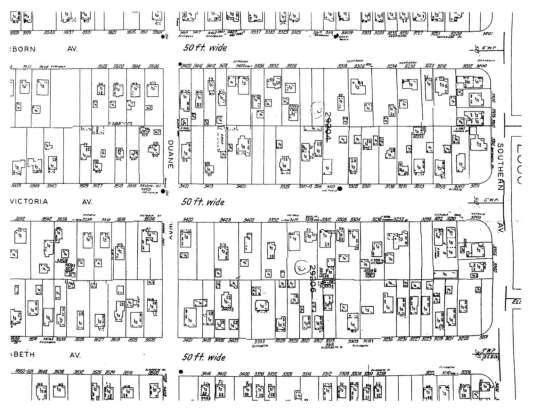

Figure 7-9 Sanborn Company fire insurance maps show that the shape and position of homes on their lots varied considerably in Home Gardens. This evidence strongly suggests the presence of unregulated owner building in the area. Copyright © 1929–1940, The Sanborn Map Company, The Sanborn Library, LLC. All Rights Reserved. Further reproductions prohibited without prior written permission from the Sanborn Library, LLC. Illustration in original, 31.

ficulty. The job itself consumed the spare hours of wage earners who worked by day, then returned at night to put in an hour or two on the house, and more on weekends. As the wife of one owner-builder remarked, "[I]f you think it easy to start from raw land with weeds as high as my head, just you try it….A lot of these folks in grand houses couldn't do this." The building process could drag on for years, forcing families to live with the discomfort and inconvenience of unsealed walls, exposed pipes, bare studs, and strewn materials. One housewife noted, "The back rooms have never been finished although we've lived here for three years. My husband works six days a week and his health hasn't been very well." And the Smith family…moved into their house before it had a roof….

The process of self-building typically involved the entire family. Juanita (Smith) Hammon recalled, "My dad was a good

builder, and he had help. My mother was just as good a carpenter as he was. She laid hardwood floors and kept up with him. They used the narrow oak floors, and that living room was 21 feet long….She helped nail those floors in….And all us kids helped. We'd hold a board while my dad was sawing, or we would climb up to take supplies to him, or help hold something. I know I climbed up that ladder many times to take him some more nails or a certain piece of wood he wanted. We all helped build that house." For the more specialized work, Juanita's father hired out a plasterer, electrician, and plumber.

These "jackknife carpenters" built as cheaply as possible, sometimes erecting nothing more than shacks. As longtime resident John Sheehy reminisced, "More than half built them themselves [laughs]. But what did they build? 600 square feet, maybe. Little tiny places. They lived in tents a lot of people….It was as common as dirt....They'd build a little garage that they slept in and cooked out of doors. That was common. We were delivering milk here, and got stiffed for a few milk bills here, I'll tell you that. They were really poor....But [out here] you had a chance, even the working people had a chance because land was cheap, they could scrounge around and buy a lot....[A]nd they'd buy a little bit of lumber every month and put in a foundation, mix it by hand. I saw hundreds of them do that." The "shack" was particularly common in Home Gardens. As Juanita (Smith) Hammon remembered, many residents built their own homes, "and a lot of them did it badly, because there was no inspection."

The typical South Gate home was a modest bungalow consisting of one bedroom, a living room, a kitchen, and a bathroom. On the smaller thirty-foot frontage lots, offset requirements meant a home could measure only eighteen feet across....To make matters worse, some of these homes were constructed of poor materials. During the 1920s, magnesite stucco was a popular type of construction material across Southern California. When the magnesite got wet, it dissolved and the walls literally crumbled. This spelled inconvenience at the least and disaster at the worst. The presence of the South Gate House Wrecking Company in a community just over a decade old was poetic testimony to the quality of local housing.

The ways residents used their homes reflected their aspiration for economic security. While property in South Gate won no prizes for appearance, it was highly valued for its function as a site of domestic production. In backyards, residents raised vegetables, fruits, and small animals for home consumption and sale. A rabbit hutch or chicken pen were common sights, as was the occasional milk goat. Even the local doctor's family raised rabbits and a home garden, critical during lean years when cash was scarce and patients couldn't pay their bills. As these practices flourished, they created a distinctly rural veneer in South Gate. "Chickens and other poultry...entering my Home Gardens properties," warned one resident in 1924, "will provide excellent short-range practice for me with my new Winchester repeating shot gun."...

Food produced in backyard gardens was consumed at home, sold, and bartered. Home consumption made good economic sense for working-class residents. Food represented 35.7 percent of the consumer spending of a typical industrial wage earner in 1929, amounting to roughly $551. (This was significantly more than the 27.8 percent spent on housing.) If a family raised fruits, vegetables, chickens, and rabbits on their property, a substantial portion of that bill could be saved. John Sheehy remembered that residents grew produce for their own use since "pennies counted in those days."

Selling homegrown produce and poultry was also common in South Gate and Los Angeles as a whole. As early as 1913, thirty-two hundred small growers peddled their produce at several thriving municipal markets....Backyard chicken growers could sell excess livestock to the many poultry farms that lined Atlantic Avenue, just north of South Gate.

As well, many neighbors participated in a local, informal barter network. Juanita (Smith) Hammon recalled the importance of this exchange for working families: "Sometimes residents would trade vegetables, they would exchange produce if someone had a big crop of this or that. Instead of money, like bartering. There was all that land around. I remember one lady saying, 'Why do they bother growing produce when it's so cheap anyway?' Well they were cheap according to her. She was buying vegetables for a penny a bunch. But when they're a penny a bunch and you don't have the penny, they're expensive."

The appearance and function of property in South Gate show how working-class aspirations for security defined the meaning of suburban living for these residents. In most cases, they favored the use value over the commodity value of their homes. While some early speculative buying occurred in South Gate mainly in the northwest section, the practice subsided by 1924, when an overwhelming majority of building permits were issued to individual homeowners. In their quest for independence, residents launched the community in a direction to best meet their needs. Ironically, South Gate's working-class residents had more control over their environment than middle-class inhabitants of the typical garden suburb. Since they couldn't afford a well-developed community, it was up to them to create one....

In the interwar years, the working-class suburb was, thus, far from the sleepy bedroom community of the postwar period. It was a bustling, coarse neighborhood where domestic property was a locus of ongoing productive labor, where rural and urban rhythms blurred, where working people struggled to make ends meet, and where space and structures often enabled them to succeed in this struggle.

ESSAY 7-2. ANDREW WIESE, *PLACES OF THEIR OWN: AFRICAN AMERICAN SUBURBANIZATION IN THE TWENTIETH CENTURY* (2004)

Source: University of Chicago Press. Copyright © 2004 by The University of Chicago.

In 1959 a writer from the *Cleveland Plain Dealer* visited a small African American community near Cleveland called Chagrin Falls Park. He described a landscape of small houses, large gardens, frame churches, and cinder-block stores as well as overgrown lots and cannibalized automobiles. To the reporter's eye, the 700 inhabitants lived in a "shantytown," but among those he interviewed were men and women who described "the Park" as a community where they had built better lives for themselves. Representative of these was Magnolia Strickland, a native of Georgia who praised the community for its open space, fresh air, gardens, and the opportunity to own a home. "I think I bettered my condition," Strickland said. "I got five rooms; they all got heat from an oil furnace. I got an electric stove and hot and cold running water from my well...and it's all paid for....I couldn't have done all that in Cleveland."

The divergent views of Strickland and the reporter illustrate common reactions to early black suburbs. To outsiders—journalists, city planners, white neighbors, and many middle-class blacks—these places were "slums," "poverty pockets," or in the case of Chagrin Falls Park a "curse." Academic observers, too, saw these communities as little more than "rural slums" or "little ghettoes" that belonged outside the legitimate suburbanization process. To residents, however, these neighborhoods represented something altogether different; they were home, places where people had bought land, built houses, nurtured families, and created communities. Moreover, Strickland's comments suggest that residents wanted many of the same things as other suburbanites, including homes of their own, bucolic landscapes, and family-centered community life. Yet they also pursued a distinctive residential ethic: a set of values and practices that affected how they perceived and used domestic space. Slums to some, these places were also suburbs shaped by the experience, aspirations, and income of the black families who made them home.

The emphasis that Strickland and her neighbors placed on the aesthetic as well as material benefits of their domestic situation underscores the importance of residential choice among black suburbanites. Evident as the point may seem, few historians have explored the domestic preferences that shaped how and where African Americans lived....Approaching suburbanization from the perspective of Magnolia Strickland, however, illustrates that African Americans' choices about how and where to live reflected not only the location of a job but social, economic, and aesthetic predilections that they brought with them from the South. Strickland and her neighbors indicate that middle-class whites were not the only Americans who sought to better their lives by moving to the suburbs.

Despite differences in the communities where they settled, early black suburbanites moved to suburbs for many of the same reasons as nonblacks. Suburban jobs and the appeal of suburban social networks were among them. So, too, were cheap land, fuel, and transportation (especially widespread automobile ownership) and a relative lack of building restrictions at the edge of town. Further, many of the normative values associated with the middle-class "suburban dream," such as the emphasis on detached single-family houses in a semi-rural environment, were widely shared among Americans in the early twentieth century. In short, black suburbanites responded to the same social, ideological, and structural forces that encouraged urban decentralization in general.

All the same, class, race, and culture influenced discrete patterns of suburban life. Facing low wages and unstable employment, African American workers used suburban property as a means of adapting to urban capitalism. In this respect, they heeded class-based imperatives that they shared with other Americans. Regardless of race, blue-collar workers were more likely than middle-class suburbanites to view their homes as a basis for economic survival—as a source of income through renting rooms, as a supplement to wages through gardening and backyard livestock, and, in the years before the welfare state, as irrevocable shelter in times of unemployment, sickness, or retirement. They were less likely than the middle class to view a house as an appreciating asset that they would later sell, and they were more likely to "underconsume" in order to obtain a home of their own, habits that included owner building, self-provisioning, delaying service improvements, and sacrificing children's education for additional wages. Consequently, working-class immigrants in many parts of North America were *more* likely to own their own homes than native-born middle-class whites, a pattern that was especially pronounced on the suburban fringe. For millions of blue-collar Americans before World War II, suburban homes represented a means to economic security and shelter from a hostile economic environment.

Like other Americans, black suburbanites also internalized images of ideal places to live, drawing inspiration not only from elite-oriented visions of suburban arcadia but from southern history and cultural inclinations they shared with other black migrants. Despite the diversity of early suburbs, working-class African Americans expressed recognizable values in regard to housing, home ownership, economic independence, open space, and family life. Where there was vacant land, they worked to buy it and build homes. Even in the most congested suburbs, they grew gardens, kept domestic livestock, and used domestic space to generate income. They relied on extended families for economic as well as emotional support, and many explicitly rejected city living, preferring, instead, rustic landscapes reminiscent of the region from which most had come. Lastly, they gravitated to black communities not only because of racial restrictions but because of the comfort and connection they felt among people like themselves. Taken together, these preferences reflect a coherent vision of better living in the metropolitan United States, what we would rightly call a working-class African American suburban dream....

Unplanned Suburb: Chagrin Falls Park, Ohio

During the spring of 1921, an agent of the Home Guardian Corporation of New York walked into the Cleveland offices of Samuel Rocker, publisher of the *Jewish World*, a Yiddish-language newspaper. Home Guardian had recently subdivided a suburban tract southeast of the city called Chagrin Falls Park. The agent proposed to Rocker that the *Jewish World* offer lots in Chagrin Falls as subscription premiums. By June 1921 full-page advertisements in the *World* announced the premiums, and readers began buying lots. Developed with a minimum of investment and no restrictions, the subdivision had no sewers, water lines, or electricity and its streets were little more than dirt lanes. Perhaps because of poor services, the buoyant expectations of Rocker and Home Guardian went unfulfilled. Lots sold slowly, and in 1924 Home Guardian sold the remainder of its lots to white real estate agents Grover and Florence Brow, who began a thirty-year career selling Chagrin Falls Park lots—mostly to African Americans in the city of Cleveland.

In marketing rustic building lots to African Americans, the Brows replicated the decision of real estate agents in dozens of American cities. Despite the professionalization of real estate practice and the spread of land-use planning, low-cost land markets serving working-class families endured in the United States and Canada before World War

II. African Americans represented a small but important segment of these markets. During the 1910s and 1920s, black newspapers brimmed with advertisements for lot subdivisions like Chagrin Falls Park. Between 1921 and 1927, New York's black press advertised subdivisions in no less than fourteen suburbs, in addition to homes and lots in a dozen more. Black papers such as the *Chicago Defender, California Eagle, Pittsburgh Courier, Cleveland Gazette,* and *Baltimore Afro-American* published advertisements for local allotments as well as subdivisions as far away as Egg Harbor and New Brunswick, New Jersey; Gainesville, Florida; and Washington, D.C.

Regardless of the region or race of the subdivider, their sales pitches were remarkably similar, reflecting agents' best understanding of their market. Insofar as families bought, these ads may offer clues to the desires of black suburbanites during the Great Migration. Reflecting migrants' southern origins, ad after ad offered a slice of country life: open space for fruit trees, garden plots, chickens, and other small livestock. Notably, they promised elements of the country in combination with urban amenities: proximity to urban jobs, convenient transportation, and community facilities such as churches, schools, and stores. In a few cases, ads appealed to race pride explicitly, encouraging readers to "join hands with your own people" by buying lots in a black subdivision. More often, they linked suburbanization to race uplift by naming subdivisions after heroes in the freedom struggle, such as Booker T. Washington, Frederick Douglass, or Abraham Lincoln. Promoting a borderland between urban and rural living, with the image of racial progress at center stage, agents above all promised the opportunity "for colored people to own a home."

Although the Brows's sales pitch is not recorded, they made inexpensive suburban land available to working-class black Clevelanders. Prices of Chagrin Falls Park lots fluctuated during the 1920s from $60

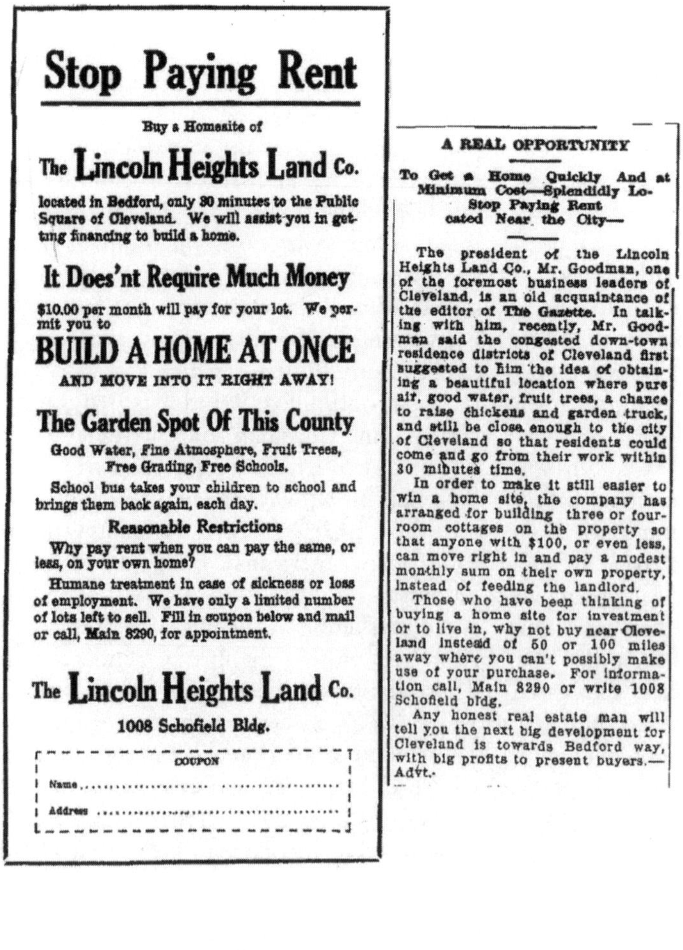

Stop Paying Rent

Buy a Homesite of

The Lincoln Heights Land Co.

located in Bedford, only 30 minutes to the Public Square of Cleveland. We will assist you in getting financing to build a home.

It Does'nt Require Much Money

$10.00 per month will pay for your lot. We permit you to

BUILD A HOME AT ONCE

AND MOVE INTO IT RIGHT AWAY!

The Garden Spot Of This County

Good Water, Fine Atmosphere, Fruit Trees, Free Grading, Free Schools.

School bus takes your children to school and brings them back again, each day.

Reasonable Restrictions

Why pay rent when you can pay the same, or less, on your own home?

Humane treatment in case of sickness or loss of employment. We have only a limited number of lots left to sell. Fill in coupon below and mail or call, Main 8290, for appointment.

The Lincoln Heights Land Co.

1008 Schofield Bldg.

COUPON

Name ....

Address ....

A REAL OPPORTUNITY

To Get a Home Quickly And at Minimum Cost—Splendidly Lo-
Stop Paying Rent
cated Near the City—

The president of the Lincoln Heights Land Co., Mr. Goodman, one of the foremost business leaders of Cleveland, is an old acquaintance of the editor of The Gazette. In talking with him, recently, Mr. Goodman said the congested down-town residence districts of Cleveland first suggested to him the idea of obtaining a beautiful location where pure air, good water, fruit trees, a chance to raise chickens and garden truck, and still be close enough to the city of Cleveland so that residents could come and go from their work within 30 minutes time.

In order to make it still easier to win a home site, the company has arranged for building three or four-room cottages on the property so that anyone with $100, or even less, can move right in and pay a modest monthly sum on their own property, instead of feeding the landlord.

Those who have been thinking of buying a home site for investment or to live in, why not buy near Cleveland instead of 50 or 100 miles away where you can't possibly make use of your purchase. For information call, Main 8290 or write 1008 Schofield bldg.

Any honest real estate man will tell you the next big development for Cleveland is towards Bedford way, with big profits to present buyers.—Advt.

Figure 7-10 Advertisement for a black subdivision in Oakwood, Ohio, not far from Chagrin Falls Park. Ads for low-cost building lots in rustic subdivisions were common in the pages of the nation's black press during the Great Migration. *Cleveland Gazette*, June 14, 1924. Illustration in original, 73.

Figure 7-11 Stephen and Ruby Hall built this house in the late 1930s with the help of Mrs. Hall's parents and other relatives. In the backyard were a cast iron pump, chicken coop, vegetable garden, and an outhouse. Photograph by Andrew Wiese, 1996. Illustration in original, 75.

to $200—two weeks' to two months' salary for the average black factory worker in Cleveland. By contrast, similar parcels in the city ran to several hundreds of dollars, and house prices reached into the thousands....

Having purchased bare lots in Chagrin Falls Park, black families built homes and community institutions in a fashion similar to working-class European immigrants in a number of cities. Clara Adams described her husband's efforts:

> When they had the sheriff's sale, he went up there and bought these three lots. He built on two lots a little three-room house. He had friends to help him. The funny part about it, he was on WPA at that time and he was talking about building a house. I said, "How you gonna build a house? You haven't got any money." And he said, "I got $50." And I said, "$50?" 'Cause that tickled me, him talking about building a house on $50. But he said, "Well, if you never start anything, you never get anything."

Buyers with greater resources hired builders, and a few rented or bought houses vacated by early white residents, but most newcomers, like Adams, came out on the weekends or evenings and built their own homes. To cut costs, many used scrap lumber, and they extended construction over long periods, building what they could afford and then waiting until the next few paychecks to proceed. Where family labor or carpentry skills proved insufficient, many builders employed the muscle of friends and neighbors. An ethic of neighborly aid pervaded the community during the early years of building. One resident, whose mother built her own house, remarked that "most everybody could do some kind of fixing, and everybody kind of helped everybody."...

Toward a Working-Class African American Suburban Vision

The most important reason early residents gave for settling in Chagrin Falls Park was the desire to own a house and property. Among early settlers, the value of property ownership ran so deep that it needed almost no explanation. Ruby Hall, for example, noted that families like hers moved to the park because "wasn't nobody could buy in

Figure 7-12 Residents of Chagrin Falls Park and other unplanned suburbs created a rustic landscape that included modest homes, large gardens, livestock pens, and plenty of open space. This landscape (ca. 1940) reflected a vision of suburban life that emphasized domestic production, thrift, and family security, while exposing a lingering ambivalence about urban industrial life. Courtesy of the Estate of Elizabeth Meade Smith. Illustration in original, 78.

the city." Others seemed to take it for granted that working-class people would buy property when the chance presented itself....To Ruby Hall, the reason people struggled to build a community in an isolated section of suburban Cleveland was simple. "Everybody at that time," she said, "wanted a little place of their own."

The desire for a place of one's own, historians have shown, has been a central feature of American suburbanization since the nineteenth century. Exactly what different groups wanted and why remains a subject for debate. Middle-class whites, for example, often invested home ownership with images of masculine independence, female domesticity, and idealized nuclear families, not to mention long-term capital appreciation and superior educational advantages to ensure the heritability of their success. Working-class whites, on the other hand, more often valued home ownership for its everyday economic usefulness as well as for economic security over the long run. African Americans, too, sought to use space for their own ends, placing high value on home ownership as well as detached housing, family-based communities, and bucolic environments. Yet in each case, they approached these as people with a history and experiences that set them apart. Looking at these aspirations more carefully reveals the outlines of a working-class black suburban vision rooted in settlers' experience

in the South as well as their expectations for life in urban areas.

As black southerners, suburbanites' value for property ownership had a long history. In the aftermath of the Civil War, property ownership was indissolubly linked with freedom in the aspiration of former slaves. Throughout the late nineteenth and early twentieth centuries, property ownership persisted among the chief values of blacks in the rural South. As the *New York Age* editorialized, "Nearly everybody who is anybody" in the South "owns something." Proprietorship symbolized hard work and ambition in a way evident to every member of the community. It provided a basis for upward mobility, shelter for immediate and extended families, and a foundation in a society that systematically marginalized African Americans. Lastly, it meant a greater degree of independence, which is to say freedom, than any form of tenancy....

In addition to fulfilling historic desires for property ownership, a house of one's own represented an economic strategy for many early suburbanites. Owner building itself was the most obvious example, as families expended their own labor power to defray the largest expense they faced. There was no single pattern. Some families built everything by themselves or with the help of friends, but many engaged some combination of paid and unpaid labor over an extended period. Rather than purchasing shelter as a commodity through savings or future earnings, residents created "sweat equity" by investing their own labor in the production of new homes.

Owner building and other economic uses of property were common class-based strategies of urban survival in the early twentieth century. Gardens and livestock helped families economize. Proprietorship allowed them to escape central city rents, and domestic spaces provided rental income that supported economic mobility and helped families weather hard times. Regardless of race or ethnicity, domestic production was a characteristic feature of working-class suburbia.

This was particularly true of black suburbs, where evidence of self-provisioning and other economic uses of property was omnipresent across the range of suburban types. In Homestead, Pennsylvania, Margaret Byington reported in 1910 that African American and white immigrant steelworkers used yards for gardening and raising small livestock whenever they could. Likewise in Pasadena [California], residents remembered that "everyone had their own garden in the backyard, and everybody had chickens and eggs." In World War II Richmond, California, black women in the city's sprawling defense housing projects regularly kept kitchen gardens, where they grew okra, collards, butter beans, sweet potatoes, and other vegetables. By growing familiar foods, they not only supplemented their incomes and diet but, through exchanges or gifts of fresh produce, reinforced community bonds and preserved tangible links to their heritage as African American southerners.

Black suburbanites not only grew food in the backyard; they also utilized interior spaces as a source of income…In Chagrin Falls Park, Estella Denson not only ran a small canteen in her house, she and her husband built an addition to their home that they rented to recent arrivals. Essie Kirklen initially rented space from another family when she moved to Chagrin Falls Park, and once she became settled, she, too, occasionally took in boarders to supplement her income. Clara Adams's husband built their own home as well as three additional houses, which the Adamses kept as rentals. Socially and economically, home ownership

in suburbs like Chagrin Falls Park supported upward mobility for many African American families.…

In other ways, too, black suburbanites adapted to life in the North by bringing parts of the South with them.…[B]lack suburbanites followed intricate migration chains to the suburbs. The kinship network of early Chagrin Falls Park resident Sallie Denson suggests the ways that extended family supported the development of suburban communities. Mrs. Denson, a widow, moved to the Park in the late 1920s and built a cinder-block house on Geneva Street with the help of her grown children. By the early 1930s, five of these children—Essie, Edith, Cornelia, Letha, and Pete—had relocated from Cleveland to Chagrin Falls with their spouses. Two other sons, John and Willie, lived in the Park with their wives for a short time before returning to Cleveland. By 1940 Essie's sister-in-law and her husband had also settled, as had two of Mrs. Denson's nephews and their wives. These wives, Annie and Mattie Pounds, attracted cousins Shepherd Beck and Nellie Lawrence to settle with their families in Chagrin Falls by the early 1940s. The Denson family had among the most extensive kin relations in the Park, but other early residents followed a similar pattern, settling with or joining family already living there. By the 1940s a strong network of kin-based suburbanization had created a web of familial relationships that bound residents to one another as a community. In a suburb where incomes and jobs were insecure, transportation inconvenient, and voluntary cooperation important for survival as well as progress, extended families were a bulwark against hardship and a foundation for upward mobility. In contrast to the middle-class suburban model of the era, characterized by child-centered nuclear families, suburbanization for African Americans in Chagrin Falls Park strengthened the bonds of extended families and friendships that stretched through Cleveland to roots in the South.

In addition to visions of home and family, residents of Chagrin Falls Park expressed normative ideas about landscape that reflected their experience in the South and shaped the community they built in the suburbs.

"My family heard about a place where they could buy them some land which reminded them of home," one woman said. "They all came from the South, and they had lived in Cleveland for many years, but they never forgot their home. They wanted a little place where they could have chickens and different little things and a little farm life and gardens." Weighing the sacrifice of city services against the benefits of country living, Clara Adams, who relocated with her husband in 1940, claimed:

> I didn't mind it [giving up a modern apartment in Cleveland]. When we came out here it was just so nice and quiet. You didn't hear nothing but the birds in the morning singing nice. It was where I could have a garden, and I liked that. So it wasn't hard at all. Plus, I was used to the country. That's where I was raised up, so it didn't bother me at all. I didn't like *in* the city—too congested. I liked *out*. I like the fresh air, and it's nice and quiet....

Based on preferences such as these, residents let side lots grow thick, cultivated extensive gardens, and planted fruit trees and even pine trees from "down home." In the evenings, they sat on front porches they had built and surveyed the quiet. Like middle-class suburbanites, they created a bucolic landscape of residence in union with nature, but with a difference. For early Park settlers, the prospect of fresh air, birdsong, open space, and "a little farm life and gardens" outweighed the desire for modern conveniences that were fundamental to middle-class suburbanization. Their landscape was more rustic, but it was no less suburban....

Beyond the legacy of southern landscape, race and shared elements of southern culture shaped the process of early black suburbanization in other ways as well. Racism as well as African Americans' efforts to overcome it ensured that most black suburbanites lived in a segregated world. Discrimination limited black incomes and prevented families from buying property in all but a few areas of the metropolis—often marginal land beset by environmental nuisance. Bias in mortgage lending encouraged working-class black families to build their own homes and to use property in economically productive ways. Although informal home building was common among working-class white suburbanites, it was a choice African Americans made from even fewer options. Race also shaped early suburbanization from the inside. Suburbanites' passion for home ownership sprang from a venerable black tradition in the South. Patterns of family migration and settlement followed lines that were common among African American migrants, and women's economic activity in many suburbs reflected the wider economic participation of black women in the wage economy....

If race and racism shaped early black suburbanization, suburban life itself tended to reinforce migrants' racial identities. Held at arm's length by white suburbanites, African Americans relied on their own resources. They established separate institutions, worshiped in separate churches, and socialized in a predominantly black milieu. Politically, they organized to overcome racial inequality as members of race- and place-based communities. In Chagrin Falls Park, black men rode to work together and labored with other blacks in segmented occupations—in the foundry at American Steel & Wire or at the back of a garbage truck with the Department of Sanitation. Women who worked as domestics had closer connections with local whites, but at best these relationships left racism unchallenged. Religious groups from the Park visited black churches in nearby suburbs such as Twinsburg and Miles Heights, and ministers from these communities as well as Cleveland preached guest sermons in local churches.... Encouraged by persisting white racism as well as their own perception of accomplishment, residents of such places as Chagrin Falls Park forged a distinct sense of themselves as both African Americans and suburbanites....

Conclusion...

The Park tripled in population during the 1940s, reaching a peak of nearly 900 in 1960 as a new wave of black southerners hit the city. However, population dwindled thereafter. As African American living standards improved, black expectations for life in an "affluent society" expanded, and strategies of working-class subsistence that had served prewar suburbanites failed to support a standard of living satisfactory to most urban-born African Americans. Pioneer suburbanites preferred a lifestyle reminiscent of the South, but their children and grandchildren often perceived these places as the boondocks. Moreover, they had greater options. By the 1990s, population in Chagrin Falls Park had shrunk to less than 500, and the average income was the lowest in Geauga County. Even so, dozens of elderly men and women lived independently in homes that they owned.

Even though many early suburbs suffered depopulation and chronic poverty, the history of these places belies the mystique of suburbia as the preserve of elite and middle-class whites. In the years before 1950, thousands of central city blacks moved to suburbs. Long ridiculed as "poverty pockets" and "suburban slums," the communities where they settled were often poor, but they were fully part of the national trend toward urban decentralization known as suburbanization. At the same time, they reflected a vision of residential, family, and community life that was at once suburban, working-class, and African American. This vision, as much as economic necessity, shaped the landscape of American suburbia in the same fashion as the well-documented dreams of middle-class whites.

NOTES

1. See for example, Richard Harris, *Unplanned Suburbs: Toronto's American Tragedy, 1900-1950* (Baltimore: Johns Hopkins University Press, 1996).
2. Richard Harris, "Working Class Home Ownership in the American Metropolis," *Journal of Urban History* 17 (November 1990), 46–69.
3. Todd Gardener, "The Slow Wave: The Changing Residential Status of Cities and Suburbs in the United States, 1850–1940," *Journal of Urban History* 27 (March 2001), 293–312, 293.
4. The "lawns for pawns" thesis is discussed in Matthew Edel, Elliott D. Sclar, and Daniel Luria, *Shaky Palaces: Homeownership and Social Mobility in Boston's Suburbanization* (New York: Columbia University Press, 1984), 169–194.

CHAPTER 8

The Tools of Exclusion

From Local Initiatives to Federal Policy

INTRODUCTION

By the early decades of the twentieth century, the pace of suburban change threatened to undermine the romantic conception of suburbia that many middle-class Americans held dear. The decentralization of industry and commerce not only altered the landscape in ways that seemed "urban," but it drew growing numbers of workers and their families to suburban areas. Improved transportation and services opened the urban fringe to a wider class of people and fueled a boom in new housing construction. Moreover, some of these newcomers built communities that reflected very different ideas about land use and landscape. Lastly, the continued subdivision of farms, forests, and meadows exposed a fundamental paradox in the suburbanization process; the construction of new homes for urban commuters, even affluent ones, inevitably eroded the bucolic atmosphere that had attracted many suburbanites in the first place. The romantic suburban ideal, it seemed, was under siege by factories, the "lower" classes, and overdevelopment.

In the first half of the twentieth century, affluent suburbanites and their advocates launched multiple efforts to reclaim a more exclusive suburban ideal. Those efforts originated on many levels, from the grassroots to the federal government. Among upper-middle-class and elite families, concerns often focused on the social profile of the new suburbanites. Their concerns mirrored the broader context of early twentieth-century American society, a period of massive immigration and African-American migration to metropolitan areas. As such, many early efforts to protect suburbia from uncontrolled change corresponded implicitly and explicitly with attempts to control the types of people who could move there. The results were a series of measures designed to ensure suburban exclusivity, which in turn created a metropolitan landscape characterized by intensifying segregation.

The first initiatives to plan and regulate suburban development were private, local efforts. Real estate promoters, seeking to secure the character of neighborhoods against unwanted changes, inserted restrictive clauses in property deeds. These conditions governed physical development—placement of buildings and fences, architectural styles, and minimum construction costs—but they also controlled the class of people who could afford to move in. Many also explicitly restricted purchase or occupancy to "Caucasians only." As black migration to metropolitan areas accelerated during the 1910s, white exclusion efforts intensified. In 1914, the recently formed National Association of Real Estate Boards, or "Realtors," adopted a code of ethics that prohibited members from "introducing into a neighborhood...members of any race or nationality...whose presence will clearly be detrimental to property values."[1] Realtors who failed to comply faced stiff professional penalties. Realtor-sponsored textbooks, in turn, emphasized the idea that nonwhites threatened the value of property. Mortgage lenders colluded by refusing to make loans to people of color outside of a few segregated districts. White residents in older neighborhoods perpetuated exclusion by signing legal agreements, or covenants, that bound one another not to sell or rent to "any person other than one of the Caucasian race."[2] When these methods failed, white neighbors took more drastic measures, resorting to violence and intimidation. By the end of World War I, a vision of metropolitan space thoroughly segregated by class and race had become a matter of common sense within the formal real estate market, the nascent city planning movement, and much of the white middle class.

Government sanction of these practices followed shortly. During the late 1910s and 1920s, municipalities across the country adopted regulations to control private land use. New building codes, subdivision regulations, and zoning ordinances gave local authorities unprecedented influence over real estate development within their borders. These powers allowed, for example, local governments to exclude practices common in working-class suburbs, such as informal home building, small-lot subdivisions, multifamily housing, and backyard livestock. The impact of these new regulations was especially far reaching in suburbs because it was there that the city was growing most rapidly and the more abundant open spaces provided a clean slate for development according to the latest fashion. Furthermore, suburban authorities served a much narrower range of local interests than most big city officials. Responding to their constituents, they delivered land use regulations that furthered race and class segregation. In 1926, the Supreme Court provided legal sanction that wrapped the whole movement in a package. In the case of *Euclid v. Ambler*, the Court upheld the right of local governments to employ zoning to control the use of privately held real estate within their borders. In a second case, *Corrigan v. Buckley*, it approved the use of race restrictive deeds and covenants, lending the weight of public enforcement to private contractual agreements. By the time the federal government intervened in the housing market to avert its collapse during the 1930s, patterns and practices of exclusion were entrenched. Federal housing policy, largely drafted and implemented by members of the real estate industry, followed a well-established path.

Before the 1890s there had been few attempts to strictly segregate urban or suburban territory along race or class lines. Within a few short decades, however, the movement to control metropolitan land use and residency evolved from a voluntary effort of private citizens on the local level to a matter of national domestic policy. Along the way, ideas about suburban homes and neighborhoods that reflected the biases of white, upper-middle-class suburbanites became codified in real estate practice, municipal regulation, federal housing programs, and the law. Reflecting the growing power of a middle-class suburban ideal, these restrictions overturned traditional attitudes toward private property rights, requiring individual property owners to sacrifice some of those rights for what proponents argued was the good of the larger community. As the suburbs boomed after World War II, these ideas and practices formed the basic infrastructure on which postwar suburbia grew. To its supporters, this new regime of metropolitan land use dramatically improved the quality of American housing and laid the foundation for vastly expanded home ownership. To its critics, it represented the essence of structural racism.

DOCUMENTS

In **Document 8-1**, magazine editor and suburbanite Frederick Allen pinpoints one of the central dilemmas of suburban life: the idealized blend of rural and urban landscapes that comprised affluent suburbia was unsustainable under market conditions. While Allen's alarm over the loss of open space foreshadows the rise of suburban environmentalism a generation later, his fears also illustrate suburbanites' concern over the social changes that development portended—apartment dwellers, high population density, social diversity, long commutes. Worries such as these underlay the movement to establish greater controls and restriction of suburban land use.

With a material stake in the marketability of suburban property, real estate developers were pioneers in formulating new suburban restrictions. **Document 8-2**, by Jesse Clyde "J. C." Nichols, offers the perspective of one such developer. Best known as the builder of Kansas City's fashionable Country Club District, and a founding member of the Realtors, Nichols was instrumental in promoting private subdivision restrictions and public land use planning nationwide. **Document 8-3** is an early example of the kind of deed restrictions that developers like Nichols would tranform into an art. Written for a 1911 subdivision near San Diego, California, this document reveals that such deeds routinely limited both the use and occupancy of property. Such prescriptions, which could last for a few years or for decades, reassured prospective buyers that the value of their property—and character of their neighborhood—would be protected from unwanted changes. By the 1920s, race restrictive deeds and neighborhood covenants (legally binding agreements among property holders established after the initial subdivision) were becoming commonplace in most suburban areas. **Document 8-4** provides a glimpse into the workings of race restrictions on the ground. The document is from the court transcript of a 1933 lawsuit brought by white residents of Evanston, Illinois to prevent the sale of a home to a black family in an area covered by a restrictive covenant. In a matter-of-fact tone, the principals describe how they had maintained an "improvement association" for more than a decade to ensure that minority homeseekers were excluded. In this case and others, the courts upheld the legality of racial covenants until the landmark Supreme Court case, *Shelley v. Kraemer*, in 1948. The sale was reversed and the black couple evicted.

By the 1930s, social scientists had translated the historical processes of metropolitan change that Allen and Nichols condemned into universal models. The concerns of real estate brokers and suburbanites with neighborhood "deterioration" and their desire for restrictions now gained the authority of academic expertise. In **Document 8-5,** a popular real estate textbook reflects this new understanding of urban and suburban growth, emphasizing the importance of neighborhood stability, "security," and social homogeneity—in other words, segregation. Written by Arthur Weimer, an economist at Indiana University, and Homer Hoyt, an economist with the Federal Housing Administration, formerly of the University of Chicago, textbooks such as this one codified ideas about how real estate thrives and declines into an industry standard that persisted through the 1960s. Hoyt's role, too, illustrates the overlapping influences of the real estate industry, academic expertise, and public policy on the housing market.

This convergence is also apparent in **Document 8-6**, the frontispiece from a report by the President's Conference on Home Building and Home Ownership. Culminating a decade of public–private partnerships to promote home ownership and better housing in America, this conference, convened by President Herbert Hoover in 1931, laid a practical basis for New Deal housing policy to come. This image visually delineates the ideal that governed the type of housing that federal programs would or would not support.

Document 8-7 shows just how the government translated this ideal into actual housing policy. This document contains four worksheets from the Home Owners Loan Corporation (HOLC) "City Survey" of Los Angeles, produced in the late 1930s. Federal officials produced similar worksheets for over 200 metropolitan areas, recording their observations about the "quality" of every neighborhood and its prospects as a "security risk" for home loans. Three of the worksheets cover different sections of Pasadena, California, a prestigious older suburb of Los Angeles. By the 1930s, Pasadena was home to wealthy Eastern transplants and Los Angeles elites, middle-class white homeowners, and a range of nonwhite suburbanites who often worked for them. These worksheets depict three different HOLC ratings—A (green), B (blue), and D (red) reflecting different catagories of supposed risk for lending. A final worksheet is from the "San Gabriel Wash & Whittier Way" section of Los Angeles, populated primarily by Mexican immigrants. This area was given a D rating, for reasons linked to the class and race of its occupants. Harsher than most such worksheets, its starkly racist language nonetheless reveals the kind of assumptions that underlay the HOLC appraisal process. This basic appraisal system would be adopted by the Federal Housing Administration and by private lenders in subsequent years.

Does class or race seem to have been more important in the formulation of new restrictions in suburbia? To what extent did ideas about race and class overlap? How did ideas about housing as an investment vs. "home sweet home" shape thinking about the need for restrictions? In what ways did the interests of suburban residents and real estate professionals diverge as well as coincide? What part did blue-collar workers, immigrants, and African Americans and other racialized minorities play in the process of expanding regulation and government intervention? How did the federal government—through the HOLC—define worthy or unworthy neighborhoods? How would you define the suburban ideal at this time, as expressed by these documents?

8-1. SUBURBANITE FREDERICK LEWIS ALLEN SHARES HIS "SUBURBAN NIGHTMARE," 1925

Source: Frederick Lewis Allen, "Suburban Nightmare," *The Independent* 114 (June 13, 1925).

I live in one of the most attractive suburbs of New York. It is built on rolling hills, with belts of woodland and outcropping ledges; excellent trains reach it in forty minutes from the city; the houses were mainly designed by architects, rather than contractors, with fortunate results; and there is not a tenement, a three-decker, or a factory within its limits. The house which I occupy looks out over several acres of open country, where on a June evening one may walk beside a little brook and hear wood thrushes singing in the thickets; and I can reach it from my office in a little over an hour. It sounds idyllic, now, but my lease will soon come to an end, and when I think of buying or building I find myself facing the problem which sooner or later confronts every New York commuter. The city is growing too fast for us.

When the late Dr. Jowett was invited to come to New York to preach, he asked for only a modest salary and a house "with a bit of green about it," not realizing that on Manhattan Island only Mr. [Henry] Frick and Mr. [J. P.] Morgan and Mr. [Charles] Schwab and two or three others can afford a bit of green. This is one of the things for which people go out to the suburbs. They want air that does not reek of motor exhaust, light instead of the grim shadow of apartment houses, quiet instead of the clatter of riveters by day and the squawk of taxicabs by night, neighbors whom they know and to whom their existence is not a matter of utter indifference, and a life whose tempo is less nerve-racking than that of the city. And some of them think it not unreasonable to hope for still other benefits: for a measure of the informality of country life; for the sight of trees that grow as God intended, and of flowers that have the

temerity to bloom outside of florists' shops; for a chance for their children to grow up knowing cows and robins by sight. The New York commuter can get these things now if he is lucky, and can, to some extent, continue to get if he is wealthy, but the odds are against him. The city is growing fast and is swallowing up the surrounding country.

Take our suburb as an example. It is growing like a boom town. Those who have lived in it for ten years are considered old inhabitants. When the trains from the city draw in at night, the crowds that swarm down on to the platform are nearly half as large again as they were a year ago. The price of land has doubled or tripled in five years. New houses are springing up everywhere, and bits of natural greenery, like that on which my windows look out, are doomed shortly for what the real-estate broker, in unconsciously ironic language, is pleased to call "improvement."

A few months ago there were four large tracts of open land, where one could ramble without interruption, within easy walking distance of my house. Last December, one of these tracts was sold to a real-estate corporation for more than a million dollars, and soon they will begin to cut streets through it, break it up into house lots, and make a village of it. They plan to build apartment houses, stores, a moving-picture theatre, and to bring in several thousand people, and they are somewhat surprised that we do not regard them as public benefactors for thus making the suburb bigger and busier.

The second tract was sold in January, also for "improvement." Real-estate men are bickering over the third, and the fourth will follow suit. The groves where we now look for anemones in spring will be sliced through with orderly little streets down which orderly little commuters will hurry to catch the seven-forty-eight train for town, while their wives look into each other's back windows and tell each other that you never would believe, my dear, what goings on there are at

Mrs. So-and-So's, right in plain sight of everybody. On Sunday afternoons, the villagers can take their children walking along Woodcrest Avenue or Kenmont Street, but there will be no pastures studded with violets to stroll in, no tumbled stone walls to climb; no lanes to follow between the apple blossoms. An innocuous community with neat oblong gardens before the doors, but a standardized community which has lost the life of the country for that of the town.

Similar things are happening to nearly all the suburbs. Last November, the population of a nearby suburb increased overnight by three thousand. Several new apartment houses were thrown open and immediately filled. That suburb is getting to have a smart metropolitan air; prices, standards of living, and complexions are highly artificial. Recently, in another suburb, I was driving with a prosperous real-estate man. "Do you see that house?" he said to me. "Bought in 1920 for twenty-three thousand dollars and sold this year for thirty-seven. A clear profit of fourteen thousand, and the owner had the use of it all that time." He assured me that the values of houses were going up all over the town, despite frantic building, and referred to them as "homes"—which suggested an interesting problem in definition. A home, to me, is a place where you intend to stay—a century or two, perhaps. To my real-estate friend, a home was an investment (with incidental shelter value) to be turned over, when the market permitted, in order that your next investment might be more pretentious, revealing to all, by the amplitude of its sun porch and the dimensions of its two-car garage, that you were a man of importance and likely to move soon again.

Yet, who can build for permanence when the face of the land is changing so rapidly? You think of buying a house that gives on an open field, and you cannot foresee what will become of that field. You can be sure that it will not stay as it is. In ten years, you may have a view of a row of identical back yards, and a swarm of neighbors not even remotely of your own choosing. All sense of security for the future is lost. With such a gamble before you, is it any wonder that you are driven to think in terms of profitable investment?

Already, we hear our friends talking of "moving farther out."…

To move to another suburb farther from New York means, for the man of the family, spending anywhere from three to four hours a day in travel. I often wonder who the champion commuter of New York is and how far he goes. He must live farther away than Philadelphia or New Haven, for the commuters from these places are numbered by the score. Probably, he spends over five hours a day *en route*; say a third of his waking time. If he keeps it up for thirty years, he will have given up ten solid years to reading newspapers in the jiggling light of a train, milling through crowds in subterranean corridors, and being half suffocated in subway cars. Thousands of New York commuters give more than four hours a day to this ordeal, in order that they may have a home not too far from station and store and school, but still in the quiet country.…

This is not a New York problem only. It has merely reached New York first. It will soon be as bad in Chicago, though Chicago has more directions to expand in. It will confront other American cities in time, unless the trend of modern life changes. So long as the rush to the cities continues, the movement into the suburbs to escape the turmoil of city life can only defeat its own end.

When I am sick of thinking of the future of our suburb, I like to contemplate Vermont, whose population is actually decreasing. At its present rate, in a few centuries Vermont will be frequented by archaeologists exhuming the remains of a defunct civilization. There are still a few railroads there, and all about are the eternal hills with never a sign of a real-estate development called Green Mountain Heights or Vermont Park, or of little streets running out into the underbrush and noisy with carpenters building imitation colonial houses and alleged English cottages. Moving to Vermont would require, on our part, a new point of view. We should have to be content with smaller spheres of business influence, but perhaps when that day came we would be glad to advertise our smallness; to put up signs reading, "Watch Vermont Dwindle," and "Move Here If You Want to Live, but for Heaven's Sake Don't Build a

Factory." Meanwhile, New York continues to grow, and I look out of my window at the maples bursting into bud in the hollow, and wonder how soon they will be cut down in all their beauty to make way for urban improvements.

8-2. J. C. NICHOLS MAKES THE CASE FOR SUBURBAN PLANNING, 1923

Source: Jesse Clyde Nichols, "When You Buy a Home Site You Make an Investment; Try to Make it a Safe One," *Good Housekeeping* 76 (February 1923).

A young man, about to be married and possessed of five thousand dollars, and a real estate man who had just opened a new subdivision, met in Kansas City some fifteen years ago. The real estate man speedily found a way to induce the young man to visit the subdivision. They rode to the end of a streetcar line, drove in a buggy for a mile or so through the nondescript outskirts of the city, passing tin-can dumps, ash-piles, hog lots, dairies, and shanties, and finally, tying the horse to a rail fence, they crossed a stream on a foot bridge, climbed a hill, and so reached the subdivision.

It was a rough, ten-acre patch of ground with nothing but a few stakes and a narrow, board sidewalk to distinguish it from a country field. A sturdy imagination was needed to picture it as an attractive home site. But the real estate man possessed imagination to spare.

"The city," he averred, flourishing a map, "is bound to move out this way. It's the logical place for homes."

"Possibly," the prospect said, "but yonder is a brickyard. I don't want a brickyard with clouds of smoke just over the hill."

"Of course you don't! But when we get a few houses up, property will advance. The ground will be too valuable for the brickyard, and it will move out."

They argued this point. The prospect finally admitted that the real estate man might be right, but he saw other objections.

"There aren't any city improvements," he said, "no city water, gas, electric light, sewers, pavements."

"You're right!" rejoined the real estate man; "and if all those things *were* in, do you know what you'd have to pay for this property?"

He went into those details earnestly.

The real estate man was honest and self-convinced, but inexperienced. He believed almost anybody buying property in his subdivision would profit by it, and the young man with five thousand dollars caught his enthusiasm and ended by buying a couple of lots. The real estate man arranged to build his house for him also.

Several years passed. There had been other buyers, all equally hopeful at the start that the investment would turn out well. But gradually they discovered they were wrong.

The real estate man had been right about one thing: the city did move in the direction of his subdivision. But he was wrong about several other things.

For one, the brickyard was not abandoned. For fifteen years it operated on the other side of the hill!

For another, the fact that city improvements were not in proved to be a serious disadvantage. When a number of people had made their homes on the subdivision, it was taken into the corporate limits of the growing city. Improvements were ordered by the municipality, but the public contract methods used were not economical.

One street, for example, ran down hill. The upper portion had to be graded down, and the lower portion graded up. It would have been economical to grade up the lower portion with the dirt removed from the upper portion. But the job was done piecemeal, and only the upper part was paved at first. Dirt was excavated and carted away for dumping. Later, when the lower part was paved, dirt had to be hauled in!

The cost of that and other operations equally shortsighted had to be met out of taxes and special assessments handled in an extravagant manner. The charges fell heavily on owners and increased the amount of money they put into their property without correspondingly increasing its value.

In due time the young man who had started with five thousand dollars—by now he had the responsibility of a family—wanted to dispose of his extra vacant lot. He could not get as much for it as he had paid, even with the improvements in. This opened his eyes. He tried to sell his house also. He managed to find a buyer but the property returned to his pockets less than it had taken out.

I happen to know the details of this transaction, because I was the real estate man. That was my first subdivision. The woes of many people who bought from me, and my discovery as time went on that unintentionally I had misled them when I induced them to invest, caused me to make a careful study of the factors that influence home values. I tried to discover when and under what circumstances the purchase of a home can be considered a reasonably good investment.

The study led to some interesting practical results, but not until I had learned that in a surprisingly large number of cases the purchase of a home in American cities does *not* turn out to be a good investment. My experiences on my first subdivision, instead of being unusual, were common and rather typical, and that seemed to me fundamentally wrong, because the purchase of a home is the one big investment in the lives of millions. For that reason alone the home investment ought to be protected in so far as possible against every kind of value-destroying encroachment.

It is not only in new developments, I found, that the home investment often shrinks. Day after day people buy homes in fully-developed sections, where they can see exactly what is around them, and there also, after a little while, they find it impossible to sell for as much as they paid.

Choose any city you please. Go into what were pleasant by-streets five, ten, or fifteen years ago, and you will find houses otherwise in good condition, but blackened with grime inside and out until they are scarcely habitable; factories have crept in among them. Go also into the part of the city that was ultra-fashionable a dozen or a score of years ago; there you will find mansions turned into boarding houses or modiste shops, or remodeled or razed for office and store buildings; or if some homes have not been used in that way, you will find their original residence values destroyed by the establishment of stores, shops, undertaking parlors, and the like, in proximity. Look over any large city

in the United States, and you will discover striking examples of abandoned or shifting residence sections where no compensating use has maintained former values.

This loss from the abandonment of homes that are still good, but undesirable because of the encroachment of business or other elements, must be measured in American cities not in millions of dollars, but in *billions*. The emotional losses to families that have to forsake their homes can not be measured, but they are not slight. These losses have been accepted for the most part as if they were inevitable.

In Kansas City we have been trying to make the purchase of homes a good investment. We have demonstrated, I believe, that by proper regulation the permanence and safety of the investment can be assured, and the emotional values can be enhanced....

This is significant, but not mysterious. The reason for it is found, briefly, in adequate restrictions, suitable development and surroundings, and a constructive community spirit....

There is a desperate need in every city of ten thousand or more for effective city planning, and the kind of city planning that means most to the individual property owner is not a handsome scheme for civic centers—these are needed, truly—but a satisfactory scheme of zoning which districts property according to the uses to which it may be put, and restricts it to those uses until the best interests of the holders of a majority of the acreage make a change imperative after certain prescribed periods of time.

When I began selling lots in that first subdivision in the tag-end outskirts of the city, I was afraid to suggest my present broad building restrictions. I thought nobody would buy rigidly restricted lots. It was hard enough, I reasoned, to sell them anyhow!

But I saw what happened to those first buyers, and I felt that I was not delivering full value to them. The situation had passed beyond my control in that subdivision. But I proposed to those interested with me that we take one hundred acres of land, thoroughly improve and beautify it, and obligate ourselves for a period of twenty-five years to sell none of it for homes costing less than three thousand dollars each, or having lots less than fifty feet wide and one hundred and fifty feet deep, with a required amount of side free space, controlled frontage, and other phases then unheard of in building restrictions.

The common plan in the city had been to restrict property deed by deed, as the land was sold, if there were any restrictions at all. A depression in the real estate market often came before the tract was all disposed of, and the owners would very likely sell the remaining lots without restrictions. Those who had already bought restricted property might protest, but that was all they could do. They had no recourse.

My proposal called for obligating ourselves in advance on the whole tract. My associates ridiculed the possibility of success, so I went ahead alone.

As I look back, those first restrictions seem extremely mild and incomplete. We go so far now as to restrict certain large tracts in two hundred foot lots, varying in depth from two hundred to three hundred feet, and limited to homes ranging in minimum cost from ten to fifty thousand dollars. We limit in many details the uses to which the land can be put. And we find that the more restrictions we can put on, the more cheerfully is the land

bought by those wishing permanent homes safeguarded with respect to the financial and other values.

At first, as the character of our restrictions became more and more elaborate, we were occasionally accused of transgressing upon property rights. It was said that we attempted to dictate the family affairs of our purchasers. Of course, that was untrue. We simply knew some factors that often tend to make property a poor investment, and we undertook to prevent their action....

A list of a few of the restrictions on a carefully protected subdivision will suggest the length to which it is practicable to go in protecting the investment. On this property every buyer agrees to the following:

Billboards may be prohibited on any lot.

Lots may be used only for private residences designed for occupancy by a single family: flats and apartment houses cannot be erected.

The cost of the houses to be built must be at least a certain amount, specified *for each lot*.

We reserve the right to approve the plans, color, and elevation of every new house or addition thereto.

Figure 8-1 1,000 Acres Restricted, View of Country Club District Sign, ca. 1910. To reassure potential buyers nervous about possible encroachments on suburban homesites—such as the intrusion of factories and working-class neighbors—community builders such as J. C. Nichols soon found deed restrictions to be a key selling point. He prominently highlighted these restrictions in his marketing of real estate. Western Historical Manuscript Collection-Kansas City, J.C. Nichols Company Records KC106.

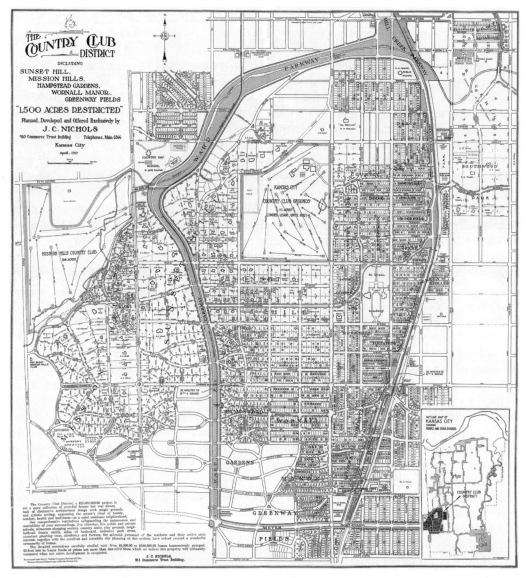

Figure 8-2 Map of Ward Parkway and Country Club District, 1917. This map of Kansas City's exclusive Country Club District reveals both the scale and the amenities of community builder, J. C. Nichols', signature development. The map also shows the parkways and greenspace that enveloped and buffered the development from neighboring properties. From the Western Historical Manuscript Collection-Kansas City, J.C. Nichols Company Records KC106.

The amount of required ground frontage and side free space are specified.

There are regulations regarding the distance houses must be set back from the street, and the distance that bay and dormer windows, cornices, chimneys, trellises, vestibules, and porches may project in the front or on the side from the main body of the house....

Certain areas are reserved for houses of English architecture, other areas for Colonial types, and so on, thus giving a harmonious grouping of homes in a given area.

No detached outbuildings are permitted in certain tracts....

I have mentioned that formerly building restrictions were imposed deed by deed. One result was that they ran out at different times; further, there was no satisfactory way of renewing them. Now the permanence of restrictions is all-important, and we designed a new type. They extend over definite periods of twenty-five years each, and are automatically self-renewing for periods of twenty years each, unless at least five years prior to each expiration period, the owners of a majority of the net acreage execute and properly record an agreement releasing the land from the restrictions at the end of the period. It is not easy to get such releases unless the change is clearly to the interest of a majority of the property owners....

There are other elements than the physical which also tend to enhance values and to make the purchase of a home a good investment. One of these, intangible and therefore too seldom considered, is of very great importance. This may be called residential morale....

Communities generally suffer from the fact that everybody's business is nobody's business—as soon as the developer has sold out. For fear of giving personal offense, a neighbor will often see a restriction violated near by without remonstrance. We organize local maintenance associations. Neighbors are selected to represent the entire community, with full responsibility for the period of their office to observe all the many little things that help to preserve desirable home surroundings and property values. We have never had any one elected who refused to serve....

My experience has been in a residential development in which the total cost of land and its development and the homes already erected is more than twenty-five million dollars. I know as a result of it that the purchase of a home can be made a good permanent investment and the sentimental and civic considerations of home-owning can be enhanced. But we have to remember that in the last fifty years cities have undergone more change than they did in the previous two thousand years, due to changes in the mode of living, the growth and change in character of traffic, the development in the size and kind of transportation units, and the extension of cities over wider areas than ever before.

This means that in the future, at least as far as residence districts are concerned, cities *must be built* according to *carefully studied plans*. The economic, civic, and moral loss is far too great when they are permitted, as in the past, to sprawl.

8-3. RESTRICTIVE DEED, EAST SAN DIEGO, CALIFORNIA, 1911

Source: Deed to lots 12 and 13, Fairmount Addition to City Heights, East San Diego, California, Office of the County Recorder, San Diego, California.

Map #1035 (#6)
Bk 544, pg 356 Dds
Fairmount Add. to Cy Hts.

We, Pacific Building Company, a corporation having its principal place of business in San Diego, County of San Diego, California, by virtue of a resolution authorizing the same, passed at a meeting of its Directors, for and in consideration of the sum of Ten and 00/100 Dollars, do hereby grant to A. R. Graeall that real property situated in County of San Diego, State of California, bounded and described as follows:

Lots Twelve (12) and Thirteen (13) in Block Twenty-five (25) of Fairmount Addition to City Heights, in the County of San Diego, State of California, according to map thereof No. 1035, filed in the office of the County Recorder of said San Diego County March 8, 1907.

Provided always that this conveyance is made upon the following express conditions:

FIRST: This property shall not be sold, leased, rented to or occupied by any person other than one of the Caucasian race.

SECOND: No intoxicating liquors of any kind shall be manufactured or sold upon these premises.

THIRD: No dwelling house shall be erected upon said premises which shall cost less than $1000.00.

FOURTH: No building shall be erected upon said premises which shall be located less than 20 feet from the line of Molino Avenue.

It is hereby expressly agreed that in case the foregoing conditions, or any thereof, be broken by the grantee, his heirs, successors or assigns, or legal representatives, this conveyance shall become and be null and void and the title to the premises herein conveyed shall revert to the grantor, and the said grantor, its legal representatives, successors or assigns, shall have the right to reenter upon and possess said premises with their privileges and appurtenances and hold the same forever.

TO HAVE AND TO HOLD the above granted and described premises unto the said Grantee, his heirs and assigns forever, subject to the above conditions.

IN WITNESS WHEREOF, said corporation has caused this deed to be signed by its President and Secretary and its corporate seal to be affixed hereto, this twenty-second day or December, 1911.

PACIFIC BUILDING COMPANY,
By O. W. Cotton, President
Attest: G. H. Frost, Secretary

8-4. A SUBURBANITE DEFENDS RACIAL EXCLUSION IN COURT, 1933

Source: *Baker v. Engstrom*, Superior Court of Cook County, Illinois. No. 578255, 1933. Gen. No. 455947.

JOHN E. WING, called as a witness on behalf of the complainants [white residents of Wesley Avenue, Evanston, Illinois], being first duly sworn, testified as follows:

DIRECT EXAMINATION By Mr. Fox:
Q   State your name, please.
A   John E. Wing
Q   Your address and occupation?
A   Business address 72 West Adams Street, Chicago; attorney; member of the firm of Isham, Lincoln, & Beale.
Q   Are you admitted to practice in the State of Illinois?
A   I am, since 1905.
Q   Did you tell where you reside?
A   1827 Asbury Avenue, Evanston, Illinois.
Q   I am showing you the originals of six contracts…and ask you what, if anything, you had to do with the preparation of those contracts.…
A   In 1922 the residents living in that locality became particularly conscious of the fact that there was a likelihood of negroes moving south of Emerson Street [Ed. note: the recognized division be-

tween white and black neighborhoods]. It was first brought to our attention in connection with the premises at 1844 Wesley Avenue, which are the premises involved in this proceeding.

In 1922 that property was about to be sold to negroes, and the residents in the district which I am speaking of arranged to have the property purchased by a white man, Mr. Winter, and at that time we paid Mr. Winter $1,000.00, in order to get him to agree to sign an agreement with other residents in that block, whenever the agreement was made and properly prepared for record.

MR. SELINGER: Q Pardon me, will you state who "we" was?
A   I say, the residents in that district. I know about it, because I assisted in collecting the money, in paying the money to Mr. Winter.…

Because of that incident, and some others, we decided that we would form some kind of an association to protect ourselves. The West Side Improvement Association was formed in 1922 and 1923, and the object of the association is to protect the neighborhood from encroachment of all kinds, and particularly to preserve it as a place for white people to live.

At this time we also founded what we called a syndicate, which was to furnish the money to back the plan of protecting the district. We proceeded with the syndicate for several years, and during that time we had several instances where property was sold to negroes, or about to be sold to negroes, and we were able to prevent the sale by the payment of money.

One incident of that kind is on Wesley Avenue, just south of Lyons Street, one block south of this property. That cost us $3500.00. Another instance was over on Dewey Avenue. Another instance was on Florence Avenue. After we had done that for a time, we saw that we could not keep on doing that, because our purse was not long enough.…

[W]e decided that the only method of real protection was to have the property restricted by a covenant, providing that none of the property could be occupied by negroes or sold to negroes; and in order to carry that out, we proceeded to have an examination made as to the ownership of the property in different blocks....That examination was carried out for the managers of the association through my office....I used the information...and prepared these agreements....

Q   Will you state to the Master whether or not at the time these agreements were executed, the persons who executed them were white persons?

A   They were.

Q   Will you state whether or not there have been any negroes occupying property in this district...since the date of the execution of these agreements, except the Waldens [Ed. note: the African-American couple who were the object of the suit]?

MR. SELINGER: You mean, collectively?

MR. FOX: Q On any one piece of property in this district, occupying any piece of property in this district.

A   None as householders of any kind....

Q   When did you, as chairman of the Board of Managers, first learn that the property at 1844 Wesley was being occupied, or about to be occupied by negroes? When did you first learn that?

A   It is my recollection it was April 8th....

Q   Of what year?

A   Of the year 1933.

Q   How did you learn of that fact?

A   Someone on Wesley Avenue called me up....

MR. FOX: Q What did you do when that was called to your attention?

A   When that was called to my attention, I went to see Mr. Ingersoll, who lives in that block....

Q   After you talked to Mr. Ingersoll, did you have any conversation with Mr. and Mrs. Walden, or either of them?

A   Mr. Ingersoll and I then went to see Mr. and Mrs. Walden....

Q   Who was present at that conversation?

A   Mr. Ingersoll, Mr. and Mrs. Walden.

Q   And you?

A   Myself.

Q   That is all?

A   Yes.

Q   Where was that conversation held?

A   ...in the house, 1844 Wesley Avenue....

Q   How long did that conversation last?

A   Oh, I should say it lasted half an hour.

Q   Without detailing everything that happened during that conversation, will you state what, if anything, was said with reference to the occupancy of that property by [the] Waldens as colored persons, or as negroes....

A   I told Mr. and Mrs. Walden that the property was restricted against occupancy by negroes, and that they were negroes, and that they could not continue to live there. Shall I go on?

Q   Yes. Tell what, if anything, Mr. Walden said.

A   Mr. Walden said in reply to that, "Why, yes, we are negroes, but why can't we live here?" "Well," I said, "there is a restrictive agreement which prohibits you living here," and I had the agreement there, and referred him to the provisions of the agreement. Mr. Walden said, "Well, we are respectable people, and we will keep our house in as good looking condition as the other people in the block," and I said, "That, Mr. Walden, is not the point. This is not directed against you individually. This is directed against general occupancy by negroes, because the people in this block know by experience that if negroes come in, their property values will be destroyed, and that is the reason, it is purely a matter of property values."

Q   Did Mr. and Mrs. Walden have anything to say to that?

A   They still said that they thought that they might be permitted to occupy the premises, but before we left they were not insistent about that....

MR. FOX: Q Have you exhausted your recollection, Mr. Wing?

A   I have not. Before we left, Mrs. Walden—I don't know whether a whimsical idea, or what it was—said to me, "Mr. Wing, are you a Christian? Do you go to church?" And I said, "Yes," and she said, "Well, Mr. Wing, what do you think is going to happen when we get to heaven? Are we negroes going to be separated from the whites? Do we have to live in a separate place from the whites?"

MR. SELINGER: Q What did you answer to that?

A I said, "I can't tell you what the answer is, and I want to tell you that I have a great deal of respect for negroes. I have no objection to them. I respect the negro as much as I do a white. But this is just a question of property values, and that is all there is to it, and for that reason we cannot let you stay here."

MR. FOX: Q Have you now exhausted your recollection as to what Mrs. Walden said?

A I think so. There may have been something more.

Q State whether or not Mrs. Walden said anything to you as to where she, as a negro, ought to live, if she cannot live there.

A Yes.

Q What?

A Mrs. Walden said, "Where can we live?" She said, "Where I came from"—it was some place in Ohio—"where I came from I lived with white people, I don't like to live with negroes. I would rather live with white people. Where can I live?" I said, "There are plenty of places in Evanston where you can live, and particularly there are some very good residences west of here, west of the railroad, and along Emerson Street. There is no difficulty with that."

Q What did she say?

A She said she did not want to live there.

8-5. WEIMER AND HOYT OUTLINE THE *PRINCIPLES OF URBAN REAL ESTATE,* 1939

Source: Arthur M. Weimer and Homer Hoyt, *Principles of Urban Real Estate,* Copyright © 1939 by The Ronald Press. Reprinted with permission of John Wiley & Sons, Inc.

Changing Character of Neighborhoods

Residential neighborhoods are seldom in a static condition but are influenced by numerous forces which are constantly in operation. These forces are of three main types: (1) physical and functional depreciation; (2) the development of nuisances and more intensive land uses; and (3) the movements of various groups of people.

Physical wear and tear is constantly tending to make existing structures less desirable places in which to live and forcing people to seek new locations. As new houses are built, the older ones usually cannot compete with them because new conveniences, designs and locations usually are more attractive.

In addition, each family attempts to better its living conditions and tends to move to the most desirable location which its income permits. As certain types of individuals move, they may be absorbed into a neighborhood without any change, or, because of special characteristics, they may tend to displace the groups already there and force them to seek new locations in turn. Usually, we find people desiring to live with neighbors whose earnings, living standards, and general social backgrounds are similar to their own. This attitude is characteristic of all income groups, as well as racial and national groups.

As a result of the operation of these forces, people are drawn to newer or more desirable neighborhoods because of the advantages which they offer and driven from older or less desirable areas because inharmonious groups have entered or because of the deterioration of older buildings....

Analysis of Neighborhoods

Because of these constant changes, which may be so slow in operation that they are not recognized by people living in areas where such changes are occurring, there is a general tendency for land values in residential areas to decline unless some "higher" or more intense use is made of the land.

If this tendency is true, and past experience indicates that it is, the problem of analyzing neighborhoods resolves itself into one of determining which areas are least likely to suffer future decline, rather than that of determining which ones are most likely to advance in value. Hence, neighborhood analysis becomes a process of evaluating the forces which are most likely to lead to future stability or militate against it. This process necessitates analysis of: (1) location with respect to main lines of city growth; (2) nearness to blighting influences; (3) age; (4) types of people in an area and extent of owner occupancy; (5) types of improvements; (6) transportation facilities; (7) nearness to schools, churches, shopping centers, amusement places and places of employment; (8) tax rates and special assessments; (9) utilities and conveniences; (10) topography; and (11) special hazards and nuisances....

Blighting influences include unfavorable land uses and inharmonious groups of people. Thus, if a neighborhood is located near a factory area which is expanding, it is likely to decline rapidly. Similarly, rapid development and expansion of commercial uses tends to undermine a neighborhood. The building of apartment houses usually detracts from the desirability of single-family areas.

Any neighborhood which is in the direct path of a lower grade area is in danger of being blighted, especially if both areas are served by the same transportation line. The presence of inharmonious racial or national groups in a nearby area also represents a force which may lead to neighborhood decline. Usually the coming in of a lower income group or types of people who will not harmonize with the present occupants in the area results in great instability.

The foreign-born who have most recently migrated from Europe tend to cluster in certain sections of every large American city, while those groups which settled in America years ago have scattered throughout our urban areas. For example, in one census tract in Greater Cleveland 65 per cent of the family heads were born in Czechoslovakia, in another 68 per cent were born in Poland, while in another 91 per cent were Negroes.

Certain national and racial groups tend to move almost as units. For example in one Cleveland census tract migration reduced the number of persons who had been born in Russia from 893 in 1920 to 15 in 1930, while the Negro population increased from 8.7 to 90.6 per cent....

The extent to which blighting influences may affect a neighborhood depends in part on the protections against them which exist.

Zoning laws usually regulate the types of uses to which various areas in a city may be put. To be adequate they must not only indicate the permitted uses in a definite manner but the uses allowed must be such as to promote harmonious and stable neighborhoods. The city plan commission or the city engineer's office are the chief sources of information of this type. Also, height and area restrictions are often helpful in promoting neighborhood stability since they protect against overcrowding and the dangers likely to result from it.

Deed restrictions represent another effective type of regulation in protecting neighborhoods against blight. Usually such restrictions can be much more detailed and definite than zoning laws and may regulate architecture, cost of buildings, setbacks, and types of people who may be allowed to live within designated areas.

In recent years certain modifications and extensions of the ideas involved in deed restrictions have been developed. One of these is the "Neighborhood Restrictive Agreement," which is a private contract entered into voluntarily by owners in a certain district. These agreements may be drawn up after the area is developed, while deed restrictions are usually imposed at the time a new subdivision is started. Another recent proposal designed to achieve the same objectives is the enactment of "Neighborhood Improving Acts." Under such acts a city may divide itself into various areas and 60 per cent of the owners of land in a neighborhood may propose a plan for developing and preserving the area. Their strength and value must be judged by reference to existing condition.

8-6. WHITE HOUSE PANEL OF EXPERTS DEPICTS THE IDEAL HOME, 1932

Copyright—The Architects' Small House Service Bureau, Inc.—Home Plan No. 6-F-8

The detached one-family house on an adequate lot in pleasant surroundings expresses the housing ideals and aspirations of most American families, particularly those with small children.

Figure 8-3 President Hoover's Conference on Home Building and Home Ownership laid the foundations for future federal housing policy. Illustrations such as this one depicted the type of homes that policy would promote. Copyright © Architects' Small House Service Bureau, republished in *Home Ownership, Income and Types of Dwellings*, ed. John M. Gries and James Ford (Washington, D.C.: President's Conference on Home Building and Home Ownership, 1932), frontispiece.

8-7. HOME OWNERS LOAN CORPORATION APPRAISES LOS ANGELES, 1939

AREA DESCRIPTIONS - SECURITY MAP OF <u>LOS ANGELES COUNTY</u>

1. POPULATION: a. Increasing <u>Rapidly</u> Decreasing _____ Static _____

   b. Class and Occupation <u>Business & professional men, retired people, Jr. executives,</u>
   <u>public officials, etc. Income $2400 to $5000 and up.</u>
   c. Foreign Families <u>None</u>% Nationalities _____ d. Negro <u>None</u> %

   e. Shifting or Infiltration <u>None apparent</u>

2. BUILDINGS:

	PREDOMINATING 85 %	OTHER TYPE %
a. Type and Size	6, 7 & 8 rooms	5 rooms 5%
b. Construction	Frame, stucco & masonry	
c. Average Age	3 years	
d. Repair	Good	
e. Occupancy	99%	
f. Owner-occupied	95%	
g. 1935 Price Bracket	$ Very few % chge	$ % chge
	constructed	
h. 1937 Price Bracket	$ 6000-10000 %	$ %
i. 1939 Price Bracket	$ 6000-10000 %	$ %
j. Sales Demand	Good	
k. Predicted Price Trend (next 6-12 months)	Static	
l. 1935 Rent Bracket	$ Not a % chge	$ % chge
m. 1937 Rent Bracket	$ rental %	$ %
n. 1939 Rent Bracket	$ district %	$ %
o. Rental Demand	—	
p. Predicted Rent Trend (next 6-12 months)	—	

   6, 7 & 8 rooms
3. NEW CONSTRCTN (past yr) No <u>125</u> Type & Price $6500-$10000 How selling <u>Readily</u>

4. OVERHANG OF HOME PROPERTIES: a. HOLC <u>None</u> b. Institutions <u>Few</u>

5. SALE OF HOME PROPERTIES (<u>3</u>yr) a. HOLC <u>None</u> b. Institutions <u>Few</u>

6. MORTGAGE FUNDS: <u>Ample (FHA)</u> 7. Total Tax Rate per $1000 (193 7/8) $48.80

8. DESCRIPTION AND CHARACTERISTICS OF AREA:
   Terrain: Level with favorable grades. No construction hazards. Land improved 60%.
   Deed restrictions provide for architectural supervision and protect against subversive racial hazards. Conveniences are all readily available. This is a recent subdivision which has grown very rapidly in the past few years under the stimulus of
   promotional effort and FHA Title II financing. While owner occupancy is very high,
   indications are that in most cases equities are low, which has a decided bearing
   upon the economic stability of the area. Construction and maintenance are of
   excellent character. Architectural designs are attractive and population is homogeneous. Improvements are noticeably larger and more imposing on Orange Grove Ave. and
   Mountain St. This, however, does not affect the harmonious appearance of the area.
   Indications are that development of the area will progress along the established
   pattern and it is therefore accorded a "low green" grade.

9. LOCATION <u>Pasadena</u> SECURITY GRADE <u>Low A</u> AREA NO. <u>A-11</u> DATE <u>4-14-39</u>

11

Figure 8-4 A Home Owners Loan Corporation appraisal worksheet for a wealthy section of Pasadena, California, 1939. This area received a favorable "Low A" rating. The
HOLC evaluated neighborhoods in cities across the country, following standards that
favored suburban communities of white middle- and upper-class residents. Los Angeles City Survey files, Area Descriptions, Home Owners Loan Corporation, Record
Group 195, National Archives, Washington, DC, 1939. Doc # A-11.

AREA DESCRIPTIONS - SECURITY MAP OF __LOS ANGELES COUNTY__

1. POPULATION: a. Increasing __Slowly__   Decreasing _____   Static _____

  .b. Class and Occupation __Business & professional men, skilled artisans, & white__ collar workers. Income $1800 to $3600 & up

   c. Foreign Families __Few__ % Nationalities __None subversive__   d. Negro __None__ %

   e. Shifting or Infiltration _____None apparent_____

2. BUILDINGS:

	PREDOMINATING	85 %	OTHER TYPE	%
a. Type and Size	_5, 6 & 7 rooms_		Large outmoded types 5%	
b. Construction	Frame, stucco & masonry		8, 9 & 10 rooms	10%
c. Average Age	16 years			
d. Repair	Good			
e. Occupancy	98%			
f. Owner-occupied	75%			
g. 1935 Price Bracket	$ 3250-5000	% chge	$	% chge
h. 1937 Price Bracket	$ 3500-5500	%	$	%
i. 1939 Price Bracket	$ 3500-5500	%	$	%
j. Sales Demand	Good			
k. Predicted Price Trend (next 6-12 months)	Static			
l. 1935 Rent Bracket	$ 25-50	% chge	$	% chge
m. 1937 Rent Bracket	$ 30-60	%	$	%
n. 1939 Rent Bracket	$ 30-60	%	$	%
o. Rental Demand	Good			
p. Predicted Rent Trend (next 6-12 months)	Static			

$4500 to $7500

3. NEW CONSTRCTN (past yr) No __35__ Type & Price __5 & 6 rooms__ How selling __Moderately__

4. OVERHANG OF HOME PROPERTIES: a. HOLC __1__ ? b. Institutions __Few__

5. SALE OF HOME PROPERTIES (3 yr) a. HOLC __None__ ? b. Institutions __Few__

6. MORTGAGE FUNDS: __Ample__   7. Total Tax Rate per $1000 (193 7/8) $49.54 Co. $37.54 Cy. $11.90

8. DESCRIPTION AND CHARACTERISTICS OF AREA: Terrain: level with favorable grades. No construction hazards. Land improved 85%. Deed restrictions have expired but movement is on foot to cover area with protective racial restrictions. Zoning is single family residential. Conveniences are all readily available. This area has been developing steadily for more than 25 years and is still comparatively active. Construction is of standard quality or better and maintenance indicates a high pride of occupancy. Population is homogeneous, the district being particularly favored by the business men of the community. Variance in size and types of improvements gives a heterogeneous aspect to parts of area. Convenience of location and stability are outstanding characteristics. Proximity to Pasadena Golf Club and Altadena Recreational Center are favorable influences. Prevalence of age and obsolescence are derogatory factors. Indications are that the area will remain desirable for a number of years to come and it is accorded a "medial blue" grade.

9. LOCATION __North Pasadena__ SECURITY GRADE __Med.__ B AREA NO. __B-29__ DATE __4-14-39__

89

Figure 8-5 In this HOLC appraisal of a neighborhood in north Pasadena, officials made open reference to "protective racial restrictions," which they believed positively enhanced neighborhood stability. These "protections" helped this area earn a favorable "B" rating, the second highest. Los Angeles City Survey files, Area Descriptions, Home Owners Loan Corporation, Record Group 195, National Archives, Washington, DC, 1939. Doc # B-29.

1. **POPULATION:** *a. Increasing*_____ *Decreasing*_____ *Static* Yes

   b. *Class and Occupation* Skilled artisans, letter carriers, laborers, & WPA workers
   Income $700-$1800

   c. *Foreign Families* Few % *Nationalities* Mexicans & Italians   d. *Negro* 5 %

   e. *Shifting or Infiltration* Indications of increasing subversive racial influences

2. **BUILDINGS:** | PREDOMINATING 90 % | OTHER TYPE ___ % |

	PREDOMINATING 90 %		OTHER TYPE ___ %	
a. Type and Size	5 & 6 room			
b. Construction	Frame & stucco			
c. Average Age	18 years			
d. Repair	Fair			
e. Occupancy	96%			
f. Owner-occupied	80%			
g. 1935 Price Bracket	$ 3000-4000	% change	$	% change
h. 1937 Price Bracket	$ 2750-3750	%	$	%
i. 1939 Price Bracket	$ 2750-3750	%	$	%
j. Sales Demand	Poor			
k. Predicted Price Trend (next 6-12 months)	Downward			
l. 1935 Rent Bracket	$ 25-35	% change	$	% change
m. 1937 Rent Bracket	$ 25-35	%	$	%
n. 1939 Rent Bracket	$ 25-35	%	$	%
o. Rental Demand	Fair			
p. Predicted Rent Trend (next 6-12 months)	Static			

3. **NEW CONSTRUCTION** (past yr.) No. 0 Type & Price -- How Selling --

4. **OVERHANG OF HOME PROPERTIES:** a. HOLC 0 b. Institutions Few

5. **SALE OF HOME PROPERTIES** (3 yr.) a. HOLC 1 b. Institutions Few

6. **MORTGAGE FUNDS:** Limited 7. **TOTAL TAX RATE PER $1000** (1937) $ 50.27
County $11.90-City $38.37 1938

8. **DESCRIPTION AND CHARACTERISTICS OF AREA:**

Terrain: Level with favorable grades. No construction hazards or flood threats.
Land improved 85%. Zoned single family residential. All conveniences. This
area is favorably located but is detrimentally affected by 10 owner occupant
Negro families located in center of area north and south of Bell St. between
Marvista and Catalina Aves. Although the Negroes are said to be of the better
class their presence has caused a wave of selling in the area and it seems
inevitable that ownership and property values will drift to lower levels.
Construction, maintenance and architectural designs while not of the highest
type are generally of good quality. The area is accorded a "high red" solely
on account of racial hazards. Otherwise a medial yellow grade would have been
assigned.

9. **LOCATION** Pasadena   **SECURITY GRADE** 4th + **AREA NO.** D-7 **DATE** 4/6/39

355

Figure 8-6 HOLC appraisal of a mixed-race section of Pasadena, 1939. The presence of racial diversity—regardless of class—automatically downgraded a neighborhood's ranking. This neighborhood received a "D" rating, the lowest score. Los Angeles City Survey files, Area Descriptions, Home Owners Loan Corporation, Record Group 195, National Archives, Washington, DC, 1939. Doc # D-7.

AREA DESCRIPTION

Security Map of___LOS ANGELES COUNTY___

1. POPULATION: a. *Increasing*_____ *Decreasing*_____ *Static* Yes___

   b. *Class and Occupation* Laborers, farm and WPA workers.- Income $700-$1000

   c. *Foreign Families* 100 % *Nationalities*___Mexicans___ d. *Negro*___0 %
      Many American born - impossible to differentiate

   e. *Shifting or Infiltration* of goats, rabbits and dark skinned babies indicated.

2. BUILDINGS:

	PREDOMINATING 100 %	OTHER TYPE %
a. *Type and Size*	2 to 5 rooms	
b. *Construction*	Shacks and hovels	
c. *Average Age*	50 or more years	
d. *Repair*	Terrible	
e. *Occupancy*	98%	
f. *Owner-occupied*	50% (formerly homesteads)	
g. *1935 Price Bracket*	$ Up to $1000 *% change*	$ *% change*
h. *1937 Price Bracket*	$ Up to $1000 %	$ %
i. 1939 *Price Bracket*	$ Up to $1000 %	$ %
j. *Sales Demand*	Poor	
k. *Predicted Price Trend* (next 6-12 months)	Static	
l. *1935 Rent Bracket*	$ Up to $10 *% change*	$ *% change*
m. *1937 Rent Bracket*	$ Up to $10 %	$ %
n. 1939 *Rent Bracket*	$ Up to $10 %	$ %
o. *Rental Demand*	Good	
p. *Predicted Rent Trend* (next 6-12 months)	Static	

3. NEW CONSTRUCTION (*past yr.*) No. None *Type & Price*___-___ *How Selling*___-___

4. OVERHANG OF HOME PROPERTIES: a. HOLC___0___ b. *Institutions*___0___

5. SALE OF HOME PROPERTIES (3 *yr.*) a. HOLC___0___ b. *Institutions*___0___

6. MORTGAGE FUNDS:___None___ 7. TOTAL TAX RATE PER $1000 (193__) 1937-8 $ 47.58

8. DESCRIPTION AND CHARACTERISTICS OF AREA:
   Terrain: Low lying level.- Some adobe soil. Land improved 90%. Many dwellings
   have small acreage adjoining. Deed restrictions and zoning are lacking. Conveniences are all readily available, including bus line on Whittier Blvd. This
   is an extremely old Mexican shack district, which has been "as is" for many
   generations. Like the "Army mule" it has no pride of ancestry nor hope of posterity. It is a typical semi tropical countryside "slum".
   The area is generously accorded a "low red" grade.

9. LOCATION San Gabriel Wash & Whittier Way___ SECURITY GRADE 4th- AREA NO. D-57 DATE 4-26-39
   405

Figure 8-7 HOLC appraisal of the "San Gabriel Wash & Whittier Way" section of Los Angeles, 1939. The harsh language on this worksheet reveals that ethnic Mexicans, too, were targeted as racially inferior by federal appraisers. This area received a "D" rating. Los Angeles City Survey files, Area Descriptions, Home Owners Loan Corporation, Record Group 195, National Archives, Washington, DC, 1939. Doc # D-57.

ESSAYS

In **Essay 8-1**, historian and city planner Marc A. Weiss underscores the critical role played by real estate developers in the movement for public planning and land use regulation in the early twentieth century. He emphasizes the importance of a group of real estate entrepreneurs that he dubs "community builders" who consolidated once separate parts of the real estate business—the purchase and subdivision of raw land, installation of infrastructure and landscaping, and the construction of housing—into the unified enterprise of "development." Out of a desire to protect their own large investments as well as those of their clients, these developers were among the leading advocates for public land use restrictions and regulations, and they influenced city planners and lawmakers to follow suit. **Essay 8-2** by historian Kenneth Jackson shows how real estate practices that had existed piecemeal in the private sector became codified into federal policy in the 1930s. Two important New Deal federal agencies—the Home Owners Loan Corporation and the Federal Housing Administration—developed policies that privileged suburban areas for federal assistance and supported restrictions that ensured segregated neighborhoods. Jackson's essay suggests that by the 1930s, real estate restrictions had fully evolved: from the haphazard use of private mechanisms like deed restrictions in the early twentieth century, to municipal tools like zoning, and finally to the housing policy of the federal government. The end result was a metropolitan landscape that increasingly favored white, middle-class suburbanites while excluding poorer and nonwhite urbanites from these same advantages.

ESSAY 8-1. MARC A. WEISS, *THE RISE OF THE COMMUNITY BUILDERS: THE AMERICAN REAL ESTATE INDUSTRY AND URBAN LAND PLANNING* (1987)

Source: Copyright © 1987 Columbia University Press. Reprinted with permission of the publisher.

Defining an Agenda for Public Action

In 1916 J. C. Nichols delivered a major address to the National Conference on City Planning....The 1916 talk, "Financial Effect of Good Planning in Land Subdivision," outlined the broad contours of the urban land planning agenda that would accompany and help foster the emerging transformation in the institutional processes of urban land development. His speech clearly underscored the crucial interconnection between the changing nature of residential development and the creation of land-use regulations and planning agencies in American cities. It also described the basis of cooperation between community builders and city planners from the developer's viewpoint....

J. C. Nichols began his address with a complaint and a lament. The complaint was that "Eighty to ninety percent of our city property is covered with residence districts, and yet ninety percent of the discussion in city planning conventions I have attended is directed to traction problems and downtown development." His own participation and that of other community builders helped to considerably change the latter percentage.

The lament was that in order for community builders to successfully develop a large subdivision, the amount of land they needed to control and the length of time it took to sell all the parcels imposed huge financing problems on the subdivider, despite the profitability of individual lot sales.... By rejecting the method of selling cheap unrestricted speculative lots for quick turnover, the developer exposed himself to the financial risk of not being able to sell high-quality restricted lots rapidly enough to stay afloat for the long haul.

Nichols then listed the various ways that good planning, including deed restrictions...generally brought much higher and more enduring property values and sales prices. "But this private planning must have municipal aid," he insisted. "Now, how in the world can the private developer, without municipal assistance, expect his property to succeed, if he is to work with unregulated development all around him?"

The solution for Nichols was quite clear: public regulation of all private development. Subdivision controls would establish different classes of property development in different locations (as part of a master plan) and then ensure that a new high-grade subdivision in an undeveloped area would eventually be ringed by like-minded neighbors, what Nichols called "the cumulative effect." "The constant effort of the operator is to try to get surroundings that are entirely congenial to what he has placed upon his property, and to do that successfully we absolutely must have municipal control of the surroundings on the adjoining lot."

In addition to the control of new subdividing, Nichols called for continuing municipal regulation of building use, size, land coverage, and setback, or what was called districting or zoning. Zoning would classify each type of development and make future development stable and predictable at any given building site. He extolled the ability of private deed restrictions to create monopoly value and hence extra profits for the developer, and asserted that public restrictions could achieve similar results:

> Now, if in developing our subdivisions, we can limit the quantity of certain classes of property, if we can create the feeling that we have a monopoly of that class of property around a little plaza or square, if we give the prospective buyer notice that if he doesn't buy that property today somebody else will buy all that is left of it tomorrow, we are assisting in the sale of that property, and the man that has it won't give it up except at an advanced price, and we can raise the prices of the adjoining property.

Finally, Nichols argued that the developer needed municipal assistance in aligning his subdivision with future plans for extension of major streets and highways, as well as the placement or extension of public parks and recreation land, schools, utilities, and the entire range of municipal improvements and services. In the next two decades this notion of coordination-based regulation between public and private development was to become the central logic of land-use planning for urban expansion: (1) the comprehensive land-use plan, (2) the capital improvements budget, (3) the Official Map of public land reservations for future uses, and (4) the staff planning agency to work with the subdivider to correlate public and private development plans and establish rules for accepting dedications of prospective streets, parks, and other land from private subdividers for public development and maintenance. Nichols also stated that community builders needed the same type of coordination-based cooperation from other key private concerns including financial institutions, street railway companies, and churches.

The essential thrust of Nichols' comments was a community builder's manifesto on the need for local government planning. He advocated a public-private partnership in the preparation and execution of private urban land development at a level of resource commitment and regulatory intervention much greater than had been applied by American local government since colonial times....

The needs described by J. C. Nichols and the policy tools which formed the basis of the planning response—Master Plan, Official Map, zoning map and laws, set-back requirements, subdivision map filing regulations and planning agency review, capital budget—defined the direction taken by both the community builders and the planners in modern U.S. city planning's first big decade, the 1920s. At first the focus was on establishing zoning laws. In 1921, Secretary of Commerce Herbert Hoover appointed an Advisory Committee on Zoning, which published *A Standard State Zoning Enabling Act* in 1924, and later in 1928, as the renamed Advisory Committee on City Planning and Zoning, published *A Standard City Planning Enabling Act*. Together these two documents outlined the basic principles for state and local governments to follow in implementing the comprehensive urban land-use planning agenda. Many state legislatures adopted one or both of the model enabling acts almost verbatim....

In 1931 President Hoover's Conference on Home Building and Home Ownership expanded the public urban land planning agenda by detailing the means by which the federal government, in association with financial institutions, building products manufacturers, utilities, and trade associations from various branches of the real estate and construction industries, could help speed the transition from subdividing to homebuilding as a large-scale, standardized, modernized, and economically integrated sector of production. Community builders were prominent participants in the Conference, and "community building" as a goal was very highly valued in the conference recommendations....

In the mid-1930s the federally owned greenbelt towns furthered the state-of-the-art in public community building that had previously been explored by the U.S. Housing Corporation. The private Radburn, New Jersey, experiment of the late 1920s, "a town for the motor age," as well as various development efforts by innovative subdividers, also broke new ground in establishing better planning standards. The last and in many ways the most effective step in tying the entire planning package together came through the federal rationalization of housing development and financing initiated by the FHA in the mid-1930s. FHA's Land Planning Division played a crucial role in institutionalizing as part of the housing tract development process the very forms of "municipal assistance" and regulatory intervention that J. C. Nichols had called for in his 1916 NCCP speech....

Deed Restrictions—Private Innovation Preceding Public Planning....

The initial step in the long march toward achieving "public control of private real estate," as the planners called it, was attaining a measure of private control. Deed restrictions legitimized the idea that private owners should surrender some of their individual property rights for the common good, including their own. By 1914, it was becoming clear that the rising land values of deed-restricted property demonstrated that it was quite beneficial for individual private owners to participate in collective land-use control, and that many prospective land purchasers, builders, and occupants understood and appreciated its advantages. As J. C. Nichols noted in his 1912 NAREB [National Association of Real Estate Boards] talk: "In the early time (1906–1908) I was afraid to suggest building restrictions; now I cannot sell a lot without them."

Deed restrictions did more than legitimate the concept of land-use control, however. They also were the principal vehicle by which subdividers and technicians tested and refined the methods of modern land-use planning. In this important activity the community builders led the economic charge, but received a great deal of guidance and assistance from leading landscape architects, civil engineers, architects, and other professionals. The finest designers frequently were the planners of the best deed-restricted private subdivisions. For example, F. L. Olmsted (Sr.) and Calvert Vaux laid out Riverside, Illinois, the Chicago residential suburb that set the early and long-held standard for excellence of planning and for the creative use of deed restrictions....

Community builders worked together with planners to privately establish the framework for most major aspects of what later became public planning-building restrictions; classification and separation of land uses; integrated planning and design of streets, blocks, and lots, such as the "superblock"; planning and design of open space between buildings and within and between subdivisions; uniform set-backs; advance reservation and dedication of subdivision land for public use—the list is long and covers a wide range of applications of zoning and subdivision regulations and urban design and engineering. Even on the commercial side, the basic concept of the modern suburban shopping center was first developed by J. C. Nichols and widely introduced as a new innovation in residential subdivision planning by community builders....

Members of the real estate business community understood that private restrictions were no panacea and could not substitute for public regulation. J. C. Nichols made this point quite forcefully in his 1916 speech to the National Conference on City Planning. Seven problematic issues rendered private restrictions inadequate: (1) They were difficult to establish once land was subdivided and sold to diverse owners. Thus they could only be easily applied to new subdivisions, and not in already built-up areas. (2) They were often difficult to enforce through the civil courts. Property owners could not depend on their future effectiveness with any certainty.

(3) They generally were only considered to be legally enforceable for a limited period of years, at which point the restrictions would completely expire and the area would be officially unprotected. (4) They were very inflexible. Once written into the original deeds, they were extremely difficult to change, even where new and unforeseen conditions clearly warranted certain modifications. (5) They only applied to whatever size parcel of land could be controlled by a single owner or subdivider. All land surrounding a restricted subdivision could remain unrestricted, subjecting the subdivision's border areas to the threat of encirclement by "undesirable" uses. (6) Even where deed restrictions were applied to a number of tracts, each subdivider used a different standard, leaving a complete lack of uniformity between each private effort. (7) In addition to the lack of coordination between privately restricted and unrestricted land uses, restricted subdivisions were not at all coordinated with public land uses and future public land-use plans.

Leading subdividers and realtors advocated public planning to overcome the deficiencies of private restrictions and to supplement their strengths. Without the visible precedent of private planning efforts by community builders and their advisers and allies within the city planning profession, the establishment of public land-use regulations would no doubt have taken longer to accomplish and the newly created public planning agencies would have been far less knowledgeable in their initial attempts to set reasonable standards for urban land development.

ESSAY 8-2. KENNETH T. JACKSON, "RACE, ETHNICITY AND REAL ESTATE APPRAISAL: THE HOME OWNERS LOAN CORPORATION AND THE FEDERAL HOUSING ADMINISTRATION" (1980)

Source: *The Journal of Urban History* 6 (1980). Copyright © 1980 by Sage Publications, Inc. Reprinted by permission of Sage Publications, Inc.

The appeal of low-density living for more than a century in the United States and across regional, class, and ethnic lines has led some observers to regard it as natural and inevitable, a trend "that no amount of government interference can reverse." Or as a senior Federal Housing Administration (FHA) official told the 1939 convention of the American Institute of Planners: "Decentralization is taking place. It is not a policy, it is a reality—and it is as impossible for us to change this trend as it is to change the desire of birds to migrate to a more suitable location."

Despite such protestations, there are many ways in which government largesse can affect where people live....

On the urban-suburban level, the potential for federal influence is also enormous. For example, the Federal Highway Act of 1916 and the Interstate Highway Act of 1956 moved the government toward a transportation policy emphasizing and benefiting the road, the truck, and the private motor car. In conjunction with cheap fuel and mass-produced automobiles, the urban expressways led to lower marginal transport costs and greatly stimulated deconcentration. Equally important to most families is the incentive to detached-home living provided by the deduction of mortgage interest and real estate taxes from their gross income. Even the reimbursement formulas for water line and sewer construction have had an impact on the spatial patterns of metropolitan areas.

The purpose of this article...is to examine the impact of two innovations of the New Deal on the older, industrial cities of the nation.

The Home Owners Loan Corporation

On April 13, 1933, President Roosevelt urged the House and the Senate to pass a law that would (1) protect small homeowners from foreclosure, (2) relieve them of part of the burden of excessive interest and principle payments incurred during a period of higher values and higher earning power, and (3) declare that it was national policy to protect homeownership....The resulting Home Owners Loan Corporation (HOLC), signed into law by the President on June 13, 1933, was designed to serve urban needs; the Emergency Farm Mortgage Act, passed almost a month earlier, was intended to reduce rural foreclosure.

The HOLC replaced the unworkable direct loan provisions of the Hoover administration's Federal Home Loan Bank Act and refinanced tens of thousands of mortgages in danger of default or foreclosure. It even granted loans at low-interest rates to permit owners to recover homes lost through forced sale. Between July 1933 and June 1935 alone, the HOLC supplied more than $3 billion for over a million mortgages, or loans for one-tenth of all owner-occupied, non-farm residences in the United States....[N]ationally about 40 percent of eligible Americans sought HOLC assistance.

The HOLC is important to housing history because it introduced, perfected, and proved in practice the feasibility of the long-term, self-amortizing mortgage with uniform payments spread over the whole life of the debt. Prior to the 1930s, the typical length of a mortgage was between five and ten years, and the loan itself was not paid off when the final settlement was due. Thus, the homeowner was periodically at the mercy of arbitrary and unpredictable forces in the money market. When money was easy, renewal every five or seven years was no problem. But if a mortgage expired at a time when money was tight, it might be impossible for the homeowner to secure a renewal, and foreclosure would ensue. Under the HOLC program, the loans were fully amortized, and the repayment period was extended to about 20 years.

Aside from the larger number of mortgages which it helped to refinance on a long-term, low-interest basis, the HOLC systematized appraisal methods across the nation. Because it was dealing with problem mortgages—in some states over 40 percent of all HOLC loans were foreclosed even after refinancing—the HOLC had to make predictions and assumptions regarding the useful or productive life of housing it financed. Unlike refrigerators or shoes, dwellings were expected to be durable—how durable was the purpose of the investigation.

With care and extraordinary attention to detail, HOLC appraisers divided cities into neighborhoods and developed elaborate questionnaires relating to the occupation, income, and ethnicity of the inhabitants and the age, type of construction, price range, sales demand, and general state of repair of the housing stock. The element of novelty did not lie in the appraisal requirement itself—that had long been standard real-estate practice. Rather, it lay in the creation of a formal and uniform system of appraisal, reduced to writing, structured in defined procedures, and implemented by individuals only after intensive training. The ultimate aim was that one appraiser's judgment of value would have meaning to an investor located somewhere else. In evaluating such efforts, the distinguished economist C. Lowell Harriss has credited the HOLC training and evaluation procedures "with having helped raise the general level of American real estate appraisal methods." A less favorable judgment would be that the HOLC initiated the practice of "redlining."

This occurred because HOLC devised a rating system which undervalued neighborhoods that were dense, mixed, or aging. Four categories of quality—imaginatively entitled First, Second, Third, and Fourth, with corresponding code letters of A, B, C, and D and colors of green, blue, yellow, and red—were established. The First grade (also A and green) areas were described as new, homogeneous, and "in demand as residential locations in good times and bad." Homogeneous meant "American business and professional men." Jewish neighborhoods, or even those with an "infiltration of Jews," could not possibly be considered "Best."

The Second security grade (blue) went to "still desirable" areas that had "reached their peak," but were expected to remain stable for many years. The Third grade (yellow) or "C" neighborhoods were usually described as "definitely declining," while the Fourth grade (red) or "D" neighborhoods were defined as areas "in which the things taking place in C areas have already happened."

The HOLC's assumptions about urban neighborhoods were based on both an ecological conception of change and a socioeconomic one. Adopting a dynamic view of the city and assuming that change was inevitable, its appraisers accepted as given the proposition that the natural tendency of any area was to decline—in part because of the increasing age and obsolescence of the physical structures and in part because of the filtering down of the housing stock to families of lower income and different ethnicity. Thus physical deterioration was both a cause and an effect of population change, and HOLC officials made no real attempt to sort them out. They were part and parcel of the same process. Thus, black neighborhoods were invariably rated as Fourth grade, but so were any areas characterized by poor maintenance or vandalism. Similarly, those "definitely declining" sections that were marked Third grade or yellow received such a low rating in part because of age and in part because they were "within such a low price or rent range as to attract an undesirable element."

The HOLC did not initiate the idea of considering race and ethnicity in real-estate appraising. As Calvin Bradford has demonstrated, models developed at the University of Chicago in the 1920s and early 1930s by Homer Hoyt and Robert Park became the dominant explanation of neighborhood change. They suggested that different groups of people "infiltrated" or "invaded" territory held by others through a process of competition. These interpretations were then adopted by prominent appraising texts, such as Frederick Babcock's *The Valuation of Real Estate* (1932) and McMichael's *Appraising Manual* (1931). Both advised appraisers to pay particular attention to "undesirable" or "least desirable" elements and suggested that the influx of certain ethnic groups was likely to precipitate price declines.

The HOLC simply applied these notions of ethnic and racial worth to real estate appraising on an unprecedented scale. With the assistance of local realtors and banks, it assigned one of its four ratings to every block in every city. The resulting information was then translated into the appropriate color and duly recorded on secret "Residential Security Maps" in local HOLC offices. The maps themselves were placed in elaborate "City Survey Files," which consisted of reports, questionnaires, and workpapers relating to current and future values of real estate.

Because the two federal agencies under analysis here [the Home Owners Loan Corporation and the Federal Housing Administration] did not normally report data on anything other than a county basis, the St. Louis area was selected as a case study. There, the city and county were legally separated in 1876, so that there was no alternative to individual reporting....

The residential security map for the St. Louis area in 1937...gave the highest ratings to the newer, affluent suburbs that were strung out along curvilinear streets well away from the problems of the city. Three years later, in 1940, the advantage of the periphery over the center was even more marked. In both evaluations, the top of the scale was dominated by Ladue, a largely undeveloped section of high, rolling land, heavily wooded estates, and dozens of houses in the $20,000 to $50,000 range. In 1940, HOLC appraisers noted approvingly that the area was "highly restricted" and occupied by "capitalists and other wealthy families." Reportedly not the home of "a single foreigner or Negro," Ladue received an "A" rating....

At the other end of the scale in St. Louis County were the rare Fourth grade areas. A few such neighborhoods were occupied by white laborers, such as "Ridgeview" in Kirkwood, where the garagelike shacks typically cost less than $1500. But the "D" regions in the county were usually black. One such place in 1937 was Lincoln Terrace, a small enclave of four- and five-room bungalows built about 1927...[E]ven though the homes were relatively new and of good quality, the HOLC gave the section...the lowest possible grade, asserting that the houses had "little or no value today, having suffered a tremendous decline in values due to the colored element now controlling the district."

In contrast to the gently rolling terrain and sparse settlement of St. Louis County, the city had proportionately many more Third and Fourth grade neighborhoods, and more than twice as many renters as homeowners....As the St. Louis Regional Planning report...concluded in 1936: "The older residential districts which are depreciating in value and in character constitute one of the most serious problems in this region.... Even if owners wished to build new homes within them, it would be inadvisable because of the present character of the districts."

But the HOLC appraisers marked other inner-city areas down not because of true slum conditions, but because of negative attitudes toward city living in general. The evaluation of a white, working-class neighborhood near Fairgrounds Park was typical. According to the description, "Lots are small, houses are only slightly set back from the sidewalks, and there is a general appearance of congestion." Although an urban individual might have found this collection of cottages and abundant shade trees rather charming, the HOLC thought otherwise: "Age of properties, general mixture of type, proximity to industrial section on northeast and much less desirable areas to the south make this a good fourth grade area."

As was the case in every city, any Afro-American presence was a source of substantial concern to the HOLC. In a confidential and generally pessimistic 1941 survey of the economic and real-estate prospects of the St. Louis metropolitan area, the Federal Home Loan Bank Board (the parent agency of the HOLC) repeatedly commented on the "rapidly increasing Negro population" and the resulting "problem in the maintenance of real estate values." The officials evinced a keen interest in the movement of black families and included maps of the density of Negro settlement with every analysis. Not surprisingly, even those neighborhoods with small proportions of black inhabitants were typically rated D, or hazardous....

The HOLC insisted that "there is no implication that good mortgages do not exist or cannot be made in Third and Fourth grade areas." And, there is some evidence to indicate that HOLC did in fact make the majority of its obligations in "definitely declining" or "hazardous" neighborhoods. This seeming liberality was actually good business because the residents of poorer sections generally maintained a better pay back record than did their more affluent cousins....

The damage caused by the HOLC came not through its own actions, but through the influence of its appraisal system on the financial decisions of other institutions. During the late 1930s, the Federal Home Loan Bank Board circulated questionnaires to banks asking about their mortgage practices. Those returned by savings-and-loan associations and banks in Essex County (Newark), New Jersey indicated a clear relationship between public and private "redlining" practices. One specific question asked: "What are the most desirable lending areas?" The answers were often "A and B" or "Blue" or "FHA only." Similarly, to the inquiry, "Are there any areas in which loans will not be made?" the responses included, "Red and most yellow," "C and D," "Newark," "Not in red," and "D areas." Obviously, private banking institutions were privy to and influenced by the government's Residential Security Maps.

Even more significantly, HOLC appraisal methods, and perhaps the maps themselves, were adopted by the FHA.

The Federal Housing Administration

Direct, large-scale Washington intervention in the American housing market dates from the adoption of the National Housing Act on June 27, 1934. Although intended "to encourage improvement in housing standards and conditions, to facilitate sound home financing on reasonable terms, and to exert a stabilizing influence on the mortgage market," the primary purpose of the legislation was the alleviation of unemployment in the construction industry....

Between 1934 and 1968, the FHA had a remarkable record of accomplishment. Essentially, it insured long-term mortgage loans made by private lenders for home construction and sale. To this end, it collected premiums, set up reserves for losses and in the event of a default on a mortgage, indemnified the lender. It did not build houses or lend money. Instead, it induced lenders who had money to invest it in residential mortgages by insuring them against loss on such investments, with the full weight of the U.S. Treasury behind the contract. And it revolutionized the home finance industry in the following ways.

First, before FHA began operation, first mortgages typically were limited to one-half or two-thirds of the appraised value of the property. During the 1920s for example, savings and loan associations held one-half of America's outstanding mortgage debt. Those mortgages averaged 58 percent of estimated property value. Thus, prospective home-buyers needed a down payment of at least 30 percent to close a deal. By contrast, the fraction of the collateral that the lender was able to lend for a FHA-secured loan was about 93 percent. Thus, large down payments were unnecessary.

Second, continuing a trend begun by the HOLC, the FHA extended the repayment period for its guaranteed mortgages to 25 or 30 years and insisted that all loans be fully amortized. The effect was to reduce both the average monthly payment and the national rate of mortgage foreclosure. The latter declined from 250,000 non-farm units in 1932 to only 18,000 in 1951.

Third, FHA established minimum standards for home construction that became almost universal in the industry. These regulations were not intended to make any particular structure fault-free, or even to assure the owner's satisfaction with the purchase. But they were designed to assure with at least statistical accuracy that the dwelling would be free of gross structural or mechanical deficiencies. Although there was nothing innovative in considering the quality of a house in relation to the debt placed against it, two features of the system were new; first, that the standards were objective, uniform, and in writing; second, that they were to be enforced by actual on-site inspection—prior to insurance commitment in the case of an existing property, and at various fixed stages in the course of construction in the case of new housing. Since World War II, the largest private contractors have built all their new houses to meet FHA standards, even though financing has often been arranged without FHA aid. This has occurred because many potential purchasers will not consider a home that cannot get FHA approval.

Fourth, in the 1920s the interest rate for first mortgages averaged between 6 and 8 percent. If a second mortgage were necessary, as it usually was for families of moderate incomes, the purchaser could obtain one by paying a discount to the lender, a higher interest rate on the loan, and perhaps a commission to a broker. Together, these charges added about 15 percent to the purchase price. Under the FHA and Veterans Administration (VA) programs, by contrast, there was very little risk to the banker if a loan turned sour. Reflecting this government guarantee, interest rates fell by two or three percentage points.

These four changes substantially increased the number of American families who could reasonably expect to purchase homes. By the end of 1972, FHA had helped nearly 11 million families to own houses and another 22 million families to improve their properties. It had also insured 1.8 million dwellings in multiunit projects. And in those same years between 1934 and 1972, the percentage of American families living in owner-occupied dwellings rose from 44 percent to 63 percent.

Quite simply, it often became cheaper to buy than to rent. Long Island builder Martin Winter recently recalled that in the early 1950s, families living in the Kew Gardens section of Queens were paying almost $100 per month for small two-bedroom apartments. For less money they could, and often did, move to the new Levittown-type developments springing up along the highways from the city.... Not suprisingly, the middle-class suburban family with the new house and the long-term, fixed-rate FHA-insured mortgage became a symbol, and perhaps the stereotype, of "the American way of life."

Unfortunately, the corollary to this achievement was the fact that FHA programs hastened the decay of inner-city neighborhoods by stripping them of much of the middle-class constituency. This occurred for two reasons. First, although the legislation nowhere mentioned an antiurban bias, it favored the construction of single-family [homes] and discouraged construction of multifamily projects through unpopular terms. Historically, single-family housing programs have been the heart of FHA's insured loan activities. Between 1941 and 1950, FHA insured single-family starts exceeded FHA multifamily starts by a ratio of almost four to one. In the next decade, the margin exceeded seven to one. Even in 1971, when FHA insured the largest number of multifamily units in its history, single-family houses were more numerous by 27 percent.

Similarly, loans for the repair of existing structures were small and for short duration, which meant that a family could more easily purchase a new home than modernize an old one....

The second and more important variety of suburban, middle-class favoritism had to do with the so-called unbiased professional estimate that was a prerequisite for any loan guarantee. This mandatory appraisal included a rating of the property itself, a rating of the mortgagor or borrower, and a rating of the neighborhood. The lower the valuation placed on properties, the less government risk and the less generous the aid to the potential buyers (and sellers). The purpose of the neighborhood evaluation was "to determine the degree of mortgage risk introduced in a mortgage insurance transaction because of the location of the property at a specific site." And unlike the HOLC, which used an essentially similar procedure, the FHA allowed personal and agency bias in favor of all-white subdivisions in the suburbs to affect the kinds of loans it guaranteed—or, equally important, refused to guarantee....

The FHA was quite precise in teaching its underwriters how to measure the quality of residential area. Eight criteria were established (the numbers in parentheses reflect the percentage weight given to each):

(1) relative economic stability (40 percent)
(2) protection from adverse influences (20 percent)
(3) freedom from special hazards (5 percent)
(4) adequacy of civic, social, and commercial centers (5 percent)
(5) adequacy of transportation (10 percent)
(6) sufficiency of utilities and conveniences (5 percent)
(7) level of taxes and special assessments (5 percent)
(8) appeal (10 percent).

Although FHA directives insisted that no project should be insured that involved a high degree of risk with regard to any of the eight categories, "economic stability" and "protection from adverse influences" together counted for more than the other six combined. Both were interpreted in ways that were prejudicial against heterogeneous environments. The 1939 *Underwriting Manual* taught that "crowded neighborhoods lessen desirability" and "older properties in a neighborhood have a tendency to accelerate the transition to lower class occupancy." Smoke and odor were considered "adverse influences," and appraisers were told to look carefully for any "inferior and non-productive characteristics of the areas surrounding the site."

Obviously, prospective buyers could avoid many of these so-called undesirable features by locating in peripheral sections. In 1939, the Washington headquarters asked each of the 50-odd regional FHA offices to send in the plans for six "typical American houses." The photographs and dimensions were then used for a National Archives exhibit. An analysis of the submissions clearly indicates that the ideal home was a bungalow or a colonial on an ample lot with a driveway and a garage.

In an attempt to standardize such ideal homes, FHA set up minimum requirements for lot size, for setback from the street, for separation from adjacent structures, and even for the width of the house itself. While such requirements did provide air and light for new structures, they effectively eliminated whole sections of cities, such as the traditional 16-foot-wide row houses of Baltimore, Philadelphia, and New York from eligibility for loan guarantees. Even apartment owners were encouraged to look to suburbia: "Under the best of conditions a rental development under the FHA program is a project set in what amounts to a privately owned and privately controlled park area."

Reflecting the broad segregationist attitudes of a majority of the American people, the FHA was extraordinarily concerned with "inharmonious racial or nationality groups." Homeowners and financial institutions alike feared that an entire area could lose its investment value if rigid white-black separation was not maintained. Bluntly warning, "If a neighborhood is to retain stability, it is necessary that properties shall continue to be occupied by the same social and racial classes," the *Underwriting Manual* openly recommended "enforced zoning, subdivision regulations, and suitable restrictive covenants" that would be "superior to any mortgage." Such covenants were a common method of prohibiting black occupancy until the U.S. Supreme Court ruled in 1948 (*Shelley v. Kraemer*) that they were "unenforceable as law and contrary to public policy." Even then, it was not until late 1949 that FHA announced that as of February 15, 1950, it would not insure mortgages on real estate subject to covenants....

As late as November 19, 1948, Assistant FHA Commissioner W. J. Lockwood could write that FHA "has never insured a housing project of mixed occupancy" because of the expectation that "such projects would probably in a short period of time become all-Negro or all-white."...

Such data as are available indicate that neighborhood appraisals were very influential in determining for FHA "where it would be reasonably safe to insure mortgages."...Of a sample of 241 new homes insured by FHA throughout metropolitan St. Louis between 1935 and 1939, a full 220 or 91 percent were located in the suburbs. Moreover, more than half of these home buyers (135 of 241) had lived in the city immediately prior to their new home purchase....

One possible explanation for the city-county disparities in these figures is that the city had very little room for development, that the populace wanted to move to the suburbs, and that the periphery was where new housing could be most easily built. But in the 1930s, many more single-family homes were constructed in the city than in the county. Moreover, more than half of the FHA policies traditionally went to *existing* rather than *new* homes, and the city of course had a much larger inventory of existing housing than did the county in the period before 1960. Even in terms of home improvement loans, a category in which the aging city was obviously more needy, only $43,844,500 went to the city, while about three times that much, or $112,315,798, went to the county through 1960....

For its part, the FHA usually responded that it was not created to help cities, but to revive homebuilding and to stimulate homeownership....

But FHA also helped to turn the building industry against the minority and inner-city housing market, and its policies supported the income and racial segregation of most suburbs. Whole areas of cities were declared ineligible for loan guarantees; as late as 1966, for example, FHA did not have a mortgage on a single home in Camden, New Jersey, a declining industrial city.

Despite the fact that the government's leading housing agency was openly exhorting segregation, throughout the first 30 years of its operation, very few voices were raised against FHA's redlining practices....

Not until the civil rights movement of the 1960s did community groups and scholars become convinced that redlining and disinvestment were a major cause of neighborhood decline and that home improvement loans were the "lifeblood of housing."...

The main beneficiary of the $119 billion in FHA mortgage insurance issued in the first four decades of FHA operation was suburbia, where approximately half of all housing could claim FHA or VA financing in the 1950s and 1960s. In the process, the American suburb was transformed from a rich person's preserve into the normal expectation of the middle class.

NOTES

1. "The Realtors Code of Ethics," *National Real Estate Journal* 40 (April 20, 1939), 64.
2. See Document 8-3 as an example.

PART II

Postwar Suburbia, 1940–1970

CHAPTER 9

Postwar America

Suburban Apotheosis

INTRODUCTION

The year 1945 represents a turning point in the history of American suburbanization. Not only did suburbs change in character, but they multiplied at breakneck speed. Within a few decades, suburbs would house more Americans than cities and rural areas, and they would leave an indelible imprint on American life. America was firmly on its way to becoming a suburban nation.

Why did suburbanization mushroom after 1945? A confluence of forces—including a tremendous pent-up demand for housing, prosuburban policies of the federal government, and new production techniques—created the motivation and means for explosive suburban development. Intensive housing demand followed a sixteen-year slump in the housing market during the Great Depression and World War II, which had severely curtailed housing production. In addition to this supply shortage, demand rose precipitously by the early 1940s, as civilians migrated to urban areas for defense jobs and birth rates climbed. By the end of the war, the housing shortage had reached crisis levels. Millions of families were forced to double up, while others found makeshift shelter in automobiles, grain bins, and converted chicken coops.

Recognizing the severity of the crisis, the federal government launched a massive national construction program that emphasized the building of single-family homes in suburban areas. New Deal liberals believed that a strengthened housing industry would not only alleviate the housing shortage, but would ensure robust economic growth after the war and avert a return to economic depression. The choice to emphasize single-family home ownership—one among several policy options—came about under tremendous pressure from real estate lobbyists and opportunistic politicians, including Senator Joseph McCarthy, who attacked public housing and planned towns as "communist" projects, an accusation that resonated during the early Cold War years. The federal government bolstered its commitment to suburban home ownership in several ways: by increasing the budget of the FHA to underwrite loans for single-family homes, by passing the G.I. Bill, which included a mortgage program for veterans, and by offering production advances to large-scale builders to minimize their economic risk. The latter policy especially helped stimulate the emergence of a new breed of large-scale developer-builders who would emerge as central players in the story of postwar suburbanization.

It is difficult to overestimate the role of private developers during this period. They not only reshaped the way homes were built, but they wielded tremendous power over the total process of design, planning, and land development. Their impact was felt first and foremost in skyrocketing housing production. Whereas only 142,000 housing units were built nationwide in 1944, just two years later builders were hammering up over a million homes annually, 1.9 million by decade's end. Between the end of World War II and 1965, the building industry constructed over 26 million nonfarm homes, most of them in the suburbs. To meet demand and maximize profits, these developer-builders reorganized the construction trade to mass produce homes, allowing them to build quickly on an unprecedented scale. While the builders of Levittown, Long Island, were most famous for this new technique—and received an inordinate share of media attention—builders across the nation were doing the same. The result was a transformed landscape on the outskirts of American cities—tract after tract of similar homes, amid infant trees and shrubs, on freshly bulldozed land. The barrenness of the landscape contributed to a popular sense that these communities were, truly, the product of an assembly line.

This new approach to suburb building had deep social repercussions. Most importantly, the affordability of mass-produced housing opened suburbia to a broad cross-section of Americans, particularly members of the expanding middle class. Indeed, suburbia played a crucial, if complex, role in the formation of this class in the postwar years. The middle-class expanded to include not just white-collar workers and professionals, but blue-collar workers whose economic standing rose, thanks to union-earned wage and benefit increases. Middle-class status came to depend less on occupation, more on possessions and way of life—what a person consumed and how he behaved were more important than what he did for a living. In this milieu, suburban home ownership became an important badge of middle-class status. If you lived in a particular place, owned a home, and fit in, you were considered middle class. Furthermore, influenced by the shared struggle against Nazism and common experiences of military service and home front hardship, Americans developed a new tolerance for religious and ethnic difference, reflected in a new willingness to accept Jews and Catholics into suburban communities. In the new suburbia, older social barriers of religion, ethnicity, and class—which had represented key social dividing lines throughout the early twentieth century—fell away. This tolerance stopped at race, however. Indeed, some argue that a shared identity of whiteness among second-generation European ethnics was a crucial element of middle-class identity, and helps explain the persistent, intractable unwillingness to open suburbia to racial minorities. This, indeed, would remain the unresolved dilemma—some would say failure—of postwar suburbia.

Advertisers and the mass media played a crucial role in publicizing the idea of an inclusive—if all-white—middle class that found its bearings in the suburbs. Much of this media attention focused on the most iconic mass-produced suburbs of the period, such as Levittown, Park Forest, Illinois, and Lakewood, California, and indeed this emphasis still exerts itself fifty years later as historians continue to focus on these sites. In advertisements, magazine articles, and television sitcoms, every suburbanite was deemed part of this democratic America, from the humble factory worker to the well-educated professional. They were the beneficiaries of an expansive postwar economy and a democratic way of life, a model for the postwar world. In the suburbs, Americans could express themselves and live their dreams through vigorous consumption of U.S.-made goods in their cheerful suburban homes.

Suburbia's historic relationship to gender, embodied in the ideal of homemaker wife, working father, and children living in a single-family home, reached a heady climax in the postwar years. As new families proliferated during the baby boom, so did private detached homes, which reinforced this "traditional" family structure. A detached single-family home catered best to the needs of the nuclear family, promoting a privatized way of handling family life and child rearing. Alternative family arrangements, such as extended kin, were not easily accommodated in the mass-produced suburban home. Suburbia, thus, continued to reinforce a narrow vision of normative family life, and this vision was publicized as never before. As part of their aggressive effort to sell suburban property and lifestyles, sellers of homes and household goods hawked a gendered image of the suburban lifestyle—the woman homemaker achieving fulfillment in the confines of her well-run, well-stocked suburban home. The extent to which this portrayal reflected reality is a question still unresolved in the historical literature. We do know that increasing numbers of women found work outside the home in the postwar years, and many who remained at home failed to find the promised fulfillment.

Yet the fact also remains that many Americans embraced the postwar suburban way of life with great fervor and enthusiasm. They waited in lines to buy homes. They boasted of new ways to keep house. They participated actively in their communities. Both literally and metaphorically, they bought what was being sold. Clearly, postwar suburbia touched a vital nerve in America.

DOCUMENTS

The nation's experience leading up to 1945, particularly the Great Depression and World War II, created the conditions for the postwar suburban housing boom. **Document 9-1** suggests the deep, emotional connection between the battlefront and the home front. To the soldier holed up in a bunker or the soldier's wife going it alone, the imagery of home was compelling: a cozy house in a peaceful suburb symbolized the end goal, the dream of life once the war was over. As this advertisement for Kelvinator kitchen appliances reveals, the makers of household products promoted this connection aggressively in their advertising, linking their products to resonating images of home, victory, and family. **Document 9-2,** a report by the *New York Times*, describes hundreds of veterans lining up days in advance to purchase the first Levittown homes. This report and the accompanying photograph illustrate the unprecedented demand for housing after the war.

Document 9-3 is a set of advertisements for postwar suburbs in Tucson, Arizona, Portland, Oregon, and, Long Island, New York. Although developments like Levittown and Park Forest received the most media attention, the mass production of suburban homes was truly a nationwide phenomenon. As these ads reveal, builders pitched similar, if not interchangeable, housing and values in suburbs across the country. It is worth noting that "Manor Homes" targeted African-American home buyers; this development, unlike the others but like many black subdivisions, did not receive FHA or VA support. **Document 9-4** is a photo gallery of postwar suburbia, highlighting three famous mass-produced developments, Levittown (Long Island), Lakewood, and Park Forest. Over the years, these neighborhoods would convey greater individuality in housing and landscapes, something the original developers hoped would happen.

The final set of documents offers insight into the new patterns of life taking shape in mass-produced suburbia. In **Document 9-5**, a Levittown housewife describes the new techniques of housekeeping she developed since moving to the suburbs. For all of the labor-saving appliances that came with many suburban homes, this housewife's daily round of chores still included labor-intensive activities such as sewing clothes and furniture covers. These practices suggest the modest means of many families who moved to mass-produced suburbs, who still had to rely on homemade, rather than store-bought, goods. Feminist writers such as Betty Friedan would later criticize this routine as "make work" that consumed women's time and constricted their opportunities. As children grew older, another task taken up by the suburban housewife was chauffeuring the family. **Document 9-6** describes the driving routine of a housewife in Westchester County, New York, an upper-class suburban area north of Manhattan. This evocative description suggests not only that women's labor was directed primarily to the intensive needs of her family, but that the spread-out design of suburban neighborhoods—and lack of public transportation between suburbs—exacerbated the workload.

In **Document 9-7**, D. J. Waldie's "suburban memoir" offers a lyrical reflection about life in Lakewood, California, a mass-produced suburb outside of Los Angeles. Developed by Ben Weingart, Mark Taper, and Louis Boyar, Lakewood reached a population of 80,000 people and 17,500 homes, surpassing even Levittown in size by the early 1950s. Waldie's memoir is a moving rumination on life "on the grid," as he puts it, weaving community history with personal memory, and offering glimpses of the inner life of the people who lived in these communities.

How did postwar suburbs differ from earlier suburbs? Consider factors like planning, development, and the social makeup and expectations of postwar suburbanites. Which earlier suburban traditions most influenced postwar suburbia—elite, middle class, or working class—in terms of ideology, social practices, and uses of residential space? How did this new suburbia affect class and gender in postwar America? What accounts for the emotional attachment that many suburbanites felt for this new world?

9-1. KELVINATOR ADVERTISES THE DREAM OF A SUBURBAN HOME, 1944

Figure 9-1 During World War II, the dream of a suburban home epitomized the hope of millions of Americans for a return to peace and family comforts. *American Home* 33 (December 1944), 55.

9-2. HUNDREDS LINE UP TO BUY A LEVITTOWN HOME, 1949

Source: "Line Forms Early in Sale of Houses," *New York Times*, March 7, 1949, 21. Copyright © 1949 by The New York Times Co. Reprinted with permission.

ROSLYN, L.I. [Long Island], March 6—If William J. Levitt, Long Island mass building contractor, had any illusions about the end of the housing shortage, they were rudely dispelled this morning when he found nearly 300 home-hungry veterans camping on the doorstep of his model home here.

In the last two months since the model home went on display at 275 Willis Avenue, 5,000 prospective buyers had indicated their interest and been put on a waiting list. Last week those on the list were notified by letter that 350 of these houses would go on sale at 9 A.M. tomorrow.

About 11 o'clock Friday night Roger Williams of Bayside, Queens, appeared at the model home and announced that he was in line for Monday's sale. Within the next two hours a dozen other veterans had followed suit and ensconced themselves in deck chairs and sleeping bags on the lawn.

By Saturday morning the number had grown to nearly fifty, and Mr. Levitt decided that the police guard, which had watched over the house since its opening, would have to be augmented. Six patrolmen were assigned to guide new arrivals and maintain order in the line.

Meanwhile, the veterans had set up an organization of their own and had assigned a number to each new home-hunter as he fell into line. In this way husbands were able to take a few hours off for sleeping, eating and seeing their wives, and still retain their priority.

As the line grew Saturday and looped around into the back yard, word arrived that the wife of one of the waiting veterans had presented him with twins in a local hospital. Unperturbed, he received the congratulations of his companions and kept right on standing in line.

This morning, after two nights and a day had produced nearly 300 persistent customers, with others to follow later, Mr. Levitt decided that enough was enough. He gave each a number, guaranteed that it would entitle the holder to buy a house, and sent all home to bed....

The arrangement broke up the encampment, but it left 4,500 buyers who had been advised of the sale with nothing to purchase when they report tomorrow. Mr. Levitt said he expected the police guard would be necessary for several days more.

The veterans who buy the $7,990 homes tomorrow and Tuesday will pay $90 down and the remainder in $58 monthly installments. This price will include a four-room house equipped with radiant heating, automatic laundry, refrigerator and stove, and will cover taxes, water and fire insurance.

The 350 homes, which will be ready for occupancy in mid-July, will bring to 1,100 the number that Mr. Levitt has sold in the last two months. They are part of 4,000 houses of a new model to be erected in Levittown, which will raise the population to 10,000 families.

Figure 9-2 Hundreds of veterans camped out over two frozen nights for the chance to buy a Levittown home in 1949, reflecting the voracious demand for housing after the war. *Architectural Forum* 90 (April 1949), 84. Photograph by Drennan Photo Service, Mineola, New York.

9-3. PHOTO GALLERY: ADVERTISEMENTS FOR POSTWAR SUBURBS

Figure 9-3 Advertisement for suburban homes in Portland, Oregon, June 1950. New suburban housing often included appliances as part of the package, a key selling point. *The Oregonian* (Portland), June 25, 1950, p. **7

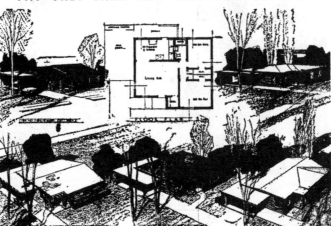

Figure 9-4 Advertisement for suburban homes in Tucson, Arizona, June 1950. The G.I. Bill made housing affordable for a broad cross section of Americans. *Arizona Daily Star*, June 18, 1950, p. 12A.

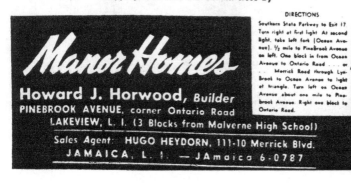

Figure 9-5 Advertisement for an African American subdivision on Long Island, New York, 1953. By the 1950s, a small number of builders marketed suburban homes to black families using similar appeals and imagery to those in ads meant for middle-class whites. Unlike the previous ads, this one makes no reference to FHA or VA assistance. *Amsterdam News*, May 16, 1953, p. 34.

9-4. PHOTO GALLERY: POSTWAR SUBURBIA

Figure 9-6 Lifting shingles, Lakewood, California, 1951. Large-scale builders, such as Lakewood developers Boyar, Weingart and Taper, divided the home production process into over two-dozen steps and relied heavily on prefabricated materials to produce houses in assembly-line fashion. Courtesy of the City of Lakewood Historical Collection.

Figure 9-7 The results of assembly-line building techniques are evident in this aerial view of Lakewood, California, 1954. Pacific Air Industries. 54-2548. Long Beach, California: PAI, 1954. 4"x 5" negative dated December 15, 1954. Courtesy of the Map and Imagery Laboratory, Davidson Library, University of California, Santa Barbara. Copyright 2006 The Regents of the University of California. All rights reserved.

Figure 9-8 Developer Philip Klutznick so admired the homes built by his friend William Levitt that he used similar designs in Park Forest, Illinois, 1997. Courtesy of Gregory C. Randall.

Figure 9-9 The architectural monotony of original postwar developments was soon transformed by renovations. To meet the changing needs of their growing families, suburbanites added rooms, converted garages, or built a second story, as in this 1997 view of an original Park Forest home. Courtesy of Gregory C. Randall.

Figure 9-10 Levittown, New York, homes, 2005. "No man who has a house and lot can be a Communist," said builder William Levitt. "He has too much to do." Levitt assumed that homebuyers would spend plenty of time on home maintenance and improvement. The results are evident in present-day Levittown, where a variegated built landscape prevails. Photograph by Becky Nicolaides.

9-5. A LEVITTOWN HOUSEWIFE DESCRIBES HOW SHE KEEPS HOUSE, 1949

Source: Elizabeth Sweeney Herbert, "This is How I Keep House," *McCalls*, April 1949.

Little Peter Eckhoff was four months old before his parents were finally able to move from their two-room walk-up in New York City to a comfortable cottage in Levittown, Long Island. Bringing a new baby into a tiny city apartment, Helen Eckhoff says, taught her as nothing else could the importance of good housekeeping equipment and careful planning before and after a baby arrives. When she and Bob discovered, shortly after they moved to Levittown, that they were going to have a second child they began planning for it months in advance. "We were determined this time to work things out far enough ahead so that there'd be no last-minute exhaustion and we'd still have time for a little social life."

While Helen now had Peter to take care of, and a house instead of two rooms, she also had the advantage in her new home of a yard, an attic and a full-size kitchen equipped with an electric refrigerator, a modern sink, an electric range with accurate heat control and an automatic washing machine.

"The first thing I did," she says, "was to arrange my kitchen so that it would save the most time and energy possible. I now have three working centers—the baby center where I keep all baby food, bottles and the like, a baking center and a cleaning center for general cleaning and washing machine supplies. It may not sound impressive, but it's amazing the steps you save if you keep all your supplies together like this."

One of Helen's greatest joys in her new home is the washing machine, which takes care of the family's regular laundry (including Peter's diapers) and is invaluable for all the slip covers, curtains, etc., that Helen plans to have spic and span before the baby comes. "I want the house to be thoroughly cleaned before I go to the hospital. Bob and I found that the first six weeks after Peter came were too busy for any intensive cleaning."

Helen does the washing every other day in two loads, one at seven o'clock just as Bob leaves to commute to his job as a sales accountant in New York, and the other about ten. As far as possible she buys washable fabrics that don't require ironing.

Besides her house cleaning economies she saves time for the weekend by carefully planning her Saturday baking and by preparing casserole dishes and quick refrigerator desserts. "It means," she says, "that Bob and I have just about as much social life as we ever did. Naturally I don't gad about, but there's always time to have people over. On Saturday night we usually have a television party. Refreshments are simple and we don't use many dishes so it's just as relaxing for me as for the guests."

Another project is the sewing and mending that must be done before the baby arrives.

NUMBER EIGHT IN A SERIES
BY ELIZABETH SWEENEY HERBERT

THIS IS HOW I KEEP HOUSE

Bob Eckhoff happily brings Peter's old bassinet back to the nursery to get it ready for a second baby

The Eckhoffs' new house isn't gigantic but it's heaven to Helen after a two-room apartment

"Housekeeping while you're expecting a baby," says Helen Eckhoff, "is the best lesson I know in saving time, money and strength"

"Two thirds of housekeeping," Helen says, "is knowing where things belong and seeing that they stay there." In this convenient kitchen-laundry-dining room combination everything has its proper place

LITTLE Peter Eckhoff was four months old before his parents were finally able to move from their two-room walk-up in New York City to a comfortable cottage in Levittown, Long Island. Bringing a new baby into a tiny city apartment, Helen Eckhoff says, taught her as nothing else could the importance of good housekeeping equipment and careful planning before and after a baby arrives. When she and Bob discovered, shortly after they moved to Levittown, that they were going to have a second child they began planning for it months in advance. "We were determined this time to work things out far enough ahead so that there'd be no last-minute exhaustion and we'd still have time for a little social life."

While Helen now had Peter to take care of, and a house instead of two rooms, she also had the advantage in her new home of a yard, an attic and a full-size kitchen equipped with an electric refrigerator, a modern sink, an electric range with accurate heat control and an automatic washing machine.

"The first thing I did," she says, "was to arrange my kitchen so that it would save the most time and energy possible. I now have three working centers—the baby center where I keep all baby food, bottles and the like, a baking center and a cleaning center for general cleaning and washing machine supplies. It may not sound impressive, but it's amazing the steps you save if you keep all your supplies together like this."

One of Helen's greatest joys in her new home is the washing machine, which takes care of the family's regular laundry (in-

Helen stocks all her cleaning supplies in this metal cabinet next to the washing machine. Supplies she uses frequently are kept in a basket there and toted from room to room on cleaning day

41

Figure 9-11 This article, published in *McCall's* magazine in 1949, profiles the new routines of a Levittown housewife. Dozens of articles such as this presented a normative portrait of suburban family life and advised housewives how to live up to this standard. Elizabeth Sweeney Herbert, "This is How I Keep House," *McCall's* 76 (April 1949), 41.

For this Helen depends on her electric sewing machine which she has already used to make slip covers and curtains for the new house. With the sewing machine and its flexible at-

tachments Helen makes clothes for herself, Peter and the baby-to-come. "I can even do most of my mending on it—a wonderful help in salvaging Peter's outgrown clothes for the baby." With it she also remodeled her own clothes to make them bigger and remade blankets and bedding for the baby's crib.

Planning so carefully for the second baby, Helen feels, has taught her many housekeeping tricks that will be just as useful when the new baby comes and she has two small children to look after. "Naturally I'll be tied down," she says, "but Bob and I know now that no matter how many children we have it's possible to plan so there'll be time left over for ourselves."

9-6. A DAY IN THE LIFE OF A SUBURBAN CARPOOL MOTHER, 1955

Source: Merrill Folsom, "Suburbia on Wheels: Around the Clock with a Mother Serving in a Typical Westchester Car Pool," *New York Times,* May 2, 1955. Copyright © 1955 by The New York Times Co. Reprinted with permission.

WHITE PLAINS, N.Y., May—The car pool has shifted into high gear as a development of modern Suburbia.

It was spawned by economics of the Depression and became a necessity during wartime shortages of fuel and vehicles. Now it is a daily mobile house party for children being taken to school and for adults going to railroad stations and offices.

It is the commuter's contrivance for having one housewife do the chauffeuring for several, for reducing congestion in downtown traffic and for sharing the mounting charges for tolls, tires and parking....

[A recent study found] that 60 per cent of the men and 26 per cent of the women rely on automobiles. As for buses, only 14 per cent of the men and 36 per cent of the women now use them. Auto travel costs, often shared by a car pool, struck a median of $12.73 a month. The median for a bus traveler was $4.69 a month.

Mr. and Mrs. Dan Donaldson of 515 Ridgeway, White Plains, are members of a car pool. They live in a pleasant home of Colonial design on an acre of lawns, fruit trees, tulip beds and split-rail fences.

They are miles from railroad stations and schools. As a carpool housewife, Mrs. Donaldson drives 300 miles a week when her full turn comes. On a recent typical day the Donaldsons' daily pinwheel began spinning at 6:30 A.M.

"Another day on the merry-go-round," Mr. Donaldson said to his wife, Noni, as he rubbed sleep from his eyes. He pondered another day of advertising soap, cup cakes, bread and beer. As a radio and television announcer in New York, he makes the sound track for thrice-a-week sports newsreels....

At 8:15 A. M. the Donaldsons and their maid, Helena Wiggins, who comes to work by bus, got the two children, Jeff, 8 years old, and Chris, 4, into the family convertible.

Then the family started on an odyssey. Mrs. Donaldson drove twenty-one miles. She encountered twenty-seven traffic lights and ten stop signs. And she took the shortest serpentine route that the job would permit.

The first stop was on Scott Circle, Purchase. There the Donaldsons picked up Paul S. Mauer, a New York textile broker, and two of the Mauer children, Douglas, 10, and Charlotte, 8.

Then they drove to the Rye Country Day School, where the Mauer children and Jeff were deposited. Cutting back through White Plains the car stopped on Gedney Park Drive to pick up William F. Luddy, head of a New York merchandise reporting bureau. At a nursery school in the Church in the Highlands, Chris was deposited, and as the 9:33 commuters' special was rounding the bend, the automobile pulled up at the White Plains railroad station to deposit the men.

Mrs. Donaldson went home to have a cup of coffee before starting the second lap.

At noon she picked up Chris, then returned at 12:30 P.M. to the Rye Country Day School to get nine children, including her own and those of the Mauers. At present she makes the midday trip to Rye three days one week, two days the next, alternating with other mothers. She handles the morning run Mondays through Fridays....

After miscellaneous driving for painters and craftsmen, Mrs. Donaldson returns most evenings to chauffeuring her husband home from the train and, finally, the maid home, too. Mr. Donaldson often is delayed by a late broadcast. If he has not arrived at the station by 11 P. M., Mrs. Donaldson lets him take a taxi.

"I've got to get some sleep sometime," she explains.

9-7. D. J. WALDIE RECOLLECTS LIFE ON THE GRID, 1996

Source: *Holy Land: A Suburban Memoir* by D.J. Waldie. Copyright © 1996 by Donald J. Waldie. Used by permission of W.W. Norton & Company, Inc.

26

The average number of houses per acre in prewar subdivisions had been about five.

In the suburb where I live, begun in 1950, the number of houses per acre is eight.

The houses were designed by an architect named Paul Duncan.

27

You leave the space between the houses uncrossed. You rarely go across the street, which is forty feet wide.

You are grateful for the distance. It is as if each house on your block stood on its own enchanted island, fifty feet wide by one hundred feet long.

People come and go from it, your parents mostly and your friends. Your parents arrive like pilgrims.

But the island is remote. You occasionally hear the sounds of anger. You almost never hear the sounds of love.

You hear, always at night, the shifting of the uprights, the sagging of ceiling joists, and the unpredictable ticking of the gas heater.

28

What is beautiful here?

The calling of a mourning dove, and others answering from yard to yard. Perhaps this is the only thing beautiful here....

43

This suburb was thrown up on plowed-under bean fields beginning in early 1950. No theorist or urban planner had the experience then to gauge how thirty thousand former GIs and their wives would take to frame and stucco houses on small, rectangular lots next to hog farms and dairies.

In Long Beach, some businessmen assumed the result would be a slum. Others wondered if it would be a ghost town.

Someone asked the eager promoter sent by the developers, "Who will you sell all those houses to—the jack rabbits?"

Had you seen the delicate houses then, going up on the tract's light gray soil, the ground scraped clean and as flat as Kansas, you might have wondered, too.

44

This is not a garden suburb. The streets do not curve or offer vistas.

The street grid always intersects at right angles. The north-south roads are avenues. The east-west roads are streets. The four-lane highways in either compass orientation are boulevards.

The city planted some of these with eucalyptus trees and red crape myrtle on narrow, well-tended medians and parkway strips.

People passing through the city often mention the trees. They never mention the pattern over which they pass....

172

The critics of suburbs say that you and I live narrow lives.

I agree. My life is narrow.

From one perspective or another, all our lives are narrow. Only when lives are placed side by side do they seem larger.

173

Mrs. R and her husband lived across the street. They had a daughter, born a few months before my brother.

They were Episcopalians.

My mother and Mrs. R were friends. They spent afternoons in each other's houses, while my mother waited through her first pregnancy.

One afternoon, Mrs. R's baby stopped breathing. Mrs. R came to my mother's front door in tears, helpless.

Neither Mrs. R nor my mother had a car. Neither could drive. Few women in the neighborhood could.

It was 1946. Neither house had a telephone.

My mother, heavy with her baby, ran across the street into Mrs. R's house.

She picked up Mrs. R's daughter. She walked into the kitchen and turned on the faucet.

She cradled the dead baby in her arm against the curve of her stomach, and cupped her hand into the stream of water.

With a little of the water, she baptized the baby.

It was all she could do.

174

I saw my father cry only once before my mother's death. I was nine or ten.

It seemed to me that my parents were arguing about my father's health. I don't think they were. Something else had unfolded in their life together.

The argument stopped. My father came into the middle bedroom, where I had gone to be as far from them as I could. In this house, the greatest distance is fifteen or twenty feet.

My father sat on the end of the small bed that took the place of a couch in the middle room. The room was crowded with a desk, bookshelves my father built, the bed, and a black-and-white television set.

We sat a short distance from each other. My father cried.

The middle room became my bedroom when I entered college. I slept there on weekends when I went to graduate school in Orange County. It was my room when I left school and began a part-time teaching job.

After my mother died in 1979, my father suggested I take the larger, back bedroom.

I said no....

205

My father believed in authority. He believed that faithfulness of a particularly knowing kind could replace moral choices.

He was a good Catholic.

My father knew that the place where he lived allowed him to be a good Catholic. It allowed him to think his life might be redeemed.

Three Jews built a faithfulness into the place where I live. They built the city where my family lived and where my mother and father died.

206

When I walk to work, thinking of these stories, they seem insignificant. At Mass on Sunday, I remember them as prayers....

208

One neighbor on my block ran a lathe. Another worked on the assembly line in a plastics plant. Another was an oil refinery worker until his death.

My father was an engineer for the Gas Company.

There was no obvious way to tell a factory worker from a business owner or a professional man when I grew up. Every house on my block looked much the same.

It's still hard to measure status. One neighbor is a cosmetics salesman. Another is a security guard at Douglas. Two more work for the city of Long Beach.

Several are now retired. Some are widows.

The man who used to live across the street owned his own painting business. He became moderately well-off repainting school buildings, and he moved away.

The family moved to Rancho Palos Verdes, a suburb with horses and swimming pools....

215

The grid limited our choices, exactly as urban planners said it would. But the limits weren't paralyzing.

The design of this suburb compelled a conviviality that people got used to and made into a substitute for choices, including not choosing at all.

There are an indefinite number of beginnings and endings on the grid, but you are always somewhere.

ESSAYS

The three essays that follow explore the phenomenon of postwar suburbanization from several angles—the central importance of federal policy and private developers in the suburbanization process, the environmental impact of mass-produced suburbia, and finally the social values reflected in the design of postwar homes. In **Essay 9-1**, historian Dolores Hayden emphasizes the fundamental, often unnoticed role of federal policy in determining the trajectory of twentieth-century suburbanization. With the help of hidden government subsidies, private developer-builders amassed tremendous power to shape postwar suburban expansion. The profit motive invariably drove the choices they made which, Hayden notes critically, could result in dismal community planning, unimaginative house designs, and stingy provisioning for public services. Collectively, federal policies promoted suburbanization on an unprecedented scale. Hayden is the author of numerous books on the history of America's metropolitan landscapes, including a recent synthesis, *Building Suburbia: Green Fields and Urban Growth, 1820–2000* (2003).

While the proliferation of suburbs may have solved the nation's postwar housing crisis, it began creating new problems. One was the enormous toll on the environment, as farmland, hillsides, and hinterlands were bulldozed to make way for suburban homes. In **Essay 9-2**, environmental historian Adam Rome explores one facet of this story: the use and impact of the suburban septic tank. The history of this single suburban apparatus illustrates how the massive scale of suburbanization intensified its impact on the land. In his larger study, *The Bulldozer in the Countryside*, Rome shows how the public's discovery of suburbia's environmental degradation—from septic tank problems to the decline of open space—ultimately led to the rise of the environmental movement. In **Essay 9-3**, historian Barbara Kelly examines how the design of postwar Levittown homes reflected the prevalent values of the period: conformity, privacy, and domesticity. Kelly's work is important for reminding us that individuals also shaped postwar suburbanization, in their choice to embrace the suburban lifestyle and in the ways they used and adapted their homes. The houses might have been mass produced at the outset, but residents eventually personalized them in multiple ways.

ESSAY 9-1. DOLORES HAYDEN, "BUILDING THE AMERICAN WAY: PUBLIC SUBSIDY, PRIVATE SPACE" (2004)

Source: Unpublished paper delivered at the International Planning History Society conference, Barcelona, Spain, July 17, 2004.

From the early seventeenth century through the 1920s, Americans created regional traditions of town design centered on public space. Residents of New England's villages grouped their houses around substantial town greens; builders of Southwestern towns and cities organized plazas with pedestrian arcades; designers of Midwestern county seats sited their public courthouses inside tree-shaded squares. Traces of these physical patterns linger in major urban centers such as Los Angeles and Boston as well as in

smaller towns and villages, but in the twentieth century, urban design in the United States largely shifted from public to private control. Since 1945, complex public subsidies have buttressed many types of private real estate development. Americans have often made the mistake of condemning the low-grade products—badly-sited tracts, enormous parking lots, or gigantic malls—rather than attacking the process which has diverted public dollars to private rather than public space.

Between the mid-1920s and the mid-1950s, the National Association of Real Estate Boards (NAREB), an influential lobby, encouraged the federal government to enact five kinds of legislation: Federal Housing Administration (FHA) and Veterans Administration (VA) programs for mortgage loan insurance; homeowner mortgage interest deductions from income tax; interstate highway subsidies funded by gasoline taxes; and tax deductions for accelerated depreciation on commercial real estate. The first three subsidies led to the tract house suburbs of the 1940s and 1950s. The other two generated interstate highways in the 1960s and edge nodes consisting of malls, offices and other commercial real estate projects at highway interchanges in the 1960s, 1970s, and 1980s. By providing subsidies indirectly, through loan guarantee programs or manipulation of the tax codes, the federal government avoided extensive scrutiny of the politics behind public funding for privately owned space. Few requirements for infrastructure (sewer systems, schools, transit), public amenities (open space), or public access accompanied indirect subsidy programs. While all of these programs have been critiqued, their cumulative impact on private and public space has not yet been fully assessed. A brief history of three postwar developments, Levittown, Lakewood, and Park Forest, outlines the devastating economic and physical consequences of private, urban-scale construction.

Making the Rules: The Department of Commerce and the Real Estate Lobby

The federal government was first drawn toward urban planning and housing through Herbert Hoover's efforts. As Secretary of Commerce from 1921–1928 and then as President from 1929–1933, he worked with the real estate lobby to promote construction. Hoover was an engineer and his Commerce Department began by establishing a Division of Building and Housing that supported banking, building, and real estate activities. It developed a model zoning ordinance, a uniform national building code, and drafted preliminary versions of legislation to establish the Federal Housing Administration. Hoover also nurtured a private non-profit group called Better Homes in America, Inc. By 1930, Better Homes had organized over 7,000 local chapters composed of bankers, subdividers, construction firms, realtors, utilities, small businesses, and manufacturers advocating government support for the private development of small houses as a way to boost mass consumption. This coalition formed a "Growth Machine," a political

machine promoting large-scale land development in many localities. In 1931, Hoover ran a National Conference on Homebuilding and Home Ownership that explored federal financing and construction of houses, subdivision layout, and the location of industry and commerce.

Under Hoover, real estate historian Marc Weiss notes that the National Association of Real Estate Boards (NAREB) became "an important and highly favored trade organization, working with Commerce and other agencies." Large developer/builders had formed NAREB in 1908, and they assisted the federal government with housing issues during World War I. Between 1921 and 1931, NAREB grew into "a key national lobbying force." Its leaders included major developers such as Harry Culver of Culver City near Los Angeles and J. C. Nichols of the Country Club District in Kansas City. In 1927 NAREB worked jointly with the American City Planning Institute (ACPI) on the document that became the Commerce Department's *Standard City Planning Enabling Act*. Interestingly, planners wanted to require subdividers to dedicate some portion of all new tracts to parks and open space for public use. The realtors thought the planners too idealistic—they wanted to get paid for every bit of land.

President Franklin D. Roosevelt followed Hoover and launched a number of New Deal programs in planning and housing during the Depression years. The National Housing Act created the Federal Housing Administration (FHA) in 1934. The realtors had worked on drafting the rules for the FHA and were active in administering the agency once it was established. Other New Deal efforts stressed public construction and public space, and the realtors fought them. The Resettlement Administration, created by Executive Order in 1935, sponsored the Greenbelt Towns, planned towns that were soon attacked by the real estate lobby as "too expensive." The U.S. Housing Act (Wagner Act) created the U.S. Housing Authority to sponsor public housing in 1937, soon attacked by the real estate lobby as "un-American." Activists such as Catherine Bauer (RPAA member) and other members of a group called the Labor Housing Conference had long campaigned for the design of multi-family housing with child care centers and recreational amenities including swimming pools and meeting rooms. Projects such as the Hosiery Workers Housing in Philadelphia and the Harlem River Houses for African Americans in New York, designed by teams of noted architects in the 1930s, pointed to what could be achieved. Nevertheless, NAREB lobbyists held to the Hoover programs and fought hard against any alternatives to the single-family tract house purchased on a long mortgage. Conservative Republicans defeated the Wagner Act in 1935 and 1936, burdening its passage in 1937 with severe cost restrictions, means testing for tenants, and slum clearance to protect private landlords. These provisions meant public housing design would be minimal and residents would be poor. FHA would be the dominant program. Kenneth T. Jackson has shown that FHA's concern for appraised value was expressed as a prohibition on people of color in white neighborhoods. As a result, postwar housing was dominated by private developers who created vast new tracts segregated by government policy.

None of this was inevitable—there was a moment after World War II when housing activists again challenged federal policy, and real estate interests fought hard to control the issue. Historians Rosalyn Baxandall and Elizabeth Ewen document the lobbying by bankers and builders behind the hearings on housing dominated by Senator Joseph McCarthy in 1947 and 1948. McCarthy developed his "sledgehammer style" hassling proponents of public housing and planned towns as socialists and communists. McCarthy also attacked building workers in traditional craft unions in the AFL as incompetents who produced slack work and would impede the postwar housing process. McCarthy found developer William Levitt an ally who would testify that only federal aid to large private builders could solve the postwar housing shortage. McCarthy and his allies also attacked the expansion of benefits for the poor in the 1949 Housing Act. FHA remained dominant in the housing area, and Title I of the 1949 housing legislation opened the way to land clearance in big cities for the benefit of private developers, later called "urban renewal."

Following the Rules: Postwar Suburbs

In the vast new tracts produced in the late 1940s and 1950s, public and private were redefined. With populations between fifty and eighty thousand, the largest of the post-World War II subdivisions were the size of cities, but they looked like overgrown subdivisions. Ten million new homes built between 1946 and 1953 were the products of a newly restructured private housing industry working closely with the federal government. Prewar the average builder made a few houses a year. By 1949, the majority of new dwelling units in the United States were produced by very large builders. Levitt and Sons of New York, Weingart, Taper, and Boyar of Lakewood, California, and Manilow and Klutznick's American Community Builders (ACB) of Park Forest, Illinois were typical. At seventy to eighty thousand residents apiece, Lakewood and Levittown, New York, were the two largest suburbs of this era. In these suburbs, the federal government provided massive aid directed at developers (whose 90% production advances were insured by the FHA). They also subsidized veterans (who could get VA guarantees for mortgages at 4% with little or nothing down) and white male homeowners (who could deduct their mortgage interest payments from their taxable income for the next thirty years).

Levittown, Nassau County, New York

William Levitt and his brother Alfred were college dropouts. Their lawyer father, Abraham Levitt, encouraged them to stay busy by forming a building company during the Depression, and after the war they emerged as major developers. Levitt and Sons promoted a brand name product to promote the community of over 17,000 houses they built on Long Island for about 77,000 people. A reporter described William Levitt as a hoarse-voiced chain smoker of three packs a day, with "a liking for hyperbole that causes him to describe his height (5 ft. 8 in.) as 'nearly six feet,' and his company as the 'General Motors of the housing industry.'" Alfred, the firm's designer, said, "As in your car, the parts in a Levitt house are standardized; each part will fit any house of the same model...the Leavitt factory...is the land on which we assemble our houses." William Levitt developed a public relations campaign promoting every last step in the house building process, as well as every supplier. Bendix washers, General Electric stoves, and Admiral televisions were installed in the houses. Levitt houses endorsed the advertised products, and the products were often selling points for Levitt houses.

Although they are often credited with this, Levitt and Sons did not originate the methods of organizing the rapid production of houses in a continuous production process. Fritz Burns in California seems to have been first, but Levitt and Sons was pushing in the same direction in a 1942 project for seven hundred and fifty FHA Title VI houses in Norfolk, Virginia, where they systematized over two dozen basic tasks of house building. Alfred Levitt styled their first Cape Cod to recall Sears, Roebuck mail order houses like "The Nantucket." Levitt and Sons stood behind the product with an unwritten one-year warranty, and began to sell 800 sq. ft. houses for $6,990 in the late 1940s. The Levitt "ranch" that followed included a carport. Levitt and Sons also relied on some sweat equity, giving veterans and their wives the chance to personalize their houses. They could convert the attics of their houses into additional bedrooms, build garages or porches, and landscape the yards. "No man who has a house and lot can be a Communist," claimed William Levitt. "He has too much to do." Stories of customers standing in line for days appeared in the press. Happy purchasers posed in front of houses. By October of 1952, *Fortune* magazine gushed over "The Most House for the Money" and praised "Levitt's Progress," publishing William Levitt's complaints about government interference, that is strict FHA and VA inspections and standards. Said Levitt, with a straight face, despite hundreds of millions of dollars of FHA financing: "Utopia in this business would be to get rid of the government, except in its proper function of an insurance agency."

Levitt and Sons never talked about urban planning. They were far more conservative than someone like NAREB's J. C. Nichols, who took pride in designing his developments well. Levittown was a large, unincorporated community of 80,000 people, straddling several towns including Hempstead and Oyster Bay. It had no master plan and no government of its own. Land purchases were not always contiguous—arterials with commercial strip development owned by others often intersected residential areas. Between 1947 and 1951, Levitt and Sons constructed seven small shopping areas, a few stores each. Also they built nine swimming pools and seven small parks with children's playgrounds and some baseball fields. What the Levitts did not build was infrastructure, according to a study made by NYU students and faculty in 1951. Levitt failed to integrate their road systems with county and state highways. Levitt and Sons did not plan for urban scale sewage disposal. They did not even use septic tanks— historian Barbara Kelly has noted they used individual cesspools attached to each house, rather than sewers. Engineers in the Nassau County Department of Public Health protested the problems of ground saturation without success. No sewers were built until the 1960s, when the federal government provided aid to suburbs around the country to eliminate health hazards and install sewers retroactively. Similarly, the Levitt firm left trash removal up to private contractors, whose private waste removal services would be paid for by the residents. Levitt and Sons boasted that they "set aside" land for schools to both towns, but they paid for nothing and built nothing. Towns had to assess the taxpayers in special districts to pay for the land, school buildings, and operations. State government provided financial aid to avoid a crisis. By 1951, Alfred Levitt learned from his mistakes, and proposed a new, planned community called Landia. Bill Levitt then claimed he and his brother could no longer make decisions together. He split from Alfred and built two more Levittowns emphasizing houses plus more shopping.

Lakewood, California

Lakewood developed a little bit more slowly than Levittown, but eventually it was slightly larger, about 80,000 people. The three developers, Ben Weingart, Mark Taper, and Louis Boyar bought ten square miles of flat land near Long Beach. The entire area was gridded with streets meeting at right angles, lined by lots of 50 by 100 feet, the smallest size permitted in Los Angeles County. It held 17,500 frame and stucco houses of 1,100 square feet. There were sewers, required by the county, and a Waste King electric garbage disposal in every kitchen. O'Keefe and Merritt gas stoves, Norge refrigerators, and Bendix "Economat" washers could be added to the purchase price at a hefty extra charge of $9 per appliance each month. Each house was provided with one small tree in the planting strip between front sidewalk and street. The developers were stingy with recreational facilities, but a county supervisor did browbeat the developers into building one swimming pool in a local park. The developers hired William Garnett, the noted aerial photographer, to fly over the land recording their progress. His chilling images of rows of houses sprouting from fields became famous, but not for the reasons he had been hired.

In contrast to Levittown, Lakewood also included, from the start, a highly profitable regional shopping mall surrounded by 10,580 parking spaces, as well as sixteen small commercial centers within walking distance— one half mile—of the houses. The shopping mall was anchored by a branch of the May Company, designed by architect Albert C. Martin with four giant neon "M's" sixteen feet high, facing north, south, east, and west. Opening in February 1952, the shopping center offered the goods new residents might need and also drew in outside customers. With the mall, a private store became a public landmark, pointing to the directions real estate would soon take across the country. The housing around it fueled controversy. In *Holy Land*, D. J. Waldie relates that in 1954 Ben Weingart and Louis Boyar were subpoenaed to testify before Homer Capeheart's Senate subcommittee on "irregularities in their federally backed mortgages and construction loans." The developers had not gotten FHA Title VI funding for a 90% guarantee. Instead, they had proceeded under the National Housing Act, Section 213, asking for 100% financing by pretending to be the organizers of "mutual homes." They got their employees to front dummy corporations, using a New Deal program planned for rural cooperatives with a maximum of 501 houses apiece. Using this deception over and over, they built the largest suburban community in America. It didn't cost them any jail time.

Park Forest, the GI Town

Some developers tried to do better. American Community Builders (ACB), a private development firm headed by Philip Klutznick, a former federal government official who had served in the Roosevelt and Truman administrations, created Park Forest, Illinois. He said: "We aren't interested in houses alone. We are trying to create a better life for people. In our view, we will have failed if all we do is to produce houses." Approached about fronting a "GI town" by Nathan Manilow, a major Chicago real estate developer, Klutznick said he would only be interested if it were a real town, not an overgrown suburban development. According to landscape architect Gregory Randall, ACB selected a site of over 3,100 acres about 30 miles south of Chicago on a railroad line. The firm added experienced public housing architects Jerrold Loebl and Norman Schlossman. Elbert Peets, the noted Washington, D.C., landscape architect, co-author of *The American Vitruvius*, and co-designer of Greendale, Wisconsin, did the basic town plan for a "garden city" with a nearby railroad station, sites for industry, a shopping center and several smaller commercial areas, parks, schools, and different types of housing.

ACB decided to begin with the construction of rental housing. Using Clarence Stein's Baldwin Hills Village as a model, a variety of two-story townhouses and flats were grouped in courtyards and superblocks. This phase included 3,010 units. By 1948, tenants were moving in, the Klutznick family first among them. At the first barbecue, the developers pressed residents to vote for incorporation as a village. Many volunteers stepped forward and began to run the town and its committees. Meanwhile the company began to develop a town center with government offices, a department store, and 44 smaller stores. By trying to build a town center (although it was similar to a mall) and setting a higher standard for postwar development, ACB attracted other developers to the fringes of their area, smaller firms who would build only houses and sell them more cheaply. Those who thought sound neighborhoods turned few profits challenged Peets' residential neighborhood concept. Under pressure to avoid slow home sales, ACB discarded Peets's elegant scheme of small residential neighborhoods with a hierarchy of streets, parks, and pedestrian circulation, in favor of Levitt-like streets with no connecting greenbelt and fewer landscape buffers. Costs were slashed at every turn: houses were moved closer to the streets to save on piping, planting strips were removed, sidewalks were combined with curbs to save on concrete work. Over time, the houses were all sold, and the town filled out to a population of 30,000. By the late 1950s and early 1960s, ACB began to dissolve, selling various parts of the village that had not been on the market before, including the rental housing. The partners became wealthy men. In time, Klutznick became the developer of Chicago's Water Tower Place, and then Secretary of Commerce in the Carter Administration.

Keeping the Postwar Boom Going

In the mid-fifties, American politicians and business people worried about how to keep mass-consumption going in a "consumer's republic" where white male citizens were encouraged to see purchasing things as a patriotic duty. Could families who owned houses, cars, and consumer goods be persuaded to keep on buying? In the 1950s, Americans owned three-quarters of the appliances and gadgets produced in the world. As the fifties wore on, the attention given to houses, appliances, and consumer products turned explicitly political in the televised 1959 Nixon/Khrushchev "Kitchen Debate" in Moscow. At this exhibition, Nixon boasted to Khrushchev that a model house, "Splitnik," an all-electric kitchen, and dozens of small appliances provided material evidence of the superiority of the way of life of an ordinary American worker.

But could one more appliance keep consumers happy? Back in the 1930s, GE and other manufacturers had lobbied the FHA to get appliance costs included in mortgages. Energy consumption soared as part of this strategy. The problem two decades later was to find novel ways to keep appliance consumption rising, and the strategy backfired. The introduction of air-conditioning in the early 1950s (first room air conditioners, then central cooling) was followed by campaigns for electric heat (to balance the cooling load in summer with a comparable demand for power in the winter). The "all-electric home" was promoted by utilities and manufacturers looking for more business. They offered so many sweetheart deals for tract builders, as well as coercive measures, that their promotional practices generated congressional hearings.

One alternative route to high consumption of appliances and energy was building bigger houses. Would families trade-up their houses the way they did with automobiles? Those families who owned houses were encouraged to spend more with the "mansion subsidy," because tax deductions for mortgage interest rose with the cost and size of the house. Average size of a new house in 1950 was 800 square feet, in 1970, 1200 square feet, and in 1990, 2100 square feet. Estimated at $81 billion in 1994, the mansion subsidy remains larger than the annual budget of the department of Housing and Urban Development. As house sizes rose, household size was decreasing and more and more mothers were engaging in paid work. By 2000, close to 60 percent of mothers of children under one were in the paid labor force. While white male-headed households were often homeowners, households headed by persons of color and women lagged in their rates of home ownership—and still do. Rather than extend housing to those not housed, the next two federal subsidies went to support more development on urban peripheries.

Highways and Edge Nodes

Historians have often suggested that from the late 1920s on, cars enabled people to move to suburbs. Another way to understand the car-house relationship is that the FHA model of hidden subsidies for private housing was, in

Figure 9-12 Cross Country Plaza, Stamford, Connecticut, 1959. Sleek, spacious shopping malls revolutionized the nature of retailing after 1945. By bringing the most fashionable stores to these centers, the suburban mall obviated the need for suburbanites to travel downtown for fine shopping. Courtesy of Library of Congress, Prints and Photographs Division, Gottscho-Schleisner Collection, LC-G613-73745 DLC (bl and white film neg).

the mid-50s, applied to asphalt, trucks, and automobiles, when the Interstate Highway Act provided for the construction of 42,500 miles of roads with 90% federal financing. Legislation specifically excluded public transportation from sharing in the subsidy.

From the mid-1950s on, developers responded to the infrastructure of Interstate highways, and the lack of planned centers in existing suburbs, by large-scale construction of commercial real estate at highway off-ramps. These anchored dozens of non-places that Joel Garreau called "edge cities" in 1991 and Robert E. Lang recently expanded to "edgeless cities." Terms such as "out-towns" and "outer cities" did not explain them. Perhaps "taxopolis" would have been better. As Tom Hanchett has shown, federal tax policies between 1954 and 1986 offered accelerated depreciation for new commercial real estate in greenfield locations. Developers received huge tax write-offs for "every type of income-producing structure," including

motels, fast food restaurants, offices, rental apartments, and of course, shopping centers. As Hanchett notes, "Throughout the mid-1950s, developers had sought locations *within* growing suburban areas. Now shopping centers began appearing in the cornfields *beyond* the edge of existing development." This tax write-off cost the federal government about $750 to $850 million per year in the late 1960s. Accelerated depreciation also encouraged cheap construction and discouraged adequate maintenance. Obsolescence was rapid.

Over time edge nodes expanded, adding new building types such as "category killers" (big box discount stores) and "power centers" (groups of big boxes), plus disguised boxes and outlet malls trying to look like villages. Less and less was local. Businesses were increasingly tied to national or international chains, part of an expanding global economy, often requiring airport access as well as access by truck. Warehouse-like buildings were dictated by management pro-tocols about "facilities" having nothing to do with the towns where they operated. Mil-lions who worked in edge nodes refused to live in places like Tyson's Corner, Virginia, or Schaumburg, Illinois. Instead, many Ameri-cans chose to drive to residences located on the rural fringe. The 2000 Census showed rural fringes as the fastest growing areas in the country. (Myron Orfield's *American Met-ropolitics* critiques the way that residents of older, inner-ring suburbs are often subject to state and local taxes which subsidize the ex-tension of infrastructure to the affluent outer fringes, but these state and local subsidies are beyond the scope of this paper.)

The American Way: Growth Machines

The Hoover era established a national pattern of urbanization based on federal subsidies to stimulate the consumption of houses, cars, and consumer goods by white, male-headed households. The visions of the "growth ma-chines" never included public space. Without a federal commitment to economic equity, without urban and regional planning, with-out design controls, growth machines sur-rounded older city centers with low-density, low-quality greenfield construction, under-mining their economic vitality. Oblique meth-ods of delivering federal financial support to private developers made frontal attack dif-ficult, so many reformers targeted narrower single issues. Since the 1950s, conservation-ists have campaigned for more open space in suburbs. Environmentalists have critiqued the wasteful use of land and energy in subur-ban development and struggled to get federal regulations to protect soil, water, and wild-life. Political activists have decried racism and campaigned for fair housing legislation. Architects have proposed pedestrian-friendly mixed-use neighborhoods. There have been relatively few critiques of the broad spatial impact of the real estate lobby, its close ties to the federal government, and its definitions of building the American way.

In *Modern Housing in America: Policy Struggles in the New Deal Era*, historian Gail Radford defines the 1930s as the time when Americans developed a "two-tier" policy to subsidize housing. Cramped multi-fam-ily housing for the poor, the elderly, female-headed families, and people of color would be constructed by public authorities, and more generous single-family housing for white, male-headed families would be constructed by the private developers with government support. The split had profound implica-tions for urban design: inadequate financial resources behind one effort and wasted ma-terial resources behind the other. And worst of all it mystified many working-class and middle-class Americans, who saw minimal subsidies for the poor but never understood their own tract housing, highways, and malls were far more heavily subsidized.

As Barry Checkoway has noted, back in the 1950s *Fortune* was fond of portraying suburbs as "exploding" over the landscape, as the happy result of consumer preferences that created a boom. But, he says, "ordinary consumers had little real choice." There were no well-designed multifamily housing proj-ects in urban settings. There were no well-de-signed single family houses in integrated new towns with substantial public space. Instead urban-scale places like Levittown, Lakewood, and Park Forest were constructed without much input from architects or urban design-ers, as if they were subdivisions of houses rather than cities. Design and construction were even worse a decade or two later, in edge nodes identified as hot spots for commercial real estate. Small town Main Streets with-ered, and urban commercial neighborhoods declined, as businesses moved to subsidized edge nodes. Although private investors made money, even the largest of these edge nodes, such as Tyson's Corner and Schaumburg, were monotonous landscapes of window-less malls, windowless big box stores, cheap office buildings, and logo-buildings housing food franchises, all designed for constant au-tomobile and truck traffic.

Coupled with earlier subsidies for mas-sive, new urban-scale housing tracts in sub-urban locations, more recent subsidies for edge nodes and rural fringes surrounding them have devastated the centers of older cities and towns. A few decades of subsidies for greenfield growth reversed centuries of concentrated, locally regulated urban development. In 2003, metropolitan regions have expanded into urbanized areas two hundred miles in diameter. Beyond the village greens of New England, the plazas of the Southwest, and the courthouse squares of the Midwest, beyond the centers of new towns established before 1920, public places built to attract citizens are scarce.

Legal scholar Carol Rose has written about "Property as Storytelling." "Property is process," argues natural resources specialist Louise Fortmann. Sketched here is the story of federal policies to stimulate the real estate and construction sectors of the economy, policies that granted large private developers a lavish sequence of subsidies without incentives to create well-designed residential neighborhoods, transit, and public space. To understand why public space is missing, Americans must remember that after 1945, most of the built environment was never planned or designed—it was shaped by old Commerce Department programs devised with the aid of the real estate industry just before the Depression. It would be funny if it were not so unfair.

ESSAY 9-2. ADAM ROME, *THE BULL-DOZER IN THE COUNTRYSIDE: SUBURBAN SPRAWL AND THE RISE OF AMERICAN ENVIRONMENTALISM* (2001)

Source: Copyright © Adam Rome 2001. Reprinted with the permission of Cambridge University Press.

Septic Tank Suburbia: The Problem of Waste Disposal at the Metropolitan Fringe

About 20 years ago, the best-selling chronicler of American middle-class culture, Erma Bombeck, offered a succinct interpretation of the rise of suburbia:

The suburbs were discovered quite by accident one day in the early 1940s by a Welcome-Wagon lady who was lost. As she stood in a mushy marshland, her sturdy Red Cross shoes sinking into the mire, she looked down, and exclaimed, "It's a septic tank. I've discovered the suburbs!"

News of the discovery of a septic tank spread and within weeks thirty million city dwellers readied their station wagons and began the long journey to the edge of town in search of a bath and a half and a tree.

In that passage from *The Grass Is Always Greener Over the Septic Tank,* Bombeck humorously noticed what more scholarly observers have overlooked: Like the automobile and the highway, the septic tank was a key element in the suburbanization of the United States. With backyard systems for waste disposal, houses did not need to be near municipal sewer lines, so the area available for suburban development expanded tremendously.

Because the census bureau did not begin to count the nation's septic tanks until 1960, historians have no sure way to gauge the increase in numbers after World War II. But the available evidence makes clear that the increase was phenomenal. In 1945, according to one government estimate, only about 4.5 million homes had septic tanks. In 1960, the first census counted nearly 14 million. If the 1945 estimate was close to the mark, then the increase in just 15 years was over 300 percent. The two figures also suggest that roughly 45 percent of the new homes built in those years had septic tanks....In some metropolitan areas, the reliance on backyard waste-disposal systems was even more pronounced: In metropolitan Phoenix, for example, a 1958 study found that more than 70 percent of subdivision homes had septic tanks. Thus, septic tanks were not found only on the large, isolated lots of the affluent. Builders installed them by the hundreds and thousands in tract developments. In one extreme case, a developer used septic tanks for a subdivision with more than 8,000 houses.

Yet the widespread use of septic tanks in suburbia proved problematic. Because a substantial number of the backyard waste-disposal systems failed in the first two or three years, homebuyers were often faced with foul and unsanitary messes. Many were stuck with steep repair bills, and some lost everything they had invested in their homes. The high failure rate also cost the nation's taxpayers, since the FHA and the Veteran's Administration insured millions of homes with septic tanks. Eventually, the federal government provided billions in subsidies to enable local governments to replace septic systems with sewers. In many areas of the country, septic tank failures were responsible for outbreaks of infectious disease. The technology also had a considerable environmental cost, since poor design, siting, and maintenance of septic tanks often led to contamination of groundwater, pollution of streams, and eutrophication of lakes....

Yet the number of homes with septic tanks continued to increase. Though the most flagrant problems caused by backyard waste disposal were overcome, septic tanks continue to pollute the nation's waters. At every stage, from the 1950s to the 1970s, the effort to regulate septic tank use demonstrated the difficulty of controlling the process of urban and suburban development.

The First Concerns about Septic Tanks

In 1945, the nation's builders saw only the benefits of using the septic tank. The long years of depression and war had led to a severe housing shortage. The title of a 1948 "March of Time" newsreel summed up the postwar demand—"Needed: More Houses." To build on a large scale and thus to build cheaply, builders flocked to the suburbs, where large tracts of inexpensive land were readily available. But much of the land at the periphery of cities was well beyond the limits of sewer service. How would builders provide for waste disposal? The septic tank seemed a reasonable solution to a fundamental problem....Septic tanks were cheap—much cheaper, at least initially, than building a neighborhood or community sewage-treatment plant. In the 1950s, the installation of a septic tank cost less than $300 in many areas, whereas the alternatives might easily be double or triple that amount per house, depending on the size and character of the development.

In engineering terms, the system also was quite simple. Household waste traveled from the house to the underground tank by a short sewer line. In the oxygen-less environment of the tank, the waste broke down through bacterial action. Some of the waste became gas, which was vented to the surface. A residue of greasy "scum"—as the experts called it— floated on the top of the tank, and

a residue of "sludge"—unbroken-down solids—settled to the bottom. But much of the waste became liquid, and moved out into a soil-absorption field through a network of underground drainage pipes....The liquid waste seeped into the soil, where it was disinfected naturally. The sludge in the tank, however, remained noxious. Periodically, both sludge and scum had to be removed for disposal elsewhere.

In ecological terms, however, septic systems were quite complex. The possible causes of failure were legion. If the soil of a yard was too dense, the effluent from the tank might back up into the house or float to the surface of the yard. If the soil was too porous, or if the water table was close to the surface, the system might contaminate underground aquifers. If the drainage field was close to a drinking well, the well might be contaminated. Similarly, septic tanks could pollute nearby lakes and streams....

Because the FHA was involved all over the country in financing housing construction, the agency became the first organization with responsibility for keeping track of hundreds of thousands of backyard waste-disposal systems. The FHA soon found that as many as one-third of the systems in suburban subdivisions failed within the first three years. Agency officials quickly understood that the failure of so many waste-disposal systems threatened both public and private investment in housing. "[We] viewed tracts of homes with failing septic-tank systems," one FHA inspector later recalled. "Children were playing in the surfaced effluents. I was told that these homes constituted the one major life's expenditure of most of the owners. They could neither sell their homes nor afford to sewer them. They could only live with their sewages or walk away from their investments and lose them." In one case, the agency had to repossess a 1,000-house development because of wholesale septic-tank failures. The tanks could not be fixed or replaced, so the houses were worthless: No one wanted to buy a home without a working toilet....

Beyond offering technical advice, city, county, and state officials were not much help to homebuyers. In 1945, the use of septic tanks was unregulated in most areas—the buyer simply had to beware. To be sure, many state health departments had issued recommendations for septic-tank installation, but apparently few cities and suburbs had made those standards binding. According to a U.S. Public Health Service survey conducted in 1948, only about 40 percent of the septic tanks in metropolitan areas were installed with any kind of regulatory oversight. Since the survey covered only communities with full-time health officials—the communities generally with the most sophisticated, best informed health departments—the number of unregulated septic tanks nationwide surely was much greater than the 60 percent reported by the PHS....

Septic Tanks and the Environment....

The FHA commissioned a review of research on groundwater contamination in 1960. The next year, the U.S. Public Health Service organized a symposium on the issue. The experts all came to a disturbing conclusion: The threat of contamination was increasing, while the nation was becoming more dependent on groundwater to meet residential, municipal, and industrial needs. Without preventive action, therefore, the pollution problem would cause a crisis.

The experts also agreed that industrial wastes were no longer the only important threat to groundwater. In many metropolitan areas, the effluent from backyard waste-disposal systems had contaminated wells and aquifers....

As public health officials had recognized for years, the effluent from septic tanks often contained a variety of organic contaminants of drinking water, including bacteria and viruses. By 1960, a number of studies had traced outbreaks of hepatitis to contamination of drinking wells by nearby septic tanks. But the danger of disease was not the primary concern of officials in the early 1960s. Instead, the attention-getting contaminant was a new chemical component of laundry detergents.

In the late 1950s, public health boards in a number of communities began to receive complaints from homeowners about foul odors and tastes in their drinking water. In many cases, people also noted a strange suds-

ing when they turned on their taps. When the authorities investigated, they found that most of the complaints came from people who lived in neighborhoods built after World War II with no public water supplies or sewers. Instead, the homes relied on backyard wells and septic tanks, and the wells were contaminated with septic-tank effluents. Though the foul odors and tastes might be attributable to the presence of unbroken-down sewage, the suds were something new. As chemical tests revealed, they were caused by synthetic detergents which had followed a liquid path from washing machines through septic tanks to drinking wells.

By 1960, a rapidly growing body of evidence indicated that the problem of detergent pollution was widespread. In a review of 30 studies from 13 states, the director of water conservation studies at the U.S. Public Health Service reported that detergents had shown up in 37 percent of the drinking wells tested for contaminants. In some subdivisions, the figure was almost 100 percent....

The detergent problem went beyond the contamination of drinking wells. The engineers in charge of water- and sewage-treatment plants reported the presence of a froth which proved to be extraordinarily difficult to remove. Across the country, suds also began to appear in rivers and lakes—in the worst cases, the detergent residue formed floating mountains of foam. Without the threat at home, however, the problem might have concerned only civil engineers and conservationists. Instead, the environmental effects of detergents became a source of anxiety for millions of Americans.

In the early 1960s, the issue received considerable attention in the popular press. "Synthetic detergents, and worse, are getting into our drinking water," warned the headline of a 1960 *Consumer Bulletin* article. In magazines devoted to the concerns of middle-class women, from *Redbook* to *Good Housekeeping* to *American Home*, the subject was especially prominent. The weekly newsmagazines also published pieces about the problem of drinking-water quality. Invariably, the popular articles pointed out the way septic tanks turned the sudsing ingredient of detergents—alkyl benzene sulfonate—into a hazard. "In areas where homes discharge sewage into septic tanks, the chemical seeps down into the underground water and then is pumped up from wells," *U.S. News and World Report* explained in 1963. "Tests have shown that ABS persists in underground water for years, and the concentration is building up rapidly."

Occasionally, the problem was the subject of black humor. "One of the more familiar beverages in suburban areas is the 'detergent cocktail'—a glass of tap water foaming with suds," wrote one critic of septic-tank subdivisions. The author of a pioneering book about water pollution titled a chapter on detergents "white beer." But the jokes always led to sober tabulations of the number of homes with contaminated wells....

Throughout the 1970s, researchers found additional evidence about the harmful impact of septic tanks on public health. By increasing the levels of nitrates in suburban drinking water, septic tanks increased the threat to infants from blue-baby syndrome. The syndrome itself was not new: In the late 1950s, a sizable body of research on the problem already existed, but researchers had focused on the threat in farm areas, where nitrate-rich manure could contaminate wells. The new research made clear that blue-baby syndrome had become a problem in suburbia too. The pollution of both ground and surface water by septic-tank effluent also caused countless cases of infectious hepatitis, typhoid fever, dysentery, and gastrointestinal illness. According to a number of estimates, septic-tank failure caused roughly 40 percent of all outbreaks of waterborne diseases from 1945 to 1980.

In addition to threats to human well-being, investigators reported disruptive effects on the nonhuman world. Salamanders and frogs seemed to be especially vulnerable. By the mid-1970s, a handful of studies pointed to septic-tank effluent as a cause of declines in suburban reptile and amphibian populations. The effluent from backyard waste-disposal systems also affected fish. In some places, septic-tank failures caused eutrophication of nearby ponds and lakes. Fed by the nutrients in urine and excrement, blue-green algae soon covered the water, and the algal bloom choked off aquatic life below. The septic tank truly was an environmental problem.

ESSAY 9-3. BARBARA M. KELLY, *EXPANDING THE AMERICAN DREAM* (1993).

Source: Copyright © 1993 by State University of New York. Reprinted by permission of State University of New York Press, Albany.

Houses Fit for Heroes

The years after the war were necessarily years of change. Soldiers who had given up the security of guaranteed military employment were seeking civilian jobs; veterans and workers shuffled for rank in employment. Women who had held well-paying nontraditional positions in all phases of the war effort were both pushed and pulled back into the home. Men who had postponed marriage "for the duration" were encouraged to begin a family. It was the time for a return to traditional values.

A close examination of the characteristics of the Levittown Cape Cod reveals the dominant values of the postwar period: conformity and privatization, as well as the revival of several nineteenth-century themes: the cult of domesticity, the doctrine of separate spheres, and the agrarian myth. Each of these themes was also related to another value of American life, the right to private property. In the America of 1947, these themes had wide appeal.

The design of the domestic space at Levittown logically follows from this preexisting set of social assumptions. Through their physical layout, the houses supported these values, and, by extension, a traditional family life. Conversely, they failed to support lifestyles that were at odds with the prevailing culture. There was little need to do so: the postwar period was marked by a strong consensus on family values, particularly among the aspiring middle class.

Moreover, the population of Levittown was unusually homogeneous in many of their most important characteristics: they were similar in age, stage in the life cycle, socioeconomic level, and race. Not only had the residents shared the war experience—as soldiers or as waiting wives and sweethearts—but most were also recently married couples, many with small children. The similarity in age was the result of the VEHP [Veterans' Emergency Housing Program] restriction that the houses be made available only to veterans of World War II, most of whom ranged in age from 21 to about 32.

The homogeneity in Levittown was also economic. The houses, all built to rent or sell for about $60 a month, were eagerly sought by people whose income level was about $3500 a year. Although there was no *de jure* income ceiling, the houses' lack of amenities limited the community's appeal for the more affluent, especially as proprietary housing. As a result, most of those who remained in Levittown when it was made available for sale were those whose purchase of a house was facilitated by the GI Bill's "no down payment" clause.

Finally, Levittown was homogeneous in race; the property came with restrictions on the racial mix of the community. Initially, some black veterans were allowed to rent, but the deeds restricted the sale of the houses to Caucasians. In this, Levitt was essentially following standard FHA practice. The FHA strongly recommended in its technical bulletin, *Planning Profitable Neighborhoods,* that builders aim at a particular market, based on similarities of age, race, and economic level.

Although the population of Levittown included members of many different national and religious groups, these variations were largely offset by the similarities in age, stage of the life cycle, economic level, and recent war experience. Social conformity was therefore predetermined to some degree by the composition of the Levittown population. It was also reinforced by the temper of American society at the time.

Comfort and Conformity: The Cape Cod

The assumptions about family life that were built into the houses of Levittown in 1947 and 1948 imposed a high degree of conformity upon Levittown and its residents. This conformity was not an uncomfortable fit for most of the families who lived there, however. After years in uniform, the American veteran was inured to uniformity in his dress and environment. Despite the popularity of the rhetoric of rugged individualism, the values of the period stressed moderation and conformity. There was a growing consensus that American workers should be encouraged neither to be overly individualistic nor to develop the collective solidarity of labor under socialism. Seeking security, many Americans had become suspicious of collective activity. Seeking stability, they had become equally suspicious of differences....

Social nonconformity was viewed as tantamount to political subversion; in 1947, to be a nonconformist was to take sides against "us." Conformity was a value shared by many of the more outspoken early residents of Levittown. In this, the Levittowners were not unusual.

Yet it was not merely political deviance to which many of the Levittown residents objected. They frequently found fault with neighbors whose lifestyles failed to conform to the community norms. Diffidence or introversion were viewed as anti-social. Their accusations against nonconforming neighbors, revealed in letters to the editors of local papers, invariably included some reference to the nonconformist as "commie," "Russkie," "Comrade," or some similar epithet....

In a world threatened by political subversion and atomic annihilation, nonconformity was interpreted as a danger signal. The Levittown Cape Cods fit this mood quite well. The single-family houses on separate plots reinforced the American myth of rugged individualism without encouraging nonconformity. Their design, plan, and setting were neither individualistic nor identical; although the interiors of the houses were identical their exteriors varied somewhat in appearance. Despite the contemporary rhetoric praising their "individuality" of design—subtle differences in color and window arrangements, along with staggered setbacks—the 6000 houses built in 1947 and 1948 were essentially indistinguishable. Their replication suited both the economic need for standardization and the political need for conformity....

Privatization

The house provided each family with the minimum space and accoutrements necessary for privatized domesticity. Indeed, there were no collective domestic facilities built into Levittown. Each house was equipped with the requisite space and appliances to serve one family's basic needs, as the designer envisioned them. Here too, the equipment served not only to reflect but to reinforce the conformity of family life that would become so much a part of the suburban scene....

The relationship of public to private space provided in the Levitt house reinforced the domestic role of the homemaker-mother in the nuclear family. The kitchen, a room that had previously been treated as not only private, but somewhat declassé, in most homes now shared the front of the house with the living room.

The washing machine opened into a small space facing the side of the kitchen stove. As a result, doing the family's wash had become a kitchen, or semipublic, activity. Yet, Levitt apparently viewed the public use of outdoor wash-lines as a marginally unacceptable practice. The wash-line was an urban icon; laundry in the suburbs was a private matter.

Although he found the outdoor wash-line offensive, Levitt provided no space within the floorplan in which to place an automatic dryer, even had the residents wanted to purchase one. Though he expected the Levittown housewife to do her own laundry, Levitt enjoined the use of any but a company-approved drying device in order to prevent the appearance of a tenement neighborhood. No permanent lines could be installed; instead, he recommended the use of a portable, umbrella-like collection of lines that his directives referred to as "dryers."

Not only did the residents have to conform to the use of this particular model, they also had to dismantle it on Saturdays, Sundays, and holidays. Since these are the days on which an employed mother would normally do her laundry, the injunction against weekend wash-lines underscores the tacit assumption that the wives of Levittown would be at home during the week to do their laundry....

In keeping with the Levitt covenant against fencing—natural or constructed—there is no division between the plots. The highly acclaimed fruit trees that Abraham Levitt had provided are still spindly, barely taller than the small shrubs which flank the door. Behind the house the lawn stretches past the utility company's right-of-way and on up to the rear of the house beyond.

The openness of the lawn area suggests a lack of privacy. Yet, despite the presence of what sociologist William M. Dobriner has referred to as "the Visibility Principle" of postwar suburbia, the houses of Levittown were designed to be very private. Each was centered on its own plot of 6000 square feet. The side door—the entrance into the kitchen—is on the right wall of the exterior of the house. (The kitchen entry was placed on the right of every house, where it faced the wall of the house next door.) A vestigial eight-foot length of split-rail fence separates this "service" area from the more formal front lawn. Trash was picked up at the street end of the service path in front of each house. There was no communal path, no common service area.

Each wife did her own laundry in her own washing machine in her own kitchen; each husband cared for his own patch of ground. Each nuclear family watched its own television in its own living room.

The privatization of the nuclear family unit did not extend to its individual members, however. Although privatized as households, the houses provided little or no internal privacy for the family members. Rather, the size, selection, and limit of four rooms combined to reinforce the values of family life that were being advocated at all levels in 1947—among them the return to the "cult of domesticity".

Domesticity

The social pressure toward homemaking for young women in the 1940s and 1950s has been explored rather thoroughly in the recent surge of interest in the history of women and the family. Less well-developed has been the concomitant pressure on the young men of the period to marry and "settle down."

The houses of the GI Bill imposed a subtle form of domesticity upon the young husbands, and by extension, the family unit, through the distribution of space. The privatization of the family through the individualization of their dwelling served to keep the nuclear unit intact, while limiting the opportunity for the rise of collective activity among the young men. There were few of the traditional male meeting places in early Levittown, and the weekend activities

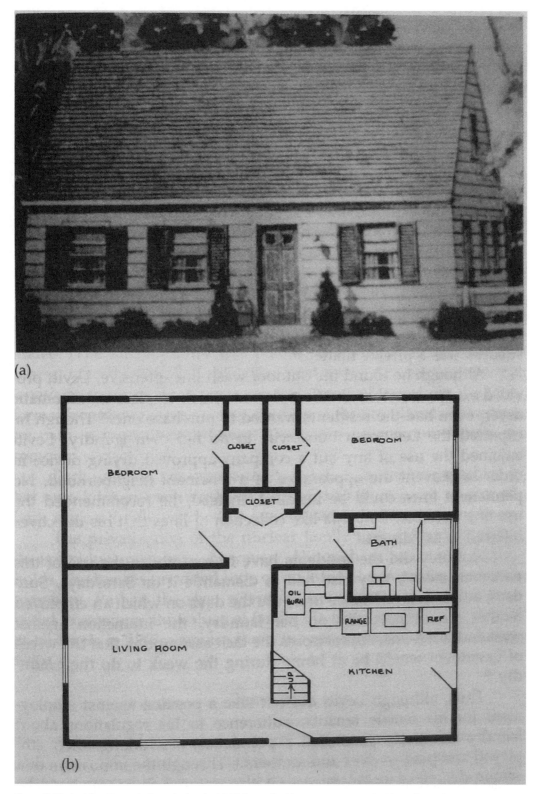

Figure 9-13 Architect's rendering of a basic 1947 Cape Cod home, accompanied by a floor plan sketch by Barbara Kelly. Illustration in original, 67.

of home maintenance limited the free time of the young residents—particularly during the rental years, when Levitt could dictate the tasks. The community facilities provided by the builder were focused on the assumed needs of women and children; "village greens" provided shopping areas with playgrounds, pools, and—later—schools. Levitt had also included a community meeting house at one of the village greens. By shaping the available recreation, these sites served to limit large-group activities in Levittown to those which were essentially domestic, that is, child- and family-centered. These institutions, predicated by the recommendations of the FHA, were oriented toward the needs of a nuclear family....

Combined with the lack of external gathering places for the men, the size of the house all but forced the young couple to spend most of their recreational time together. The design of the house contained all that was necessary for suburban living, but it was not sufficient. The houses lacked the standard equipment like garages, basements, dining rooms, or pantries, as well as the accessory spaces like dens, family rooms, libraries, solariums, or porches associated with upper middle-class suburban homes.

The lack of separate male space in both the houses and the community (den, garage, or game room in the houses; bars, pool halls, or clubs in the community) reinforced the emphasis on togetherness. There was simply no place else to go—at least in the beginning. Within months, the front lawn would begin to pinch-hit as the suburban equivalent of the corner bar....

The houses encouraged a second form of male domesticity. This was the promotion of do-it-yourself home production. Due in part to the shortage of labor induced by the postwar building boom, manufacturers instituted a marketing strategy to move such materials as paint, flooring, plumbing fixtures, and the like that encouraged the homeowner to "do it Yourself!"...

The original size of the Levittown houses virtually demanded that they be enlarged in order to correspond to the customary middle-class homes of the period. Although the earliest residents were not expected to have adolescent children when they moved in, the probability that they would still be in Levittown when their children reached that stage demanded at least the opportunity for separate gender-ordered bedrooms. American children, when of different gender, were (and are) expected to have separate sleeping quarters before puberty. The expansion attic was therefore included—to be finished by the residents at such time as it became necessary or affordable. In December, Levitt's press release "suggested" that the tenants might be allowed to turn the attic into bedrooms. Indeed, Levitt expected the residents, whether homeowners or tenants, to do some form of remodeling. His press releases, allowing the tenants to build garages and finish the attics, were clear invitations to enlarge the houses....

Market and Design: The Ranch

In the fall of 1948, the housing market was changing. With 6000 Cape Cods already built and more projected, the Levitt Corporation faced a new challenge. The FHA had been sending signals of concern about "market saturation" for several months. Its officials believed that the market was becoming glutted with mass-produced, small-scale houses that were no longer satisfying the needs of the target population. They began to question the advisability of funding any further projects of the nature of Levittown. Such signals indicated changes to come, both in policy and in funding. Whether or not the housing crisis had been solved, the market for Levitt-type rental housing appeared to be softening, and the government was rethinking its role in the housing market....

In order to continue building and selling, Levitt designed the next generation of houses—the 1949 through 1951 ranch models—for the buying market, modifying both the exterior styling and the floor plan. The firm spent "upwards of $50,000" in research and redesign before they brought out their 1949 models of the Levittown house....

The redesign began with the layout of the house lots and roadways. The 1947 street pattern of mildly curved streets ending in T-intersections had been called for by the FHA as a means of reducing the flow and

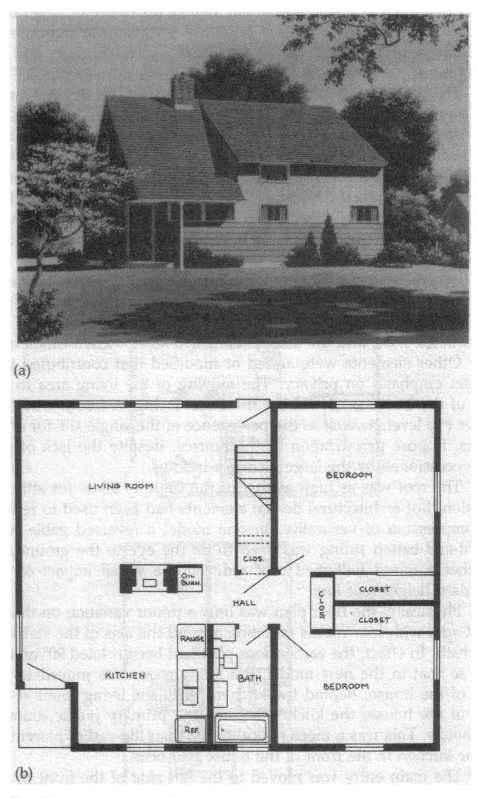

Figure 9-14 Architect's rendering of a basic 1949 ranch model home, accompanied by a floor plan sketch by Barbara Kelly. Illustration in original, 81.

speed of traffic. In 1949 this pattern was replaced by one with much more strongly curved streets and cul-de-sacs. The new street layout resulted in irregular plot shapes and sizes, a more expensive but more marketable use of available land…. On the vast flat expanses of the Hempstead Plain, the curvilinear street is an artifice. As Robert Stern put it, the grid, curved gently, "adapts the reality of real estate to the illusion of country living." By mimicking the street pattern of his more affluent North Shore communities, Levitt added an upscale illusion to a low-cost development. The new pattern did not actually produce an increase in pedestrian safety. Instead, the safety factor was exaggerated to enhance product appeal….

Levitt understood his market; the young lower-income white- and blue-collar workers who would perceive Levittown as their permanent home. It was to these people that Levitt addressed his weekly press conferences, filled with advice, admonitions, and suggestions for better living in Levittown—young people who worked in the service sector as clerks or teachers, or in factories on the assembly lines of Long Island's aircraft industry.

In his discussions of Levittown, Levitt stressed the firm's total "redesign" of their 1949 models. Although they remained, like the Cape Cods, one-and-a-half story cottages, there are significant differences between the 1947 Cape Cod and the model he called "the forty-niner."…

The house itself was 50 square feet larger than the Cape. The additional footage provided for larger bedrooms. The remaining changes primarily involved the public/semi-public areas of the house: the exterior elevation, the kitchen, and the living room….

Other elements were added or modified that contributed to a greater emphasis on privacy. The moving of the living area to the rear of the house while raising the street-facing bedroom windows above eye level, as well as the persistence of the single site for entry doors, impose privatization of the houses, despite the lack of privacy occasioned by the large picture windows….

Physically, the floor plan was only a minor variation on that of the Cape, with four rooms radiating around the axis of the stairway and bath. In effect, the earlier floor plan had been rotated 90' on this axis so that in the new model, the living room was moved to the rear of the house, behind the kitchen. With the living room at the rear of the house, the kitchen became the primary public room of the house. This was a more radical move than the earlier placement of the kitchen in the front of the house had been….

The rear wall of the living room contained a large floor-to-ceiling picture window and a door to the rear yard….

The window…was commercial in scale: eight feet high and 16 feet wide. The postwar windows of this size and scale were billed as picture windows by most manufacturers, suggesting that the homeowner could look out at the sylvan view beyond the walls. The picture window of the suburban house, however, most often looked out into the windows of another house just like itself. The picture, therefore, became the interior of the house, which gradually became more and more like a stage—or in 1949, a television—setting….

Although many of the innovations that Levitt included in the ranch models contained elements which addressed some of the needs of the women of Levittown, the house was still primarily designed for those women who played the traditional role as home-maker/wife. Moreover, they were consistently marketed to her husband. The redesign included no accommodations for working mothers; the pools and playgrounds were not set up to provide day care. Similarly, the houses were not receptive to single mothers; the house-and-grounds maintenance all but demanded the heavy labor of a husband.

The restrictions on wash-lines, fences, and shrubbery imposed by the Levitts in the lease agreements, and later covenanted into the deeds, as well as the introduction of the family hearth, reinforced Levittown as a document for what most Americans believed a home and community should be. The young, nuclear families, in their similar (but distinct), privatized (but conforming) houses, living in their do-it-yourself domesticity, were the ideal model for the young, American family of modest means in the postwar period.

CHAPTER 10

Critiques of Postwar Suburbia

INTRODUCTION

The proliferation of postwar suburbs touched off a heated national debate in the 1950s and 1960s over one basic question: were suburbs good or bad for America? This public discussion attracted numerous participants—journalists, academics, novelists, artists, filmmakers, advertisers, and real estate developers—whose opinions swung between the two extremes of utopia and dystopia. Suburbia was imagined as either the happy realization of the American dream or a cesspool for every American neurosis and social pathology. By the 1960s, a group of sociologists sought to test these hyperbolic assertions by exploring life on the ground in suburbia. Despite their efforts, the extremist rhetoric captured the public imagination, influencing public understand of suburbia even to our own day.

To its boosters, suburbia was the very embodiment of the middle-class American dream. These advocates included an array of interests who shared a stake in selling suburban homes and the goods to fill them—developer-builders, mortgage lenders, real estate agents, television networks, women's magazines, and advertisers. In their portrayals, suburbia was a warm idyllic place. Families lived the dream of upward mobility in an economically robust America, enjoying the good life replete with all the latest gadgets. This imagery appeared in advertisements for property and household products—such as those depicted in chapter 9—as well as 1950s and 1960s television sitcoms like *Ozzie and Harriet, Leave It to Beaver,* and *Father Knows Best.* These similarities were no accident. Advertisers recognized suburbia as a vast and lucrative market. The average suburban family was 70 percent richer than the national average and it was poised to make major purchases. Television, in turn, was highly dependent on advertising revenues. It thus made economic sense for both TV programs and their sponsors to celebrate and even romanticize the suburban lifestyle.

By the mid-1950s, a much darker view of suburban life began to emerge. According to the critics—including academics, novelists, filmmakers, and designer-planners, among others—the mass-produced landscape of suburbia was a breeding ground for the most troubling social trends of the era: conformity, materialism, a blind embrace of corporate culture, excessive mobility, and female oppression. Critics chastised suburbia for promoting the trivialization of life. In their view, homogeneous neighborhoods sheltered suburbanites from the diverse experiences and needs of the broader population, while an overemphasis on family life and pocketbook politics destroyed a sense of civic obligation. Even kids—the presumed beneficiaries of suburbanization—suffered. They were portrayed variously as coddled, infantilized by overbearing mothers, cut off from "the real world," or headed for juvenile delinquency.It is worth noting the contradictions among some of these critiques. Scholars such as Lewis Mumford and the urban critic Jane Jacobs emphasized suburbia's social isolation, its tendency to cut people off from one another. Others, like William Whyte, drew a portrait of restless socializing and nosy neighbors. The one common denominator among them was a belief that suburbia was somehow responsible for these problems. In some cases, this attack was an indirect defense of a more pastoral and exclusive suburbia, where tasteful landscaping emphasized the union of family and nature, safely distant from factory workers and urban ethnics. Even for those who had once seen suburbanization as the salvation of the city, the reality of mass suburbia was a shock. Planning proponents who had envisioned a ring of co-operative garden cities saw instead hungry capitalism and state-sponsored sprawl. Whatever their perspective, the landscape became a disturbing symbol for the society that inhabited it. Stirred by this critique, a handful of planner-developers initiated a short-lived movement for New Towns in the 1960s and early 1970s, most notably in Reston, Virginia, Columbia, Maryland, and Irvine, California. Their aim was to counter the purportedly lifeless and irra-tional development of most suburbs with comprehensively planned suburban cities, designed to reinvigorate civic engagement and community life.

Strikingly enough, in this broad body of criticism, the white middle-class suburbanite emerged as a kind of victim, a casualty of mass society and corporate greed. This assessment took its cue from other cultural criticism of the 1950s, which lambasted mass culture as a source of manipulation and oppression. At the same time, suburban critics were curiously silent on the most pressing domestic conflict of the decade—the civil rights campaign to overturn the color barrier in the suburban north and Jim Crow south. Acknowledging this conflict would have required the critics to recognize suburbia as a site of rich resources and opportunity, a desirable place that many "outsiders" were clamoring to enter. Few critics bothered to reconcile the drive for equality in housing with their own portrayals of oppressive life in the "burbs," which ended up rendering whites the victims and people of color invisible.

How did reality stack up with the images of dream or nightmare? The simple answer is, it lay somewhere in the middle. This was the finding of several sociologists in the 1960s who set out to challenge what they called "the myth of suburbia," a reference to the polemics dominat-ing the public discourse. Scholars like Bennett Berger, Herbert Gans, and William Dobriner found that a move to suburbia did not change people as drastically as either the boosters or critics claimed.[1] Rather, people continued to make life choices based on factors like class, eth-nicity, religion, and personal preference. Collectively, the work of these scholars challenged the notion of environmental determinism.[2] Historians have been slower to document the social history of postwar suburbia, but we do know several things that counteract some of the stereotypes: suburbs continued to vary widely by class, suggesting a multiplicity of sub-urban experiences rather than a single one; suburban women were entering the workforce in substantial numbers even by 1960, and they were often highly engaged in local politics; and suburbia was characterized by religious and ethnic—and to a lesser extent racial—diversity.

Despite what we are learning about everyday life in postwar suburbia, the extreme images generated by postwar critics have had remarkable staying power. In popular culture espe-cially, the depiction of suburbia as an oppressive place, waiting for protagonists to break out and express themselves, is a theme oft repeated, particularly in films like *American Beauty,* *Pleasantville, The Truman Show,* and *Far From Heaven.* Even the television series *Desperate Housewives* plays on the image of corruption lying just beneath a picture-perfect surface. Even though more and more Americans live suburban lives that bear little resemblance to these portrayals, the myth of suburbia continues to resonate in the popular imagination.

DOCUMENTS

The notion that the environment of mass suburbia homogenized the people who lived there was a central theme of postwar suburban critiques. In **Document 10-1**, folksinger Malvina Reynolds ex-presses this idea in the song, "Little Boxes," evoking an image of a "soulless landscape producing a soulless populace," in the words of scholar Robert Beuka.[3] The song became a national hit when Pete Seeger recorded it in 1964. **Document 10-2** comes from perhaps the most important work of suburban criticism of the 1950s, William Whyte's *Organization Man.* Whyte, an editor at *Fortune* magazine, explores what he perceived as a broad, dangerous postwar trend toward conformity and "group think" at the expense of individualism. He attributes this shift partly to increased mobility among organization men, who endured numerous job transfers which made them desperate for social ties. These tendencies were most apparent in the mass-produced suburbs, which he calls the "dormitories" of organization man. Whyte devotes the final third of his book to an analysis of life in suburbia, based mainly on his observations of Park Forest, Illinois. His work had tremendous influence on subsequent suburban critics—journalists, novelists, filmmakers, and urban scholars—who portrayed suburbia as a place defined, above all, by conformity. **Document 10-3**, Dan Weiner's 1953 photograph of commuters returning to Park Forest, Illinois from Chicago, captures the everyday faces of William Whyte's organization men (and women). In **Document 10-4**, the renowned urbanist, Lewis Mumford, wages a deep, multilayered critique of mass-produced suburbia, offering a remarkably different reading of suburban social life from that of Whyte. Mumford was an enthusiastic proponent of Ebenezer Howard's "Garden City" idea, perceiving it as the solution to the ills of the modern metropolis. Yet mass suburbs, he believed, were a distorted, disastrous outcome of that original concept. Mumford ultimately poses a chilling *1984*-like scenario, where suburbanites in their mass-produced homes become captive to automation, mass media, and excruciating isolation.

The condition of women in suburbia was also a key concern of postwar critics. The central text was Betty Friedan's *Feminine Mystique* (1963), considered by many the bible of the 1960s woman's liberation movement. In **Document 10-5,** Friedan describes the "problem that has no name," a reference to the deep unease of the dutiful suburban housewife, and its devastating consequences—from psychological damage to civic disengagement. Friedan also explores the colluding role of suburbia, which she argues fostered an environment that maximized busywork and minimized opportunity for female privacy and autonomy. **Document 10-6**, which accompanied a 1961 *Reader's Digest* article entitled "Why Young Mothers Feel Trapped," graphically depicts many of the ideas synthesized by Friedan. **Document 10-7** reports on how women in one suburban community, Great Neck, New York, began a tentative exploration of feminism. While this *McCall's* magazine article confirms many of Friedan's claims, it also suggests that women were not passive witnesses to their circumstances as suburban housewives. This article was one among many that appeared in the national press by the early 1970s, reporting on the emergence of female activism and feminism in suburbia.

A whole genre of fiction that probed suburban dysfunction was another influential strand of the suburban critique. Writers such as John Keats, Sloan Wilson, John Marquand, Richard Yates, and John Cheever became famous for works depicting a superficial suburban world. **Document 10-8** is a compelling example of this fiction by the writer perhaps most closely associated with the genre, John Cheever. Cheever's numerous short stories, many set in the imaginary suburb of Shady Hill, explored the nuances and contradictions of middle-class identity in suburbia. His tales are notable for their complex characterizations and themes, often probing tensions between the external and internal lives of suburbanites. The story reprinted here, "O Youth and Beauty!", originally appeared in *The New Yorker* in 1953. **Document 10-9** offers images from Peter Blake's influential book, *God's Own Junkyard*. Juxtaposing images of natural wonder with garish sprawl, Blake's work epitomized the aesthetic critique of postwar suburbia and heralded the rise of suburban environmentalism. **Document 10-10** is a biting satire of suburbia from the writers of *Mad Magazine*. Spoofing Carl Sandburg's poem "Chicago," a majestic ode to the "City of the Big Shoulders," *Mad* presents "Chicago Suburb," home of the shallow and absurd.

By the 1960s, the onslaught of suburban criticism prompted a backlash among sociologists, who approached their work with skepticism about the power of suburbia to shape behavior. They asked basic empirical questions: Did moving to the suburbs change people? Can we accurately speak of "a suburban way of life"? In **Document 10-11**, sociologist Bennett Berger answers "no" to both queries, and he offers an astute explanation for why the suburbs had become the target of such intense criticism. His article, "The Myth of Suburbia," remains one of the most cogent statements on this topic even forty years after its publication. Berger grounded his understanding of postwar suburbia in a book-length study of Milpitas, California, a suburb in San Francisco's East Bay. In that work, *Working-Class Suburb: A Study of Auto Workers in Suburbia* (1960), he found that residents retained the lifeways and outlooks of their former city life. While it represented an important counterpoint to works on white-collar suburbia, *Working-Class Suburb* received much less attention—and had less public impact—than works like *Organization Man,* a fact that attests to the immense influence of the suburban critique on the public imagination. **Document 10-12** is an excerpt from sociologist Herbert Gans's study, *The Levittowners*, which he wrote as a participant-observer after living in

Levittown (now Willingboro), New Jersey from 1958 to 1960. While Gans observed some of the same social patterns that Whyte described in Park Forest, he interpreted those patterns very differently, seeing in suburbia a healthy, humane, and legitimate way of life.

Why were social critics so vehemently against suburbia? What was it about suburbia that provoked such an emotional reaction? What underlying factors may have motivated their critiques? What role did the democratization—or the opening up of suburbia to a broad class of Americans—play in inciting these criticisms? In your opinion, what was the worst offense of the suburban way of life? Can we safely speak of a suburban way of life? Do you think the critics were right—and still are—about life in suburbia? What aspects ring true, or not?

10-1. FOLKSINGER MALVINA REYNOLDS CRITIQUES SUBURBIA IN SONG, 1962

Source: From the song, *Little Boxes*. Words and music by Malvina Reynolds. Copyright © 1962 Schroder Music Co. (ASCAP). Renewed 1990. Used by permission. All rights reserved.

"Little Boxes"
Little boxes on the hillside,
Little boxes made of ticky tacky,
Little boxes on the hillside,
Little boxes all the same.
There's a green one and a pink one
And a blue one and a yellow one,
And they're all made out of ticky tacky,
And they all look just the same.

And the people in the houses
All went to the university,
Where they were put in boxes
And they came out all the same,

And there's doctors and lawyers,
And business executives,
And they're all made out of ticky tacky,
And they all look just the same.

And they all play on the golf course
And drink their martinis dry,
And they all have pretty children
And the children go to school,
And the children go to summer camp,
And then to the university
Where they are put in boxes
And they come out all the same.

And the boys go into business
And marry and raise a family
In boxes made of ticky tacky
And they all look just the same.
There's a green one and a pink one
And a blue one and a yellow one,
And they're all made out of ticky tacky
And they all look just the same.

Figure 10-1 Conformity was the central complaint of many suburban critics in the postwar years. This cartoon by Claude Smith, Jr. originally appeared in *The New Yorker,* 1956. Reprinted by Permission of the Estate of Claude Smith, Jr.

10-2. WILLIAM WHYTE DESCRIBES THE "ORGANIZATION MAN" IN SUBURBIA, 1956

Source: William H. Whyte, Jr., *The Organization Man* (New York: Simon and Schuster, 1956). Used by permission of Alexandra Whyte.

This book is about the organization man. If the term is vague, it is because I can think of no other way to describe the people I am talking about. They are not the workers, nor are they the white-collar people in the usual, clerk sense of the word. These people only work for The Organization. The ones I am talking about *belong* to it as well. They are the ones of our middle class who have left home, spiritually as well as physically, to take the vows of organization life, and it is they who are the mind and soul of our great self-perpetuating institutions. Only a few are top managers or ever will be...most are destined to live poised in a middle area that still awaits a satisfactory euphemism....

The corporation man is the most conspicuous example, but he is only one, for the collectivization so visible in the corporation has affected almost every field of work. Blood brother to the business trainee off to join Du Pont is the seminary student who will end up in the church hierarchy, the doctor headed for the corporate clinic, the physics Ph.D. in a government laboratory,...the engineering graduate in the huge drafting room at Lockheed, the young apprentice in a Wall Street law factory....

The organization man seeks a redefinition of his place on earth—a faith that will satisfy him that what he must endure has a deeper meaning than appears on the surface. He needs, in short, something that will do for him what the Protestant Ethic did once. And slowly, almost imperceptibly, a body of thought has been coalescing that does that.

I am going to call it a Social Ethic....

By Social Ethic I mean that contemporary body of thought which makes morally legitimate the pressures of society against the individual. Its major propositions are three: a belief in the group as the source of creativity; a belief in "belongingness" as the ultimate need of the individual; and a belief in the application of science to achieve the belongingness....

The New Suburbia: Organization Man at Home

I now turn to the Organization Man at home...I am going to examine him in the communities that have become his dormitories—the great package suburbs that have sprung up outside our cities since the war....

For they are not merely great conglomerations of mass housing. They are a new social institution, and while the variations in them are many, wherever one goes—the courts of Park Forest [Illinois], the patios of Park Merced in San Francisco, Philadelphia's Drexelbrook, the new Levittown, Pennsylvania—there is an unmistakable similarity in the way of life.

It is a communal way of life, and the residents are well aware of it. They are of many minds how to describe it. Sometimes they lean to analogies like the frontier, or the early colonial settlements. Other times they are a little more wry; "sorority house with kids,"...or...a lay version of Army post life. But no matter how sharp the coinages—"a womb with a view," "a Russia, only with money"—it is a way of life they find suited to their wants, their needs, and their times....

Park Forest, the community I studied most intensively, has its unique features, but its most salient characteristic is that it is virtually a controlled sample of organization people. As elsewhere, there are other kinds of people too, and for many a newcomer from the city such communities are an education in middle-class values. What might be called the modal man, however, is a twenty-five-to-thirty-five-year-old white-collar organization man with a wife, a salary between $6,000 and $7,000, one child, and another on the way....

The people who went to Park Forest went there because it was the best housing for the money.... The space for the money, the amenities not elsewhere available, and, most important, the fact that it was so well set up for children have been in most cases the dominant factors.

Park Foresters, in short, went there for quite rational, and eminently sensible, reasons. Once there, however, they created something over and above the original bargain. Together, they developed a social atmosphere of striking vigor…. The developers were quick to recognize it. At first they had advertised Park Forest as housing. Now they began advertising happiness….

Here's the way they went:

You Belong
in PARK FOREST!
The moment you come to our town you know:
You're welcome
You're part of a big group
You can live in a friendly small town instead of a lonely big city.
You can have friends who want you—and you can enjoy being with them.
Come out. Find out about the spirit of Park Forest…

The ads are quite right. Let's take, for example, a couple we shall call Dot and Charlie Adams. Charlie, a corporation trainee, is uprooted from the Newark office, arrives at Apartment 8, Court M-12.[4] It's a hell of a day—the kids are crying, Dot is half sick with exhaustion, and the movers won't be finished till late.

But soon, because M-12 is a "happy" court, the neighbors will come over to introduce themselves. In an almost inordinate display of decency, some will help them unpack and around suppertime two of the girls will come over with a hot casserole and another with a percolator full of hot coffee. Within a few days the children will have found playmates, Dot will be *Kaffeeklatsching* and sunbathing with the girls like an old-timer, and Charlie, who finds that Ed Robey in Apartment 5 went through officers' training school with him, will be enrolled in the Court Poker Club. The Adamses are, in a word, *in*—and someday soon, when another new couple, dazed and hungry, moves in, the Adamses will make their thanks by helping them to be likewise.

In the court, they find, their relationships with others transcend mere neighborliness. Except for the monastic orders and the family itself, there is probably no other social institution in the U.S. in which there is such a communal sharing of property. Except for

the $200 or $300 put aside for the next baby, few of the transients have as yet been able to accumulate much capital or earthly possessions, and so they share to make the best of it. One lawn mower (with each man doing his allotted stint) may do for the whole court. For the wives there may be a baby-sitting "bank" (i.e., when one wife baby-sits for another she is credited with the time, and when she wishes to draw on it one of the wives who has a debit to repay will sit for her). To hoard possessions is frowned upon; books, silverware, and tea services are constantly rotated, and the children feel free to use one another's bikes and toys without asking. "We laughed at first at how the Marxist society had finally arrived," one executive says, "but I think the real analogy is to the pioneers."

But the court social life, important as it is in rooting the transient, is only part of the acclimation. Before long, Charlie Adams may feel the urge to shoot out a few extra roots here and there and, having normal joining instincts, may think a mild involvement in some community-wide organization just the thing. When the matter is bruited to him he may be tentative—nothing strenuous, understand, awfully busy with company work; just want to help out a little. Instantaneously, or no longer than it takes one person to telephone another, the news is abroad. Charlie will never be quite the same again.

He has plunged into a hotbed of Participation. With sixty-six adult organizations and a population turnover that makes each one of them insatiable for new members, Park Forest probably swallows up more civic energy per hundred people than any other community in the country….

On the matter of privacy, suburbanites have mixed feelings. Fact one, of course, is that there isn't much privacy….[P]eople don't bother to knock and they come and go furiously. The lack of privacy, furthermore, is retroactive. "They ask you all sorts of questions about what you *were* doing," one resident puts it. "Who was it that stopped in last night? Who were those people from Chicago last week? You're never alone, even when you think you are."

Less is sacred. "It's wonderful," says one young wife. "You find yourself discussing all your personal problems with your neighbors—things that back in South Dakota we would have kept to ourselves." As time goes on, this capacity for self-revelation grows; and on the most intimate details of family life, court people become amazingly frank with one another. No one, they point out, ever need face a problem alone....

But there is another side to the coin. Contemporary prophets of belongingness point out the warmth and security the tight-knit group produces for the individual, but they generally stop short at diagnosing some of the other things it produces.... It is not the question of conformity, though many speak of it as such. It is, rather, the question of determining *when* one is conforming, when adjustment is selflessness, or surrender. It is a moral dilemma—the one, I believe, central to the organization man....

In the tight-knit group...each member feels an equity in others' behavior. With communication so intensive, the slightest misunderstanding can generate a whole series of consequences. If Charley ducks his turn at the lawn mower, if little Johnny sasses Mrs. Erdlick just once more, if Gladys forgets to return the pound of coffee she borrowed, the frictions become a concern of the group and not just of the principals.

The more vigorous the search for common denominators, the stronger the pressure to alikeness. Sometimes this extends even to house design. The architects have tried to vary the facades of each house, and one might assume that in putting up aluminum awnings, making alterations, repainting and the like, residents try hard to enlarge the differences. This is not always so; in some areas residents have apparently agreed to unify the block with a common design and color scheme for garages and such.

In such blocks an otherwise minor variation becomes blatant deviance; if a man were to paint his garage fire-engine red in a block where the rest of the garages are white, he would literally and psychologically make himself a marked man. So with fences; if they are obviously designed to keep the children safe, eyebrows are not raised. But if the height or elaborateness of the fence indicates other motives, there will be feeling....

Reprisal is inevitable. The sanctions are not obvious—indeed, people are often unconscious of wielding them—but the look in the eye, the absence of a smile, the inflection of a hello, can be exquisite punishment, and they have brought more than one to a nervous breakdown. And the more social the block, the rougher it is on those who don't fit in....

It is frightening to see the cruelty with which an otherwise decent group can punish the deviate, particularly when the deviate is unfortunate enough to be located in the middle of the group, rather than isolated somewhat out of benevolence's way. "Estelle is a case," says one resident of a highly active block. "She was dying to get in with the gang when she moved in. She is a very warmhearted gal and is always trying to help people, but she's, well—sort of elaborate about it. One day she decided to win over everybody by giving an afternoon party for the gals. Poor thing, she did it all wrong. The girls turned up in their bathing suits and slacks, as usual, and here she had little doilies and silver and everything spread around. Ever since then it's been almost like a planned campaign to keep her out of things. Even her two-year-old daughter gets kept out of the kids' parties. It's really pitiful. She sits there in her beach chair out front just dying for someone to come and *Kaffeeklatsch* with her, and right across the street four or five of the girls and their kids will be yakking away. Every time they suddenly all laugh at some joke she thinks they are laughing at her. She came over here yesterday and cried all afternoon. She told me she and her husband are thinking about moving somewhere else so they can make a fresh start." (The woman in question has since moved.)...

Is this simple conformity? I am not for the moment trying to argue that yielding to the group is something to be admired, but I do think that there is more of a moral problem here than is generally conceded in most discussions of American conformity....

The group is a tyrant; so also is it a friend, and *it is both at once*. The two qualities cannot easily be separated, for what gives the group its power over the man is the same cohesion that gives it its warmth. This is the duality that confuses choice.

10-3. THE COMMUTERS OF PARK FOREST, ILLINOIS, 1953

Figure 10-2 Commuters crowded on platform returning from work in Loop in Chicago, Dan Weiner, January 1, 1953. Like the era's myriad photographs of mass-produced suburban housing, this image of commuters clad in business attire conveys the impression of sameness that social critics derided. Courtesy of Time Life Pictures/Getty Images, Image #50603608. All Rights Reserved.

10-4. LEWIS MUMFORD POINTS TO THE FAILURES OF MODERN SUBURBIA, 1961

Source: Lewis Mumford, *The City in History: Its Origins, Its Transformations, and Its Prospects* (New York: Harcourt, Brace & World, 1961). Copyright © 1961 and renewed 1989 by Lewis Mumford, reprinted by permission of Harcourt, Inc.

To be your own unique self; to build your unique house, mid a unique landscape: to live in this Domain of Arnheim a self-centered life, in which private fantasy and caprice would have license to express themselves openly, in short, to withdraw like a monk and live like a prince—this was the purpose of the original creators of the suburb. They proposed in effect to create an asylum, in which they could, as individuals, overcome the chronic defects of civilization while still commanding at will the privileges and benefits of urban society. This utopia proved to be, up to a point, a realizable one: so enchanting that those who contrived it failed to see the fatal penalty attached to it—the penalty of popularity, the fatal inundation of a mass movement whose very numbers would wipe out the goods each individual sought for his own domestic circle, and, worse, replace them with a life that was not even a cheap counterfeit, but rather the grim antithesis.

The ultimate outcome of the suburb's alienation from the city became visible only in the twentieth century....In the mass movement into suburban areas a new kind of community was produced, which caricatured both the historic city and the archetypal suburban refuge: a multitude of uniform, unidentifiable houses, lined up inflexibly, at uniform distances, on uniform roads, in a treeless communal waste, inhabited by people of the same class, the same income, the same age group, witnessing the same television performances, eating the same tasteless pre-fabricated foods, from the same freezers, conforming in every outward and inward respect to a common mold, manufactured in the central metropolis. Thus the ultimate effect of the suburban escape in our time is, ironically, a low-grade uniform environment from which escape is impossible....

The Suburban Way of Life

As an attempt to recover what was missing in the city, the suburban exodus could be amply justified, for it was concerned with primary human needs. But there was another side: the temptation to retreat from unpleasant realities, to shirk public duties, and to find the whole meaning of life in the most elemental social group, the family, or even in the still more isolated and self-centered individual. What was properly a beginning was treated as an end....

[T]oo soon, in breaking away from the city, the part became a substitute for the whole, even as a single phase of life, that of childhood, became the pattern for all the seven ages of man. As leisure generally increased, play became the serious business of life; and the golf course, the country club, the swimming pool, and the cocktail party became the frivolous counterfeits of a more varied and significant life. Thus in reacting against the disadvantages of the crowded city, the suburb itself became an over-specialized community, more and more committed to relaxation and play as ends in themselves. Compulsive play fast became the acceptable alternative to compulsive work: with small gain either in freedom or vital stimulus....

Families in Space

On the fringe of mass Suburbia, even the advantages of the primary neighborhood group disappear. The cost of this detachment in space from other men is out of all proportion to its supposed benefits. The end product is an encapsulated life, spent more and more either in a motor car or within the cabin of darkness before a television set....Every part of this life, indeed, will come through official channels and be under supervision. Untouched by human hand at one end: untouched by human spirit at the other. Those who accept this existence might as well be encased in a rocket hurtling through space, so narrow are their choices, so limited and deficient their permitted responses. Here indeed we find "The Lonely Crowd."...

Does this not explain in some degree the passiveness and docility that has crept into our existence?...Suburbia offers poor facilities for meeting, conversation, collective debate, and common action—it favors silent conformity, not rebellion or counter-attack. So Suburbia has become the favored home of a new kind of absolutism: invisible but all-powerful.

10-5. BETTY FRIEDAN, *THE FEMININE MYSTIQUE*, 1963

Source: *The Feminine Mystique* by Betty Friedan. Copyright © 1983, 1974, 1973, 1963 by Betty Friedan. Used by permission of W.W. Norton & Company, Inc.

The Problem That Has No Name

The problem lay buried, unspoken, for many years in the minds of American women. It was a strange stirring, a sense of dissatisfaction, a yearning that women suffered in the middle of the twentieth century in the United States. Each suburban wife struggled with it alone. As she made the beds, shopped for groceries, matched slipcover material, ate peanut butter sandwiches with her children, chauffeured Cub Scouts and Brownies, lay beside her husband at night—she was afraid to ask even of herself the silent question—"Is this all?"...

The suburban housewife—she was the dream image of the young American women and the envy, it was said, of women all over the world. The American housewife—freed by science and labor-saving appliances from the drudgery, the dangers of childbirth and the illnesses of her grandmother. She was healthy, beautiful, educated, concerned only about her husband, her children, her home. She had found true feminine fulfillment. As a housewife and mother, she was respected as a full and equal partner to man in his world. She was free to choose automobiles, clothes, appliances, supermarkets; she had everything that women ever dreamed of.

In the fifteen years after World War II, this mystique of feminine fulfillment became the cherished and self-perpetuating core of contemporary American culture. Millions of women lived their lives in the image of those pretty pictures of the American suburban housewife, kissing their husbands goodbye in front of the picture window, depositing their stationwagonsful of children at school, and smiling as they ran the new electric waxer over the spotless kitchen floor. They baked their own bread, sewed their own and their children's clothes, kept their new washing machines and dryers running all day. They changed the sheets on the beds twice a week instead of once, took the rug-hooking class in adult education, and pitied their poor frustrated mothers, who had dreamed of having a career. Their only dream was to be perfect wives and mothers; their highest ambition to have five children and a beautiful house, their only fight to get and keep their husbands. They had no thought for the unfeminine problems of the world outside the home; they wanted the men to make the major decisions. They gloried in their role as women, and wrote proudly on the census blank: "Occupation: housewife."...

If a woman had a problem in the 1950's and 1960's, she knew that something must be wrong with her marriage, or with herself. Other women were satisfied with their lives, she thought. What kind of a woman was she if she did not feel this mysterious fulfillment waxing the kitchen floor? She was so ashamed to admit her dissatisfaction that she never knew how many other women shared it....

But on an April morning in 1959, I heard a mother of four, having coffee with four other mothers in a suburban development fifteen miles from New York, say in a tone of quiet desperation, "the problem." And the others knew, without words, that she was not talking about a problem with her husband, or her children, or her home. Suddenly they realized they all shared the same problem, the problem that has no name. They began, hesitantly, to talk about it. Later, after they had picked up their children at nursery school and taken them home to nap, two of the women cried, in sheer relief, just to know they were not alone.

Gradually I came to realize that the problem that has no name was shared by countless women in America. As a magazine writer I often interviewed women about problems with their children, or their marriages, or their houses, or their communities. But after a while I began to recognize the telltale signs of this other problem....Sometimes I sensed the problem, not as a reporter, but as a suburban housewife, for during this time I was also bringing up my own three children in Rockland County, New York....

Just what was this problem that has no name? What were the words women used when they tried to express it? Sometimes a woman would say "I feel empty somehow...incomplete." Or, she would say, "I feel as if I don't exist." Sometimes she blotted out the feeling with a tranquilizer. Sometimes she thought the problem was with her husband, or her children, or that what she really needed was to redecorate her house, or move to a better neighborhood, or have an affair, or another baby. Sometimes, she went to a doctor with symptoms she could hardly describe: "A tired feeling...I get so angry with the children it scares me...I feel like crying without any reason." (A Cleveland doctor called it "the housewife's syndrome.")...

A mother of four who left college at nineteen to get married told me:

I've tried everything women are supposed to do—hobbies, gardening, pickling, canning, being very social with my neighbors, joining committees, running PTA teas. I can do it all, and I like it, but it doesn't leave you anything to think about—any feeling of who you are. I never had any career ambitions. All I wanted was to get married and have four children. I love the kids and Bob and my home. There's no problem you can even put a name to. But I'm desperate. I begin to feel I have no personality. I'm a server of food and a putter-on of pants and a bedmaker, somebody who can be called on when you want something. But who am I?...

If I am right, the problem that has no name stirring in the minds of so many American women today is not a matter of loss of femininity or too much education, or the demands of domesticity. It is far more important than anyone recognizes....It may well be the key to our future as a nation and a culture. We can no longer ignore that voice within women that says: "I want something more than my husband and my children and my home."

Housewifery Expands to Fill the Time Available....

One of the great changes in America, since World War II, has been the explosive movement to the suburbs, those ugly and endless sprawls which are becoming a national problem. Sociologists point out that a distinguishing feature of these suburbs is the fact that the women who live there are better educated than city women, and that the great majority are full-time housewives.

At first glance, one might suspect that the very growth and existence of the suburbs causes educated modern American women to become and remain full-time housewives. Or did the postwar suburban explosion come, at least in part, as a result of the coincidental choice of millions of American women to "seek fulfillment in the home?" Among the women I interviewed, the decision to move to the suburbs "for the children's sake" followed the decision to give up job or profession and become a full-time housewife, usually after the birth of the first baby, or the second, depending on the age of the woman when the mystique hit....

When the mystique took over...a new breed of women came to the suburbs. They...were perfectly willing to accept the suburban community as they found it (their only problem was "how to fit in"); they were perfectly willing to fill their days with the trivia of housewifery. Women of this kind...refuse to take policy-making positions in community organizations; they will only collect for Red Cross or March of Dimes or Scouts or be den mothers or take the lesser PTA jobs. Their resistance to serious community responsibility is usually explained by "I can't take the time from my family." But much of their time is spent in meaningless busywork. The kind of community work they choose does not challenge their intelligence—or even, sometimes, fill a real function. Nor do they derive much personal satisfaction from it—but it does fill time.

So, increasingly, in the new bedroom suburbs, the really interesting volunteer jobs—the leadership of the cooperative nurseries, the free libraries, the school board posts, the selectmenships and, in some suburbs, even the PTA presidencies—are filled by men. The housewife who doesn't "have time" to take serious responsibility in the community, like the woman who doesn't "have time" to pursue a professional career, evades a serious commitment through which she might finally realize herself; she evades it by stepping up her domestic routine until she is truly trapped.

The dimensions of the trap seem physically unalterable, as the busyness that fills the housewife's day seems inescapably necessary. But is that domestic trap an illusion, despite its all-too-solid reality, an illusion created by the feminine mystique? Take, for instance, the open plan of the contemporary "ranch" or split-level house, $14,990 to $54,990, which has been built in the millions from Roslyn Heights [Long Island] to the Pacific Palisades [Los Angeles]. They give the illusion of more space for less money. But the women to whom they are sold almost *have* to live the feminine mystique. There are no true walls or doors; the woman in the beautiful electronic kitchen is never separated from her children. She need never feel alone for a minute, need never be by herself. She can forget her own identity in those noisy open-plan houses. The open plan also helps expand the housework to fill the time available. In what is basically one free-flowing room, instead of many rooms separated by walls and stairs, continual messes continually need picking up....

For the very able woman, who has the ability to create culturally as well as biologically, the only possible rationalization is to convince herself—as the new mystique tries so hard to convince her—that the minute physical details of child care are indeed mystically creative; that her children will be tragically deprived if she is not there every minute; that the dinner she gives the boss's wife is as crucial to her husband's career as the case he fights in court or the problem he solves in the laboratory. And because husband and children are soon out of the house most of the day, she must keep on having new babies, or somehow make the minutiae of housework itself important enough, necessary enough, hard enough, creative enough to justify her very existence....

It is the mystique of feminine fulfillment, and the immaturity it breeds, that prevents women from doing the work of which they are capable.... That housewifery can, must, expand to fill the time available when there is no other purpose in life seems fairly evident. After all, with no other purpose in her life, if the housework were done in an hour, and the children off to school, the bright, energetic housewife would find the emptiness of her days unbearable.

10-6. THE TRAPPED SUBURBAN MOTHER, 1961

Why Young Mothers Feel Trapped

Today's housewife, trying to serve children, husband, home and community, has taken on an impossible number of tasks. To get out of the squirrel cage calls for resolute decision

Condensed from Redbook

JHAN AND JUNE ROBBINS

"ROBLEMS? *What* problems?" The young husband we were talking with suddenly lost his temper. "My wife is well educated and in perfect health. We have three fine children and a home of our own. My wife has 16 push-button machines to do her housework. She has a car. I take her out to dinner. We give parties and go on vacations. What's more, all her friends and neighbors have the same advantages. No women in the world's history have ever had it so good! I'm getting sick and tired of hearing about the problems of today's married woman!"

Many young American husbands feel this same sense of resentment and impatience. More important,

Redbook (September '60), © 1960 by McCall Corp., 230 Park Ave., New York 17, N. Y.   99

Figure 10-3 By the early 1960s, writers began to question the apparent privileges of suburban housewives, revealing a level of dissatisfaction that soon exploded in the women's movement. The monotony of housework, chauffering kids and husbands, and the isolation felt by some suburban housewives underlay this unhappiness. *Reader's Digest* 78 (January 1961), 99.

10-7. SUBURBAN WOMEN IN GREAT NECK, NEW YORK, EXPLORE FEMINISM, 1973

Source: Jean Pascoe, "Suburban Women's Lib: Turning Mrs. into Ms.," *McCall's* 100 (September 1973).

This fall one of the hottest items in the adult-education sphere will be women's liberation. Although courses in fem-lib have been sweeping college campuses for years, they have just begun to catch on among housewives in the suburbs.

Women's studies, of course, encompass all the feminist territory, from personal consciousness-raising to the History of Women in America. Are these courses worth taking? Do they really help women reevaluate their life situations? Provide new solutions for their discontent?

"Yes," say almost every one of 32 suburban wives just finishing the fifth and final session of a course called "Ms.: The New Status of Women," in Great Neck, New York. The course, typical of those offered in many parts of the country, cost $12 and featured four speakers—all professional women—who talked on sex, money, law and jobs and what they mean to women. Finally, a group of housewives demonstrated a consciousness-raising session to the class.

By the end of the course, a few enrollees still felt that they had found no place for themselves in women's lib. "My husband puts no restrictions on me," commented one such woman. "I do clean the house and cook, but this requires minimal time and I have a lot left over to be what I want." All but five of the class members, however, did change their views about women's traditional roles as wife, mother and sexual being. Many had also started to change their lives.

Typically the Ms.-class member at Great Neck's night school was slightly over 40 and married, with children still living at home. Frequently she was inspired to take the course by her young feminist-minded daughter. She did not have to work to supplement the family exchequer. In fact, she had it so good that she felt she had forfeited—for a certain security—her right to be her own person. "I'm somebody's wife and somebody's mother rather than a separate human being" was the general thought that cropped up again and again. One woman of 50 put it specifically: "I had come to the realization that for too many years I had been an expendable person—filling whatever niche I was placed in. In doing so, I had negated myself completely."

For these women, the adult-education course seemed a more respectable way to find out what the women's movement might hold for them than plunging directly into a consciousness-raising group. Besides, most of them already knew what response that would get from their husbands: negative.

As they began to think about becoming more assertive and making demands of their own, guilt feelings were the first to surface. "I feel that I must have more discussion about women's lib at home, yet I'm fearful of making waves," one 38-year-old mother confessed.

"I was leery of many liberated attitudes and afraid of exposing myself to too much freedom," said another wife, 40, "because I felt it could pose a danger to a marriage based on 'old' ways. It could disturb too much between my husband and me if I went all out—which is truly the way I feel." But many decided anyway "to try to free myself and then work out the guilt feelings that would engender," as one of them said.

Although for some the course provided the necessary nudge to start making plans for going back to school or to work, it was at home that the Great Neck housewives actually began expressing long-buried feelings and discarding long-held attitudes. After a session on women and sex many began talking more openly with their husbands about sexual needs they had been too embarrassed to acknowledge or sometimes even to recognize before. After a session on money, several realized that they had been downright irresponsible in leaving the management of the family's finances entirely to their husbands.

At the end of the course, Great Neck men, by and large, were still somewhat less than enthusiastic. Typical was this description by a class member of her husband's reaction: "He felt very angry and threatened during the early stages. He made deriding remarks. Now he is beginning to accept it, but not joyously."

Gradually, however, many of the women noticed that "speaking more openly with husband, children and friends about my feelings all along the line—from sex to work" was having positive results. "It got both my husband and me thinking and talking," said one woman.

There will be no bra-burning, either real or symbolic, in Great Neck—at least not among these women. For the most part, they have chosen to work quietly on their own heads, leaving drastic changes for later—if ever.

10-8. JOHN CHEEVER'S SHORT STORY, "O YOUTH AND BEAUTY!" 1953

Source: *The Stories of John Cheever* by John Cheever, copyright © 1978 by John Cheever. Used by permission of Alfred A. Knopf, a division of Random House, Inc.

AT THE TAG END of nearly every long, large Saturday-night party in the suburb of Shady Hill, when almost everybody who was going to play golf or tennis in the morning had gone home hours ago and the ten or twelve people remaining seemed powerless to bring the evening to an end although the gin and whiskey were running low, and here and there a woman who was sitting out her husband would have begun to drink milk; when everybody had lost track of time, and the baby-sitters who were waiting at home for these diehards would have long since stretched out on the sofa and fallen into a deep sleep, to dream about cooking-contest prizes, ocean voyages, and romance; when the bellicose drunk, the crapshooter, the pianist, and the woman faced with the expiration of her hopes had all expressed themselves; when every proposal—to go to the Farquarsons' for breakfast, to go swimming, to go and wake up the Townsends, to go here and go there—died as soon as it was made, then Trace Bearden would begin to chide Cash Bentley about his age and thinning hair. The chiding was preliminary to moving the living-room furniture. Trace and Cash moved the tables and the chairs, the sofas

and the fire screen, the woodbox and the footstool; and when they had finished, you wouldn't know the place. Then if the host had a revolver, he would be asked to produce it. Cash would take off his shoes and assume a starting crouch behind a sofa. Trace would fire the weapon out of an open window, and if you were new to the community and had not understood what the preparations were about, you would then realize that you were watching a hurdle race. Over the sofa went Cash, over the tables, over the fire screen and the woodbox. It was not exactly a race, since Cash ran it alone, but it was extraordinary to see this man of forty surmount so many obstacles so gracefully. There was not a piece of furniture in Shady Hill that Cash could not take in his stride. The race ended with cheers, and, presently the party would break up.

Cash was, of course, an old track star, but he was never aggressive or tiresome about his brilliant past. The college where he had spent his youth had offered him a paying job on the alumni council, but he had refused it, realizing that that part of his life was ended. Cash and his wife, Louise, had two children, and they lived in a medium-cost ranch house on Alewives Lane. They belonged to the country club, although they could not afford it, but in the case of the Bentleys nobody ever pointed this out, and Cash was one of the best-liked men in Shady Hill. He was still slender—he was careful about his weight—and he walked to the train in the morning with a light and vigorous step that marked him as an athlete. His hair was thin, and there were mornings when his eyes looked bloodshot, but this did not detract much from a charming quality of stubborn youthfulness.

In business Cash had suffered reverses and disappointments, and the Bentleys had many money worries. They were always late with their tax payments and their mortgage payments, and the drawer of the hall table was stuffed with unpaid bills; it was always touch and go with the Bentleys and the bank. Louise looked pretty enough on Saturday night, but her life was exacting and monotonous. In the pockets of her suits, coats, and dresses there were little wads and scraps of paper on which was written: "Oleomargarine, frozen spinach, Kleenex, dog biscuit, hamburger, pepper, lard...." When she was still half awake in the morning, she was putting on the water for coffee and diluting the frozen orange juice. Then she would be wanted by the children. She would crawl under the bureau on her hands and knees to find a sock for Toby. She would lie flat on her belly and wiggle under the bed (getting dust up her nose) to find a shoe for Rachel. Then there were the housework, the laundry, and the cooking, as well as the demands of the children. There always seemed to be shoes to put on and shoes to take off, snowsuits to be zipped and unzipped, bottoms to be wiped, tears to be dried, and when the sun went down (she saw it set from the kitchen window) there was the supper to be cooked, the baths, the bedtime story, and the Lord's Prayer. With the sonorous words of the Our Father in a darkened room the children's day was over, but the day was far from over for Louise Bentley. There were the darning, the mending, and some ironing to do, and after sixteen years of housework she did not seem able to escape her chores even while she slept. Snowsuits, shoes, baths, and groceries seemed to have permeated her subconscious. Now and then she would speak in her sleep—so loudly that she woke her husband. "I can't afford veal cutlets," she said one night. Then she sighed uneasily and was quiet again

By the standards of Shady Hill, the Bentleys were a happily married couple, but they had their ups and downs. Cash could be very touchy at times. When he came home after a bad day at the office and found that Louise, for some good reason, had not started supper, he would be ugly. "Oh, for Christ sake!" he would say, and go into the kitchen and heat up some frozen food. He drank some whiskey to relax himself during this ordeal, but it never seemed to relax him, and he usually burned the bottom out of a pan, and when they sat down for supper the dining space would be full of smoke. It was only a question of time before they were plunged into a bitter quarrel. Louise would run upstairs, throw herself onto the bed and sob. Cash would grab the whiskey bottle and dose himself. These rows, in spite of the vigor with which Cash and Louise entered into them, were the source of a great deal of pain for both of them. Cash would sleep downstairs on the sofa, but sleep never repaired the damage, once the trouble had begun, and if they met in the morning, they would be at one another's throats in a second. Then Cash would leave for the train, and, as soon as the children had been taken to nursery school, Louise would put on her coat and cross the grass to the Beardens' house. She would cry into a cup of warmed-up coffee and tell Lucy Bearden her troubles. What was the meaning of marriage? What was the meaning of love? Lucy always suggested that Louise get a job. It would give her emotional and financial independence, and that, Lucy said, was what she needed.

The next night, things would get worse. Cash would not come home for dinner at all, but would stumble in at about eleven, and the whole sordid wrangle would be repeated, with Louise going to bed in tears upstairs and Cash again stretching out on the living-room sofa. After a few days and nights of this, Louise would decide that she was at the end of her rope. She would decide to go and stay with her married sister in Mamaroneck. She usually chose a Saturday, when Cash would be at home, for her departure. She would pack a suitcase and get her War Bonds from the desk. Then she would take a bath and put on her best slip. Cash, passing the bedroom door, would see her. Her slip was transparent, and suddenly he was all repentance, tenderness, charm, wisdom, and love. "Oh, my darling!" he would groan, and when they went downstairs to get a bite to eat about an hour later, they would be sighing and making cow eyes at one another; they would be the happiest married couple in the whole eastern United States. It was usually at about this time that Lucy Bearden turned up with the good news that she had found a job for Louise. Lucy would ring the doorbell, and Cash, wearing a bathrobe, would let her in. She would be brief with Cash, naturally, and hurry into the dining room to tell poor Louise the good news. "Well, that's very nice of you to have looked," Louise would say wanly, "but I don't think that I want a job any more. I don't think that Cash wants me to work, do you, sweetheart?" Then she would turn her big dark eyes on Cash, and you could practically smell smoke. Lucy would excuse herself hurriedly from this scene of depravity, but never left with any hard feelings, because she had been married for nineteen years herself and she knew that every union has its ups and downs. She didn't seem to leave any wiser, either; the next time the Bentleys quarreled, she would be just as intent as ever on getting Louise a job. But these quarrels and reunions, like the hurdle race, didn't seem to lose their interest through repetition.

ON A SATURDAY NIGHT in the spring, the Farquarsons gave the Bentleys an anniversary party. It was their seventeenth anniversary. Saturday afternoon, Louise Bentley put herself through preparations nearly as arduous as the Monday wash. She rested for an hour, by the clock, with her feet high in the air, her chin in a sling, and her eyes bathed in some astringent solution. The clay packs, the too tight girdle, and the plucking and curling and painting that went on were all aimed at rejuvenation. Feeling in the end that she had not been entirely successful, she tied a piece of veiling over her eyes—but she was a lovely woman, and all the cosmetics that she had struggled with seemed, like her veil, to be drawn transparently over a face where mature beauty and a capacity for wit and passion were undisguisable. The Farquarsons' party was nifty, and the Bentleys had a wonderful time. The only person who drank too much was Trace Bearden. Late in the party, he began to chide Cash about his thinning hair and Cash good-naturedly began to move the furniture around. Harry Farquarson had a pistol, and Trace went out onto the terrace to fire it up at the sky. Over the sofa went Cash, over the end table, over the arms of the wing chair and the fire screen. It was a piece of carving on a chest that brought him down, and down he came like a ton of bricks.

Louise screamed and ran to where he lay. He had cut a gash in his forehead, and someone made a bandage to stop the flow of blood. When he tried to get up, he stumbled and fell again, and his face turned a terrible green. Harry telephoned Dr. Parminter, Dr. Hopewell, Dr. Altman, and Dr. Barnstable, but it was two in the morning and none of them answered. Finally, a Dr. Yerkes—a to-

tal stranger—agreed to come. Yerkes was a young man—he did not seem old enough to be a doctor—and he looked around at the disordered room and the anxious company as if there was something weird about the scene. He got off on the wrong foot with Cash. "What seems to be the matter, old-timer?" he asked.

Cash's leg was broken. The doctor put a splint on it, and Harry and Trace carried the injured man out to the doctor's car. Louise followed them in her own car to the hospital, where Cash was bedded down in a ward. The doctor gave Cash a sedative, and Louise kissed him and drove home in the dawn.

CASH was in the hospital for two weeks, and when he came home he walked with a crutch and his broken leg was in a heavy cast. It was another ten days before he could limp to the morning train. "I won't be able to run the hurdle race any more, sweetheart," he told Louise sadly. She said that it didn't matter, but while it didn't matter to her, it seemed to matter to Cash. He had lost weight in the hospital. His spirits were low. He seemed discontented. He did not himself understand what had happened. He, or everything around him, seemed subtly to have changed for the worse. Even his senses seemed to conspire to damage the ingenuous world that he had enjoyed for so many years. He went into the kitchen late one night to make himself a sandwich, and when he opened the icebox door he noticed a rank smell. He dumped the spoiled meat into the garbage, but the smell clung to his nostrils. A few days later he was in the attic, looking for his varsity sweater. There were no windows in the attic and his flashlight was dim. Kneeling on the floor to unlock a trunk, he broke a spider web with his lips. The frail web covered his mouth as if a hand had been put over it. He wiped it impatiently, but also with the feeling of having been gagged. A few nights later, he was walking down a New York side street in the rain and saw an old whore standing in a doorway. She was so sluttish and ugly that she looked like a cartoon of Death, but before he could appraise her—the instant his eyes took an impression of her crooked figure—his lips swelled, his breathing quickened, and he experienced all the other symptoms of erotic excitement. A few nights later, while he was reading *Time* in the living room, he noticed that the faded roses Louise had brought in from the garden smelled more of earth than of anything else. It was a putrid, compelling smell. He dropped the roses into a wastebasket, but not before they had reminded him of the spoiled meat, the whore, and the spider web.

He had started going to parties again, but without the hurdle race to run, the parties of his friends and neighbors seemed to him interminable and stale. He listened to their dirty jokes with an irritability that was hard for him to conceal. Even their countenances discouraged him, and, slumped in a chair, he would regard their skin and their teeth narrowly, as if he were himself a much younger man.

The brunt of his irritability fell on Louise, and it seemed to her that Cash, in losing the hurdle race, had lost the thing that had preserved his equilibrium. He was rude to his friends when they stopped in for a drink. He was rude and gloomy when he and Louise went out. When Louise asked him what was the matter, he only murmured, "Nothing, nothing, nothing," and poured himself some bourbon. May and June passed, and then the first part of July, without his showing any improvement.

THEN IT IS a summer night, a wonderful summer night. The passengers on the eight-fifteen see Shady Hill—if they notice it at all—in a bath of placid golden light. The noise of the train is muffled in the heavy foliage, and the long car windows look like a string of lighted aquarium tanks before they flicker out of sight. Up on the hill, the ladies say to one another, "Smell the grass! Smell the trees!" The Farquarsons are giving another party, and Harry has hung a sign, WHISKEY GULCH, from the rose arbor, and is wearing a chef's white hat and an apron. His guests are still drinking, and the smoke from his meat fire rises, on this windless evening, straight up into the trees.

In the clubhouse on the hill, the first of the formal dances for the young people begins around nine. On Alewives Lane sprinklers continue to play after dark. You can smell the water. The air seems as fragrant as it is dark—it is a delicious element to walk through—and most of the windows on Alewives Lane are open to it. You can see Mr. and Mrs. Bearden, as you pass, looking at their television. Joe Lockwood, the young lawyer who lives on the corner, is practicing a speech to the jury before his wife. "I intend to show you," he says, "that a man of probity, a man whose reputation for honesty and reliability...." He waves his bare arms as he speaks. His wife goes on knitting. Mrs. Carver—Harry Farquarson's mother-in-law—glances up at the sky and asks, "*Where* did all the stars come from?" She is old and foolish, and yet she is right: Last night's stars seem to have drawn to themselves a new range of galaxies, and the night sky is not dark at all, except where there is a tear in the membrane of light. In the unsold house lots near the track a hermit thrush is singing.

The Bentleys are at home. Poor Cash has been so rude and gloomy that the Farquarsons have not asked him to their party. He sits on the sofa beside Louise, who is sewing elastic into the children's underpants. Through the open window he can hear the pleasant sounds of the summer night. There is another party, in the Rogerses' garden, behind the Bentleys'. The music from the dance drifts down the hill. The band is sketchy—saxophone, drums, and piano—and all the selections are twenty years old. The band plays "Valencia," and Cash looks tenderly toward Louise, but Louise, tonight, is a discouraging figure. The lamp picks out the gray in her hair. Her apron is stained. Her face seems colorless and drawn. Suddenly, Cash begins frenziedly to beat his feet in time to the music. He sings some gibberish—Jabajabajabajaba—to the distant saxophone. He sighs and goes into the kitchen.

Here a faint, stale smell of cooking clings to the dark. From the kitchen window Cash can see the lights and figures of the Rogerses' party. It is a young people's party. The Rogers girl has asked some friends in for dinner before the dance, and now they seem to be leaving. Cars are driving away. "I'm covered with grass stains," a girl says. "I hope the old man remembered to buy gasoline," a boy says, and a girl laughs. There is nothing on their minds but the passing summer nights. Taxes and the elastic in underpants—all the unbeautiful facts of life that threaten to crush the breath out of Cash—have not touched a single figure in this garden. Then jealousy seizes him—such savage and bitter jealousy that he feels ill.

He does not understand what separates him from these children in the garden next door. He has been a young man. He has been a hero. He has been adored and happy and full of animal spirits, and now he stands in a dark kitchen, deprived of his athletic prowess, his impetuousness, his good looks—of everything that means anything to him. He feels as if the figures in the next yard are the specters from some party in that past where all his tastes and desires lie, and from which he has been cruelly removed. He feels like a ghost of the summer evening. He is sick with longing. Then he hears voices in the front of the house. Louise turns on the kitchen light. "Oh, here you are," she says. "The Beardens stopped in. I think they'd like a drink."

Cash went to the front of the house to greet the Beardens. They wanted to go up to the club, for one dance. They saw, at a glance, that Cash was at loose ends, and they urged the Bentleys to come. Louise got someone to stay with the children and then went upstairs to change.

When they got to the club, they found a few friends of their age hanging around the bar, but Cash did not stay in the bar. He seemed restless and perhaps drunk. He banged into a table on his way through the lounge to the ballroom. He cut in on a young girl. He seized her too vehemently and jigged her off in an ancient two-step. She signaled openly for help to a boy in the stag line, and Cash was cut out. He walked angrily off the dance floor onto the terrace. Some young couples there withdrew from one another's arms as he pushed open the screen door. He walked to the end of the terrace, where he hoped to be alone, but here he surprised another young couple, who got up from the lawn, where they seemed to have been lying, and walked off in the dark toward the pool.

Louise remained in the bar with the Beardens. "Poor Cash is tight," she said. And then, "He told me this afternoon that he was going to paint the storm windows," she said. "Well, he mixed the paint and washed the brushes and put on some old fatigues and went into the cellar. There was a telephone call for him at around five, and when I went down to tell him, do you know what he was doing? He was just sitting there in the dark with a cocktail shaker. He hadn't touched the storm windows. He was just sitting there in the dark, drinking Martinis."

"Poor Cash," Trace said.

"You ought to get a job," Lucy said. "That would give you emotional and financial independence." As she spoke, they all heard the noise of furniture being moved around in the lounge.

"Oh, my God!" Louise said. "He's going to run the race. Stop him, Trace, stop him! He'll hurt himself. He'll kill himself!"

They all went to the door of the lounge. Louise again asked Trace to interfere, but she could see by Cash's face that he was way beyond remonstrating with. A few couples left the dance floor and stood watching the preparations. Trace didn't try to stop Cash—he helped him. There was no pistol, so he slammed a couple of books together for the start.

Over the sofa went Cash, over the coffee table, the lamp table, the fire screen, and the hassock. All his grace and strength seemed to have returned to him. He cleared the big sofa at the end of the room and instead of stopping there, he turned and started back over the course. His face was strained. His mouth hung open. The tendons of his neck protruded hideously. He made the hassock, the fire screen, the lamp table, and the coffee table. People held their breath when he approached the final sofa, but he cleared it and landed on his feet. There was some applause. Then he groaned and fell. Louise ran to his side. His clothes were soaked with sweat and he gasped for breath. She knelt down beside him and took his head in her lap and stroked his thin hair.

CASH had a terrible hangover on Sunday, and Louise let him sleep until it was nearly time for church. The family went off to Christ Church together at eleven, as they always did. Cash sang, prayed, and got to his knees, but the most he ever felt in church was that he stood outside the realm of God's infinite mercy, and, to tell the truth, he no more believed in the Father, the Son, and the

Holy Ghost than does my bull terrier. They returned home at one to eat the overcooked meat and stony potatoes that were their customary Sunday lunch. At around five, the Parminters called up and asked them over for a drink. Louise didn't want to go, so Cash went alone. (Oh, those suburban Sunday nights, those Sunday-night blues! Those departing weekend guests, those stale cocktails, those half-dead flowers, those trips to Harmon to catch the Century, those postmortems and pickup suppers!) It was sultry and overcast. The dog days were beginning. He drank gin with the Parminters for an hour or two and then went over to the Townsends' for a drink. The Farquarsons called up the Townsends and asked them to come over and bring Cash with them, and at the Farquarsons' they had some more drinks and ate the leftover party food. The Farquarsons were glad to see that Cash seemed like himself again. It was half past ten or eleven when he got home. Louise was upstairs, cutting out of the current copy of *Life* those scenes of mayhem, disaster, and violent death that she felt might corrupt her children. She always did this. Cash came upstairs and spoke to her and then went down again. In a little while, she heard him moving the living-room furniture around. Then he called to her, and when she went down, he was standing at the foot of the stairs in his stocking feet, holding the pistol out to her. She had never fired it before, and the directions he gave her were not much help.

"Hurry up," he said, "I can't wait all night."

He had forgotten to tell her about the safety, and when she pulled the trigger nothing happened.

"It's that little lever," he said. "Press that little lever." Then, in his impatience, he hurdled the sofa anyhow.

The pistol went off and Louise got him in midair. She shot him dead.

10-9. PETER BLAKE PORTRAYS SUBURBIA AS *GOD'S OWN JUNKYARD*, 1964

Source: Reprinted by the permission of Russell & Volkening as agents for the author. Copyright © 1963, 1964 by Peter Blake, renewed in 1991, 1992 by Peter Blake.

This book is not written in anger. It is written in fury—though not, I trust, in blind fury. It is a deliberate attack upon all those who have already befouled a large portion of this country for private gain, and are engaged in befouling the rest....

This is perhaps a rather naïve book. It is based on the assumption that our national purpose, or purposes, are somewhat more than idealistic. It is based on the further assumption that it is not too late for us to learn to see again, and to learn to care again about the physical aspects of our environment. And it is based, finally, on the assumption that ours could be a ___ civilized society—if ___ stirred into action.

This ___ book, not because ___ rly enjoyable acti ___ ms to be so much r ___ be raked so that th ___ it again to live in.

Figure 10-4 In his book *God's Own Junkyard*, Peter Blake paired images that emphasized the environmental destructiveness of suburbanization. These pairs—implying "before" and "after" perspectives—heightened the visual impact of his critique. In this couplet, we see images from two different places: Trousdale Estates, in Beverly Hills, California, where the land is being graded for suburban homes. Below it, the wilderness of Grant County, Oregon. Top: Pacific Air Industries, 56-2966, Long Beach, California: PAI, 1956, 4 x 5", negative dated October 8, 1956. From collections of the Map and Imagery Laboratory, Davidson Library, University of California, Santa Barbara. Copyright © 2006 The Regents of the University of California. All rights reserved.

Figure 10-4 Bottom: Grant County, Oregon, Malheur National Forest, Valley of the Canyons, Russell Lee, 1942, Courtesy of Library of Congress, Prints and Photographs Division, FSA-OWI Collection, LC-UYSF34-073417-D DLC. Illustrations in original, figs. 64-65.

10-10. *MAD MAGAZINE* SATIRIZES SUBURBIA, 1974

CHICAGO SUBURB

by Carl Sandbag

Hog Barbecuer for the World,
School Segregator, Mower of Lawns,
Player with Golf Clubs and the Nation's Wife Swapper;
Bigoted, snobbish, flaunting,
Suburb of the White Collars.
They tell me you are lazy, and I believe them; for I have seen your
  women in the super-market parking lots, tipping box boys to load
  their station wagons.
And they tell me you are brutal, and my reply is: At the stations of
  your commuter trains, I have seen old ladies trampled by men in
  quest of seats on the shady side.
And they tell me your soil is rotten and vengeful, and I answer: Yes,
  it is true, for I have seen crab grass killed and rise up to grow
  again.
But still, I turn to those who sneer at this, my suburb, and I give
  them back the sneer and say to them:
Come and show me another town with eight drive-in mortuaries and a
  Colonel Sanders on every block;
Show me a suburb with mortgage payments so high that men worry
  themselves into heart attacks at forty,
  Debt-ridden,
  Overdrawn,
  Embezzling,
  Financing, defaulting, re-financing,
But pleased as punch to be Hog Barbecuers for the World, School
  Segregators, Mowers of Lawns, Players with Golf Clubs and
  Champion Wife Swappers of the Nation.

Figure 10-5 Chicago Suburb, 1974. This satire, a spoof on Carl Sandberg's poem "Chicago," appeared in the pages of *Mad Magazine.* From MAD #165 © 1974 E.C. Publications, Inc. All Rights Reserved. Used with Permission.

10-11. SOCIOLOGIST BENNETT BERGER CHALLENGES THE "MYTH OF SUBURBIA," 1961

Source: Bennett M. Berger, "The Myth of Suburbia," *Journal of Social Issues* 17 (1961). Used by permission of Blackwell Publishing.

In recent years a veritable myth of suburbia has developed in the United States. I am not referring to the physical facts of large-scale population movement to the suburbs: these are beyond dispute. But the social and cultural "revolution" that suburban life supposedly represents is far from being an established fact. Nevertheless, newspapers and magazines repeatedly characterize suburbia as "a new way of life," and one recent textbook refers to the rise of suburbia as "one of the major social changes of the twentieth century."

To urban sociologists, "suburbs" is an eco-logical term, distinguishing these settlements from cities, rural villages, and other kinds of communities. "Suburbia," on the other hand, is a cultural term, intended to connote a way of life, or, rather, the intent of those who use it is to connote a way of life. The ubiquity of the term in current discourse suggests that its meaning is well on the way to standard-ization—that what it is supposed to connote is widely enough accepted and implicitly enough shared to permit free use of the term with a reasonable amount of certainty that it will convey the image or images it extends. Over the last dozen years, these images have coalesced into a full blown myth, complete with its articles of faith, its sacred symbols, its rituals, its promise for the future, and its resolution of ultimate questions. The details of the myth are rife in many popular maga-zines as well as in more highbrow periodicals and books....

The Elements of the Myth

Approaching the myth of suburbia from the outside, one is immediately struck by rows of new "ranch-type" houses either identical in design or with minor variations built into a basic plan, winding streets, neat lawns, two-car garages, infant trees, and bicycles and tricycles lining the sidewalks. Nearby is the modern ranch-type school and the even more modern shopping center dominated by the department store branch or the giant supermarket.... Beneath the television antenna and behind the modestly but charmingly landscaped entrance to the tract home resides the suburbanite and his family. I should say *"temporarily* resides" because perhaps the most prominent element of the myth is that residence in a tract suburb is temporary; suburbia is a "transient center" because its breadwinners are upwardly mobile, and live there only until a promotion or a company transfer permits or requires something more opulent in the way of a home. The suburbanites are upwardly mobile because they are predominantly young (most commentators seem to agree that they are almost all between 25 and 35), well educated, and have a promising place in some organizational hierarchy.... They are engineers, middle-management men, young lawyers, salesmen, insurance agents, teachers, civil service bureaucrats— groups sometimes designated as Organization Men, and sometimes as "the new middle class." Most such occupations require some college education, so it comes as no surprise to hear and read that the suburbanites are well educated. Their wives too seem well educated; their reported conversation, their patois, and especially their apparently avid interest in theories of child development all suggest exposure to higher education.

According to the myth, a new kind of hyperactive social life has developed in suburbia. Not only is informal visiting or "neighboring" said to be rife, but a lively organizational life also goes on. Clubs, associations, and organizations allegedly exist for almost every conceivable hobby, interest, or preoccupation. An equally active participation in local civic affairs is encouraged by the absence of an older generation....

This rich social and civic life is fostered by the homogeneity of the suburbanites; they are in the same age range, have similar jobs and incomes; their children are around the same age, their problems of housing and furnishing are similar. In short, a large number of similar interests and preoccupations promotes their solidarity. This very solidarity and homogeneity, on top of the physical uniformities of the suburb itself, is often perceived as the source of the problem of "conformity" in suburbia....The "involvement of everyone in everyone else's life" submits one to the constant scrutiny of the community, and everything from an unclipped lawn to an unclipped head of hair may be cause for invidious comment. On the other hand, the uniformity and homogeneity make suburbia classless, or one-class (variously designated as middle or upper-middle class). For those interlopers who arrive in the suburbs bearing the unmistakable marks of a more deprived upbringing, suburbia is said to serve as a kind of "second melting pot" in which those who are on the way up learn to take on the appropriate folkways of the milieu to which they aspire.

During the day, suburbia is almost wholly given over to the business of child rearing. Manless during the day, suburbia is a female society in which the young mothers, well-educated and without the interference of tradition (represented by doting grandparents), can rear their children according to the best modern methods....

Part of the myth of suburbia is the image of suburbanites as commuters. Much has been deduced about suburbia from the fact of commuting. For father, commuting means an extra hour or two away from the family— with debilitating effects upon the relationship between father and children. Sometimes this means that Dad leaves for work before the children are up and comes home after they are put to bed. Naturally, these extra hours put a greater burden upon the mother, and has implications for the relationship between husband and wife.

The commuter returns in the morning to the place where he was bred, for the residents of suburbia are apparently former city people who "escaped" to the suburbs. By moving to suburbia, however, the erstwhile Democrat from the "urban ward" becomes the suburban Republican. The voting shift has been commented on or worried about at length; there seems to be something about suburbia that makes Republicans out of people who were Democrats while they lived in the city. But the political life of suburbia is characterized not only by the voting shift, but by the vigor with which it is carried on. Political *activity* takes its place beside other civic and organizational activity, intense and spirited.

The Sources of the Myth

This brief characterization is intended neither as ethnography nor as caricature, but it does not, I think, misrepresent the image of suburbia that has come to dominate the minds of most Americans, including intellectuals. Immediately, however, a perplexing question arises: why should a group of tract houses, mass produced and quickly thrown up on the outskirts of a large city, apparently generate so unique and distinctive a way of life? What is the logic that links tract living with suburbia as a way of life?

If suburban homes were all within a limited price range, then one might expect them to be occupied by families of similar income, and this might account for some of the homogeneity of the neighborhood ethos. But suburban developments are themselves quite heterogeneous. The term "suburbia" has not only been used to refer to tract housing developments as low as $8,000 per unit and as high as $65,000 per unit, but also to rental developments whose occupants do not think of themselves as homeowners....

If we limit the image of suburbia to the mass produced tract developments, we might regard the fact of commuting as the link between suburban residence and "suburbanism as a way of life." Clearly, the demands of daily commuting create certain common conditions which might go far to explain some of the ostensible uniformities of suburban living. But certainly commuting is not a unique feature of suburban living; many suburbanites are not commuters; many urban residents are. It may be true that the occupations of most suburbanites presently require a daily trip to and from the central business district of the city, but it is likely to be decreasingly true with the passage of time. For the pioneers to the suburban residential frontier have been followed not only by masses of retail trade outlets, but by industry also....

If the occupations of most suburbanites were similar in their demands, then this might help account for the development of a generic way of life in suburbs. And, indeed, if suburbia were populated largely by Organization men and their families, then one could understand more readily the style of life that is ascribed to it. Or, lacking this, if Organization men, as Whyte puts it, give the prevailing *tone* to life in suburbia, then one could more readily understand the prevalence of his model in the writing on suburbia. But there is no real reason to believe that the Organization man dominates the suburbs. Perhaps the typical Organization man is a suburbanite. But it is one thing to assert this and quite another thing to assert that the typical tract suburb is populated by Organization men and their families or dominated by an Organization way of life.

Clearly then one suburb (or *kind* of suburb) is likely to differ from another not only in terms of the cost of its homes, the income of its residents, their occupations and commuting patterns, but also in terms of its educational levels, the character of the region, the size of the suburb, the social and geographical origin of its residents, and countless more indices—all of which, presumably, may be expected to lead to differences in "way of life."

But we not only have good reason to expect suburbs to *differ* markedly from one another; we have reason to expect striking *similarities* between life in urban residential neighborhoods and tract suburbs of a similar social cast. In large cities many men "commute" to work, that is, take subways, buses, or other forms of public transportation to their jobs which may be over on the other side of town. There are thousands of blocks in American cities with rows of identical or similar houses in them within a limited rental or price range, and presumably occupied by families in a similar income bracket. The same fears for massification and conformity were felt regarding these urban neighborhoods as are now felt for the mass produced suburbs....

In continually referring to "the myth of suburbia" I do not mean to imply that the reports on the culture of suburban life have been falsified.... *I mean only to say that the reports of suburbia we have had so far have been extremely selective.* They are based for the most part, upon life in Levittown, N.Y., Park Forest, Ill., Lakewood, near Los Angeles, and, most recently (the best study so far) a fashionable suburb of Toronto, Canada. The studies that have given rise to the myth of suburbia have been studies of *white collar suburbs* of large cities. If the phrase "middle class suburb" or "white collar suburb" strikes the eye as redundant, it is testimony to the efficacy of the myth. Large tracts of suburban housing, in many respects indistinguishable from those in Levittown and Park Forest have gone up and are continuing to go up all over the country, not only near large cities, but near middle sized and small ones as well. In many of these tracts, the homes fall within the 12,000 to 16,000 dollar price range, a range well within the purchasing abilities of large numbers of semi-skilled and skilled factory workers in unionized heavy industry. Many of these working class people are migrating to these new suburbs—which are not immediately and visibly characterizable as "working class," but which, to all intents and purposes, look from the outside like the fulfillment of the "promise of America" symbolized in the myth. Even more of them will be migrating to new suburbs as increasing numbers of factories move out of the city to the hinterlands. Many of these people are either rural-bred, or urban-working class bred, with relatively little education, and innocent of white collar status or aspiration. And where this is true, as it is in many low-price tracts, then one may expect sharp differences between their social and cultural life and that of their more sophisticated counterparts in white collar suburbs.

This should be no surprise; indeed, the fact that it should have to be asserted at all is still further testimony to the vitality of the myth I have been describing. My own research among auto workers in a new, predominantly "working class" suburb in California demonstrates how far removed their style of life is from that suggested by the myth of suburbia. The group I interviewed still vote 81% Democratic; there has been no "return to religion" among them—more than half of the people I spoke to said they went to church rarely or not at all. On the whole, they have no great hopes of getting ahead in their jobs, and an enormous majority regard their new suburban homes not as a temporary resting place, but as paradise permanently gained. Of the group I interviewed, 70% belonged to not a single club, organization, or association (with the exception of the union), and their mutual visiting or "neighboring" was quite rare except if relatives lived nearby....[T]he group of auto workers I interviewed has, for the most part, maintained its working class attitudes and style of life intact in the context of the bright new suburb.

The Functions of the Myth

Similar conditions probably prevail in many of the less expensive suburbs; in any case, semi skilled "working class" suburbs probably constitute a substantial segment of the reality of suburban life. Why, then, is the myth still so potent in our popular culture?...

One source of the peculiar susceptibility of "suburbia" to the manufacture of myth is the fact that a large supply of visible symbols are ready at hand. Picture windows, patios and barbecues, power lawn mowers, the problems of commuting, and the armies of children manning their mechanized vehicles down the sidewalks, are only secondarily facts; primarily they are symbols whose function is to evoke an image of a way of life for the non-suburban public. These symbols of suburbia can be fitted neatly into the total pattern of the "spirit" of this "age."...[T]he myth of suburbia is enabled to flourish precisely because it fits into the general outlook of at least four otherwise divergent schools of opinion whose function it is to shape the "judgment of history."

To realtor-chamber of commerce defenders of the American Way of Life suburbia represents the fulfillment of the American middle-class dream; it is identified with the continuing possibility of upward mobility, with expanding opportunities in middle-class occupations, with rising standards of living and real incomes, and the gadgeted good life as it is represented in the full-color ads in the mass circulation magazines.

To a somewhat less sanguine group, for example, architects, city planners, estheticians, and designers, suburbia represents a dreary blight on the American landscape, the epitome of American standardization and vulgarization, with its row upon monotonous row of mass produced cheerfulness masquerading as homes, whole agglomerations or "scatterations" of them masquerading as communities. To these eyes, the new tract suburbs of today are the urban slums of tomorrow.

Third, the myth of suburbia seems important to sociologists and other students of contemporary social and cultural trends.... [T]he myth of suburbia conceptualizes for sociologists a microcosm in which some of the apparently major social and cultural trends of our time (other-direction, social mobility, neoconservatism, status anxiety, etc.) flow together, and may be conveniently studied.

Finally, for a group consisting largely of left-wing and formerly left-wing critics of American society, the myth of suburbia provides an up-to-date polemical vocabulary. "Suburb" and "suburban" have replaced the now embarrassingly obsolete "bourgeois" as a packaged rebuke to the whole tenor of American life. What used to be condemned as "bourgeois style," "bourgeois values," and "bourgeois hypocrisy," are now simply designated as "suburban."...

[H]eaping abuse on suburbia instead of on the classic targets of American social criticism ("success," individual and corporate greed, corruption in high and low places, illegitimate power, etc.) has its advantages for the not-quite-completely-critical intellectual. His critical stance places him comfortably in the great tradition of American social criticism, and at the same time his targets render him respectable and harmless—because, after all, the critique of suburbia is essentially a "cultural" critique; unlike a political or economic one, it threatens no entrenched interests, and contains no direct implications for agitation or concerned action. Indeed, it

may be, as Edward Shils has suggested, that a "cultural" critique is all that is possible today from a left-wing point of view; the American economy and political process stand up fairly well under international comparisons, but American "culture" is fair game for anyone.

Despite the epithets that identify suburbia as the citadel of standardization and vulgarization and conformity, suburbia is also testimony to the fact that Americans are living better than ever before. What needs emphasis is that this is true not only for the traditionally comfortable white collar classes but for the blue collar, frayed collar, and turned collar classes also. Even families in urban slums are likely to be paying upward of $85 a month in rent these days, and for this or only slightly more, they can "buy" a new tract home in the suburbs. There is an irony, therefore, in the venom that left-wing critics inject into their discussions of suburbia because the criticism of suburbia tends to become a criticism of industrialization, "rationality," and "progress".... It is almost as if left-wing critics feared the seduction of the working class by pie—not in the sky, not even on the table, but right in the freezer....

Nothing I have said about suburbs gives us the right to doubt the truth of what many observers have said about places like Park Forest and Levittown. I do, however, question the right of others to generalize about "suburbia" on the basis of a few studies of selected suburbs whose representative character has yet to be demonstrated....—as if these two communities could represent a nationwide phenomenon that has occurred at all but the very lowest income levels and among most occupational classifications. If "suburbia" is anything at all unique, we'll never know it until we have a lot more information about a lot more suburbs than we now, unfortunately, have.

10-12. SOCIOLOGIST HERBERT GANS EXPLORES LIFE IN LEVITTOWN, 1967

Source: *The Levittowners* by Herbert J. Gans, copyright ©1967 by Herbert J. Gans. Used by permission of Pantheon Books, a division of Random House, Inc.

Social Life: Suburban Homogeneity and Conformity

Some critics charge that suburban life is socially, culturally, and emotionally destructive, and that the causes are to be found in the nature of suburbia and the move from the city. Testing their charges requires evaluation of the quality of Levittown life and measurement of Levittown's impact on its residents to determine what changes in behavior and attitudes have actually resulted from the move....

Perhaps the most frequent indictment of suburban life has been leveled against the quality of social relationships. The critics charge that the suburbs are socially hyperactive and have made people so outgoing that they have little time or inclination for the development of personal autonomy. The pervasive homogeneity of the population has depressed the vitality of social life, and the absence of more heterogeneous neighbors and friends has imposed a conformity which further reduces the suburbanite's individuality....Because many suburbanites are Transients or Mobiles, they have been accused of wanting social companions only for the duration of their stay, disabling them for more intimate friendship.

Evidence from Levittown suggests quite the opposite. People report an accelerated social life, and in fact looked forward to it before moving to Levittown. The major reason for the upswing is indeed homogeneity, but an equally appropriate term might be "compatibility." Propinquity may initiate social contact but it does not determine friendship. Many relationships are indeed transient, but this is no reflection on their intensity. Finally, conformity prevails, although less as malicious or passive copying than as sharing of useful ideas. In short, many of the *phenomena* identified by the critics occur in Levittown but their alleged *consequences* do not follow. Levittowners have not become outgoing, mindless conformers; they remain individuals, fulfilling the social aspirations with which they came. To be sure, social life in Levittown has its costs, but these seem minor compared to its rewards.

About half the Levittowners interviewed said that they were visiting more with neighbors than in their former residence; about a quarter said less, and the remaining quarter reported no change. The greatest increase was reported by the people who said they had wanted to do more visiting, particularly those who had had little opportunity for it in their previous residence....

In addition to the desire to do more neighboring, the increase resulted initially from the newness of the community and the lack of shopping facilities and other places for daytime activities. But these reasons were mentioned far less often than the "friendliness" of the neighbors, and this in turn was a function of population homogeneity. One Levittowner, describing her next-door neighbor, said, "We see eye to eye on things, about raising kids, doing things together with your husband, living the same way; we have practically the same identical background." Conversely, the people who reported less neighboring were those who could not find compatible people on the block....

Of course, some friendliness was built into the neighbor relationship, for people needed each other for mutual aid. In a community far from the city, women are cut off from relatives and old friends—as well as from commuting husbands—so that readiness to provide mutual aid is the first criterion of being a good neighbor. This includes not only helping out in emergencies, but ameliorating periodic loneliness by being available for occasional coffee-klatsching and offering informal therapy by being willing to listen to another's troubles when necessary. Helping out also offers an opportunity—rare in everyday life—to practice the dictates of the Judeo-Christian ethic, and brings appropriate emotional rewards. The reciprocity engendered by mutual aid encourages—and allows—neighbors to keep a constant watch on each other, as they do in established neighborhoods everywhere....

[D]espite a fairly high building density—five to six houses to the acre—there was no pressure to be sociable. Neighboring rarely extended more than three or four houses away in each direction, so that the "functional neighborhood" usually consisted of about ten to twelve houses at the most, although people did say hello to everyone on the block....

The critics' charge that suburbanites indulge in hyperactive visiting to counteract boredom and loneliness brought on by the lack of urbanity in their communities is...mistaken. Coming from academia where the weekend brought parties, and having just lived in an Italian working class neighborhood in Boston where people maintained an almost continual "open house," I was surprised at how little entertaining took place among Levittowners. Although people often had visitors on Sunday afternoons, weekend evenings were not differentiated from the rest, a fact that should be obvious from the high ratings of television programs on the air at that time. I would guess that, on the average, Levittowners gathered informally not more than two or three times a month and gave formal parties about once a year, not counting those around Christmas and New Year's Eve. Social life in Levittown was not hyperactive by any stretch of the imagination, except perhaps in the first few months of putting out feelers. I suspect that the critics either confuse the early hyperactivity with the normal pattern once life had settled down, or they generalize from observations in upper middle class suburbs, where partying is a major leisure activity.

Admittedly, the critics could question my assumption that an increase in social life is equivalent to an improvement in its quality, and argue that it represents instead an escape from pervasive boredom. If the Levittowners had found their social life boring, however, they would either have cut it down or complained about greater boredom. The data indicate just the opposite, for those visiting more were less bored (and vice versa), and besides, if social life had been as dull as the critics claim, why would the interview respondents have been so enthusiastic about the friendliness of their fellow residents?

The suburban critique is quite emphatic on the subject of demographic homogeneity. For one thing, homogeneity violates the American Dream of a "balanced" community where people of diverse age, class, race, and religion live together. Allegedly, it creates dullness through sameness. In addition, age homogeneity deprives children—and adults—of the wisdom of their elders, while class, racial, and religious homogeneity prevent children from learning how to live in our pluralistic society. Homogeneity is said to make people callous to the poor, intolerant of Negroes, and scornful of the aged. Finally, heterogeneity is said to allow upward mobility, encouraging working and lower class people to learn middle class ways from their more advantaged neighbors.

There is no question that Levittown is quite homogenous in age and income as compared to established cities and small towns, but such comparisons are in many ways irrelevant. People do not live in the political units we call "cities" or "small towns"; often their social life takes place in areas even smaller than a census tract. Many such areas in the city are about as homogeneous in class as Levittown, and slum and high-income areas, whether urban or suburban, are even more so....

By ethnic and religious criteria, Levittown is much less homogeneous than these other areas because people move in as individuals rather than as groups, and the enclaves found in some recently built urban neighborhoods, where 40 to 60 per cent of the population comes from one ethnic or religious group, are absent. Nor is Levittown atypically homogeneous in age; new communities and subdivisions always attract young people, but over time, their populations "age" until the distribution resembles that of established communities.

Finally, even class homogeneity is not as great as community-wide statistics would indicate. Of three families earning $7000 a year, one might be a skilled worker at the peak of his earning power and dependent on union activity for further raises; another, a white collar worker with some hope for a higher income; and the third, a young executive or professional at the start of his career. Their occupational and educational differences express themselves in many variations in life style, and if they are neighbors, each is likely to look elsewhere for companionship. Perhaps the best way to demonstrate that Levittown's homogeneity is more statistical than real is to describe my own nearby neighbors. Two were Anglo-Saxon Protestant couples from small towns, the breadwinners employed as engineers; one an agnostic and a golf buff, the other a skeptical Methodist who wanted to be a teacher. Across the backyard lived a Baptist white collar worker from Philadelphia and his Polish-American wife, who had brought her foreign-born mother with her to Levittown; and an Italian-American tractor operator (whose ambition was to own a junkyard) and his upwardly mobile wife, who restricted their social life to a brother down the street and a host of relatives who came regularly every Sunday in a fleet of Cadillacs. One of my next-door neighbors was a religious fundamentalist couple from the Deep South whose life revolved around the church; another was an equally religious Catholic blue collar worker and his wife, he originally a Viennese Jew, she a rural Protestant, who were politically liberal and as skeptical about middle class ways as any intellectual. Across the street, there was another Polish-American couple, highly mobile and conflicted over their obligations to the extended family; another engineer; and a retired Army officer. No wonder Levittowners were puzzled when a nationally known housing expert addressed them on the "pervasive homogeneity of suburban life."

Most Levittowners were pleased with the diversity they found among their neighbors, primarily because regional, ethnic, and religious differences are today almost innocuous and provide variety to spice the flow of conversation and the exchange of ideas....

Critics of the suburbs also inveigh against physical homogeneity and mass-produced housing. Like much of the rest of the critique, this charge is a thinly veiled attack on the culture of working and lower middle class people, implying that mass-produced housing leads to mass-produced lives. The critics seem to forget that the town houses of the upper class in the nineteenth century were also physically homogeneous; that everyone, poor and rich alike, drives mass-produced cars without damage to their personalities; and that today, only the rich can afford custom-built housing. I heard no objection among the Levittowners about the similarity of their homes, nor the popular jokes about

being unable to locate one's own house. Esthetic diversity is preferred, however, and people talked about moving to a custom-built house in the future when they could afford it. Meanwhile, they made internal and external alterations in their Levitt house to reduce sameness and to place a personal stamp on their property....

Levittown and America

I began this study with [several] questions, the answers to which can be generalized to new towns and suburbs all over America. *First*, a new community is shaped neither by the builder, planner, and the organizational founder, nor by the aspirations with which residents come. A builder creates the physical shell of the community; a founder, the social one; but even when organizations and institutions are initiated by national bodies outside the community, they can only survive by attracting people, and responding to their demands....

These choices are not made in a vacuum, but involve values and preferences which people bring with them. Perhaps the most significant fact about the origin of a new community is that it is not new at all, but only a new physical site on which people develop conventional institutions with traditional programs. New towns are ultimately old communities on new land, culturally not significantly different from suburban subdivisions and urban neighborhoods inhabited by the same kinds of people, and politically much like other small American towns.

Second, most new suburbanites are pleased with the community that develops; they enjoy the house and outdoor living and take pleasure from the large supply of compatible people, without experiencing the boredom or malaise ascribed to suburban homogeneity. Some people encounter unexpected social isolation, particularly those who differ from the majority of their neighbors. Who will be socially isolated depends on the community; in Levittown, they were older couples, the well educated and the poorly educated, and women who had come from a cohesive working class or ethnic enclave or were used to living with an extended family. Such people probably suffer in every suburb; even though they want to escape from the close life of the "urban village," they miss their old haunts, cannot find compatible people, or do not know how to make new friends. But the least happy people are always those of lowest income and least education; they not only have the most difficulty in making social contacts and joining groups, but are also beset by financial problems which strain family tempers as well as family budgets. And if the suburb is designed for young adults and children, the adolescents will suffer from "nothing to do" and from adult hostility toward their youth culture and peer groups.

People's lives are changed somewhat by the move to suburbia, but their basic ways remain the same; they do not develop new life styles or ambitions for themselves and their children. Moreover, many of the changes that do take place were desired before the move. Because the suburb makes them possible, morale goes up, boredom and loneliness are reduced, family life becomes temporarily more cohesive, social and organizational activities multiply, and spare-time pursuits now concentrate on the house and yard. Some changes result from the move: community organizational needs encourage some people to become joiners for the first time, ethnic and religious difference demands more synagogue attendance, and social isolation breeds depression, boredom, and loneliness for the few who are left out. But change is not unidirectional; different people respond differently to the new environment, and the most undesirable changes usually stem from familial and occupational circumstances.

Third, the sources or causes of change are not to be found in suburbia per se, but in the new house, the opportunity for home ownership, and above all, the population mix—the people with whom one now lives. They bring about the intended increase in social life, the unintended increase in organizational activity, and, of course, the equally unintended social isolation. Some changes can be traced to the openness of the social structure in a new community and people's willingness to accept and trust each other, as well as to the random settling pattern which requires them to make friends with strangers next door or to leave the block for the larger community to find compatible people. But most result from the homogeneity of age and class of the population that buys into a new suburb. Indeed, the basic sources of change come from goals for home ownership, a free-standing house, outdoor living, and being with people of similar age and class, which have long been basic aspirations of American working and middle class cultures. Even unintended changes could be traced finally to national economic trends and cultural patterns that push people out of the city and provide incentives for builders to construct communities like Levittown. Ultimately, then, the changes people undergo in the move to the suburbs are only expressions of more widespread societal changes and national cultural goals.

NOTES

1. See Bennett Berger and Herbert Gans, this chapter. William Dobriner, *Class in Suburbia* (Englewood Cliffs, N.J. : Prentice-Hall, 1963).
2. For elaboration of this argument, see J. John Palen, *The Suburbs* (New York: McGraw-Hill, 1995), 82–84.
3. Robert Beuka, *SuburbiaNation: Reading Suburban Landscape in Twentieth-Century American Fiction and Film* (New York: Palgrave Macmillan, 2004), 112.
4. Editors' note: The early phase of Park Forest's development included extensive rental housing, designed as apartment courts that were grouped around "superblocks."

CHAPTER 11

Postwar Suburbs and the Construction of Race

INTRODUCTION

Mass suburbanization had inescapable repercussions for the history of race in postwar America. The suburban housing boom opened opportunities for property ownership and upward mobility to millions of white Americans, but this housing was rigidly segregated. Blacks and other racial minorities faced hostility at every level of the suburban housing market. Behind these defensive ramparts, an expansive sense of white identity and privilege took shape, supported by federal largesse, protected by local government and private enterprise, and pampered by economic abundance to which whiteness was the key. At the same time, however, growing numbers of African-American, Asian-American, and Latino families battled to enter the suburbs, and by transgressing racial boundary lines, they challenged not only the presumed whiteness of suburbia but the principle of white supremacy implicit in postwar suburban ideology. Contrary to popular stereotypes of placid consensus, the 1950s was a period of intensive, high-stakes, sometimes violent conflict over suburban space that pivoted squarely around the issue of race. That struggle would continue in subsequent years with outcomes that not only inscribed race on the metropolitan landscape, but also communicated powerful messages about belonging in America.

As detailed in chapter 9, mass suburbanization played an important role in expanding the white middle class after World War II. Federal programs made it possible for millions of European Americans to attain symbols of middle-class status such as college educations, small businesses, and homes of their own. At the same time, mass suburbia tied these benefits together in a coherent spatial package. The mushrooming suburbs became the setting for common aspirations, shared lifeways, and similar political and economic interests, all of which—because these new communities were premised on the principle of racial exclusion—reinforced solidarities of race while downplaying the significance of ethnic, religious, and occupational differences. Cementing this conflation of race and suburbia were the ever-present images in the national media of happy, white families celebrating the postwar suburban dream.

Yet the making of whiteness in postwar America also reflected darker, more fearful currents. As middle-class status was increasingly defined by one's possessions—rather than one's occupation—the home emerged as a critical class marker. The quality and value of one's home reflected on the family's status itself. A further presumption—encouraged by public policy and years of promotion by the real estate industry—was that racial mixing lowered property values. The logic thus extended full circle: if integration occurred, property values would drop, a family's status and very identity as part of the middle class would be destroyed. Individual and class identities, thus, became intertwined with the expectation of all-white neighborhoods. For families newly arrived in the middle class—recently unionized blue-collar workers earning a good wage or low-level white-collar workers in their first jobs—the stakes were highest. Their gains were fresh, and the fear of loss strong.

Underlying this sense of unease was the fast-changing population of many metropolitan areas. Concurrent with the white exodus to the suburbs, new waves of nonwhites were moving to the cities. Three million African Americans moved to urban areas during the 1940s and 1950s, the peak of decades of migration from the rural South. Joining them were more than 500,000 Puerto Ricans, who settled primarily in the urban Northeast. And in cities stretching from Chicago to Los Angeles, Mexican-American communities grew, augmented by a slowly growing current of immigration and by domestic migration from the *colonias*, ranches, and labor camps of the rural Southwest. Asian-American populations also swelled after passage of the 1965 Immigration Act, especially in cities along the west coast. During the postwar years, a growing middle class emerged in these communities. While comparatively few in number, they had economic resources to buy well-built homes in outlying urban and suburban neighborhoods. Moreover, in the aftermath of World War II, many were determined to challenge domestic racism. They quickly found themselves on a collision course with whites in the postwar metropolis.

To ward off these challenges, whites created a web of discrimination that secured the ties between race, social advantage, and metropolitan space. Mechanisms of segregation included collusion by real estate brokers, homebuilders and lenders, the influence of federal housing guidelines, action by local neighborhood associations, and municipal land use controls. These practices had a long history, but in the context of postwar suburbia—marked by the mass production of housing, federal subsidies, and expanded territory under the control of like-minded suburban governments—they represented something new, a regime of land use control and racial exclusion deployed on an unprecedented scale. Where these defenses failed, whites in cities and suburbs alike resorted to violence. Thus, house bombings, arson, death threats, physical assaults, and mob demonstrations became an ugly commonplace in postwar suburbia. African Americans were targeted in most of these attacks, but discrimination also affected Asian Americans and Latinos, though in less predictable, capricious ways. This bleak side of postwar urban history led historian Arnold Hirsch to refer to the 1940s and 1950s as "an era of hidden violence."[1]

Despite these obstacles, African Americans and other minority families carved footholds in postwar suburbia. Between 1940 and 1960, the number of black suburbanites alone increased by over a million, amounting to 2.5 million by 1960—about 5 percent of the total suburban population.[2] Regional variations typified this movement. In the South, where African Americans had lived outside the city for generations, developers built more than 200,000 new homes and apartments for black households during the 1950s. In many cities, construction reflected explicit planning for "Negro expansion," so that black communities could grow without upsetting segregation or provoking neighborhood violence. Ongoing annexation by southern cities brought most of these areas within the city limits, but otherwise the process of new construction on the rural margins of town mirrored suburban trends nationwide, creating a kind of suburbanization in the city that was characteristic of the Sunbelt region. Outside the South, by contrast, the proliferation of new suburban governments limited construction for minority families. There, African Americans and other nonwhite households battled for housing in existing neighborhoods. In every region, however, most of these suburbanites settled in the vicinity of older minority communities, confined there by fierce resistance in adjacent white sections. Their communities faced ongoing public and private incursions—school segregation, service cutbacks, redlining, lax zoning enforcement, and reckless urban renewal programs—that forced them to mobilize politically as racial communities and sharpened the connection between race and residence.

Even as pundits emphasized the universality of suburbia as the "American way of life," white and nonwhite suburbanites mobilized as members of local communities defined by race. Postwar suburbanization upheld, and even intensified, racial segregation in the metropolitan United States. For whites and nonwhites alike, race became naturalized by the separate and often unequal spaces that they occupied.

DOCUMENTS

Before the end of World War II, people of color began to challenge the limits that confined them to separate and unequal neighborhoods, and national civil rights organizations mobilized to support their efforts. Their first important target was race restrictive covenants. Suburbanites had used these agreements for decades to keep neighborhoods white. Legal suits, brought by black homebuyers with the support of the NAACP, reached the Supreme Court in 1948. In the case of *Shelley v. Kraemer*, the Court ruled that state enforcement of such restrictions violated the 14th Amendment guarantee of equal protection under the law for all citizens. The Court was equally clear, however, that discrimination by private individuals and groups was beyond the reach of the law.

Document 11-1 reflects the outpouring of hope with which black communities greeted the *Shelley* decision. This editorial in the nation's most influential black newspaper, the *Chicago Defender*, reveals the central role that many people attributed to covenants in preserving racial segregation, clearly a misjudgment of the depth of structural support for segregation in housing.

Proponents of segregation were quick to devise means to circumvent the ruling. **Document 11-2** appeared in *U.S. News & World Report* magazine just eleven days after *Shelley*. It outlined more than a dozen methods that white neighborhoods might use to preserve racial exclusivity. The report not only demonstrates the tenacity of white Americans' support for racial segregation but it illustrates basic assumptions that they made about race, property values, and neighborhoods. It also points obliquely to the advantages that suburbs held over city neighborhoods in maintaining future segregation. Civil rights advocates immediately assailed the piece as a "how to" guide for sidestepping the Court's decision.

U.S. News & World Report's predictions about the tenacity of segregation proved accurate. **Document 11-3, Document 11-4, and Document 11-5** illustrate ongoing struggles over urban and suburban territory that followed the *Shelley* decision. On the heels of their court victory, civil rights groups and other liberal organizations challenged federal support for builders who refused to sell houses to "nonwhites." Two articles from the *New York Times* in **Document 11-3** expose the struggle over racial restrictions at Levittown, New York. Like most postwar builders, the Levitts refused to rent or sell housing to blacks or other minorities, and they claimed no responsibility for racial segregation. That, they said, was what consumers wanted. Not long after this interchange, the FHA announced that it would stop underwriting new developments that contained race restrictive deeds, and it eliminated references to the desirability of such agreements, which had been part of its guidelines since the 1930s. Nonetheless, the FHA did not withhold its support for homebuilders like Levitt, who simply refused to sell to nonwhites. That policy would not be enacted until the early 1960s, by which time the FHA alone had underwritten more than 7 million new homes, most of them in the suburbs and about 98 percent of which were limited to "Caucasians only." **Document 11-4** is an excerpt from housing activist Charles Abrams's 1955 book *Forbidden Neighbors,* an impassioned attack on housing discrimination. Abrams exposed a more drastic tactic deployed by white suburbanites to resist integration: the use of violence and intimidation. In addition to documenting countless acts of racial terrorism against African Americans who tried to move into all-white neighborhoods, Abrams excoriated the FHA and the white real estate industry for their roles in promoting segregation. Abrams's comprehensive and biting critique has served as the point of departure for many contemporary scholars who have examined the role of race in the postwar metropolis. **Document 11-5** offers a personal perspective on suburban housing discrimination. In testimony before the U.S. Commission on Civil Rights, baseball pioneer Jackie Robinson recounts his own family's difficulty in finding a place to live in the suburbs of New York. Robinson's struggle, despite his wealth and fame as a national sports hero, underscores the barriers that faced all black families seeking suburban homes. **Document 11-6** reveals the capricious nature of housing discrimination and the arbitrary manner in which "race" lines were drawn, especially as they applied to Latinos. Ralph Guzman of the Alianza Hispano-Americana of Los Angeles, a Latino service organization, spotlights an effort by local Realtors to block the sale of a suburban home to a Mexican-American couple. The attempt failed, but the agent who listed the home faced severe financial repercussions.

Document 11-7 and **Document 11-8** shed light on parallel struggles in the South where explicit racial planning had strong roots. **Document 11-7** records a proposal by African-American civic leaders in Atlanta to establish a separate place for themselves in the postwar suburbs. Rather than challenge white homeowner resistance, they pressed local officials for the green light to build "self-contained" neighborhoods on the city's edge. By the mid-1950s, construction of houses and apartments for black families had begun in most of these proposed areas. Many Southern cities pursued a similar strategy in the 1940s and 1950s, though none achieved Atlanta's level of new construction. **Document 11-8** reflects the intensity of white fears about black encroachment in Atlanta's newly annexed suburban fringe. Letters from residents of these areas point to a sense of white ownership over neighborhoods and institutions and to the obvious, almost natural connections that Americans drew between race and metropolitan space in the postwar years.

In contrast to the widespread efforts to maintain segregation, a handful of communities sought to undermine the equation of race and space by working for stable racial integration. As more minority families moved to suburbs in the 1960s, neighborhood-based integration groups sprang into being across the country. **Document 11-9**, a 1957 profile of Teaneck, New Jersey, one suburb that led the way in this movement, describes the difficulties, conflicts, and ambiguous motives that characterized many of these efforts. Looking ahead to chapter 13, the document also illustrates a level of civic engagement and locally based political mobilization that characterized many suburban places during the postwar decades—regardless of whether residents' politics leaned toward the left or the right.

Finally, as civil rights demonstrations, urban rioting, and neighborhood violence shook the nation in the late 1960s, the artist Norman Rockwell chose a suburban driveway to represent the challenge of racial equality to the nation. **Document 11-10**, which appeared on the cover of the weekly magazine *Look* in May 1967, offered a hopeful image of racial parity in America, using a color-blind rendering of the suburban good life as the ultimate answer to the nation's problems.

Compare and contrast the assumptions that various Americans expressed about race and neighborhoods in the postwar period. Why did whites react to racial integration in the ways they did? What factors were most important in the persistence of racial segregation during this period? In what ways did the separation of American neighborhoods affect ideas about race? How did ideas about class intermingle with those about race? What aspects of this history surprise you the most?

11-1. THE *CHICAGO DEFENDER* CELEBRATES THE SUPREME COURT'S RULING ON RESTRICTIVE COVENANTS, 1948

Source: "Let Freedom Ring," *Chicago Defender*, May 15, 1948.

The United States Supreme Court has made perhaps, the greatest contribution to American democracy that is within its power to make. The unanimous decision of the Justices prohibiting judicial enforcement of restrictive covenants brings to a dramatic close one of the ugliest developments in American history.

These covenants have been responsible for more human misery, more crime, more disease and violence than any other factor in our society. They have been used to create the biggest ghettoes in history. They have been used to pit race against race and to intensify racial and religious prejudices in every quarter.

In outlawing these covenants the Supreme Court has not only upheld the Constitutional rights of Negro citizens, it has laid the ground work for the building of interracial peace and goodwill. It has given substance to the dream of democracy.

Tribute must be paid to the Negro Press, the National Association for the Advancement of Colored People and to all the organizations and their leaders, white and colored, who have fought so valiantly to abolish restrictive agreements. Special honors must go to Thurgood Marshall [who argued the case before the Court] and the legal department of the NAACP which he heads.

In this gallant fight, however, we found an ally in the Federal government itself. It was Solicitor General Philip Perlman at the bidding of Attorney General Tom Clark and President Truman who opened the argument against restrictive covenants in the hearings before the Supreme Court.

The Solicitor General declared "They have been told, time and again, by this Court, that this is a Government of laws and not of men, and that all men are equal before the law. They wait—millions of them—outside this courtroom door, to learn whether these great maxims really apply to them."

The profound and eloquent appeal of the Federal government before the court on behalf of full citizenship for all Americans marked a high point in this historic struggle. President Truman threw the whole weight of the Executive branch of the government behind the fight to emancipate us from these restrictions which have for so long despoiled our lives and impeded our progress.

In some quarters the decision of the high court is being viewed with great alarm. The professional bigots who exploit native racism for their own profitable ends have been struck a serious blow. By the same token the apostles of defeatism on the left who would overthrow our democratic system have been routed.

Today it must be clear even to the most skeptical among us that we can and will achieve full citizenship by working within the framework of our constitutional democracy.

We salute Chief Justice Vinson and the Associate Justices of the Supreme Court who, without dissent, have condemned the restrictive covenant to the "limbo of things as dead as slavery."

11-2. *U.S. NEWS & WORLD REPORT* REVIEWS STRATEGIES TO PRESERVE SEGREGATION, 1948

Source: "Real Estate: 'Exclusive…Restricted,'" *U. S. News & World Report* 24 (May 14, 1948). Copyright © U.S. News & World Report, L.P. Reprinted with permission.

A property owner today is legally free to sell or rent his property to anyone, regardless of racial restrictions that may have governed what he did with that property in the past. A court no longer will enforce covenants that have barred sale or rental of property in some neighborhoods to Negroes or Chinese or other racial or religious groups.

The Supreme Court, in denying court enforcement to real estate covenants that restrict sale on the basis of race or color, upset a property restriction that has been imposed upon real estate in many parts of the country….

A mild revolution, therefore, is in sight. It now is to be more difficult for exclusive neighborhoods to protect their status. Occasional moves by Negroes into white neighborhoods, even exclusive neighborhoods, may be expected.

Widespread and immediate changes in the character of neighborhoods are not likely, however….Besides, alternative methods are expected to be used to try to maintain the status quo. These will be based in some instances on new plans and in others upon pressures that can be brought to accomplish indirectly what formerly was done directly through covenants.

Plans that have the effect of restricting neighborhoods and that apparently are within the law, under the ruling of the Supreme Court, already are in use here and there. These plans are being studied by property owners who now want to figure out exactly where they stand. Any of these plans that prove practical as well as legally valid are expected to come into more general use.

Self-enforcement of a covenant that limits property ownership in a neighborhood to the members of a racial or religious group is one such plan. Covenants still can be written into deeds, and signers of a covenant can be required to deposit cash or give bond, as a guarantee that they will abide by its terms.

The Supreme Court, in its decision, specifically declared that "private restrictive agreements" of property owners are legal, so long as the purposes of these agreements are achieved through "voluntary adherence to the terms" and without the aid of governmental action through the courts. Thus, if a restrictive covenant is violated by one of the signers, he may be penalized through forfeiture of the cash he deposited when he signed the covenant. Whether the courts would uphold such a forfeiture, however, still is considered an open question….

Requiring membership in a club or a cooperative as a condition for owning or occupying property is a second plan, already in use, by which sale of property is restricted to certain groups. In one type of club, the property is owned by the club itself. The householder-member simply owns shares of stock and is assigned certain property for occupancy. This type of club is considered legal, without any question. But it has the drawback that the householder never has individual title to the property he occupies.

Legal opinion is not so unanimous on the question of whether requiring membership in a club as a condition for individual ownership of property would be enforceable in the courts....

Meanwhile, many real estate subdivisions probably will be platted and sold in connection with golf clubs, tennis clubs, gardening clubs, and a great variety of other clubs based on some common activity or interest....

High occupancy standards, now in effect in many communities, are being used as a means of maintaining the general character of a neighborhood and of indirectly achieving, to a high degree, the same ends sought by racial restrictions. Such requirements as the minimum cost of dwellings and number of occupants per room are considered legal and enforceable.... Plans under which a college degree or other education is required of an occupant, however, appears [sic] to be in the same category, from a legal standpoint, as those involving club membership or approval of neighbors.

Damage suits, or the threat of damage suits, may possibly be used by one or more signers of a covenant to discourage any other signer from selling his property in violation of the covenant's terms. The Supreme Court's decision on covenants clearly says that courts cannot invoke the racial restrictions of covenants to invalidate transfers of property or to evict occupants of property. But the decision does not specifically debar breach-of-contract suits for damages brought by covenant signers against other signers who have violated the covenant....

None of these plans is entirely free from legal or practical weaknesses as a means of controlling occupancy of a residential area. But their widespread use will tend to minimize or to postpone any general lowering of property values or change in the character of neighborhoods.

Pressures of various kinds also will play a part in maintaining the status quo of neighborhoods and communities where ownership restrictions have been based on race or color.

Social pressure—that is, a hostile attitude on the part of neighbors to unwanted newcomers—will operate to a certain extent. But experience has shown that social pressure by itself will not keep a community's gates entirely closed to members of minority groups.

Financial pressure is expected to give much greater leverage over transfers and rentals of property. Private lending institutions, often interested in maintaining property values in a community, can exercise a high degree of control over the sale or rental of residential property in the community. This is exercised sometimes through giving or withholding mortgage or other loans to an individual, and sometimes through the giving or denying of credit to a builder.

Customs of real estate dealers in many communities will reinforce the financial pressure exerted by lending institutions. Real estate dealers usually are interested in maintaining property values in neighborhoods in which they do business. Therefore they may avoid selling to persons whose presence they think will lower values.

Methods of harassment by police and other local authorities may be employed to some extent to maintain residential segregation. In the South, where fewer property covenants have been adopted than in other areas, such methods have been a factor in keeping Negroes from becoming residents of sections where white persons have their homes.

In one way or another, plans or pressures of many types are likely to be utilized by community groups, in order to build up resistance to sudden or widespread changes in the residential areas they occupy....

Ramifications.... Years will elapse before property owners can be absolutely sure what methods of restricting neighborhoods are enforceable in the courts and what methods are not. Most of the plans now being studied can be applied much more easily to new real estate projects than to neighborhoods already settled. Changes in these older neighborhoods probably will be slow in coming, but the basis of property values in many of them appears to have been fundamentally altered.

11-3. THE *NEW YORK TIMES* RE-PORTS ON RACIAL EXCLUSION AT LEVITTOWN, 1949

"FHA Asked to Curb Negro Housing Ban," March 12, 1949.

Copyright © 1949 by The New York Times Co. Reprinted with permission.

The Federal Housing Administration was asked yesterday to forbid the exclusion of Negroes from any housing insured by that agency.

Specific target of a delegation that called at the FHA offices, 90 Church Street, was William J. Levitt, whose organization has built thousands of small homes for veterans on Long Island.

Besides members of the American Labor Party [ALP], National Association for the Advancement of Colored People, Civil Rights Congress, and Nassau-Suffolk Consumers Council, the group of eleven persons included James Mayweathers. Mr. Mayweathers said that although he is a veteran, he has been excluded, as a Negro, from a group of prospective purchasers of homes Mr. Levitt's organization is building under FHA commitments.

Mr. Mayweathers conducts a floor-polishing service from his home at 88 Rosell Street, East Williston, L.I. [Long Island]. He said he had applied for one of 350 houses, the first of 4,000 to be built in Roslyn, L.I. To do this, he said, he had stood in line outside the model home there from 7 a.m. Saturday until 7:30 o'clock the following morning.

On Sunday morning, he said, Mr. Levitt told him that a Negro could not buy one of the houses. This statement was confirmed by John S. Fells, a real estate broker of Great Neck....

Henry Doliner, executive secretary of the ALP in Nassau and Suffolk Counties, said that speedy action was urgent. He requested that the FHA hold up processing of sales of the 350 houses in Roslyn, pending determination of the right of Negro veterans to be considered equally with white veterans.

Harold M. Clay, FHA district director who received the group, said that matters of policy could not be decided here. He said

that a meeting had been arranged for next Friday at 3 p.m. with Thomas G. Grace, state FHA director to discuss the question with Mr. Fells and the others.

Meanwhile, the district director agreed to pass on to Mr. Grace the delegation's request. This was that Mr. Grace recommend to his superiors in Washington that all existing and future FHA commitments be adjusted to forbid sale or rental of homes to "white Caucasians only." It was requested also that Mr. Grace recommend that Negro veterans be placed on the same footing with white veterans, as applicants for sale or rental of home [sic].

"FHA Can't Prevent Housing Ban," March 19, 1949.

Copyright © 1949 by The New York Times Co. Reprinted with permission.

The Federal Housing Administration lacks the powers to bring builders to terms with Negro buyers on FHA-backed projects, Thomas G. Grace, state director, told a protesting group yesterday in a discussion of the Levittown, L.I. race discrimination problem.

In a conference at 90 Church Street with about thirty persons who represented veterans, tenants, labor unions, cooperative buyers and civil rights organizations, headed by the National Association for the Advancement of Colored People, the FHA director said Federal approval of a mortgage cannot be withdrawn if the owner writes into a lease or deed a clause barring occupancy to any race, religious or national group.

He said that in August, 1947, he had gone to some length to have William J. Levitt, Long Island builder, eliminate from a prospectus an objectionable clause barring Negroes. The clause read:

"No dwelling shall be used or occupied except by members of the Caucasian race, but the employment and maintenance of other than Caucasian domestic servants shall be permitted."

Mr. Grace said his office was restricted to a survey of the plans, materials and financial backings of FHA-backed projects.

Persons in the discussion who were

introduced as representatives of the NAACP, the American Jewish Congress, the American Jewish Committee, the Civil Rights Congress, the National Lawyers Guild, the American Labor Party of Long Island and a local of the United Automobile Workers, CIO, were unanimous in condemning the policy that the Federal Government was concerned with no social values, "only brick and mortar."...

Mr. Grace said that on more than one occasion his office had approved "interracial" projects seeking federal loans. He told the group they were wrong "in asking me to be impertinent or insubordinate" in approaching his superiors in Washington....

11-4. CHARLES ABRAMS ATTACKS HOUSING DISCRIMINATION, 1955

Source: Selection from pages 103-119 from *Forbidden Neighbors* by Charles Abrams. Copyright © 1955 by Harper & Brothers. Reprinted by permission of HarperCollins Publishers.

On Thursday, July 12, 1951, Governor Adlai Stevenson declared martial law in Cicero [Illinois], a city adjoining Chicago, after police and sheriff's forces declared themselves unable to cope with a mob of 4000 which had assembled to keep Harvey E. Clark, Jr., a Negro war veteran, from moving his family into a $60 apartment. The rioting had started the previous Tuesday and raged without interruption up to early Friday morning. Law and order collapsed as the mob ran free and the police looked on. Flares, bricks, and burning torches were thrown into the $100,000 apartment house; radiators and walls were ripped out; furniture was thrown from the windows, and trees were torn up by the roots to be burned as the mob cheered. Policemen joked with the mobsters as though it were a prank. The mayor and the chief of police were "out of town." When the militia tried to push back the mob at bayonet point, four militiamen were felled and only the superb discipline of the others as they saw their men go down kept the riot from turning into massacre.

The implications of the riot were too ugly for many people to face. The riot was variously held to be a nasty incident that does not happen too often, a wicked occurrence in a wicked city that is the haunt of Al Capone's former mob, an eruption provoked by "alien" Czechs and Poles who have not yet learned the American way of life, a teenagers' lark that got out of control, and a rumpus started by communists. It was not at all surprising that a Cook County grand jury even added the interpretation it was all a "Negro plot."

Yet behind the Cicero affair lies one of the most disturbing violations of civil rights in American history. Its most ominous aspect is the growing use of legal processes to flout civil rights. The Cicero riot was only a recent phase of this development.

The Cicero rioting started when a Mrs. DeRose, who owned the apartment house, got into a controversy with her tenants and was ordered to refund a portion of the rent. Shortly after, out of spite, profit, or both, she rented an apartment to Clark, a graduate of Fisk University. Movement of Negroes into white areas is nothing new in Chicago. But it was new in Cicero which, like...many similar communities, had successfuly resisted Negro settlement.

When it was learned that a Negro was moving into the apartment house, a high Cicero official arrived to warn Mrs. DeRose there would be "trouble" if Clark moved in. The city, he said, could not be responsible for keeping order. Two policemen then came to tell Mrs. DeRose she could not "get away with it." At 2:30 P.M. on June 8 a moving van containing $2000 worth of Clark's furniture drove up to the house and was halted by the police. The rental agent was ushered out with a drawn revolver at his back. A jeering crowd had gathered and Clark was then told to get out or he would be arrested "for protective custody." A detective warned him, "I'll bust your damned head if you don't move."

"At about 6 P.M.," reads Clark's affidavit, "the chief of police of Cicero rushed out of the alley nearby followed by twenty men and grabbed my arm." The chief told him to "'get out of here fast. There will be no moving into this building.'...He hit me about eight times while he was pushing me ahead of him toward my car which was parked across the street. I was trying to walk but he was trying to make me move faster. When we reached my car, I opened the door and the chief shoved me inside and said 'Get out of Cicero and don't come back in town or you'll get a bullet through you.'"

When suit was brought against the Cicero police through the National Association for the Advancement of Colored People, United States District Judge John P. Barnes, on June 26, enjoined the city from "shooting, beating or otherwise harassing Clark"—one of the most unusual injunctions in legal annals. "You are going to exercise the same diligence in seeing that these people move in as you did in trying to keep them out," said the judge.

When Clark moved in, word was passed along that there would be "fun" at the apartment house. Crowds gathered, tensions rose, and a rock smashed the window of Clark's apartment.

On Wednesday, July 11, some of the white families in the apartment house, warned of impending trouble, stored their furniture and moved out. By dusk a crowd of 4000 cut the ropes put up by the police. Only 60 policemen were assigned to the scene. The uniformed policemen in front of the building stepped out of the way when the crowd moved forward; the plainclothesmen simply mixed with the crowd as fires were set inside the building. Women carried stones from a nearby rockpile to bombard the windows while policemen stood by.

A few state police and twenty deputy sheriffs under County Sheriff John E. Babb, who arrived Wednesday evening, were at the scene, but little was done to disperse the mob. When the sheriff's deputies asked Cicero firemen to turn hoses on the crowd, the firemen refused to do so without orders from their lieutenant, who was unavailable. After $20,000 in damage had been done to the building, Babb requested the Governor to send in the state militia. The troops arrived and finally pushed back the mob at bayonet point. Four of the militiamen were felled in the process.

The Cicero riot received more than usual notice in Chicago, although for two days the news had been played down. In fact, most Chicagoans saw the riot on television before they read it in their newspapers. But when the Governor called out the National Guard, the news broke all over the country, forcing the grand jury to investigate.

On January 18, 1952, the grand jury brought in its findings. Instead of indicting the hoodlums responsible for the vandalism which denied Clark the right to live where he chose, it indicted the NAACP attorney who was defending his right. It also indicted the owner, her lawyer, and her rental agent, charging them all with conspiracy to injure property by causing "depreciation in the market selling price." The right of a Negro to buy or rent a home, which is guaranteed by the federal Civil Rights Law of 1866, was thus declared to be null and void in Illinois.

Ultimately, after protest by civic groups, the indictments were dropped and the United States Attorney General ordered an investigation. Indictments were then obtained against the town president, the fire chief, the police chief, the town attorney, and three policemen. The charges were dismissed against the town president and fire chief. Later the police chief and two policemen were fined a total of $2500.

The federal prosecution was hailed as a courageous step forward. It could more accurately be called rare, since incursions upon civil rights in housing have not often stirred action by federal officials.

Also forgotten was the fact that the Cicero riot was only the most recent of a series in Cook County. The other riots were either not publicized, or were reported like local fires. From July, 1949, to July, 1952, there were four such riots in Chicago, and there have been nine altogether from 1945 to 1954. In addition, from 1949 to the day of the Cicero outbreak there were more than a hundred lesser incidents in the Chicago area: bombings, fires, or organized assaults against Negro families, one of these by a hit-and-run incendiary who started a fire that cost ten lives. Another incident was the bombing [in the suburb, Oak Park] of the home of Dr. Percy Julian, the eminent Negro scientist....

The immediate cause of the flare-ups differs in each case, but the underlying cause is always the same: Negroes try to move out of their overcrowded slum areas and are met with violence, or the presence of an occasional Negro is interpreted as signalizing an influx. Groups are permitted to gather around the target; they draw larger groups, including the subnormal, the prejudiced, the emotionally immature, and youth seeking "fun." These are encouraged to take the lead. Rumors begin to fly, emotion rises, order breaks down, and normally law-abiding citizens become part of the mob action. Frustrated by not being able to get at the target, the mob looks for a scapegoat—Negroes, Jews, communists, strangers, intellectuals. In five of the recent outbreaks, police showed no willingness to protect the Negroes in their rights, and in some their forces were even deployed to let the victims take their beatings. The potential for similar miniature race wars exists in other parts of urban America....

The Cook County outbreaks were no isolated incidents chargeable to local conditions or to some single criminal segment of the population. They are only one of the most recent symptoms of a major disease in the American scene. The police that stood by as Negroes were beaten and their homes burned were echoing the sentiments of those they thought were the "good people." The Cook County jury that accused the landlady, her lawyer, her agent, and the NAACP lawyer was not corrupt but only converting those sentiments into a formal indictment. Nor were the rioters all vandals or gangsters. They often had the sanction of their elders, of the community, of the police, and of parts of the press. The Cicero police who tried to prevent the Negro family from moving in undoubtedly believed they were acting in the interests of their community. When the mayor and the chief of police "couldn't be found," it was because they knew that if they stopped the riot they would lose any chances of reelection. The sheriff of Cook County felt politically embarrassed when he tried to enforce the law....

Chicago and Cicero are cities where opposition to housing for Negroes may pay off politically. It is one of the outstanding examples of two cities where too many people have lost their ethical sense on the race issue. It will take a long and laborious effort to restore it. Nor will it ever succeed until its press and enlightened citizenry, its responsible businessmen and its public officials, all shift from their attitudes of indifference and give the cause leadership.

11-5. JACKIE ROBINSON TESTIFIES TO DISCRIMINATORY "BEANBALLS" IN HOUSING, 1959

Source: U.S. Commission on Civil Rights, *Hearings before the United States Commission on Civil Rights: Housing*, vol. I, *Hearings Held in New York, February 2-3, 1959* (Washington, D.C.: Government Printing Office, 1959).

As you know, discrimination in housing deeply affects millions of Americans here in New York and elsewhere in the United States. I speak as a personnel executive of a company with some 1,000 employees and as a director of a building company and as an American Negro.

I read in a page 1 story of the *New York Times* on January the 28th that—and I quote: "The Commission has received no complaints from New York about housing bias." Well, I am sure you learned members of the Commission are not naive, and I am sure you are aware that directly and indirectly discrimination in renting or purchasing apartments and homes does exist in New York, and I guarantee you, gentlemen, that beanballs are still being thrown in the housing field as well as on the ballfield....

When my wife and I decided to move from St. Albans, Long Island [ca. 1956], we were put through the usual bag of tricks right in this State. At first we were told the house we were interested in had been sold just before we inquired, or we would be invited to make an offer, a sort of a sealed bid, and then we'd be told that offers higher than ours had been turned down. Then we tried buying houses on the spot for whatever price was asked. They handled this by telling us the house had been taken off the market. Once we met a broker who told us he would like to help us find a home, but his clients were against selling to Negroes. Whether or not we got a story with the refusal, the results were always the same. Because of these tactics, we began to look in Connecticut; and we finally were able to settle in Stamford due to the strong efforts of some very wonderful people there.

Now, this leads to a basic truth about ending segregation in housing, as in any other phase of our life: That is, Government regulations alone are not enough. Public housing operated on an open-occupancy basis by itself is not enough. True, we need both of these; but we also need positive action by individuals to spur bias-free, privately built housing.

I went to Washington about 10 times in recent years to confer with officials, seeking action which would grant Negroes some progress toward equal rights in housing. The officials have been very polite to me but, regardless of the reason, nothing has been done.

In the 25 years that the FHA has been in existence a grand total of some 200,000 dwelling units available to Negroes have been built with FHA assistance. Meanwhile, builders have constructed a million units a year or better for quite awhile. Now, 200,000 units may sound like quite a bit of housing, but it is a tiny fraction compared with the 25-year total of housing built with FHA aid. FHA is not necessarily at fault. It is just that hardly anyone has built private housing open to Negroes until very recently.

We use such words as "discrimination" and "equality," but they don't tell the story.

There is a builder in New York whose conscience was troubled about housing discrimination against Negroes. Nevertheless, he was afraid that if he would let just one Negro buy a home it would spoil his business success. So, with a guilty conscience, he stalled a Negro buyer for just about a year and a half. Things came to a head when the Negro broke into tears in the builder's office and left. The builder said, "If he had waited just another minute, I would have sold him the house." The builder now sells to Negroes, but he had to first feel some measure of the harm that he was working on another human being.

We know that for many charity begins at home. So do hate, hostility, and delinquency, especially when the home environment is a slum, lacking adequate space, lacking facilities, but not lacking for high rentals, while infested with insects and rodents....

Because of discrimination in housing, the end result for many is mental and physical suffering, ofttimes personal tragedy, domestic difficulties, discouragement, a waste of human potential, and, finally, an abundance of community problems...

11-6. CIVIL RIGHTS ADVOCATE RALPH GUZMAN REVEALS DISCRIMINATION'S "NEW LOOK," 1956

Source: Ralph Guzman, "The Hand of Esau: Words Change, Practices Remain in Racial Covenants," *Frontier* 7 (June 1956). Reprinted with permission from the June, 1956 issue of *Frontier*.

When a home was refused to the famous Dr. Sammy Lee, the Olympic diving champion, newspapers throughout the country and the world carried the story. Indignation blazed from all directions, and leaders of the country denounced the small town of Garden Grove, Calif., because it had refused a home to a famous Olympic star.

Minority groups watched. The cynics said: "He will get a home. After all, he is Sammy Lee." In Lynwood, Calif., a similar case involving a Mexican family and a courageous realtor received little attention. There were no famous names and consequently no Vice-Presidential pronouncements.

Yet, the Lynwood incident is more important than the Lee case for it exposes the "new look" in restrictive covenants. It uncovers for the first time how the real estate boards have successfully continued "lily white" policies—in spite of the U.S. Supreme Court's 1950 [sic] decision in *Shelley v. Kraemer* outlawing the enforcement of restrictive covenants.

Lynwood, Compton, and South Gate are three small cities lying south of the downtown Los Angeles area. They are generally neat communities with well kept lawns and painted homes. The residents for the most part are Anglos of the Protestant faith.... But, Mr. and Mrs. Average American do not live in those towns.

There are no Negroes, few Mexicans and fewer Orientals. Minority people, living in the crowded districts of Los Angeles, have been excluded.

Two years ago, Manuel and Mary Portugal commenced escrow proceedings with Merle and Dorothea Stevens for a property on 10851 Alexander Street, Lynwood. Both families knew and liked each other. Their teen-age daughters were friends, and the Stevens were delighted to sell to the Portugals because "We would be glad to have them for neighbors ourselves."

The Stevens had listed their property for sale through the realty firm of Harry Beddoe, who was a member in good standing of the South Gate Realty Board. Beddoe placed the Stevens property on a multiple listing service, which meant that other members of the Realty Board could also advertise the home. This is a lucrative, cooperative system which provides the seller with good fast service. When the property is sold commissions are split between the realtor who first took the listing and the one made the actual sale.

The Realty firm of Ardell Thomas found the Portugals interested in the Stevens place and proceeded to show them the property. The transaction moved along its normal course until it suddenly hit a snag—someone had passed the word that the Portugals were Mexican. Agreement had already been reached between the Stevens and the Portugals, but still other prospective customers were being brought around to see the property.

"The place is sold," said Dorothea Stevens. She insisted that no one else be allowed to visit the property.

"They were trying to substitute a buyer," said Merle Stevens.... "I thought they were stalling for time in hopes that the Portugals would get disgusted and not take the place," Stevens stated.

Neighbors' Protest Halts Sale

When the word was passed, in the form of a letter signed by the neighbors, the transaction came to a halt. An indignant Stevens wrote a letter to the Realty Board demanding that the deal be permitted to proceed.... Beddoe, with whom the Stevens family had originally listed the property, agreed to stand by the wishes of his client to sell....

Sale of the Stevens place was completed in spite of the discovery that the Portugals were Mexican. A year ago, the members of the board of directors of the Southeast Realty Board held a meeting to discuss the transaction. The board summoned its own chairman, Ardell Thomas, whose firm had sold the property to the Portugals; John H. Schroeder, a salesman for the Thomas Realty, and Harry Beddoe.

A fine was levied against Thomas and Beddoe amounting to $310.85 apiece. Schroeder, the salesman, lost his commission. Thomas promptly paid, but Beddoe refused and unsuccessfully appealed the decision to the same board. Six months later, Beddoe was expelled from membership in the South Gate Realty Board for violating Article 35 of the Code of Ethics of the National Association of Real Estate Boards [Ed. note: known as Realtors, for short].

The article reads:

"A realtor should not be instrumental in introducing into a neighborhood a character of property or use which will clearly be detrimental to property values in a neighborhood."

This is the little known enforcement aspect which keeps realtors from selling to anyone who is not of the proper pigmentation, religious faith or national background. If the realtor insists on his right to sell to anyone he is fined, suspended, and possibly expelled from the realty board....

Before *Shelley v. Kraemer* the same article 35 read:

"A realtor should not be instrumental in introducing a character or use of property for occupancy by members of any race or nationality or any individual whose presence will be detrimental to the neighborhood."

Membership in the realty board brings important economic security through the multiple listing service. To be expelled means a considerable loss of business. The realtor can continue his business, but few people will risk dealing with someone who has been expelled....Beddoe, one of the most outstanding and reputable realtors in the state, was hard hit. Friends quietly urged him to keep up the fight, but few stepped forth to say it publicly....

There is one happy note to this incident: the neighbors who signed the letter opposing the presence of the Portugals have changed their minds. They now say the Portugals "are nice people." However, Harry Beddoe continues his struggle for economic survival....

11-7. ATLANTA HOUSING COUNCIL PROPOSES "NEGRO EXPANSION AREAS," 1947

Source: Atlanta Housing Council, "Proposed Areas for Expansions of Negro Housing in Atlanta, Georgia," May, 1947, Box 252, file 1, Papers of the Atlanta Urban League, Robert W. Woodruff Library, Atlanta University Center, Atlanta, Georgia.

During the war years and the ten depression years preceding it, far fewer houses were built in Atlanta and the rest of the nation than were needed for our expanding population. The war emergency and the present postwar period have brought increasing pressure for expansion of white housing facilities, but little attention has yet been given to adequate housing for the colored population. Of the many thousands of Atlanta's Negro veterans of this war, nearly forty percent are living doubled up in rooms without adequate sanitary and cooking facilities. The Negro population has overflowed the maximum possible use of present facilities with the result that colored families have been forced to move into housing areas in white fringe sections. Increasing friction between races and small scale attempts to rectify the situation have come about only because the Negro families involved have had no assistance and direction in determining which areas were most suitable for Negro housing and which areas could be used by them as their very own. The present overcrowding of central areas has resulted in a blight that tends to lower values of adjacent properties and is a direct menace to health, safety, morals, and the prosperity of the entire community....

All areas now being developed either for white or Negro occupancy should be properly planned not only with relation to the entire plan of the metropolitan area but also as individual integrated neighborhoods, each with its own park and recreational facilities, commercial areas, and schools. Greenbelts or strip parks should be provided along the delineating roads and highways of the various proposed sites, and additional greenbelts to separate neighborhoods within these communities. The design of the street pattern within each development should provide a continuous circulation system, so arranged as to discourage through traffic which would be a neighborhood safety hazard. All streets should be of ample width for free movement of local traffic, with off-street parking facilities provided at community shopping centers and at all multiple-dwelling areas. The size of single family lots should be 60x100 feet, with setback and lot coverage restrictions to assure sufficient open space for light and air, and to encourage gardening. Parks and playgrounds, with bathing facilities, should be incorporated in plans, and completed as soon as possible. All building and structures should be of approved type, carefully controlled by deed restriction and zoning.

The Proposed Areas for New Negro Housing—The following areas have been selected as the most logical and appropriate areas for expansion of Negro housing, to provide adequate residential accommodations from the point of view of employment of the group, extension of present Negro areas, and to round out the growth of the city to a more practical and economically sound concentric pattern:

1. Simpson, Hunter, and Gordon Roads Area—This is a westerly extension of the present Negro section centering around Ashby Street, north of West View. It is bounded by 150 to 300 ft, greenbelts north of West View to Chicamauga north to Hunter and around to the north side of Mozley Park, thence continuing west on the north side of the A. B. & C. railroad to or near Gordon Road. On the north the greenbelt should be located along the south side of Simpson Road (and the proposed Simpson super highway) continuing on a straight westerly line to meet the Gordon Road boundary. Much of this area is already occupied by Negroes and expansion in the area would consist primarily of filling

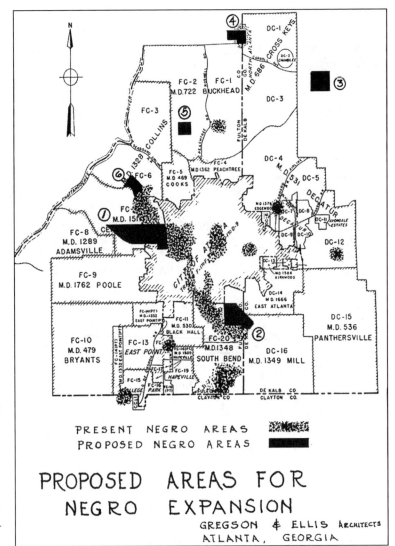

Figure 11-1 Proposed Areas for Negro Expansion, Atlanta, Georgia, 1947. This map locates the areas proposed by black civic leaders for the development of new African American housing. With few exceptions, they were adjacent to existing black neighborhoods in outlying areas not immediately attractive to whites. Illustration in original.

in the still vacant land in properly planned neighborhood developments.

2. Federal Penitentiary Area—The present large Negro settlement south and southeast of the prison should be extended (and is now being extended on a small scale) between McDonough Boulevard and the Southern Railroad as far south as the Fulton County line to fill in the undeveloped gap between East Atlanta and Hapeville and to provide housing for Negro employees at Candler Field, Ford Motor Company, and the many other industries which are located or are developing in and around Hapeville, College Park, East Point, and the southern section of Atlanta.

3. Doraville area—An initial Negro settlement of more than 100 families was established in the vicinity of the General Motors Plant to provide Negro workers now being utilized at that plant. There is considerable land around this Negro community which should be developed in several greenbelt neighborhoods to accommodate Negro workers who will be needed at the General Motors Plant and in other industries locating in and around Doraville and northeast of Atlanta....

5. Nancy Creek Area—There are several scattered Negro settlements in the vicinity of Peachtree and Nancy Creeks, Moores Mill Road, Howell Mill Road, Arden Road,

Wesley Road, West Paces Ferry Road, Northside Drive, and the New Marietta Highway. Although it may not be practical to fill in this entire section with new planned Negro neighborhoods, considerable expansion of residential greenbelted sections is not only possible but is urgently needed throughout this section to provide homes for workers in this area and to accomodate [sic] those Negro families who are gradually being squeezed out of the Bagley Park area in Buckhead....

Conclusions—It is recognized that the above areas cannot legally be designated as areas for expansion of Negro housing. However, in order to provide adequate housing in complete self-contained neighborhoods, to raise the standard of living for the minority group, to permit subsistence gardening, and to make possible the reclamation of the present blighted areas, all properly guided for accomplishment by private enterprise, it is hoped that business and civic groups alike will recognize and endorse the above recommended areas as being in fact, if not law, the proper areas in which Negroes may build and live without racial or economic conflict to strive with all of us for a more prosperous and more democratic community.

Figure 11-2 Robert Norwood—Norwood Manor Billboard, ca. 1955. Under the leadership of the Atlanta Urban League, Atlanta's black business elite mobilized to develop homes for African Americans in the city's suburban fringe. Here, land owner Robert Norwood poses before the subdivision that bears his name. Atlanta Urban League Papers, Box 326 Folder 7, Robert W. Woodruff Library of the Atlanta University Center.

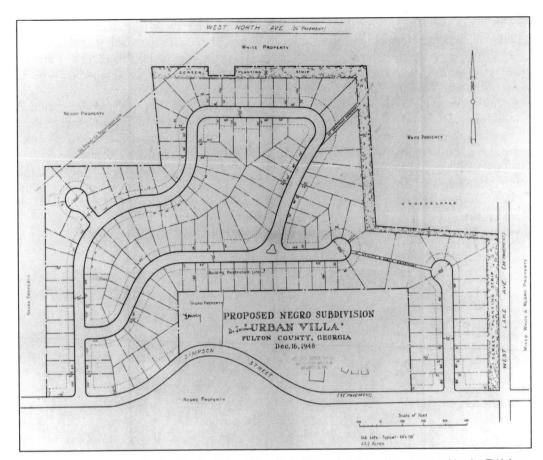

Figure 11-3 Proposed Subdivision Plan for Urban Villas, 1948. This subdivision plan, prepared by the FHA for a black veterans' group in Atlanta, bears the hallmarks of segregated suburban planning in the South. To secure white support, black civic leaders accepted and even emphasized the fifty-foot "screen planting strip" that separated the development from white neighbors. Atlanta Urban League Papers, Box 251 Folder 7, Robert W. Woodruff Library of the Atlanta University Center.

11-8. WHITES REACT TO FEARS OF BLACK ENCROACHMENT IN WEST ATLANTA, 1950s

Source: Open Letter, Southwest Citizens Association, Inc., January 28, 1954, and Atlanta Resident to Mayor William Hartsfield, September 28, 1956, Papers of the Atlanta Bureau of Planning, Box 3, files 5 and 6, Kenan Research Center at the Atlanta History Center, Atlanta, Georgia.

January 28, 1954

This letter is an appeal to your sense of fair play.

You are probably aware of the attempt made by a minority of the property owners in Collier Heights [a recently annexed neighborhood on Atlanta's west side] to force the sale of houses in this all white area to Negroes....

We have reliable information that the majority of the home owners do NOT want to sell their homes to colored. We sincerely believe that there is no real cause for alarm that this community will ever go colored. It is true that a Negro developer has purchased land west of Collier Heights. Actually, this tract is separated to some extent by natural lines, and eventually will be well separated by the proposed future highway pattern included in the Major Street Master Plan for Atlanta.

We believe that a few persons have deliberately agitated the situation by spreading false rumors concerning the aforesaid tract. In order to acquire the land west of Collier Heights, the developer had to take several unsold vacant lots in Collier Heights.

He has offered in good faith to hold these

vacant lots for sale to whites only. His development will not infringe on Collier Heights.

He has refused to handle the sales of white owned houses in this area. The Empire Real Estate Board of Negro realtors has repeatedly agreed that Collier Heights should remain a white community.

We have been very pleased to note the excellent cooperation of the Empire Board and their willingness to respect the integrity of white communities. This has been shown by their actions in respecting the "Gentlemen's Agreement" worked out by the Fourth Ward delegation of City Council in 1952, along Westview Drive, S. W. It also has been demonstrated by their refusal to invade Collier Heights.

We ask all members of the Atlanta Real Estate Board and all white Real Estate agents and brokers to demonstrate that they, too, can play fair. Let us not be a party to the grasping of a few Collier Heights people at the expense of the majority.

We ask you, as a fair-minded individual, to refuse to make a fast dollar at the expense of the majority of the 150 or more home owners in this always white community. If our Negro real estate people can play fair, certainly our white real estate men can do as much. Please refuse to have anything to do with sales of white owned homes in Collier Heights to colored.

We believe that Atlanta City Officials will be very pleased to learn that you will cooperate with us in this situation.

Sincerely yours,
S.B. Avery
President [Southwest Citizens Association, Inc.]

Atlanta, Georgia
September 28, 1956
Mr. Mayor Hartsfield,

I'm writing you to see if you can help us in trying to keep our Homes[.] [W]e own our Home here and the Colored are coming in on us and they don't want to give us nothing for our Home. They have already taken 2 Schools here so what can be done[?] 2 Families of Colored people have already moved in[.] [W]e don't go around trying to take what they got. My Husband is sick all

the time not able to work or to hunt a place to move. There are widow women around here with children and they have to walk for miles to schools [s]ince the Colored taken our School. [T]he people around are talking and have just about taken all they can[,] and I don't want no trouble[.] I love peace. Can you [help] us please[?] Will you help us[?] [P]lease let me know.

Mrs. W. L. Peters

11-9. *REDBOOK* EXAMINES INTEGRATION EFFORTS IN TEANECK, NEW JERSEY, 1957

Source: Selwyn James, "'We're Learning to Live Together,'" *Redbook Magazine* 109 (June 1957).

Two years ago, the residents of a quiet, tree shaded neighborhood of middle-income homes in Teaneck, New Jersey, were faced with the unexpected arrival of Negroes as neighbors.

"You'll soon be living in a Negro slum," real-estate agents told nervous homeowners. "Better sell your house now while you can still get a good price for it."

FOR SALE signs began sprouting like crabgrass after a heavy rain. Frightening rumors caused dozens of families to sell their homes for $1,000 to $3,000 below their true market value.

Faced with this situation, a group of level-headed young residents rallied their neighbors and halted panic sales. At a series of block meetings, they exposed the scare tactics of the real-estate agents and went to work on the fears, doubts, prejudices and outright misconceptions that threatened to destroy the community.

This turn of events,...was a heartening example of community action against race prejudice, and a model for hundreds of other traditionally all-white communities confronted with Negro home ownership.

But stories rarely have completely happy endings in real life. Indeed, they rarely end at all. The people of this Teaneck neighborhood, white and colored, have been living together now for two years....

What then, has happened to this Teaneck neighborhood since its well-publicized victory over bigotry? Are its residents still convinced that people of different races can live harmoniously together? Has panic selling recurred? Is the area indeed becoming a slum? ...

"You won't be able to say we have licked all our problems," Ed Schick, the 36-year-old homeowner who headed the campaign against panic selling, told me. "But nobody can say we have failed either." ...

Today, the community's white residents are pondering an inescapable fact. During 1956, more than 40 white families moved away, all of them selling their homes to Negro buyers. Now, about one-fifth of the 500 odd homes in the area are owned by Negroes. "Nothing has really changed," says Katherine Schick, Ed's 32-year-old wife. "We still live in a comfortable middle-class community. We have proved that Negroes and whites can live harmoniously together.

"But this is what puzzles me, proof doesn't seem to be enough. Although white residents now admit that most of their former fears were baseless, they are still moving. No, they're not panic selling, as a matter of fact, they're getting good prices for their homes. They seem ashamed of what they're doing; they stop talking to neighbors who have always said they are going to stay. They even get in touch with families who've already moved out to draw strength from them. I guess. What gets me is this, why have no white families moved into our neighborhood in the past year? *Where are the white buyers?*"

Many of the remaining white residents foresee the slow development of an all-Negro community. "What we would like to see is whites and Negroes moving into the neighborhood in approximately equal numbers," says a housewife with three young children. "Maybe that's asking too much, but we don't want to be a minority here."

Most concerned of all are the executive members of the Teaneck Civic Conference (TCC), the citizens' group formed to assure that neighborhood changes would be as painless as possible. In an informal survey of departing families, they are constantly seeking the reasons for what some despairing white residents call the "white exodus." About half of the families who sold out during 1956 seem to have had honestly nonracial motives for quitting the neighborhood. Husbands who had switched jobs wanted to live in an area more convenient to their place of work. Growing families needed additional living space, which was unavailable in the immediate neighborhood.

However, most other families were frankly unable to adjust to interracial living for a variety of reasons: bigoted, vindictive, irrational and merely human. A middle-aged couple, who for years had complained of a bellowing Saturday night (white) drunk next door, announced they were leaving when a Negro social worker and his wife moved in on the other side of them. A mother of two pretty teen-age daughters was worried about the prospect of mixed marriages. The people next door were plagued by the same fears, even though their daughter was not yet three-years-old. The parents of a nine-year-old boy who parroted street-corner gossip about race riots left out of simple anxiety for the lad's safety. A young factory executive was told by his boss that the house he lived in reflected badly on his company. For others the social pressure of friends tipped the balance against staying.

The TCC also discovered that many residents seem to set their own private limits to racial tolerance. One young couple announced they were "perfectly satisfied" with their Negro neighbors. "They watered our lawn for us every day while we were at the seashore," they reported. "And just take a look at their back yard—it's always spick-and-span. Why, they even keep *us* on our toes! We don't let our kids mess up the yard with their toys as they used to. Of course, we'll have to leave if another Negro family moves on the other side. We don't want to be hemmed in."

Residents with less tolerance have moved when a Negro bought a house on the same street; some families have arbitrarily set the presence of Negroes five houses away as a reason for leaving. "Live and let live is what I say," a 27-year-old salesman told the TCC, "but when they move into my block, I'm getting out fast. Next thing you know, they'll be inviting themselves into my living room." ...

The majority of families have adopted a wait-and-see attitude. They remain, not because they *prefer* interracial living, but because in the past two years they have discovered no serious objections to it. They simply refuse to leave pleasant homes in a neighborhood that has served them well for years.

Most of these remaining white famlies have long forgotten their worst fears—that the neighborhood would deteriorate while they watched, become shabby and littered before the year was out; that Negro owners would subdivide their homes, cramming two or three families into single-family houses, or even converting them into rooming houses for Negro bachelors; that they would allow their properties to run down, fail to pay their taxes promptly and default on mortgage payments.

A tour of the neighborhood—which comprises homes, new and old, in the $12,000-$30,000 bracket—reveals it to be as well-kept, tranquil and pleasant as ever. Indeed, many new Negro residents have made repairs on properties which the former white occupants had neglected, and at least a dozen Negro-owned homes show such solid improvements as new garages, concrete pathways, retaining walls to prevent erosion, new landscaping and basements converted into finished playrooms.

Public services remain unaffected by the interracial character of the neighborhood; garbage collection, street cleaning and repair, and police protection are as efficient as in other areas of Teaneck. The sharp increase in crime, the rodent invasions and epidemics which fainthearted residents predicted have not materialized. Nor have the day-to-day irritations and resentments many white residents expected would arise from having Negro neighbors. On the contrary, the experience has changed the racial attitudes of many remaining white families who, as recently as a year ago, never bothered to keep their prejudices a secret....

A minority of Teaneck homeowners constitutes a kind of moral dike which keeps the neighborhood from being inundated by a sudden flood of panic and prejudice. As Mrs. Harold Eby, a local dentist's wife, puts it, "Even if we had a legimate reason for leaving, it would be difficult to go now. It's like a marriage pact—you and your house are joined together till death do you part."

It is this embattled minority—the same tough-minded people who mobilized resistance to panic selling back in 1955—who today are reduced almost to despair every time a white homeowner puts his house up for sale. Despondently shouldering the blame, they ask themselves, "Could we have prevented it? Have we made mistakes? What have we failed to do? Is our cause hopeless?"...

Looking back over the past two years, [leaders of the TCC] could point to some solid achievements. To begin with, since Negroes moved in, white residents have become more community-conscious than ever before. Together with their Negro neighbors, they persuaded the Teaneck city government to build two additional playgrounds for their children. One block petitioned for the city to provide better street lighting; another called in a tree surgeon to treat ailing elms, and shared the cost of new trees. Recently at the request of homeowners, the police put a stop to cars speeding through neighborhood streets. Both Negro and white women attend Mrs. Harold Eby's ceramics classes. An interracial team shows up Friday evenings at a nearby bowling alley, and last summer 65 neighborhood youngsters of both races enjoyed a picnic and sports day organized by their parents at a local park.

Now, after admitting past errors, the TCC committee has drawn up a new program which combines grass-roots democracy with expert counsel for the first time since the panic selling of 1955. This program, approved by the TCC membership, includes:

- A visual education program, featuring films, booklets and posters prepared by national organizations in the field of human relations. These will be presented at neighborhood block meetings and will be offered to local women's clubs, church groups, Chambers of Commerce and other civic organizations.
- A continuing war against unscrupulous real-estate agents, with no delays in forwarding complaints to the proper state agency.

- A school program to acquaint children with the customs and cultures of the world's different peoples. The Parent-Teachers Association will introduce the program to school faculties.
- A Clean-Up-and-Fix-Up Week twice a year to keep homeowners conscious of high neighborhood standards.
- An interracial baby-sitting service as a means of bringing parents of both races together....

Before I left Teaneck, I discussed this program with several Negro residents. Most of them belong to the same income group as former white homeowners, and by and large they are as well-educated. Did they think the program would succeed and, if so, would it stop the movement of white homeowners from the neighborhood? Most believed it would and were pleased, for they hope their neighborhood will remain interracial.

11-10. NORMAN ROCKWELL DEPICTS SUBURBAN INTEGRATION, 1967

Figure 11-4 New Kids in the Neighborhood, Norman Rockwell, 1967. This image appeared on the cover of *Look* magazine in May 1967. Its placid depiction of suburban race relations was a hopeful vision that belied reality in many metropolitan areas. Printed by permission of the Norman Rockwell Family Agency, Copyright © 1967. The Norman Rockwell Family Entities.

ESSAYS

Beginning in the 1990s, scholars began to examine connections between suburbanization and the making of racial identities in twentieth-century America. Following the lead of historians such as Kenneth Jackson and Arnold Hirsch, who demonstrated the deep racial biases that underlay postwar federal housing policies, most have emphasized the role of government in shaping the meaning of race.[3] **Essay 11-1**, by American Studies scholar George Lipsitz, was one of the first to link suburbia to an expanded sense of "whiteness" in postwar America. In this pathbreaking essay, Lipsitz argues that racial formation is an ongoing social process sustained by concrete social advantages and disadvantages, especially those supported by the state. Access to suburban home ownership, he argues, represented a very important kind of social privilege that was readily available to European Americans and largely denied to African Americans and other racialized minorities. In this restricted milieu, European ethnics—once derided as members of inferior races—became ever more invested in a racial identity as "white" people. While Lipsitz offers a theory and outline of the forces shaping whiteness, **Essay 11-2**, examines race and class formation among African-American suburbanites through a case study of Nepperhan-Runyon Heights, a neighborhood of Yonkers, New York. Sociologist Bruce Haynes explores the politics of race, class, and space that shaped life in this suburb. Like many early black suburban communities, Runyon Heights attracted members of a growing black middle class after World War II. Haynes examines how local political struggles surrounding schools, busing, zoning, and housing both challenged and bolstered residents' sense of racial and class identities.

ESSAY 11-1. GEORGE LIPSITZ, "THE POSSESSIVE INVESTMENT IN WHITENESS: RACIALIZED SOCIAL DEMOCRACY AND THE 'WHITE' PROBLEM IN AMERICAN STUDIES" (1995)

Source: *American Quarterly* 47: 3 (1995), 218-224, 232-233. Copyright © The American Studies Association. Reprinted with permission of The Johns Hopkins University Press.

Shortly after World War II, a French reporter asked expatriate Richard Wright his opinion about the "Negro problem" in the United States. The author replied "There isn't any Negro problem; there is only a white problem." By inverting the reporter's question, Wright called attention to its hidden assumptions—that racial polarization comes from the existence of blacks rather than from the behavior of whites, that black people are a "problem" for whites rather than fellow citizens entitled to justice, and that unless otherwise specified, "Americans" means whites. But Wright's formulation also placed political mobilization by African Americans in context, attributing it to the systemic practices of aversion, exploitation, denigration, and discrimination practiced by people who think of themselves as "white."

Whiteness is everywhere in American culture, but it is very hard to see. As Richard Dyer argues, "white power secures its dominance by seeming not to be anything in particular." As the unmarked category against which difference is constructed, whiteness never has to speak its name, never has to acknowledge its role as an organizing principle in social and cultural relations....

In recent years, an important body of American studies scholarship has started to explore the role played by cultural practices in creating "whiteness" in the United States. More than the product of private prejudices, whiteness emerged as a relevant category in American life largely because of realities created by slavery and segregation, by immigration restriction and Indian policy, by conquest and colonialism. A fictive identity of "whiteness" appeared in law as an abstraction, and it became actualized in everyday life in many ways. American economic and political life gave different racial groups unequal access to citizenship and property, while cultural practices including wild west shows, minstrel shows, racist images in advertising, and Hollywood films institutionalized racism by uniting ethnically diverse European-American audiences into an imagined community—one called into being through inscribed appeals to the solidarity of white supremacy....

In these accounts..., cultural practices have often played crucial roles in prefiguring, presenting, and preserving political coalitions based on identification with the fiction of "whiteness."...This impressive body of scholarship helps us understand how people who left Europe as Calabrians or Bohemians became something called "whites" when they got to America and how that designation made all the difference in the world.

Yet, while cultural expressions have played an important role in the construction of white supremacist political alliances, the reverse is also true (i.e., political activity has also played a constitutive role in racializing U.S. culture). Race is a cultural construct, but one with sinister structural causes and consequences. Conscious and deliberate actions have institutionalized group identity in the United States, not just through the dissemination of cultural stories but also through systematic efforts from colonial times to the present to create a possessive investment in whiteness for European Americans....

From the start, European settlers in North America established structures encouraging possessive investment in whiteness. The colonial and early-national legal systems authorized attacks on Native Americans and encouraged the appropriation of their lands. They legitimated racialized chattel slavery, restricted naturalized citizenship to "white" immigrants, and provided pretexts for exploiting labor, seizing property, and denying the franchise to Asian Americans, Mexican Americans, Native Americans, and African Americans.... [P]ossessive investment in whiteness pervades public policy in the United States past and present—not just long ago during slavery and segregation but in the recent past and present as well....

Contemporary racism is not just a residual consequence of slavery and de jure segregation but rather something that has been created anew in our own time by many factors including the putatively race-neutral liberal social democratic reforms of the past five decades. Despite hardfought battles for change that secured important concessions during the 1960s in the form of civil rights legislation, the racialized nature of social democratic policies in the United States since the Great Depression has, in my judgment, actually increased the possessive investment in whiteness among European Americans over the past half-century.

The possessive investment in whiteness is not a simple matter of black and white; all racialized minority groups have suffered from it, albeit to different degrees and in different ways. Most of my argument here addresses relations between European Americans and African Americans because they contain many of the most vivid oppositions and contrasts, but the possessive investment in whiteness always emerges from a fused sensibility drawing on many sources at once—on antiblack racism to be sure, but also on the legacies of racialization left by federal, state, and local policies toward Native Americans, Asian Americans, Mexican Americans, and other groups designated by whites as "racially other."

During the New Deal, both the Wagner Act and the Social Security Act excluded farm workers and domestics from coverage, effectively denying those disproportionately minority sectors of the work force protections and benefits routinely channeled to whites. The Federal Housing Act of 1934 brought home ownership within reach of millions of citizens by placing the credit of the federal government behind private lending to home buyers, but overtly racist categories in the Federal Housing Administration's (FHA's) "confidential" city surveys and appraisers' manuals channeled almost all of the loan money toward whites and away from communities of color. In the post-World War II era, trade unions negotiated contract provisions giving private medical insurance, pensions, and job security largely to the mostly white workers in unionized mass-production industries rather than fighting for full employment, universal medical care, and old age pensions for all or for an end to discriminatory hiring and promotion practices by employers.

Each of these policies widened the gap between the resources available to whites and those available to aggrieved racial communities, but the most damaging long-term effects may well have come from the impact of the racial discrimination codified by the policies of the FHA.

By channeling loans away from older inner-city neighborhoods and toward white home buyers moving into segregated suburbs, the FHA and private lenders after World War II aided and abetted the growth and development of increased segregation in U.S. residential neighborhoods. For example, FHA appraisers denied federally supported loans to prospective home buyers in the racially mixed Boyle Heights neighborhood of Los Angeles because it was a "'melting pot' area literally honeycombed with diverse and subversive racial elements." Similarly, mostly white St. Louis County secured five times as many FHA mortgages as the more racially mixed city of St. Louis between 1943 and 1960. Home buyers in the county received six times as much loan money and enjoyed per capita mortgage spending 6.3 times greater than those in the city.

In concert with FHA support for segregation in the suburbs, federal and state tax monies routinely provided water supplies and sewage facilities for racially exclusive suburban communities in the 1940s and 1950s. By the 1960s, these areas often incorporated themselves as independent municipalities in order to gain greater access to federal funds allocated for "urban aid." At the same time that FHA loans and federal highway building projects subsidized the growth of segregated suburbs, urban renewal programs in cities throughout the country devastated minority neighborhoods.

During the 1950s and 1960s, federally assisted urban renewal projects destroyed 20 percent of the central city housing units occupied by blacks, as opposed to only 10 percent of those inhabited by whites. Even after most major urban renewal programs had been completed in the 1970s, black central city residents continued to lose housing

units at a rate equal to 80 percent of what had been lost in the 1960s. Yet white displacement declined back to the relatively low levels of the 1950s. In addition, the refusal first to pass, then to enforce, fair housing laws, has enabled realtors, buyers, and sellers to profit from racist collusion against minorities without fear of legal retribution.

During the decades following World War II, urban renewal helped construct a new "white" identity in the suburbs by helping destroy ethnically specific European-American urban inner-city neighborhoods. Wrecking balls and bulldozers eliminated some of these sites, while others became transformed by an influx of minority residents desperately competing for a declining number of affordable housing units. As increasing numbers of racial minorities moved into cities, increasing numbers of European-American ethnics moved out. Consequently, ethnic differences among whites became a less important dividing line in American culture, while race became more important. The suburbs helped turn European Americans into "whites" who could live near each other and intermarry with relatively little difficulty. But this "white" unity rested on residential segregation and on shared access to housing and life chances largely unavailable to communities of color....

Although the percentage of black suburban dwellers also increased during this period, no significant desegregation of the suburbs took place. From 1960 to 1977, four million whites moved out of central cities, while the number of whites living in suburbs increased by twenty-two million. During the same years, the inner-city black population grew by six million, but the number of blacks living in suburbs increased by only 500,000 people. By 1993, 86 percent of suburban whites still lived in places with a black population below 1 percent. At the same time, cities with large numbers of minority residents found themselves cut off from loans by the FHA; in 1966, because of their growing black and Puerto Rican populations, Camden and Paterson, New Jersey, received no FHA-sponsored mortgages between them....

Group interests are not monolithic, and aggregate figures can obscure serious differences within racial groups. All whites do not benefit from the possessive investment in whiteness in precisely the same way; the experiences of members of minority groups are not interchangeable. But the possessive investment in whiteness always affects individual and group life chances and opportunities. Even in cases where minority groups secure political and economic power through collective mobilization, the terms and conditions of their collectivity and the logic of group solidarity are always influenced and intensified by the absolute value of whiteness in American politics, economics, and culture.

In the 1960s, members of the Black Panther Party used to say that "if you're not part of the solution, you're part of the problem." But those of us who are "white" can only become part of the solution if we recognize the degree to which we are already part of the problem—not because of our race, but because of our possessive investment in it....

ESSAY 11-2. BRUCE HAYNES, *RED LINES, BLACK SPACES: THE POLITICS OF RACE AND SPACE IN A BLACK MIDDLE-CLASS SUBURB* (2001)

Source: Copyright © 2001 by Bruce D. Haynes. Reprinted by permission of Yale University Press.

Red Lines, Black Spaces is a case study of Nepperhan-Runyon Heights, one of the first middle-class black suburbs in the New York metropolitan region. Runyon Heights is nestled in the northeast section of Yonkers, New York, on the banks of the Hudson River, in the southwest corner of Westchester County, just north of New York City....

Runyon Heights, located on the east side of Yonkers amid predominantly white communities, is home to some thirteen hundred middle-class African Americans. As such, it is more than a historical anomaly. The community is the product of eight decades of black suburbanization, from the period just before World War I, which greatly expanded housing opportunities and initiated the first period of private home ownership by the

American working class, through the middle-class suburban expansion of the post-World War II era. As a result, the community's history sheds light on the ways in which contemporary suburban residential development was shaped by race and class.

The neighborhood of Nepperhan-Runyon Heights is, in many respects, like other suburban home-owning communities. Residents are mostly concerned with maintaining good schools, safe and clean streets, and their middle-class suburban lifestyle. Racial subordination created unique problems for the African-American middle class in Yonkers, however, and the residents of Runyon Heights have had to resist political, economic, and social forces that threatened to transform their neighborhood into a ghetto. They have fought against school gerrymandering, employment and housing discrimination, and attempts by city government to address public housing needs by repeatedly targeting the area for low-income housing projects. Paradoxically, these political battles have tended to promote both class solidarity and racial pride, as residents seek political power and residential stability through the community. Strong community ties have been forged in the heat generated by conflicts involving race and class.

The case of Runyon Heights also details how the creation of racially defined residential space after the turn of the [twentieth] century helped racialize American society in general and provided the foundation for racially segregated educational, social, and religious institutional life. The organization of communities by race, in turn, meant the politicization of racial identity. Residents had little choice but to identify common political interests, and thus the community became the framework for exercising political power. Racial consciousness provided a basis for social solidarity and mobilization, while partially insulating residents from the daily slights of overt racism.

Although racialization encouraged a sense of community that at times transcended residential boundaries, the material interests of this home-owning middle class also made it necessary to maintain a degree of physical and social distance from the black masses who came to dominate the west side of Yonkers. Runyon Heights residents were in the awkward position of negotiating the politics of race and class while relying on both for constructing community....

The Color Line and the Postwar Suburb....

Prosperity during the postwar years brought changes to Nepperhan....Black and white real estate investors built ever more costly homes for sale in an expanding market. The newcomers differed from earlier settlers in that many were college-educated, as only a few of the children of the first settlers had been. Together, they constituted the first black workers to be employed in white-collar jobs as clerks, salesmen, teachers, and nurses. Overall, the socioeconomic status of newcomers tended to be higher than that of children of the original settlers, many of whom had had only a high school education. The working-class black residential suburb of Nepperhan was beginning to become gentrified by a more traditionally middle-class group....

While the occupational color line began to fade slowly after World War II, race took on added significance in local community conflicts. When school district lines were redrawn, Runyon Heights children were isolated in School 1, and community boundaries were aligned with school zone boundaries....[R]esidents' shared experiences with the Yonkers Board of Education helped reinforce racial solidarity as well as prompt community political involvement. Residents mobilized around what they perceived to be their material self-interest, defined in racial terms. Education, they believed, was the ticket to middle-class prosperity, and racial barriers prevented a free market from operating. They concluded that racial consciousness and political solidarity were prerequisites to their mobility, for race subordination linked them together in a community of fate.

Since the earliest days, School 1 had served elementary schoolchildren from Runyon Heights and neighboring areas. As in other suburban communities, the school was the heart of civic life. Children walked to the school on Dunbar Street; the parents knew

the teachers, and the teachers knew the community. The Parent Teacher Association had even sponsored the reactivated Boy Scout Troop #34, which ran from the early 1950s through the early 1960s.

School 1 was the only truly integrated elementary school in Yonkers, drawing pupils from a broad geographic area. Black students constituted an estimated one-third to one-half of the student body. The majority of Runyon Heights senior residents had attended School 1, and strong and lasting bonds developed among classmates....

School 1 retained its interracial character until 1938, when school district lines were first redrawn. White students who had previously attended School 1 were slowly relocated to the already predominantly white Schools 5 and 22. The rezoning made School 1 the smallest school zone in Yonkers and effectively isolated the Runyon Heights children....

While Schools 5 and 22 became overcrowded, School 1 became underutilized and racially concentrated. By 1950, School 1 enrolled a mere 100 students in a facility designed to hold 240 and was 91 percent black. Underutilization resulted in mergers of the first- and second-grade classes and the third- and fourth-grade classes. According to informants, the assignment of the first three black Yonkers schoolteachers to School 1 during this period further emphasized the school's racial identity and marginal status.

By 1953, Runyon Heights formed a solid Negro community, having been cut off from adjoining, predominantly white communities in the religious, educational, and occupational spheres. In the hope of securing their children's educational and financial futures, parents in the community petitioned the Yonkers Board of Education to reexpand the School 1 district lines, thus reintegrating the school. One woman who served on the committee of concerned Runyon Heights residents remembers: "Number 1 had become a nothing. Number 1 had become just a place to put black children. Number 1 had become totally an all-black school. I think they had white teachers there that were pulling in a salary who really had no interest in our children...."

The NAACP joined the petition, but the board decided instead to close the school and assign Runyon Heights children to Schools 5 and 22. This decision immediately followed the May 1954 ruling by the Supreme Court in the case of *Brown v. Board of Education of Topeka, Kansas*, which declared racially separate schools unconstitutional. The board's decision solved the immediate problem created by the all-black School 1, while marginally improving the racial balance at Schools 5 and 22, but it also compounded the problem of overcrowding at those schools.

The closing of School 1 not only dispersed the Runyon Heights children to other schools and thus weakened community bonds but also undermined efforts to control deviant behavior among youths. Local Boy Scout troops had been typically sponsored by the local school. With the closing of the local school, the Men's Club began to sponsor the Runyon troop. By the 1960s, the local troop was disbanded, and Runyon children participated in troops based in their new schools. A community tradition had been lost.

Runyon Heights parents who favored a community school and opposed busing their children, had challenged the board's decision legally. To their dismay, their challenge was rejected by the New York State commissioner of education. Even the local NAACP supported the commissioner's decision, in light of the Yonkers School Board's rejection of the parents' initial proposal to expand district lines. The parents, never satisfied with the busing solution, were obliged to comply with the state's decision. Runyon children would be bused....

Public education for Runyon children remains unresolved. Since the 1970s, the children have been shuffled from school to school in a vain attempt to create racial balance in the Yonkers school system. Prospects for racially balanced schools remain elusive, as the minority population in Yonkers has grown while the percentage of white school children has steadily declined. Efforts to create racial balance have annoyed parents and heightened racial tensions, but they have also inspired newer Nepperhan residents to become involved in local politics and community organization....

Negotiating Race and Class: Dilemmas of Public Housing....

In 1956, community members mobilized to challenge the city council's plan to build 335 rental units of low-income public housing on the southern end of Ridgeview Avenue. The reborn Runyon Heights Improvement Association [RHIA] was called into action to organize residents. A project of this scale would have radically transformed the economic composition of the community, by housing more families than were currently living in the entire area. Residents wished to maintain the low population density as well as the level of city services available to their middle-class single- and two-family housing. The addition of 335 units would have overwhelmed the area and transformed it into a ghetto. As one former president of the association commented, "This is the reason why you see a community house. This is the reason why you see us organized now—because we had to get organized. That was it."

Their common concerns also brought Runyon Heights residents into alliance with the [historically white] neighboring Homefield community, which believed that the proposed low-income development was too close to home. Both groups protested to the city government. Paradoxically, after having created and maintained [since the 1920s a] four-foot reserve strip [of land] as an artificial border separating them from black Nepperhaners, the Homefield community now made common cause with their black neighbors. Both groups of residents wanted to maintain the middle-class character of the area. The paradox of this class alignment was that the initial fight for low-income housing in Yonkers had been championed by the local NAACP, an organization widely supported by Runyon Heights residents. In fact, numerous leaders of the Yonkers Branch of the NAACP have been community residents. Initiatives for low-income housing would disproportionately benefit the poor and working-class black populations of Yonkers, and the middle-class of Runyon Heights, in taking on the fight against racial oppression, supported local NAACP activities with both financial and intellectual resources. But residents also sought to protect their own class interests by resisting the placement of low-income housing in or near their community. They hoped to prevent the ghettoization of their neighborhood....

Unlike the white suburbanites, Runyon Heights residents were obviously not troubled by the presumed race of prospective low-income residents. Their concern focused on the class position of the newcomers and the impact a multiple-dwelling unit might have on community life.

The "why us?" syndrome was manifested in the way Nepperhaners interpreted events. They believed race to be the motivating factor behind the site selection. "Why us?" became "Why us blacks in Runyon Heights?" Their motivation for resistance was material and not specifically racial: avoid ghettoization at all costs.

An attorney for the RHIA told the city council that the national trend was "away from putting housing sites in minority areas, as it has a tendency to create slums" and that the placement of a public housing project in Runyon Heights would have similar consequences. Speaking to the city council, representatives of the Yonkers branch of the NAACP and the Urban League of Westchester County voiced similar apprehension about black residential concentration, segregation, and community deterioration.

The initial housing proposal was defeated, but another, much smaller proposal was put forth in 1958. After vociferous debates and numerous city council meetings, the community won the battle but lost the war. Nepperhan succeeded in blocking the original proposal for 335 units, but a 48-unit housing project was slated for Dunbar and Kenmore Streets. The Hall Court Housing Complex...was finally completed in 1962. The bitter irony for residents was that the project was constructed on the old School 1 site....

The Defended Community....

The 1960s brought other changes to Nepperhan that threatened the character of the area.... Businesses took advantage of earlier zoning designations and began moving in.

This brought congestion, air pollution, and noise to the community, as well as a transient population with little commitment to quality of life in Runyon Heights....

During the 1960s, residents, led by the RHIA, began a long fight with city hall and the City Planning Bureau to ensure that land use in the area would retain a suburban character....

After numerous battles with local businesses over parking, trucks, and noise, the RHIA urged the city to upgrade the [east side of the community]...to allow only detached single-family units on fifty-foot lots. A large portion of east-side residential real estate in Yonkers is currently in this category. The remaining Runyon Heights area west of the railroad, excluding the Runyon Avenue [business] strip, was also upgraded to a "T" district in 1968. From the standpoint of preserving the suburban character of the community, the "T" district designation was an improvement over the old "B" designation, which had permitted apartment buildings and neighborhood businesses. Through active negotiations with city government, the RHIA helped ensure the middle-class, detached, single-home character of much of the community....

Defining Black Space...

Early on, the Nepperhan-Runyon Heights community came to resemble what sociologist Gerald Suttles describes as a defended community. Community cohesion had been determined by the structural constraints placed on local residents by the larger environment. Residents who shared local territory also came to share a common fate. The common fate of Runyon Heights residents was, however, shaped by race and class. Residential segregation encouraged social solidarity and fostered a community identity and a common history that tied Nepperhan residents to the belief in a shared fate.

By the 1920s, the community found it necessary to organize to oppose outside forces that threatened its way of life. School and labor issues came first. By the mid-1960s, business development and low-income housing challenged the area's suburban character....

Community issues have been further compounded by solutions that have often brought unforeseen negative consequences. Although it is the socioeconomic character of the area that is threatened by outside forces, the mechanism for the production of social, economic, and political inequality has been explicitly racial....

[T]ogether race and class provide the sentiments necessary for community solidarity and defense. The invocation of racial sentimentality, which has often mistakenly been labeled primordial, takes place amid the structural forces that push and pull individuals into specific residential localities. Racialization has been a major force in shaping suburban development. Thus, in Runyon Heights, race makes place. Opposition from outside forces rather than "primordial" sentiments gives the defended community its solidarity. Racial consciousness is informed by the physical boundaries that define the community. Consequently, the reverse is also true: place makes race. The need for common history links race and place across time and space. Race becomes reified, disembodied, and ahistorical. Racial affinities and residential segregation seem natural.

NOTES

1. Arnold Hirsch, *Making the Second Ghetto: Race and Housing in Chicago, 1940–1960* (New York: Cambridge University Press, 1983).
2. In addition to 2.5 million African American suburbanites in 1960, there were 355,000 "other nonwhites" in suburbia, most of them Asian Americans. Reliable figures for Latinos do not exist before 1970, since the Census did not begin collecting coherent data until that date. By that time, just over 3 million persons of "Spanish Heritage" lived in suburban areas.
3. Kenneth T. Jackson, *Crabgrass Frontier: The Suburbanization of the United States* (New York: Oxford University Press, 1985); Hirsch, *Making the Second Ghetto*.

CHAPTER 12

The City–Suburb Divide

INTRODUCTION

In the decades after World War II, cities and suburbs underwent a tectonic shift in prestige and power. Before 1950, central cities had exerted clear economic, political, and social dominance over their peripheries, but after the war, urban and suburban trajectories diverged. Across the old manufacturing belt, urban fortunes declined. By the 1960s, observers were speaking of a full-fledged "urban crisis." Meanwhile suburbs boomed, reaping the majority of metropolitan growth in manufacturing, retail sales, and office employment, not to mention population. Cities and suburbs remained inseparably linked as parts of a single metropolitan system, yet the gravitational pull of the center had loosed its hold, or even reversed polarity altogether. In an era of national economic prosperity, two warring images of suburban abundance and urban decline defined both popular discourse and certain realities of life in the postwar metropolis.

Underlying these shifts were several interrelated factors. The first was suburbanization itself. As population and jobs decentralized, they sapped economic vitality from urban neighborhoods. Reflecting a national trend toward deindustrialization in the postwar decades, thousands of central city factories relocated to cheaper suburban or exurban sites—or shut their doors altogether. Job losses drained wages that had flowed through surrounding urban communities, sustaining mom and pop stores, saloons, and groceries, as well as banks, churches, synagogues, and other institutions. Major retailers followed their customers and pioneered stores in sleek suburban shopping malls that sprouted along the expanding network of metropolitan highways. Even downtown offices began to heed the advantages of outlying locations, trading city skyscrapers for low-rise suburban office parks. The cumulative result was a shift in human and monetary capital from central cities to their suburbs that greatly intensified by the 1970s.

Exacerbating this trend was the distinctive political structure of American metropolitan areas. As chapters 5 and 8 illustrate, independent municipalities exercise significant powers to control land use and levy taxes. As growing numbers of higher-income taxpayers and businesses moved beyond the city limits, they shifted tax dollars from one jurisdiction to another, creating a drain on city revenues and forcing cutbacks in services and/or tax rate increases. Both options encouraged additional taxpayers to leave. By contrast, many suburbs wooed businesses and people to relocate by keeping tax rates down. Property taxes on business enterprises afforded a high level of local services and amenities while keeping the overall tax burden low for ordinary suburbanites. Over time, many cities entered a potentially lethal fiscal spiral of falling tax revenues, declining services, rising tax rates, and a steady outflow of taxable property. The results were apparent in disinvested urban landscapes: pockmarked streets, unkempt parks, uncollected garbage, and failing schools. By the 1970s, fiscal crises pushed older industrial cities like Cleveland, Detroit, Baltimore, and St. Louis to the brink of bankruptcy, while New York City—the nation's largest city and financial capital—actually went bankrupt. One notable counterweight to this trend was among cities of the so-called Sunbelt, which grew in both size and population throughout this period. In part, these cities gained by attracting economic activities fleeing the Northeast and Midwest. But they also benefited by political and historical context. Unconstrained by rings of incorporated suburbs, cities like Atlanta, Dallas, Houston, and Phoenix evaded the suburban fiscal crunch by annexing hundreds of square miles of suburban territory during the postwar decades, much as northeastern cities had done in the nineteenth century.

State and federal policies deepened the division of metropolitan fortunes while exacerbating this regional shift. Despite large government investments in central city highways, slum clearance, public housing, and urban renewal programs, these inputs paled in comparison to federal bounty for the suburbs. As Kenneth Jackson shows in chapter 8, federal housing programs funneled over $100 billion into metropolitan areas in the postwar decades, three-fourths of it to the suburbs. In addition, federal investments in suburb-based defense firms and interstate expressways, tax breaks for central city plant closures, and mortgage interest deductions for homeowners together amounted to federal and state subsidy to suburban areas that outstripped investment in cities by billions of dollars every year. The disproportionate location of defense enterprises in the South and West and the rapid, suburban-style growth of sunbelt cities also meant that these regions picked up a disproportionate share of this largesse.

A final feature of the emerging city–suburb divide was racial. As the twin streams of white suburbanization and black and brown urbanization flowed, they produced growing racial differences between city and suburban populations. Like generations of migrants before them, the urban newcomers were younger, poorer, and less educated than many of those who were leaving. They placed greater demands on city services—especially schools and medical facilities—while they contributed less per capita to the city's tax coffers. Unlike earlier European immigrants, however, the new arrivals inherited cities weakened by the outflow of jobs and taxable property, while simultaneously facing unique levels of discrimination that blocked their economic and spatial mobility. Central city woes merely compounded the racial and economic inequality that already beset these new migrants. Moreover, confounding efforts to craft metropolitan solutions, white suburbanites increasingly identified the "inner city" as a racialized space, a decrepit "other" juxtaposed against the progressive, advantageous, "white spaces" they had crafted in the suburbs. For many whites, central city black neighborhoods, often stereotyped as "the ghetto," or "inner city," became the dominating symbol of the city as a whole.

The urban crisis did not represent the end of urban history, of course. Since the 1980s, in fact, central cities, and especially central business districts have undergone various waves of revival. Moreover, millions of Americans continued to work and make their homes in the central city. The point is not that people stopped living in cities, but that they often did so at a disadvantage. Older cities lived in a world of limits that contrasted sharply with the opulent centers of suburban economic growth and power.

Through the 1950s, central city officials and civic leaders remained upbeat that they could solve the cities' problems—that they would rebuild aged housing, rein in pollution, construct highways to accommodate the automobile, attract new industrial jobs, and incorporate new migrants into the larger civic body, just as they had done with earlier migrants. For all of their optimism, however, these predictions proved naive. Urban renewal programs destroyed more units of housing than they replaced, accelerating the depopulation of the center city. Highways sliced through vibrant neighborhoods even as they reduced the economic advantages of central locations and made it easier for commuters to reach distant suburbs. Working-class and minority neighborhoods bore the brunt of disorder and displacement, fomenting ongoing discontent. And in postwar America the balance continued to tip, year after year, from city to suburb.

DOCUMENTS

As early as the 1940s, some urban boosters read troubling signs in the growing suburban trend. In **Document 12-1,** editorialist William Laas foresees fiscal catastrophe for cities looming in the ongoing trend of political balkanization in metropolitan areas. Echoing the prescription of political scientist Thomas Reed two decades earlier, Laas proposes the consolidation of metropolitan governments as the solution to the fiscal "strangulation" of cities by their surrounding suburbs.

Suburban expansiveness, on the other hand, often resulted from aggressive efforts by suburban leaders to attract business and investment, which created rivalries among competing municipalities. In **Document 12-2,** the *Wall Street Journal* approvingly profiles one such suburb, San Leandro, California. Revealing an ideology characteristic of the growing suburbs themselves, the *Journal* links San Leandro's bounty not merely to the arrival of several hundred business enterprises but to administrative foresight, budgetary restraint, rejection of direct federal aid, and racial homogeneity.

By the 1960s, a discourse of "urban crisis" had become a common theme of public debate. Increasingly, observers perceived this crisis in racial terms, in light of the ongoing demographic shift of whites to suburbs and minorities to cities. In **Document 12-3**, the U.S. Commission on Civil Rights, an investigative body created by Congress in 1957, defines the growing division between the nation's cities and suburbs as a civil rights issue—and as the foundation for racial inequality outside the South. Widespread discrimination in the housing market, reinforced by the invisible barriers of suburban municipal power, had created, in the memorable words of one witness, a "white noose" of suburbia around the throat of the cities.

Events of the decade only strengthened this racial critique. **Document 12-4** is an excerpt from the report of National Advisory Commission on Civil Disorders, better known as the Kerner Commission after its chairman, Illinois governor Otto Kerner. Created by President Lyndon Johnson to uncover the causes of urban rioting, the commission blamed the widening socioeconomic gap between black Americans, confined in central city ghettoes, and whites, increasingly resident in prosperous suburbs. The report concluded ominously that the nation faced a permanent division based on race and residence. To redress this imbalance, the commission urged the federal government to promote metropolitan economic and racial integration. A startled Johnson repudiated the report. Just weeks later, the murder of Martin Luther King, Jr. ignited rioting in dozens of U.S. cities. Congress, in response, passed a Fair Housing Bill, outlawing most forms of housing discrimination, one of few recommendations in the report to be enacted.

Document 12-5 looks ahead to the late twentieth century, exploring the repercussions of continued metropolitan inequality, twenty years after the Kerner Report. In this excerpt from his book, *Savage Inequalities*, journalist Jonathan Kozol compares conditions in the nation's urban and suburban schools. Kozol's findings—a grim portrait of continued city–suburb inequity—indicates the extent to which the Kerner Commission's prescriptions went unfilled. Despite celebrated examples of central city revival, Kozol reveals that the city–suburb divide remained one of the most significant features of metropolitan life at century's end.

What responsibilities should citizens of different jurisdictions in a metropolitan area share? Why did suburban residents defend the existing arrangement? Was there anything that governments could—or should—have done to prevent this trend? Which factor was most significant in creating this urban-suburban divide? What role, if any, did individual suburbanites play in creating this division? To what extent did the dire predictions of postwar urban observers come to pass? How important are questions of fairness in evaluating metropolitan growth? Should declining central cities continue to exist?

12-1. WILLIAM LAAS PROMOTES CONSOLIDATION AS THE CURE FOR "SUBURBITIS," 1950

Source: William Laas, "The Suburbs Are Strangling the City," *New York Times Magazine*, June 18, 1950.

Shortly before the Civil War, when the boundaries of New York City did not extend beyond Manhattan Island, a Democratic member of the park board named Andrew Haswell Green suggested that the time had come to unite "our harbor islands" into a greater city. To his shocked surprise the idea was savagely attacked....

But Green was a persistent fellow. In 1898,...Manhattan, Brooklyn, Queens, Staten Island and the part of Westchester known as the Bronx were consolidated into the five-borough City of New York. It was a triumph of social foresight, but by the time it came about it was barely adequate even for the New York of fifty years ago.

Today New York City and its circle of satellite communities stand in urgent need of another Andrew Haswell Green. Since 1900 the metropolis...has exploded over the surrounding landscape. As O'Henry's four million swelled into Damon Runyon's seven, they pushed still other millions ahead of them into the open country. New suburbs boomed along rails and highways. Trade and industry followed.

Preliminary figures from the new 1950 census make this trend strikingly clear. They show a relatively small rate of growth for New York and other major cities *within* the city limits, and a huge growth *outside* the city limits in surrounding suburban areas. The suburban population of most large cities in this country now averages about 50 per cent of the population within the municipal boundaries. Director of the Census Roy V. Peel recently took note of the phenomenal suburban growth. He said: "If cities want their population to keep going up, they are going to have to expand their city limits."

His observation goes to the heart of one of New York's biggest problems. During the twentieth century everything has changed in New York except the city limits...a fact which may ultimately spell ruin for the greatest city on earth.

Why, one may ask, is it it essential to expand New York City's limits and authority? What is the danger in our horse-and-buggy political set-up?

The answers have to do with handicaps placed on the whole of the metropolitan community—not just the core of it—by the myriad of political barriers. These handicaps are strangling the central city and at the same time are preventing any effective planning for development of the suburbs.

Today, New York City is the lifegiving focus for an area larger than Connecticut and more populous than Canada. Five-borough New York covers 385 square miles of land and has a resident population approaching 8,000,000. Around it in a fifty-mile circle is a suburban territory comprising nearly 500 separate communities....The...metropolitan "region" consists of twenty-two counties covering about 7,500 square miles and more than 14,000,000 people, of whom at least 6,000,000 live outside the city proper....

By the peculiarities of local government, the outer neighborhoods of commuting New Yorkers—comprising 40 per cent of the total population and increasing daily—are living on the lifeblood of the central city without contributing the nourishment so necessary to sustain it. The city must provide costly facilities that are used by nearly twice its own population, but it can tax only those persons and properties within its limits. Moreover, it can organize and control only the rather small part of the area's public services which function within the five boroughs, although its life may depend upon what happens outside this area of control....

No modern city is immune to suburbitis, but few can match New York's complication. The basic complication is the split of the metropolitan district among three state sovereignties—New York, New Jersey and Connecticut. The most baffling is the number and variety of the suburbs, comprising 418 separate municipal authorities and additional unincorporated centers.

The confusion has been further compounded by an intricate system of private and public pseudo-governments. These are the so-called *ad hoc*, or special-purpose authorities, set up in efforts to meet the most pressing needs of the hodge-podge of small comunities. Superimposed on the suburban municipal patchwork is a maze of taxing districts; school, library, water, sewage, highway, park, hospital and welfare districts; parkway and public service commissions; the Port Authority and other technical bodies; police; fire, paving and sanitation jurisdictions, building codes, zoning laws, and heaven knowS what else. The typical suburbanite seldom can say where one boundary ends and the other begins; he is sometimes hard put to explain just where he lives.

Such is the nature of the disease. Let us now examine some of its effects.

The Central City

The political "atomization" of the metropolitan district has steadily piled increasing burdens on New York proper in both fiscal and administrative fields. Taxes are high, especially in Manhattan, in part because of the necessity of providing facilities for suburbanites who pay little or nothing toward their cost. At the same time many of the city's basic facilities are subject to outside [state] control....

The political disunity is responsible, at least in part, for the fact that New York City's billion-dollar budget—second in size only to the Federal budget—is chronically a deficit operation. Some of the more expensive projects, such as highways, water supply, transit improvements and public housing, have had to be heavily subsidized by state and Federal funds or by huge borrowings. Thus most of the 6,000,000 non-resident users of the city's facilities pay their way only indirectly, through state and Federal taxation. Bridge tolls, the increased subway fare, the hotel tax, and the city sales tax are efforts—all with grave disadvantages—to shift some of the crushing burden to those who make their living in the city but pay their taxes elsewhere.

The city's resulting high tax is an incentive, in turn, for intensive land use, meaning bigger buildings and more congested industries. While some sections of the city suffer blight and loss of tax values from the exo-dus of population to the suburbs, other sections are perforce overdeveloped to take care of the daytime non-resident workers. The end products are more traffic, more subway jams, more smoke, more packing in of people—and additional expensive facilities to ease the strain. Manhattan, with a resident population of 2,000,000, is host every weekday to 3,500,000 others whose goings and comings not only create the paralyzing traffic and transit congestion but add immensely to the problems of water and food supply, waste disposal, police protection, and all the rest....

New York's one real hope lies in the almost forgotten example of Andrew Haswell Green. Common sense always has its faithful and persistent advocates. In the end even the strongest obstacles established by custom give way to progress when the handicaps become intolerable to a sufficient number of enlightened and influential citizens....

Perhaps experience as a world capital will eventually prod Greater New York into governing its own huge urban empire. Year by year traffic congestion, smelly rivers, fiscal squeezes, business difficulties and just plain discomfort produce more glaring evidence of the inability of petty governments to serve a modern people well. Things probably will have to get a good deal worse before they get better. But in a democratic society there is always reason to believe that time and pressures will force a workable compromise between isolationist home rule and metropolitan necessity in this air and atomic age.

12-2. THE *WALL STREET JOURNAL* HIGHLIGHTS INDUSTRY, THRIFT AND RACIAL HOMOGENEITY IN A "MODEL MUNICIPALITY," 1966

Source: Lew Phelps, "Model Municipality: San Leandro, Calif., Manages to Surmount Many of the Problems That Plague Cities," *Wall Street Journal*, March 4, 1966. Copyright ©1966 by Dow Jones & Co., Inc. Reproduced with permission of Dow Jones & Co, Inc. in the format Other Book via Copyright Clearance Center.

It's almost an urban dweller's dream. New city facilities spring up like mushrooms, yet property taxes decrease. The city refuses to expand the police force, yet the crime rate drops. The city rejects Federal aid, yet the downtown facelifting that aid would have paid for proceeds apace. And somebody builds a municipal golf course free of charge.

It's all happening in [San Leandro, California] this prosperous little city (pop. 72,000) just south of Oakland on the eastern side of San Francisco Bay. While most cities suffer the seemingly unending cycle of bigger budgets, rising taxes and still bigger budgets, San Leandro has somehow managed to get all the benefits of lavish public spending while putting a surprisingly small bite on the local taxpayers.

It's true the effort has included wooing a little more industry to town than some of the local citizenry would like to see—but most cities would envy such success. Equally important, this growth has been accompanied by some inventiveness in holding down costs. Furthermore, the city has engaged in some of the long-range planning critics say many of the nation's cities continue to lack.

The planning started way back in 1947 when San Leandro was a semi-agricultural community of 20,000 population. The key step was passage of a bond issue to finance installation of sewer lines. Where? Through acres of otherwise cherry orchards and to-mato fields on the city's outskirts. With land still cheap and the sewers already in, industry came flocking from Oakland and San Francisco, where land was already dear....

"We moved our plant to San Leandro because we needed some room for expansion, and didn't have it where we were before," says Russell L. McGinnis, plant manager for International Harvester Co. "We've found other benefits. Besides lower tax rates than any other city in the area that could provide utilities, San Leandro has a city government that really works with industry. For instance, they've been holding off tract development and saving a lot of their available land for industry, to keep the tax base strong and taxes low."

Industry Helps on Costs

Since 1947, some 600 companies; have moved to town, adding about $200 million in property to the tax roles. Industry now pays more than a third of the cost of government in San Leandro, 57% of the sales taxes and 45% of the property taxes.

With such growth, and the tax revenue potential that has come with it, it's all the more surprising that the city fathers have kept such a tight rein on costs. They've avoided borrowing—there's been only one bond issue, for a library, since the 1947 sewer bonds. And typical of the close watch they keep on expenses are these moves:

When a new public safety building is completed early next year the city will pool the dispatching teams for fire and general communications. Compared with present separate facilities, this cut the communications staff to six men from 10.

When an addition to the 30-year-old city hall was built in 1964, offices were arranged so that clerks and typists could work in several departments rather than being pigeonholed in one. The saving: "Several" jobs, a city official says....

To get a second public golf course, the city struck a deal with a rubbish disposal firm, allowing the firm to dump for free on useless bayside tideland. The disposal firm is even compacting the fill and contouring the area to golf course design. "All we'll have to do is put on a little topsoil and plant some grass," says Mayor Jack Maltester. "Otherwise, we'd have had to buy all that fill, and dirt cheap isn't cheap at all these days."

San Leandro has even saved money by appearing to spend it. The salaries it pays its police and firemen are among the best in the state.... At the same time, San Leandro's police force numbers ... [are] roughly two-thirds the average for cities of its size....

The acid test: San Leandro's crime rate, already below state averages, fell 10% in fiscal 1965 while the statewide rate increased by about the same amount.

What all this means is that the city has managed to keep its spending well within what the city's population and industrial growth can support. While real estate property taxes are rising in all of Alameda County, which embraces Oakland as well as San Leandro, San Leandro's share of that tax has been declining steadily for 18 years. One typical middle income homeowner is paying $51 in property taxes to the city now, compared with $66 back in 1947....

Where the Money Goes

The city's budget in the current fiscal year is $5.7 million, a far cry from the $613,000 of 1947, but still slightly below the record $5.9 million of 1962.... The spending is going for such things as city parks, development of all the city's San Francisco Bay waterfront into beaches and a marina, a $2 million library, and a new civic center complex, including the police and fire station, a new city hall, a courthouse, and headquarters for the Chamber of Commerce.

San Leandro even has afforded itself the luxury of turning down $2.5 million of Federal funds. Back in 1959 the city started planning a Federally financed urban renewal project. But local citizens got up in arms about it—they didn't want land condemnation power [in] the hands of non-elected officials—so the city gave Washington back its money.

Then Wesley McClure, the city manager since 1947, came up with a new plan, locally financed. The city, invested $1 million in the five-block renewal area, but it is utilizing a little-known California statute called the tax increment law. This allows the redevelopment agency to recover its investment by keeping any increased tax revenues stemming from the increased value of the face-lifted buildings....

In some respects, San Leandro has been lucky. Unlike some cities, it hasn't been forced to absorb a heavy influx of minority groups and unskilled workers. Combined with rapid growth in industry, jobs have been plentiful and the city's welfare load well below average. Too, officials of some neighboring cities see San Leandro facing more problems in the future than it has in the recent past.

"Nobody thinks badly of San. Leandro," says a city administrator in Oakland. "It's a progressive city." But, he contends, sooner or later San Leandrans are going to run out of land for industrial expansion. "Then they'll be facing the same problems everybody else does[.]"...

But San Leandrans think otherwise. "We've only used 40% of our land," contends Frank King, manager of the active Chamber of Commerce. "And while we don't have many really large industrial locations left, that's not the type of business we want. We're after white collar industry—clean, middle-sized and beneficial to the economy."

12-3. U.S. CIVIL RIGHTS COMMISSION DESCRIBES SUBURBIA AS A "WHITE NOOSE," 1961

Source: U.S. Commission on Civil Rights, *Housing: 1961 Commission on Civil Rights Report* (Washington, D.C.: Government Printing Office, 1961).

In 1959 the Commission found that "housing...seems to be the one commodity in the American market that is not freely available on equal terms to everyone who can afford to pay." Today, 2 years later, the situation is not noticeably better.

Throughout the country large groups of American citizens—mainly Negroes, but other minorities too—are denied an equal opportunity to choose where they will live. Much of the housing market is closed to them for reasons unrelated to their personal worth or ability to pay. New housing, by and large, is available only to whites. And in the restricted market that is open to them, Negroes generally must pay more for equivalent housing than do the favored majority. "The dollar in a dark hand" does not "have the same purchasing power as a dollar in a white hand."

As a consequence there is an ever-increasing concentration of nonwhites in racial ghettos, largely in the decaying centers of our cities—while a "white noose" of new suburban housing grows up around them. This racial pattern intensifies the critical problems of our cities: slums whose growth is abetted by the racial ghetto; loss of tax revenue and community leadership through flight to the suburbs of those financially (and racially) able to leave—all this in the face of growing city needs for transportation, welfare, and municipal services.

These problems are not limited to any one region of the country. They are nationwide and their implications are manifold. Attorney General [Stanley] Mosk of California told this Commission: "It is most appropriate in our concern with these [civil rights] problems to concentrate on housing, for here we have…what in most instances outside of the South is the root of the evil." Commissioner [Theodore] Hesburgh outlined the difficulty in these terms:

"I think this is the condition that we face…—the central city throughout the United States in all of our large metropolitan areas is a rundown, dismal, most depressed and antiquated part of our city…completely backward in all its facilities, and these include the homes, the schools, the recreational facilities.…It is not just a question of houses and bricks and mortar and businesses and loans and all the rest. It is a problem of people, and unless we can find some answers to this problem on all levels we are in real trouble as a Nation.…"

Just as the problem of housing inequalities must be considered in deeper terms than blueprints and mortgages, so its effects cannot be understood merely in terms of statistical tables. It is a problem of people and its effects on the human spirit cannot so readily be calculated.

As the Commission noted in 1959: "Some of the effects of the housing inequalities of minorities can be seen with the eye, some can be shown by statistics, some can only be measured in the mind and heart."

12-4. THE KERNER COMMISSION PREDICTS "TWO SOCIETIES," 1968

Source: *Report of the National Advisory Commission on Civil Disorders* (Washington, D.C.: Government Printing Office, 1968).

The summer of 1967 again brought racial disorders to American cities, and with them shock, fear and bewilderment to the nation.

The worst came during a two-week period in July, first in Newark and then in Detroit. Each set off a chain reaction in neighboring communities.

On July 28, 1967, the President of the United States established this Commission and directed us to answer three basic questions:

What happened?

Why did it happen?

What can be done to prevent it from happening again?

To respond to these questions, we have undertaken a broad range of studies and investigations. We have visited the riot cities; we have heard many witnesses; we have sought the counsel of experts across the country.

This is our basic conclusion: Our nation is moving toward two societies, one black, one white—separate and unequal.

Reaction to last summer's disorders has quickened the movement and deepened the division. Discrimination and segregation have long permeated much of American life; they now threaten the future of every American.

This deepening racial division is not inevitable. The movement apart can be reversed. Choice is still possible. Our principal task is to define that choice and to press for a national resolution.

To pursue our present course will involve the continuing polarization of the American community and, ultimately, the destruction of basic democratic values.

The alternative is not blind repression or capitulation to lawlessness. It is the realization of common opportunities for all within a single society.

This alternative will require a commitment to national action—compassionate, massive and sustained, backed by the resources of the most powerful and the richest nation on this earth. From every American it will require new attitudes, new understanding, and, above all, new will.

The vital needs of the nation must be met; hard choices must be made, and, if necessary, new taxes enacted.

Violence cannot build a better society. Disruption and disorder nourish repression, not justice. They strike at the freedom of every citizen. The community cannot—it will not—tolerate coercion and mob rule.

Violence and destruction must be ended—in the streets of the ghetto and in the lives of people.

Segregation and poverty have created in the racial ghetto a destructive environment totally unknown to most white Americans.

What white Americans have never fully understood—but what the Negro can never forget—is that white society is deeply implicated in the ghetto. White institutions created it, white institutions maintain it, and white society condones it.

It is time now to turn with all the purpose at our command to the major unfinished business of this nation. It is time to adopt strategies for action that will produce quick and visible progress. It is time to make good the promises of American democracy to all citizens—urban and rural, white and black, Spanish-surname, American Indian, and every minority group....

II. Choices for the Future

The complexity of American society offers many choices for the future of relations between central cities and suburbs and patterns of white and Negro settlement in metropolitan areas....

For purposes of analysis, the Commission has defined three basic choices for the future....

The Present Policies Choice

Under this course, the nation would maintain approximately the share of resources now being allocated to programs of assistance for the poor, unemployed and disadvantaged. These programs are likely to grow, given continuing economic growth and rising federal revenues, but they will not grow fast enough to stop, let alone reverse, the already deteriorating quality of life in central-city ghettos....

The Enrichment Choice

Under this course, the nation would seek to offset the effects of continued Negro segregation and deprivation in large city ghettos. The Enrichment Choice would aim at creating dramatic improvements in the quality of life in disadvantaged central-city neighborhoods—both white and Negro. It would re-

quire marked increases in federal spending for education, housing, employment, job training, and social services.

The Enrichment Choice would seek to lift poor Negroes and whites above poverty status and thereby give them the capacity to enter the mainstream of American life. But it would not, at least for many years, appreciably affect either the increasing concentration of Negroes in the ghetto or racial segregation in residential areas outside the ghetto....

The Integration Choice....

The third and last course open to the nation combines enrichment with programs designed to encourage integration of substantial numbers of Negroes into the society outside the ghetto.

Enrichment must be an important adjunct to any integration course. No matter how ambitious or energetic such a program may be, few Negroes now living in central-city ghettos would be quickly integrated. In the meantime, significant improvement in their present environment is essential....

[I]n any event, what should be clearly recognized is that enrichment is only a means toward the goal; it is not the goal.

The goal must be achieving freedom for every citizen to live and work according to his capacities and desires, not his color.

We believe there are four important reasons why American society must give this course the most serious consideration. First, future jobs are being created primarily in the suburbs, but the chronically unemployed population is increasingly concentrated in the ghetto. This separation will make it more and more difficult for Negroes to achieve anything like full employment in decent jobs. But if, over time, these residents began to find housing outside central cities, they would be exposed to more knowledge of job opportunities. They would have to make much shorter trips to reach jobs. They would have a far better chance of securing employment on a self-sustaining basis.

Second, in the judgment of this Commission, racial and social-class integration is the most effective way of improving the education of ghetto children.

Third, developing an adequate housing supply for low-income and middle-income families and true freedom of choice in housing for Negroes of all income levels will require substantial out-movement. We do not believe that such an out-movement will occur spontaneously merely as a result of increasing prosperity among Negroes in central cities. A national fair housing law is essential to begin such movement. In many suburban areas, a program combining positive incentives with the building of new housing will be necessary to carry it out.

Fourth, and by far the most important, integration is the only course which explicitly seeks to achieve a single nation rather than accepting the present movement toward a dual society. This choice would enable us at least to begin reversing the profoundly divisive trend already so evident in our metropolitan areas—before it becomes irreversible....

12-5. JONATHAN KOZOL DESCRIBES INEQUALITY IN URBAN AND SUBURBAN SCHOOLS, 1991

Source: *Savage Inequalities* by Jonathan Kozol, copyright © 1991 by Jonathan Kozol. Used by permission of Crown Publishers, a division of Random House, Inc.

"Drive west on the Eisenhower Expressway," writes the *Chicago Tribune*, "out past the hospital complex, and look south." Before your eyes are block after block of old, abandoned, gaping factories. "The overwhelming sensation is emptiness....What's left is, literally, nothing."

This emptiness—"an industrial slum without the industry," a local resident calls it—is North Lawndale. The neighborhood, according to the *Tribune*, "has one bank, one supermarket, 48 state lottery agents...and 99 licensed bars and liquor stores." With only a single supermarket, food is of poor quality and overpriced. Martin Luther King, who lived in this neighborhood in 1966, said there was a 10-to-20-percent "color tax" on produce, an estimate that still holds true today. With only a single bank, there are few loans available for home repair; private housing therefore has deteriorated quickly.

According to the 1980 census, 58 percent of men and women 17 and older in North Lawndale had no jobs. The 1990 census is expected to show no improvement. Between 1960 and 1970, as the last white families left the neighborhood, North Lawndale lost three quarters of its businesses, one quarter of its jobs. In the next ten years, 80 percent of the remaining jobs in manufacturing were lost.

"People carry a lot of crosses here," says Reverend Jim Wolff, who directs a mission church not far from one of the deserted factories....

As the factories have moved out, he says, the street gangs have moved in. Driving with me past a sprawling redbrick complex that was once the world headquarters of Sears, Roebuck, he speaks of the increasing economic isolation of the neighborhood: "Sears is gone. International Harvester is gone. Sunbeam is gone. Western Electric has moved out. The Vice Lords, the Disciples and the Latin Kings have, in a sense, replaced them.

"With the arrival of the gangs there is, of course, more violence and death. I buried a young man 21 years old a week ago. Most of the people that I bury are between the ages of 18 and 30."...

As spring comes to Chicago, the scarcity of [teacher] substitutes [in the city schools] grows more acute....On Mondays and Fridays in early May, nearly 18,000 children—the equivalent of all the elementary students in suburban Glencoe, Wilmette, Glenview, Kenilworth, Winnetka, Deerfield, Highland Park and Evanston—are assigned to classes with no teacher.

In this respect, the city's dropout rate of nearly 50 percent is regarded by some people as a blessing. If over 200,000 of Chicago's total student population of 440,000 did not disappear during their secondary years, it is not clear who would teach them.

In 1989, Chicago spent some $5,500 for each student in its secondary schools. This may be compared to an investment of some $8,500 to $9,000 in each high school student in the highest-spending suburbs to the north. Stated in the simplest terms, this means that any high school class of 30 children in Chicago received approximately $90,000 less each

Figure 12-1 Near West Side of Chicago, 1995. Deindustrialization, fiscal decline, and the decentralization of population and jobs produced a hollowed urban landscape and sharp social disparities across the nation's former manufacturing belt. Photograph by Andrew Wiese.

year than would have been spent on them if they were pupils of a school such as New Trier High [in suburban Winnetka].

The difference in spending between very wealthy suburbs and poor cities is not always as extreme as this in Illinois. When relative student needs, however, have been factored into the discussion, the disparities in funding are enormous. Equity, after all, does not mean simply equal funding. Equal funding for unequal needs is not equality. The need is greater in Chicago, and its children, if they are to have approximately equal opportunities, need more than the children who attend New Trier. Seen in this light, the $90,000 annual difference is quite startling.

Lack of money is not the only problem in Chicago, but the gulf in funding…is so remarkable and seems so blatantly unfair that it strikes many thoughtful citizens at first as inexplicable. How can it be that inequalities as great as these exist in neighboring school districts?

The answer is found, at least in part, in the arcane machinery by which we finance public education. Most public schools in the United States depend for their initial funding on a tax on local property. There are also state and federal funding sources…, but the property tax is the decisive force in shaping inequality. The property tax depends, of course, upon the taxable value of one's home and that of local industries. A typical wealthy suburb in which homes are often worth more than $400,000 draws upon a larger tax base in proportion to its student population than a city occupied by thousands of poor people. Typically, in the United States, very poor communities place high priority on education, and they often tax themselves at higher rates than do the very affluent communities. But, even if they tax themselves at several times the rate of an extremely wealthy district, they are likely to end up with far less money for each child in their schools....

Cities like Chicago face the added problem that an overly large portion of their limited tax revenues must be diverted to meet non-school costs that wealthy suburbs do not face, or only on a far more modest scale. Police expenditures are higher in crime-ridden cities than in most suburban towns. Fire department costs are also higher where dilapidated housing, often with substandard wiring, and arson-for-profit are familiar problems. Public health expenditures are also higher where poor people cannot pay for private hospitals. All of these expenditures compete with those for public schools. So the districts that face the toughest challenges are also likely to be those that have the fewest funds to meet their children's needs.

Many people, even those who view themselves as liberals on other issues, tend to grow indignant, even rather agitated, if invited to look closely at these inequalities. "Life isn't fair," one parent in Winnetka answered flatly when I pressed the matter. "Wealthy children also go to summer camp. All summer. Poor kids maybe not at all....Wealthy children have the chance to go to Europe and they have the access to good libraries, encyclopedias, computers, better doctors, nicer homes. Some of my neighbors send their kids to schools like Exeter and Groton. Is government supposed to equalize these things as well?"

But government, of course, does not assign us to our homes, our summer camps, our doctors—or to Exeter. It does assign us to our public schools. Indeed, it forces us to go to them. Unless we have the wealth to pay for private education, we are compelled by law to go to public school—and to the public school in our district. Thus the state, by

requiring attendance but refusing to require equity, effectively requires inequality. Compulsory inequity, perpetuated by state law, too frequently condemns our children to unequal lives.

In Illinois, as elsewhere in America, local funds for education raised from property taxes are supplemented by state contributions and by federal funds, although the federal contribution is extremely small, constituting only 6 percent of total school expenditures. State contributions represent approximately half of local school expenditures in the United States; although intended to make up for local wealth disparities, they have seldom been sufficient to achieve this goal. Total yearly spending—local funds combined with state assistance and the small amount that comes from Washington—ranges today in Illinois from $2,100 on a child in the poorest district to above $10,000 in the richest. The system, writes John Coons, a professor of law at Berkeley University, "bears the appearance of calculated unfairness."...

Far from the worst school in Chicago, Goudy [Elementary School]'s building is nonetheless depressing. There is no playground. There are no swings. There is no jungle gym.

According to Bonita Brodt, a writer for the *Chicago Tribune* who spent several months at Goudy during 1988, teachers use materials in class long since thrown out in most suburban schools. Slow readers in an eighth grade history class are taught from 15-year-old textbooks in which Richard Nixon is still president. There are no science labs, no art or music teachers. Soap, paper towels and toilet paper are in short supply. There are two working bathrooms for some 700 children.

These children "cry out for something more," the *Tribune* writes. "They do not get it."

"Keisha, look at me," an adult shouts at a slow reader in a sixth grade class. "Look me in the eye." Keisha has been fighting with her classmate. Over what? As it turns out, over a crayon. The child is terrified and starts to cry. Tears spill out of her eyes and drop onto the pages of her math book. In January the school begins to ration crayons, pencils, writing paper....

The bleakness of the children's lives is underlined by one of Goudy's third grade teachers: "I passed out dictionaries once.... One of my students started ripping out the pages when he found a word. I said, 'What are you doing? You leave the pages there for the next person.' And he told me, 'That's their problem. This is my word.'"

Children who go to school in [suburban] towns like Glencoe and Winnetka do not need to steal words from a dictionary....By the time they get to sixth or seventh grade, many are reading at the level of the seniors in the best Chicago high schools. By the time they enter ninth grade at New Trier High, they are in a world of academic possibilities that far exceed the hopes and dreams of most schoolchildren in Chicago.

"Our goal is for students to be successful," says the New Trier principal. With 93 percent of seniors going on to four-year colleges—many to schools like Harvard, Princeton, Berkeley, Brown and Yale—this goal is largely realized.

New Trier's physical setting might well make the students of Du Sable High School [on the South Side of Chicago] envious. The *Washington Post* describes a neighborhood of "circular driveways, chirping birds and white-columned homes." It is, says a student, "a maple land of beauty and civility." While Du Sable is sited on one crowded city block, New Trier students have the use of 27 acres. While Du Sable's science students have to settle for makeshift equipment, New Trier's students have superior labs and up-to-date technology. One wing of the school, a physical education center that includes three separate gyms, also contains a fencing room, a wrestling room and studios for dance instruction. In all, the school has seven gyms as well as an Olympic pool.

The youngsters, according to a profile of the school in *Town and Country* magazine, "make good use of the huge, well-equipped building, which is immaculately maintained by a custodial staff of 48."

It is impossible to read this without thinking of a school like Goudy, where there are no science labs, no music or art classes and no playground—and where the two bathrooms, lacking toilet paper, fill the building with their stench.

"This is a school with a lot of choices," says one student at New Trier; and this hardly seems an overstatement if one studies the curriculum. Courses in music, art and drama are so varied and abundant that students can virtually major in these subjects in addition to their academic programs. The modern and classical language department offers Latin (four years) and six other foreign languages. Elective courses include the literature of Nobel winners, aeronautics, criminal justice, and computer languages.... The school also operates a television station with a broadcast license from the FCC, which broadcasts on four channels to three counties.

Average class size is 24 children; classes for slower learners hold 15. This may be compared to Goudy—where a remedial class holds 39 children and a "gifted" class has 36....

The ambience among the students at New Trier, of whom only 1.3 percent are black, says *Town and Country*, is "wholesome and refreshing, a sort of throwback to the Fifties." It is, we are told, "a preppy kind of place." In a cheerful photo of the faculty and students, one cannot discern a single nonwhite face.

New Trier's "temperate climate" is "aided by the homogeneity of its students," *Town and Country* notes. "Almost all are of European extraction and harbor similar values."...

The wealth of New Trier's geographical district provides $340,000 worth of taxable property for each child; Chicago's property wealth affords only one-fifth this much. Nonetheless, *Town and Country* gives New Trier's parents credit for a "willingness to pay enough...in taxes" to make this one of the state's best-funded schools....Families move here "seeking the best," and their children "make good use" of what they're given. Both statements may be true, but giving people lavish praise for spending what they have strikes one as disingenuous. "A supportive attitude on the part of families in the district translates into a willingness to pay...," the writer says. By this logic, one would be obliged to say that "unsupportive attitudes" on the part of Keisha's mother and the parents of Du Sable's children translate into fiscal selfishness, when, in fact, the economic options open to the parents in these districts are not even faintly comparable. *Town and Country* flatters the privileged for having privilege but terms it aspiration.

"Competition is the lifeblood of New Trier," *Town and Country* writes. But there is one kind of competition that these children will not need to face. They will not compete against the children who attended Goudy and Du Sable. They will compete against each other and against the graduates of other schools attended by rich children. They will not compete against the poor.

It is part of our faith, as Americans, that there is potential in all children. Even among the 700 children who must settle for rationed paper and pencils at Goudy Elementary School, there are surely several dozen; maybe several hundred, who, if given the chance, would thrive and overcome most of the obstacles of poverty if they attended schools like those of Glencoe and Winnetka. We know that very few of them will have that opportunity. Few, as a result, will graduate from high school; fewer still will go to college; scarcely any will attend good colleges. There will be more space for children of New Trier as a consequence.

The denial of opportunity to Keisha and the superfluity of opportunity for children at New Trier High School are not unconnected. The parents of New Trier's feeder districts vote consistently against redistribution of school funding. By a nine-to-one ratio, according to a recent survey, suburban residents resist all efforts to provide more money for Chicago's schools....

ESSAYS

Essay 12-1 is geographer Peter Muller's classic analysis of the economic ascendance of suburbia. Writing at the height of the "urban crisis" in the mid 1970s, he heralds the suburbs as a new kind of "outer city." Muller not only catalogues the patterns of suburban economic growth, but reveals the emerging landscape and spatial arrangements to which they have given rise—the giant shopping malls, high-tech industrial parks, corporate campuses, and high-rise suburban "minicities," which have alternately astonished and confused suburban observers in the decades since. While the decentralization of economic activity had been taking place since the late nineteenth century, as chapter 4 details, the heightened scale, diversity, and visibility of this activity caused many to treat this as a new trend.

While Muller attributes this shift in economic clout from cities to suburbs primarily to market forces and the impact of technology—especially the "locational pull" of outer-city expressways—in **Essay 12-2**, historian Robert Self situates the postwar transformation of metropolitan America squarely in the arena of politics and political economy. In this excerpt, a case study of the Oakland suburb of San Leandro, California, Self illuminates the fiscal, territorial, and racial policies that produced competition between industrial cities and their suburbs after the war. Like Muller, Self approaches the whole metropolis as his unit of analysis. In this context, he emphasizes connections between "development" in some places and "underdevelopment" in others.

12-1. PETER O. MULLER, *THE OUTER CITY: THE GEOGRAPHICAL CONSEQUENCES OF THE URBANIZATION OF THE SUBURBS* (1976)

Source: Copyright © 1976 by the American Association of Geographers. Used by permission of the American Association of Geographers.

I. The Outer City in Space and Time...

Urbanization trends in the United States today indicate suburbia to be the essence of the contemporary American city. It is now patently evident that the suburbs are no longer "sub" to the "urb" in the traditional sense. Chiefly as a result of the recent intrametro-

Figure 12-2 This view toward the Irvine Town Center in Orange County, California, exemplifies the multi-nodal "outer city"—a mix of suburban housing, offices, retail, and manufacturing that has helped shift the balance of power from central cities to outlying suburban centers. In the right distance is a second growth "node" focused around Disneyland in Anaheim. Photograph by Andrew Wiese, 2005.

politan deconcentration of economic activity following in the wake of the enormous population exodus from the central cities in the last quarter century, suburbia in the late 1970s is emerging as *the outer city*. Expressed geographically, this transformation involves a shift from the tightly focused single-core urban region of the past to the widely dispersed multi-nodal metropolis of today. As a result, large new outlying urban centers of considerable locational pull have rapidly emerged in the seventies, and such suburban minicities as Newport Center (Los Angeles), Schaumburg (Chicago), Cherry Hill (Philadelphia), and the Galleria (Houston) are already widely known....

The 1970 census clearly documents the vast scale and new dominance of America's suburbs. Although these data are already several years old..., the suburban trends they indicate persist into the 1970s, and they still paint a vivid portrait of a decidedly suburban nation:

- 37.6 percent (76.3 million) of the U.S. population resided in the suburbs in 1970, with 31.4 percent (63.8 million) living in central cities and 31.0 percent (63.0 million) in rural areas; the latest 1975 population estimates show these proportions to be 39.1 percent suburban, 29.6 percent central city, and 31.3 percent rural

- 54.2 percent of the nation's 1970 metropolitan population lived outside central cities; in the 25 largest metropolitan areas 62.7 percent resided in the suburban ring

- in the 1960s suburbs grew more than five times faster than the central cities, capturing 84 percent of all urban population growth....

- in the 1960s the suburban share of metropolitan employment in the largest metropolitan areas grew by 44 percent compared to a seven percent decrease for the central cities;...by the end of 1973 suburban employment nationwide exceeded the cities' job total for the first time

- suburban political power has expanded to the point where it now accounts for the largest bloc of seats in the U.S. House of Representatives (131 suburban; 130 rural; 102 central city; and 72 mixed districts with many partially suburban) as well as control of several key state legislatures....

However one regards the data, it all adds up to the ongoing urbanization of the suburbs. Old distinctions between city and suburb are disappearing. In fact, America's largest "city" in 1970 was suburban New York (8.9 million). In partial recognition of that status, the federal government designated Greater New York's Long Island salient (Nassau and Suffolk Counties) the nation's first all-suburban SMSA in 1972....

The deconcentration of [economic] activities appears to be one of the strongest forces in sustaining the current urbanization of the suburbs....Contemporary suburbia offers an attractive locational alternative for most metropolitan activities and now shares, and even usurps, nearly all the exclusively downtown-bound functions of the past. A few of these functions which are currently decentralizing successfully are international corporation headquarters, financial institutions with extensive regional operations, major league sports, and musical and theatrical events of national importance. To be sure, urbanization has also had its negative side-effects in suburbia as the outer city now shares many of the central city's social, political, environmental, and transportation problems.

As the suburbs approach self-sufficiency increasing numbers of its residents avoid the central city altogether. Understandably, this trend is having a devastating impact on big cities because those catalytic activities and talented leaders needed to reverse the present exodus are themselves pulling up stakes for destinations beyond the city line....

III. The New Role of the Suburbs in Metropolitan Economic Geography...

The suburbanization of commerce and industry, underway for the first two-thirds of this century, has accelerated strikingly since the mid-sixties, and its intensification in the 1970s has reshaped the economic geography of the metropolis. Retailing and the rapid rise of the catalytic regional shopping center led this latest and most vigorous episode of intraurban activity deconcentration. Following close behind was the dramatic upsurge in the suburbanization of employment, not only in manufacturing but increasingly in office-based...functions. Originally content to locate at any interchange or other site convenient to the expressway network,

suburban economic activities are now gravitating toward each other. Accordingly, multifunctional urban cores (minicities) have emerged swiftly in the outer city, and these major nodes are now beginning to confer a greater degree of spatial order on the heretofore centerless distribution of production in the suburbs....

The Suburbanization of Manufacturing Since 1960...

As the metropolis is transforming [due to highway construction] into an all but frictionless area vis-á-vis goods movement, transportation costs no longer shape the spatial structure of its manufacturing activity.... [I]ndustrial entrepreneurs are free to move to the "best" urban site they can find. Noneconomic factors come to the fore in such locational decision-making, and the perceived advantages of suburban sites are accentuated for just about every kind of industrial operation. Overriding these non-cost-related forces today is the prestige factor in suburban industrial location, which is fast becoming central to an understanding of the contemporary spatial organization of urban manufacturing....

Thus firms increasingly avoid low status areas such as the blighted inner city, much of the urban waterfront, and even the older suburban rail corridors whereas they covet prestigious outlying locations. Until recently high amenity residential suburbs were most prized for several obvious reasons, not the least of which was the chief executive's desire to minimize his personal commuting time....Much more important has been the gravitation of suburban industry to freeway corridors, not only for their superior accessibility but also for their priceless visibility, advertising, and image enhancement opportunities. Practically every suburban expressway in the nation is lined with prominently displayed modern plants where site amenities (at least on the side facing the freeway) are given greater weight in facility design than production-related needs. Lately, industrial plants have indicated a stronger preference for expressway nodes, particularly those possessing the most glamorous suburban addresses in the proximity of superregional shopping malls....

Selected Data On the Deconcentration of Intrametropolitan Economic Activity in the Fifteen Largest SMSAs

SMSA	Percent Suburban Share Total Jobs		Percent Suburban Share Total SMSA Retail Sales		Percent Suburban Share Total SMSA Manufacturing Employment	
	1960	1970	1963	1972	1963	1972
New York	28.8	35.9	32.9	N.A.	19.1	53.4
Los Angeles*	47.8	54.3	58.7	60.0	63.9	64.0
Chicago	32.2	47.5	43.1	56.8	41.0	57.4
Philadelphia	37.0	51.8	56.6	66.7	50.5	59.3
Detroit	43.3	61.4	57.3	74.1	59.3	67.6
San Francisco	44.9	50.0	52.0	63.3	53.3	62.3
Washington DC	36.2	54.9	57.9	76.3	55.8	64.7
Boston	55.5	62.2	68.8	76.3	71.8	78.2
Pittsburgh	64.0	63.7	65.9	77.0	70.0	76.1
St. Louis	39.3	58.0	62.5	77.2	50.3	62.0
Baltimore	34.1	49.9	41.9	61.5	45.4	68.3
Cleveland	28.3	46.0	45.2	69.0	39.7	51.3
Houston*	15.7	24.4	17.6	29.0	28.8	34.3
Minneapolis-St. Paul	23.6	41.1	38.5	62.9	32.7	45.3
Dallas*	24.4	29.0	28.8	58.6	21.2	53.6
Average	37.0	47.6	48.5	64.9	46.8	59.9

* Annexation of suburban territory since 1960.

Current Trends in the Location of Suburban Office Activity

Many of the same processes contributing to the prestige-related deconcentration of manufacturing are also working to reshape the intraurban distribution of office-based employment. After modest postwar beginnings, suburbanization of the office industry has accelerated since the mid-1960s. Pioneering sales offices of manufacturers were followed by large routine-operation insurance and other companies; they in turn were pursued by a myriad of smaller computer, research, and other service firms. In the next stage, regional offices of large national companies arrived, followed closely by a steadily rising number of major corporate headquarters. Finally, the dispersal of supposedly exclusively downtown-bound elitist office functions began....

The Suburbanization of Corporate Headquarters

[T]he ongoing intrametropolitan deconcentration of major corporate headquarters has signalled a new phase in the suburbanization of the office industry. Nowhere is this spatial behavioral trend more apparent than in the decentralization of traditionally downtown-bound international corporation headquarters from Manhattan to New York's suburbs....

From 1969 to 1974, suburban New York registered a spectacular increase of from five to 50 corporate headquarters listed in *Fortune*'s annual directory of the nation's 500 largest industrial firms; at the same time, New York City's share of these home offices has dwindled from 140 in the mid-1960s to just over 90 in 1976....

Although metropolitan New York has received the most publicity, the recent suburbanization of corporate head offices is a nationwide phenomenon....Boston lost 75 large companies to its suburbs in 1970–71 and St. Louis 43 in 1970 alone; Los Angeles saw several major banks desert its CBD; and in Detroit, which recently lost S.S. Kresge, Bendix, Budd, and both of its daily newspaper offices to the suburbs, things are so depressing that former mayor [Jerome] Cavanaugh refers to "Detroit's sister cities—Nagasaki and Pompeii," and a sign at a business banquet not long ago read "Will the Last

Company to Leave Detroit Please Turn Out the Lights."...

Suburban Office Location Types...

Early postwar suburban offices, like manufacturing plants, were usually isolated and scattered widely among outlying sites offering good highway access. Although the high-amenity, single-company business campus concept was developed before 1950 (most notably by Reader's Digest in New York's Westchester suburb of Pleasantville), the innovation was slow to catch on until the late 1960s. A parallel trend...involved the growth of specialized centers containing concentrations of smaller offices. By the early 1970s..., both locational types came to dominate the suburban office scene. With the recent wave of major corporate headquarters decentralization, the business campus (now frequently dominated by high-rise structures) has been developed to a sophisticated and prestigious architectural level. Smaller centers have also proliferated rapidly since 1970 particularly in the form of office parks, the newest locational concept in the industry.

Suburban office parks include many of the same attractions as industrial parks, especially prestigious addresses, self-contained concentrative economies, and easy access to other business centers....Office park development in recent years has...been considerable and is typified by suburban Atlanta which grew from one facility in 1964 to 40 office parks employing nearly 25,000 workers in 1974. The internal structure and range of supporting services in newer office parks emphasizes the ultimate in prestige and luxury: imaginative combinations of high- and low-rise buildings designed by famous architects; elegant restaurants and visitor reception areas; and such frills as swimming pools, tennis courts, saunas, and jogging and bike trails....

As office parks multiply and grow ever larger, they enhance the position of the suburbs as a site for complete white-collar business concentrations. Nearly every metropolis now contains at least one such high-prestige suburban office cluster, typified by Westchester's "Platinum Mile" of glamorous business complexes which line the central section of that county's major east-west expressway. As was the case with intraurban manufacturing activity, suburban moves by major office firms are now beginning to affect the location decisions of others: More than one corporation has recently shifted to the suburbs because its competitors have found it advantageous to do so....

Minicities and Suburban Spatial Organization

Integration of the location trends shaping the suburban distribution of retailing, manufacturing, and the office industry shows a growing propensity for economic activities to gravitate toward each other. Pacesetting superregional shopping centers with their myriad social activities, complete attunement to the automobile, and regionwide drawing power via freeway, have become such focal points in the outer city. Their immediate vicinities assume an equally glamorous aura, and attract manufacturing and office employers whose current locational desires are fully satisfied at these prestigious sites highly accessible to labor and established suburban business facilities. The result has been the emergence of major multi-functional urban cores which are rapidly coming to dominate the economic geography of contemporary suburbia....

Thus we are now witnessing the rise of a continuous unitary curvilinear outer city whose circumferential freeway spine funcions as both lifeline and main street of suburbia....

[One example is the] remarkable development along suburban Baltimore's Beltway. Known locally as the "Golden Horseshoe," this corridor is capturing much of the productive activity in the metropolis. Several important suburban facilities were already located close to its path (e.g., Bethlehem Steel's vast Sparrows Point complex which employs more than 30,000 workers); and major employers such as the U.S. Social Security Administration (13,000 employees), which recently relocated from the central city to its new headquarters office complex adjacent to the Beltway..., continue to be attracted in rising numbers. Moreover, the Golden Horsehoe is unique in that it lies within the single political jurisdiction of suburban Baltimore County, thus overcoming the development conflicts which frequently occur among municipalities....

The success of suburban Baltimore's circumferential expressway corridor has been equalled and surpassed in the adjoining suburbs of the District of Columbia to the southwest where the Capital Beltway has truly become the main street of metropolitan Washington....

Since 1960, nearly one million new residents have settled in the Capital Beltway corridor. A dozen regional malls as well as several other major suburban activity nuclei have sprung up at nearly every one of the 38 exits along the freeway's 66-mile length. New employment is burgeoning with the federal government playing a leading role in the economic development of the corridor. Nearly half the region's federal jobs have dispersed from the District of Columbia, with a sizeable proportion of them now located along the Beltway....

As the huge office complexes of the federal government disperse to the Maryland and Virginia suburbs, they create an enormous impact on the communities to or from which they move. Since many employ thousands of modestly skilled workers who reside in Washington's inner city, the social consequences of the suburbanization of these facilities are generally negative. Despite the rising protest of the District's blacks and other disadvantaged groups about their greatly reduced access to these suburban jobs which are frequently relocated from central city neighborhoods, the federal government seems to be acting no differently from other employers who abandon the city with little regard for the problems of the labor force left behind.

Perhaps the most far-reaching impact of the Capital Beltway and its sister circumferential freeways is that they foster suburban self-sufficiency and independence. With multi-functional minicities offering the full array of urban goods and services and with driving times such that half the Beltway can be traversed in less time than it takes to travel from any point on it into downtown Washington, a steadily increasing number of suburban residents are avoiding the central city altogether.

Suburban Avoidance of the Central City and the Metropolitan Future...

A sampling of recent press reports reveals an emerging consensus of suburban perception of the central city: irrelevant. Everything the suburban resident requires now lies within easy automobile reach in the outer city, and when a rare good or service is not available a close suburban substitute is usually accepted in place of the undesirable trip to center city; not surprisingly, most suburbanites interviewed either could not remember their last visit downtown or recalled only a single trip there in connection with a special occasion....

Detachment from the central city can be interpreted according to the demographic composition of today's suburban population. The postwar generation is to a large degree suburban-born without first-hand experience in true city living. Moreover, the lion's share of recent migration to the suburbs has come not from the adjacent central city but from largely suburban origins in other metropolitan areas. Thus, "[m]ost new suburbanites have no ties whatsoever to the old [central] city. It is not the hub of their cultural, economic, material, or social lives; it is not their previous home; it is nothing to them—just another place (not even a relatively large place) in their sprawling metropolitan home territory. What impact do arguments of moral responsibility or abstract dependency have for these people? Virtually none."...

Given this suburban attitude, what, then, is to become of the central cities? The intra-metropolitan deconcentration of the most vital population groups and a critical mass of economic activities cannot continue for much longer before we become a nation with no important cities. Though many urban planners and other enthusiastic proponents of city living insist that central cities are recoverable, trends shaping the metropolitan reality as the twentieth century ends would dictate otherwise. The big city is not yet dead, but its economic and cultural raisons d'etre are disappearing.

12-2. ROBERT O. SELF, *AMERICAN BABYLON: RACE AND THE STRUGGLE FOR POSTWAR OAKLAND* (2003)

Source: Copyright © 2003 Princeton University Press. Reprinted by permission of Princeton University Press.

Driving South from Oakland [California] into the adjacent suburban community of San Leandro, an observer in 1948 would have found it impossible to know when he or she had crossed from one city into the other. The tree-lined streets and 1920s-era bungalows common to both would have offered no clue. Even the industrial landscape would have struck the casual observer rolling past small machine shops and warehouses as a single piece. Not far from the fading brown brick of the General Motors Durant plant on East Fourteenth Street in Oakland was the red brick Caterpillar Tractor plant in San Leandro. Both would have hummed with activity and spilled workers onto the streets at shift change.... San Leandro looked like a good deal of East Oakland in 1948, but their postwar histories would be very different. To understand why, we must cross Oakland's boundary and move into the expanding neighboring suburbs....

Between 1945 and the early 1960s, cities south of Oakland, between East Oakland and San Jose, emerged as the industrial garden imagined in the Metropolitan Oakland Area Program [MOAP, a local economic development campaign begun in Oakland in 1935]. By the 1970s one could trace a straight line on a map following this landscape from Oakland's southern edge through San Leandro, Hayward, Union City, Newark, Fremont, and Milpitas to San Jose's northern boundary forty miles away in the South Bay. San Leandro and Hayward alone existed as corporate cities prior to the mid-1950s. The others incorporated during that decade, as civic entrepreneurs from the scattered towns, farms, and orchards of the East Bay flatlands forged new municipalities. Conceived as lo-

cations of both employment and residence, of factories and homes, the suburbs they created were designed locally but depended on national developments: the unprecedented postwar federal mortgage guarantee program, new federal interstate highways, and capital mobility. This pattern of growth elaborated the MOAP's suburban vision, but it also undermined Oakland, creating cities and economic networks that would compete with, as much as complement, the presumed "center" of the new industrial West.

Postwar suburbanization in the United States was driven by the politics of making markets in property and in maintaining exclusionary access to those markets.... In the postwar decades, three primary sets of interests came together to shape suburbanization and...suburban markets:...the federal state, local city-builders, and white homeowners. Each brought an ideological and material investment in the process of market creation. The resulting "compact" between these different agents, worked out over more than a decade, made the postwar suburb possible....

First, postwar homeownership developed with the assistance of massive state subsidies. The federal government dramatically democratized the housing market for whites while simultaneously enforcing a racial segregation that resembled apartheid. State intervention in the housing market made financing single-family homes more profitable to lenders, more accessible to white buyers, and virtually unobtainable for African Americans.... [F]or more than thirty years, the Federal Housing Administration and the Veterans Administration...underwrote segregation. Because of the enormous sums of capital involved—billions of dollars annually—their actions gave contour to the entire national housing market....

The second architect of suburbanization, local city-builders, came in the East Bay from a broad, diffuse entrepreneurial political class that managed municipal incorporation campaigns between Oakland and San Jose. Unlike California's celebrated "community builders," who constructed entire cities from a single massive property—and made famous such places as Irvine, Rancho

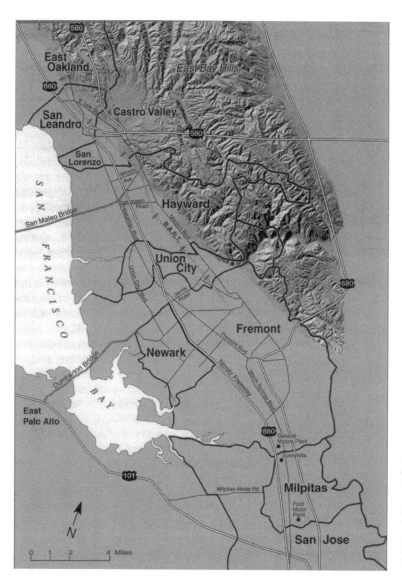

Figure 12-3 Suburban Alameda County in the 1960s. The dark lines indicate new municipal boundaries. Between 1945 and 1958 all of the available unincorporated land between Oakland and San Jose, west of the hills, was incorporated into existing or altogether new cities. Only San Lorenzo and Castro Valley, bedroom communities with no industry, resisted this process. Altogether it was an extraordinary land rush with few equals in California. Cartography Lab, University of Wisconsin. Illustration in original, 123.

California, Huntington Beach, and Foster City—the East Bay's suburban civic founders were neither large landholders nor, with a few exceptions, major developers. They were almost universally middle-class professionals, industrialists, modest landholders, and merchants, men and women who had smaller, though no less real, financial stakes in incorporation....[C]ity-builders set out to create and maximize two kinds of property markets, one in industrial land the other in residential. They did so in order to finance public services, maintain home equity, and, in the optimistic and market-driven logic of American development, to ensure future economic growth. This city building was politi-

cal because interests differed over how those markets would be created and racialized, and territorial because the way municipal boundaries were drawn, how the tax burden was distributed, and where people lived in relation to where they worked depended on both an imagined and real geography.

The third agent of suburban city building, white homeowners, was also the most diverse group....They were diverse in class background and place of origin, but the structure of the housing markets into which they entered in the postwar decades would begin to give them a common identity, to shape for them a set of concerns and interests that would unite more than divide them. These issues started with the concrete economics of taxes and home values. No investment an average family in midcentury America would make in their lifetime was larger than that in their home, and in California, perhaps more than anywhere else in the nation, the detached, single-family home had been elevated in popular culture as the preeminent symbol of both independence and assimilation. Together, markets and culture—and later, electoral politics—encouraged homeowners in suburban California to identify property ownership first and foremost in terms of their own individual financial interests.

Over time, the product of the suburban compact between the federal state, city-builders, and homeowners in the East Bay was a set of expectations and ideologies that could be mobilized politically. Three key elements lay at the core of those expectations. First, homeowners came to expect, and later demand, low property taxes. Second, they came to expect and rationalize racial segregation. Finally, they came to accept as natural the conflation of whiteness and property ownership with upward social mobility.... In these suburbs, homeownership stood at the core of political identification, and small property holders emerged as the most important social class and political constituency.... Far from the cradle of republican independence and American voluntarism its proponents proclaimed, homeownership among white families was one of the most state-subsidized features of the postwar national economy....

San Leandro: The Industrial Garden Realized

San Leandro entered the national iconography of suburban industrial growth in 1966 when it was named a "model municipality" by the *Wall Street Journal*. In the 1920s San Leandro had served as a bedroom community for both San Francisco and Oakland commuters and as a truck farming center that provided vegetables, fruit, and cut flowers to nearby cities—the "land of sunshine and flowers," boosters bragged. Its streets and neighborhoods were indistinguishable from those of East Oakland, where the modest homes of skilled workers, merchants, and

semiprofessionals blended into San Leandro's northern edge in a suburban menage typical of the East Bay's flatland geography. Despite its size (22,903 in 1940) and semirural orientation, however, San Leandro had attracted a few notable industries—a Caterpillar Tractor assembly plant and Frieden Calculators, in particular—before the war. After 1945 the city's civic leaders, developers, and wartime newcomers added to that industrial base by converting nearby agricultural land into cheap factory and housing sites in pursuit of what they termed "balanced development." San Leandro's choices underline how "model municipality" was understood, not just by the *Journal* but by those who built the city. Civic leaders and homeowners chose industrial growth led by low taxes as one foundation and racial segregation as another.... Through their choices and politics, San Leandro residents realized one version of suburbanization: dynamic industrial job growth and pastoral neighborhoods enclosed behind the exclusionary walls of apartheid. It was a civic space that would profoundly influence the future of both Oakland and suburban Alameda County.

Between 1946 and 1948 the San Leandro City Council hotly debated the direction and pace of industrial development.... On the one hand, the city could encourage industrial investment by allowing companies to build new factories on unincorporated land outside of the municipal tax district. On the other, the city could require industry to locate within San Leandro while expanding its municipal boundaries to incorporate existing and future factories. In the latter instance, according to [local newspaper editor George] Thompson, "with industry paying its full pro-rata share of city government costs, and thereby in the long run reducing all city taxes," the results would "make this community a better place in which to live and work." In 1947, however, the council struck a deal with Chrysler Motor Parts in which the latter received a full slate of municipal services—including water, sewer, fire, and police—while remaining outside San Leandro's city limits, its properties off the tax rolls. Thompson and others fumed.... "The average homeowner should not be expected to underwrite the costs of industry," Thompson editorialized. "Those same industries, sharing in the benefits which the community has to offer them…must be made to realize their community responsibility."

Thompson's language was bursting with a largely inchoate, but nonetheless powerfully persuasive, discourse that championed homeowners by echoing American traditions of populism.… In places like the East Bay suburbs, populism was refashioned in the postwar decades in the form of a homeowner-centered faith in the righteousness of the "small taxpayer." Homeowner populism brought property taxes to the fore of local politics and tied the fulfillments of suburban living to the tax revenues generated by corporate industrial property owners.… In this period, under the conditions of city building, a low tax burden was understood by people like Thompson as part of a common-sense "fair" distribution of local economic burdens.

Civic leaders, neighborhood associations, industrialists, and politicians all understood the enormous relevance and long-term consequences of mundane decisions about sewer bond measures, municipal boundaries, and the siting of industrial property. The East Shore Park Civic League, a neighborhood association representing new wartime residential development, emerged as the city's most vocal advocate of using industrial property taxes to improve municipal services and the physical infrastructure of the city—especially sidewalks, sewer lines, street lights, and other amenities in East Shore Park itself. Between 1946 and 1948 the League grew disenchanted with the existing city council, which was composed of an established generation of San Leandro businessmen…who, so it appeared to the organized newcomers, overburdened new homeowners to accommodate corporations like Chrysler. Barbara Burbank, a self-declared "scribe" for the East Shore Park Civic League, asked her readers if they "know how much of the city taxes come from your neighborhood?" and "how much of that is spent in your neighborhood?" The league was not antitax in an absolute sense, but…believed that neighborhoods should be shielded from high taxes by shifting the

city's fiscal burden onto those businesses and industries that could, in Thompson's words, "well afford to pay."

In 1948 the East Shore Park Civic League translated these concerns into electoral politics, when they swept the incumbent city councilmembers from office with a reform slate pledged to "let the people decide and know where their tax dollar is spent."…According to the *News-Observer*, the city's governing clique "forgot to remember that there are thousands of little property owners who were not impressed with the desirability of underwriting the manufacturing costs of such enterprises as the Chrysler corporation."…

The electoral victory of 1948 set the stage for a political and administrative consensus in San Leandro that carried the city through a remarkable period of industrial and residential growth. With plenty of neighboring "vacant" agricultural land for new and expanding factories, San Leandro enjoyed what its boosters liked to call "natural advantages." The new city council, the city manager appointed by the 1948 reform slate, and the Chamber of Commerce developed an industrial strategy designed to transform San Leandro from the "city of sunshine and flowers" into the "city of industry." As long as new businesses located within the municipal boundaries, taxes on industrial property would fund city services. Yet the property tax rate would be deliberately low, both to accommodate the "thousands of little property owners" who voted and to attract new industrial capital seeking entry into the Bay Area's rapidly expanding postwar markets. There could hardly have been a more ironic reformulation of the Metropolitan Oakland Area Program than this low-tax industrial strategy. Regional East Bay growth "with Oakland at the center"…yielded in reality to intercity competition. Between 1948 and the late 1960s, San Leandro competed for new investment with nearby Oakland, Hayward, and Fremont, as well as with the South Bay and San Francisco Peninsula, by driving its property tax rate to the lowest level in California.

While San Leandro's city manager coordinated with business and political leaders on an industrial strategy, homeowners and real estate developers articulated a related, but still distinct, exclusionary racial strategy. Prior to World War II in San Leandro, as in the southern East Bay generally, a hierarchy of social status delineated people according to race, nation of origin, and religion. The city's large Catholic Portuguese population, for instance, included a sizable middle class of merchants and professionals who had achieved some social standing in the eyes of the city's residents of northern European, Protestant background. Nonetheless, working-class Portuguese often found themselves denigrated by Anglos, because of the latter's distaste for the "Spanish" or "Mexican" workers who provided much of the region's agricultural labor. Ethnic Mexican laborers and Japanese truck farmers experienced housing discrimination and other abuses, as did the fewer Chinese American residents. Middle-class Mexican, Japanese, and Chinese American merchants and professionals, however, could occasionally break into civic leadership circles....This hierarchy of race and nation did not disappear, but after the war San Leandrans specifically targeted newly arrived African Americans in Oakland for legal exclusion....

Homeowners in San Leandro defended their rights against corporate property owners while trampling on the rights of African Americans at the same time. They crafted a populism, which, like its nineteenth-century counterpart, embraced both the possibility of an inclusive progressive politics of the "little guy" and an exclusionary racism mobilized against blacks. For San Leandro's real estate brokers and homeowners, racial restriction was rationalized as a way to maintain low property taxes and high property values. Segregation was reinforced by the fact that the federal government had promoted white-only suburbanization since the 1930s, first through the Home Owners Loan Corporation, then through the Federal Housing Administration (FHA).... Between the end of World War II and the 1960s, the FHA and VA guaranteed more than $3.3 million in home loans in San Leandro, an enormous subsidy for white homeownership denied to African Americans. The view that African Americans

lowered the value of property became widely accepted by whites and encouraged both homeowners and real estate agents to utilize an array of devices to maintain racial exclusivity even as federal policy slowly changed in the postwar era.

Immediately after the war, San Leandro residents erected a figurative white wall along the city's border with Oakland. M. C. Friel and Associates, a Hayward real estate firm with expertise in racial covenants, became the East Bay's leading consultant on shoring up segregation. In 1947 Friel developed a plan to place as much of San Leandro's residential property under restrictive covenants as possible, limiting future property sales to "members of the Caucasian race." Such restrictions had been used in San Francisco and parts of the East Bay for decades to contain the mobility of Chinese and Japanese residents, and while Friel's postwar covenants perpetuated such exclusions, his 1947 tactics were aimed at newly arrived African Americans. The *San Leandro News-Observer* reported in the autumn of 1947 that Friel outlined his "plan for protecting property values" in an address "before the board of directors of the Chamber of Commerce," which concluded with "the board giving its approval of the program...." In undisguised language the *News-Observer* announced that the "sudden increase in the East Bay Negro population" meant that "local neighborhoods are spontaneously moving to protect their property values and calling upon Friel's company to assist them."

San Leandro's campaign of racial exclusion earned the city a regional reputation. The *San Francisco Chronicle*, reporting on Friel's efforts in early 1948, lamented that the "closed door" policy of cities like San Leandro had exacerbated the postwar housing crisis in the "Bay Area's non-white districts." Such liberal lamentations, however, did little to disrupt patterns of racial segregation. Even the U.S. Supreme Court's ruling against covenant enforcement in 1948 (*Shelley v. Kraemer*) slowed but did not halt the process. Already known in the East Bay for designing racial covenants that could survive close legal scrutiny, Friel responded to the Court's landmark decision by reconfiguring San Leandro's covenant agreements into "neighborhood protective associations," pseudo-corporations of homeowners that could legally select acceptable homebuyers through "corporation contract agreements" as long as "race and creed" were not taken into account....

San Leandro's zealous pursuit of racial homogeneity and rising property values in the late 1940s and into the 1950s, as well as its policy of racial restriction, occurred under no pressure from actual African American mobility. African Americans could not purchase homes anywhere in East Oakland until 1950 because of policies enforced by the real estate industry in Oakland. During 1947 and 1948, Friel's most active period in San Leandro, no black homebuyers could purchase property within miles of the city. Yet its residents pursued restrictions with fervent determination. As parts of East Oakland opened to black families in the 1950s and 1960s, San Leandro remained firmly closed.... During those same decades, San Leandro's industrial growth and its obvious prosperity contrasted sharply with East Oakland's deindustrialization (including the closing of two automobile factories) and the emergence there of the city's poorest African American neighborhoods. Such consequences were not the product of white "backlash." They were the product of an assertive, aggressive segregation policy pursued by the federal state and supported by local white consensus before African Americans had even arrived in nearby neighborhoods....

San Leandro residents shared a sense of participating in the creation of a civic space that excluded African Americans, which gave at least one concrete meaning to the otherwise impressionistic terms "Caucasian" and "white."

San Leandro's postwar development illustrates the social production of space in postwar metropolitan America.... In this structure, political boundaries became economic boundaries. Because San Leandro was a municipality—and not, for instance, a neighborhood within a larger city like Oakland—it could deploy the powers of a municipality to set tax policy, annex outlying industry, and establish zoning patterns to create potential markets for investment and to leverage property taxes into public services and infrastructure. These public powers, unavailable to big-city neighborhoods, were crucial components and tools of postwar suburbanization, because they reified physical boundaries and made them markers of profit potential and indicators of safe investment. At the same time, real estate brokers and homeowners mobilized private contracts and agreements among property holders into an apartheid-like set of racial restrictions on mobility. These restrictions enjoyed official local support through the San Leandro Chamber of Commerce and city council and federal support through FHA and VA redlining, but their most fundamental characteristic was an agreement among local property holders on how to construct and organize the city as racial space.

Between the late 1940s and the late 1960s, two great rivers of public and private capital surged through the nation, enriching and developing certain kinds of places, primarily suburban, and contributing to the underdevelopment of others, primarily urban. San Leandro had positioned itself well in relation to these currents and stood to benefit enormously from them. The first was the unprecedented federal underwriting of private home construction through the mortgage guarantee programs of the VA and the FHA.... The second river had two forks. One was federal military contracts that fed private companies like Lockheed, Boeing, Douglas Aircraft, Convair, and dozens of others. California received more than an ample share of these contracts—upon which entire communities were built in places like Sunnyvale, Pasadena, and Long Beach—but San Leandro and the East Bay were minor recipients of this kind of largess. A second fork, however, did flow through San Leandro: manufacturing capital decentralizing from the nation's older industrial heartland in the East and Midwest and seeking new, moderate-sized facilities to produce consumer products for southern and West Coast markets.... [I]ndustries based in the East or Midwest opened branch plants in California employing between 150 and 500 workers throughout the 1940s and 1950s. Other local businesses followed, some looking to leave older facilities and high taxes in cities like Oakland, others looking for land on which to build a first plant or warehouse.

Having positioned itself to capture these postwar capital flows, San Leandro enjoyed a two-decade boom envied by its East Bay civic rivals. Between 1948 and 1957 the city added 15,000 industrial jobs and over $130 million in capital investment in property and facilities.... In just five years, between 1951 and 1956, the city's assessed property valuation nearly tripled, from just over $31 million to just over $85 million; by the early 1960s industry in San Leandro paid more than one-third of the cost of city government....San Leandrans had created a working-class city with middle-class amenities: the industrial garden....

San Leandro's public officials navigated the city according to the logic encouraged by postwar American growth economics: expand the pie and everyone's piece is bigger. The city avoided the potential pitfalls of its low-tax development strategy—underfunded schools and poor city services—with two conservative fiscal tactics based on an inflationary property market. First, with the exception of the 1947 bonds for sewer facilities, between the early fifties and mid seventies the city never went into bonded debt, adopting instead a "pay-as-you-go" philosophy. With no debt payments, the city could dedicate tax revenues solely to schools, fire and police, and other basic municipal responsibilities. Second, as the value of existing property in the city increased, and as new property was added through annexation and capital investment in plants and factories, the city could lower its tax rate annually without decreasing its overall revenue. These tactics worked well for thirty years because of the spatial context in which they were deployed. The total amount of property tax paid by both individual homeowners and industries remained stable or increased slightly, but because the city in turn reduced the property tax rate every year—and did so with a consistency unmatched by any other comparable city in the region or state—San Leandro property holders and industry enjoyed a comparative advantage over those in

nearby cities. Cutting the tax rate was both an economic incentive to attract industry and a socio-political tactic designed to incorporate local homeowners into an ideological and political consensus about the benefits of growth....

San Leandro was touted in both local and national planning and development circles in the 1960s as a "model municipality." It modeled to the nation a combination of fiscal conservatism and racial exclusivity that made the city's property markets and industry the envy of Bay Area cities. "Since 1947 some 600 companies have moved to town," gushed the *Wall Street Journal* in its effusive 1966 article..., "adding some $200 million in property to the tax roles." Articulating a cornerstone of postwar U.S. ideology, the *Journal* even argued that the city was successful because "it hasn't been forced to absorb a heavy influx of minority groups and unskilled workers." In a cultural construction of far-reaching implications, the *Journal* presented racial diversity as self-evidently bad for business. In San Leandro, industry paid the taxes, the federal government guaranteed mortgages, and racial exclusivity confined this industrial garden to whites only. With homeowner populism elevated to a civic creed, San Leandrans had made the California industrial garden a national model....

The emergent classes at the center of this story, city-builders and suburban homeowners of moderate income, invested not simply in new towns and homes but in a cultural-economic compact of national historical significance.... [T]hey participated in a regional and ultimately national redistribution of public resources and public responsibility. In simplest terms, the property tax base moved to the suburbs, indeed certain suburbs, while the greater proportion of social problems, and financial responsibility for them, remained in the central city. Suburbanization thus turned on the role of property and development in distributing a social surplus and social debt—the costs and benefits of capitalist economic growth....

This chapter has told two overlapping stories, each extraordinarily important to the postwar narrative of Oakland and the East Bay. In the first, suburban entrepreneurs created new investment markets with the assistance of the federal state. The spatial political economies of places like San Leandro…were constructed to attract capital and growth—in the form of homeowners, industry, commerce, and the like. In the first two postwar decades, these places offered privileges and advantages to an array of groups, but especially to middle-class, white homeowners. Postwar suburbanization was driven by this development process, not by people "fleeing" Oakland. This East Bay story reaches beyond California to a national dynamic of the second half of the twentieth century: in the frantic competition for private capital investment, cities, trapped in the capitalist marketplace, entered into a savage rivalry with each other, the end result of which was the development of some places and the underdevelopment of others. Second, the postwar suburban compact among the federal state, city-builders, and homeowners lay the groundwork for the emergence of a political identity rooted in homeownership. This identity, and the ideological work done on its behalf, would emerge as a profound force in East Bay and California politics in the 1960s and 1970s. In those decades, that identity would become increasingly parochial and would be mobilized to preserve the suburban "good life" from a range of democratic challenges by excluded groups. Both of these stories take us back to Oakland, because the history and evolution of property markets ensure that as people and capital create places, those places in turn shape the possibilities and opportunities of other places.

PART III

Recent Suburbia, 1970 to the Present

CHAPTER 13

The Political Culture of Suburbia

INTRODUCTION

In the second half of the twentieth century, the strong, steady pull of suburbia gradually tilted the nation's demographic balance until suburbanites emerged as the majority in 2000. Inevitably, this monumental shift transformed the nation's political landscape. Suburbanites continued to place great emphasis on local politics, and indeed formulated many of their central ideas within this context. The political culture they forged locally would soon impress itself on the national political stage, forcing the major parties to reorient their ideas and policies. As early as the 1970s, national politicians—from presidential candidates on down—had come to recognize the "suburban bloc" as decisive to victory, a trend that intensified as the century wore on. The American electorate had, in a word, suburbanized.

This transformation was deeply interlinked to two broader phenomena in American politics—the rise and fall of the liberal state and the emergence of an influential conservative movement. Indeed, the confluence of suburbia's and liberalism's ascendance in the 1960s proved a combustible mixture. For not only did suburban political ideas directly challenge central tenets of an urban-based liberal agenda—such as civil rights legislation and Great Society programs to help minorities and the poor—but it exposed the limits of liberalism itself and forced its fundamental reorientation. The postwar metropolis was, in many ways, the product of liberal growth policies. These same policies helped create the structural inequalities and segregation that shaped all American cities. The irony of the liberal state helping to create, then seeking to redress, metropolitan inequality represented a volatile backdrop for postwar suburban politics, galvanizing suburbanites to solidify their political identity, press new agendas, and ultimately reshape both the Republican and Democratic parties. In the process, conservative politicians melded traditional concerns with small government and the promotion of free enterprise with the local and nuclear family oriented social concerns of suburban and rural voters to produce a new electoral majority by the century's end.

Localism continued to play an essential role in shaping suburban political culture in the postwar decades, as it had since the nineteenth century. Many suburbanites derived their core political identity—as middle-class, taxpaying homeowners—within the context of their own suburban neighborhoods, often politically separate and independent. In this milieu, suburbanites made a direct connection between their role as taxpayers and their right to a particular quality of life, delivered partly through services like good schools and safe streets. Suburbanites came to see themselves as entitled to these things, an expectation bolstered by a broader federal (and liberal) promise of security and economic well-being in the postwar years, as well as by the web of development practices that privileged white homeowners. The notion of homeowner/taxpayer entitlement would emerge as a core element of suburban political culture—one that transcended party lines and made suburbanites highly tax-sensitive and prone to interpret politics through the lens of taxation: who paid them, who levied them, who benefited from them. Using taxes as their political touchstone, suburbanites often mobilized to protect their suburban "good life"—and local fiscal resources—from perceived threats by free-spending liberals, the urban poor and excluded minorities, and inefficient government. By the late 1970s, these concerns began to boil over, first at the state and then the national levels. In 1978, California taxpayers led the way by enthusiastically passing Proposition 13, a measure that placed severe limits on property tax rates. Two years later, the former governor of California, Ronald Reagan, a proponent of Prop 13 and a long-time critic of the liberal state, won election to the presidency on a domestic platform of tax cuts, limited government spending, and the assurance that less government would enhance both the personal freedom and personal finances of Americans.

Even before this moment, suburban politics had found a national voice. Not only did political observers take notice of the growing suburban bloc of voters with every successive postwar election, but suburban political demands began to shape both federal policy and the national parties. Suburban opponents of school desegregation, fair housing, and public housing, for example, became so large and vocal a group that they influenced federal policy on these issues. The Republican Party was first to connect with this voting bloc, using it to win electoral majorities in seven of the ten Presidential elections after 1968. By the 1990s the Democrats too—traditionally an urban-based party—came to recognize the importance of the middle-class suburban vote, and adjusted their ideology and platforms accordingly. For the Democrats, this adjustment has been enormous, forcing the party to reconcile its traditional commitment to the urban poor, minorities, and the disadvantaged (and their need for public programs), with a new commitment to middle-class suburban voters (and their aversion to taxes and social welfare spending). Some see this adjustment—known variously as the "third way" or the "New Democrats—as the effective death of liberalism, others as a realistic shift toward the political center. Either way, the impact of suburban political culture on this process is indisputable.

In the past decade, historians have focused on documenting the emergence, substance, and impact of postwar suburban political culture. This research largely assumes active political engagement by suburbanites. Curiously missing from most of this work, however, is a sense of overall participation levels among suburbanites. In other intellectual circles, this has been a point of focus. Indeed, from the suburban critics of the 1950s to political scientists of our own time, writers have fretted over the influence of suburbia on political life—many fearing that suburbia's culture of privatism has disengaged people from political and civic involvement, a case of private self-interest taken to the extreme. While the jury is still out on this question, what does remain clear is the profound impact that suburban political culture—whether defined as the politics of self-interest, the politics of the middle-class taxpayer, or the politics of antiliberalism—has had on both metropolitan and national life. Born of lived experiences rooted deeply in suburban soil, suburban political culture has reshaped our national civic life.

DOCUMENTS

The first set of documents centers around California's Proposition 13, one of the most famous and controversial outcomes of suburban homeowner politics in the postwar era. Known variously as the "Tax Limitation Initiative" and the "Jarvis-Gann Initiative" after the men who authored it, this 1978 measure proposed to limit property tax to 1 percent of the assessed value of the home in 1975–76 and limit property tax increases to 2 percent per year. In effect, it would sharply reduce property taxes and then put a tight lid on future increases. After passing by a two-to-one majority, the measure had the short-term effect of stimulating the state economy. Over the years, however, the impact of Prop 13 began to register more negatively. As home prices in California raced upward, potential tax revenues sheltered by Prop 13 reached the billions, with multiple effects on life in the state.

The first set of documents presents several perspectives on this measure, reflecting the tenor of debate at the time as well as recent thought on the effects of Prop 13. At the time, many Californians believed that some kind of tax relief was necessary, as soaring real estate prices caused property tax bills to balloon under the old system. Yet supporters of the measure turned this concern with rising property taxes (tied as they were to rising property values) and redirected it toward a broad critique of government. **Document 13-1**, a collection of letters to the editor printed in the *Los Angeles Times* just before the election, captures the flavor of the contemporary debate. Pro-Prop 13 citizens frequently expressed dissatisfaction with inefficient politicians and their penchant for spending—particularly on social welfare programs. Public opinion polls at the time, in fact, found that California voters favored cutbacks in government spending, smaller government, *and* additional services—as long as those services were directed at the "general public" (like roads, schools, and fire protection), and not at specialized clienteles (like the urban poor). **Document 13-2** and **Document 13-3** offer opposing editorials on Proposition 13, published around the time of the election. They set out the general arguments being waged on both sides. **Document 13-4** is a journalistic account of the impact of Proposition 13, twenty years later. It points to numerous consequences—some intended, others unintended—and indicates the continued high levels of popular support for the measure, making it a politically untouchable issue.

The second set of documents traces the evolution of suburban influence on national politics. **Document 13-5**, from political scientist Robert Wood's classic book *Suburbia: Its People and Their Politics* (1958), is a wide ranging analysis conducted in the vein of other sociological studies of the decade. In this excerpt, Wood begins by reviewing two prominent theories of suburban politics at the time—the theory of conversion (people change politically when they move to the suburbs) and the theory of transplantation (people bring their politics with them)—which paralleled differing sociological approaches to postwar suburbia. While Wood ultimately downplayed the influence of suburbanization on national party politics—a view that future analysts and events would challenge—he did describe an emerging suburban political ethos with some accuracy. Wood, a professor at MIT, went on to serve as head of the U.S. Department of Housing and Urban Development from 1965 to 1969. By the late 1960s, there was growing recognition in academia, the media, and political backrooms of the power of the suburban vote. In **Document 13-6,** political analyst Kevin Phillips outlines the ascendance of both suburbanites and Republicans over the postwar years, drawing out their connections. Careful to recognize suburban diversity, Phillips nonetheless sees a strong conservative streak among suburban voters, especially among the new middle class. By 1992, suburbia reached center stage in the political arena, prompting writer William Schneider to declare the beginning of "the Suburban Century." **Document 13-7** is an excerpt from Schneider's essay making this case and detailing the profound impact of suburban voters on the two political parties. While Schneider and other analysts tend to conflate political culture across the range of suburban types, recent evidence indicates much greater variation, from older inner suburbs (more liberal) to the outer suburban fringe (more conservative). Even historian Sylvie Murray, in Essay 13-1, detects political diversity in suburbia in the 1950s. By 2004, the outer suburbs had increased in number and political clout. **Document 13-8** reports on the impact of these suburbs on the presidential election of that year. At the furthest edges of suburban sprawl, voters embraced solidly conservative values that were crucial to George W. Bush's victory.

What is the substance of the suburban political ethos? What factors have shaped it? Is there just one? What are the pros and cons of a measure like Prop 13? Who benefited and who lost? What might be an alternative to such a measure? Can we make safe generalizations about partisanship in suburbia; that is, have suburban voters tended to be liberal or conservative? Do these labels apply accurately to the suburban political mentality? What sorts of issues linked various levels of suburban political life from local to national? What impact has suburbia had on national political life?

13-1. CALIFORNIANS AIR THEIR OPINIONS ON PROP. 13, 1978

Source: Letters to the Editor, *Los Angeles Times*, May 15, 1978 and June 3, 1978.

On D-day, June 6, 1944, many Americans (of which I was proud to be one) stormed the shores of Normandy to free the world of a tyrant and a madman. It was a day of deliverance.

On June 6, 1978 we, the homeowners, will engage in another D-day to seek deliverance from incompetent, insensitive and inept politicians.

We shall, this time, storm the election booths to seek deliverance from tyrannical assessments, torturous taxes and porcine politicians.

DAN FELLER
Beverly Hills

The clichés fly thickly in the Proposition 13 countdown. Most of them are merely irritating. One is a real crybaby.

I hear over and over from my fellow middle-class persons that the present tax structure is squeezing the life out of the middle class. The poor middle class. It just can't get ahead any more. It doesn't pay to work hard, etc.

This is the most privileged middle class in the history of the world, and the most spoiled. The price it's paid for its incredibly well-to-do way of life is tiny. It should quit whining.

JAMES R. MOORE
Claremont

The outpouring of emotional rhetoric, as evidenced by your letters column, obscures the real issue of the Jarvis-Gann initiative: ever-increasing government spending.

We should look at Proposition 13 not as the final solution to fair property taxes; nor as a benefit to landlords or to any other special interest group, but as the only vehicle available to carry a message to our elected and appointed government representatives that enough is enough when it comes to spending our money....

The most shocking part of the debate over Proposition 13 is that practically every elected and appointed official has threatened us with dangerously reduced police and fire protection, firing of an unbelievable number of teachers, closing of libraries, loss of other critical services, and complete fiscal disaster, but we have yet to hear any of them tell us how they could cut their spending by reducing overhead, increasing efficiency, improving management, cutting featherbedding, taking the free-loaders off welfare, and correcting the many other wasteful practices that we read about daily and observe in government offices and field projects.

In face of official apathy towards our concern over the excessive cost of government, we have no choice but to ignore the "bad" features of Proposition 13 and vote for it because a vote against it is a vote for business as usual from Sacramento down to the lowest local level.

CLAY TICE JR.
Rolling Hills Estates

Proposition 13 on the June ballot is not essentially a tax-relief measure. It is instead, a crucial test of the civic maturity of property owner-voters. Most profoundly, it is a test of whether we are worthy of self-government through ballot processes. Statement after statement from otherwise responsible citizens reveal a level of selfishness and disregard for the public good that suggests that we may not meet the test.

Of course, property taxes are excessive and painful. To be sure, property taxes may not be the best way to finance many public services. Yes, basic tax reform is a crying need. Unfortunately, legislators have failed to institute needed tax changes. Consequently a taxpayers' revolt of some sort might be expected. But, the public disaster promised by Proposition 13 makes this radical measure a far worse "cure" than the ills it is supposed to treat.

If California goes for Proposition 13, we will have demonstrated that personal greed is more important than civic responsibility and public good. We will have demonstrated that we are incapable of studying a complex economic, political, and social issue, understand it, and vote in an intelligent responsible manner. We will have demonstrated that we are incapable and unworthy of governing ourselves.

RALPH GRAWUNDER
San Diego

13-2. UCLA BUSINESS PROFESSOR ARGUES THAT PROP. 13 WOULD REDUCE BLOATED GOVERNMENT, 1978

Source: Neil H. Jacoby, "Would Prop. 13 Really Lighten the Load? Yes: Bloated Government Will Be the Only Loser," *Los Angeles Times*, June 4, 1978.

Heroic surgery is needed if we are to excise the cancerous growth of government spending and relieve the intolerable tax burdens now borne by homeowners.

That is why Proposition 13 has received unprecedented backing from the residents of California. It is both sweeping and based on sound economic principles. If it passes, it can launch a new era of efficient and responsible financing of state and local government and, at the same time, promote social stability and economic expansion through just and equitable taxation.

If the initiative should fail, California's politicians will feel free to pursue their present course of wanton spending, which encumbers our economy and threatens the material security of many homes.

Economic theory and practical experience both suggest that reducing tax revenues is the most effective way to compel politicians and public administrators to reorder their outdated priorities and weed out obsolete and unnecessary spending. So long as tax revenues continue to swell, these people can afford to avoid facing the hard decision such essential reforms entail.

California's state and local governmental spending has gone up twice as rapidly as the rate of inflation during the past decade. Government employment has increased three times as fast as the general population…California also has the highest per capita state and local taxes in the nation, with the exceptions of New York and Alaska.

But Proposition 13 will create powerful pressures to end overspending by the government because it will lower total tax revenue collected within the state by approximately $6 billion, from the present total governmental income of $40 billion, including federal grants. Since government spending has been going up at the rate of 10% a year, most of the adjustment for this cut can be made simply by holding the line on expenditures for a year and a half….

At present, California's tax system unfairly wrings many welfare, health and school costs from taxes on property. This state collects 50% more revenue from its property taxes than the nationwide average percentage. Yet in today's urban, industrialized economy, ownership of property is not a true measure of an individual's ability to pay. And since taxation of property is based on the principle of benefits received, the taxes should cover the costs of governmental services that are actually utilized by homeowners, such as police and fire protection, sewers, street lighting and maintenance, and rubbish collection….

Given the upward spiral toward economic and social betterment of all Californians that Proposition 13 is capable of setting in motion, it is not surprising that so many of the state's residents are enthusiastically behind it….As an economist—and taxpayer—I sincerely hope that on June 6 my fellow Californians overwhelmingly encourage them to continue along that path.

13-3. *COMMONWEAL* CRITICIZES PROP. 13, 1978

Source: "The Message from California," *Commonweal* 105 (August 4, 1978). Copyright © 1978 Commonweal Foundation, reprinted with permission.

The reaction to the passage two months ago by a two-to-one margin of California's Proposition 13—limiting property taxes to one percent of the property's 1975–76 assessed value, holding assessment increases to two percent a year, and restricting the legislature's ability to increase other taxes—should give the nation several things to worry about.

First we must acknowledge that some

Californians voted for Proposition 13 with a valid complaint. The state has an unusually high proportion of homeowners and taxes on houses have risen spectacularly in the last few years. For example, a three-bedroom house assessed at $44,000 in 1972 was assessed at $91,000 in 1977. Middle-income families have been paying property taxes of between $2000 and $3000 a year. Also, scare tactics by the Proposition's opponents may have backfired and driven angry voters into the Proposition's camp. Finally, in some strange way, the vote may have been a symbolic rejection of the country's leadership.

Nevertheless, the consequences of the vote for the national welfare are bad. What has been interpreted as a "taxpayers' revolt," "sending a message" to every politician in the country, seems also to be, on another level, a product of one of the populace's lower emotions—the politics of resentment. Resentment by the dominant, relatively-well-off majority who feel bewildered and shortchanged by state and federal programs that have modestly redistributed resources and services to the disadvantaged over the past 15 years. Resentment susceptible, at different times, to manipulation by demagogues of every stripe: Richard Nixon's "law and order," George Wallace's "send them a message," Howard Jarvis's vulgar appeals to public distrust of bureaucrats....

Meanwhile, what was sold to the voters as tax relief for the little-man homeowner was actually a boon to big-business property owners, many of whom live outside the state, a cloak for the racism of those who thought they were voting against welfare loafers, and a blow to the weakest members of the community—old people, the disabled, those who need free health-care clinics, drug-abuse programs, free museums and libraries.

But, worst of all, the broad-based support for Proposition 13 raises the fundamental social-moral question about the function of taxation in a democratic society. The American system since the Progressive Era and the New Deal has used taxation to help fulfill the promises of the American dream of equal opportunity for all citizens. This means, in a happy coincidence of Christian principles and democratic theory, that everyone, through the government, assumes some responsibility for the welfare of everyone else. The tax revolt, in its gut-level expression, is a throwback to the most primitive nineteenth century individualism.

The only proper response to this attitude, which Senator George McGovern has correctly called "a degrading hedonism," is a strong moral, not pious, political leadership that confronts the real injustices in both the tax system and the economy.... The most frightening "message" from California is that, through the opportunism of business and political leaders, the deepest principles of democratic equality may be sacrificed while, just when we are struggling for some understanding of poverty both at home and in the Third World, the attention of America is focused on the swimming pool in some middle-class Californian's backyard.

13-4. THE *LOS ANGELES TIMES* REFLECTS ON PROP. 13'S IMPACT TWO DECADES LATER, 1998

Source: Stephanie Simon, "20 Years Later, Prop. 13 Still Marks California Life," *Los Angeles Times*, May 26, 1998. Copyright © 1998 by Stephanie Simon, *Los Angeles Times*. Reprinted with permission.

Does your car bump from pothole to pothole on ragged city streets? Blame it on Proposition 13.

Is your neighborhood stable, full of old-timers enjoying low property taxes? Credit Proposition 13.

The San Fernando Valley secession movement. O.J. Simpson's acquittal. The outlet malls gulping up strawberry fields on the Oxnard Plain. The fee for running a red light. The Wal-Mart by the freeway. The waiting list for John Grisham's latest at your local library.

Proposition 13, according to the experts, has had a hand in it all.

Which is no doubt why Howard Jarvis' famous tax-hacking initiative provokes such passion still, 20 years after it won at the polls and began to transform California's economic, political and social landscape.

"Prop. 13 was the beginning, not the end," said Rick Cole, regional director of the Local Government Commission, a nonprofit research firm. "It has affected our roads. It's affected our jobs. It's affected our schools. It's affected our neighborhoods. It's affected our democracy itself."

Or, as urban planner William Fulton put it: "Prop. 13 was supposed to change the relationship between people and their government. That was the goal. And that goal was achieved. But it was achieved in all sorts of weird ways that were never anticipated.".…

In the end, the initiative—which passed on June 6, 1978—did both more and less than anticipated. And it's not done doing, not by a long shot. It continues to reverberate in many key areas:

- Property taxes. It's the most basic, and most widely praised, effect of the Jarvis-Gann revolution: Thanks to Proposition 13, property taxes have for the past two decades been capped at 1% of a home's assessed value.…

  Analysts from all camps agree that California homeowners have saved billions of dollars since 1978, when taxes in some jurisdictions were running at 3% of a home's assessed value. But no one can say exactly how much.
- Proliferating fees. After Proposition 13, politicians became creative in their hunt for new sources of revenue to keep government running. They added parking meters and began charging soccer leagues for use of public parks. They raised utility taxes or slapped fees on tourists staying in local hotels. Above all, they created hundreds of new special districts to tax property owners in exchange for providing services from lighting streets to fighting fires.

  Though some of these fees had existed before, many were new—and most did not require voter approval.
- Public services. Jean Ross, executive director of the nonprofit California Budget Project, a liberal research group, sums up Proposition 13's impact this way: "It has fundamentally weakened the whole public infrastructure of the state, from education to roads and everything in between."

Conservatives disagree—loudly. Yes, public schools have slipped badly. (California, which ranked 22nd in the nation in per-pupil spending before the Jarvis-Gann initiative, had dropped to 37th by this school year.) And yes, other public services, from street maintenance to local libraries, may well be on the skids. But for that, they blame government waste—not the Proposition 13 guarantee of lower taxes.…

- Local development. Barred from raising property taxes, politicians have turned to sales tax as the best way to pad city coffers. Dangling incentives from cheap land to new roads, they woo big retailers to town. Many see nothing wrong with the sales tax rush. That's capitalism, they say.

  But critics fret that in their lust for Targets and auto malls, local pols are promoting suburban sprawl. They fear, too, that cities are overloading their economies with dead-end, minimum-wage jobs instead of bringing in factories or building affordable housing.
- Voter clout. Proposition 13 gave the state the power to allocate property tax. The Legislature divides the revenue among cities, counties and special districts according to a convoluted formula established in 1978.…Each jurisdiction's share of the property tax is based on how much it got before Proposition 13 passed.

Even Proposition 13's biggest boosters concede that shifting so much power to Sacramento was a mistake. An "unintended consequence," Fox calls it. But reform has so far proved elusive. And no wonder.

In a *Los Angeles Times* poll of 1,409 Californians last month, two-thirds approved of Proposition 13 after they were reminded of its provisions. Conservatives, the elderly and the middle class liked the initiative's impact even more.…

Block Parties and Bridge Clubs

It might sound a bit farfetched to assert that Mike Grassi is chummy with his neighbors because of Proposition 13. But he absolutely believes it.

Sure, Proposition 13's biggest winners—

in raw dollar terms—were big corporations. Though many business leaders opposed the initiative out of fear the tax cuts would decimate public services, they cheerfully pocketed big gains when it passed. Southern California Edison Co., for instance, saved $54 million a year in property tax. And $130 million was scratched off the tax bill of Pacific Telephone & Telegraph, a precursor of Pacific Bell.

Yet while the big savings went to big business, little guys like Grassi felt they got a darn good deal as well. In Grassi's Chatsworth neighborhood, bright with flowers and perky painted mailboxes, homeowners saw their tax bills drop by $2,000 a year or more.

Plus, as long as Grassi and his neighbors remained in their homes, their taxes would be based on their 1975 property values. That provision has proved a powerful incentive to stay put. Across Los Angeles County, for example, nearly 27% of single-family homes are still taxed on their 1975 value. (Not all of those homes have been in the same hands for two decades; owners can pass their low tax rate on to children or spouses.)

As most homeowners realize, this system has led to startling inequities throughout the state. Grassi and others who have lived in his neighborhood since the Jarvis-Gann revolt pay less than $1,000 a year in property taxes. But more recent arrivals face annual bills of $3,000 and up.

Newcomers may gripe, but Grassi maintains that the incentive not to sell creates more stable neighborhoods. In his own patch of cul-de-sacs, old-timers have bonded over the past 30 years, getting together for block parties, bridge clubs and Friday night dinners of pan-fried chicken at Skoby's, a local restaurant....

As for economics, Grassi and many others believe that without Proposition 13 they would have been taxed out of their homes. If the initiative had not passed, Grassi jokes, high taxes would have driven out so many seniors that kids in his neighborhood "wouldn't have known what elderly people looked like."...For all his enthusiasm, Grassi is quick to add that Proposition 13 was not an absolute success.

It was supposed to teach politicians to make do with less. But consider the latest property tax bill his neighbors, Eunice and Bob McTyre, received.

The basic 1% levy on the Chatsworth home they've owned for three decades amounts to $938. Then there's $115 for light maintenance. For flood control, $62. There are fees for schools and paramedics and a 911 fund. Even mosquitoes get their own line item: $2.10 a year to control them.

Calculating how much those fees have jumped since Proposition 13 can be tough. Should hikes in University of California fees—which increased from $671 in 1978 to more than $3,600 this year—be counted? What about the steep new $270 fine for running a red light?...

Since every academic study sets different parameters, their conclusions vary. But a general drift is clear: Government has made up much, though not all, of the revenue it lost to Proposition 13 by imposing a variety of fees. The Public Policy Institute of California estimates that state and local governments take in about 85% as much revenue today as they did in 1978, adjusted for inflation....

Proposition 13 has been made a scapegoat for much that ails California.

Obese kids? Blame Proposition 13: Budget crunches forced cities to cancel after-school sports. The Orange County bankruptcy? Proposition 13, of course: Bare coffers make risky investments look good. O.J. Simpson's acquittal? There, too, some analysts find a link: If it had not been for Proposition 13, they say, Los Angeles County would have had the money to put together a competent case....

Sales Tax Seductions...

To Proposition 13's foes, the rush for sales tax dollars is one of the initiative's most distressing legacies. They worry that cities are perverting good planning principles to build what urban analyst William Fulton calls "sales tax canyons...bleak, relentless, lifeless [zones] designed not to encourage or facilitate community, but simply to empty passing wallets."

In Duarte, however, City Manager Jesse Duff contends that the drive for sales tax has made his working-class San Gabriel Valley town of 22,000 a safer, more enjoyable place to live.

After attracting Wal-Mart, Target and several auto dealers in the past six years, Duarte was able to cancel a 3% tax on all utility bills. And it nearly doubled its contract with the Los Angeles County Sheriff's Department, hiring additional deputies and building a local substation....

Not every city, of course, can boast the same success as Duarte.

Competition for sales-tax dollars has been so intense in some regions that cities have been criticized for giving away huge concessions with only marginal returns. And it's been hard to stop the giveaways....

The sales tax rush has other consequences, too, besides instigating battles between neighboring cities. Cole, a former mayor of Pasadena, blames the rise of freeway-friendly malls for decimating downtowns and wiping out the mom-and-pop shops that used to sponsor Little League teams, take out ads in school yearbooks and help build a sense of community.

As catalog and Internet sales eat into the traditional retail market, Cole said, it makes less and less sense for cities to depend on sales tax. Yet they do so, more and more. "Cities have become addicted to this drug of sales tax," he said.

Purse Strings and Power...

Since Proposition 13...all property tax has been funneled through Sacramento. By law, the state can't use the money for its own purposes. But it can dictate how local governments use it. So over the years, the state has added more and more mandates that the county must fund from property tax revenue, such as specific health care programs for the poor.

The mandates and other factors have squeezed the county budget to the point where [County] supervisors control just over 3.3% of the general fund....

Indeed, it's one of Proposition 13's big ironies that a populist movement fueled by anti-government slogans—"It's them or us," Jarvis used to chant—ended up boosting Sacramento's power....

The resulting sense of disenfranchisement—the feeling that voters lack influence on local spending—fuels cynicism, apathy and rebellions such as the San Fernando Valley secession movement, analysts say. And when that happens, Yaroslavsky warns: "The democracy we're all part of can unravel in a hurry."...

Whether the taxpayers did right by passing Proposition 13 is still open to debate—and probably always will be.

"Prop. 13 was not perfect. No initiative is," Gov. Pete Wilson said. "But it was the classic expression of what occurs when, finally, people have had enough. Never has there been a more vehement expression of the people's will."

13-5. POLITICAL SCIENTIST ROBERT WOOD CHARACTERIZES SUBURBAN POLITICS, 1958

Source: Robert C. Wood, *Suburbia: Its People and Their Politics* (Boston: Houghton Mifflin Co, 1958).

The Theory of Conversion

Suburbanites, according to this analysis, escaping from big city politics, are ready converts to the small town set of political values. They may have precious little equity in their houses, but they think of themselves—and are thought of—as homeowners. They may fail to find the suburb where their own kind already lives, but wherever they locate, they seek eagerly to be accepted. The first property tax bills they receive reinforce the voters' recognition of their new status. The first local organizations to which they are admitted enhance their desire to belong to the community *in toto* and erase latent tendencies for deviation. Green grass, fresh air, and new social status, in Louis Harris' words, work their magic; class and ethnic appeals lose their potency. Differences in nationality, religion, and occupation become submerged by a predominant identification with locality. The ownership of land, the symbol of community, these provide the sources for suburban loyalty and interest....

The proof of this process of assimilation,

according to its advocates, shows up in the ballots—in the overwhelming shift to Republicanism that has taken place in metropolitan areas since 1946. The Republican Party lays claim to the suburban vote, it is argued, because it better protects their new interests and status and because it is the political faith of the old-time residents whose friendship is cultivated by the newcomer. Why retain allegiance to the Democrats, with their big city machines, corruption, and handouts? Loyalty to the party of the city conjures up memories of personal problems of the city—"a thousand images of an indecent, uncivilized past, perhaps necessary for the poor and ignorant" but not for the suburbanite. As homeowner and taxpayer, he is the man "economically coming up."…

In New York, the *Times* reports the settled convictions of suburban politicians that a change in allegiance has taken place: "A sense of property rights and a concern for tax rates comes with the key to a suburban home…a feeling that local conditions require a Republican enrollment if there is any hope of a consequent political career or political favors."

The Theory of Transplantation

But do suburbanites change their votes *because* they live in suburbia? Perhaps the process of assimilation is the dominant force at work, or perhaps the newcomers seek out suburbia because other forces earlier changed their political outlook and disposition.… Suburbia and Republicanism may both be symptoms of other changes taking place in the American scene.…

Connections exist between locality and party affiliation, but they also exist—and probably even more closely—between party and social characteristics, religious affiliations, occupational status, and simple historical accident. Unraveling the relative importance of each of these factors in political behavior is a complicated job.…

[In a study of Boston from 1940 to 1954,] when the social and economic composition of the fastest-changing suburbs were compared, the expected differences showed up: the increasingly Republican suburbs have higher educational levels, higher incomes, higher rents, more homeowners, and better jobs.… Suburbs closest to Boston, with either stable or declining populations, were most heavily Democratic. Suburbs with no change in political disposition or with an increasing Democratic vote occupied the second ring or extended along a transportation route in which housing and income patterns corresponded to those in the second ring. The Republican towns occupied the outer fringe of the metropolitan area; they displayed the highest income and professional characteristics and the fastest rate of growth.…

Somewhere along the "old tenement trail," former political loyalties may break, and a shift to the Republican ranks may be made. Yet the critical reason for the switch is the individual family status that has been achieved and, depending on the generation involved, the break may never come at all. Whatever the political outcome, the change—or lack of change—is precipitated by reasons quite apart from residence. The suburbs merely reflect a more pervasive transformation of American society.…

Politics at the Local Level: Symbols and Beliefs

If no spectacular discoveries of suburban influence in state and national elections can be seen, the same does not hold true for local elections. Especially at the municipal level, suburban politics appear to differ, at least in degree, and probably in substance, from those of other American communities.…In the end, this difference has important implications for the state and national pattern.

One indication of this difference…is the relative respectability and restraint of suburban politics at the local level—the yearning to shed the disreputable political habits of the big city. Another bit of evidence…is the strong sense of community consciousness and civic responsibility that impels active participation in local affairs. Deeply concerned with the quality of schools, conscious of their new status, suburbanites are inclined to "care" about local affairs—zoning regulation, recreational plans, garbage collection, school curricula, street paving—in an especially intense way. As the logical converse of their apathy toward strong party affiliations, suburbanites approach the politics of the community on the basis of individual preferences; they are, more and more frequently, nonpartisan, sharply distinguishing their local public preferences from their views of national and state affairs....

The Grassroots of Suburbia

From this general discussion an impression of highly individualistic political behavior emerges. It is doubtful that any one suburb fits exactly the pattern that has been described and it is quite certain that some suburbs do not fit it at all. The possibilities of different combinations of forces, exceptions, and aberrations approach infinity....

The evidence that is available, however, suggests that the distinguishing mark of suburban politics is not a difference in partisan attitudes between suburbanites and other Americans. If any conclusion is possible in this respect, it is that the suburbs, as such, have no significant influence on the fortunes of the two parties. The real point appears, rather, to be the way in which they intensify and exaggerate the traditional politics of small localities. More completely nonpartisan than one-party small towns in rural areas, and with the activities of the party leader more severely limited, the suburban municipalities represent the principle of direct popular political participation.... Each suburbanite is expected to undertake the responsibilities of citizenship on his own initiative and determine the common good by himself. He is called upon to rise above personal interest and avarice so far as the affairs of the suburb are concerned, and, largely unorganized and unled, to manage his local government in company with his neighbor. Whatever conflict in interest exists in the suburb must express itself informally, secretly, and without the sanction of law.

Under these circumstances, the importance of the professional public servant— the expert and the bureaucrat—obviously increases.... The nonpartisan vacuum places him in a strategic position to assume a role as community leader, especially since political leaders are suspect....

In the final analysis, the suburban man may become apolitical altogether. He has escaped from the divisive conflicts and hostilities of the great city in search of peace and fellowship among his own kind. The theory is that he has created a democratic haven in which a consensus of right-thinking men replaces a compromise among partisan-thinking men. This theory wraps him in a cloak of nonpartisanship and no politics, which makes active expression of political views socially unacceptable, if not immoral. If faithfully followed, the theory would demand so much of his time, so great a communion with his neighbors, so high a competence in public affairs, as to be nearly all-consuming. For most suburbanites, the feasible way out is indifference, as revealed by apathy in local elections. If the expert is entrusted with the really tough problems, the suburbanite has the best of all possible worlds: grassroots government run by automation. Under these circumstances, the purest theory of democracy requires no democratic action or responsibility at all.

13-6. POLITICAL ANALYST KEVIN PHILLIPS DOCUMENTS SUBURBIA'S ROLE IN THE REPUBLICAN ASCENDANCY, 1969

Source: Kevin P. Phillips, *The Emerging Republican Majority* (New Rochelle, N.Y.: Arlington House, 1969).

At one extreme, suburbia resembles prosperous urban blue-collar precincts; at the other, silk-stocking strongholds. The suburbia of crabgrass and commuter fame falls more or less in the middle. Back in the Nineteen-Twenties, suburbs were few in number, limited in importance and silk-stocking in character. Since that time, suburbia has multiplied twentyfold and its socioeconomic character has been revolutionized by a middle-class and increasingly non-Anglo-Saxon exodus from the cities.... Most of today's suburbanites live and vote more in the fashion of their friends and cousins still residing in The Bronx or Jamaica Plain....

During the Nineteen-Fifties, suburbia did not burgeon at the record rate of 1948–52;

nevertheless it continued to expand rapidly. Around Boston and New York, one half of the persons moving to lawn-mower country were Catholics, and in New York perhaps another quarter were Jews. By the end of the decade, these displaced Democrats threatened the hegemony of entrenched town and county Republican officialdoms throughout most of suburban New York. Irish and Italian voters formed the bulwark of suburban Democratic strength....The great Republican hero of the suburban new middle class was Dwight Eisenhower. In 1956, he further increased his suburban vote share over the already high levels of 1952. Not only was Eisenhower popular in his own right, but Adlai Stevenson, his Democratic opponent, was an alien being to upwardly mobile suburban Catholics. Locally, however, the Catholic new middle class was more likely to take sociocultural umbrage at an old-line Protestant Republican village trustee. For this reason, the years between 1958 and 1964 saw a large number of suburban offices and patronage fall to the Democrats....

But although the great exodus to suburbia was filling up station-wagonland with longtime urban Democrats and dethroning old-line and typically unresponsive Republican local administrations, it was not, in the ultimate context of the Nineteen-Sixties, a liberal movement. On the contrary, much of the suburban exodus was prompted by the changing demography of the cities—Southern Negroes were moving to the Northeast in large numbers—and thus when the politics of the Nineteen-Sixties began to pivot more and more on the Negro socioeconomic revolution, the newer reaches of suburbia proved highly unresponsive. To many new suburbanites, their relocation represented a conscious effort to drop a crabgrass curtain between themselves and the increasingly Negro central cities....[P]sychologically, the suburban boom is an anti-urban phenomenon—an attempt to escape crime, slums and slum-dwellers....

[N]otwithstanding Johnson's 1964 victory and Democratic claims of a new middle-class majority following, suburbia and Great Society social programs were essentially incompatible. Suburbia did not take kindly to rent subsidies, school racial balance schemes, growing Negro immigration or rising welfare costs. A few silk-stocking suburbs joined in experimental racial balance or pupil-exchange schemes—actual integration was obviously no threat at all to such rich communities—but the great majority of middle-class suburbanites opposed racial or welfare innovations. In general, suburbia voted Republican in the 1966 elections....

Despite the seeming suburban orientation of Richard Nixon's 1968 presidential appeal to the "forgotten man," suburbia did not respond with one approving voice....Middle-class suburbia showed a heavy conservative shift in comparison with both 1960 and 1964, but silk-stocking suburbia (and Jewish suburbs of all income levels) gave the Republican nominee a much smaller vote share than he had won in 1960....

Contemporary suburban demography is very much on the conservative side. Across the nation, suburban growth is centered in middle-class locales—the suburbs of the South and Southwest—which gave Nixon and Wallace vast leads over Humphrey. Each year, the environs of Los Angeles, San Diego, Houston, Dallas and many Southern cities add 10 per cent to 20 per cent to their populations, whereas the leading silk-stocking suburban counties around New York and Philadelphia—storied Westchester and Main Line Montgomery County—are showing little or no growth. Even within the Northeast, there is considerable suburban growth, but it is coming in low-middle and middle-income tracts in counties far beyond the parent city, while the close-in, old-line suburban counties are gripped by unchanging, manicured (and unsubdivisible) estate sections and decaying urbanized areas increasingly attractive to Negroes....

A new suburbia is being built across America by many millions of blue-collar and middle-level white-collar families in their twenties and thirties. This is the new young America on the move, and from Southern California to Richmond, Virginia to Long Island's Suffolk County, the movement is conservative....[T]he old, liberal cities are casting an ever-lower percentage of the vote in their states and nation. The power is shifting to this new suburbia; some call it the "white noose" around the increasingly Negro cities.... A generation after Al Smith and Franklin Roosevelt, the burgeoning middle-class suburbs are the logical extension of the new popular conservatism of the South, the West and the Catholic sidewalks of New York.

13-7. *THE ATLANTIC MONTHLY* HERALDS THE SUBURBAN CENTURY, 1992

Source: William Schneider, "The Suburban Century Begins: The Real Meaning of the 1992 Election," *The Atlantic Monthly*, July 1992.

The United States is a nation of suburbs. The 1990 Census makes it official. Nearly half the country's population now lives in suburbs, up from a quarter in 1950 and a third in 1960. This year will see the first presidential election in which a majority of the voters will in all likelihood be suburbanites—the first election of the suburban century.

That explains the obsessive focus on the middle class in the 1992 campaign. The middle class is who lives in the suburbs. The word that best describes the political identity of the middle class is "taxpayers." Democrats have been talking about "the forgotten middle class," and for good reason. For the past twenty-five years the Democrats have forgotten the middle class. And they have paid dearly.

They can't afford to do that anymore. The third century of American history is shaping up as the suburban century....

The Suburban View of Government...

Suburbanization means the privatization of American life and culture. To move to the suburbs is to express a preference for the private over the public. The architects Andres Duany and Elizabeth Plater-Zyberk offer this disdainful characterization:

"The classic suburb is less a community than an agglomeration of houses, shops, and offices connected to one another by car, not by the fabric of human life.... The structure of the suburb tends to confine people to their houses and cars; it discourages strolling, walking, mingling with neighbors. The suburb is the last word in privatization, perhaps even its lethal consummation, and it spells the end of authentic civic life."

There is a reason why people want to be confined to their houses and their cars. They want a secure and controlled environment. Suburban commuters show a determined preference for private over public transportation. Automobiles may not be efficient, but they give people a sense of security and control. With a car you can go anywhere you want, anytime you want, in the comfort of your own private space....

Suburbanites' preference for the private applies to government as well. Suburban voters buy "private" government—good schools and safe streets for the people who live there. They control their local government, including taxes, spending, schools, and police.

There are rich suburbs (Fairfax County, Virginia) and poor suburbs (Chelsea, Massachusetts); black suburbs (Prince Georges County, Maryland) and Hispanic suburbs (Hialeah, Florida); liberal suburbs (Marin County, California) and conservative suburbs (Orange County, California). Can suburban voters, then, be said to have a defining characteristic? Yes: suburban voters are predominantly property owners. And that makes them highly tax-sensitive.

A major reason people move out to the suburbs is simply to be able to buy their own government. These people resent it when politicians take their money and use it to solve other people's problems, especially when they don't believe that government can actually solve those problems. Two streams of opinion seem to be feeding the anti-government consensus as American politics enters the suburban era. One is resistance to taxes, which is strongest among middle-class suburban voters. The other is cynicism about government, which is strongest among the urban poor and the poorly educated.

Upscale voters are the most likely to say that government has too much power and influence, that taxes should be kept low, and that people should solve their problems for themselves. That's the "elitist" suburban view. Downscale voters express doubts about what government can do. They are the most likely to say that public officials don't know what they are doing, that most of them are crooks, that they don't pay attention to what people think, that government is run by a few big interests, and that you can't trust the government to do what is right. That's the cynical, "populist" view. Put the two together and you have a powerful, broad-based, anti-government, anti-tax coalition.

Polls show that people want government to do more about education, the environment, the infrastructure, and health care. But they trust it less than ever. The more expansive view of what government should do has been canceled out by the more constricted view of what government can do. No one wants to give politicians more money to spend, even if the nation's problems are becoming more serious.

The last time the nation was in this kind of anti-political frenzy was during the Progressive era, in the early decades of this century. Progressives, however, were anti-political but pro-government. The reforms of that era were aimed at curbing the power of political parties by expanding what Progressives saw as the rational, managerial authority of government (for example, having cities run by professional city managers instead of politicians). They used the attack on politics to justify an essentially liberal agenda: making government more professional.

Today the attack on politics serves an essentially conservative agenda: taking government out of the hands of a professional political elite and making it more responsive to the people. How? By limiting terms, limiting pay, limiting spending, and limiting taxes. In the suburban era, unlike the Progressive era, opposition to politics and opposition to government go hand in hand.

Spend Broadly, Tax Narrowly

The suburbanization of the electorate raises a big problem for the Democrats: How can they sell activist government to a constituency that is hostile to government? The answer is, they have to learn how to talk about taxes and spending in ways palatable to the middle class. There are two lessons the Democrats should have learned by now. One is that the only social programs that are politically secure are those that benefit everybody. Medicare, for example, is the principal enduring legacy of Lyndon Johnson's Great Society. Like Social Security, Medicare helps everybody, not just those in greatest financial need. The Democrats found it impossible to sustain support for LBJ's War on Poverty, however, precisely because it was not a universal entitlement. It was targeted at the poor.

Consider two kinds of government spending. Public-works spending is salable to middle-class voters. Social-welfare spending is not. Public-works spending involves benefits that are available to everyone and that people cannot provide for themselves—things like good schools, fast highways, safe streets, and a clean environment.

Social-welfare spending is targeted by need. It helps disadvantaged people get things that others are able to provide for themselves, like housing, food, and medical care. That is fine with middle-class voters, as long as they are persuaded that the benefits are going to the "truly needy" and that no one is taking advantage of the system. But middle-class voters tend to be suspicious of programs aimed at creating social change rather than providing public services....

The other lesson for Democrats comes from the Reagan era: Don't raise taxes that hurt everybody....

The message to Democrats is: In order to compete for a suburban electorate, keep spending as broad as possible and make taxes as specific as possible.

That, of course, is the exact reverse of urban priorities. The urban agenda consists of broad-based taxes and targeted spending programs: tax as many people as possible in order to provide for the needs of specific disadvantaged groups.... To middle-class voters, a program that helps the few and taxes the many is an outrage. A program that helps the many and taxes the few seems eminently fair....

A Southern or a Suburban Strategy?...

Bill Clinton, the presumptive Democratic nominee, pitches his message directly at what he calls "the forgotten middle class." He calls on Democrats to abandon the "tax and spend" policies of the past. He criticizes congressional Democrats for contributing to the mismanagement of the economy during the 1980s. He talks about restoring a sense of personal responsibility. That's a subtle way of trying to change the Democratic Party's image. More personal responsibility means less government responsibility. It's a way of saying, "We're not going to have a program for every problem. People are basically responsible for themselves. That's the middle-class way...." In fact, the three Democrats who have done best this year, Clinton, [Paul] Tsongas, and Jerry Brown, share a skeptical, pragmatic view of government.... Clinton's message, like that of Tsongas, is aimed squarely at the suburban middle class....

The Democrats have to break into the suburbs by proving that they understand something they have never made an effort to understand in the past—namely, the values and priorities of suburban America.

13-8. GEORGE W. BUSH WINS WITH CRITICAL SUPPORT FROM SUBURBAN FRINGE, 2004

Source: Ronald Brownstein and Richard Rainey, "GOP Plants Flag on New Voting Frontier," *Los Angeles Times*, November 22, 2004. Copyright © 2004 by Ronald Brownstein and Richard Rainey, *Los Angeles Times*. Reprinted with permission.

The center of the Republican presidential coalition is moving toward the distant edges of suburbia.

In this month's election, President Bush carried 97 of the nation's 100 fastest-growing counties, most of them "exurban" communities that are rapidly transforming farmland into subdivisions and shopping malls on the periphery of major metropolitan areas.

Together, these fast-growing communities provided Bush a punishing 1.72 million vote advantage over Democrat John F. Kerry, according to a *Times* analysis of election results. That was almost half the president's total margin of victory....

These growing areas, filled largely with younger families fleeing urban centers in search of affordable homes, are providing the GOP a foothold in blue Democratic-leaning states and solidifying the party's control over red Republican-leaning states....

These are places defined more by aspiration than accumulation, filled more with families starting out than with those that have already reached their earnings peak.

They include Union County, N.C., 25 miles southeast of Charlotte, where poultry farms are being converted into new developments so quickly that nearly one-seventh of the population is employed in construction. In Douglas County, Colo., about 20 miles south of Denver, so many young families have relocated that the budget for the local Little League is estimated at $500,000 a year....

"It's possible that the nature of these places changes people," said [Mark] Mellman, the Kerry pollster. "If you are in, say, Montgomery County [Maryland], you are talking to other Democrats, your friends and family. Then all of a sudden you move to Loudon County, Va., and your social networks are dominated by Republicans."...

Most analysts agree that the basic sociology of these counties provides the GOP an advantage. The high-growth counties are not especially affluent....

Instead, they are filled with young families, most of them white, many of modest means, willing to trade time for space—accepting longer commutes into urban areas so they can afford homes.

"If there is an Ozzie and Harriet-ville in America today, these are the places where it is," said William H. Frey, a demographer at the Brookings Institution.

That basic demography ensures a leg up for Republicans, who typically run well with married parents. "I think people are never as conservative as they are when they have kids," said Rep. Thomas M. Davis (R-Va.), the former chairman of the National Republican Congressional Committee.

Adding to the GOP advantage, many of those who relocate to these high-growth counties tend to be more socially conservative and eager to distance their children from urban cultural influences—and, in some cases, from the heavy concentration of minorities and new immigrants in urban areas.

Republican messages about lower taxes also find a receptive audience in these edge communities, and some analysts believe Democrats are faced with the perception that they disapprove—at some intrinsic level—of families who abandon the urban centers and flock to developments that pave the distant countryside.

"I think their conservatism is born out of a feeling that Bush looks like a regular guy, and the Democrats are all snots and they are not addressing my concerns," said analyst [Robert] Lang.

Democrats don't necessarily need to win these places in order to win the competitive states. Their problem is more the size of the margins that Bush amassed. His advantages in these high-growth edge counties helped him blunt the most important Democratic advance of the 1990s—the party's breakthrough into metropolitan suburbs.

Under Clinton, the Democrats broke the GOP hold on the more mature inner-tier suburbs (in places other than the South)....

Politically and socially, these inner-tier suburbs have become "an extension of the cities" they surround, said Lang. Increasing concentrations of ethnic minorities, generally liberal attitudes on social questions like gun control and abortion, a greater presence of singles in high-rise and condominium developments and a receptivity to arguments for environmental protection and planned growth have all made them increasingly valuable terrain for Democrats....

The problem for Democrats is that in almost all metropolitan areas the distant Republican strongholds are growing much faster than either the cities or the inner suburbs....

Democrats haven't focused nearly as much on these areas. Mellman, the Kerry pollster, said that "nobody has been willing to spend the time and money to figure out why" the party is running so poorly there....

But Bush's enormous margins in the fast-growth counties suggest that, if anything, these places are growing even more solidly Republican.

And in some of the most hotly contested states—Michigan, Ohio, Florida and Colorado—that trend could leave the Democrats trying to squeeze out even more votes from static or shrinking urban centers and inner-tier suburbs, while Republicans are dominating the counties exploding in population several exits down the interstate.

Even in several states Kerry won, Democratic blue was concentrated in urban areas, with Republican red covering almost everything else.

"The Democrats just need to look at the map: Their constituency is very concentrated," said demographer Kasarda. "It's a wake-up call."

ESSAYS

In **Essay 13-1**, historian Sylvie Murray outlines a middle-class suburban political culture that emerged in the 1950s and endured over the next fifty years. She emphasizes three main components: a focus on local issues, an ideology of taxpayer entitlement, and a sense of civic obligation. Murray's study, which focuses on outlying neighborhoods of Queens, New York—a section characterized by high rates of home ownership and a low-density "suburban" landscape despite its location within the municipal limits of New York City—reveals several other trends worth noting: the key role of women as neighborhood activists, the presence of liberal activism in suburbia, and a suburban citizenry that was highly engaged in politics. These findings challenge stereotypes of postwar suburban politics—especially the claim that suburbia fostered alienation, privatization to the point of noninvolvement, and apolitical women unconcerned with the world beyond their homes.

In **Essay 13-2**, historian Lisa McGirr explores the strong, familiar connection between suburban and Republican politics. Focusing on Orange County, California, which she considers a "prototype" of the suburban conservative milieu, McGirr identifies a potent breeding ground of modern-day conservatism, characterized by high-tech industry, a well-educated populace, and a vested interest in the military–industrial complex. These suburbanites cut their political teeth on local issues, then moved into national political activism. McGirr's larger study traces the evolution of this process in terms of conservative ideas and strategies: the initial focus was on public, political and international enemies (namely, communism), then shifted to enemies within (namely, secular humanists, women's liberationists, and later homosexuals). The selection here focuses on the late 1950s and early 1960s, when anticommunism was paramount. McGirr notes that Orange County was nearly all-white in this period, eliminating race as a potential issue while allowing others to take precedence. The opposite was true in Charlotte, North Carolina, the subject of **Essay 13-3.** Here, historian Matthew Lassiter expands the scope of suburban political influence beyond the Republican Party. In Charlotte, the explosive politics of race and busing galvanized homeowner suburbanites of both parties to oppose mandatory busing. Their actions—and the suburban ideology it represented—impacted not only federal policy, but forced both political parties to take notice of this "volatile center" of the American electorate. The result, he argues, has been a reshaping of national politics.

ESSAY 13-1. SYLVIE MURRAY, *THE PROGRESSIVE HOUSEWIFE: COMMUNITY ACTIVISM IN SUBURBAN QUEENS, 1945–1965* (2003)

Source: Reprinted by permission of the University of Pennsylvania Press.

Citizenship and Middle-Class Politics in the Postwar Era

They are strangers to politics. They are not radical, not liberal, not conservative, not reactionary; they are inactionary; they are out of it. If we accept the Greeks' definition of the idiot as a privatized man, then we must conclude that the U.S. citizenry is now largely composed of idiots.

C. Wright Mills, *White Collar* (1951)

Dear President Truman:

We, a group of Alley Pond citizens, gathered at a barbecue picnic celebrating our first anniversary of the founding of our community, are gravely concerned at the delays and this weekend's breakdown in the Korean War truce talks. We are a group of veteran families who know well the horror and futility of war. We urge you to use your presidential power to hasten the successful conclusion of the talks so that our next barbecue may be held in a world of peace and prosperity and world amity.

Letter to the Editor, *Meadow Lark*,
August 9, 1951

Ironically, Betty Friedan could have written both statements, albeit at different times of

her life. The famous author who in 1963 described the female citizenry in terms similar to those used by Mills had lived in northeastern Queens in the early 1950s. Like her neighbors from Alley Pond, she was a politically active resident of suburbia, not a "privatized" woman. Indeed in 1952, at a time when she lived in a garden apartment in the area, Friedan led a collective protest to stop a steep rent increase which threatened to destroy her racially and culturally integrated community. Of course, the young and radical Friedan has been eclipsed by the feminist best-selling author of *The Feminine Mystique.* Similarly, and not coincidentally, the political history of her suburban neighbors has been ignored, in fact, denigrated to serve as a foil for a renewed feminist movement. This book is an attempt to recapture this lost past....

This study stems from a set of questions about women's public activism in the 1950s, and a conviction that it coexisted with the postwar domestic ideology—just as the two had coexisted in earlier times. It evolved into an analysis of community politics in the neighborhoods of northeastern Queens, New York City, a newly developing suburban area in the immediate postwar period. Full-time mothers and housewives were a driving force among community activists who sought to build residential neighborhoods of quality in which to raise their families....

The political culture in suburban Queens was infused with a celebration of the virtues of active citizenship. Men and women alike were encouraged to get involved in the public life of their community, and many did. An extensive network of community activists worked tirelessly to promote the interests of their residential neighborhoods. They organized collectively and fought political battles to build a better life, one that they expected as members (or aspiring members) of an upwardly mobile postwar middle class. By doing so, they shaped their living and political environment, although within constraints, and they revealed their political consciousness.

The definition of postwar suburban citizenship that I analyze here was centered on the local residential community (albeit one that was never seen as divorced from the broader national and international debates of the day). Second, suburban residents had a clear perception that as middle-class citizens they were deserving of certain social and economic rights (namely, the right to a residential neighborhood of quality) and that their government had an obligation for their welfare and that of their community. Third, this sense of entitlement was paired with a clear understanding of their obligations as citizens to participate in the collective life of their communities. These three elements, which defined their relationship to their fellow citizens and to the state, deserve further elaboration.

The focus on the residential community is perhaps the element that most clearly identifies these citizens as "middle class." This elusive socioeconomic category has been defined, historically, according to a number of criteria, including income level, occupation, education, even character. But students of the twentieth century, especially of the postwar era, have highlighted the importance of one's place of residence as a defining characteristic of social status: the home (along with its material goods and surrounding neighborhood) has become a crucial marker of one's location in the socioeconomic structure. For middle-class suburbanites, the home or, more accurately, the residential neighborhood was the defining element of their civic and political lives.

The second core characteristic of suburban citizenship—the belief that "the good

life" was an entitlement—has to be understood in the context of the right to economic well-being and security that entered the vocabulary of Western political culture following the Great Depression and World War II. In T. H. Marshall's words, this refers to the right "to live the life of a civilised being according to the standards prevailing in the society." What these standards were for postwar Americans who claimed, or aspired to, a middle-class status varied slightly. But they could be summarized as the right to a residence of quality in an environment congenial to family and community living: this included sufficient and quality schools, safe and pleasant neighborhoods, parks, libraries, and the like. Compared with other racial and socioeconomic groups, the residents of suburban Queens had achieved a relative access to such material comfort. Yet the reality of a fast-developing residential area posed problems of its own. Schools were generally of good quality in northeastern Queens, but they were overcrowded. The neighborhoods were greener and less dense than elsewhere, but increased traffic on high-speed highways made them unsafe for pedestrians. Public transportation and libraries were insufficient by the residents' standards. Securing what they considered the "basic needs" of their communities was an ongoing preoccupation.

Third, along with an assertion of their rights to "the good life," Queens citizens had a clear and explicitly articulated sense of their obligations as active, or "good," citizens. The term *good citizen*, according to political scientist Judith Shklar, describes "the people of a community who are consistently engaged in public affairs." They "are public meeting-goers and joiners of voluntary organizations who discuss and deliberate with others about the politics that will affect them all." This applies to a large number of Queens suburbanites, as it does to the residents of many postwar suburban communities. Queens citizens joined home owners', tenants', and parents' associations, political parties and clubs, veterans' and religious groups. The issues that they discussed ranged from local to national and international affairs. Most important, participation in community associations reflected more than a commitment to abstract civic duties (although this was certainly part of the local political rhetoric); it served the more direct purpose of shaping the "good life" that these families aspired to.

Indeed, in contrast with an ideal version of disinterested civic participation, suburbanites' sense of civic obligation was directly related to their concerns for the immediate needs of their residential communities. Participation in community associations was necessary to lobby city officials for the construction of public services, such as schools....

As was the case for the American citizenry as a whole, Queens citizens were a diverse group and disagreed at times over what the well-being of their communities entailed. Some, for instance, strongly believed that it was inextricably tied to national issues of racial justice, and their struggle to preserve the multicultural and multiracial nature of their neighborhoods was cast in this light. Others, like the group of Alley Pond residents cited above, believed that their own suburban peace and security were ephemeral in a world at war. The commitment to racial justice or world peace expressed by some was by no means shared by the majority of their neighbors. Yet in spite of their differences and disagreements they were united in their determination to shape their living environment.

One last point brings us back to the centrality of the residential community in the political lives of suburban citizens. Not only was it the object of their political activism but it constituted the public forum from which they acted as well. The residents' homes and neighborhood streets, their schools and places of worship, their community organizations and newspapers were all sites where public discussions took place.... It was thus in the heart of their residential communities and with their neighbors, with whom they alternately disagreed and devised concerted action, that middle-class men and women acted as "good" citizens....

The experience of Queens suburbanites profoundly challenges our image of postwar middle-class life. The Alley Pond citizens who met in the comfort of their backyard and discussed the Korean War effectively belied the academic wisdom on the period. Their example forces us to discard old stereotypes. But realizing that middle-class Americans were not Greek idiots is only the beginning. More challenging is the task of understanding their political views and reassessing the period in light of that new knowledge....

ESSAY 13-2. LISA MCGIRR, *SUBURBAN WARRIORS: THE ORIGINS OF THE NEW AMERICAN RIGHT* (2001)

On March 4, 1964, Estrid Kielsmeier, a mother of two young children and the wife of an accountant, rose bright and early at her home on Janet Lane in one of the newer suburban developments of Garden Grove, California. She made her way into the kitchen to set out coffee, putting dozens of cups on the table. Mrs. Kielsmeier was expecting visitors. But this was not to be an ordinary suburban coffee klatch. Next to the coffee, she placed blank nominating petitions to qualify Barry Goldwater as a candidate for president in her state's Republican primary. Starting at six o'clock, the first neighbors arrived to sign the petitions. Throughout the morning they came alone, as families, and in small groups. Goldwater was their candidate....

Kielsmeier's effort on behalf of Goldwater that early spring morning was just one step in her deepening conservative activism—an activism spurred by her strong conviction that the world's first "Christian Republic" was in danger. America was, in her eyes, on a course of political, economic, and moral decline; a course steered by the nation's liberals. To counter the tide, Kielsmeier, and many men and women like her, sought to create, as she put it, a "mini-revolution...in the true sense of the word...a revolving back...to the foundations of the country." It was a revolution quite different from those we usually associate with the 1960s.

Indeed, Kielsmeier and "suburban warriors" like her built a vibrant and remarkable political mobilization during the 1960s....It was in suburbs such as Garden Grove, Orange County (the place Kielsmeier called home), in conjunction with the backing of regional entrepreneurs, that small groups of middle-class men and women met in their new tract homes, seeking to turn the tide of liberal dominance. Recruiting the like-minded, they organized study groups, opened "Freedom Forum" bookstores, filled the rolls of the John Birch Society, entered school board races, and worked within the Republican Party, all in an urgent struggle to safeguard their particular vision of freedom and the American heritage. In doing so, they became the ground forces of a conservative revival—one that transformed conservatism from a marginal force preoccupied with communism in the early 1960s into a viable electoral contender by the decade's end....

These conservative activists and the movement they forged are essential to understanding the rightward shift in American politics since the 1960s. Far outside the boundaries of respectable politics in the early 1960s, the Right expanded its influence on the national scene in the late 1960s and 1970s and vaulted to national power with the Reagan landslide of 1980. Since that time, conservatives in Washington have transformed the relationship between federal and state power, limited the regulatory capacity of the central state, and altered the fundamental structure of the New Deal welfare state. Conservatives' successes, to be sure, were due in no small part to liberalism's foundering on the shoals of race, economic discontent, and its own internal contradictions. But just as significantly, conservatives' ability to build a powerful movement enabled them to pick up the pieces and profit politically from liberal failures....

Conservatives in Orange County enjoyed the fruits of worldly success, often worked in high-tech industries, shared in the burgeoning consumer culture, and participated in the bureaucratized world of post-World War II America. Their mobilization, then, was not a rural "remnant" of the displaced and maladapted but a gathering around principles that were found to be relevant in the most modern of communities. Post-World War II American conservatism thus explodes any easy dichotomies between tradition and modernity. Indeed, an exploration of this movement highlights the dual nature of modern American conservatism: its strange mixture of traditionalism and modernity, a combination that suggests the adaptability, resilience, and, thus perhaps, intractability of the Right in American life....

[C]onservatives in the 1960s shared a number of concerns. First, they were united in their opposition to liberal "collectivism"— the growing tendency of the state to organize social and economic life in the name of the public welfare and the social good. Libertarians sought to limit the intrusiveness of the nation-state in economic matters (although their antistatism stopped at the door of a strong-armed defense), and normative conservatives opposed what they perceived to be a decline in religiosity, morality, individual responsibility, and family authority—a decline, they argued, that went hand in hand with the growth of centralized federal power. In Orange County, both groups championed virulent anticommunism, celebrated laissez-faire capitalism, evoked staunch nationalism, and supported the use of the state to uphold law and order. America, they believed, had an organic, benevolent order that would function well if not for tampering by liberal elites....

In the wake of conservative upheavals— from the fundamentalist mobilizations of the 1920s and the Red-baiting crusades of the 1950s to the Goldwater movement in the 1960s—liberal commentators argued that the Right was in disarray and retreat. With the spread of national liberal culture, education, and modernization to the rural areas and small towns that had once formed the heartland of conservative mobilizations, so the argument went, the Right would become increasingly marginalized. But conservative forces have instead flourished, and they have done so most recently in areas considered least conducive to them: modern suburban regions....

The Setting...

[Orange] County officials largely left the control of development in private hands. This resulted in a built environment that reinforced privacy, individual property rights, home ownership, and isolation at the expense of public space and town centers that could have created a sense of public and community responsibility. While many communities throughout the United States embraced similar models of development without becoming strongholds of the Right, the built landscape is nonetheless the stuff of one's everyday environment, not only reflecting an ethos but also affecting the consciousness of its inhabitants. This was even more the case for women and men who had left friends, family, and old associations behind and consequently were more likely to be looking to establish new community ties. The physical landscape, therefore, contributed to creating a hospitable terrain for the Right by reinforcing a search for alternative forms of community. A segment of its middle class found a sense of community in the politics and social interaction proffered by local businessmen, right-wing ideologues, and conservative church leaders. Thus, one woman said of conservative activism that "it became…a social thing."

Much of the county followed the "planned sprawl" model of development. This led to chaotic spatial arrangements, with one tract developed after another. Streets were bisected by new housing tracts, increasing a perception of discontinuity and chaos. This form of growth created what one may term "free-enterprise cities," with a strong emphasis on private development and growth and little regard for public and community spaces. By neglecting public space in favor of growth, such arrangements weakened the sense of community. In fact, even the existing central spaces in the old downtowns were undermined in favor of convenience, privacy, and shopping malls. The most extreme result of this pro-growth attitude was the eventual demolition of the old downtown city center in Anaheim to make room for development.…

The result of development along these lines, of both the corporate and the free-market models, was spatial isolation and an absence of community, which, in a complicated way, helped to reinforce a conservative ethos. One Santa Ana resident, for example, who in 1961 criticized the lack of neighborliness in housing developments and called for "more community recreational activity…where people can get to know one another," linked the depletion of community to government centralization. He believed that the growing scale and scope of the federal government was "being born in a community that don't [sic] care what happens to Joe Smith or Bill Jones who just happen to live in the same block as us but we never had the time to be neighborly." He called, as a result, for "getting government back in the hands of the people."

The peculiar form of mixed-market anarchy and corporate planning that shaped the built landscape also created an exceptional degree of economic and racial homogeneity, which further contributed to a favorable setting for the Right.…

"A Sleeping Giant is Awakening": Right-Wing Mobilization, 1960–1963

In La Palma Park Stadium in Anaheim, more than 7,000 Orange County young people gathered to attend a special session of Fred Schwarz's School of Anti-Communism. It was an early spring morning in 1961, and the students, many of them excused from regular classes by their school boards, listened to Schwarz and other national right-wing figures rail against communist subversion in the schools, the government, and the nation. The event had been planned for months by prominent local citizens with the help of such organizations as the Kiwanis Club, and it culminated a five-day Orange County School of Anti-Communism. At the weeklong school, "educational" sessions detailed the Communist Party's "treasonous" networks in the United States, classified communist philosophy as "Godless materialism," linking it with a "faith" in progress and change, and outlined the networks in Washington that purportedly had contributed to Soviet gains since World War II. In a concluding session, participants were treated to a dinner banquet with the program theme "Design for Victory." Attendance at the "school" surpassed its organizers' expectations. "The tremendous response" required them to hold "double sessions" and to send overflow crowds from the original site at the Disneyland Hotel to the Anaheim High School auditorium. According to the [Orange County] *Register,* the school "brought the largest attendance ever reported in an effort of this type.

Fred Schwarz's school was just one sign of the awakening in Orange County to the perceived dangers of "communism" in the early 1960s, an awakening that initially drew on the legacy of 1950s McCarthyism for its language, targets, and ideology. Before the school arrived, and even more so in its wake, local anticommunist initiatives flourished. These initiatives cloaked conservative concerns with American liberalism—fears of federal government centralization and apprehensions over the penetration of liberal ideas into the nation's schools, churches, and communities—under an overarching discourse of "communist subversion." Numerous organizations were formed to thwart the "Red menace"...Orange Countians also swelled the ranks of the John Birch Society, opened numerous right-wing bookstores, and worked within their churches, schools, and communities to roll back liberal gains that, in their eyes, threatened the nation....

Orange County doctors, dentists, housewives, and engineers, in effect, gave birth in the early 1960s to a movement that would help shape the future of the American Right and, eventually, the political direction of the nation. It was here, in the mundane yet complex world of school battles, evangelical churches, and local politics, that the grassroots New Right asserted itself.

On June 24, 1960, the first spark of grassroots mobilization ignited when Joel Dvorman, an Anaheim resident and an elected school board trustee, held a meeting of the Orange County chapter of the American Civil Liberties Union (ACLU) in his backyard. The ACLU had earned the wrath of the Right in the past for its defense of liberals and nonconformists and now came under fire for its opposition to the activities of the state and federal investigating committees on un-American activities. The meeting Dvorman had called centered on a proposal to abolish the committees. Long a thorn in the side of progressive organizations, the committees were

under increasing attack by a vocal group of Southern California liberals. Joel Dvorman had invited Frank Wilkinson,...a leader in the national effort to abolish the House Un-American Activities Committee (HUAC), to speak on the issue. The response was swift and forceful: Angry neighbors denounced Dvorman for importing "communist ideas" into their suburban enclave. Heeding their neighbors' call, citizens whose lives had previously revolved around work, church, and family became involved in a contentious political battle....

The politics of these two men and, above all, their hostility to HUAC provoked bitter opposition among many Orange Countians who considered the committees a sacred cow, their chief protection against "internal subversion" and an appreciated way of attacking liberal and progressive organizations....

Meetings of the ACLU were not new to Anaheim, but the affront of an "identified communist," bent on abolishing HUAC, speaking in their community outraged a number of residents who heard about the meeting and decided to attend. James Wallace, a production supervisor at Autonetics, a local aerospace firm, was one of them. He learned of the meeting about an hour before it started: "Having heard many derogatory things about the ACLU, and being mildly curious about what an identified communist might have to say, I decided to attend. I was very upset to find this thing going on in our neighborhood." Returning home, he wrote a letter to the editor of the *Register* in which he described the meeting, calling Wilkinson a "traitor" and issuing a call to action: "I wonder what we would have done in 1942 if Mr. Dvorman had a German-American Bund meeting at his home."

Concerned Anaheim residents heeded Wallace's call. Aware that Dvorman was a school board trustee, they descended on school board meetings, demanding that Dvorman reveal whether he was or had "ever been a member of the Communist Party." Declaring that his ACLU activities were incompatible with his service as a trustee, opponents requested that the school board censure Dvorman and put a halt to his political activities. Rebuffed by the board, they formed a committee for the recall of Dvorman from the school board. R. Dickson Miles, an engineer at Nortronics, another local aerospace firm, became the leader of this group. Arguing that "Dvorman embraces opinions to which most loyal Americans are vigorously opposed," the group claimed that "it was the duty of all Americans to recognize the...threat to our heritage, to expose it and to combat it with every weapon at our command." And fight they did—organizing meetings, petitions, and, on November 4, 1960, a "ladies auxiliary," whose purpose was to carry the recall petition block by block through the Magnolia School District. One resident remembers answering her doorbell to find a person with petition in hand, informing her that a "comm-symp" was on the school board and requesting that she offer her signature. Hundreds of letters poured in to the *Register*, explaining why Joel Dvorman was "guilty" and how this sort of vigilance was necessary to defend the nation against subversion.

Many of these activists had, until then, led quiet suburban family lives. This is not to say that they had not held strong anticommunist beliefs. But it was only during the 1960s that they saw the need to actively involve themselves in the struggle against "subversion," and they left a deep institutional impact. According to its founder, the first Anaheim chapter of the right-wing John Birch Society was born as a result of the Dvorman conflict and grew so rapidly that it eventually split into several chapters. Underlining his newfound activism, James Wallace asserted that his only earlier civic engagements were professional activities: "The only ultra-conservative radical right-wing reactionary organizations in which I held membership at that time were the National Management Association and Precision Measurements Association." By the fall of 1960, a group of Orange Countians were thanking God and Robert Welch, the founder of the John Birch Society, for "awaken[ing] us out of our selfish apathy and indifference to what is happening in America...."

Entering their first political battles in the early 1960s, these suburban Americans came to perceive of themselves as part of a broader national conservative movement. This sense was fostered by national political organizations such as the John Birch Society and by a burgeoning conservative intellectual culture that helped to shape their initial impulses into a coherent rightwing ideology. Orange County conservatives were, for example, avid readers of magazines like *National Review* and *Human Events*....

Many right-wing tracts, books, and magazines were passed from hand to hand through a network of friends, neighbors, and family. A core group of conservatives spread the message within their communities, bringing new recruits to the cause and, in the process, generating a movement culture. One young mother recalled how an illness led to her inadvertent introduction to conservatism: A relative promised to care for her two young children if she, in turn, would read a number of conservative books. She later attended a John Birch Society meeting and soon embarked on a career of activism on the Right.... Bridge clubs, coffee klatches, and barbecues—all popular in the new suburban communities—provided some of the opportunities for right-wing ideas to spread literally from home to home throughout the county. One neighborhood meeting could produce several recruits to the cause....

The grassroots dissatisfaction with the trend of national politics may have come to naught, had it not been for the institutional support provided by strategically placed local organizations. Successful mobilization needs access to resources and information, and although it is conceivable that grassroots activists could have built their own institutions, they did not have to; instead, local businessmen, churches, and the libertarian *Register* provided the infrastructure and ideas essential to the movement's success....

This institutional backing helped a galvanized group of citizens to build a strong local movement, which, because of its striking vitality, gained national attention. Although relative to the entire population of Orange County only a small band of men and women became active, their numbers were significant, and they swam within broader supportive waters. With the later upheavals of the decade, they would adjust their rhetoric and their concerns to attract more citizens to their cause. Mobilized in the early 1960s by single issues within their school districts and communities, they soon saw that political power could most easily be exerted through an established institution—the Republican Party. Using their networks and experiences to reinvigorate Republican volunteer organizations, these activists worked within the party to achieve their goals. Here, they joined forces with others throughout the nation to become part of a burgeoning conservative resurgence.

ESSAY 3-3. MATTHEW D. LASSITER, "SUBURBAN STRATEGIES: THE VOLATILE CENTER IN POSTWAR AMERICAN POLITICS" (2003)

Source: *The Democratic Experiment: New Directions in American Political History,* eds. Meg Jacobs, William J. Novak, and Julian E. Zelizer (Princeton: Princeton University Press, 2003). Copyright © 2003 Princeton University Press. Reprinted by permission of Princeton University Press.

The Politics of Middle-Class Consciousness

During the late 1960s and early 1970s, a populist revolt of the Silent Majority rippled upward into national politics and established powerful constraints on Great Society liberalism and civil rights reform. In an opening phase, suburban parents in the Sunbelt South launched grassroots uprisings to defend their children's neighborhood schools against the legal challenge of court-ordered busing. White-collar home owners who claimed membership in the Silent Majority invented a potent "color-blind" discourse that portrayed residential segregation as the product of economic stratification rather than historical racism. This political formula eventually gained national traction as a bipartisan defense of middle-class consumer privileges and suburban residential boundaries. The rise of the Silent Majority reflected broader trends spreading throughout metropolitan America, a politics of middle-class consciousness based in subdivision associations, shopping malls, church congregations, PTA branches, and voting booths. The political culture of

suburban populism—from taxpayer revolts and antibusing crusades to home owner movements and antisprawl campaigns—galvanized a top-down response marked by the persistent refusal of all three branches of the federal government to address the historical legacies of residential segregation through collective remedies for metropolitan inequality. From the "conservative" subdivisions of southern California to the "liberal" townships of New England, the suburbanization of American society and politics has empowered a bipartisan ethos of private-property values, individual taxpayer rights, children's educational privileges, family residential security, consumer freedom of choice, and middle-class racial innocence.

The growth policies of New Deal liberalism and the rise of the Cold War military-industrial complex shaped the patterns of postwar residential expansion and transformed the South and West into the booming Sunbelt. The Federal Housing Administration and the GI Bill subsidized the "American Dream" of middle-class home ownership for millions of white families who moved from rural regions and urban centers to the sprawling suburbs. By excluding racial minorities from new suburban developments and "redlining" racially mixed urban neighborhoods, federal mortgage policies during the initial postwar decades systematically enforced residential segregation and reinforced marketplace discrimination. The 1956 Interstate Highway Act facilitated automobile-based commuting and corporate mobility in the outlying suburbs and simultaneously enabled municipal governments to concentrate racial minorities within inner-city ghettos....

Suburban decentralization and Sunbelt development ultimately produced a volatile political climate in which neither the Democrats nor the Republicans could maintain a stable electoral majority. The upward mobility subsidized by the middle-class entitlement programs of the federal government...turned suburban voters into a vital demographic that came to drive the electoral strategies of both parties. When the civil rights movement launched a direct assault on residential and educational segregation in suburban jurisdictions, the Silent Majority responded with a localist politics of home owner rights and middle-class warfare. In the affluent white-collar suburbs that have commanded the attention of national politicians, the celebratory ideology of the free market and the "color-blind" ethos of meritocratic individualism effectively concealed the role of the state in forging metropolitan patterns of residential segregation and structural inequality. Although the Republican party initially benefited from the grassroots surge of middle-class consciousness, the populist revolt of the center transcended the conservative mobilization of the New Right. The reinvention of the "New Democrats" as the champions of quality-of-life issues in suburban swing districts and the fiscally responsible managers of the "new economy" has revitalized the competitiveness of the center in a postliberal political order....

The Silent Majority

During the 1970s, a grassroots suburban strategy that revolved around a "color-blind" defense of the middle-class rights and residential privileges of the Silent Majority succeeded where the overtly racialized tactics of the top-down "southern strategy" had failed.... In response to the civil rights movement's concerted attack on metropolitan patterns of residential segregation and educational inequality, a series of grassroots uprisings in the white-collar suburbs appropriated the populist discourse of the Silent Majority and forced a new class-driven version of "colorblind" politics into the national arena. The collective debut of the Silent Majority came during the summer of 1970, when representatives from antibusing movements throughout the New South suburbs gathered in Atlanta to forge a political alliance called the National Coalition of Concerned Citizens. The leaders of the grassroots revolt included physicians, dentists, attorneys, and other upper-middle-class professionals—the most affluent tier of the white parents and home owners mobilizing under the national banner of the Silent Majority. Claiming a membership of one million supporters of "neighborhood schools" in twenty-seven states, the confederation adopted a "color-blind" stance that demanded political protection for the socioeconomic and residential privileges of the middle-class suburbs.... "We are going on the offensive," promised a Miami Beach attorney named Ellis Rubin. "We are going to organize the largest, most effective lobby this country has ever seen."

The rise of the Silent Majority demonstrates the dynamic interplay between the local and the national in postwar political culture. By the mid-1970s, the grassroots protests of the white-collar suburbs and the top-down reaction of the federal government produced a new public policy framework that reshaped desegregation case law and circumscribed civil rights reform on the metropolitan landscape.... The collective politics of middle-class consciousness defined "freedom of choice" and "neighborhood schools" as the core privileges of home owner rights and consumer liberties, and rejected as "reverse discrimination" any collective integration remedies or affirmative action mandates designed to provide redress for historical structures of inequality. The mobilization of the Silent Majority ultimately pushed the White House and the Supreme Court to adopt explicit policies of suburban protection that rejected metropolitan remedies for metropolitan inequities and effectively placed residential segregation beyond the reach of constitutional law....

The New South metropolis of Charlotte, North Carolina, a white-collar banking center with a reputation for racial moderation, became the national test case for large-scale busing between the sprawling suburbs and the crowded ghettos. In the spring of 1969, the National Association for the Advancement of Colored People (NAACP) reopened desegregation litigation based on the pathbreaking contention that the prevailing distinction between "de jure" and "de facto" segregation was artificial, and therefore the Constitution required the school system to take affirmative action to overcome residential patterns shaped by government policies and reinforced by private discrimination.... Between 1950 and 1970, when the metropolitan population doubled to include more than 350,000 residents, almost all white-collar families drawn into the corporate economy moved into newly developed subdivisions located to the south and east of the downtown business district. During the same period, the municipal government displaced more than 10,000 black residents through federal urban renewal and highway construction programs and relocated almost all of these families in public housing projects invariably located in the opposite quadrant of the city. Official planning policies meticulously separated the middle-class white suburbs of southeast Charlotte from the overwhelmingly black neighborhoods of northwest Charlotte through industrial zoning buffers and interstate highway placement. By the time of the busing litigation, about 96 percent of the African-American population lived in the highly segregated northwest sector, and more than 14,000 black students attended completely isolated public schools. In April 1969, in *Swann v. Charlotte-Mecklenburg,* district judge James McMillan issued an unprecedented and explosive remedy: the two-way exchange of students from the black neighborhoods of the central city and the white subdivisions on the metropolitan fringe, a comprehensive busing formula designed to integrate every facility throughout the consolidated metropolitan school system.

Tens of thousands of middle-class white families immediately joined forces in the Concerned Parents Association (CPA), a powerful grassroots organization based in the outer-ring suburbs of southeast Charlotte. From the beginning, the CPA rallied around a "color-blind" platform of middle-class respectability and insisted that opposition to busing had nothing to do with racial prejudice or segregationist preference.... Tom Harris, an insurance executive who headed the CPA, explained that the membership did not represent either right-wing ideologues or the "upper crust" of the city but rather "essentially the middle class, and we have every intention of maintaining the proper dignity and respect." The petitions circulated by the group defended the rights of hardworking families who had purchased homes based on "proximity to schools and churches of their choice" and condemned busing as a violation of the equal protection clause of the Four-

teenth Amendment and the original spirit of the *Brown* decision. "I am not opposed to integration in any way," claimed one suburban father during a CPA demonstration. "But I was 'affluent' enough to buy a home near the school where I wanted my children to go. And I pay taxes to pay for it. They can bring in anybody they like to that school, but I don't want my children taken away."...

The antibusing movement in Charlotte represented a populist revolt of the center, as white-collar parents from secure suburban neighborhoods responded to the racial crisis of metropolitan desegregation through a "color-blind" politics of middle-class consciousness. "I couldn't believe such a thing could happen in America," Don Roberson explained. "So many of us made the biggest investment of our lives—our homes—primarily on the basis of their location with regard to schools. It seemed like an absurdity that anyone could tell us where to send our children." In a way, *Swann* plaintiff James Polk agreed with this class analysis of Charlotte's racial showdown: "We were smacking against the whole American dream. To whites, that meant pull yourself up by your bootstraps, buy a nice home and two cars, live in a nice neighborhood and go to a nice church, send your kids to the appropriate school.... We understood that a lot of white people would raise holy hell." During Charlotte's protracted busing crisis, the CPA platform never acknowledged the judicial finding that federal and municipal policies had shaped the methodical patterns of residential segregation that produced school segregation. The white parents who joined the antibusing movement thought of the location of their homes and the proximity of quality schools as nothing more and nothing less than the individual rewards for their willingness to work hard and make sacrifices for their children's future. This philosophy of middle-class accomplishment obscured the centrality of the state in the process of suburbanization and finessed the internal contradictions in the meritocratic ethos through an unapologetic defense of the rights of children to enjoy the fruits of their parents' success....

During the winter and spring of 1970, as antibusing movements spread from the suburban South to metropolitan centers such as Denver and Los Angeles, the Concerned Parents Association pioneered the emergence of the Silent Majority on the national political landscape. After taking control of the local board of education, the antibusing movement in Charlotte embraced a compromise position that reluctantly accepted one-way busing of black students to suburban facilities but fiercely rejected the transportation of white students away from their neighborhood schools. When the district court set a firm deadline for two-way busing, the CPA immediately demanded White House intervention in the judicial process. CPA leaders promptly secured private audiences with senior members of the executive branch, and the foot soldiers of the movement sent thousands of letters and telegrams to President Nixon. One suburban physician...asked the president why prosperous communities should be punished simply because their residents worked hard and bought respectable homes in safe neighborhoods near quality public schools. After clarifying that his views had "nothing to do with race or integration," this father insisted that the "thought that this course is un-American is simply untenable."... "As a member of the silent majority," yet another Charlotte parent declared, "I have never asked what anyone in government or this country could do for me; but rather have kept my mouth shut, paid my taxes and basically asked to be left alone.... I think it is time the law abiding, tax paying white middle class started looking to the federal government for something besides oppression."

The suburban uprising of the Silent Majority established the busing controversy as an urgent and unavoidable crisis in national politics. The White House quickly responded to the pleas and demands of upper-middle-class voters with a major policy statement on school desegregation, released under President Nixon's signature in March 1970. The address attempted to stake out the middle ground.... [I]n a direct appeal to suburban voters throughout the nation, the president adopted the "color-blind" framework of the grassroots antibusing movement and defended an inviolable right to attend neighborhood schools even if they reflected residential segregation. In accord with his vocal constituents, Nixon argued that most school segregation in both the metropolitan South and the urban North resulted from "de facto" market forces beyond the jurisdiction of the federal courts.... [T]his policy represented a calculated effort to shift the heat for desegregation enforcement from the executive branch to the federal judiciary, and a prescient recognition that suburban hostility toward racial busing transcended partisan, class, and regional boundaries.

Court-ordered busing in Charlotte became a conspicuous exception to the national rule.... In the case of *Swann v. Charlotte-Mecklenburg* (1971), the United States Supreme Court rejected the "color-blind" defense and approved busing as a legitimate remedy for state-sponsored racial discrimination....After several years of "white flight" caused by the foreseeable flaws in this plan, Judge McMillan ordered the school district to prevent racial resegregation through an affirmative action commitment to "socioeconomic integration." In the most significant feature of the new approach, the board reluctantly agreed to reassign white students from the upper-middle-class suburbs to stabilize school enrollment in the black residential areas of northwest Charlotte.... The favorable conditions created by the class-based busing compromise eventually turned Charlotte-Mecklenburg into a national success story, a New South showcase that boasted a greater degree of racial integration and a lower percentage of "white flight" than most other large cities in the nation....

The antibusing movement in Charlotte lost the local battle but won the national war. In the wake of *Swann*, the NAACP launched a campaign to overcome urban school segregation through city-suburban integration formulas and metropolitan consolidation remedies. During the same period, President Nixon appointed four justices to the Supreme Court, and the grassroots resistance of the Silent Majority converged with the top-down defense of suburban autonomy....In 1974, in the landmark case of *Milliken v. Bradley,* a narrow majority on the Burger Court invalidated a three-county busing formula designed to stem "white flight" from the city schools of Detroit by including the entire metropolitan region in the quest for stable integration and equal opportunity. The majority opinion in *Milliken* immunized most suburbs throughout the nation from the burdens and opportunities of meaningful integration and foreshadowed the hypersegregation by race and income in large urban school districts across the United States....

The New Metropolitan Dilemma

The grassroots revolt of the Silent Majority accelerated the reconfiguration of national politics around programs to protect the rights and privileges of the affluent suburbs.... Since the 1970s, the bipartisan battle for the volatile center has increasingly pursued shifting groups of middle-class swing voters in the sprawling metropolises of an increasingly suburban nation. The Reagan coalition in the 1980s included the white-collar home owners who launched the tax revolts in southern California, the corporate Republicans in wealthy Northeast counties such as Westchester [New York] and Fairfield [Connecticut] and Bergen [New Jersey], the blue-collar populists in the Rust Belt suburbs of the Midwest, and the evangelical Protestants whose organizational base rests in Sunbelt "edge cities" such as Colorado Springs and Virginia Beach. The resurrection of the "New Democrats" during the 1990s revolved around an operational suburban strategy of social and fiscal moderation that included targeted entitlement programs for "soccer moms" and working women, cultural tolerance for suburban moderates alienated by the New Right....In the 1992 election, the first in which suburban voters represented an outright majority, Bill Clinton launched his populist "third way" with an unattributed homage to the Nixon era and the Silent Majority: a "campaign for the future, for the forgotten hard-working middle class families of America."...

The United States became politically and geographically a definitively suburban nation during the final decades of the twentieth century, increasingly dominated by the priorities and anxieties of voters in the broad middle-class spectrum, persistently unreceptive to policy initiatives designed to address the structural disadvantages facing central cities and impoverished communities....

The federal government never launched a sustained assault on the structural forces undergirding residential segregation, and the persistent suburban resistance to collective remedies for educational and housing inequality has spanned regional boundaries and partisan affiliations. Despite the explosive impact of court-ordered busing, the transportation remedy addressed only the symptoms and not the causes of school segregation in metropolitan regions: the public policies that simultaneously constructed the middle-class suburbs and contained the urban ghettos....

In the absence of a federal commitment to tackle metropolitan structures of "economic segregation" and residential inequality, civil rights organizations and low-income plaintiffs have increasingly turned to state courts to challenge discriminatory features such as suburban zoning policies and school funding formulas. In the *Mount Laurel* cases of the 1970s, the New Jersey Supreme Court agreed that exclusionary zoning violated the equal protection clause of the state constitution and ordered suburban municipalities to provide a "fair share" affordable housing remedy. The political backlash began immediately—grassroots resistance by affluent neighborhoods, obstructionist tactics by the legislature—and a powerful wedge issue emerged for the suburban Republicans who gained control of the state government....The chastened Democrats in New Jersey regained power only through reinvention as a culturally liberal, fiscally responsible party that will hold the line on property taxes and defend suburban quality of life at all costs. While the political bellwethers of New Jersey and Connecticut, which also resisted court-ordered school funding equalization, began trending away from the GOP during the 1990s, it is not incidental but intrinsic to the electoral strategy of the "New Democrats" that they represent the two most racially segregated, income-stratified, corporate-clustered, and demographically suburbanized states in the nation....

A comprehensive assessment of the grass-roots ferment of the political center and the metropolitan dilemmas of the contemporary landscape requires attention to the population shift to the middle-class suburbs and the power shift to the Sunbelt economy. For more than three decades, from the collective revolt of the Silent Majority in the 1970s to the bipartisan accommodation of middle-class consciousness in the 1990s, suburban home owners and their political and judicial champions have naturalized residential segregation and defended metropolitan inequality through an explicit discourse of socioeconomic privilege and free-market meritocracy. For just as long, civil rights activists and progressive scholars have challenged the foundational mythology of suburban racial innocence and the "color-blind" ethos of middle-class individualism by exposing the de jure roots of almost all cases of allegedly "de facto" residential segregation—a historical verdict based on overwhelming evidence that has proved to be singularly unpersuasive in the political and legal spheres. The dominant ethos of American suburbia has always idealized the present and celebrated the future at the expense of any critical reflection on the past. The search for…new approaches in public policy should begin by expanding traditional models of analysis through a metropolitan framework that confronts…the pervasive politics of class in the suburban strategies of the volatile center.

CHAPTER 14

Recent Suburban Transformations, 1970–2000

INTRODUCTION

After 1970, the complexity and variety of American suburbs continued to grow. The multi-nucleated outer city, with its landscape of offices, high-end retailing, and high-tech manufacturing, increased by an order of magnitude. So, too, did the size and heterogeneity of the suburban population. In 1970, 37 percent of Americans lived in suburbs; by 2000, the proportion was 50 percent. Sweeping changes in the economy and society—the shift from a manufacturing- to service-based economy, the aging of baby boomers, profuse immigration, changing family structures, and the culmination of diverse movements for civil rights, among others—played out on the suburban stage. The result was a striking diversification of the suburban population. Suburbanites now included young singles, one-parent families, empty-nesters, retirees, gays and lesbians, and a growing share of African-Americans, Latinos, and Asian-Americans. By 2000, middle-class white families with a male breadwinner and a stay-at-home mom—the stereotype of 1950s suburbia—had become the minority. By the end of the century, suburbia looked more and more like America as a whole. And, of course, the reverse was also true.

Among the most notable changes in recent suburbia has been its racial and ethnic diversification. In contrast to 1970, when "minorities" made up just under 10 percent of the suburban population, African Americans, Latinos, and Asian Americans comprised 28 percent of all suburbanites by 2000. In over half of the nation's 100 largest metropolitan areas, according to demographer William Frey, "minorities were responsible for the bulk of suburban population gains."[1] In a variety of suburban areas, the number of whites actually declined, leaving for parts ever more distant and more homogenous.

Suburbanization by African Americans, which had been growing for decades, accelerated sharply during these years. Between 1970 and 2000 the number of black suburbanites rose from 3.5 million to nearly 12 million, and by century's end, 38 percent of African Americans lived in suburbs. Underlying this change were civil rights-inspired gains in housing and jobs. The Civil Rights Act of 1964 and the Fair Housing Act of 1968 led to improving job prospects for well-educated and highly-skilled blacks and to declines in housing discrimination. Both trends translated into real gains in the housing market. Equally important, black suburbanization increased due to the simple physical growth of black urban neighborhoods. By the 1960s, many expanding communities reached the municipal limits and pushed outward into inner-ring suburbs, setting off a process of white flight and racial turnover. Thus, the results of black suburbanization were mixed. At the leading edge, members of a growing black middle class exercised unprecedented residential freedom. Their suburban journeys often ended in spacious new homes, with good schools and public services. On the other hand, many lower-middle-class and working-class families inherited suburbs that faced significant social and economic problems. Overall, the suburbs where most African Americans lived were poorer, older, and less financially secure than those of other groups. Black suburbanites were likely to pay higher taxes, receive poorer services, and reap less property appreciation than white suburbanites. Even in places like Prince George's County, Maryland, where middle-class blacks formed a majority by 1990, 45 percent of county schoolchildren in 2000 were eligible for subsidized meals, a benefit tied to low-income status. Finally, while levels of racial segregation declined, they remained higher for blacks than for any other group. In 2000, the average black suburbanite lived in a neighborhood that was 46 percent black—and in a number of metro areas the majority lived in predominantly-black suburbs. As the twentieth century came to a close, African-American suburbanites still contended with separate and, in many ways, unequal suburban spaces.

During these same years, Latinos and Asian Americans, whose numbers swelled through growing immigration, also moved to suburbs in large numbers. By 2000, Latinos had surpassed African Americans as the nation's largest "minority" group, and more than half (54%) of the nation's 35 million Latinos lived in the suburbs. Asian-American suburbanization likewise blossomed; by 2000, about 58 percent of Asian Americans (almost 6 million people) lived in suburbs. In part, this suburban boom reflected the rise of an American-born middle class in both groups, but the driving factor was immigration from Asia and Latin America. As among African Americans, differences in socioeconomic circumstances among Latinos and Asian Americans—natives as well as newcomers and people with diverse national origins—produced varying suburban experiences.

By 2000, for the first time ever, suburbs were home to a majority (52%) of foreign-born residents in the United States. Just as immigrants a century earlier gathered near central city jobs, recent immigrants followed employment opportunities to the suburbs. In fast-growing, physically sprawling cities, such as Atlanta, Dallas-Ft. Worth, Washington, Las Vegas, and Orlando, as many as 75 percent of immigrants lived in the suburbs. As in earlier eras, many immigrant families clustered together, creating suburban "Chinatowns" (Monterey Park, California), "Little Saigons" (Westminster, California), or "Little Havanas" (Hialeah, Florida). Other metropolitan areas saw the rise of multinational "ethnoburbs": Silver Spring and Langley Park, Maryland (Washington, DC); Palisades Park, New Jersey (New York City); and Doraville and Chamblee, Georgia (Atlanta) attracted immigrants from nations including Mexico, El Salvador, and Bolivia, as well as Cambodia, Korea, India, Sierra Leone, Jamaica, and Ethiopia.

Emblematic of this trend, many of the nation's immigration controversies boiled over in the suburbs. Tensions over outdoor day-labor markets flared in formerly insulated white suburbs such as Hoover, Alabama (Birmingham); Hearndon and Woodbridge, Virginia (Washington, D.C.); and Farmingville, New York (New York City). Baldwin Park, California near Los Angeles drew demonstrations by anti-immigrant groups to protest a public monument that celebrated the suburb's Latino majority. In suburbs of Los Angeles and Phoenix, authorities raided immigrant "drop houses," where smugglers held as many as 150 undocumented migrants hostage while awaiting payment. And conflicts erupted over Chinese-language signage in Monterey Park, California.

The social diversity of suburbia increased in other ways as well, with implications for suburban social, economic, and political life. As the baby boom ended and boomers aged, so did the suburban population as a whole. This trend was most obvious in suburban retirement havens across the Sunbelt, but suburbs nationwide became "grayer" as the baby boom generation "aged in place."[2] Changes in work and family patterns also affected suburban life. Two-income families became the norm in post-1970 suburbia (as they did nationwide), and suburbs saw upswings in the number of single-parent and gay and lesbian households. All of these trends drove changing demands for local goods and services; as one example, some suburban taxpayers have re-prioritized spending on schools and healthcare.

The fate of individual suburbs varied widely as well. Many older, inner-ring suburbs faced the same challenges that had beset inner cities a generation earlier: aging housing and infrastructure, fat taxes and slender services, growing rates of unemployment, poverty and crime. As the economy shifted away from manufacturing in the 1970s and 1980s, older industrial suburbs, especially, were devastated; many slipped into municipal default, their streets lined with shuttered factories, retail businesses, and abandoned housing. Many first-ring suburbs also experienced sweeping white flight after the arrival of blacks and other minorities. As middle-class pioneers continued moving up and out, these places became home to increasingly poor populations, little able to afford to update the aging infrastructure of their communities. At the same time, affluent suburbs continued to proliferate, some in new developments—or "greenfields"—on the metropolitan margins, others adjacent to highway interchanges that became growth nodes in the outer metropolis.[3]

While diversity of many kinds has characterized suburbia's history, the years since 1970 have seen an intensification of this trend in ways that captured new public attention. Almost inevitably, as America both suburbanized and diversified with growing speed, the two trends have merged. Yet even as more and different Americans find their way into suburban homes, the larger pattern of "segregated diversity" continues to define this social landscape—much as it did a century ago. Class, race, and ethnicity remain important pillars of a stubbornly polarized suburban landscape.

DOCUMENTS

The first three documents reflect on ethnic and racial diversification in suburbia. In **Document 14-1**, journalist David Dent reports on the transformation of Prince George's County, Maryland, east of Washington, DC, into the nation's first affluent majority-black suburban county. By the mid-1990s, the county had become a locus for black political and economic power in the region, and, like similar suburbs nationwide, its well-educated middle class became a symbol for black progress in post-civil-rights America. Depicting these changes in a humorous way in **Document 14-2**, Aaron McGruder's cartoon strip, "The Boondocks," tracks the suburban adventures of two boys, the politically conscious Huey Freeman and his streetwise little brother Riley, who move from Chicago to live with their grandfather in a mostly white suburb. "The Boondocks" not only offers incisive commentary on the state of American and suburban society, but it highlights pressing issues and dilemmas of African-American life—political and cultural awareness, tensions over generational values, complexion and biracialism, hip hop and the mass media, and depictions of women—all juxtaposed against the backdrop of a changing suburbia.

In **Document 14-3**, the *Atlanta Journal and Constitution* reports on growing ethnic diversity in the suburbs of metropolitan Atlanta during the 1990s. As the primary destination for new immigrants, the suburbs became home to Latino, East Asian, Pakistani, and Indian immigrants. In this account, the reporter describes some of the ways these newcomers have restyled local suburban commerce and culture.

The next set of documents reveals suburban shifts that hit squarely in the realm of the white middle class. Suburban youth has been the focal point for periodic national hand-wringing since the 1950s, but by the 1980s and 1990s, suburban (and especially white) teenagers became the focus of ever more shocking incidents, calling into question the premise that suburbia was a better place "for the kids." Episodes included a crime spree by a group of popular teens in Lakewood, California, a gang rape by well-known high-school athletes in Glen Ridge, New Jersey, rising rates of teen pregnancy and suicide, as well as violence by white-supremacist skinheads. In the 1990s, an epidemic of suburban school-ground shootings trained a national spotlight on the subject once again. Why had suburbia—supposedly the best place to raise children—become a site of nihilism, rage, and violence? What had gone so wrong? What role did suburbia play in these events? In **Document 14-4**, journalist and social worker Donna Gaines explores suburbia's "teenage wasteland" in Bergenfield, New Jersey, in the late 1980s. Gaines went to the suburb after four teenagers died there in a "suicide pact." In this excerpt, she examines class and status rivalries among teenagers, focusing on so-called "burnouts." Written before the wave of school shootings rocked suburbia in the 1990s, Gaines uncovered a world of teenaged enmity, disappointment, and self-destruction largely invisible to most adults. In **Document 14-5**, published in the conservative journal, the *National Review,* columnist Christopher Caldwell questions whether teenage alienation and violence might be related to a suburban landscape that promotes children's isolation, loneliness, and dependence on parents.

In **Document 14-6,** writer James Kaplan reflects on the effects of gentrification, climbing housing prices, and high tax burdens on the grown children of suburbia. Especially in metropolitan areas with tight housing markets, many suburbanites have found themselves unable to afford to live in the towns where they grew up. Once the refuge of middle-class family life, recent suburbia exposes the declining fortunes of the American middle class after 1970, in some cases contributing to the dispersal of these families. Kaplan reflects on many of these same themes in his suburban novel, *Two Guys from Verona* (1998).

In **Document 14-7**, metropolitan reformer Myron Orfield suggests another way of measuring suburban diversity. In the late twentieth century, he argues, the key similarities and differences among suburbs reflected their capacity to pay for basic services. In the largest U.S. metro areas, more than half of suburbanites lived in municipalities facing severe financial stress. Another quarter resided in booming outer suburbs whose ability to build infrastructure and schools relied largely on future growth. Meanwhile, a disproportionate share of metropolitan wealth clustered in a handful of "affluent job centers," home to just 7 percent of the population. As we will see in chapter 16, Orfield contends that these changes may form the basis for a new "metropolitics" that joins the interests of tax-strapped suburbs and central cities in a coalition to defeat sprawl and redress metropolitan inequalities. **Document 14-8** visually illustrates the suburban fiscal polarization that Orfield describes. East Cleveland, Ohio, like many older, inner suburbs, fell on hard times during the 1970s and 1980s. Once home to Cleveland's upper crust, the suburb began to attract upwardly mobile African-American families in the 1960s. White residents and businesses fled the area, leading to nearly complete racial turnover by 1980. Many middle-class blacks also moved away as opportunities opened up elsewhere. With rising poverty and unemployment rates and a dwindling tax base, the community struggled to maintain infrastructure and services. By contrast, suburbs such as Overland Park, Kansas, west of Kansas City, boomed, attracting both white-collar businesses and upper-middle-class residents, who enjoyed top-flight schools, abundant recreational amenities, and spacious housing in close proximity to work.

What aspects of recent suburban diversification seem new, compared to patterns described in chapters 4 and 7? Given the multiplicity of suburban experiences in recent decades, can we still talk of "suburbia" or a suburban ideal? How do expectations about suburban life measure up to reality? How does suburbia contribute to teenage angst? In what ways are Bergenfield and Littleton the same, or different, from a young person's perspective? What role, if any, does the suburban environment play in recent school shootings, such as Columbine?

14-1. THE *NEW YORK TIMES MAGAZINE* SPOTLIGHTS BLACK SUBURBANIZATION, 1992

Source: David J. Dent, "The New Black Suburbs," *New York Times Magazine,* June 14, 1992. Copyright © 1992 by The New York Times Co. Reprinted with permission.

A generation ago, peaceful civil rights demonstrators faced violent resistance in the fight for a racially integrated society. Years later, Barron and Edith Harvey, who are black, would embody the hopes of that struggle. In 1978, the couple moved into a white, upper-middle-income neighborhood in Fairfax County, Virginia, a suburb of Washington. During their seven years there, no crosses were burned in their yard and no racial epithets were muttered at them within earshot. There were a few incredulous stares, a few stops by the police, who had mistaken Barron for a criminal, and a run-in with an elementary school principal over the absence of blacks in the curriculum at the Harveys' daughter's school.

"You expect those kinds of things in a white neighborhood, and, all things being equal, we would have stayed," says Barron Harvey, chairman of the accounting department at Howard University and an international business consultant.

But the Harveys left in 1985—not because Fairfax was inhospitable, but because they wanted to become part of another

Washington suburb, Prince George's County in Maryland. Prince George's—a county that George Wallace won in the 1972 Presidential primary—was fast becoming the closest thing to utopia that black middle-class families could find in America.

What some consider the essence of the American dream—suburbia—became a reality for a record number of blacks in the 1980's. In 1990, 32 percent of all black Americans in metropolitan areas lived in suburban neighborhoods, a record 6 percent increase from 1980....As an increasing number of black Americans head for the suburban dream, some are bypassing another dream—the dream of an integrated society. These black Americans are moving to black upper- and middle-class neighborhoods, usually pockets in counties that have a white majority....

Black suburbs have sprung up across the country. In the Miami area, there is Rolling Oaks in Dade County. Around St. Louis, black suburbs exist in sections of Black Jack, Jennings, Normandy and University City in St. Louis County. In the Atlanta suburbs, black majority communities include Brook Glen, Panola Mill and Wyndham Park in DeKalb County. And in the Washington area, Prince George's County itself has a black majority.

Racial steering, though illegal, may lead some blacks in the Washington area to the predominantly black neighborhoods of Prince George's. But for most, it is a deliberate, affirmative choice.

"I don't want to come home and always have my guard up," says David S. Ball, a senior contract administrator....Ball and his wife, Phillis, moved from Washington to a predominantly black subdivision in Fort Washington, Maryland. "After I work eight hours or more a day," he says, "I don't want to come home and work another eight."...

Barron Harvey adds: "We always wanted to make sure our child had many African-American children to play with, not just one or two. We always wanted to be in a community with a large number of black professionals, and to feel part of that community. We never really felt like we were part of Fairfax."

For some Prince Georgians, like Radamase Cabrera, 39, one reason for the move was a profound sense of disillusionment.

"I think the integration of black folks in the 60's was one of the biggest cons in the world," says Cabrera, an urban planner for the city of Washington. Cabrera was one of a small number of blacks attending the University of Connecticut at Storrs in 1970. "I was called a nigger the first week there and held by the police until this white girl told them I hadn't attacked her. You want to call me a separatist, so be it. I think of myself as a pragmatist. Why should I beg some cracker to integrate me into his society when he doesn't want to? Why keep beating my head up against a wall, especially when I've been there."

While the racial balance of Prince George's population of 729,268 may indicate an integrated county—50.7 percent black, 43.1 percent white, 6.2 percent other—census data suggests a segregated county. More than half of all the census tracts in Prince George's are at least 70 percent white or 70 percent black. Some experts predict the county will be two-thirds black by the end of the century....

Radamase Cabrera and his wife, Denise, a reporter for The Associated Press, moved to Prince George's County in 1987, settling in a formerly all-white working-class neighborhood where blacks were becoming the majority. "It was about 50-50 then, and I knew it was only a matter of time before the white folks would leave and you'd have yourself a nice suburban African-American community."

For Cabrera, life in Prince George's County has become part of a mission. Though he works in Washington, he has become an outspoken activist in his community—consumed with its demographic, political and economic statistics. "Prince George's County will be, if it is not already, the most educated and affluent African-American community on the planet, and it has the opportunity to be a model of how black folks can control their political, economic and social institutions," Cabrera says. "This place is unique because usually black folks inherit things like a Newark or a Gary when it's depressed and all the wealth is gone and it has no potential."

Prince George's now has more than 8,000 black-owned businesses....Although commercial development in the county has grown, many retailers have declined the county's invitations to open stores there while entering counties with a lower median income but a larger white population. Nordstrom and Macy's have opened stores in Baltimore County, which had a median household income of $38,837, compared with $43,127 in Prince George's County in 1989. But Baltimore County is 85 percent white. Many Prince George's shoppers, like Linda Williams-Brown often ride two counties away to shop, pouring tax dollars into other communities. "For me to go to a nice mall with a Saks and a Macy's, I have to go all the way to Virginia," Williams-Brown says. "When they put new stores in the shopping centers here, they put in a T. J. Mack, in a place like Mitchellville, across the street from $200,000 and $300,000 homes that black people own. Why?"...

[S]ays Prince George's county executive, Parris N. Glendening,..."The market hasn't caught up to us. But it will."

However, Douglas Massey, a professor of sociology at the University of Chicago, would not be surprised if it did not. "I think that a group that raises residential segregation to be an ideal is going to cut itself off from many of the benefits of society," he says. "You make it easier for the larger white population to eventually decapitalize it, and

it basically becomes an easy target for racist attitudes. It becomes isolated politically....

The decision to live in a black community should not be equated with a desire to live in a one-race world....

Most residents of the black neighborhoods in Prince George's County work or function in other ways in the integrated American culture. "One of things black folks never really have to worry about in America is being outside the realm of integration," says Harvey. "We will always have to interface with the other culture."

The rise of affluent black neighborhoods could enhance the relationship between the races, [sociologist, Bart] Landry says. "I think to the extent that it strengthens feelings of self-worth, it's good for integration, because you have to believe you are O.K. first before you can mingle with others."...For the Harveys, the move to Prince George's may not be a step away from the Rev. Dr. Martin Luther King Jr.'s dream, but a step toward the realization of that dream. "We are advancing," says Barron Harvey. "We were fighting for the right to go where we want to go, to make the choice to live where we want to live. We have the freedom of choice, which we have exercised."

Figure 14-1 Home in Woodmore South, Mitchellville, Maryland, 2001. Suburbanization by affluent and well-educated African Americans after 1960 transformed Prince George's County, Maryland, into the nation's first majority black and middle-class suburban county. Photograph by Andrew Wiese.

14-2. AARON MCGRUDER SHAKES UP SUBURBIA ON THE COMIC PAGE, 1999

Figure 14-2 Since its national debut in 1999, Aaron McGruder's cartoon strip, *The Boondocks* has reviewed American society, politics, and culture through a black suburban lens. The Boondocks ©1999 Aaron McGruder. Dist. By Universal Press Syndicate. Reprinted with permission. All rights reserved. Aaron McGruder.

14-3. A REPORTER DOCUMENTS ETHNIC DIVERSITY IN ATLANTA'S SUBURBS, 1999

Source: Mark Bixler, "Latest Counts Released Today: Asians, Latinos making mark in area; rising populations give metro Atlanta, Georgia a cultural diversity that was missing eight years ago," *Atlanta Journal and Constitution*, September 15, 1999. Copyright © 1999 by The Atlanta Journal-Constitution. Reprintde with permission.

Corn tortillas were hard to find in 1990. And there wasn't much of a market for movies in the Hindi language. Now automatic teller machines ask whether you want instructions in English or Spanish, fast food restaurants have signs in Spanish and thousands of Indians and Pakistanis turn out for Hindi movies in the suburbs north and south of Atlanta.

Immigration from Latin America and Asia to Georgia and metro Atlanta has soared in the 1990s, outpacing the growth rate of all other groups.

Figures released today by the U.S. Census Bureau show that while Georgia's population increased 17.5 percent since 1990, the number of Hispanics and Asians rose 100.2 percent and 91.6 percent, respectively.

Hispanics and Asians still represent small segments of the total population—2 percent of Georgians are Asian and 2.9 percent Hispanic—but the numbers go up every year.

Jose Altamirano sees the change in his College Park store, Los Angeles Mexican Market. It sells Mexican salsas and beans that Altamirano had trouble finding after coming to Atlanta from Mexico in the late 1980s.

"It was very difficult to find in the stores," he said. "But now you can go to Buford Highway or Chamblee. If you go there—every street, every corner you can find every Mexican product."

It's not just Buford Highway, the historic heart of many of Atlanta's immigrant communities, that has changed as a result of new arrivals. The census figures show counties in metro Atlanta, such as Cherokee, Coweta, Henry, Forsyth and Paulding, made the biggest percentage gains in Hispanics and Asians from July 1990 to July 1998.

Hispanic and Asian growth in those counties ranged from 161 percent to 271 percent. One reason the gains seem so big is that there were so few Hispanics and Asians to begin with. Most of those counties remain overwhelmingly white.

African-American numbers also continued to rise, with a 27.9 percent increase in the 16 counties. Behind Florida, Georgia had the second-biggest increase in African-Americans, adding nearly 420,000 people.

The census numbers out today estimate 1998 county populations by race or Hispanic origin. They are the last such estimates before the federal government mails out the 2000 Census next spring.

Experts say the 1990 Census undercounted thousands of Georgians and that the undercount was particularly acute in minority communities.

The state lost millions of dollars in federal money as a result. Asian and Hispanic leaders and the Census Bureau are working to avoid an undercount next year. Last week, Gov. Roy Barnes appointed a committee to suggest ways to get an accurate count.

The surge in the immigrant population has affected the way many people in metro Atlanta do business. Ethnic entrepreneurs have tapped into the immigrant market by opening banks, restaurants and other businesses.

A few months ago, Hari Singh, 52, an accountant with a relative in the movie distribution business, saw dollar signs when he looked at the booming Indian and Pakistani population in metro Atlanta. He decided to play movies in the Hindi language without subtitles.

The first screening was last fall at Lefont's Marietta Star Cinemas on Roswell Road in Marietta. The movie was "Kuch Kuch Hota Hai," a musical love story whose title, Singh said, translates loosely into "When you fall in love, you get a funny feeling." Singh said more than 7,500 Pakistanis and Indians paid $7 apiece to see the film during its four-week run.

"They were from all over Atlanta all the way down to Macon. Some people came from the Carolinas. Some came from Tennessee," he said. "The Indian population is growing very fast in Atlanta."

Singh still shows movies in Marietta and recently began showing them at a six-screen cinema in Jonesboro. He said many people going to see hits such as "Big Daddy" and "Wild Wild West" do a double-take when they see the movie poster in Hindi alongside the other features.

"They find it amazing that someone could be running an Indian movie here," he said.

Metro governments also have noticed the changes. The Atlanta-Fulton County Public Library, for example, has materials in 22 languages, including Chinese, Farsi, Cambodian and Yiddish as well as the high school standards of Spanish, German, French and Italian, said Judith Lunsford, a spokeswoman for the library.

"As the Hispanic population has grown, we've tried to bring up more of that collection," she said.

The increases in the immigrant populations have brought tension this decade. A few months ago in Norcross, city officials fined a grocery store catering to Hispanic immigrants because the store did not prominently display its name in English.

The city said it would be hard for firefighters and other emergency personnel to find the store quickly.

In Cobb County, the Smyrna City Council decided in 1996 all store signs must be in English. And the Marietta City Council voted this year to bar construction crews from picking up day laborers—Hispanic men who wait for work in the morning—from city property.

Immigrant community leaders have been talking with government officials to work out such problems, working through groups such as the Latin American Association and the Asian-American Coalition.

14-4. DONNA GAINES SURVEYS SUBURBIA'S "TEENAGE WASTELAND," 1991

Source: Donna Gaines, *Teenage Wasteland: Suburbia's Dead End Kids* (New York: Pantheon Books, 1991).

Bergenfield [New Jersey] is an "upper-poor" American town, an anomaly stuck in the midst of scenic, wealthy Bergen county. To get to Bergenfield from Route 4, you turn off into Teaneck. Teaneck is right next to Bergenfield, but with its affluent homes and multicultural face, it's really another America....

Like many American towns in recent years, Bergenfield has experienced its share of economic pressure. In one of the wealthiest counties in the nation, the average income in 1984 was $37,236, placing Bergenfield forty-ninth from the top among seventy Bergen County towns. When interviewed by reporters, Bergenfield residents had described their town as "upper-poor" or working-class, even blue-collar....

From an adult's point of view, Bergenfield

appears as a warm, modest, close-knit community of well-kept, compact single-family homes....

Now, from a teenager's point of view, Bergenfield looks especially cool: six pizza places, four record stores, two car washes, two billiard halls, a dozen hair and beauty places; the walls of dark, narrow alleys testifying to immortal true loves and to the greatness of bands, remnants of prior generations that have ruled these streets. There are grand parking lots; most famous is the one in front of Foster Village Shopping Center and then the one behind the 7-Eleven....

With approximately 25,700 residents in Bergenfield, there are always plenty of kids hanging around. Washington Avenue, the main commercial street, has two lanes and clocks about two miles if you're driving north from Teaneck to Dumont. The kids call this strip of turf "the Ave" because of its notoriety and centrality among the towns of North Bergen....

It's the "burnouts" who own the streets of Bergenfield. For those inclined toward hanging around, the best thing about living in Bergenfield is that within minutes, you can find your friends. On foot! It is a terrific advantage, offering an urban sense of independence often missing in sprawling suburbs. With typically inadequate public transportation systems, local mobility in the 'burbs is always difficult. But everything is central in Bergenfield. That means you never have to hit your parents up for rides if you want to see your friends. You just go out.

But there is a downside. The particular geography of Bergenfield is such that by car or on foot, you always feel highly visible. In fact, you are highly visible. And if you've got a mark of any sort, if you're known, you cannot hide from it. Ever. This is a small town. People know who you are. Unless you have a car, plans, and money for gas, you're shipwrecked here, you're under suspicion, under surveillance.

I felt this cloying sensation immediately. At first I dismissed it as my own paranoia—I was an intruder, a spy on assignment. Bergenfield felt weird because of the suicide pact, because I knew it had happened here. It was impossible not to think about all the kids who had died in this little town. But it wasn't "the haunts" or even "the vibes."

Bergenfield simply has this horribly oppressive geography that makes it different. Different from my town, different from Levittown, and from the town I grew up in. It is just too fucking close. There is no reprieve, no refrain from the burden of this relentless landscape. With only two lanes for cars, Bergenfield's corridor of teens can get narrow pretty quickly. The town just moves in on you. After a while, it is suffocating you....

It's Thursday afternoon. After-school activities are in progress. A group of about seven teenagers are sitting around a truck in front of the 7-Eleven. Burnouts. I know from the pose, the clothes, the turf. Yep, in another age they'd be hitters or greasers or hippies or heads or freaks. On another coast—they'd be stoners. Archenemies of jocks, dexters, rahrahs, or socs for all eternity.

Guys with earrings, crucifixes, long hair hanging over a concert shirt or a hooded sweatshirt. Walking in threes with boom boxes blasting AC/DC, Bon Jovi, or Zep. Suburban rocker kids are patriotic—everyone wears denim jackets (a prized commodity among international rocker youth, proof of America's pop-cultural world supremacy). Back panel is painted, a shrine to one's most beloved band: Iron Maiden, Metallica, the Grateful Dead.

Ladies have bi-level haircuts. Long shags blown, sprayed, clipped to one side, teased, sometimes bleached. Grease & glamour. Where Farrah and Madonna meet Twisted Sister....

Street-corner society in suburbia. Hanging around minding your business until you get banished by the cops....

Spend a few minutes outside of any American public school, and you can figure out who makes up the enemy camps. It's visually apparent: different races, ethnic groups, classes. And subcultural affiliations are expressed through clothing and music, coded in signs. So at the high school in Glen Clove, Long Island, white Italian-American and black African-American teenagers play out their adjacent communities' racial and territorial rivalries. Like any place, Bergenfield had its social schisms.

Of course there were many smaller rifts, and many "unaffiliated" kids around. But the principal rivalry among the youth of Bergenfield was played out along lines of participation and refusal in adult-orchestrated athletic activity.

In most high schools the politics of conformity and defiance are not this clearly articulated. At Bergenfield, in political terms, the jocks were "hegemonic," and their arch rivals, the burnouts, were "transgressive." So the closer Bergenfield's burnouts were to the adult-prescribed action, the worse they felt about themselves. The further away from the mainstream they could get, the greater their self-respect. Whether that meant nonparticipation, obliteration through drugs, or contemplating suicide, it was a matter of psychic survival.

The burnouts' point of reference was their "scene"—whatever subcultural activity they had going after hours, outside of Bergenfield, apart from the status hierarchy expressed at school. So something like a night at an Iron Maiden show was not only weekend fun, or a thrilling pop-cultural experience.... It could also help get you through the next six months by restoring your dignity. When Maiden's lead singer, Bruce Dickinson, bleats out, "Run to the hills, run for your lives," in a huge arena to thousands of suburban refugee kids, he's singing about the American Indian under siege....But the kids identify. Who cares if arena shows are corporate, commercial, or mass, Dickinson's singing their anthem too.

For the duration of my stay, in almost every encounter, the outcast members of Bergenfield's youth population would tell me these things: the cops are dicks, the school blows, the jocks suck, Billy Milano (lead singer of now defunct S.O.D.—Stormtroopers of Death) was from a nearby town, and Iron Maiden had dedicated "Wasted Years" to the Burress sisters [two of the teens who died in the suicide pact] the last time the band played Jersey. These were their cultural badges of honor, unknown to the adults.

Because the myth of a democratized mass makes class lines in the suburbs of the United States so ambiguous to begin with, differences in status become the critical lines of demarcation. And in the mostly white, mainly Christian town of Bergenfield, where there are neither very rich nor very poor people, this sports thing became an important criterion for determining "who's who" among the young people.

The girls played this out too, as they always have, deriving their status by involvement in school (as cheerleaders, in clubs, in the classroom). And just as important, by the boys they hung around with. They were defined by who they were, by what they wore, by where they were seen, and with whom. Like any other "Other," the kids at the bottom, who everybody here simply called burnouts, were actually a conglomerate of several cliques—serious druggies, Deadheads, dirtbags, skinheads, metalheads, thrashers, and punks. Some were good students, from "good" families with money and prestige. In any other setting all of these people might have been bitter rivals, or at least very separate cliques. But here, thanks to the adults and the primacy of sports, they were all lumped together—united by virtue of a common enemy, the jocks....

The "burnouts" and "dirtbags" occupied a specific place in the status hierarchy of the 1980s high school. Where some of their equally alienated but more politically motivated peers—rads, skins, and punk/hardcore kids—shunned drugs, and practiced nihilism with purpose, the "burnouts" and "dirts" didn't ascribe their actions to some higher principle.

As stereotyped by their peers, "burnouts" are in the zombie zone of existence. Their main activity is getting high, being oblivious. It is this, not their clothing or music, that sets them apart as a clique....

Dirts defy the mainstream game through rituals of style and attitude. Anger is expressed in random episodes of violence—vandalism, fighting. Burnouts, on the other hand, are more passive, inert. They withdraw, they just wanna get wasted....

Both the dirts and the burnt may understand how they are being fucked over and by whom. And while partying rituals may actually celebrate the refusal to play the game, neither group has a clue where to take it beyond the parking lot of 7-Eleven.

So they end up stranded in teenage wasteland. They devote their lives to their bands, to their friends, to partying: they live in the moment. They're going down in flames, taking literally the notion that "rust never sleeps," that it is "better to burn out than fade away." While left-leaning adults have valorized the politically minded punks and right-wing groups have engaged some fascistic skins, nobody really thinks too much about organizing dirts or burnouts. Law enforcement officials, special education teachers, and drug treatment facilities are the adults who are concerned with these kids....

Small in numbers, isolated in decaying suburbs, they aren't visible on any national scale until they are involved in something that really horrifies us, like a suicide pact, or parricide, or incest, or "satanic" sacrifice. For the most part, burnouts and dirt bags are anomic small-town white boys and girls, just trying to get through the day. Their way of fighting back is to have enough fun to kill themselves before everything else does.

14-5. CHRISTOPHER CALDWELL LINKS TEEN ALIENATION TO THE ENVIRONMENT OF NEW SUBURBIA, 1999

Source: Christopher Caldwell, "Levittown to Littleton: How the Suburbs Have Changed," *The National Review*, May 31, 1999. Copyright © 1999 by National Review, Inc., 215 Lexington Avenue, New York, NY 10016. Reprinted by permission.

The day after the shootings at Columbine High, many newspapers ran a 2″ × 2″ inset map of the school neighborhood in Littleton, Colorado [a Denver suburb]. There was a grid of high-speed roads a mile to a block. There were residential cul-de-sacs squiggling into empty quadrants. And looming up in the corner like a 747 hangar was the monolithic high-school building.

Such brand-new landscapes, almost wholly unfamiliar to northeasterners, make up virtually all of the middle-class neighborhoods in any western metropolis—Phoenix, Albuquerque, Houston. What was odd was that the Littleton map generally ran amid columns of copy seeking out the root causes of the shooting, and seeking them most everywhere: guns, television, affluence, big schools, divorce, Hollywood, the Internet, Goth music. Looking for simple explanations for a tragedy like Littleton is probably a fool's errand. But if one is going to engage in the exercise, the suburban layout described in the little map belongs on the list.

In the weeks following the massacre, many Americans have begun to think so too. News articles and television specials have cast towns like Littleton as un-"nurturing" at best, an adolescent hell on earth at worst. People are once again deeply troubled by "suburbia." Fifty-five percent of Americans live in suburbs now—but only 25 percent of that number mention the suburbs as the place they'd most like to live.

Well, yeah, yeah, one might say. People have been beating up on suburbs since Bill Levitt developed his first neighborhood on Long Island in 1947. So what else is new?

As it turns out, *everything* is new.

The argument over the sterility of suburban developments like the various Levittowns was thrashed out decades ago, and largely settled in favor of suburbia. Witnesses for the prosecution began appearing in the 1950s: Allen Ginsberg's poetry, the Pete Seeger folk song (written by Malvina Reynolds) called "Little Boxes" ("...made of ticky-tacky/And they all look the same"), novels of corporate anomie like Sloan Wilson's *Man in the Gray Flannel Suit*. For the campus protestors of the 1960s, the suburbs were synonymous with conformity, repression, and racism. For the radicals' largely conservative opponents, they meant family, patriotism, and decency. In retrospect, we can view this as an early sign of the Left's conversion to elite snobbery: What really bothered the Left about Levittowns was that they were so *working class*. Happily, and unsurprisingly, conservatives won this battle.

But the Littleton problem is not the Levittown problem. And conservatives' victory in earlier battles has made them too quick to dismiss the complaints that have spawned dozens of panicky books in the past two years and have come to a boil in the wake of the shootings....

The problem with Levittown was its physical monotony, a problem that diminishes over time, as trees grow and suburbanites modify their homes. What's more, since Tocqueville we've been told that a tendency to uniformity comes with the democratic territory. The problem in affluent "McMansion" suburbs like Littleton is that children grow up in almost hermetic seclusion—a newer and more soul-destroying condition, with dismal implications for democracy. Large lots, dead-end streets, and draconian zoning laws mean that there are vast distances to travel to reach any kind of public space. For parents, this means dependence on cars. For children unlucky enough to inhabit a dead-end that has no children on it, this means: No friends for you. Until adolescence, not even a child who is an ambitious walker can escape, since other neighborhoods are separated from his not by streets but by highways. (Town planners may christen them "avenues" or "boulevards," and real-estate agents may sell them as such, but they're highways.) No child in Levittown faced this problem.

This seclusion, in turn, creates an abject dependence on parents for automobile travel, and with it, a breakdown in any socialization of children that could be called normal. In the largely suburban eastern town where I grew up, a 5-year-old could walk about the neighborhood, and a 10-year-old could walk all over town. Twelve-year-olds could ride their bikes most places, and 14-year-olds could ride them to other towns. When you were 16, you could take the car if you really needed it. Entry into adult mobility was gradual and supervised. By contrast, a 15-year-old Littleton resident lives in a state of dependence considerably greater than that of my 5-year-old neighbors—or of 5-year-olds in any Levittown, for that matter. When a child of the western suburbs reaches driving age, his parents face a choice: either maintain the kid in his infantile seclusion until you send him off to college (where he can go nuts) or buy him a car and unleash him as a demigod of the highways....

The ghastly solitude of much of the American upper-middle class was well evoked by Edward Luttwak in his recent book *Turbo-Capitalism*: "There is a lot of lonely space not only between but inside the ideal dwellings of the American dream, the veritable mansions of the richest suburbs, which could house parents, grown children and their children in familial communion if only all were poor enough, but which mostly house only one ever-so-busy male and as busy a female, with surviving parents in their own retirement abodes, distant children pursuing their budding careers, and few friends, whose degree of loyal commitment might rate them as mere acquaintances in other climes."

Littleton is perhaps best described as Levittown plus affluence plus limitless buildable land—and the result is something qualitatively different, even unprecedented. If in Levittown the issue is conformity, in Littleton it's identity. In Levittown, you get kids banding together lamenting that their life is less heroic than that of their parents: It's *Rebel Without a Cause*. In Littleton, you get kids building the wildest fantasies in their interminable solitude, with the help of their computers, their televisions, and their stereos: It's a high-tech version of *The Wild Boy of Aveyron*....

Critics of the Fifties complained that Levittown's sameness could lead to conformity—altogether there was never much proof that it did. Today's critics warn that the loneliness of Littleton produces something very like the opposite of conformity. We can only hope that the evidence they're right doesn't continue to mount.

14-6. SUBURBS OUTGROW LONG-TIME RESIDENTS, 2000

Source: James Kaplan, "Too Rich for Their Blood," *New York Times Magazine*, April 9, 2000.

Pete Cross bought the big white house on Ridgewood Terrace in Maplewood, New Jersey, in 1972. It was a good time. He had just made the jump from teaching phys ed at Maplewood's Columbia High School to being a guidance counselor, his lifelong dream. He and his wife, Jeanmarie, his high school sweetheart...had four healthy children, three boys and a girl, ages 5 to 12. They'd been bursting the seams of their old house....So, in the midst of a brewing energy crisis and a down housing market, they pulled off a bit of real estate prestidigitation, selling the old place for $35,500 and buying the white 1910 Colonial with two-story pillars on the front porch, a stained-glass window on the stair landing and a big backyard, in an equally good neighborhood, for $33,000. Taxes were $4,000 a year—a stretch, but Pete and Jean figured they could just make it.

Twenty-eight years later, Pete and Jean Cross still live in the big white house. "We were lucky," Jean Cross says. "We raised a family." These days, though, taxes are $9,000 per annum—a bigger stretch than ever, now that Pete is retired. Three of their children have moved away....Only the youngest, David, 34, still lives in Maplewood. He's the town's K-9 police officer. He still lives in his old bedroom upstairs, just across the hall from a room occupied by Maplewood's police dog, a 110-pound German shepherd named Britz.

Ridgewood Terrace is a long, wide street gently ascending the low crest known somewhat grandiosely as the first of the Orange Mountains, and flanked by wide lawns and big, solid houses of the same vintage as the Crosses': Victorians and Queen Annes and Dutch Colonials. It is a beautiful street in a picture-perfect suburb, and the houses are the kind that every upwardly mobile young couple moving out from Brooklyn Heights or Hoboken desperately wants to own. People stick handwritten notes in the Crosses' storm door, offering them cash for their place. Lots of cash—a similar house around the corner just sold for $610,000. And Pete Cross is puzzled and amused by his situation: he can no longer afford not to move from this house. "I'd like to give it to David, but I can't," he says. "And even if I could, he couldn't afford the taxes."

On the surface, Maplewood, population 21,000, looks much as it did 30 years ago, when Pete Cross was my gym teacher at Columbia High....

[B]ut these days, when school lets out, many of those shining faces are faces of color. Columbia High's most famous recent alumna is the hip-hop genius Lauryn Hill, and the school is more than 50 percent black. Most of this shift happened over the last decade, as upward-aspiring African-Americans from Newark, Irvington, East Orange and Orange moved in, drawn by the beautiful houses but even more by the community's renowned school system. Maplewood's black population, less than 5 percent in the 1970 census, had grown to 13 percent by 1990....

Downtown Maplewood feels as poky as it did in the 60's, but most of its stores have turned over several times since then. Food businesses, both restaurants and takeout shops, are everywhere—a subtle sign that the reign of the single-commuter household is over. This is the age of the commuting couple, both incomes necessary to afford the mortgage and taxes, both husband and wife too busy to do much cooking.

Pete Cross and I are sitting in one of the town's less chi-chi eating establishments, the Maple Leaf diner, where the waitress and a good deal of the clientele, not to mention many of the people we passed on the street on our way to lunch, know him by first name. Cross has lived in Maplewood all his life....

He takes out a sheaf of pictures. One of them is of the brown fish-scale-shingled Victorian his grandfather built on Prospect Street. "My parents had their wedding reception in that house," he says. "I lived there my whole childhood. Maplewood feels very similar to when I was young."...

"Hey," Cross says, "Want to see the house on Prospect Street?" Lunch is done. We've walked to town—Pete doesn't like to drive anywhere if he can help it. So we amble back toward Ridgewood Terrace, past the video store and yuppie caterers, past the pizza parlor where Pietz Hardware used to be, past a clutch of old gaffers standing around, one of them, florid-faced, wearing a U.S.S. New Jersey baseball cap. "Hi, Pete; hi, Pete," everyone says.

The houses get bigger as we cross Ridgewood Road. Cross's place is just two up from the corner. We climb into his gold Chrysler minivan and head back through town, past the grand municipal building, with stars-and-stripes bunting on its sandstone pillars. And there, at the corner of Prospect and Oakland, is the fishscale-shingled brown Victorian, perfectly preserved and unbearably sweet in its proportions, a snapshot of a softer time.

"There it is," Pete says.

It's beautiful, I tell him. But it's beautiful, I realize, because someone a lot newer to town than the Crosses has put a lot of money into restoring it.

David Cross repeats his father's sentiments about Maplewood. "It truly hasn't changed that much since I was young," he insists. "Kids still gather in town every weekend the way they always have. There's never really any trouble."

Would this tend to make his police work—boring?

"Nah," he says, grinning lopsidedly. He's sitting at his parents' dining-room table, a solid young man with a weight lifter's torso, a brush cut and warm brown eyes. "There's always something going on." What he means, he elaborates, is not crime but planned events like the Fourth of July. He mentions the dropping car theft and burglary statistics.

Why, then, does Maplewood need a police dog?

"He's a deterrent," Cross says, smiling. The town's K-9 program, he tells me, was modeled after that of Irvington, which has—and needs—eight dogs. The fact that Maplewood has only one says something about both its smallness and its relatively low crime rate. Yet there's an ambiguity about the presence here of such a menacing creature. David Cross tells a story of apprehending eight kids in a stolen car who were about to scatter on foot when he gave the required verbal warning: "Stop or I'll release the canine!"

He adds dryly, "They chose to give up." ...

Asked about the racial changes in Maplewood, David Cross gives a no-big-deal shrug. Where does the nearest black family live? He points a thumb over his shoulder. "Next door," he says. There are a lot more black families, though, near the Newark/Irvington/Union borders, on the other side of town, far from Ridgewood Terrace.

David Cross has traveled around a bit—he's driven half the Pacific Coast Highway. Has he ever seen anyplace like Maplewood? He shakes his head. "Some people might take it as a knock, but it's Mayberry," he says.

"Everybody knows everybody. A lot of the places I go are resorts—nobody knows nobody. You're just a tab. The goodness is gone. Not here."

Still, a town's goodness is rarely simple—or cheap. "I'm thinking about condos," Pete Cross tells me. "Maybe South Jersey. I want to get thinner on the taxes." David Cross is looking at small houses out along the Route 78 corridor in Morris County. The future is irresistible. But how much will Maplewood and the Crosses miss each other?

14-7. MYRON ORFIELD OUTLINES THE NEW DIVERSITY IN AMERICAN SUBURBIA, 2003

Source: Myron Orfield, *American Metropolitics: The New Suburban Reality* (Washington, D.C.: Brookings Institution Press, 2002). Excerpt taken from Summary Edition (Minneapolis: Amerigis Corporation, Metropolitan Area Research Corporation, 2003).

The New Suburban Reality

The Inner-ring Chicago suburb of Cicero, where a visit by Martin Luther King once precipitated a violent protest against housing integration, nonwhite students are now in the majority. In the mid-1990's in Cherokee County, an Atlanta suburb comprised largely of bedroom developing communities, students often attended schools set up in trailers as their communities had neither the tax base nor other resources to build new schools for a growing population. At the same time, schools were closing for lack of students in the region's core. Lopatcong Township, New Jersey, an area at the fringes of the New York region making the transition from rural to suburban, is defending its 2003 ordinance to limit multifamily dwellings to two bedrooms, effectively zoning out families with children in order to keep school enrollment (and costs) down. The proliferation of large-lot housing developments in suburban Macomb County, Michigan, has contaminated a nearby lake due to a rash of failed septic systems, which will cost between $2 billion and $4 billion to convert to sewer.

These examples reflect the fragmentation

that lies at the heart of America's new suburban reality. If the suburbs were ever a homogeneous bastion of untroubled prosperity, they certainly are no longer. Evidence for this goes well beyond the anecdotal: An analysis of the 25 largest metropolitan areas demonstrates that varying social and economic pressures have led to the emergence of distinct types of suburban communities that differ from one another in identifiable ways.

A method known as cluster analysis was used to group suburban areas according to several measures of their fiscal characteristics (specifically, their ability to raise tax revenue and the change over time in that ability) as well as key factors that directly or indirectly affect the cost of providing local services (including poverty levels, population density and growth, age of housing, and racial composition). The cluster analysis identified six types of communities, three of which face economic or social challenges severe enough to be considered "at risk."

The health of any community is largely a function of whether it has adequate resources to meet its particular needs. Two of the most significant factors used in the cluster analysis are school populations, which affect the "needs" side of the ledger, and tax capacity, on the "resources" side.

Schools are a powerful indicator of a community's current health and of its future well-being. As the number of poor children in a community's schools grows, middle-class families' demand for housing in the community softens, and housing prices reflect this decline. Families with school-age children are likely to leave first because changes in the schools affect them most. Some non-poor families may choose to stay in the community but put their children in private schools, though few households can afford the additional expense for long. A community with schools in transition may also draw "empty-nesters" and other non-poor households without school-age children. Poverty rates among school-age children therefore tend to rise more quickly than the overall poverty rate....

Although poverty and its consequences underlie economic segregation, it is difficult to separate poverty from race and ethnicity—particularly for African Americans and Latinos, who are strongly discriminated against in the housing market. Sadly, an analysis of racial data for elementary school students in the 25 largest metropolitan areas shows that once the minority share in a community's schools increases to a threshold level (10 to 20 percent), racial transition accelerates until minority percentages reach very high levels (greater than 80 percent).

While trends in a community's school population indicate critical local needs, local tax capacity is a good measure of the ability to raise revenues to meet those needs. Communities with copious tax resources have low tax rates and great services. Resource-poor communities have just the opposite. Why is this? Think of it this way: if a community's tax wealth per household is $100, a 10 percent tax rate raises $10 per household for services; if tax wealth is $1,000 per household, the same rate raises $100. No matter how smart administrators are, and no matter how much reorganization they do, they cannot avoid this basic math.

One of the three at-risk suburban types...is comprised of aging communities that have very low tax capacity, high municipal costs, and—most distinctively—high concentrations of minority children in the public schools. As a group, these *at-risk segregated communities* had per-household tax capacities that were less than two-thirds of the metropolitan area average, and the slowest growth in tax capacity of all the suburban types. On the cost side, this group had very high poverty rates (nearly twice the regional average), lower-than-average population growth, aging housing stock, a population density almost four times the regional average, and a higher percentage of minority children in the public schools than even the central cities.

The at-risk segregated communities are some of metropolitan America's worst places to live. Poor and segregated, they have a fraction of the resources of the central cities they surround. In 1994, the taxes on a $100,000 house in the at-risk segregated suburb of Maywood, Illinois, were $4,672. This level of taxation would support local school spending of $3,350 per pupil. In Kenilworth, an affluent suburb to the north, the taxes would be $2,688, yet this lower rate, applied to the whole tax base, would support almost three times the level of spending per pupil. Similarly, business taxes on a 100,000-square-foot office building in booming DuPage County were $212,639, compared with $468,000 in south suburban Cook County.

A second category of at-risk communities—made up mostly of inner-ring suburbs and outlying cities that have been swallowed up by metropolitan growth—has older housing stock than any of the other suburban groups. Like the at-risk segregated communities, these *at-risk older communities* have relatively low tax capacity and tax-capacity growth, and even higher density, but they also have relatively low levels of poverty and of minority children in public schools. These places often stand cheek by jowl with the at-risk segregated suburbs, and there is often a strongly defended racial line between them. In fact, though, the at-risk segregated and older communities have many common concerns. Both groups have slow (or even negative) population growth, relatively meager local resources, and struggling commercial districts. Their main street corridors and commercial districts cannot attract new, big businesses that could easily build on greenfield sites. Despite these commonalities, segregated and older at-risk suburbs have not formed a cohesive political whole, probably because they are often divided on the issue of race.

Many communities included in the third at-risk group are exurbs on the fringes of the metropolitan areas that are making the transition from rural to suburban. These *at-risk low-density communities* share the characteristics of low tax capacity and low-tax-capacity growth with the other at-risk suburbs, but they differ in other important ways. Many are just beginning the transition from rural or farm land to suburban development patterns. Their relatively low fiscal resources are thus stretched thin by demands for new infrastructure and the other accoutrements of growth. Compared to most other suburban areas, they must also cope with significantly higher-than-average poverty.

The fourth suburban type represents what many would regard as the quintessential suburb. *Bedroom-developing communities* have rapidly growing populations that tend to be white and relatively affluent. Density is low, housing is new, and tax capacity is just below average but growing at an average rate. Although this group contained about a quarter of the population of the metropolitan areas studied, it had nearly 60 percent of the population growth in those areas. Though not experiencing the social stress of some of the at-risk communities, bedroom-developing suburbs must manage the costs of a high rate of population growth with only average (or below-average) local resources.

Both the at-risk low-density and the bedroom-developing suburbs share fiscal pressures arising from school and infrastructure finance. In all the large metropolitan areas, the student-to-household ratio in these two types of communities is much higher than the regional average. Because of this ratio and their (at best) average tax base, these suburbs often have the lowest per-pupil spending in

Characteristics of the Community Types

Municipality Type	Number of Muni's	Tax Capacity	Change in Tax Capacity	Free Lunch Eligible	Density	Population Growth	Age of Housing	Minority Percentage
At-risk, segregated	348	66%	93%	175%	369%	97%	108%	209%
At-risk, older	391	74	96	59	735	98	110	35
At-risk, low-density	1,104	66	96	103	104	102	97	65
Bedroom-developing	2,152	90	100	32	83	106	85	16
Affluent job center	625	212	105	27	97	105	88	26
Very affluent job center	91	525	102	39	46	101	91	38
Central cities	30	101	97	193	452	94	125	207
All suburban	4,711	106	99	61	164	104	92	45

All variables except number of municipalities are expressed as percentages of metropolitan area averages. Population growth and change in tax capacity were calculated as the ratio of 1998 levels to 1993 levels.

metropolitan America. Developmental infrastructure such as roads and sewers can also present large challenges for the at-risk and bedroom-developing suburbs.

The last two classifications include many of the so-called "edge cities": suburban communities with vast amounts of office space and more jobs than bedrooms. Affluent job centers (and the even more prosperous very affluent job centers) reap the benefits of extraordinary tax bases—capacities of more than two and five times the regional averages, respectively—that are growing at rates outstripping regional averages. Collectively, they have more than four times the office space per household of any other group of suburbs, more even than central cities. At the same time, cost factors such as poverty and age of housing are well below regional averages. As might be expected, the political and business leaders in these communities work hard to maintain their quality of life, and, of all types of suburbs, they are the ones that have revolted

most successfully against growth and sprawl.

These places might seem to have it all: affluent residents, a high tax base, an average number of children, and very low poverty. However, the mass of jobs and commercial activity also has its downside. First, because many workers cannot afford the local housing, these beehives of local activity generally have intense traffic congestion. Second, because land becomes so valuable it is often difficult to maintain open space.

Well over half (56 percent) of the suburban population of the metropolitan areas included in the study lived in at-risk communities. Yet they controlled only 38 percent of local tax capacity in the suburbs. Conversely, the two clusters of affluent job centers accounted for less than 10 percent of the suburban population, but had 22 percent of the local tax capacity. Poverty levels and other cost factors diverge in equally dramatic fashion. These disparities point to a widening gulf between "have" and "have not" suburbs.

14-8. PHOTO GALLERY: "HAVE" AND "HAVE NOT" SUBURBIA, 1989 AND 1995

Figure 14-3 At-risk inner suburb: East Cleveland, Ohio, 1989. Neighborhoods such as this illustrate the tremendous economic range of recent suburbia. Photograph by Andrew Wiese.

Figure 14-4 Affluent job center: Overland Park, Kansas, 1995. Outer city office centers like Overland Park, near Kansas City afforded a rich tax base that supported a high level of municipal services and amenities. Photograph by Andrew Wiese.

ESSAYS

Two essays reflect the new importance of immigration to the changes in contemporary suburbia, but they also reveal startling variety and disparities among recent immigrants and the suburbs they call home. In **Essay 14-1**, ethnic studies scholar Timothy Fong catalogues the extraordinary transformation of Monterey Park, California, a Los Angeles suburb, from a mostly white to mostly Chinese-American suburb. Known locally as the "Chinese Beverly Hills," Monterey Park was the second most popular destination for Chinese immigrants to the United States during the 1980s, second only to New York City. Fueled by booming immigration of well-educated and professional families from Asia, Monterey Park became a gateway for overseas investment and settlement. Its transformation also revealed the varied social, economic, and political tensions attendant to the arrival of millions of newcomers throughout the United States. In this excerpt, Fong explores the reasons why so many Chinese newcomers settled in Monterey Park and the perceptions and controversies that marked their initial relations with long-time residents.

In **Essay 14-2**, anthropologist Sarah Mahler exposes the lives and aspirations of a very different group of immigrants who moved to New York's Long Island in the 1980s: Central Americans (mostly Salvadorans) and South Americans, who found work in the burgeoning low-wage manufacturing and service sectors. In contrast to the upwardly mobile Chinese in Monterey Park, these newcomers lived at the margins of American society. In this section, Mahler describes immigrants' strategies to find work and housing in one of the nation's most expensive suburban areas, documenting patterns of hope and disillusionment that were common in the nation's changing suburbs. One striking feature on Long Island was the persistence of a racialized housing market; many new immigrants settled in communities once pioneered by African-American suburbanites.

ESSAY 14-1. TIMOTHY P. FONG, *THE FIRST SUBURBAN CHINATOWN: THE REMAKING OF MONTEREY PARK, CALIFORNIA* (1994)

Source: Timothy P. Fong, *The First Suburban Chinatown: The Remaking of Monterey Park, California*. Used by Permission of Temple University Press. © 1994 by Temple University. All Rights Reserved.

On an early morning walk to Barnes Memorial Park, one can see dozens of elderly Chinese performing their daily movement exercises under the guidance of an experienced leader. Other seniors stroll around the perimeter of the park; still others sit on benches watching the activity around them or reading a Chinese-language newspaper.

By now children are making their way to school, their backpacks bulging with books. They talk to each other in both English and Chinese, but mostly English. Many are going to Ynez Elementary, the oldest school in town.

When a nearby coin laundry opens its doors for business, all three television sets are turned on: one is tuned to a Spanish novella, another to a cable channel's Chinese newscast, and the third to Bryant Gumbel and the Today show.

Up the street from the park a home with a small stone carved Buddha and several stone pagodas in the well-tended front yard is an attractive sight. The large tree that provides afternoon shade for the house has a yellow ribbon tied around its trunk, a symbol of support for American troops fighting in the Persian Gulf. On the porch an American flag is tied to a crudely constructed flagpole. Next to it, taped to the front door, Chinese characters read "Happiness" and "Long Life" to greet visitors.

These sights and sounds are of interest not because they represent the routine of life in an ethnic neighborhood but because they signal the transformation of an entire city. Monterey Park, California, a rapidly growing, rapidly changing community of 60,000 residents, is located just eight miles east of downtown Los Angeles. An influx of immigrants primarily from Taiwan, Hong Kong, and the People's Republic of China has made Monterey Park the only city in the continental United States the majority of whose residents are of Asian background [Ed. Note: by 2000 there were five more, all in California]. According to the 1990 census, Asians make up 56 percent of the city's population, followed by Hispanics with 31 percent, and whites with 12 percent.

In the early 1980s Monterey Park was nationally recognized for its liberal attitude toward newcomers. In fact, on June 13, 1983, *Time* magazine featured a photograph of the city council as representative of a successful suburban melting pot. The caption read, "Middle-class Monterey Park's multiethnic city council: two Hispanics, a Filipino, a Chinese, and, in the rear, an Anglo." Another national public relations coup came in 1985 when the National Municipal League and the newspaper *USA Today* named Monterey Park an "All-America City" for its programs to welcome immigrants to the community. Nicknamed "City with a Heart," it took great pride in being a diverse and harmonious community. But despite these accolades, there were signs that the melting pot was about to boil over.

Tensions had begun to simmer with the arrival in the late 1970s of Chinese immigrants, many of whom were affluent and well educated. New ethnic-oriented businesses sprang up to accommodate them: nearly all the business signs on Atlantic Boulevard, the city's main commercial thoroughfare, conspicuously displayed Chinese characters with only token English translations. In 1985, the same year Monterey Park received its "All-America" award, some three thousand residents signed a petition attempting to get an "Official English" initiative on the municipal ballot; a local newspaper printed an article accusing the Chinese of being bad drivers; and cars displayed bumper stickers asking, "Will the Last American to Leave Monterey Park Please Bring the Flag?"

In April 1986 the two Latinos and the Chinese American on the city council were defeated in their bids for reelection. Voted into office were three white candidates, one a proponent of controlled growth, the other two closely identified with the official-English movement in Monterey Park and the state. In June the new council passed Resolution 9004, which, among other things, called for English to be the official language of the United States of America. Though the resolution was purely symbolic and carried no legal weight, it was immediately branded as a deliberate slap at the city's Chinese and Latino population. Undaunted, the council continued to take controversial actions that critics labeled "anti-Chinese," among them adopting a broad moratorium on new construction and firing the city planning commission that had approved many Chinese-financed developments. But it was rejection of the plans proposed by a Taiwanese group to build a senior housing project that prompted a rare display of public protest by the usually apolitical Chinese community. Four hundred people, mostly elderly Chinese, marched to City Hall carrying American flags and signs reading, "Stop Racism," "We Are Americans Too," and "End Monterey Park Apartheid."

These high-profile controversies, lasting throughout the 1980s were not isolated or incidental cases of cultural conflict. Indeed, events in this community have received publicity in local, national, and even international media.... Close study of the community is important for several reasons. To begin with, Monterey Park's Chinese residents reflect the changing pattern of Chinese immigration nationwide. Chinese newcomers to Monterey Park and elsewhere are not analogous to the historically persecuted and oppressed male laborers who came to this country in the mid-nineteenth century; they are men and women generally much better educated and more affluent than either their Chinese predecessors or their white counterparts. Further, similar demographic and economic changes are occurring not just in Monterey Park but throughout southern California's San Gabriel Valley and Orange County, and in the northern California cities of San Francisco, Mountain View, and San Jose. Increasing Chinese influence is felt also in New York City's boroughs of Manhattan and Queens (particularly Flushing), in Houston, Texas, and Orlando, Florida....

Next, because demographic change and economic development issues have created a complex controversy in Monterey Park, the intersection of ethnic, racial, and class conflict shows up quite clearly there. One prominent aspect of the social, economic, and political dynamics in Monterey Park is the popular call for controlled growth combined with a narrow nativist, anti-Chinese, anti-immigrant tone in debates that crossed ethnic lines throughout the community....[T]hese developments too are relevant nationwide, occurring as they did at a time of increasing concern over immigration: over statistics showing that almost 90 percent of all legal immigrants coming to the United States since 1981 have been from non-European countries, and over the numbers of undocumented immigrants crossing the southern U.S. borders. Documented and undocumented immigrants are rapidly changing the face of many urban centers....

The first wave of Chinese Americans who moved to Monterey Park [in the 1960s] were commonly young professionals eager to move out of the Los Angeles Chinatown and assimilate into an integrated suburban life. [Howard] Jong, like many others, found Monterey Park's proximity to major freeways an important attraction. "My dad and sister bought houses in South Pasadena, but I'd rather be here," he said. "McDonnell-Douglas [Aircraft] moved to Long Beach, so it was more convenient.... It is a straight shot to work down the 710 freeway."

After he retired, Jong became a volunteer police officer.... Jong served as a police block captain, organizing residents to participate in a Neighborhood Watch program. Obviously proud of having established himself in his career and in the Monterey Park community, Jong strongly believes that America is a land of opportunity and meritocracy. Though he has faced racial discrimination in his life, he feels he has overcome it—no small accomplishment for Chinese Americans of his generation. "The truth is, we proved ourselves. Despite hardship, we got in and we produced. That was the main thing, and they respected us."...

The Immigrant Chinese Period

Beginning in the early 1970s, immigrant Chinese became the predominant newcomers in Monterey Park, though both the city's population and its ethnic diversity continued to grow. The 1980 census recorded for the first time that Monterey Park was a "majority minority" city: Latinos were 39 percent of some 54,000 residents; the Asian population had mushroomed to 35 percent (with Chinese outnumbering Japanese 8,082 to 7,533); whites now represented just 25 percent [down from 50.5 percent in 1970]; African Americans, 1 percent.

Three factors contributed to the influx of immigrant Chinese to Monterey Park: changes in federal immigration policy; changes in international politics; and the work of a man named Frederic Hsieh....

The fourth period [of Chinese immigration to the U.S.], which continues to the present, began when President Lyndon Johnson signed the landmark 1965 Immigration Act, which revised the quota system for non-European applicants. The new law, basing admission policy on needed skills and family reunification, allowed as many as 20,000 quota immigrants per sending country per year; in addition, the spouses, unmarried minor children, and parents of U.S. citizens could enter as nonquota immigrants. Between 1961 and 1970 the number of immigrants from China (including Taiwan and Hong Kong) approached 110,000; it more than doubled between 1971 and 1980, and from 1981 to 1989 it jumped to almost 390,000.

These increases were at least partly due to changes in international politics—United Nations recognition of the People's Republic of China and ouster of Taiwan in 1971; talks between the British and the PRC on the return of Hong Kong to China by 1997—which drove many Chinese from their homelands....

Changes in U.S. immigration policy and international politics, then, help explain the overall increase of Chinese immigrants to the United States. But one individual accounts in large measure for the influx of Chinese specifically to Monterey Park. In 1977 Frederic Hsieh, then a young realtor, boldly announced to a gathering of the city's Chamber of Commerce the reason he was buying so much property in Monterey Park: the city, he said, was going to be a "modern-day mecca" for the new Chinese who, because of political insecurity in Asia, were looking for a place in the United States to invest their money and their future. For several years Hsieh had not only been buying property but, in Chinese-language newspapers throughout Hong Kong and Taiwan, aggressively promoting Monterey Park as the "Chinese Beverly Hills." Though some established local business owners took his comments to the Chamber of Commerce as a threat of a Chinese takeover of the town, Hsieh claims he was only stating the truth. "It was not a takeover, but what was going to happen, nobody could prevent it," he explains. "I came here in 1972. The movement of Chinese immigrants has been taking place ever since then. So by the [late 1970s] the tide, or the trend, [had] already formed. But the [Monterey Park] business leaders were not aware of it. They were not as sensitive."...

Many of the first wave of Chinese immigrants to come to Monterey Park arrived in the United States with education, professional skills, strong political and class ideologies, and, in some cases, capital to help them on their way into the economic mainstream. From personal experience, Hsieh knew that the crowded and unattractive Los Angeles Chinatown would not suit these affluent newcomers: "There's no place to live. By word of mouth they came to Monterey Park. We did some promotion, such as advertisement in the magazines [and] in the newspapers over there in Hong Kong and Taiwan to encourage people to come and invest and patronize our company. Pretty soon everybody knows San Francisco's Chinatown, Monterey Park, and New York's Chinatown. We became famous."...

The 1990 census counted more than 60,000 residents living in Monterey Park, with Asians in the majority at 56 percent of the population. Among them, Chinese far outnumber Japanese by 21,971 to 6,081, and make up 63 percent of the 34,898 Asians counted. Hispanics number 19,031, or 31 percent of the total population; the 7,129 whites make up 12 percent; African Americans and others were less than 1 percent. In cities throughout the San Gabriel Valley, Asians showed impressive population gains since 1980: 289 percent growth in Alhambra; 371 percent in Rosemead. And even these gains are modest compared to those in some of the more affluent outlying areas of the valley: Asians increased 732 percent in the city of Walnut, 684 percent in Diamond Bar, and 543 percent in Arcadia. Today, roughly one-third of San Marino's population is of Asian ancestry.

Many of the Chinese who have lived in Monterey Park for a number of years are now beginning to move to other areas, often to more affluent communities away from the first suburban Chinatown. Even the less affluent Chinese who replace them see Monterey Park as a way station....

Effects of Chinese Immigration

As the influx of Chinese to Monterey Park began, most community leaders and residents compared the newcomers with the American-born Japanese *nisei* who had moved to the community twenty years earlier and quickly assimilated. Together they welcomed the Chinese as yet another group of hardworking people who would naturally be more than happy to settle into the established wholesome life of the community. But because these Chinese were new immigrants, expectations for their immediate assimilation proved unrealistic, and several areas of friction developed—involving business and social organizations, schools, and even supermarkets....

Asian Markets

The prominence of Chinese-owned and -operated businesses in town became [a great] source of resentment. Non-Asians in Monterey Park commonly complain that Chinese merchants quickly replaced many established businesses and catered almost exclusively to an Asian and Chinese-speaking clientele. The best examples are food stores and eateries.

Chinese have taken over all but two of the town's major chain supermarkets. Bok choy is more common than lettuce in produce departments, and dim sum and tea more readily available than a hamburger and coffee in the restaurants.

The first Asian grocery in Monterey Park was opened in 1978 by Wu Jin Shen, a former stockbroker from Taiwan. Wu's Diho Market proved to be an immediate success because the owner hired workers who spoke both Cantonese and Mandarin, and sold such popular items as preserved eggs and Taiwan's leading brand of cigarettes. Wu built the Diho Market into a chain of stores with 400 employees and $30 million in sales. Likewise, the Hong Kong Supermarket and the Ai Hoa, started in Monterey Park, were so successful that today they operate satellite stores throughout the San Gabriel Valley.

In Monterey Park there are now half a dozen large Asian supermarkets and about a dozen medium-sized stores. Their proprietors also lease out small spaces to immigrant entrepreneurs who offer videos, newspapers, baked goods, tea, ginseng, and herbs. Together, these enterprises attract Chinese and other Asian residents in large numbers to shop for the kinds of groceries unavailable or overpriced in "American" chain stores: fifty-pound sacks of rice, "exotic" fruits and vegetables, pig parts (arranged in piles of ears, snouts, feet, tails, and innards, as well as buckets of fresh pork blood), live fish, black-skinned pigeon, and imported canned products used in Chinese, Vietnamese, Indonesian, Thai, Philippine, and Japanese menus. In these markets, Chinese is the dominant language of commerce, and much of the merchandise is unfamiliar to non-Asian shoppers.

Growth and Resentment

For many residents, the redevelopment and replacement of businesses...seemed sudden and dramatic. In January 1979, under the headline "Monterey Park Is Due for Big Facelift," the Monterey Park *Progress* reported that a northern portion of Atlantic Boulevard was set to "be transformed so it's unrecognizable." Construction there was to

Figure 14-5 Chinese-language signage in Monterey Park, California, 2005. The rapid influx of Chinese-owned businesses in the 1980s sparked resentments among long-time residents of this suburb. Photograph by Becky Nicolaides.

include the completion of a shopping center, office, and theater complex developed by the Kowin Development Company; groundbreaking for a new office building at the northeast corner of Atlantic and Newmark Avenue; and a hillside condominium project on the west side of Atlantic Boulevard. The article went on to state with great anticipation that "a large international concern" planned to "locate its international service center in Monterey Park," that substantial construction in anticipation of new tenants was to be done at McGaslin Industrial Park in the eastern section of town, and that several street and park improvement projects were in the works....

Between the influx of new Chinese immigrants, the infusion of large amounts of capital, the rapid introduction of Chinese-owned and -operated businesses, and the disruptions caused by construction crews tearing up the city and starting new projects, rumblings of

discontent among long-time established residents became quite audible.

"I Don't Feel at Home Anymore!"

At first the new Chinese-owned businesses seemed novel, innocuous, even humorous. "The gag was that if it wasn't a bank, it was going to be a real estate office, or another Chinese restaurant," says [former city manager] Lloyd de Llamas. But as these and other Chinese businesses proliferated rapidly from 1978 on—taking over previously established merchants, displaying large Chinese-language signs, and seeming to cater only to a Chinese-speaking clientele—residents became increasingly hostile....

For "old-timers" the loss of a familiar business could be akin to the loss of an old friend. "Just a few years before they sold Paris' Restaurant [for many years the site of daily social gatherings by the city's Anglo business and political leaders] I walked in there for lunch alone," remembers Ed Rodman, "and…there wasn't a single person in there that I knew by name! That describes the changes in Monterey Park."

Such losses were compounded when many long-time residents felt they were not welcomed by new businesses because they were not Chinese. Avanelle Fiebelkorn…told the *Los Angeles Times*: "I go to the market and over 65 percent of the people there are Chinese. I feel like I'm in another country. I don't feel at home anymore." Emma Fry…agreed: "I feel like a stranger in my own town. You can't talk to the newcomers because many of them don't speak English, and their experiences and viewpoints are so different. I don't feel like I belong anymore. I feel like I'm sort of intruding."…

[W]hite flight has been the most obvious reaction to the changes in the community. While the Asian population in Monterey Park has grown and the Latino population has remained relatively stable, the white population has plummeted. In 1960 the 32,306 white residents made up 85 percent of the population; by 1990 the number of whites had dropped to 16,245, or just 12 percent. When former Monterey Park resident Frank Rizzo moved out, he cited the large condominium complexes on either side of his house and the people in them as reasons he could no longer stay. Prior to the influx of Chinese, Rizzo said, his neighborhood had been a quiet and friendly block of mostly single-family homes with expansive yards. But his new neighbors lived in large extended families in cramped quarters, spoke little English, and seemed unwilling to give up their traditions and settle into an American way of life. Rizzo, who sold his home to a Chinese developer, was emphatic about leaving Monterey Park: "What I might do is hang a little American flag on my truck and drive through town on my way out and wave goodbye to all my old friends.…I'm moving far away from here."

Latinos in Monterey Park too were concerned that they were losing the integrated community they thought they'd moved into. David Barron has lived in the city since 1964 and raised his family there. Previously, he attended nearby East Los Angeles Community College and California State University, Los Angeles. He still remembers when Monterey Park was referred to as the "Mexican Beverly Hills." Fluent in Spanish and proud of his heritage, Barron thought he had found the ideal integrated community. He is still involved in many of the city's social and civic activities and has no immediate plans to move, but he misses the diversity he initially found in the town. "I would like to see a balance maintained," he explains. "I cannot live in a mono-ethnic community. I wouldn't want to live in an all-Hispanic…or all-Chinese…or all-white community. I want to live in a mixed community."…

Like the Latinos who had settled in Monterey Park, long-time Asian American residents had lived their entire lives believing in the "American Dream" that proclaimed just rewards for hard work and initiative. It was an affront to their sensibilities to see so many newcomers acquire the fruits of a material society seemingly without having to struggle. The newcomer Chinese were simply not playing by the rules of assimilation: they bought property, started businesses and banks, and built shopping malls as soon as they arrived—and many of them didn't even speak English! John Yee—whose great-great-grandfather had come to California during the gold rush, whose great-grandfather died building the transcontinental railroad, and whose grandfather and father owned a Chinese laundry business that served steel factory workers in Midland, Pennsylvania—is particularly articulate in this regard. "When I first came to L.A., I lived in Chinatown, went into the service, came out, worked in a lot of jobs, and step by step I moved to Monterey Park. It took how many years? Thirty, forty years? It seems like these immigrants…want to live in Monterey Park as soon as they get off the boat. Not the boat, now they come by airplane. Give them another forty years, they'll be in Beverly Hills. I won't ever get to that point.…Maybe I'm jealous like everybody else."…

Particularly for Asian Americans born in the United States, the appearance of Chinese immigrants raised questions about their assumed assimilation and acceptance into American society. "When there were just

Japanese people in Monterey Park, it was no problem because we were just like them [whites]," explains long-time resident Kei Higashi. "But now all of a sudden [with the arrival of the new immigrant Chinese] when we walk into a place and start talking perfect English, they [non-Asians] look at us like we're some foreign creature," he laughs. "That's what happened in Monterey Park."

In the middle of all this are many of the Chinese immigrant professionals, who found themselves lumped together with the development- and business-oriented newcomers. Many express appreciation for the large Chinese population that makes them feel welcome, but at the same time, they say, had they wanted to live in a crowded, exclusively Chinese environment, they never would have left home....

It is difficult for an outsider to appreciate the whirlwind of emotions experienced by Monterey Park residents who saw so many changes in their community....Long-established residents, even those who recognized that the coherence of a homogeneous small town could not be restored, were resentful when their past and their plans for the future were pushed aside in the dramatic restructuring taking place in the city. The result was controversy and political conflict extending into the present....

A New Era of Transition

[B]y the end of the century, Chinese immigrants will likely have completed their shift from marginal to mainstream population in the city.

An obvious sign of this transition came on February 8, 1992, when Monterey Park and neighboring Alhambra jointly sponsored the first Chinese New Year parade ever held in the area. An estimated 35,000 spectators showed up to celebrate the Year of the Monkey—smaller than the number who attended the parade in Los Angeles' Chinatown but far larger than the number who attend the annual "Play Days" parade marking Monterey Park's birthday....

Though race and ethnicity issues have clearly been used as political organizing tools and weapons, what sets Monterey Park apart

are the new class dynamics and the diversity of the Chinese living there, within a rapidly shifting global economy....Old theoretical dichotomies of black versus white, minority versus majority, do not adequately address the rising inter- and intra-ethnic differences brought about in part by the infusion of highly affluent Asians from Pacific Rim localities since 1965.

Globalization of the economy and long-term U.S. partnership with Asian people and nations are facts that will not go away. The worst case scenario would be the triumph of economic and social nativism. The challenge in this era of transition is to develop responsible public policy through a better understanding of the international, multiracial, multicultural, and dynamic class reality exemplified by Monterey Park.

ESSAY 14-2. SARAH J. MAHLER, *AMERICAN DREAMING: IMMIGRANT LIFE ON THE MARGINS* (1995)

Do not look for Noemi Orellana by ringing the bell on the small, two-story clapboard house where she lives in Wyandanch, Long Island. Go down the dusty driveway dotted with glass shards, broken plastic, and bits of car parts to the back of the house where the yard yields to a large car on cinder blocks adorned by greasy tools and hand cloths. Turn right and descend the thick cement steps to the basement door. Knock loudly. This is where Noemi and her year-old daughter live. On a scorching July afternoon the door opens to reveal a stove, several large pots boiling away on the burners, and a small table covered with a plastic tablecloth. It is difficult to see further into the windowless interior. There is a hall light glowing a few feet past the old refrigerator and a flickering television glued to the Spanish-language channel that illuminates through the darkness as best it can. On the right is a door latched tight to a tether on the wall lest it swing open and obstruct the hallway. Inside the door there is a toilet with no seat, a sweaty floor leading to a slim shower. No window, no fan. Next to the bathroom is another room, small and so opaque that only dim outlines of beds and clothes are intelligible. In Noemi's bedroom a twin-size mattress abuts the wall on one side and piles of worldly goods hug the other walls and embrace the small playpen in the middle.

The apartment entombs Noemi; she emerges from the stairwell only rarely during the day—to retrieve her daughter from the driveway or to get into her decrepit Chevrolet Chevette (for which she has no license or insurance) for short junkets nearby. Before she became pregnant, she worked as a maid for an American family in the distant town of Hempstead. After the baby was born, Noemi found a factory job but was laid off several months ago. Now she supports herself and her daughter through splicing together income from several sources. She awakes early, shifting the sleeping baby from the bed to the playpen, and drives a friend with no car to work for a weekly fee. She cooks for her entire household, does the cleaning, and manages affairs while the men who occupy the other bedroom work during the day as landscapers. They pay her rent and additional cash for board. And during the weekends and evenings she scours among her friends and their acquaintances for clients to buy the Mary Kay cosmetics she stores in a large cardboard box in the hatchback of her car. She does not recreate at the movies or in restaurants but under the shade of the large maple tree beside the driveway. And her big excursions entail going to the grocery store and to the office where she renews her permit to work every six months—although it has been of little use since she got it.

From Noemi's front door, mainstream America cannot be seen. She does not hide from it—indeed she would like to find it—but she only glimpses it at the grocery store or post office, and then only when she leaves Wyandanch. This town, a quintessential Long Island minority pocket, is 85 percent African-American and the rest Latino, mostly Puerto Ricans and Salvadorans like Noemi. Noemi's world, the world in which most of my informants live, has evolved parallel to the world of the larger society, and there are few links between the two. Immigrants yearn for a taste of what they know exists beyond their thresholds and beyond their reach. Time after time my presence would ignite their passions to see the "real" America or, particularly among women who worked as maids or provided child care for middle-class families, to understand "real" Americans' behavior. White and blonde (at least according to them), I looked "real" American to them but, unlike most other "real" Americans they came across, could speak Spanish. Alfredo was particularly keen on deciphering the America of his dreams. As soon as I drew near, he would drill me with so many questions about "real" American life that I could barely get a question of my own in edgewise.

From Alfredo and the others I learned to interpret their yearning for inclusion in the mainstream through their language of exclusion. Alfredo told me one day, for instance, that "for me Americans are non-communicative, but not because they don't want to be communicative, rather because I can't talk to them because I don't speak English. I can't, I can't communicate. And I observe their customs only from very far away. I haven't seen real American family life. I notice that they go to work every morning; they take a train or their cars and they come back at night. But I know nothing more because, frankly, I don't live with Americans. I live with Latins. And these are [Salvadoran] peasants, they're from the countryside, not even people from towns. So I can't tell you what the customs of North Americans are because I haven't gone into their homes. I see you once in a while but you're not going to act [like a "real" American] when you come visit us as you would in your own house. You're not going to act like you do every day."

In this chapter I examine the structural, economic, and demographic conditions of Long Island that created niches of low-wage jobs and attracted immigrants, especially undocumented immigrants, to fill many of them. These people enter a very restricted sector of the local economy, taking jobs that Long Islanders shun and that offer little opportunity for advancement. Immigrants are also shunted into marginal neighborhoods populated almost exclusively by members of poor minority groups. This residential segregation…exacerbates immigrants' feelings of isolation from the mainstream. Immigrants also suffer as linguistic and cultural outsiders and from skills mismatches. They lack English and other skills and credentials required by jobs in the mainstream, formal economy…. All of these disadvantages make immigrants an ideal labor source for employers seeking cheap—and often exploitable—workers. Additionally, since immigrants are saddled with the need to produce surplus income, they are less likely than other workers to complain about their working conditions or about abuses such as nonpayment.

The exploitation of immigrant labor is not unique to Long Island nor is it exclusively a contemporary phenomenon. However, the late-twentieth-century economy, with its emphasis on service sector jobs, differs sharply from the economy that immigrants encountered at the turn of the century, when there were far greater opportunities in manufacturing. Many of these migrants were able to rise within industries owing to a constricted labor supply (immigration was severely regulated in the 1920s), an expanding economy, and unionization. The prospects for such upward mobility are much less bright for today's immigrants because they enter an economy increasingly polarized between high wage earners and low wage earners. My informants are quick to recognize that life in the United States, and particularly their ability to produce surplus income, is not as easy as they envisioned. Not surprisingly, most are unaware of the structural economic conditions that impinge on them, but they do understand that their wages will barely cover their basic necessities, let alone stretch to meet remittance, debt, and other obligation….

Why Long Island?…

For many readers it may seem strange to hear about people migrating to an area popularly stereotyped as the archetypal white, middle-class suburb. Why would they not migrate to the inner city, where presumably they would encounter more job opportunities and acceptance? First, it is key to note that Long Island has received numerous waves of migrants over the past decades; Italians and Puerto Ricans figure prominently among other groups. More recently, however, immigrants have been flowing onto the island in ever-increasing waves. Salvadorans constitute the largest single group in this wave, estimated to number ninety thousand, but Asians, Middle Easterners, and other Latin Americans have also arrived. It may also seem strange that so many immigrants from developing countries come to Long Island. An area where there is a high cost of living, where the median price of a single-family house is over $200,000, would seem to be within the reach only of families with higher-than-average incomes.

Long Island is an expensive area that has a history of thriving off high-technology, defense-related industries demanding an educated, skilled, and well-paid workforce. Why should such an area become a magnet to immigrants? The answer lies in the fact that during the 1980s the Long Island economy produced many thousands of low-wage, dead-end jobs that few natives would take. Natives spurned these jobs either because they had better opportunities available to them, or because the low wages fell short of the cost of living and they left the island to find a more economical place to live. The new jobs were created by three trends: (1) the predominance of defense industries, which spawned peripheral manufacturing industries requiring large quantities of low-cost labor, and which kept Long Island from experiencing the deindustrialization so common elsewhere, (2) a rising demand for services, particularly to households, and (3) a decline in the native-born youth and young worker population that would normally fill the jobs created. In short, a dynamic economy and a tight labor market opened niches for immigrant laborers….

Struggling Up from the Margins

When my informants reached Long Island, they found themselves on the fringes of U.S. society and at the bottom of the Long Island economy. Learning that you "earn in dollars and pay in dollars," they realized that five dollars per hour would barely permit them to survive on Long Island, let alone pay back their debts, send remittances home, and save up a nest egg. Furthermore, even five-dollar-an-hour jobs do not fall from heaven like manna; there is always someone eager to take any job. "One person told me in a conversation that here people begged you to come and work," Manuel reflected, reminiscing about the misconceptions he had held of life in the United States before he emigrated from Peru. "They told me that they invited you to their house to ask you to work, so that they would have you with them. But, with all the people who have come from Central America and so on, there's a lot more competition than I imagined." Manuel learned quickly that he might find work, but not necessarily stable work. "More than anything else, there is no security in your job. Work is not guaranteed," he explained.

"But what kind of job did you expect to get here?" I asked him.

"Anything," he responded, "but I wanted a stable job. Because here you have to pay rent, eat, send money home to the family, and you get a tremendous surprise when one day you work and the next day there is no work. Right there everything practically ends. You don't get any benefits and you begin to despair here. You look for work and during this time you have to spend the money you had saved up. And if you don't get money, you look *afligido* [anguished]. Whatever you have you have to spend on basic things—to eat, to pay the rent, and you are desperate because you don't have anything to send home."

The feeling of failure nipping his heels spurred Manuel, much as it does many other immigrants, into adopting strategies for increasing income and decreasing expenses in order to meet short- and long-term goals. The tactics immigrants employ to increase their income are varied, ranging from standard approaches, like working more jobs or hours, to more extreme methods such as get-rich-quick schemes. People often switch from strategy to strategy, or—like Noemi…they juggle several at the same time. As they experiment they learn valuable lessons about which tactics work and for what reasons; they are acquiring "immigrant capital."…

Work Breeds Isolation

The strategies most regularly used to boost income, increasing working hours or taking on additional jobs, have the unpleasant effect of further isolating immigrants from one another. Sonia, [a] peasant woman from eastern El Salvador, expressed her isolation this way. "[In El Salvador] you don't live very far away from your relatives. Rather, you build your house very close to your relatives….Here, no; even if you want to be together you can't. Because there are people who in our country were from the same town and who lived closely together—even sharing the same patio—but here they don't have time to visit each other because of their jobs. Days, months, and years pass by and you can't get together with other people because of your work. For example, here I don't see my cousin each week. There, you visit every couple of days….When I was working I wouldn't see my brothers even though I lived in the same apartment with them. We would run into each other sometimes, or I would see them only when they were asleep. When I was asleep they would come home because they worked at night. They would see me but I wouldn't see them because I was asleep! We didn't even say hello and we lived together in the same apartment!" For Sonia, the exigencies of work precluded socializing even with her close family, limiting the kind of interchange they were accustomed to back home. Even holidays, when one might expect immigrants to be free, tend to be workdays. One Fourth of July I tried to see Juanita and her toddler son. I called a week beforehand and learned that she would be available Sunday morning. On Friday evening I called to confirm this plan and was told that she was working. I called again on Saturday and stopped by. She was out working, and it was the same story on Sunday. Capitalizing on Long Islanders' desire to take the weekend off she was working their shifts; meanwhile her sisters also worked constantly, serving food at holiday parties thrown by the families for whom they normally cleaned houses. The Fourth of July was a bonanza of extra income but no day of rest.

Indeed, I found that the only day to expect to find immigrants at home was Sunday. These days were anything but relaxing, however, as the shopping and wash had to be done. But by late afternoon, pots of boiling soup and beans and rice would signal the onset of social time. Women gathered in the kitchen preparing the food and exchanging the week's small talk; men lounged on their beds or on couches drinking beers and watching sporting events. Often, men's social time actually started on Saturday night, and by Sunday morning the living area would be strewn with Budweiser bottles. These few moments of relaxation provided a respite from the psychological and physical stress of the week; they also were the forum for exchanging information about jobs and used cars, baby-sitters and locations of cheap goods....

The strategies immigrants employ to lighten their expense burdens are varied and too numerous to mention in detail here. Overall, they prove less useful to immigrants than strategies that increase income because there is little fat to slice off to begin with. Like Noemi, immigrants tend to live minimalist lives and endure conditions that most people strive to avoid. They occupy overcrowded and substandard housing, with little or no privacy, where hygiene is difficult to maintain. Children scurry across floors where the linoleum has peeled away and on grass strewn with debris. Deprivation is highly visible in their housing because rent is the single greatest expense they incur and it is the easiest to manipulate....Rarely is money squandered on entertainment; videos are swapped, not rented, and few people ever go to the movies since there are none in Spanish on the island. A case of beer, a birthday celebration, or an afternoon at the beach suffices. People eat well by their standards, however—much better than they did in their homelands. Meat is coveted and immigrants can be seen in supermarket aisles pushing shopping carts laden heavily with packages of beef and chicken. But they economize by preparing at home the food

they take to work. Landscapers learn quickly that a sandwich and a soda purchased at the deli with the boss easily consumes one hour's pay. They reduce expenditures on clothing by obtaining much of it from charities, although immigrants always have a change or two of "Sunday" clothes that are store-bought and much more presentable.

There are dozens of other methods people employ, not only to make ends meet, but to conserve income for repaying debts and making remittance payments. Only in rare cases do the strategies listed above, both for augmenting income and for capping outlays, prove sufficient to enable immigrants to save their nest egg. One of Roberto's roommates, Amilcar Sorto, a landscaper, was lucky. He returned to El Salvador after only five years with $5,000 in his pocket. With his remittances he had bought his family a piece of land. They had been landless before but now had their own soil to till. All of Amilcar's roommates remarked upon his departure that he had been extremely ascetic, never wasting a penny on entertainment or unnecessary expenses like a new change of clothes. But he is the exception, not the rule, and he recently returned to the United States—an indication that Salvadorans are adopting a circular migratory pattern highly characteristic of Mexican and many Caribbean migrants. Most of my informants show modest improvements in their lives over the years I have known them, but few would be the subjects of a Horatio Alger story. Some buy old cars and move into their own apartments; but they cannot afford to insure the cars or to live alone....

Long Island Housing:
Scarce, Expensive, and Segregated

Newly arrived immigrants encounter one of the most expensive and restricted housing markets in the country. Constructed for middle-class-to-affluent white homeowners, Long Island's residential neighborhoods consist predominantly of single-family homes, and only 18 percent of the housing stock is rental units....During the 1980s, Long Island faced such a critical shortage of affordable housing, particularly for young families, that an estimated 90,000 illegal apartments were carved out of single-family homes through the conversion of basements, attics, and the like into rentable space. The illegal market represents one-third of the entire rental market, according to conservative estimates, and urban planners forecast that the island will need to build some 100,000 units of affordable housing by the end of the decade to meet demand....

These aggregate figures do not adequately express the rental market faced by blacks and Latinos on Long Island who for decades have been subject to systematic segregation. A 1991 *Miami Herald* investigation ranked Long Island as the fifteenth most segregated metropolitan area in the United States out of 318 studied. Segregation is most extreme for African-American Long Islanders: two-thirds of Long Island neighborhoods are less than 1 percent black, and one-half have no blacks at all. The average white resident of Nassau County lives in a census tract where only 8 percent of the neighbors are black or Latino. Towns experiencing white flight, such as Freeport and Uniondale in Nassau County, found their populations replaced by blacks and Latinos. Indeed,...Latino immigrants tend to find their housing options restricted largely to communities with significant minority populations.

The living situation my informants found themselves in shocked them for two principal reasons: (1) either the practice of paying rent was new to them or the amount they needed to pay on Long Island far surpassed what they had paid at home; and (2) they found themselves severely isolated from mainstream America, the "real America," in their words, that they only glimpsed at work or from the confines of public transportation....

[T]he latter complaint is most common among middle-class and urban immigrants. The former, however, is ubiquitous....

The miscalculation immigrants make about their projected earnings versus expenses is quickly recognized and corrected once they arrive. But the pressure of housing costs, in particular, weighs heavily on everyone. They realize immediately that they can afford neither their own apartment nor even

their own room. Don Jose explained it to me, saying, "What you think is that life here is different, that you are going to live well here, in peace....Here rents are expensive, everything is expensive. Of course, if you earn in dollars you spend dollars too. So you don't save what you thought you would. I had made a plan like this: If I earn three hundred dollars then I will spend so much and save so much. So after so much time I will have saved so much money. You think that you can save. But it's not so. Here you come to find out that your expenses are two or three times what you thought they'd be. This is the great disillusionment that you carry with you. You think that if you earn a good salary you will be happy but it's not true. You can earn what they told you that you would earn, but they never tell you how much your expenses will be, especially rent. No one tells you about this. They only tell you what they earn, not what they spend. That's the problem. So when you start to see how much you spend, you begin to feel deceived."

If immigrants merely conformed to neoclassical economic rules, they would flow out of areas that they could not afford to live in. But immigrants, particularly the undocumented, are very dependent upon finding jobs, and the labor market they face, as discussed previously, is so constricted that they do not enjoy the same flexibility as natives enjoy. As a result, they leave areas such as Houston, Texas, where housing is cheap and abundant but jobs are scarce, and head for areas offering employment, despite the costs. They resort to the only other technique available to them: finding ways to minimize their housing expenditures by living in overcrowded, substandard housing in the least expensive neighborhoods....

NOTES

1. William Frey, *Melting Pot Suburbs: A 2000 Census Study of Suburban Diversity*,(Washington, D.C.: Brookings Institution, 2001).
2. William Frey, "The New Urban Demographics: Race, Space, and Boomer Aging," *Brookings Review* 18 (Summer 2000), 20–24, 20.
3. "Greenfield," see Dolores Hayden with aerial photographs by Jim Wark, *A Fieldguide to Sprawl* (New York: W. W. Norton & Co., 2004), 42.

CHAPTER 15

Our Town

Inclusion and Exclusion in Recent Suburbia

INTRODUCTION

As the suburbs diversified economically and socially after 1970, concerns about local control and regulation remained ever present. Even as the courts and legislatures struck down explicit racial barriers in the housing market, opening the way for growing numbers of African-American, Latino, and Asian-American families to move to the suburbs, many suburban communities sought new ways to control residential space—particularly in terms of population composition, land use, and local fiscal resources. In the face of growing diversity in the public realm, many Americans called into question the assumption of shared values and shared responsibility to the commonweal. In response, some suburbanites withdrew into privately owned and governed residential enclaves. At the end of the twentieth century, suburbanites still searched for secure, comforting definitions of "our town," but distinctions between who belonged and who did not remained matters of intense concern. An exclusionary sensibility continued to shape the suburban landscape.

Suburbanites deployed a range of legal, administrative, and eventually physical mechanisms to maintain this sense of control. Local zoning and building regulations were among the most common tactics. Even as the civil rights movement peaked, developers and suburbanites were already refining new ways to protect suburban exclusivity. Already, in the early 1960s, housing and civil rights activists recognized a trend toward what they called "exclusionary"—or "snob"—zoning. Such ordinances mandated large lots and floor areas, and limited construction to free-standing single-family homes, while disallowing apartments, attached housing, and manufactured homes. By the mid-1960s, lots of one-half acre or more were required to build a home in huge portions of American suburbia, and the trend was toward even larger minimums. By contrast, during the suburban boom of the 1920s, lot sizes of one eighth of an acre were commonplace, and Levittown properties of the late 1940s measured just slightly larger. By the 1960s, the development of such modest properties was prohibited by law across a growing swathe of suburbia. One result was a crisis in affordable housing, with special ramifications for African Americans and other minorities who on average earned less money than whites. In those higher-end suburbs where economic resources and potential for growth were greatest, land use policies precluded settlement by all but the most affluent segments of the metropolitan population. Thus, even as racial bias came under increasing legal assault, class bias in suburbia gained strength.

During the 1970s, the U.S. Supreme Court upheld these broad municipal powers, defining "general welfare"—the basis for government power to restrict property rights—in terms of the existing residents of a given suburb (*Village of Belle Terre v. Boraas*, 1974). In addition, the Court held that only zoning ordinances designed with the explicit intent (not just the effect) to discriminate on the basis of race were invalid (*Arlington Heights v. Metropolitan Housing Development Corp.*, 1977). Not surprisingly, race evaporated from the rhetoric of suburban exclusion, to be replaced by a class-oriented lexicon of property values, landscape aesthetics, tax rates, congestion, and even traffic safety. Suburban residential segregation thus endured under a new apparatus.

A related development during these decades was the rise of large-scale Common Interest Developments, or CIDs. Blending a number of long-standing trends in real estate development, these communities were characterized by master planning, the provision of shared facilities, extensive contractual restrictions governing the use of property, and "government" by a private association. CIDs were novel in the 1960s—in 1970, approximately 2 million Americans lived in such places. But they soon became the dominant form of suburban real estate development in the United States. By 2005, according to an estimate by the Community Associations Institute, more than 54 million Americans lived in CIDs—most of them in the suburbs.

CIDs met several challenges of the post-1970 real estate market. As suburbs intensified their zoning requirements, many large developers had difficulty finding profitable places to build. With CIDs, municipalities permitted development of higher housing densities, sometimes including attached homes and apartments (though not necessarily affordable ones), while in exchange, developers and residents paid for services and amenities that the municipality would otherwise have provided. For home seekers, CIDs offered facilities, such as pools and recreational areas, that few could afford otherwise, and a level of services that a growing number of suburbs found it hard to provide. CIDs marked the triumph of private "community building," increasing residential densities and the communal ownership of facilities at the same time that they intensified trends toward suburban privatism, a separate way of life restricted to select groups defined by ownership as opposed to citizenship.

Among the most controversial aspects of CIDs was the role of homeowner associations and condominium boards as a form of private government. As specified in the covenants, conditions, and restrictions (CC&Rs), to which residents agreed as a condition of purchase, these associations exercised wide latitude to enforce their own rules, employ private security and maintenance workers, and control the flow of association fees—a kind of private tax devoted to the benefit of the development. Ironically, as national political rhetoric assailed intrusive government, residents of CIDs submitted to private restrictions that were more intrusive than any real government could constitutionally impose. The popularity of CIDs, however, suggests an impulse among suburbanites to withdraw into privately owned, governed, and maintained residential enclaves, reinforcing wider trends in U.S. political culture toward privatism, localism, and resistance to taxation for public services that benefited anyone outside the local community.

Finally, as urban crime rates peaked in the early 1990s and media coverage of crime reached new heights, real estate developers began marketing enhanced safety and security through the construction of private gated communities. Sustained by continuing economic and social uncertainties, the trend accelerated even as actual crime rates fell after the mid-1990s. Gating became the latest tool in a long tradition of marketing suburbia as a private refuge from a hostile world, and in that same tradition, it contributed to continuing suburban exclusivity at the end of the twentieth century. By 2001, an estimated 16 million Americans (6% of the population) lived in private gated communities, a trend particularly strong in Sunbelt states like Florida, Texas, Arizona, and California.

As the twentieth century came to an end, more and more suburbanites sought the security of predictable and well-maintained physical environments, reliable social behavior, and the hope of stable or appreciating property values. They were willing to sacrifice a range of personal freedoms in order to secure these promises. Read another way, it also appeared that among the freedoms suburbanites cherished most was the freedom from free neighbors.

DOCUMENTS

Despite federal fair housing legislation and court rulings in the late 1960s, minority families continued to face stringent barriers to suburban living, and especially to those suburbs with the greatest fiscal attributes. **Document 15-1**, an influential essay by suburban legal activists Paul Davidoff and Neil Gold, pinpoints exclusionary zoning as the cause of continuing racial segregation in housing, schools, and employment. In the early 1970s, Davidoff and Gold's Suburban Action Institute brought suit against numerous suburbs with restrictive zoning ordinances, hoping to use the courts to "open up the suburbs" to minority residents. Though their efforts achieved limited success, one place the argument did carry was New Jersey, the nation's most suburban state. **Document 15-2** shares the opinion of the Supreme Court of New Jersey in the landmark Mount Laurel case. The suit stemmed from the refusal of a suburbanizing township near Philadelphia to permit a local group to build thirty-six apartments for working-class black residents of the community. Although local African Americans could trace their roots in the area to the colonial era, a town committeeman explained the new reality: "If you people can't afford to live in our town, then you'll just have to leave."[1] Writing for a unanimous court, Justice Frederick Hall argues that Mount Laurel's zoning ordinance represented a form of economic discrimination and "affirmative action" for middle- and upper-income people. Exclusionary, fiscal zoning, which paid no heed to its human consequences, the court concluded, was invalid. The case established the responsibility of New Jersey's growing suburbs to redraw their zoning maps to permit construction of a "fair share" of affordable housing. A companion decision (known as Mount Laurel II) in 1983 established a formula to accomplish this. In the next twenty years, builders constructed some 40,000 units of "fair share" housing across the state, although the distribution of that housing was a mixed bag. The court allowed municipalities to trade or sell fair share allotments to other communities. As a result, many of these new homes were built in the state's ailing central cities, improving residential opportunities there, but doing little to open growing suburbs to the working poor. **Document 15-3** and **Document 15-4** reveal the outcome of the struggle in Mount Laurel itself. After more than thirty years of resistance and millions of local tax dollars spent on legal fees, Mount Laurel allowed construction to proceed on 140 apartments for low- to moderate-income families. The Ethel R. Lawrence homes, named in memory of the woman who spearheaded the Mount Laurel struggle, opened in November 2000. Journalist Michelle Molz reports in **Document 15-3** that when the final forty units became available, hundreds of people, many of them African Americans and Puerto Ricans from the nearby city of Camden, waited in line over night for the chance to apply. **Document 15-4** gives a human face to the families that Mount Laurel and other suburbs fought decades to exclude: residents at leisure in front of their tastefully designed new homes.

The increasing trend toward privatism and regulation in the suburbs was reflected in the proliferation of community interest developments covered by covenants, conditions, and restrictions. **Document 15-5** assesses the reach (and occasional overreach) of these agreements, revealing varying opinions on the trend in suburban Philadelphia.

As suburbs diversified after 1970, African-American, Latino, and Asian-American families, too, confronted the appeal and dilemmas of private homeowner governments. In **Document 15-6,** Susan Saulny, a reporter for the *Washington Post*, examines the controversy over use of private basketball courts by nonresidents in one Prince George's County, Maryland subdivision. Complicating the issue, both the ball players and home owners in this majority black suburban county were African American.

As private, gated communities became increasingly popular in the late 1990s, they provoked heated public debate. Not surprisingly, this latest suburban trend became fodder for larger social and political critiques. In **Document 15-7,** David Boaz of the libertarian Cato Institute, explains the trend toward gated communities as a logical response to urban crime and the failures of municipal government. Gated communities, he writes, represent an example of people drawing a new social contract. Ironically, Boaz sees these communities as an outgrowth of "the failures of big government," despite suburbs' long-standing emphasis on small-scale home rule. In contrast, urban planner Edward Blakely attacks the trend toward gated living in **Document 15-8**, blaming it for contributing to segregation, the decline of community, and drains on public life. **Document 15-9** offers images of two recent gated communities, one in affluent, mostly white northern San Diego County, California, and the second in affluent, mostly African-American Prince George's County, Maryland.

In your opinion, why did so many Americans in the late twentieth century move into these access-controlled, increasingly private worlds? How do these new communities differ from earlier suburbs? In what ways are they similar? Why do they provoke such intensity of debate? To what extent do these places restrict the rights or opportunities of other Americans? In your opinion, should suburbs have a responsibility to zone a fair share of land for affordable housing? Why or why not? Where does the responsibility of citizens for the health and well-being of their neighbors begin and end?

15-1. LEGAL ACTIVISTS PAUL DAVIDOFF AND NEIL GOLD ATTACK "EXCLUSIONARY ZONING," 1970

Source: Paul Davidoff and Neil Newton Gold, "Exclusionary Zoning," *Yale Review of Law and Social Action* 1 (Winter 1970). Reprinted with permission from Yale Law School.

The Suburban Shift...

Underlying the movement of jobs, housing and population from central cities to their surrounding suburbs is the availability of a relatively vast supply of vacant land. Indeed, in the nation's twenty largest urban areas, 99 per cent of the vacant land lies outside of core cities. The unavailability of vacant land within central cities necessarily sets reasonably firm limitations on the employment and population capacities of these areas. Conversely, the existence of a seemingly limitless supply of vacant land on the urban periphery practically insures that future urban growth will take place in the fringe areas....

Exclusionary Zoning

Blacks and other minority groups have not moved out of central cities to the surrounding suburbs. Only the white population has benefitted from the availability of suburban job and housing opportunities. By 1966, as a result of the suburbanization of the white population, only 42 per cent of urban whites remained in central cities. On the other hand, more than 82 per cent of urban nonwhites lived in central cities in 1966—a higher proportion than in 1950....

These remarkable population shifts and growth patterns have resulted in severely imbalanced population distribution in our metropolitan areas. The cities of the United States are rapidly becoming ghettos of the poor and the black, while the suburbs appear likely to remain affluent and white.... This growing separation of white and black in U.S. metropolitan areas is a direct result of the nation's acknowledged failure to insure that all social and racial groups are able to gain access to suburban land.

Exclusionary suburban zoning is that complex of zoning practices which close suburban housing and land markets to all but the wealthy. Such practices include the following:

(1) zoning vacant residential land for large minimum-lot size, thereby reducing the supply of developable land and increasing its cost;
(2) zoning for excessively large minimum-house size, without regard to the size of families occupying the house or a generally accepted minimum standard of floor area;
(3) prohibiting all forms of multifamily housing from an entire municipality, thereby zoning out the people who cannot afford their own homes;
(4) spot-zoning land for multifamily housing through the use of special or conditional permits, thereby allowing only expensive apartments in the suburbs; and,
(5) imposing unduly expensive subdivision requirements which increase the cost of land development by shifting the burden of public improvements from the public at large to new homeowners.

If only a small amount of the vacant land of a particular region were controlled through exclusionary practices, the public harm might be very limited. The example of the suburban region surrounding New York City, however, indicates just the opposite. The 1962 *Spread City* report of the Regional Plan Association pointed out that in 1960, two thirds of the vacant land in the New York Region was zoned for lot sizes of more than one-half an acre, and less than one per cent of the vacant land in the New York metropolitan area (New York City plus four suburban counties) was zoned for multifamily housing....

[T]he publicly imposed cost of land, land development and construction cost in the exclusionary suburb prohibits development of houses selling below $45,000. If these restrictions were abolished, however, developers in the private market could build single-family housing for less than $25,000. Additional savings could be realized through construction of attached housing and garden apartments.

To understand the full meaning of these zoning-imposed costs of new housing, it is necessary to indicate the per cent of families in the region who can afford housing priced at the $45,000 level....[D]ata show that less than 2.8 per cent of white households and .04 per cent of non-white households in the United States are in the income range necessary to purchase new housing in the New York region. The data also suggest that housing priced at $35,000 would be beyond the financial reach of 90 per cent of the nation's households....

Racial Segregation

Exclusionary zoning is largely responsible for the fact that segregation by race and economic class has, over the past few decades, become accepted social policy in large metropolitan areas around the nation. What is special about the use of zoning to this end is that it is accomplished through public law. We are not examining private agreements to discriminate. Rather, we are dealing with public mapping which determines where different classes may reside—with segregation flowing directly and predictably from the enforcement of these ordinances.

For this reason, current efforts to distinguish *de facto* and *de jure* school segregation are not only beside the point but also falsely premised. The segregation that exists in northern schools is *de jure* segregation. It is produced through the use of local zoning ordinances—adopted pursuant to state enabling legislation—which prevent all but a few urban non-whites from leaving ghetto and poverty areas. For New York State, the results have been graphically portrayed....Eighty-five per cent of the 495,000 black school children in New York State were enrolled in only eight school districts....[T]he concentration of Puerto Ricans is even more intense: 93 per cent of the 280,000 Puerto Rican school children in New York State were enrolled in the New York City school system....

Policy Issues...

In our view, the decentralizing forces of American economic life are not reversible. The absence of vacant land within central cities, coupled with the existence of an enormous supply of vacant land on the urban periphery, will not permit a major expansion of the employment or housing capacity of central cities. Public programs that seek only to rebuild the central city housing stock and to encourage industry to locate within central cities and ghettos run counter to the movement of the private economy....

To renew [central city] neighborhoods, we must open opportunities for outmigration to new, decent housing outside the ghetto.

Restrictive zoning and land-use controls in suburban areas constitute the principal barriers to the development of job-linked, moderate-cost housing in the suburbs. These measures have been remarkably effective in preventing low- and moderate-income families from penetrating suburban housing and land markets, in greatly limiting the matching of jobs and workers in urban areas and in raising the cost of new housing in the suburbs to all home-seeking families. If this nation is to provide for the housing and job needs of its minority citizens, the power of government must be used to break the land-use barriers erected by suburban communities. This challenge may soon be recognized as the new frontier of the civil rights movement.

15-2. THE NEW JERSEY SUPREME COURT REJECTS EXCLUSIONARY ZONING IN ITS DEVELOPING SUBURBS, 1975

Source: *Southern Burlington County N.A.A.C.P. v. Mount Laurel*, 67 N.J. 151; 336 A.2d 713; 1975 N.J. LEXIS 181 (1975)

The Facts

Mount Laurel is a flat, sprawling township, 22 square miles, or about 14,000 acres, in area, on the west central edge of Burlington County....[T]he township is about seven miles from the boundary line of the city of Camden and not more than 10 miles from the Benjamin Franklin Bridge crossing the river to Philadelphia....

After 1950, as in so many other municipalities similarly situated, residential development and some commerce and industry began to come in. By 1960 the population had almost doubled to 5,249 and by 1970 had more than doubled again to 11,221.... 65% of the township is still vacant land or in agricultural use....

Under the present [zoning] ordinance, 29.2% of all the land in the township, or 4,121 acres, is zoned for industry.... At the time of trial no more than 100 acres...were actually occupied by industrial uses....

The amount of land zoned for retail business use under the general ordinance is relatively small—169 acres, or 1.2% of the total....

The balance of the land area, almost 10,000 acres, has been developed until recently in the conventional form of major subdivisions. The general ordinance provides for four residential zones.... All permit only single-family, detached dwellings, one house per lot.... Attached townhouses, apartments (except on farms for agricultural workers) and mobile homes are not allowed anywhere in the township under the general ordinance....

The general ordinance requirements, while not as restrictive as those in many similar municipalities, nonetheless realistically allow only homes within the financial reach of persons of at least middle income. [Ed. note: Mount Laurel's least restrictive zone

required a minimum lot size of about one-quarter acre; about 50 percent of the Township was zoned for half acre lots.]...

[A]ffirmative action for the benefit of certain segments of the population is in sharp contrast to the lack of action, and indeed hostility, with respect to affording any opportunity for decent housing for the township's own poor living in substandard accommodations, found largely in the section known as Springville....In 1968 a private non-profit association sought to build subsidized, multi-family housing in the Springville section with funds to be granted by a higher level governmental agency. Advance municipal approval of the project was required. The Township Committee responded with a purportedly approving resolution, which found a need for "moderate" income housing in the area, but went on to specify that such housing must be constructed subject to all zoning, planning, building and other applicable ordinances and codes. This meant single-family detached dwellings on 20,000 square foot lots. (Fear was also expressed that such housing would attract low income families from outside the township.) Needless to say, such requirements killed realistic housing for this group of low and moderate income families....

There cannot be the slightest doubt that the reason for this course of conduct has been to keep down local taxes on property (Mount Laurel is not a high tax municipality) and that the policy was carried out without regard for nonfiscal considerations with respect to people, either within or without its boundaries....

This pattern of land use regulation has been adopted for the same purpose in developing municipality after municipality. Almost every one acts solely in its own selfish and parochial interest and in effect builds a wall around itself to keep out those people or entities not adding favorably to the tax base, despite the location of the municipality or the demand for varied kinds of housing.... One incongruous result is the picture of developing municipalities rendering it impossible for lower paid employees of industries they have eagerly sought and welcomed with open arms (and, in Mount Laurel's case, even some of its own lower paid municipal employees) to live in the community where they work....

The Legal Issue

The legal question before us...is whether a developing municipality like Mount Laurel may validly, by a system of land use regulation, make it physically and economically impossible to provide low and moderate income housing in the municipality for the various categories of persons who need and want it and thereby, as Mount Laurel has, exclude such people from living within its confines because of the limited extent of their income and resources. Necessarily implicated are the broader questions of the right of such municipalities to limit the kinds of available housing and of any obligation to make possible a variety and choice of types of living accommodations.

We conclude that every such municipality must, by its land use regulations, presumptively make realistically possible an appropriate variety and choice of housing. More specifically, presumptively it cannot foreclose the opportunity of the classes of people mentioned for low and moderate income housing and in its regulations must affirmatively afford that opportunity, at least to the extent of the municipality's fair share of the present and prospective regional need therefor....

We reach this conclusion under state law and so do not find it necessary to consider federal constitutional grounds urged by plaintiffs....

[I]t is fundamental and not to be forgotten that the zoning power is a police power of the state and the local authority is acting only as a delegate of that power and is restricted in the same manner as is the state. So, when regulation does have a substantial external impact, the welfare of the state's citizens beyond the borders of the particular municipality cannot be disregarded and must be recognized and served....

It is plain beyond dispute that proper provision for adequate housing of all categories of people is certainly an absolute essential in promotion of the general welfare required in all local land use regulation. Further the universal and constant need for such hous-

ing is so important and of such broad public interest that the general welfare which developing municipalities like Mount Laurel must consider extends beyond their boundaries and cannot be parochially confined to the claimed good of the particular municipality. It has to follow that, broadly speaking, the presumptive obligation arises for each such municipality affirmatively to plan and provide, by its land use regulations, the reasonable opportunity for an appropriate variety and choice of housing, including, of course, low and moderate cost housing, to meet the needs, desires and resources of all categories of people who may desire to live within its boundaries. Negatively, it may not adopt regulations or policies which thwart or preclude that opportunity....

In other words, such municipalities must zone primarily for the living welfare of people and not for the benefit of the local tax rate.

15-3. SOUTH JERSEY RESIDENTS STAND IN LINE FOR AFFORDABLE SUBURBAN HOUSING, 2003

Source: Michelle Molz, "Hundreds Apply for Low-Cost Homes," [Cherry Hill, New Jersey] *Courier-Post*, September 16, 2003. Reprinted by courtesy of the Courier-Post.

Priscilla Perry and her two daughters want to get out of South Camden [New Jersey].

"There are too many drugs where I live," said Perry, 42, a nursing assistant at the Cadbury Home in Cherry Hill. "I want to raise my kids in a safe, quiet, clean place with no drugs and no crime."

Perry and her daughter Tyisha, 22, brought lawn chairs and joined a snaking line of 1,525 people who applied Monday for a chance to live in 40 new townhomes at the Ethel R. Lawrence Homes on Moorestown-Mount Laurel Road.

Juanita Carmona, six months pregnant with her first child, waited in her car overnight Sunday so she could be among the first in line. She was 19th.

"I like the environment here," said Carmona, 20, of Magnolia, as she rubbed her swollen belly. "It'll be better for my baby."

Shortage of Homes

Cars jammed streets named Tolerance and Equality as hopeful tenants from Philadelphia, Trenton, Camden, and all points between lined up across the parking lot for a chance to live here. The townhomes will be finished in December, joining 100 units built nearly three years ago.

The one-, two- and three-bedroom units—all rentals—are carpeted, with central heat and air, all appliances and a washer/dryer. Rent ranges from $125 per month to about $825.

Eighty percent are reserved for those with low or moderate incomes. The rest are rented at market rates.

In the tri-county region, low income means a family of four earns less than $34,110 annually. Moderate income is a family of four earning between $34,111 and $54,560 a year.

"We have a severe shortage of homes," said property manager Deborah Del Grande. "It's very competitive. We could do 100 of these developments."

Tenants must meet strict criteria to qualify, including a credit check, five-year landlord history, criminal background check, employment verification and an in-home visit.

Anyone with a felony conviction is excluded due to state funding laws.

The development is the product of a 32-year legal battle with the township over its zoning laws.

Known as the Mount Laurel I decision, the state Supreme Court mandated in 1975 that all towns must provide a realistic opportunity for low- and moderate-income housing. It reaffirmed that decision in 1986.

The case started in 1971, when the township was sued by Ethel Lawrence, a homemaker with nine children who lived on Elbo Lane.

Lawrence was horrified by the condition of low-cost homes rented by her friends and family. As large homes began replacing farmland in the 1960s and 70s, there was no provision for less-costly housing and poor families were forced to move out.

"Field of Dreams"

Today, the battle is about access to opportunity, said attorney Peter O'Connor, who represented Lawrence and now operates Fair Share Housing Development Inc. from an office building in the development.

"This is our "Field of Dreams," O'Connor said. "If you build it, they will come. We're trying to provide access to better schooling, a low crime rate, a better environment and more employment opportunities. These exist in this region, not in segregated urban areas."

Despite a strong need, more communities like the Ethel R. Lawrence Homes are not being built, said Ethel Lawrence-Halley, a paralegal from Southampton who continued her mother's cause after her death in 1994.

"The fact that there are lines as long as this is a sad commentary about how the state is addressing affordable housing," Lawrence-Halley said. "A lot of towns just still fight it unless they are legally challenged. We really need to educate our politicians and their constituents that affordable housing is not a dirty word."...

In addition to 140 townhomes, there will be a recreation complex with basketball, tennis and handball courts, an amphitheater and a $5 million community center....

15-4. RESIDENTS OF MOUNT LAUREL, NEW JERSEY ENJOY FAIR SHARE HOUSING, 2002

Figure 15-1 Residents of Ethel R. Lawrence Homes, Mt. Laurel, New Jersey, 2002. For a generation, Mount Laurel symbolized the obstacles to building affordable housing in suburbia. When the Ethel Lawrence apartments opened in 2000, hundreds of people waited in line for the chance to apply. Photograph by Tina Markoe Kinslow, Courtesy of Camden/South Jersey Courier-Post.

15-5. THE *PHILADELPHIA INQUIRER* EXAMINES CC&RS, 1991

Source: Steve Goldstein, "Don't Even Think of Pink Flamingos: Own a Home in the Suburbs? Chances Are You Gave Something Up When You Moved In. And Not Just the Right to Bad Taste," *Philadelphia Inquirer*, October 27, 1991. Copyright © 2005 by The Philadelphia Inquirer. Reprinted by permission. Reprinted by Reprint Management Services.

Question: What would you call a suburban Philadelphia subdivision that forbids you from hanging wash out to dry, swimming in an above-ground pool or storing your lawnmower in an outdoor shed?

Answer: Typical.

There's more. Most subdivisions built in the last 20 years impose restrictions on: fences; satellite dishes; parking commercial vehicles, boats or Winnebago-type RVs in the driveway; lawn "sculptures"; mailbox styles; outside propane tanks, and play gyms.

Want to wash a car? Sorry, not in front of your home. Fond of dogs? No problem, but let's weigh Terminator to make certain he's not over the 25-pound limit. A basketball hoop? Well, perhaps. But the backboard has to be transparent.

And, by the way, no signs. Except "The Smiths" or "For Sale."

These are not township ordinances. These are rules and restrictions adopted and enforced by homeowners associations.

Chances are, if you are buying a home in any suburban subdivision built in the Philadelphia area in the last two decades, you are buying into a community that not only regulates how you can alter the appearance of your home with paint and other decorations, but also prescribes the kind of life you live on your property.

"This is extremely widespread," said West Chester [Pennsylvania] lawyer John D. Snyder, who represents developers and municipalities. "People do not own their yards in the strict sense. Traditional ownership is not the way it used to be."

Sure, your home is still your castle. But hold the moat and turrets, please.

"The good news is that your neighbor can't do anything obnoxious. The bad news is you lose some expression of individuality," said W. Joseph Duckworth, president of Realen Homes, the region's second-largest homebuilder.

"Most customers prefer protection against someone else's poor taste to the freedom," said Duckworth.

Developers, real estate lawyers and municipal officials agree that the number of covenant-restricted communities is growing.

Virtually all townhouse-condominium communities are governed by homeowners associations that impose restrictions. Such rules are most readily accepted as necessary when you share walls, roofs and grounds with your neighbors.

But rules also abound in communities that consist almost entirely of single-family detached homes, *even* those where the houses are built on one-acre lots....

There are more than 1,000 such association-communities in the eight-county Philadelphia region alone....Nationally, one person in eight lives in such a community.

The trend is driven by a need for conformity and fears that property values could be degraded in the absence of "standards."

"If you are a purchaser in this community, then you want to know that the largest capital investment of your life will be protected and not subject to the taste and judgment of your neighbor," said Ken Brookman, a lawyer...who has written many covenants....

Brookman described the restrictions as contractual obligations that cannot be violated unless a court finds the rules deny a constitutional right or unlawfully discriminate against race, religion or physical condition.

"Almost everything else is enforceable because you agreed to it when you bought the house," Brookman said....

Covenants and restrictions are recorded with the deeds to the property, so they are publicly available to prospective buyers.

"The buyer has no one to blame but himself when they do something against the covenant," said Brookman. "However, in the case of non-condominium sales, there is no obligation to present the buyer with these restrictions before closing on the house."

In fact, the evidence suggests that many home buyers don't bother to investigate whether it's OK to let their flamingos perch in front of their dream house.

"One of our major problems is people buy into associations without being informed," said Pamela Bennett, executive director of the Delaware Valley chapter of the national Community Associations Institute. "Then they get in and it upsets them."

People don't ask for the rules and they don't know to ask, said Bennett. Then they are presented with the rules as part of the blizzard of documents at settlement.

"Who is going to sit there and read these rules and regulations at a closing?" Bennett said....

[Lawyer, Harry] Dunn, who once lived in a covenant-restricted community, is in favor of what he calls "reasonable" regulations. There are those that overreach, he said, but "by and large they are good for homeowners and good for developers."

Urban designer Ruth Durack, an associate at [a] Philadelphia architectural firm..., has written codes that prescribe uniformity in appearance, but finds "behavioral" restrictions distasteful....

As the number of restrictive communities grows, some developers are feeling a backlash. Realen Homes pushed a hot button in several developments when it limited the number of pets.

"That was a mistake," concedes marketing chief David Della Porta, "and we won't do it again."

In a few cases the regulations are creeping under the door. At Hillcrest, a development in Middletown Township, Delaware County, the rules state: "Interior drapery linings will be limited to the following colors: whites, creams and beiges."

In his book, *Edge City: Life on the New*

Frontier, author Joel Garreau, who terms these homeowners associations "shadow governments," cites a community outside Phoenix that banned "pornographic" films, books, magazines and devices from homes.

"There is somewhat of a legitimate purpose (for these covenants), but it's a fuzzy area," said Ron Bednar, director of the regional office of the state Department of Community Affairs. "Where do you draw the line?"

Not in the sandbox. Absolutely a no-no.

15-6. A BLACK SUBURB DEBATES PRIVACY, 1996

Source: Susan Saulny, "On the Inside and Looking Out; Black Suburb Rebuffs Uninvited Black Visitors," *The Washington Post*, July 8, 1996. Copyright © 1996, The Washington Post. Reprinted with permission.

At dusk, the black teenagers rolled into the Perrywood community of Upper Marlboro [Maryland]. They came in cars and on bikes, some from as far away as the District [of Columbia], to play basketball. By 7:15 p.m., there wasn't enough room on the court, so the players spilled onto the streets, sat on cars, played music and chilled.

This nightly ritual disturbed residents who found it increasingly difficult to cut through the teenage bramble at the entrance to their suburban Prince George's County neighborhood, where homes sell for $180,000 to $300,000.

The homeowners association, concerned about what members called an eyesore and recent break-ins and vandalism, hired off-duty Prince George's police officers. They were instructed to stop people at the basketball court and ask for some proof that they "belong in the area," said Anthony Jaby, the neighborhood watch chairman.

That decision sounded a familiar and unpleasant chord with some residents for one reason: Perrywood is virtually all black. And the idea of black people asking police to keep other black people from their neighborhood, for whatever reason, has left some residents ill at ease.

"We started having problems with the young men, and unfortunately they are our people," said Greta Scott, who has lived in Perrywood for two years. She agrees with the measures, but "it becomes pretty uncomfortable, because I resent the fact that black males are already singled out. Here we are singling them out again. But what can you do?"

Well-to-do black neighborhoods such as Perrywood—eight miles east of the District—are sprouting all across central and southern Prince George's, the richest black-majority suburb in the nation. As they do, some residents are worried about protecting their property values without adopting the same separatist, elitist attitudes that many blacks have accused suburban whites of having.

Perrywood, which is about four years old, consists of 350 single-family homes and town houses, but eventually it will grow to 1,400 units. An Olympic-size swimming pool, tennis courts, ball fields and hiking trails are all part of the community. Volvos, minivans and Mercedes-Benzes line its driveways....

Perrywood is far from the county's high-crime neighborhoods, but lately, car thefts, loitering, break-ins and graffiti on gazebos have become concerns. In late May, a homeowners association newsletter denounced the scene around the basketball court.

"Unfortunately, we have already experienced violence and property damage in our community...not to mention the 'eyesore' at the basketball court every night," said the recent newsletter....

Although the homeowners board "does not directly connect the outsiders with security problems," Jaby said, some residents say cracking down on the uninvited guests around the court, as well as erecting stop signs and posting speed limits, will help curtail the problems.

The resulting conflict of emotions is complex.

"I have a major problem with this decision," said Perrywood resident Robert Lewis, 29. "When I found out...I was mad. I was angry. I don't think I'm better than any other blacks."

Lewis, a producer for Electra Records, said he learned of "the foul situation" when he saw a white officer stop a youth he knows "while he was just walking home, not spray-painting anything."

"I thought our kids shouldn't have to grow up feeling that they're a security threat just because they're black," Lewis said.

Richard Vaughan, a music teacher in the Prince George's schools, said the security stops "send a negative message to the kids, that I don't care who you are or what you do. If you are a minority person, you still are considered the lowest and most dangerous. And that is a terrible thing to feel."

Ben Froman, 18, drove from the District one June day looking forward to an evening of basketball and movies with a friend from school who lives in Perrywood. As he searched for his buddy's address, he said, an officer "roadblocked" him and asked him to leave the community.

"I didn't do anything wrong, except that I had D.C. plates on my car," said Froman, who is black. "It's not fair. We should have the right to come over here and play."

The homeowners board and the police don't see it that way.

"We're not trying to hassle anybody. The police are here to make everybody feel better, safer," Jaby said. "The security seems harsh because it seems that we are trying to patrol our own people, but in reality, we're just asking to live in an environment where you can feel free. We want our kids to know the officers. We want them to talk together and have a relationship."

Other options, such as a gate for the community, were discarded because "that would imprison the neighborhood," Jaby said....

[According to] Bart Landry, a sociology professor at the University of Maryland..."Today, we're seeing the black middle class do what the white middle class has long done: carve out residential space for themselves."

Perrywood resident Ed Connor, who is black and recently moved with his family from Atlanta, put it this way: "People who don't live here might not care about things the way we do. Seeing all the new houses going up, largely unprotected, someone might be tempted."

Bryan Davis, 14, a resident of another well-to-do black Prince George's neighborhood, Lake Arbor, sometimes visits Perrywood. He doesn't object to the security checks.

"White neighborhood or black neighborhood—it doesn't matter," he said. "People start to act the same whatever color they are. If they see somebody suspicious, it really doesn't matter where they are. They just want to protect what's theirs."...

But, Landry said, "middle-class blacks have a hard time doing the same thing whites do without it appearing harsh and insensitive. Because of the racial tension in this society, there is some pressure within the black community to stick together in opposing racism and ignoring class differences."

Still, some said, there are times when the ties that bind tightest are those among economic equals.

"People have a tendency to stick together because they want to maintain their property values, their homes—class issues," said James Newborn, a resident of Perrywood for two years. "We're just strong working people who want something nice. Race never entered the picture."

15-7. COMMENTATOR DAVID BOAZ EXPLAINS THE VIRTUES OF GATED COMMUNITIES, 1996

Source: David Boaz, "Gates of Wrath; Angry About Crime, Communities Have Good Reason to Fence Out the World," *The Washington Post*, January 7, 1996.

Private, gated communities are coming under intense media scrutiny, from the front page of the *New York Times* to prime-time magazine shows on television. An article in *The Washington Post* by architectural critic Roger K. Lewis recently deplored the trend this way: "Welcome to the new Middle Ages. We are building a kind of medieval landscape in which defensible, walled and gated towns dot the countryside."

As it happens, I read those words the morning after my car had been broken into—yet again—on a Friday evening, in the busy Dupont Circle area a mile or so from my home in Washington. Perhaps I will be forgiven if

I have more sympathy for walled cities than critics from the ivory tower could muster.

Last fall, as it also happens, I visited some of the walled medieval cities of Spain and southern France. I said to my companion then, "Look at the width and strength of these walls. Imagine how dangerous the world outside must have been for people to spend so much effort building them." I added a speculation: "What do you think history will record as the period in which cities didn't need walls around them—about 1500 to 1995?"

People are flocking to gated communities for a very good reason: Cities are failing to provide the basic necessities for civilized life, notably physical safety.

In a sense, the rise of communities that increasingly rely on their own, private services is a peaceful but extreme response to the failure of big government. Like their federal counterpart, local governments today tax us more heavily than ever but offer deteriorating services in return. Not only do police seem unable to combat intolerable levels of crime, but the schools get worse, garbage and litter don't get picked up, potholes aren't fixed, panhandlers confront us on every corner.

Why pay taxes to a local government that can't provide basic services and physical safety?

Some fight city hall. Others just leave, as have 60,000 D.C. residents since the beginning of the 1980s, both black and white. Around the country, the trend is much the same: Residents are heading for the suburbs or for the safe confines of private communities. Experts estimate that 4 million Americans have chosen to live in some 30,000 private communities—28 million if you count privately guarded apartment houses, which are, after all, small gated communities.

In these communities, the homes, the streets, the sewers, the parks are all private— that is, independently owned and operated by the residents or a development company, not the local government. After buying a house or condominium there, residents pay a monthly fee that covers security, maintenance and management. Many of the communities are both gated and guarded, with entrance limited to residents and approved visitors. Guards patrol the area, with full authority to expel unauthorized persons.

Many have rules that would range from annoying to infuriating to unconstitutional if imposed by a government—regulations on house colors, shrubbery heights, on-street parking, even gun ownership. People choose such communities partly because they find the rules, even strict rules, congenial.

Private developments are often in the suburbs, on previously undeveloped land. But some are in the heart of major cities....

In some cities, neighborhoods are petitioning to privatize themselves or at least to erect gates on public streets. In Los Angeles, for instance, several dozen communities are closed off, and more are petitioning for barriers....

Many social critics don't like these communities. They complain that fortressed enclaves are the essence of classism, a retreat from diversity. Los Angeles City Council member Rita Walters calls the demand for gates "Balkanization of the city." Writer Mike Davis says that gates will "Brazilianize Los Angeles," while a few miles south the nightmare analogy seems closer to home: San Diego resident Bill Dean says that gated communities reflect "the Los Angelization of San Diego."

The answer, according to many of these naysayers, is to tax people more, to put more money into the hands of government so that residents won't take it upon themselves to provide services they once considered the purview of government.

Listen again to the words of council member Walters: "If you're willing to pay the money it takes to wall off your community, to pay for private security, why not be willing to pay for an extra measure of tax that may not be as much, that will benefit the city as a whole and then you don't have to have these guards and walls?"

She continues, "It's like people who... won't vote for a bond issue for a public school but will pay to send their kids to private schools."

Indeed it is. But the fact that public officials are so willing to see more money as the solution is, in fact, exactly the problem. As the urban flight and rise of gated communities makes clear, people don't think they can improve city schools, for example, by giving them more money or by "getting involved" in a bloated system that operates hundreds of schools....[I]nstead of paying more for less, people who can afford to move, or to send their children to private school, don't try make the D.C. schools work, they simply get their kids out.

Nor do people believe that giving city governments more money will improve the quality of other basic services. Instead, many believe that smaller, more responsive private communities are better equipped to spend money in a way that will improve the residents' quality of life. The issue isn't frugality, it's practicality; often people pay association fees that are higher than the taxes in neighboring cities. The difference is that they see the tangible benefit of those payments.

Economists Donald J. Boudreaux and Randall G. Holcombe offer a theoretical explanation for the growing popularity of private communities..., "The establishment of a contractual government appears to be the closest thing to a real-world social contract that can be found because it is created behind something analogous to a veil [of ignorance], and because everyone unanimously agrees to move into the contractual government's jurisdiction."

University of Maryland professor Roger K. Lewis complains that residents of private communities are "abandoning the whole 'idea' of city," seeking a homogeneous community in which "their neighbors act and think much as they do."

Well, one might ask, what's wrong with that? Why shouldn't people live among people with whom they're comfortable? Even those of us who like the dynamism and diversity of the big city want some standards. When I dine at a sidewalk cafe, I revel in the vibrancy of the city even when it occasionally means enduring the rantings of a street person passing by. But when my car is broken into, when I feel unsafe sitting in the neighborhood park on a Sunday afternoon, I'm less tolerant.

Like most urban residents, I'm not trying to avoid people of a different color or socioeconomic status. I'm trying to avoid the culture of crime and social decay that I seem increasingly to find everywhere around me. Anybody who accepts basic social customs— don't rob, don't hit, don't urinate on the sidewalk—is welcome in my city. But when I pay high taxes to a city that can't pick up the garbage, maintain public civility, or keep my home, my car and my person safe from injury, living in a gated community starts looking mighty appealing....

[A]s long as city governments can't keep their citizens any safer than did medieval governments, we can expect Americans to respond just as the people of the Dark Ages did: by taking responsibility for our own safety by walling ourselves off from barbarian threats.

15-8. PLANNER EDWARD BLAKELY CRITICIZES "FORTRESS AMERICA," 1998

Source: Edward J. Blakely, "Am I My Brother's Gatekeeper? The Fortressing of Private Communities Contributes to the Increasing Fragmentation of American Society," *The Daily News of Los Angeles*, March 1, 1998.

It has been more than three decades since this nation legally outlawed all forms of public discrimination—in housing, education, public transportation and public accommodations. Only one year ago the state [California] passed Proposition 209, banning affirmative action and quotas on the basis that our state needs only equal protection under the law.

Yet in the last decade we are seeing one of the visible forms of discrimination—the gated, walled, private community. Californians are increasingly electing to live behind walls with active security mechanisms to prevent intrusion into their private domains.

In every part of our state, a frightened middle class that moved to escape school integration, to secure appreciating housing values, now must move to maintain its economic advantage. California's middle class is fortressing up.

Many gated communities are residential areas with restricted access such that normally public spaces have been privatized.

More than 1 million of our fellow Californians are seeking this new refuge from the problems of urbanization. A 1991 poll of the Los Angeles metropolitan area found 16 percent of respondents living in some form of secured-access environment.

While many of these are traditional security apartment buildings, a conservative estimate that one-third are gated communities provides a rough figure of 530,000 residents, with many more such developments having been built since then.... [M]ore than 40 percent of all new housing developments in our state are inside walls.

California leads the nation in gated developments, but they are found across the country and are very common in Florida, Arizona, Texas and New York. I have estimated that there are 30,000 gated communities nationwide, or close to 4 million people living in walled security compounds.

Economic segregation is scarcely new. In fact, zoning and city planning were designed in part to preserve the position of the privileged by subtle variances in building and density codes.

But the gated communities go further in several respects. They create physical barriers to access and privatize community space, not merely individual space.

Many of these communities also privatize civic responsibilities such as police protection and communal services such as schools, recreation and entertainment. The new developments create a private world that shares little with its neighbors or the larger political system.

This fragmentation undermines the very concept of civitas—organized community life.

The fortressing phenomenon also has enormous policy consequences for all Californians. By allowing some residents to internalize and to exclude others from sharing in their economic privilege, it aims directly at the conceptual base of community and citizenship in America. The potential for our melting pot of a state to realize the dream of social and economic equality is torn apart by these changes in community patterns.

What is the measure of nationhood when the divisions between neighborhoods require armed patrols and electric fencing to keep out other residents? By gating our neighborhoods, are we just carrying the street-gang mentality to its fullest extent—that is, adults marking their territory and hiring people to protect it? When public services and even local government are privatized, when the community of responsibility stops at the subdivision gates, what happens to the function and the very idea of democracy?

In short, can California develop and fulfill its social contract in the absence of social contact? Will we develop a new and frightening form of geographic segregation that destroys the paradise that we all came here—regardless of race or national origin—to seek? Surely the sunshine will not be enough to keep the Golden State together in the next century.

15-9. PHOTO GALLERY: CONTEMPORARY GATED COMMUNITIES

Figure 15-2 Gates of Vezelay, North San Diego County, California, 2005. San Diego, like other parts of southern California saw a boom in gated developments as concerns with prestige mixed with latent social fears in a metro area marked high immigration but low rates of crime. Photograph by Andrew Wiese.

Figure 15-3 Gates of Woodmore, Mitchellville, Maryland, 2001. While suburban gated communities were disproportionately white, in Prince George's County, Maryland, the gated Woodmore subdivision, which featured a private country club and golf course, attracted an affluent black majority. Photograph by Andrew Wiese.

ESSAYS

Essay 15-1 is an excerpt from political scientist Evan McKenzie's path-breaking book, *Privatopia*, which explores the history and implications of Common Interest Developments (CIDs). McKenzie traces the roots of this phenomenon back to innovative suburbs like Radburn, New Jersey, Kansas City's Country Club District and even Ebenezer Howard's Garden City, which proposed not only master planning for the built environment but communal ownership of property and a form of private self-government to oversee it. In McKenzie's view, CIDs have affected American politics as well as landscape, promoting an ideal of citizenship in which rights and responsibilities depend on how much tax or fees one pays and where. In this excerpt, McKenzie examines one of the most remarked-upon features of these developments, the covenants, conditions, and restrictions (CC&Rs) that govern the use of property and other behavior in these communities. In **Essay 15-2**, anthropologist Setha Low goes *Behind the Gates* of gated communities to investigate the motivations and aspirations of residents. In addition to the fact that gated communities are not demonstrably safer than unenclosed communities nearby, Low finds, ironically, that life behind walls may actually increase the level of insecurity that residents—and especially children—feel. The book offers a balanced, empathetic appraisal of the impulses that underlie the popularity of these controversial communities.

ESSAY 15-1. EVAN MCKENZIE, *PRIVATOPIA: HOMEOWNER ASSOCIATIONS AND THE RISE OF RESIDENTIAL PRIVATE GOVERNMENT* (1994)

Source: Copyright © 1994 by Yale University. Reprinted by permission of Yale University Press.

Morning in Privatopia

If Ebenezer Howard could awaken…and look about him at the America in which his ideas have had so much impact, he might react with astonishment and disappointment. He would see more than thirty million Americans, or some 12 percent of the U.S. population, living in about 150,000 common-interest developments. These developments are Americanized, third-generation descendants of Howard's utopian garden city idea. Our garden cities are a hybrid of Howard's utopian ideas and American privatism, and I use the term privatopia to capture the two concepts.

Rancho Bernardo

If Ebenezer Howard happened to awaken twenty-five miles north of downtown San Diego, California, he would see a commu-

nity of 33,250 known as Rancho Bernardo. Started in 1961 by builder Harry L. Summers, Rancho Bernardo typifies the large CID and has served as a model for many smaller developments. Summers began, like Howard, with 6,107 acres of undeveloped land, mainly rolling hills, on which he built a planned community that included housing, streets, recreation facilities, commercial areas, and light industry. It is easily distinguishable from the town of Poway to the east by the red tile roofs that top every building, the most notable of many tight architectural restrictions.

There are now about fourteen thousand dwellings in Rancho Bernardo, of which some eight thousand are single-family detached homes; the remainder is made up of single-family attached homes (generally called townhouses), condominiums, and apartments. When it is fully developed…Rancho Bernardo will house 41,200 people in about 17,900 dwellings. Rancho Bernardo is legally part of the city of San Diego, but it is to a large extent self-sufficient. A fifty-three-acre town center houses a large supermarket, many retail businesses, banks, and a retirement home. Two other parcels…accommodate a post office, library, fire station, movie theaters, financial institutions, auto service centers, hotels, and restaurants....Four smaller neighborhood commercial centers offer convenience goods and services. Two industrial parks...house such high-tech employers as UNISYS..., National Cash Register, Hewlett Packard, Sony....

The development is divided into a variety of "neighborhoods"—which offer distinct architectural styles, housing prices, and lifestyles—that were created during the different phases of the project. For example, Seven Oaks is a retirement community. Oaks North is for people age forty-five and older. Westwood includes apartments and a large "family area" with playground. The Trails offers larger lots, more privacy, a bit more individuality, and prices in the high six figures.

The plan includes complex and detailed architectural restrictions for each of the neighborhoods—restrictions that are rigidly enforced by the more than one dozen neighborhood homeowner associations run by elected directors. Even the most minute changes in the restrictions require the approval of the association. Richard Louv, who studied Rancho Bernardo for his book *America II*, describes the restrictions as follows:

"Even vegetable gardens are frowned upon—though some people do grow tiny ones out of their neighbors' view. Fences, hedges, or walls require approval, and may not be more than three feet tall. Signs, other than for-sale signs, are prohibited. Trees must be kept trimmed and may not grow above the level of the roof, which must be covered with red tiles. Residents are not allowed to park recreational vehicles or boats in their driveway; a special communal parking area is set aside for them. One village, designed for seniors, prohibits grandchildren from using the recreation center, and home visitation by grandchildren is strictly limited. The owners of patio homes (semidetached houses that share common grounds, except for patio areas) must gain their neighbors' approval before altering the patio, planting a rosebush, or raising a canopy."

Restrictions in some neighborhoods are so detailed as to regulate the color of curtains. The rigidity with which these restrictions are interpreted and enforced is illustrated by a matter that had to be resolved by the California courts. One phase of the development had a restriction providing that "no truck, camper, trailer, boat of any kind or other form of recreational vehicle shall be parked" in the project. One of the residents bought a new pickup truck with a camper shell to use for personal transportation. The association, through its management company, took him to court to enjoin him from parking the truck under his own carport and to recover $2,060 in fines for this "violation." After losing in the trial court, the management company appealed, only to see the appellate court side with the resident and hold the company's action unreasonable.

Yet this sort of action does not seem unreasonable to many Rancho Bernardo residents. They place a high value on the restrictions, feeling that the infringement on one's own freedom is a small price to pay for protection from the potential misdeeds of one's neighbors. Louv quotes one resident as saying, "Sure, they have some rules, like the one that regulates campers. But the community associations are here to protect our interests, not let the community deteriorate. That's not regulation; it's common sense. I don't know why anyone would look at it differently than I do, do you?"

In addition to the neighborhood associations that enforce architectural restrictions, there are projectwide committees and corporate entities that perform other functions.... At the top is the Rancho Bernardo Town Council, which has numerous specialty commissions within it to deal with such matters as senior services, civic-community relations, public services, and community appearance. The Rancho Bernardo Community Planning Board communicates directly with the San Diego Planning Commission to maintain control over the gradual build-out of the project.

Through these groups Rancho Bernardo residents are better represented before the San Diego city government than virtually any other part of the city. The Bernardo Home Owners Corporation not only maintains an official liaison with the San Diego City Council, it also provides buses that transport hordes of residents to City Council meetings at which topics in which they have an interest are being addressed.

Figure 15-4 The Villas at Rancho Bernardo, San Diego, California, 2005. Begun in 1961, Rancho Bernardo, known for its required red-tile roofs, became a model for other Common Interest Developments (or CIDs) across the nation. Photograph by Andrew Wiese.

The political clout of San Bernardo [sic] is increased through the concentration of wealthy and skilled professionals among its residents, many of whom are retired and have not only the skills but the time to act as community advocates....Talent, wealth, and position are found in extraordinary abundance among Rancho Bernardo residents.

Figure 15-5 Private Playground in Rancho Bernardo, San Diego, California, 2005. CIDs often provide common areas, which are collectively owned by residents. Because they are private property, only residents can use them. Photograph by Andrew Wiese.

Moreover, journalist Harold Keen notes, "the community's affluence is reflected in its sociological makeup and political leanings—predominantly white Anglo, conservative Republican, overwhelmingly pro-Reagan."

No More Pink Flamingos

Rancho Bernardo is larger than most CIDs, but it is not unique in exalting private rules and regulations for their own sake and in emphasizing property values over considerations of individual privacy and freedom.

Some community associations have banned political signs, prohibited distribution of newspapers, and forbidden political gatherings in the common areas.

In Ashland, Massachusetts, a Vietnam War veteran was told that he could not fly the American flag on Flag Day. The board backed down only after the resident called the press and the story appeared on the front page of a local newspaper.

In Monroe, New Jersey, a homeowner association took a married couple to court because the wife, at age forty-five, was three years younger than the association's age minimum for residency. The association won in court, and the judge ordered the sixty-year-old husband to sell, rent the unit, or live without his wife.

In Houston, Texas, a homeowner association took a woman to court for keeping a dog in violation of the rules of her CID. The association won, but she kept the dog anyway. The judge sent her to jail for contempt of court.

In Fairbanks Ranch, an affluent CID in Southern California that lies behind six locked gates, there are forty-five private streets patrolled by private security officers who enforce a private speed limit. First-time speeders get a warning; the second offense brings a hearing and a reprimand; a third offense means a five-hundred-dollar fine, and the car and driver are banned from the private streets for a month....

In Fort Lauderdale, Florida, condominium managers ordered a couple to stop entering and leaving their unit through their back door, claiming that they were wearing an unsightly path in the lawn by taking a short cut to the parking lot. The couple retained an attorney who filed a lawsuit seeking a court's permission for the couple to use their own back door.

In Boca Raton, Florida, an association cited a homeowner and took her to court because her dog weighed more than thirty pounds, a violation of association rules. A court-ordered weighing ceremony was inconclusive, with the scales hovering between just under and just over the limit. After the story made national news, the association settled the suit on undisclosed terms....

In Santa Ana, California, the Townsquare Owners' Association posted notices throughout the complex accusing a resident of "parking in circular driveway kissing and doing bad things for over 1 hour." She was warned that she would be fined if another such incident happened. The woman denied the charge, retained legal counsel, and threatened a lawsuit for defamation, invasion of privacy, and infliction of emotional distress. The association issued an apology through its attorney, explaining it as a case of mistaken identity....

These examples illustrate the peculiar internal dynamics of these heirs to the garden city legacy. American CIDs are both like and unlike the garden city. The similarities include master planning of large-scale communities; isolation of the development from its surroundings and protection against change; capitalization on dislike of city life to attract residents; development of a government based on a corporate charter and attempts to replace politics with management; and creation of a government with greater powers than that of the city.

The differences, however, are profound. Designers of American CIDs dwell on the physical plan but slight the social and economic structure of the community, particularly Howard's quasi-socialist reforms; base land tenure on private ownership rather than rental from a public landlord; and do not create real, self-sufficient communities with a full economic base. American CIDs are not intended first and foremost as a vehicle for reforming society, as was the garden city. But the American CID may have greater potential for achieving Howard's goal of undermining the city than did the English new towns.

For these and other reasons, the American CID falls short of Howard's expectations regarding both the nature and the quality of relations between homeowners and their boards of directors—what could be called their micropolitics—and in their apparent impact on society, or macropolitics.

The Micropolitics of Private Governments

Instead of having a benevolent public landlord, as Howard anticipated, CIDs feature a form of private government that takes an American preference for private home ownership and, too often, turns it into an ideology of hostile privatism. Preservation of property values is the highest social goal, to which other aspects of community life are subordinated. Rigid, intrusive, and often petty rule enforcement makes a caricature of Howard's benign managerial government, and the belief in rational planning is distorted into an emphasis on conformity for its own sake.

To many residents, association boards often seem to operate as though wearing blinders, rigidly enforcing technical rules against people's use of their own homes and ignoring the consequences of such intrusive behavior. Many CID residents casually accept the rationality of such management-mania, but others become angry and file lawsuits or refuse to obey and find themselves sued by the association. A California study found that 44 percent of board members had been harassed or threatened with lawsuit during the preceding year. The CID resident must choose between conformity and conflict.

This predilection toward litigation is primarily the result of the particular kind of private government found in CIDs....

[CIDs] have three distinct legal characteristics that set their residents apart from other Americans: common ownership of property, mandatory membership in the homeowner association, and the requirement of living under a private regime of restrictive covenants enforced by fellow residents.

First, residents own or exclusively occupy their own units, but they share ownership of the "common area" of the development used by all (hence the term "common interest")....
[T]he common area may include recreation centers, streets, front lawns, parks, and parking lots. Residents are assessed fees to pay for these facilities and for private services that range from police protection to local self-government services that were once the province of cities. Because these amenities are privately supported, only residents are allowed to use them.

Second, because common property ownership requires organization of some sort, everyone who buys a home in a CID automatically becomes a member of a homeowner association, or HOA. These are nearly always nonprofit corporations. They are set up on paper by the developer of the project while the project is in the planning stage, not voluntarily organized by the residents after they move in. The only way to resign from the association is to sell one's home and move out.

Third, because the homeowner association itself needs organization if it is to function, all residents are governed by a corporate board of directors elected by the unit owners, renters being disenfranchised.... The operation of the development involves collecting assessments from all owners, handling the association's finances, maintaining the common property, filing and managing lawsuits on behalf of all owners, and enforcing against the owners and renters a set of private laws drawn up by the developer and known as "covenants, conditions and restrictions," or CC&Rs. Empowered by this quasi-constitution, the board is a private government....

The CC&Rs enforced by the board are a complicated system of private covenants, known generically as "deed restrictions," built into the deeds to all the homes. This device...permits a seller of land—such as the original developer and his successor, the board—to retain control over how the land is used after he sells it. The sale is conditional on the buyer's agreement to abide by certain restrictions on the way he may use or dispose of the property. The promises "run with the land," meaning that all successive buyers are bound by the same covenants as the original purchaser.

Certain particular covenants, such as racial restrictions or covenants banning children, are invalid everywhere or in some states.…But…today restrictive covenants are an approved legal device.

Today's real estate developers do not merely insert into the deeds a covenant or two, as sellers did in earlier times, such as a promise not to build a slaughterhouse or soap factory.…Instead, they have lawyers draft a fat package many pages long and full of elaborate restrictions that, taken as a whole, dictate to a large extent the lifestyle of everybody in the project.

The rigidity that seems to characterize CID rule enforcement was deliberately institutionalized by developers. It is maintained through the rules and laws under which CID boards operate. Even if individual board members wish to use prudent discretion in the enforcement of restrictions, and make exceptions, it is often difficult for them to do so. Individual association members can sue the board for failing to enforce the rules. Moreover, attorneys and property managers who specialize in servicing CIDs advocate strict rule enforcement in order to avoid setting precedents that could be used to justify further exceptions, and, ultimately, undermine the entire regime. Even if many residents and board members wish to change a rule, the task is made especially difficult by developers' "super-majority" requirements, which mandate approval from 75 percent of *all* owners, not just those voting.

This form of private government is strikingly different from that of cities. In a variety of ways, these private governments are illiberal and undemocratic. Most significantly boards of directors operate outside constitutional restrictions because the law views them as business entities rather than governments. Moreover, courts accept the legal fiction that all the residents have voluntarily agreed to be bound by the covenants by virtue of having bought a unit in the development.

Macropolitics: Secession of the Successful?

Rather than offering a solution to the problems of big cities, as Howard intended, CIDs exacerbate them. The developments take over many municipal functions for those who can pay the price, offering a competing sector of pay-as-you-go utilities.…This privatization was undertaken without consideration of its implications and consequences, however.…Most important, it carries with it the possibility that those affluent enough to live in CIDs will become increasingly segregated from the rest of society.…

Instead of housing people from all walks of life, as Ebenezer Howard envisioned, CIDs compete with cities for the affluent, siphoning off their tax dollars, their expertise and participation, and their sense of identification with a community. Such developments have come to be invoked as part of a disturbing trend called the "secession of the successful" by liberal economist Robert Reich, who…[was] Secretary of Labor under President Clinton. "In many cities and towns, the wealthy have in effect withdrawn their dollars from the support of public spaces and institutions shared by all and dedicated the savings to their own private services," Reich writes.…

Similar observations have been made by conservative social scientist Charles Murray, who views the growth of CIDs as a symbol of America becoming "a caste society" with "utter social separation" of the rich from the rest of society. Murray envisions a day when this growing sector of rich Americans will come to view cities as the internal equivalent of Indian reservations—places of deprivation and dysfunction for which they have no responsibility.

ESSAY 15-2. SETHA LOW, *BEHIND THE GATES: LIFE, SECURITY, AND THE PURSUIT OF HAPPINESS IN FORTRESS AMERICA* (2003)

Felicia—"Fear Flight": Safety, Community, and Fear of Others

I climb into Felicia's Volvo station wagon, carefully setting my tape recorder on the dashboard. Outside, the twisted junipers and gray-green cottonwoods of San Antonio flash by.… New gated developments with partially constructed houses and bulldozers leveling wild grass fields…suddenly disappear, leaving countryside that looks like it's been untouched for the past hundred years.

The contrast between the small-town past and suburban present is demarcated as we speed north.

Felicia is a tall, thin woman in her mid-forties who sits straight upright in the driver's seat. Her long fingers clutch the steering wheel as she drives; she is telling me about her college and graduate degrees. Even with the amount of education she has accumulated, she decided to stay home to take care of her seven-year-old daughter. They moved from California because of her husband's job and the opportunity to have a more comfortable life with a bigger house. They now live on an attractive cul-de-sac in a two-story, four-thousand-square-foot Scottsdale model located within a gated subdivision on the northern edge of the city.

She is articulate and gets right to the point. When they were shopping for a house, school district and aesthetics were important considerations. In fact, she had some reservations about living in a gated community, including the fact that it only has one exit if there is a fire. But they were concerned for their child's safety, and now feel that it was a good choice because it allows her to go outside and play. As Felicia puts it, "We're in San Antonio, and I believe the whole country knows how many child-kidnappings we've had.…My husband would not ever allow her outside to play without direct adult supervision unless we were gated." It allows them the freedom to walk around the neighborhood at night, and their daughter and her friends from nongated neighborhoods are able to ride their bicycles safely.

Felicia, however, thinks it has a flip side in that it produces a false sense of safety. The guards aren't "Johnny-on-the-spot," and anybody who wants to could jump the gate. There's a perception of safety among residents that may not be real and could potentially leave one more vulnerable "if there was ever an attack."…

Their development is made up of people who are retired and don't want to maintain large yards, or people who want to raise families in a more protected environment. There is a lot [of] "fear flight," people who have moved in the last couple of years as the crime rate, or the reporting of the crime rate, has

become such a prominent part of the news. She knows people who are building because they want to get out of their exclusive subdivisions that don't have gates; she mentions one family that was shopping for a house in the gated community because they had been robbed many times.

Their neighbors are upper middle and middle class, white, Christian, and, apart from one Jewish family, quite homogeneous—businessmen and doctors, with stay-at-home wives, many without college educations. On their street, they know everyone by sight and visit with neighbors who have children; but they no longer have a party when new people move in. The houses are "very nice," architecturally designed and custom built, and she worries that the new ones will not be as tasteful or beautiful.

Felicia feels safe inside the community, but expresses considerable anxiety about living in San Antonio:

"When I leave the area entirely and go downtown [little laugh], I feel quite threatened just being out in normal urban areas, unrestricted urban areas.…Please let me explain. The north central part of this city [San Antonio], by and large, is middle class to upper-middle class. Period. There are very few pockets of poverty. Very few. And therefore if you go to any store, you will look around and most of the clientele will be middle class as you are yourself. So you're somewhat insulated. But if you go downtown, which is much more mixed, where everybody goes, I feel much more threatened."

Her daughter was four years old when they first moved, and I wonder about the psychological impact of moving from a rambling, unfenced Californian suburb to a gated community. Felicia says her daughter feels threatened when she sees poor people, because she hasn't had enough exposure:

"We were driving next to a truck with some day laborers and equipment in the back, and we were stopped beside them at the light. She wanted to move because she was afraid those people were going to come and get her. They looked scary to her. I explained that they were workmen, they're the 'backbone of our country,' they're coming from work, you know, but…"

So living in a secured enclave may heighten a child's fear of others. It's unclear, though, whether Felicia's observation reflects many children's experience of growing up in a gated community, or simply her daughter's idiosyncracy and modeling of her mother's anxiety.

Felicia and her husband wanted to buy the nicest house in the best school district, while providing a safe environment for their daughter, one where they can be cloistered from any class differences. They consider the neighborhood "a real community" where you know your neighbors, although it is not as friendly as where they used to live. For them, the gated community provides a haven in a socially and culturally diverse world, offering a protected setting for their upper-middle-class lifestyle.

Desire for safety, security, community, and "niceness," as well as wanting to live near people like themselves because of a fear of "others" and of crime, is not unique to this family, but expressed by most residents living in gated communities. How they make sense of their new lives behind gates and walls, as well as the social consequences of their residential choices, are the subjects of this book. The emergence of a fortress mentality and its phenomenal success is surprising in the United States, where the majority of people live in open and unguarded neighborhoods. Thus, the rapid increase in the numbers of Americans moving to secured residential enclaves invites a more complex account of their motives and values. Like other middle-class Americans, residents of gated communities are looking for a place where they feel comfortable and secure, but this seemingly self-evident explanation reflects different underlying meanings and intentions. And collectively, their individual decisions are transforming the American dream of owning a suburban home in a close-knit community with easy access to nature into a vision that includes gates, walls, and guards....

One explanation for the gated community's popularity is that it materially and metaphorically incorporates otherwise conflicting, and in some cases polarized, social values that make up the moral terrain of middle-class life. For example, it reflects urban and suburban tensions in the United States regarding social class, race, and ethnicity and at the same time represents the perennial concern with creating community. The gated community's symbolic power rests on its ability to order personal and social experience.

Architectural symbols such as gates and walls also provide a rationale for the moral inconsistencies of everyday life. For instance, many residents want to feel safe in their homes and argue that walls and gates will keep out criminals; but gated communities are not safer than nongated suburban neighborhoods, where crime rates are already low. Instead, the logic of the symbolism satisfies conventional middle-class understandings of the nature of criminal activity—"it makes it harder for them to get in"—and justifies the choice to live in a gated community in terms of its moral and physical consequences—"look at my friends who were randomly robbed living in a nongated development."

Living in a gated community represents a new version of the middle-class American dream precisely because it temporarily suppresses and masks...the inherent anxieties and conflicting social values of modern urban and suburban life. It transforms Americans' dilemma of how to protect themselves and their children from danger, crime, and unknown others while still perpetuating open, friendly neighborhoods and comfortable, safe homes. It reinforces the norms of a middle-class lifestyle in a historical period in which everyday events and news media exacerbate fears of violence and terrorism. Thus, residents cite their "need" for gated communities to provide a safe and secure home in the face of a lack of other societal alternatives.

Gated residential communities, however, intensify social segregation, racism, and exclusionary land use practices already in place in most of the United States, and raise a number of values conflicts for residents. For instance, residents acknowledge their misgivings about the possible false security provided by the gates and guards, but at the same time, even that false security satisfies their desire for emotional security associated with childhood and the neighborhoods where they grew up. Living in a gated development contributes to residents' sense of well-being, but comes at the price of maintaining private guards and gates as well as conforming to extensive homeowners association rules and regulations. Individual freedom and ease of access for residents must be limited in order to achieve greater privacy and social control for the community as a whole. These contradictions—which residents are aware of and talk about—provide an opportunity to understand the psychological and social meaning-making processes Americans use to order their lives.

Defining the Gated Community

A gated community is a residential development surrounded by walls, fences, or earth banks covered with bushes and shrubs, with a secured entrance. In some cases, protection is provided by inaccessible land such as a nature reserve and, in a few cases, by a guarded bridge. The houses, streets, sidewalks, and other amenities are physically enclosed by these barriers, and entrance gates are operated by a guard or opened with a key or electronic identity card. Inside the development there is often a neighborhood watch organization or professional security personnel who patrol on foot or by automobile.

Gated communities restrict access not just to residents' homes, but also to the use of public spaces and services—roads, parks, facilities, and open space—contained within the enclosure. Communities vary in size from a few homes in very wealthy areas to as many as 21,000 homes in Leisure World in Orange County, California.... Many include golf courses, tennis courts, fitness centers, swimming pools, lakes, or unspoiled landscape as part of their appeal; commercial and public facilities are rare....

In many ways, buying a home in a gated residential community is a microcosm of the contemporary American dream. It reflects the social concerns and conflicts as well as the pleasures and desires of modern middle-class life. But it is the American dream with a twist, one that intentionally restricts access and emphasizes social control and security over other community values. Thus, by exploring the lives of gated community residents, we learn about ourselves, and at the same time we glimpse an increasingly secured and segregated world—a fortress America.

Kerry—Remembering a Childhood Home...

Kerry is an attractive woman, in her mid-thirties, wearing navy slacks and a starched white blouse.... George, her husband, works at a well-known financial center in Manhattan and just left for the day. She offers me ginger muffins and tea from a silver teapot, while describing their decision to move to Manor House [a gated community of 4,000 to 6,000 square foot homes on Long Island, New York] from their first home.

"We lived in Sunnyside Gardens, Queens, which was a planned community built in 1928. It was designed to imitate English garden communities with two- and three-family attached and semiattached brick houses. Everyone has a private front and back yard with a communal garden behind. We paid a yearly maintenance fee and sometimes volunteered to help with the garden.

The garden and volunteers made it a community. There's a street fair once or twice a year, and there's a local [neighborhood] organization. We were involved and had a great sense of a community.

So why did we leave? First of all, it's like what's happening to New York City. Things change, neighborhoods change, the makeup of the population changes. I was raised on Long Island, and missed the security of living there. And my husband was born in Portugal and was used to the openness of the land outside of Lisbon where he used to go climbing with his friends....

She knew that she would never find another community where she could walk down the block and say hi to most of the people she passed."...

"But here," she says, "I'm free and clear." She doesn't have to worry about raking leaves, watering the garden, or plowing the driveway. But she does miss walking into the shops and seeing her friends.

The most important thing, though, is that it is a gated community, "and there is a guard. I can't believe I'm leaving this till the end, that I feel safe and secure. I mean, I walk around the house sometimes and the door is open. It feels like when I was growing up on the south shore [of Long Island]....[And] it fulfills my husband's desire to have open space like when he was a child." The fact that Manor House is gated, has open space, and does the outside maintenance seems to make all the difference.

Florence Ladd, an environmental psychologist, says we re-create aspects of our childhood in distant communities wherever we resettle. We unconsciously remember places from our early childhood...and these place memories reappear in our homes and landscapes. We turn to this window on the past to perpetuate settings where we were happy as children, and by discovering characteristics of remembered places we replicate them for ourselves and our children....

How could it be otherwise? Our earliest spatial and environmental relationships are to our homes and local communities. These places are imprinted in our imaginations as given, even natural, and taken for granted until we grow up and begin to question them. Is it so surprising, then, that when we search for a home, community, or design concept we return time and again to this resource?

But why are these residents moving to a type of community that did not exist when they were young? The answer lies in how gated community residents infuse their desire to re-create a childhood place with the feelings of emotional security and protection of childhood. Gated community residents want to recapture physical elements of their childhood landscapes, just like other people, but this desire is entangled with an unconscious longing for security they identify with living behind gates and walls....

So what exactly do residents mean when they say "I feel secure in my community"? At an emotional level, it means feeling protected and that everything is right with the world; unconsciously it is associated with a sense of childhood trust and protection by parents.

Socially it means "I feel comfortable with my friends and neighbors." "I feel secure in my community" also means feeling physically safe, not just psychologically or socially comfortable. These meanings—and many others—are evoked whenever they talk about security. This simultaneity and ambiguity of meaning gives the concept the power to evoke a complex and ever-shifting set of feelings, feelings that become encoded in a variety of symbolic forms, including the built environment....

Protecting the Children and Safety for All

"Interview me, interview me," clamors Alexandra as we walk toward her friend's house, "I want to be in the book."

"The book will be about you," I try to console her, "but I'm only interviewing parents, not children."

"Why aren't you asking me?" she counters. "I live in a gated community too."...

[T]his is my nine-year-old niece; surely I can have a casual conversation with her.

"Tell you what....I'll ask you one question, okay?"...

"If you could live anywhere, in any house, where would you live?" I ask.

"Do you mean here in San Antonio?" Alexandra looks at the curb.

"Yes, but in any neighborhood or kind of house you can think of."

"Okay...," she pauses....

"Take your time," I reassure her, "this is not a test."

Her face relaxes. "Well..." she drawls. "I want a two-story house on a hill with a stable nearby where I can keep my horse. It must be a safe neighborhood, new, with green all around and lots of flowers. The backyard has a swing set and a pool. Behind the house is water and a boat." She is combining the fantasies of her father, mother, and even her aunt.

"Would it be gated?"

She hesitates. "Only if needed."

"How would you know?"

"If there were robbers."...

Walking slowly, Alex tagging behind, I think about what I have just learned. The children say they want more protection—higher walls and patrol cars. What are they afraid of? Robbers, Alex said. Why should she be so afraid of "robbers"? As far as I know her family has never been burglarized. Her friend's older brother is afraid that people can get into his house, while the younger one imagines someone climbing over the wall. Yet they live so far from other people, out on the suburban fringe. Are they repeating what they hear their parents say or is this some childhood fascination with guns and robbers?

Fear is a part of every child's life and varies over the course of a child's normal development and as a consequence of emotional vulnerability to perceived dangers. The content changes: a four-year-old may fear the dark, large animals, and imaginary creatures, while an eight-year-old's fears are a mix of ghosts and tigers and more realistic fears about bodily harm. Until recently it was thought that it was not until the teenage years that children begin to focus on societal violence and failure at school.

A study of San Antonio, Texas, schoolchildren between the ages of seven and nine, however, found that most of their fears were related to personal threats and injury, including societal danger such as street drugs, drive-by shootings, guns, gangs, and nuclear weapons. Girls reported more fears than boys did, and poorer children expressed more fears than middle-income children did. Clearly, the fears of children under ten in San Antonio resemble those of older children documented in earlier eras. In our increasingly violent society, young children may be prematurely encountering "an array of fears for which they may be neither cognitively nor emotionally prepared."...

Karen—Worrying About Surveillance and Safety...

Karen, a young-looking woman in her midthirties, greets me at the door [of her two story house in a gated community north of San Antonio] dressed in pink Bermuda shorts and matching silk golf shirt....She starts by talking about problems with their security company, complaining that they do not do a very good job. I ask if there is a block watch or other surveillance organization. "Just the security that patrols the golf course. They're supposed to come down here once an hour. [They] drive through, and monitor the gates with security cameras. I mean, it's limited, but

that's unfair to say: [at least] it's controlled-access entry." I ask her to be more specific about the kinds of dangers she imagines.

"[The kids] getting hit by a car [while] playing in the road. That's one of my biggest fears, because they're not into watching and being cautious. Since we live on a cul-de-sac and in a gated community, you falsely have the security that no one is going to hit you. Probably my biggest fear is that there is all this construction going on because the construction workers draw a lot of illegal aliens working out here. I guess, not to stereotype it, but it's like that's the way typically you see lots of burglaries going on. The house next to you is being built, and then you have a burglary at your house. And they can take something and watch when you come and go. During construction I would be very, very cautious."

She emphasizes how the gates restrict traffic and make it possible for children to ride their bicycles around the neighborhood at an early age. She lets her older child ride anywhere inside the community:

"But he always tells me, 'I'm going to ride my bike.' So that I know he's out there, and I can look for him. He really rarely goes off, and he won't go too far. Or he'll come and tell me, or he'll be with a group of kids doing it. I assume that my kid must have a real fear of a lot of things. One day, he says, 'You know, Mom, I wish our school made us go through one of those things like they have...'

'What are you talking about?' I ask him.

And he says, 'You know, he has to walk through and if he had a gun, then....'

I just says, 'Metal detector?' He says, 'Yeah.'...

Where is that [fear] coming from?

The thing that I see about the gates [is that] you're going to see very different kinds of gated communities. You're going to see this kind of gate, where it's controlled but it's very limited. If you want to come in here, you just sit there, and you wait, and when the gate opens you tailgate somebody. You know, we're told if somebody does that, get on the phone and call security, say somebody followed me in. But, you know, I don't think everybody does, all the time. I know it's happened to me, and I have not done it, even when I didn't know the person. Because there are so many workers, you've got people coming and going. And I guess the way I look at the security issue out here is those gates are not going to stop a burglar if he really wants to come in here. They're going to deter him, though. He's going to drive up and he's going to say, 'You know, I'm going to go across the street here because the houses are just as nice, you know, they all look just as nice. But it's not gated, and there are other ways to get out.'

Statistics show a burglar does not come down a dead-end road. They want two exits. Now, we've had a handful of burglaries out here…in two of the houses, but they were probably inside jobs. The kid had a party, the parents were gone, the party got totally out of control, [and] it turns out there was $2,000 in cash missing. Another house, the same sort of situation, where she's got teenage girls and a teenage son. They've got all kinds of people coming and going from their house with those kids.…[They] had some jewelry stolen. Not that you shouldn't take it seriously, but those kinds of things don't matter to me.… "

I find it interesting that Karen draws a distinction between burglaries within the community and her general concern about protecting her family from crime. It's as if a burglary by someone from within the neighborhood is not as dangerous or threatening as crime committed by outsiders. Sally Merry, an anthropologist who studies perceptions of danger, found that familiarity—familiarity with other residents and with the locations where crime usually occurred—reduced residents' sense of fear. In Karen's case, familiarity seems a reasonable explanation.

I ask her how she would characterize this community in comparison with other neighborhoods in San Antonio.

"It's not the real world out here, although that may not be true, because if you look around in all the new developments, 90 percent of them have gates.…More and more, all the new communities that are built are all pretty much gated. And it's almost as a form of competition.

I think it's [gating] one of those nice things.

I don't think people are so afraid. I think they have that same attitude that I originally had that crime doesn't really affect me. I think people have that sense of security, although it's probably false if you look at personal property crimes like we have here…[but] if you asked me tomorrow if I was going to move, it would be only to a gated community. I think that the safety is most important; I really like knowing who's coming and going…I love knowing my kids can get on their bicycles and ride around the block, and I don't have to wonder are they gonna come back home."…

Whether it is Mexicans, black salesmen, workers, or "ethnic changes," the message is the same: residents are using the walls, entry gates, and guards in an effort to keep perceived dangers outside of their homes, neighborhoods, and social world. Contact incites fear and concern, and in response they are moving to exclusive, private, residential developments where they can keep other people out with guards and gates. The walls are making visible the systems of exclusion that are already there; now the walls are constructed in concrete.…

Residents talk about their fear of the poor, the workers, the "Mexicans," and the "newcomers," as well as their retreat behind walls, where they think they will be safe. But there is fear even behind the walls. There are workers who enter the community every day, and residents must go out in order to buy groceries, shop, or see a movie. The gates provide some protection, but residents would like more. Even though the gates and guards exclude the feared "others" from living with them, "they" can slip by the gate, follow your car in, crawl over the wall, or, worse, the guard can fall asleep. Informal conversations about the screening of guards and how they are hired, as well as discussions about increasing the height and length of the protective walls as new threats appear, are frequent in the locker room of the health club, on the tennis court, and during strolls in the community in the evening.

The discourse of fear encompasses many social concerns, about class, race, and ethnic exclusivity and gender. It provides a verbal component that complements—and even reinforces—the visual landscape of fear created by the walls, gates, and guards....

Civic engagement and social connectedness...[have] declined over the last thirty years; Americans are now less trustful and more isolated. Gated communities are not the cause or even indirectly the result of these societal changes, but they amplify these tendencies, further reducing the possibilities of social interaction between people, and the symbiosis between city and suburb.

Gated communities—in California, as well as in San Antonio, and Long Island—participate in this transformation by redefining the meaning of "community" to include protective physical boundaries that determine who is inside and who is outside....

Gated community residents are interested in "community," but a specific kind of community that includes protecting children and keeping out crime and others while at the same time controlling the environment and the quality of services. The "community" they are searching for is one imagined from childhood or some idealized past. In a variety of ways, these residents are all searching for their version of the perfect community, one where there is no fear, no crime, no kidnapping, no "other" people, where there is a reassuringly consistent architectural and physical landscape, amenities and services that work, and great neighbors who want exactly the same things....

Architecture and the layout of towns and suburbs provide concrete, anchoring points of people's everyday life. These anchoring points reinforce our ideas about society at large. Gated communities and the social segregation and exclusion they materially represent make sense of and even rationalize problems Americans have with race, class,

and gender inequality and social discrimination. The gated community contributes to a geography of social relations that produces fear and anxiety simply by locating a person's home and place identity in a secured enclave, gated, guarded, and locked....

The reasons people give for their decision to move to a gated community vary widely, and the closer you get to the person and his or her individual psychology, the more complex the answer. At a societal level, people say they move because of their fear of crime and others. They move to secure a neighborhood that is stable and a home that will retain its resale value. They move in order to have control of their environment and of the environment of those who live nearby. Residents in rapidly growing areas want to live in a private community for the services. And retirees particularly want the low maintenance and lack of responsibility that come with living in a private condominium development.

At a personal level, though, residents are searching for the sense of security and safety that they associate with their childhood. When they talk about their concern with "others," they are splitting—socially and psychologically—the good and bad aspects of (and good and bad people in) American society. The gates are used symbolically to ward off many of life's unknowns, including unemployment, loss of loved ones, and downward mobility. Of course, gates cannot deliver all that is promised, but they are one attempt to resurrect aspects of the American dream that many people feel they have lost.

NOTES

1. David L. Kirp, John P. Dwyer, and Larry A. Rosenthal, *Our Town: Race, Housing, and the Soul of Suburbia* (New Brunswick, NJ: Rutgers University Press, 1997), 2.

CHAPTER 16

The Future of Suburbia

INTRODUCTION

Contemporary America is shaped by large-scale suburbanization. In every region of the nation, metropolitan areas seem to look more and more alike: miles of freeways, vast tracts of suburban housing, strip malls and big box stores, multiple "downtowns," and sprawling office parks. Not everyone agrees on how to best characterize this built landscape—"technoburb," "edge city," and "burbopolis," are just a few of the names coined to describe it; others just call it sprawl. Some claim we've reached a "postsuburban" era altogether, because what we see around us today no longer resembles the classic suburbs of years past—the Riversides, Llewellyn Parks, and Kenilworths, where homes dominated, nature imbued neighborhoods with a sense of peace and seclusion, and residents commuted to downtown jobs. As we have for at least a century, Americans continue to debate what "suburbs" are and more importantly what shape they should take.

In our own day, urban experts are grappling with the challenges posed by this pervasive landscape. Like the reformers and planners a century ago who envisioned a better, more livable city, today a renewed effort is underway to reimagine the metropolis, to reshape it into a place that best meets human and environmental needs. Ironically, one hundred years ago, reformers conceived of suburbanization as a *solution* to the problems of the modern industrial city. Today, many reformers see suburbanization as the *problem* that needs repair. Critics blame the sprawling form of contemporary suburbs for exacerbating segregation and social inequalities between older and newer parts of the metropolis, for destroying productive farmland and rural ways of life, for the loss of natural habitat, for air and water pollution, for high rates of death and injury on metropolitan highways, and for the waste of resources spent developing new neighborhoods and infrastructure while mature areas languish (a condition that analyst Myron Orfield calls, "growing against ourselves"). To many contemporary observers, suburbia has failed to provide a successful or sustainable living environment, although it continues to dominate how metro areas are developed and to attract numerous home seekers. Two key questions have emerged: how can we fix the problems of the suburban metropolis? And can we do so without jeopardizing the qualities that make current suburbs so popular?

Answers to these questions have varied enormously. Today's reformers are largely responding to the challenges posed by mass suburbanization and its evolution since World War II. Ironically, many draw inspiration from earlier suburban initiatives. The garden city movement, planned suburbs like Radburn, speculatively built streetcar suburbs, and the 1960s new town movement have all become models for contemporary reform.

Today, the impetus for reform comes from diverse quarters and offers multiple solutions. Some emphasize neighborhood design and planning, others politics and policy choices. Different approaches target different scales, from the local to the regional, state, and national levels. The reformers themselves represent a multitude of interests: professional planners, environmentalists, academics, mass-transit advocates, business leaders, farmers, suburban citizens, and politicians of various stripes—from proponents of regional government to antitax conservatives. On the most basic level, the common challenge has been to alleviate the problems caused by relentless, low-density development farther and farther into the periphery of metropolitan areas. Reform solutions focus on restraining or reshaping this sprawling growth through such means as better, more coordinated regional planning and tax sharing; revised state and federal subsidies for transportation, housing, and infrastructure; higher density, mixed-use development; preservation of open space for agriculture, parks, and native habitat; projects to "fill in" the empty and underutilized spaces within current metropolitan limits; and political measures to slow peripheral development. Several states and metropolitan areas have become leaders in this movement. In 1973, Oregon passed a statewide land use act that established growth boundaries for metropolitan areas, such as Portland. Maryland's 1997 Smart Growth Act placed limitations on state infrastructure spending outside established population areas, and in the Minneapolis–St. Paul area, the state established a strong metropolitan planning body in 1994 to coordinate infrastructure and land use development throughout the region. In other states, such as Utah, Ohio, New Jersey, and Pennsylvania, antisprawl initiatives passed or were under consideration.

As these examples suggest, many experts embrace "regionalism" as a means for tackling the problems of suburban sprawl. As earlier chapters show, suburbanization historically has had a fragmenting effect on politics and fiscal resources. In the view of critics, political atomization has paralyzed problem solving efforts, because when small, politically independent suburbs wield the power of local control, they too often act in the narrow interests of their constituents alone while avoiding a wider metropolitan perspective. Urban analysts such as David Rusk, Myron Orfield, Peter Calthorpe, William Fulton, and Eric Oliver all emphasize the importance of a regional framework for metropolitan problem solving—from issues of design and planning to resource allocation and even civic engagement.[1] They emphasize the interconnectedness of *all* metropolitan problems—from the fiscal strains on fast-growing outer suburbs to the disinvestment of inner cities and suburbs. Their solutions propose a coordinated effort at the regional level to confront these issues simultaneously.

This chapter offers a range of perspectives on these questions. The first cluster of readings includes descriptions of recent suburban growth, commonly labeled "sprawl." The second cluster surveys some of the solutions that reformers have proposed. The final cluster offers differing perspectives on social and political life in a suburbanizing America. As might be expected, consensus is elusive. Americans offer a multitude of opinions and visions about the future of suburbia—how it should be fixed, or whether it needs fixing at all. The examples here only scratch the surface of a rich, deep, and prolific debate, which we encourage readers to explore further on their own. This is a debate that impacts us all, as it will define the way we build our cities, suburbs, and communities today and well into the future.

DOCUMENTS

The first five documents name and describe the contemporary metropolitan landscape. One phrase that has entered the popular lexicon is "edge city," which refers to the constellation of outlying economic centers that now spread across most metropolitan areas. *Washington Post* reporter Joel Garreau, who coined the term, describes the characteristics of edge cities in **Document 16-1**. Using a functional—rather than social or cultural—definition of edge cities, Garreau points to their importance as places that now eclipse the traditional, singular downtown. The difference is that not only are edge cities proliferating, but they are decidedly "suburban" in character. While Garreau claims that this is a new phenomenon, in fact it follows the pattern of diverse deconcentration evident since the late nineteenth century. In **Document 16-2**, journalist James Howard Kunstler issues a biting indictment of suburban sprawl. In this 1994 speech, he summarizes many of the themes in his book, *The Geography of Nowhere* (1993), which reignited a popular, critical dialogue about the shape of "our everyday environment." While Kunstler's critique focuses mainly on the design failures of suburban areas, in **Document 16-3** historian Dolores Hayden condemns suburban sprawl for the deep inequality it produces. For Hayden, the victims of suburban sprawl are not the people who live in these new environments, but the residents of older, declining urban areas who are robbed of the resources diverted to new suburbs. **Document 16-4** presents a tongue-in-cheek proposal by Euclid, Ohio, Mayor Paul Oyaski to combat sprawl: post "Sprawl Warnings" on buildings guilty of promoting the trend. Though humorous in tone, Oyaski's missive articulates several common critiques of suburban sprawl, and it indicates growing concern in many inner-ring suburbs with the consequences of continued decentralization. **Document 16-5** presents images of recent development on the northern edges of suburban Denver, where high plains range land is fast giving way to suburbia and where battles over growth have loomed for years. These aerial views illustrate such classic sprawl patterns as: highway-oriented big box developments; "greenfield" subdivisions, where new development occurs on previously rural land in the absence of existing services or public facilities; the construction of transportation lines into undeveloped areas; and the emergence of suburban "edge cities" anchored by regional shopping malls.

The next five documents survey how some urbanists today are devising plans to address these many issues. **Document 16-6** captures a range of perspectives on the question of sprawl—and how the public might begin thinking about solutions. It comes from a roundtable discussion on suburban sprawl held in 1996, with participants that included academics, environmental activists, and politicians, among others. In **Document 16-7** lawyer and legislator Myron Orfield prescribes a comprehensive set of regional reforms based on initiatives enacted in the Minneapolis-St. Paul metropolitan area during the 1990s, while he was a member of the Minnesota State Legislature. Drawing on his analysis of shared interests among a diverse set of American suburbs (outlined in his essay in chapter 14), Orfield pushes for greater regional tax sharing, coordinated planning of housing and infrastructure, and strengthened institutions of regional governance, in an effort to reduce incentives for sprawl that exist in the current fragmented structure of metropolitan governance. In a nod to the realities of the political process, Orfield appeals to bipartisan concerns—such as conservative attention to fiscal efficiency and liberal concerns about equity and environmental health—and he proposes a new coalition of city and suburban voters based on shared interests. **Document 16-8** and **Document 16-9** highlight The New Urbanism, a movement of planners, designers, and architects begun in the 1980s. Miami-based architects Andres Duany and Elizabeth Plater-Zyberk helped launch the Congress for the New Urbanism in 1994, whose charter is presented in **Document 16-8**. It sets out the core principles of New Urbanism, which begins with a critique of sprawl as a wasteful, socially detrimental urban form, and calls for small-scale, mixed-used, high density, and pedestrian friendly development, with plenty of public space—all in an effort to reconnect work, homes, and leisure in more compact communities. Hundreds of self-styled New Urbanist projects have been launched in the past decade, from small scale urban and suburban infill projects and downtown redesigns to whole new towns like Seaside, Florida and Kentlands, Maryland. **Document 16-9** presents images from Kentlands, a suburb of Washington, D.C., designed by the firm of Duany, Plater-Zyberk, and Co.

In **Document 16-10**, urban scholar Robert Bruegmann offers a provocative critique of contemporary antisprawl reform, which he characterizes as a movement dominated by experts and devoid of ordinary citizens. Imploring readers to take a broad historical perspective on the current debate, Bruegmann charges that the latest rash of antisprawl criticism and reform suffers from vagueness, class bias, faulty evidence, and, ultimately, irrelevance.

For years, commentators have debated the impact of suburbanization on political and social life—some seeing an invigorating effect and others blaming suburban privatism for eroding community and civic life. In **Document 16-11**, social scientist Robert Putnam implicates sprawl in the decline of community life over the past several decades. In this excerpt from his book *Bowling Alone*, he outlines the ways that suburban life impedes civic and social engagement, particularly in robbing commuters of time for community participation. While Putnam, along with writers like Eric Oliver, emphasizes suburbia's erosion of civic and social participation, another body of literature explores the ways that suburbanites *are* forging community by deploying new technologies such as the Internet.[2] Readers might wish to explore these works on their own to compare arguments.

In the final excerpt—**Document 16-12**—journalist Charles McGrath offers a poignant coda to the suburban dream. This essay eloquently describes one man's gradual, begrudging acceptance of the suburban way of life, capturing well the continuing allure of this landscape for millions of Americans and offering a powerful counterpoint to critics who insist that suburbs need an overhaul.

Do you agree that today's metropolitan areas need fixing? What aspects work, and which don't? Do the solutions proposed here seem effective and realistic to you? What are their strengths or limitations? Do you believe that most metropolitan citizens would support such reforms? Why or why not? Do you agree that social and civic life are harmed by suburbanization? How does suburbanization promote or impede community life? What might be done to improve it?

16-1. JOURNALIST JOEL GARREAU NAMES AND DEFINES THE EDGE CITY, 1991

Source: *Edge City* by Joel Garreau, copyright © 1991 by Joel Garreau. Used by permission of Doubleday, a division of Random House, Inc.

Americans are creating the biggest change in a hundred years in how we build cities. Every single American city that *is* growing, is growing in the fashion of Los Angeles, with multiple urban cores.

These new hearths of our civilization—in which the majority of metropolitan Americans now work and around which we live—look not at all like our old downtowns. Buildings rarely rise shoulder to shoulder, as in Chicago's Loop. Instead, their broad, low outlines dot the landscape like mushrooms, separated by greensward and parking lots. Their office towers, frequently guarded by trees, gaze at one another from respectful distances through bands of glass that mirror the sun in blue or silver or green or gold, like antique drawings of "the city of the future."

The hallmarks of these new urban centers are not the sidewalks of New York of song and fable, for usually there are few sidewalks. There are jogging trails around the hills and ponds of their characteristic corporate campuses. But if an American finds himself tripping the light fantastic today on concrete, social scientists know where to look for him. He will be amid the crabapples blossoming under glassed-in skies where America retails its wares....[M]alls usually function as the village squares of these new urbs.

Our new city centers are tied together not by locomotives and subways, but by jet-ways, freeways, and rooftop satellite dishes thirty feet across. Their characteristic monument is not a horse-mounted hero, but the atria reaching for the sun and shielding trees perpetually in leaf at the cores of corporate headquarters, fitness centers, and shopping plazas. These new urban areas are marked not by the penthouses of the old urban rich or the tenements of the old urban poor. Instead, their landmark structure is the celebrated single-family detached dwelling, the suburban home with grass all around that made America the best-housed civilization the world has ever known.

I have come to call these new urban centers Edge Cities. Cities, because they contain all the functions a city ever has, albeit in a spread-out form that few have come to recognize for what it is. Edge, because they are a vigorous world of pioneers and immigrants, rising far from the old downtowns, where little save villages or farmland lay only thirty years before.

Edge Cities represent the third wave of our lives pushing into new frontiers in this half century. First, we moved our homes out past the traditional idea of what constituted a city. This was the suburbanization of America, especially after World War II.

Then we wearied of returning downtown for the necessities of life, so we moved our marketplaces out to where we lived. This was the malling of America, especially in the 1960s and 1970s.

Today, we have moved our means of creating wealth, the essence of urbanism—our jobs—out to where most of us have lived and shopped for two generations. That has led to the rise of Edge City....

Good examples of our more than two hundred new Edge Cities are:

- The area around Route 128 and the Massachusetts Turnpike in the Boston region that was the birthplace of applied high technology;
- The Schaumburg area west of O'Hare Airport, near which Sears moved its corporate headquarters from the 110-story Sears Tower in downtown Chicago;
- The Perimeter Center area, at the northern tip of Atlanta's Beltway, that is larger than downtown Atlanta;
- Irvine, in Orange County, south of Los Angeles.

By any functional urban standard—tall buildings, bright lights, office space that represents white-collar jobs, shopping, entertainment, prestigious hotels, corporate headquarters, hospitals with CAT scans, even population—each Edge City is larger than downtown Portland, Oregon, or Portland, Maine, or Tampa, or Tucson. Already, two thirds of all American office facilities are in Edge Cities, and 80 percent of them have materialized in only the last two decades. By the mid-1980s, there was far more office space in Edge Cities around America's largest metropolis, New York, than there was at its heart—midtown Manhattan. Even before Wall Street faltered in the late 1980s there was less office space there, in New York's downtown, than there was in the Edge Cities of New Jersey alone.

Even the old-fashioned Ozzie and Harriet commute from a conventional suburb to downtown is now very much a minority pattern....Most of the trips metropolitan Americans take in a day completely skirt the old centers. Their journeys to work, especially, are to Edge Cities. So much of our shopping is done in Edge Cities that a casual glance at most Yellow Pages shows it increasingly difficult in an old downtown to buy such a commodity item as a television set.

These new urban agglomerations are such mavericks that everyone who wrestles them to the ground tries to brand them. Their list of titles by now has become marvelous, rich, diverse, and sometimes unpronounceable. The litany includes: urban villages, technoburbs, suburban downtowns, suburban activity centers, major diversified centers, urban cores, galactic city, pepperoni-pizza cities, a city of realms, superburbia, disurb, service cities, perimeter cities, and even peripheral centers. Sometimes it is not clear that everybody is talking about the same thing. My heart particularly goes out to the San Francisco reporter who just started calling whatever was seething out there, past the sidewalks, Tomorrowland....

That is why I have adopted the following five-part definition of Edge City that is above all else meant to be functional.

Edge City is any place that:

- *Has five million square feet or more of leasable office space—the workplace of the Information Age.* Five million square feet is more than downtown Memphis. The Edge City called the Galleria area west of downtown Houston—crowned by the sixty-four-story Transco Tower, the tallest building in the world outside an old downtown—is bigger than downtown Minneapolis.
- *Has 600,000 square feet or more of leasable retail space.* That is the equivalent of a fair-sized mall. That mall, remember, probably has at least three nationally famous department stores, and eighty to a hundred shops and boutiques full of merchandise that used to be available only on the finest boulevards of Europe. Even in their heyday, there were not many downtowns with that boast.
- *Has more jobs than bedrooms.* When the workday starts, people head toward this place, not away from it. Like all urban places, the population increases at 9 a.m.
- *Is perceived by the population as one place.* It is a regional end destination for mixed use—not a starting point—that "has it all," from jobs, to shopping, to entertainment.
- *Was nothing like "city" as recently as thirty years ago.* Then, it was just bedrooms, if not cow pastures. This incarnation is brand new.

An example of the authentic, California-like experience of encountering such an Edge City is peeling off a highway thruway, like the Pennsylvania Turnpike, onto an arterial, like 202 at King of Prussia, northwest of downtown Philadelphia. Descending into

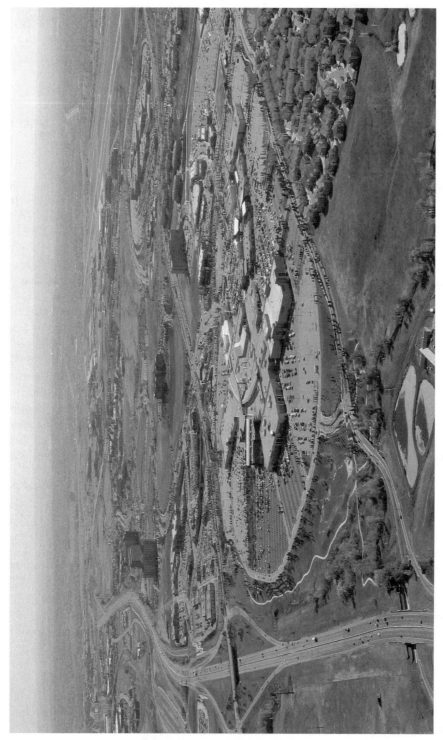

Figure 16-1 Flatirons Mall and US36 in Broomfield, Colorado, north of Denver, 2005. Sprawling shopping plazas and office complexes tied to ribbons of highway characterize the new landscape of America's "Edge Cities." Photograph by Andrew Wiese.

traffic that is bumper to bumper in both directions, one swirls through mosaics of lawn and parking, punctuated by office slabs whose designers have taken the curious vow of never placing windows in anything other than horizontal reflective strips. Detours mark the yellow dust of heavy construction that seems a permanent feature of the landscape....

Edge City is the crucible of America's urban future. Having become the place in which the majority of Americans now live, learn, work, shop, play, pray, and die, Edge City will be the forge of the fabled American way of life well into the twenty-first century.

There are those who find this idea appalling. For some who recognize the future when they see it, but always rather hoped it might look like Paris in the 1920s, the sprawl and apparent chaos of Edge City makes it seem a wild, raw, and alien place. For my sins I once spent a fair chunk of a Christmas season in Tysons Corner, Virginia, stopping people as they hurried about their holiday tasks, asking them what they thought of their brave new world. The words I recorded were searing. They described the area as plastic, a hodgepodge, Disneyland (used as a pejorative), and sterile. They said it lacked livability, civilization, community, neighborhood, and even a soul.

These responses are frightening, if Edge City is the laboratory of how civilized and livable urban American will be well into the next century. Right now, it is vertigo-inducing. It may have all the complexity, diversity, and size of a downtown. But it can cover dozens of square miles, and juxtapose schools and freeways and atria and shimmering parking lots with corporate lawns and Day-Glo-orange helicopter wind socks. Its logic takes a while to decode.

Will we ever be proud of this place? Will we ever drag our visiting relatives out to show off our Edge City, our shining city on the hill? Will we ever feel—for this generation and the ones that follow—that it's a good place to be young? To be old? To fall in love? To have a Fourth of July parade? Will it ever be the place we want to call home?

16-2. JAMES HOWARD KUNSTLER CONDEMNS SUBURBAN SPRAWL, 1994

Source: James Howard Kunstler, "A Crisis in Landscape and Townscape," in *Moving to Corn Fields: A Reader on Urban Sprawl and the Regional Future of Northeast Ohio*, ed. David Beach (Cleveland: EcoCity Cleveland, 1996).

Walt Disney had America's number. Walt Disney was so optimistic about the way things were going in postwar America that his attitudes about the past and the future were equally sentimental. It was possible for him to believe that an organization like his own, operating freely in a free country, could only bring wonderful benefits to a free people. So, the underlying message of Disney's Main Street USA was that a big corporation could make a better Main Street than a bunch of rubes in a real small town. And Walt was right!

Through the postwar decades, Americans happily allowed their towns to be dismantled and destroyed. They'd flock to Disneyland and walk down Main Street and think, gee, it feels good here. Then they'd go back home and tear down half the old buildings downtown, so they could have more parking lots, and they'd throw a parade to celebrate the new K-Mart opening—even when it put ten local merchants out of business—and they'd turn Elm Street into a six-lane expressway, and outlaw corner grocery stores in the residential neighborhoods because they caused "traffic problems," and they'd build all the new schools three miles out of town so the kids couldn't walk or bike there—they'd do every fool thing possible to destroy good existing relationships between things in their towns, and put their local economies at the mercy of distant corporations whose officers didn't care whether these towns lived or died. And then, when vacation time rolled around, they'd flock to Disneyland to feel good about America.

I just wrote a book called *The Geography of Nowhere*, about the mess we have made out of our everyday environment here in America. The public discussion of this issue has been nearly nonexistent. We apparently don't understand, for instance, that there's a connection between our economic predicament and the physical arrangement of life in this country. Yet I believe when you scratch just below the surface, Americans keenly sense that something is wrong with the places where we live and work and go about our daily business. We hear this unhappiness expressed in phrases like "the loss of community" or "no sense of place."

We drive up and down the gruesome tragic suburban boulevards of commerce, and we wince at the fantastic, awesome, overwhelming, stupefying ugliness of absolutely everything in sight—the fry pits, the Big Box stores, the office units, the lube-joints, the carpet warehouses, the parking lagoons, the jive-plastic townhouse clusters, the uproar of signs, the highway itself clogged with cars—as though the whole thing had been designed by some diabolical force bent on making human beings miserable. And naturally, this experience can make you feel kind of glum about the nature and *future* of our civilization.

Some—though certainly not all—of these terrible things were designed by architects, and many of the other common features of our everyday environments were designed by their brethren in related design fields like landscaping and traffic engineering, and administered by creatures called planners. What's out there is not out there by accident. We created Nowhere by a definite set of rules, and if we're going to fix this mess, and take ourselves from nowhere to someplace, we'll have to reexamine and change these rules.

So, we drive around and look at all this cartoon architecture and other junk we've scattered across the landscape and our response is, in some form or other, "YUK." I believe that the ugliness we see is the mere surface expression of a whole range of deeper problems; problems that go to the issue of our national character. The highway strip is not just a sequence of eyesores. The pattern it represents is also economically catastrophic, environmentally calamitous, socially devastating, and spiritually degrading. And all this is what we sense when we look at it and go "YUK."

We built a nation of scary places and became a nation of scary people.

In our manner of building since the end of World War II, we have managed to fill our land with things that are unworthy of our affection, and these add up to thousands of places that are not worth caring about. In the process of filling our landscape with these loveless and unlovable structures, we have thrown our civic life into the garbage can. And as a final consequence of all this, we are putting ourselves out of business as a civilization.

16-3. HISTORIAN DOLORES HAYDEN CONSIDERS, "WHAT IS SPRAWL?" 2004

Source: Dolores Hayden, "What is Sprawl?" *Hartford Courant*, July 1, 2004.

Visualize six shopping centers, an office park, and two subdivisions next to a roaring six-lane interstate highway. You could be in any of the eight counties of Connecticut, where cell towers pierce smoggy air, logo buildings advertise fast food or gas, and big box stores draw customers who navigate parking lots the size of ten football fields. There are no sidewalks. Along the roadsides, billboards tout vacations in unspoiled places. These cheap, disposable, automobile-dependent development patterns are often termed "sprawl." Sprawl is a verb, transitive, "to cause to spread out carelessly or awkwardly." Sprawl in the built environment means excessive growth expressed as careless, awkward, unsustainable use of land.

Sprawl is promoted by political alliances of developers and government officials who believe in constant construction as a source of profits and prosperity. Alliances of boosters who thrive on new building have been called "growth machines" by sociologist Harvey Molotch. Many have roots in the post-World War II era, when the federal government, lobbied by real estate and automobile interests, began to provide direct and indirect financial subsidies for builders of residential tracts, interstate highways, and greenfield commercial projects such as shopping malls. Growth machines created landscapes at a scale more suitable for automobiles and trucks than humans, places characterized by wide highways, endless automotive strips, large areas of single-use development (such as shopping malls or vast residential subdivisions), and little public space. If the sprawling environments of the 1950s were shocking, many Americans excused them as responses to pent-up consumer demand from the 1930s and 1940s. Today there is a more sustained critique of wasteful, careless building.

While many Americans despise about the visual blight of sprawl, fewer of us realize that across the country, the economic process of sprawl affects older urban neighborhoods and people of color most severely. The physical products of sprawl are most obvious to the eye at the fringes of urban regions where new construction is common. Older downtowns also show the consequences of sprawl because in an economy organized around new construction, existing places are often left to fall apart. For this reason, sprawl has been defined by Gregory Squires of The Urban Institute as "exclusionary new development on the fringe of settled areas often surrounding a deteriorating city." Think of Hartford, Bridgeport, or New Haven. Inner city populations are shrinking, schools are closing, services are being cut back, housing is shabby, jobs are disappearing. Then think of affluent places in those same counties, suburbs that are building new schools, planning services, creating housing, and adding jobs.

In most American metropolitan areas today, there are many reasons why residents of older, declining areas are excluded from easy access to the good schools, services, housing, and jobs in newer areas. Historically, the federal government did not insure loans to developers of 1950s suburban subdivisions unless the residents were white. And while men could get mortgages, women could not. Today, there are laws about fair lending, but we still have not seen fair growth. Some of Connecticut's locational problems are political—"residents only" requirements for schools or services. Some problems are economic—housing costs many be inflated by large-lot zoning or compounded by commuting costs. And frequently there is no public transit to reach a job in a new office building or a new mall located at a highway exit ramp. The physical distance between deteriorating older urban fabric and affluent, private new growth creates one more barrier. Sprawl intensifies the existing, intersecting difficulties of class, race, and gender by adding spatial separation.

Throwing away older neighborhoods while constructing new ones is an expensive practice that taxpayers in the United States cannot afford. In the 1950s, economic growth was based on mass-consumption of houses, automobiles, and manufactured goods designed for rapid turnover. General Motors' Harley Earl promoted exaggerated tail fins because he wanted Americans to reject last year's models and demand a new car every year. He called his appeal to acquisitiveness and status-seeking "dynamic obsolescence." Half a century later, obsolescence has become a stupid routine. Old cars fill junkyards as new cars sit in gridlock. Old neighborhoods decline as new ones echo with the sounds of hammers. But what about the residents?

In older metropolitan areas, taxpayers endure boarded-up Main Streets, broken sidewalks, poorly maintained public schools and playgrounds, declining public transit, aging energy infrastructure, and dead malls. Meanwhile public subsidies for roads and infrastructure are directed to newer developments in more affluent areas. Most Americans hate sprawl as a product in the form of scattered, cheap, new buildings. But we should criticize sprawl as a national process of discarding older neighborhoods and even entire cities as obsolete. The political and economic consequences of sprawl as a process are even more appalling than the aesthetic failures of sprawl as a product.

16-4. INNER-SUBURB MAYOR PROPOSES "SPRAWL WARNING," 2003

Source: Paul Oyaski, "Warning: Sprawl is Hazardous to Your Health." Copyright © EcoCity Cleveland, 2002. Reprinted from Smart Growth Section of www.ecocitycleveland.org.

If something as trifling as hot coffee carries a warning, why not something as significant as urban sprawl? The following tongue-in-cheek suggestion comes from Euclid [Ohio] Mayor Paul Oyaski—a proposed warning notice to be displayed on sprawl-causing structures.
WARNING: The new house you have purchased on this site (or the new business you

are visiting on this site) has been found and determined to cause urban sprawl, a deleterious regional affliction with some if not all of the following symptoms.

- Disinvestment and loss of property values in older neighborhoods nearby, probably where your parents or grandparents used to live.
- Damage to soil and water resources brought about by building on virgin land or in forested areas in rural watersheds.
- An increase in air pollution brought about by the increased use of automobiles occasioned by this previously remote and undeveloped location.
- The overbuilding of expensive infrastructure so that this property can be reached and serviced, thereby placing this region and this state at a competitive disadvantage by necessitating more taxes to be raised so that more infrastructure can be maintained at a time when the population of this region is decreasing.
- Unjust enrichment to you, the builder and the developer of this site due to the fact that its development and the infrastructure and utilities that serve it were subsidized in large part by the residents of older neighborhoods.

IMPORTANT NOTE: Commuting long distances in gasoline-powered autos has been shown to shorten life expectancy, as well as being wasteful and boring!

It is expected that very soon the development you are currently visiting will, due to the detrimental environment, economic and social consequences it entails, be declared a public nuisance, and there will be Hell to pay to the future resident of the great State of Ohio.

16-5. PHOTO GALLERY: RECENT SUBURBAN DEVELOPMENT, DENVER, COLORADO

Figure 16-2 Aerial view of New Cloverleaf and Shopping Plaza, I-25 corridor north of Denver, 2005. To afford the costly infrastructure underlying suburban housing, many municipalities compete for big box retail stores and the high tax revenues they generate. Their location here (top center) is a clear indication of development on its way. Photograph by Andrew Wiese.

Figure 16-3 Aerial view of subdivision and farms, I-25 corridor north of Denver, 2005. Construction on "green-field" sites is cheaper for developers and often welcomed by rural municipalities, but inadequate planning frequently leads to ill-matched neighbors, such as these orderly housing tracts and large-scale livestock containments. Photograph by Andrew Wiese.

Figure 16-4 New housing in Lafayette, Colorado, near Denver, 2004. Decried by critics as a "placeless" or "disposable" landscape, for many residents, new suburban developments provided a functional and attractive place to live—especially while open spaces remained between them. Photograph by Andrew Wiese.

Figure 16-5 Suburbia under construction, Lafayette, Colorado 2004. The once largely rural counties north of Denver gained more than 100,000 people during the 1990s, facilitated by the subdivision and development of ranch and farm properties. Photograph by Andrew Wiese.

16-6. URBAN EXPERTS DISCUSS THE FUTURE OF SPRAWL, 1996

Source: "Solutions: Under Development," *Amicus Journal* 18 (Fall 1996), 21. Copyright © 1996 by The Amicus Journal. First published in The Amicus Journal. Reprinted by permission.

On May 20, shortly before the nations of the world met in Istanbul for the UN "Habitat II" conference on the future of human living conditions, NRDC [National Resources Defense Council] and the Urban Assembly held a forum on the future of American cities....

Below, *Amicus* offers excerpts from the panelists' remarks, which ranged widely over the causes of and possible solutions to suburban sprawl.

Robert Bullard, Professor of Sociology and Director of the Environmental Justice Center, Clark Atlanta University:

One of the consequences of sprawl is a pattern of residential apartheid, particularly in major urban centers: racial segregation and institutionalized housing discrimination; redlining by banks, other lending institutions, insurance companies; segmentation of schools; and public dollars such as transportation dollars, actually subsidizing this segmentation, this differentiation.

Atlanta is a classic example. MARTA, the modern rail system, stops at the county lines and doesn't go into suburbs that are rapidly growing. And that didn't just happen. It was planned that way. In the mid-1960s, a couple of counties basically said they didn't want public transit coming into their area because it would bring black people.

Jim Crow is alive in many Southern towns and cities. It's hard to dismantle that type of system. But whether it's by choice or whether, as for some people, it's a forced choice, the point where justice, fairness, and equality enter in is the point at which public dollars are subsidizing it.

Harriet Tregoning, Director, Urban and Economic Development Division, U.S. Environmental Protection Agency:

There are many national tax policies that promote sprawl. But local governments also subsidize development in some significant ways. Most communities have a master plan for development that they could choose to improve at almost any time. Instead, many promote sprawl. Typically, a developer attains a permit to develop land—not a building permit that grants the right to develop. That right, in most places, never expires. And it immediately creates tremendous value for the land. The developer can then turn around and finance other projects by taking out loans based on the market value of land that's now developable.

Local governments could be taxing at that market rate. Instead, they generally tax at the value of the current use—which is agricultural or something taxed even less. This amounts to a massive property tax abatement to attract developers.

Robert Yaro, Executive Director, New York City Regional Plan Association:

We've done quality-of-life polls for two years now that show that residents of the suburbs in the New York City region tend to be more satisfied with the quality of their communities, their transportation options, and so forth, than do urban residents. I think you'd find the same thing across the country. What's frustrating is that conferences like this one were held thirty years ago, with people like us—urban intellectuals, early environmentalists—saying, "We've got to put a stop to this." And nothing happened. Because, fundamentally, we have not bothered to understand what it is that motivates people to make these choices, to live and work in the suburbs.

There is no question that we have chosen, as a nation, to subsidize those choices—but that's because there is a suburban majority that is calling the shots in this country. We have to be prepared, first, to understand what motivates them, and second, to produce alternatives that fit their needs, or what they perceive to be their needs. That means building communities and transportation alternatives that provide them with a level of service, amenities, and a range of choices that respect their interests. And I would argue—I think everyone would argue—that they do not have those choices right now....

Carl Anthony, President, Earth Island Institute:

A number of people are working on very promising innovations. In the Minneapolis region, for instance, Myron Orfield is working on a tax-sharing concept. The basic idea is that as development spreads outwards, the inner-ring suburbs are beginning to face many of the same issues that people in the inner city have faced. They're looking at the problem of not having a tax base large enough to support basic services. So Myron and his colleagues have been documenting the costs of our tax structure on these inner-ring suburbs, and developing a tax strategy that would actually put them on the side of the urban poor. This would allow us to move forward with a coalition among the inner city, blue-collar suburbs, and environmentalists.

But there is a larger context here. As a civilization, we have to make a decision about whether people ought to have the right to be racist. People have been leaving the inner city because they do not want to be in neighborhoods with black people. As we move to the twenty-first century, we need to face up to the fact that this oversimplified view of community life is driving us into a corner. The question is: Do people have the right to choose to be racist, and then to dominate the political life of the nation because they have built their lives around that choice? ...

Nancy Connery, Community Development Consultant:

We are going to see a rise in the cost of gasoline, because the world market has exploded. People are driving cars now in places where they were never expected to be. And market forces are going to make us pay. It's in the U.S. interest to begin raising the price of gasoline now. If we continue to develop as we do now, we're going to be in an increasingly vulnerable position in global political terms.

And the rising cost of gasoline will change the development equation. Banks will begin looking at access to transit, because the ability to drive will depend on income. The environmental and social costs of auto-centered development are very great, but ultimately, they won't be the compelling argument for the middle class, who are out there in the suburbs with 3.2 cars. When the middle class sees their financial vulnerability, that will be what shakes their confidence.

16-7. MYRON ORFIELD PROPOSES A REGIONAL APPROACH TO METROPOLITAN PROBLEMS, 2003

Source: Myron Orfield, *American Metropolitics: The New Suburban Reality* (Washington, D.C.: Brookings Institution Press, 2002). Excerpt taken from Summary Edition (Minneapolis: Ameregis Corporation, Metropolitan Area Research Corporation, 2003).

The many challenges facing America's metropolitan areas can be attacked effectively only through a coordinated, regional approach. Concentrated poverty and community disinvestments, among the most important of the countless factors feeding metropolitan sprawl, are related to incentives built into public policies for metropolitan development. These incentives include tax policies that promote wasteful competition among local governments, transportation and infrastructure investment patterns that subsidize sprawling development, and fragmented governance that makes thoughtful and efficient land-use planning more difficult.

Fortunately, the foundations for positive change are, to a large extent, already in place....

Tax Reform

Under the fiscal system that currently holds sway in most regions of the country, local governments have strong incentives to adopt policies and regulations designed to serve their own short-term economic interest at the expense of their own long-term health and the well-being of the region as a whole.

One way that local governments do this is through "fiscal zoning," a deliberate attempt by a government to reap fiscal dividends from new development by limiting the types of land uses within its jurisdiction. Because property taxes are the most significant form of revenue for most local governments, they have a direct incentive to tailor their land-use regulations to encourage development of high-value commercial, industrial, and residential properties that generate relatively little in public costs, and to discourage development of lower-value properties such as affordable housing that create a need for higher public expenditures. When played out over an entire metropolitan area, this fiscal zoning process can significantly influence where people can afford to live, the types and quality of public services they receive from their local government, and the presence or absence of employment opportunities near their homes.

Another aspect of local governments' short-sighted pursuit of positive fiscal dividends is the wasteful and biased competition for desirable commercial and industrial properties....

Fiscal zoning and tax-base competition tend to concentrate families and individuals with the greatest need for public services in communities that are the least able to generate the revenue to provide those services. Conversely, those who can afford to live where they choose (and therefore are less in need of public services) are increasingly concentrated in communities that have managed to successfully attract the development of large, expensive homes and other revenue-generating land uses. The result is a widening gap between communities with low tax capacities and high costs, on the one hand, and those with high tax capacities and low costs on the other.

The arguments for tax reform are primarily efficiency arguments. Attenuating the link between growth in particular types of local land uses and the tax base available to produce local services reduces wasteful competition. Providing financial incentives for particular types of development that provide regional benefits but do not generate local fiscal dividends can improve the functioning of regional housing and labor markets.

An essential part of creating a stable, cooperative region is to gradually equalize the resources of local governments with land-use planning powers. In addition to improving equity, which will allow central cities, at-risk suburbs, and many bedroom-developing suburbs to lower taxes and improve services, it

will reduce the competition between places, give communities real fiscal incentives to cooperate, and make regional land-use planning easier to achieve....

Tax-base sharing, an alternative way to reduce tax-base inequities, has several advantages over the patchwork quilt of aid programs common to most states. Unlike separate programs that distribute state revenues to counties, cities, townships, and special districts, tax-base sharing simply redistributes the common base from which each local jurisdiction derives its revenues. It also helps to equalize the resources available to local governments without removing local control over tax rates....

Land-Use Reform

Individual communities can do little to deal with the underlying regional forces contributing to sprawling development patterns. While local development moratoriums, slowdowns, or other local restrictions may seem like a good strategy for reducing the negative impacts of increased development, ultimately they only throw development farther out to surrounding communities eager to attract additional development to add to their tax base and help them keep up with the costs of their residential growth. In many cases, these surrounding communities are at-risk low-density and bedroom-developing communities trying to keep up with their growing costs.

A number of states have tried to tackle the difficulties associated with purely local land-use planning through some form of statewide planning. At present, 16 states have a land-use planning system in place; 10 of these states actually require comprehensive local planning, while the other 6 encourage it. Oregon led the way with the passage of its Land Use Act in 1973. This landmark legislation requires each of the state's cities and counties to adopt a long-range, comprehensive plan for development consistent with the state's specified planning goals.

Another popular strategy employed by states to combat sprawling development has been to authorize and encourage the use of various "smart growth" tools. Common growth-management tools include the urban growth boundary, which prevents or limits development outside a designated area; the urban service area, which limits provision of public services such as sewerage and water to a designated area; designated areas where growth will be focused; and concurrency, which requires adequate public infrastructure to be in place before or at the same time as development occurs. These can be effective tools. Misused or used in isolation without complementary policies in the non-developing portions of regions, however, they can contribute to low-density, dispersed development instead of preventing it.

Smart-growth planning also attempts to protect agricultural lands and open space from development, maintaining the amenity value of such areas and preserving them for future generations....These land-preservation tools, though well-intentioned, are extremely costly and cannot on their own truly change the nature of U.S. development patterns.

Effective regional land-use reform hinges on three elements: coordinated infrastructure planning, a regional housing plan, and regional review and coordination of local planning.

Coordinated Infrastructure Planning. Piecemeal provision of the basic infrastructure that guides regional investment and development patterns is a major contributor to inefficient, sprawling development, congested roadways, and environmental strains. Regionalizing infrastructure provision and planning helps guide development in more efficient and equitable ways. It can, for instance, help reduce per capita costs throughout the region by creating an orderly pattern of development....

Regional Housing Plan. A regional strategy to reduce zoning, financial, and other barriers to the development of affordable housing is the logical first step toward the goal of mixed-income housing in every community within a region....Fair-share requirements ensure that all places contribute to the regionwide supply of affordable housing. These programs allocate to each city a part of the region's affordable housing, on the basis of the jurisdiction's population, previous efforts to create affordable housing, and job availability. An effective fair-share housing program seeks a sustainable balance of lower-cost and more expensive housing in all areas of the region, whether they are greenfield suburban sites or gentrifying neighborhoods.

Regional Review and Coordination of Local Planning. Because much land-use and infrastructure planning is best provided at the local level, regional land-use reform requires a coordinated framework in which local governments develop comprehensive land-use plans that are consistent with state or regional planning goals....

Metropolitan Governance Reform

The fragmentation of metropolitan areas into many local governments is not only a barrier to effective growth management, but also a leading cause of racial and economic segregation, sprawl, and fiscal disparities within those areas....

Recognizing fragmentation's negative effects, a number of regions have acted to bring a greater regional focus to local governance. Metropolitan planning organizations are the most widespread form of regional governance in the U.S. today. MPOs were created by Congress in the 1970s to address the growing transportation challenges in metropolitan regions....

However, MPOs are not directly accountable to voters and do not always make their transportation investments with social separation, sprawl, and fiscal inequities in mind....

A strong, accountable regional governing body is an essential part of a comprehensive regional reform plan. The following strategies will help to ensure the longterm viability of any regional governing body, whether an MPO with expanded authority or some other regional body.

Strategy 1: Apportion voting membership by population....

Strategy 2: Hold direct elections for voting members....

Strategy 3: Broaden and deepen public awareness of how transportation investments
contribute to or alleviate social separation and sprawl....

Strategy 4: Broaden the scope of land-use
planning....

Today's metropolitan politics are based on
an inaccurate model of poor cities and rich
suburbs. It does not acknowledge that almost
half of the U.S. population lives in places that
have finished developing and have increasing
urban problems. Nor does it come to terms
with the fiscal pressure of growth and the
public's increasing discontent with sprawl
and loss of open space. A new metropolitics
must understand the diversity of U.S. suburbs
and build a broad bipartisan movement for
greater regional cooperation. If metropolitics
does not succeed, our metropolitan regions
will continue to become more unequal, and
more energy will be spent growing against
ourselves.

16-8. CHARTER OF THE CONGRESS FOR THE NEW URBANISM, 1996

The Congress for the New Urbanism views di-
vestment in central cities, the spread of placeless sprawl, increasing separation by race
and income, environmental deterioration,
loss of agricultural lands and wilderness, and
the erosion of society's built heritage as one
interrelated community-building challenge.

We stand for the restoration of existing
urban centers and towns within coherent
metropolitan regions, the reconfiguration
of sprawling suburbs into communities of
real neighborhoods and diverse districts, the
conservation of natural environments, and
the preservation of our built legacy. We recognize that physical solutions by themselves
will not solve social and economic problems,
but neither can economic vitality, community stability, and environmental health be
sustained without a coherent and supportive
physical framework.

We advocate the restructuring of public
policy and development practice to support
the following principles: neighborhoods
should be diverse in use and population;
communities should be designed for the pedestrian and transit as well as the car; cities
and towns should be shaped by physically
defined and universally accessible public
spaces and community institutions; urban
places should be framed by architecture and
landscape design that celebrate local history,
climate, ecology, and building practice.

We represent a broad-based citizenry,
composed of public and private sector leaders, community activists, and multidisciplinary professionals. We are committed to
reestablishing the relationship between the
art of building and the making of community, through citizen-based participatory planning and design.

We dedicate ourselves to reclaiming our
homes, blocks, streets, parks, neighborhoods,
districts, towns, cities, region and environment.

We assert the following principles to guide
public policy, development, practice, urban
planning, and design:

The Region: The Metropolis, the City and the Town

1. Metropolitan regions are finite places
with geographic boundaries derived from
topography, watersheds, coastlines, farm-
lands, regional parks, and river basins. The
metropolis is made of multiple centers that
are cities, towns, and villages, each with its
own identifiable center and edges.

2. The metropolitan region is a fundamental economic unit of the contemporary
world. Governmental cooperation, public policy, physical planning, and economic
strategies must reflect this new reality.

3. The metropolis has a necessary and
fragile relationship to its agrarian hinterland
and natural landscapes. The relationship
is environmental, economic, and cultural.
Farmland and nature are as important to the
metropolis as the garden is to the house.

4. Development patterns should nor blur
or eradicate the edges of the metropolis. In-
fill development within existing urban areas

conserves environmental resources, economic investment, and social fabric, while reclaiming marginal and abandoned areas. Metropolitan regions should develop strategies to encourage such infill development over peripheral expansion.

5. Where appropriate, new development contiguous to urban boundaries should be organized as neighborhoods and districts, and be integrated with the existing urban pattern. Noncontiguous development should be organized as towns and villages with their own urban edges, and planned for a jobs/housing balance, not as bedroom suburbs.

6. The development and redevelopment of towns and cities should respect historical patterns, precedents, and boundaries.

7. Cities and towns should bring into proximity a broad spectrum of public and private uses to support a regional economy that benefits people of all incomes. Affordable housing should be distributed throughout the region to match job opportunities and to avoid concentrations of poverty.

8. The physical organization of the region should be supported by a framework of transportation alternatives. Transit, pedestrian, and bicycle systems should maximize access and mobility throughout the region while reducing dependence upon the automobile.

9. Revenues and resources can be shared more cooperatively among the municipalities and centers within regions to avoid destructive competition for tax base and to promote rational coordination of transportation, recreation, public services, housing, and community institutions.

The Neighborhood, the District, and the Corridor

1. The Neighborhood, the District, and the Corridor are the essential elements of development and redevelopment in the metropolis. They form identifiable areas that encourage citizens to take responsibility for their maintenance and evolution.

2. Neighborhoods should be compact, pedestrian-friendly, and mixed use. Districts generally emphasize a special single use, and should follow the principles of neighborhood design when possible. Corridors are regional connectors of neighborhoods and districts; they range from boulevards and rail lines to rivers and parkways.

3. Many activities of daily living should occur within walking distance, allowing independence to those who do not drive, especially the elderly and the young. Interconnected networks of streets should be designed to encourage walking, reduce the number and length of automobile trips, and conserve energy.

4. Within neighborhoods, a broad range of housing types and price levels can bring people of diverse ages, races, and incomes into daily interaction, strengthening the personal and civic bonds essential to an authentic community.

5. Transit corridors, when properly planned and coordinated, can help organize metropolitan structure and revitalize urban centers. In contrast, highway corridors should not displace investment from existing centers.

6. Appropriate building densities and land uses should be within walking distance of transit stops, permitting public transit to become a viable alternative to the automobile.

7. Concentrations of civic, institutional, and commercial activity should be embedded in neighborhoods and districts, not isolated in remote, single-use complexes. Schools should be sized and located to enable children to walk or bicycle to them.

8. The economic health and harmonious evolution of neighborhoods, districts, and corridors can be improved through graphic urban design codes that serve as predictable guides for change.

9. A range of parks, from tot-lots and village greens to ballfields and community gardens, should be distributed within neighborhoods. Conservation areas and open lands should be used to define and connect different neighborhoods and districts.

The Block, the Street, and the Building

1. A primary task of all urban architecture and landscape design is the physical definition of streets and public spaces as places of shared use.

2. Individual architectural projects should

be seamlessly linked to their surroundings. This issue transcends style.

3. The revitalization of urban places depends on safety and security. The design of streets and buildings should reinforce safe environments, but not at the expense of accessibility and openness.

4. In the contemporary metropolis, development must adequately accommodate automobiles. It should do so in ways that respect the pedestrian and the form of public space.

5. Streets and squares should be safe, comfortable, and interesting to the pedestrian. Properly configured, they encourage walking and enable neighbors to know each other and protect their communities.

6. Architecture and landscape design should grow from local climate, topography, history, and building practice.

7. Civic buildings and public gathering places require important sites to reinforce community identity and the culture of democracy. They deserve distinctive form, because their role is different from that of other buildings and places that constitute the fabric of the city.

8. All buildings should provide their inhabitants with a clear sense of location, weather, and time. Natural methods of heating and cooling can be more resource-efficient than mechanical systems.

9. Preservation and renewal of historic buildings, districts, and landscapes affirm the continuity and evolution of urban society.

For information: Congress for the New Urbanism; 140 S. Dearborn St., Suite 310; Chicago, IL 60603; 312 551-7300 phone; www.cnu.org

16-9. PHOTO GALLERY: NEW URBANIST SUBURBIA: KENTLANDS, MARYLAND

Figure 16-6 Porchfronts at Kentlands, Maryland, near Washington, D.C. Begun in 1988, Kentlands incorporated traditional design features such as alleys behind homes, short set-backs, front porches, and nearby commercial areas to encourage a pedestrian-oriented community. Courtesy of Duany, Plater-Zyberk & Co.

Figure 16-7 Aerial view of Kentlands, Maryland. Built around a historic farm and home (left center), Kentlands merges a variety of architectural and residential types with man-made lakes and open space. Courtesy of Duany, Plater-Zyberk & Co.

16-10. URBAN SCHOLAR ROBERT BRUEGMANN CRITIQUES THE "ANTISPRAWL" MOVEMENT, 2000

Source: Robert Bruegmann, "The Paradoxes of Anti-Sprawl Reform," in *Urban Planning in a Changing World: The Twentieth Century Experience*, ed. Robert Freestone (New York: Routledge, 2000).

One of the most conspicuous developments in the realm of planning thought during the last decades of the twentieth century has been a concerted attack on urban 'sprawl'. Although this word was first commonly used in something like its present sense in Britain in the interwar years and was imported to the United States in the 1950s, it has been primarily in the 1990s that it has served as the focus of a broad-based reform movement. According to many reformers today, sprawl, which has typically been described as low-density and unplanned development at the periphery of large cities, is ugly, inefficient, inequitable, and environmentally damaging. To combat sprawl, a large, if loose, coalition of activ-

ist planners, architects, environmentalists, historic preservationists and other reformers, has come together to promote policies encouraging what they believe will be more carefully planned, more efficient, compact and environmentally friendly cities....

I will...argue that because these ideas were never clearly defined, are biased by class attitudes, and have been extrapolated from insufficient and out-of-date data, the results are likely to be irrelevant, ineffectual or even counter-productive. Anti-sprawl efforts will almost certainly not stop the development of the new multi-centered and highly dispersed urban settlements that are appearing in cities throughout the world....

Aesthetic Objections

The first and most persistent strain of attack on sprawl has been based on aesthetic objections....

During the postwar years, as many cities continued to decentralize rapidly, the fight against blight gradually receded and the fight against sprawl came to the fore....

In the 1950s, [William H.] Whyte organized what was probably the first conference on sprawl. This conference resulted in a widely read little book entitled *The Exploding Metropolis*. In his own contribution, an essay simply entitled 'Urban Sprawl', Whyte's chief criticisms were, as usual, aesthetic, but he also remarked, almost parenthetically, that sprawl was not only bad aesthetics but bad economics. This was a theme that would soon be taken up by others in a serious way. Closely associated with Whyte in the magazine and the conference was Jane Jacobs. Although she did not use the term sprawl in any conspicuous way in her enormously influential 1962 work, *Death and Life of Great American Cities,* she did provide a classic defence of high-density inner city living and critique of contemporary low-density suburban settlement patterns. Jacobs, like many others before and since, used Los Angeles as an example of all that was wrong with American cities, curiously attributing to that city exactly the kinds of high crime levels and urban pathology that observers at the beginning of the century had associated with the overcrowded centres of the great industrial cities.

A clear indication that 'sprawl' had arrived as a standard term by the beginning of the 1960s can be found in Lewis Mumford's magisterial work *The City in History....* In his concise epigrammatic history, Mumford revealed the powerful class-bound aesthetic biases that he probably inherited from his British planning mentors:

> Whilst the suburb served only a favored minority it neither spoiled the countryside nor threatened the city. But now that the drift to the outer ring has become a mass movement, it tends to destroy the value of both environments without producing anything but a dreary substitute, devoid of form and even more devoid of the original suburban values....

The postwar American discussion of sprawl was closely connected with attacks on 'mass culture', 'middle-brow' taste, and on suburbia generally, which was often described as socially stifling and culturally barren....

During the 1960s and 1970s, the debate over sprawl and the suburbs raged. 'This book is not written in anger. It is written in fury', wrote architect Peter Blake on the first page of his book *God's Own Junkyard.* He went on to say that Americans were about to turn their beautiful country into the 'biggest slum on the face of the earth'. The anti-suburban and anti-sprawl crusade did find its own vigorous critics. Sociologist Herbert Gans mounted an extremely effective defence of suburbia....On the matter of sprawl he wrote, 'I have never seen any persuasive evidence that sprawl has bad effects or high-density development significant virtues'....Despite these rebuttals, the criticisms of suburbia have continued unabated.

Efficiency Arguments

A second main track of argument about sprawl, more measured in tone, has been about efficiency. By the mid-1960s, most of the elements of the 'costs of sprawl' debate had been put in place. Although sprawl might be very efficient for the new arrival buying cheap land at the city edge, these critics argued, it was actually inefficient for society at large because it spreads people out, induces longer commuting, eats up valuable farmland, and requires more infrastructure. Although for various of these writers sprawl might mean low-density scattered settlement patterns, ribbon development along roads leading out of towns, and leapfrog development—that is development that skipped over areas of land that remained undeveloped—there were, from the very start, major disagreements on which elements constituted sprawl and which were harmful....

The landmark study was a report entitled *The Costs of Sprawl* prepared for several American government agencies in the early 1970s. In this study the authors devised a theoretical model to analyse six different kinds of neighbourhood prototype, ranging from low-density unplanned development (sprawl) to high-density planned (meaning increased clustering and compactness) development. They concluded that planned communities were less costly to build and operate than unplanned communities and that high and moderately high densities (for example walk-up apartments) were less expensive than low densities. Altogether, the authors found, a moderately high-density planned community would cost 41 per cent less than a low-density sprawl community. In addition, the report found that unplanned low-density development produced undesirable environmental effects, led to longer commuting, higher fuel consumption and pollution, and meant an increased cost burden on municipalities.

These findings drew immediate rebuttals. Reviews and subsequent studies fatally undermined many of the key points....In actual practice, argued Richard Peiser, planned development did not present anything like the savings the report predicted, and Helen Ladd has shown that increasing suburban density does not necessarily lower municipal service costs. Over the years the objections to the findings of the *Costs of Sprawl* report have continued to pile up....

Equity Arguments

The third strain of anti-sprawl argument, one that has been particularly important in the United States, has been based on issues of equity. These arguments were clearly modeled directly on the anti-suburban literature of the 1960s and 1970s. Following the logic of this literature, the contemporary urban pattern could be explained by the flight of affluent white citizens to the suburbs which in turn caused an increasing concentration of poor non-white residents in the centre city and, at the same time, siphoned tax funding away from the central city (which needed it most) to the suburbs.

Among the many difficulties in sustaining this argument was the question, if one believed that race was a primary cause of suburban growth, of why metropolitan areas with small minority populations have decentralized just like those with large minority populations....How can one prove that low-density settlement at the edge caused deterioration at the core, particularly when some of the cities with the most robust centres also have a great deal of low-density growth at the edge? In the hands of the sprawl reformers, these connections did not have to be proved. They were self-evident....

Environmental Arguments

The most recent, and certainly most contentious, aspect of the sprawl debate relates to environmental issues and to 'sustainability'. Like many of the other strands of this debate, this is a reformulation of issues that were hotly debated in the 1960s. In this instance, it has been the concept of global warming that has revivified earlier environmental reform efforts that had lost much of their urgency as urban air and water got noticeably cleaner in almost all Western cities since World War Two and the energy crises of the early 1970s failed to have their predicted dire impact on urban patterns.

The factual basis for the current environmental attack on sprawl is an observation that low-density cities use more energy than high-density cities. The conclusions usually drawn are that this is inequitable because small numbers of people are using a fixed amount of energy and that it is unsustainable because mankind will run out of energy or greenhouse gases will damage the Earth's ecosystem....

A major problem...is the shaky causal link between the perceived problem and observed phenomena....What makes the current environmental arguments more difficult to sustain is the unresolved debate over whether mankind is in any danger of running out of energy or whether there is potentially unlimited energy that can be tapped using new technology. There is also, even if one assumes that global warming is a long-term condition and not a statistical blip, a fundamental lack of agreement on whether it could be reversed by changing land use patterns, or, indeed, whether the effects of global warming might not be good rather than bad for at least some parts of the world....

Although the debate is far from played out, and scientists may, indeed, prove conclusively that it will be necessary to alter urban development patterns in ways advocated by anti-sprawl critics, it seems more likely that with the latest environmental objections, the arguments about sprawl have merely come back full circle to the highly subjective grounds on which they were initially founded, that is to the realm where answers to the question of proper city form flow more or less directly out of deep personal belief and conviction rather than from any empirical evidence....

The Anti-Sprawl Coalition

It is in the United States that the anti-sprawl rhetoric is loudest and the anti-sprawl coalition most developed. The current coalition consists of a large group of academics, architects and planners, historic preservationists, land conservationists, environmentalists as well as advocates for farmland protection, the central city and public transportation. Each of these groups believes the anti-sprawl fight can be used effectively to further its mission. The coalition unites individuals on the political and artistic right who would like to return to an earlier, more orderly, even authoritarian world, with individuals who consider themselves liberals in the 1960s tradition who would like to use government powers to promote what they view as a more efficient, equitable society. Among the assumptions shared by many individuals on both sides is an upper middle-class disdain for the messy reality of the middle-class fringes of large cities and a common desire to move control upward in the governmental hierarchy away from ordinary citizens and into the hands of professional experts....

Conclusion

If history is any guide, it is unlikely that the current anti-sprawl coalition will survive for any length of time given the very different, even warring, assumptions that lie behind the agendas of the constituent groups. History suggests, moreover, that even if the coalition were successful, the measures might well backfire, at least as perceived by reformers of the next generation. Here the medical analogy is suggestive. Many doctors, while admitting that certain measures of previous eras—bloodletting, for example—could have been counter-productive, rarely admit that their current prescriptions are just as liable to be condemned in a subsequent generation. So, too, the dams and atomic energy plants, championed by many environmentalists of a previous era to cut down on fossil fuel use and pollution, came to be the objects of emotional attacks by the same constituency a generation later.

The same kind of reversal of opinion has characterized many if not most of the large scale attempts in modern urban planning. Urban renewal, public housing, urban expressways and pedestrian main streets, all advocated by some planners as a way for the central city to compete effectively with the suburbs in the postwar years, came, by the 1960s, under attack by the very reform groups that had pushed hardest for them in the first place. The same is true with planning for the urban periphery. Although many of the planning devices to control growth at the metropolitan fringe, notably England's green belts and satellite cities, did have some of the effects intended, it is quite likely that they also had side effects like increased housing prices and driving growth out beyond the greenbelt, that could, for significant parts of the population, be considered worse than the initial problem.

The same might be said of the growth management, slow-growth and antigrowth efforts of the 1970s and 1980s in the United States that are the direct precursors for the 'Smart Growth' and 'Sustainable Growth' mantras of today. In these decades, the mechanisms to stop, slow or channel growth included building moratoria, growth boundaries, large-lot zoning, and 'concurrency' regulations that made building contingent on having sufficient infrastructure in place before development could proceed. Although these did do some of the things they were designed to do, they also tended to drive up the price of land, thus hurting those least able to afford housing, and they were mostly unsuccessful on a larger scale since growth usually just moved to areas beyond the regulations, meaning that it might easily spread even further out than it would have without them.

Although current reformers often decry important aspects of these previous policies, the popular appeal of the current wave of anti-sprawl efforts appears to be based on exactly the same desire to stop change where it will be most visible to current inhabitants. Instead of stopping peripheral growth entirely, which proved impossible, the new ideal is to make it invisible by channeling it as much as possible into existing areas. However, just as 'sprawl' is always almost used to refer to places other than where the speaker lives, so, too, do most people using the term appear to imagine that densification will happen in neighbourhoods other than their own. So far most of the anti-sprawl measures have not had much bite, even in places like Portland, Oregon, where anti-sprawl has been public policy for decades. The moment that they do and the abstract principles become reality, when apartment buildings replace single family homes in established neighbourhoods, and when automobile congestion inevitably increases because of the greater density and the refusal to build new roads, the enthusiasm for these measures will almost certainly decline.

These historical reversals and policy backfires underline one of the critical weaknesses of the current anti-sprawl crusade: the flimsy evidence on which it is based. Our urban systems are simply too large and complicated for us to understand, let alone to 'fix'. The vast literature on the key question of the land use-transportation connection, for example, has been mostly based on home-to-work commuting patterns of single household members at a given moment in time in cities that are understood as having a single dominant centre. None of this even remotely reflects current urban reality. Almost all of the projections into the future, moreover, tend to accept a steady state of technology, rather than the probability that our urban world will have quite different technology and functions in 50 years.

Does the record of paradoxes, backfires and unintended consequences suggest that professional planning can accomplish nothing, that there is no way to solve any urban problem? Definitely not: planners and reformers have had important places in the management of the city, if only in their efforts to make understandable the impacts of changes on various parts of the society. They have also undoubtedly helped in creating courses of action that have minimized some of the negative impacts on those hurt by urban change. It is mostly a matter of

perspective and stance. If reforms are seen as temporary and makeshift solutions to specific conditions that cannot be defined very precisely and will probably have changed by the time the reform takes place, it will be easier to resist the temptation to rush to broad-brush solutions. It will also be easier to realize that many of our frustrations are not the result of things getting worse, at least in cities in developed countries. It is, in fact, because conditions have got so much better for such a large part of the urban population so quickly and such a large part of the population has been able to enjoy the privacy, mobility and choice that were once the privilege of only the wealthy that expectations on the part of citizens often run ahead of current realities. The agitation against sprawl is a clear indication of the dynamism and resiliency of urban systems.

16-11. ROBERT PUTNAM CONNECTS SUBURBANIZATION TO THE DEMISE OF COMMUNITY, 2000

Source: Reprinted with the permission of Simon & Schuster Adult Publishing Group from *Bowling Alone* by Robert D. Putnam. Copyright © 2000 by Robert D. Putnam.

No one is left from the Glenn Valley, Pennsylvania, Bridge Club who can tell us precisely when or why the group broke up, even though its forty-odd members were still playing regularly as recently as 1990, just as they had done for more than half a century. The shock in the Little Rock, Arkansas, Sertoma club, however, is still painful: in the mid-1980s, nearly fifty people had attended the weekly luncheon to plan activities to help the hearing- and speech-impaired, but a decade later only seven regulars continued to show up.

The Roanoke, Virginia, chapter of the National Association for the Advancement of Colored People (NAACP) had been an active force for civil rights since 1918, but during the 1990s membership withered from about 2,500 to a few hundred. By November 1998 even a heated contest for president drew only fifty-seven voting members.... VFW Post

2378 in Berwyn, Illinois, a blue-collar suburb of Chicago, was long a bustling "home away from home" for local veterans and a kind of working-class country club for the neighborhood, hosting wedding receptions and class reunions. By 1999, however, membership had so dwindled that it was a struggle just to pay taxes on the yellow brick post hall....

It wasn't so much that old members dropped out—at least not any more rapidly than age and the accidents of life had always meant. But community organizations were no longer continuously revitalized, as they had been in the past, by freshets of new members. Organizational leaders were flummoxed. For years they assumed that their problem must have local roots or at least that it was peculiar to their organization, so they commissioned dozens of studies to recommend reforms. The slowdown was puzzling because for as long as anyone could remember, membership rolls and activity lists had lengthened steadily.

In the 1960s, in fact, community groups across America had seemed to stand on the threshold of a new era of expanded involvement. Except for the civic drought induced by the Great Depression, their activity had shot up year after year, cultivated by assiduous civic gardeners and watered by increasing affluence and education. Each annual report registered rising membership. Churches and synagogues were packed, as more Americans worshiped together than only a few decades earlier, perhaps more than ever in American history....

What happened next to civic and social life in American communities is the subject of this book. In recent years social scientists have framed concerns about the changing character of American society in terms of the concept of "social capital." By analogy with notions of physical capital and human capital—tools and training that enhance individual productivity—the core idea of social capital theory is that social networks have value....

[S]ocial capital refers to connections among individuals—social networks and the norms of reciprocity and trustworthiness that arise from them. In that sense social capital is closely related to what some have called "civic virtue." The difference is that "social capital" calls attention to the fact that civic virtue is most powerful when embedded in a dense network of reciprocal social relations....

The dominant theme is simple: For the first two-thirds of the twentieth century a powerful tide bore Americans into ever deeper engagement in the life of their communities, but a few decades ago—silently, without warning—that tide reversed and we were overtaken by a treacherous rip current. Without at first noticing, we have been pulled apart from one another and from our communities over the last third of the century....

Before October 29, 1997, John Lambert and Andy Boschma knew each other only through their local bowling league at the Ypsi-Arbor Lanes in Ypsilanti, Michigan. Lambert, a sixty-four-year-old retired employee of the University of Michigan hospital, had been on a kidney transplant waiting list for three years when Boschma, a thirty-three-year-old accountant, learned casually of Lambert's need and unexpectedly approached him to offer to donate one of his own kidneys.

"Andy saw something in me that others didn't," said Lambert. "When we were in the hospital Andy said to me, 'John, I really like you and have a lot of respect for you. I wouldn't hesitate to do this all over again.' I got choked up." Boschma returned the feeling: "I obviously feel a kinship [with Lambert]. I cared about him before, but now I'm really rooting for him." This moving story speaks for itself, but the photograph that accompanied this report in the *Ann Arbor News* reveals that in addition to their differences in profession and generation, Boschma is white and Lambert is African American. That they bowled together made all the difference. In small ways like this—and in larger ways, too—we Americans need to reconnect with one another. That is the simple argument of this book....

Mobility and Sprawl...

Could disengagement perhaps be linked not to urbanization, but to suburbanization?...

Initially, the postwar wave of suburbanization produced a frontierlike enthusiasm for civic engagement. The booster mythology fostered by suburban developers was positively communitarian. Ran one ad for Park Forest, the Chicago suburb closely studied by urbanist William Whyte for *The Organization Man*:

You belong in PARK FOREST!
The moment you come to our town you
 know:
 You're welcome
 You're a part of the big group
You can live in a friendly small town
 Instead of a lonely big city
You can have friends who want you—
 And you can enjoy being with them.
Come out. Find out about the spirit of
 Park Forest.

This was not mere hype, for Whyte reported that Park Forest was a "hotbed of participation..." A few years later sociologist Herbert Gans, who had actually moved into Levittown, New Jersey, to study its social life, reported that Levittowners were "hyperactive joiners." The image of suburban life that emerged from studies of the 1960s was one of unusually active involvement in neighborhood activities. Americans, it seemed, were rediscovering the civic virtues of small-town life.

As suburbanization continued, however, the suburbs themselves fragmented into a sociological mosaic—collectively heterogeneous but individually homogeneous, as people fleeing the city sorted themselves into more and more finely distinguished "lifestyle enclaves," segregated by race, class, education, life stage, and so on. So-called white flight was only the most visible form of this movement toward metropolitan differentiation. At century's end some suburbs were upper-middle-class, but many others were middle-middle, lower-middle, or even working-class. Some suburbs were white, but others were black, Hispanic, or Asian. Some were child focused, but others were composed predominantly of swinging singles or affluent empty nesters or retirees. Many suburbs had come to resemble theme parks, with uniform architecture and coordinated amenities and boutiques. In the 1980s "common interest developments" and "gated communities" began to proliferate, in which private homeowner associations and visible physical barriers manned by guards supplemented the invisible sociological barriers that distinguished each community from its neighbors....

One might expect the numbing homogeneity of these new suburban enclaves to encourage a certain social connectedness....

Most evidence, however, actually points in the opposite direction. Not only are canvassing politicians and Girl Scouts selling cookies excluded from exclusive communities, but the affluent residents themselves also appear to have a surprisingly low rate of civic engagement and neighborliness even within their boundaries....

When ethnographer M. P. Baumgartner lived in a suburban New Jersey community in the 1980s, rather than the compulsive togetherness ascribed to the classic suburbs of the 1950s, she found a culture of atomized isolation, self-restraint, and "moral minimalism." Far from seeking small-town connectedness, suburbanites kept to themselves, asking little of their neighbors and expecting little in return....

One inevitable consequence of how we have come to organize our lives spatially is that we spend measurably more of every day shuttling alone in metal boxes among the vertices of our private [commuter] triangles [of home, work, shopping]. American adults average seventy-two minutes every day behind the wheel, according to the Department of Transportation's Personal Transportation Survey. This is, according to time diary studies, more than we spend cooking or eating and more than twice as much as the average parent spends with the kids. Private cars account for 86 percent of all trips in America, and two-thirds of all car trips are made alone, a fraction that has been rising steadily....

We are also commuting farther. From 1960 to 1990 the number of workers who commute across county lines more than tripled. Between 1983 and 1995 the average commuting trip grew 37 percent longer in miles....

In short, we are spending more and more time alone in the car. And on the whole, many of us see this as a time for quiet relaxation, especially those of us who came of age in the midst of this driving boom....

The car and the commute, however, are demonstrably bad for community life. In round numbers the evidence suggests that *each additional ten minutes in daily commuting time cuts involvement in community affairs by 10 percent*—fewer public meetings attended, fewer committees chaired, fewer petitions signed, fewer church services attended, less volunteering, and so on. In fact, although commuting time is not quite as powerful an influence on civic involvement as education, it is more important than almost any other demographic factor. And time diary studies suggest that there is a similarly strong negative effect of commuting time on informal social interaction....

To be sure, suburbs, automobiles, and the associated sprawl are not without benefits. Americans *chose* to move to the suburbs and to spend more time driving, presumably because we found the greater space, larger homes, lower-cost shopping and housing—and perhaps, too, the greater class and racial segregation—worth the collective price we have paid in terms of community.... Whatever our private preferences, however, metropolitan sprawl appears to have been a significant contributor to civic disengagement over the last three or four decades for at least three distinct reasons.

First, sprawl takes time. More time spent alone in the car means less time for friends and neighbors, for meetings, for community projects, and so on. Though this is the most obvious link between sprawl and disengagement, it is probably not the most important.

Second, sprawl is associated with increasing social segregation, and social homogeneity appears to reduce incentives for civic involvement, as well as opportunities for social networks that cut across class and racial lines....

Third, most subtly but probably most powerfully, sprawl disrupts community "boundedness." Commuting time is important in large part as a proxy for the growing separation between work and home and shops. More than three decades ago, when (we now know in retrospect) civic engagement was at full flood, political scientists

Sidney Verba and Norman Nie showed that residents of "well-defined and bounded" communities were much more likely to be involved in local affairs. In fact, Verba and Nie found commuting itself to be a powerful negative influence on participation. Presciently, they wrote that "communities that appear to foster participation—the small and relatively independent communities—are becoming rarer and rarer." Three decades later this physical fragmentation of our daily lives has had a visible dampening effect on community involvement.

16-12. JOURNALIST CHARLES MCGRATH OFFERS A CODA FOR THE SUBURBAN DREAM, 2000

Source: Charles McGrath, "We Stayed for the Kids...and Stayed and Stayed: The Pleasures of Tending an Empty Nest," *New York Times Magazine*, April 9, 2000. Copyright © 2000 by The New York Times Co. Reprinted with permission.

I know all the arguments against suburbia. I invented some of them: that the suburbs literally shrivel the brain, for example. I also know that suburbs have become aluminum-sided theme parks—celebrations of sameness—and that nowhere else on earth can you find architecture of such awfulness and pretension. "Get me out of here!" I used to announce periodically when the children were small. "I can't last a minute longer." My wife and I would look through the Manhattan real estate ads, in search of some steerage-size apartment that might fit our budget. Then we'd factor in the cost of private schools and of an occasional weekend trip, because we thought we deserved to see grass and trees at least once in a while, and even before we totaled it all up, I'd slink off, my heat spent. We had to stay for the kids, we told ourselves, and because we couldn't afford anything better.

But the kids have been gone for years now—they both live in New York City, in fact—and we're still here. Without my noticing, my heels have dug in. It's not that the suburbs have improved. The New Jersey town I live in is, if anything, a little less lovely than it was when we moved here, with much of its open space having succumbed to the bulldozer. The horse farm two doors down from us, whose neighings and whickerings we could sometimes hear on a still morning, has been paved over for condos. Nor have I noticed an efflorescence of cultural life. A few years ago, I would occasionally spot some of my fellow commuters reading books. Now they're poring over the stock tables, or else they're jabbering on their cell phones.

The change has been in me, not in my surroundings. I have become attached to this place, and to my own three-quarters of an acre in particular. I like all my stuff. Over the years, I have acquired not one, or even two, but three (more or less) functioning automobiles. The queen of the fleet is a 1984 Volvo with 220,000 miles on the odometer; it sometimes starts when the newer cars won't. I also have an invaluable collection of gasoline-powered yard tools—mower, edger, leaf blower, weed whacker and chain saw—and my idea of a perfect Saturday is one when I get to crank them all up. When I'm done, I like to sit on my deck with a beer and oversee my kingdom. As the sun goes down, the bats begin to flit across the yard, the geese start honking, preparing for a splashy descent into the pond out back; pretty soon the woodchuck will come nosing out of his hole, and though I can't see them, I know the raccoons are out there too, plotting how to get into the trash cans. If I'm lucky, I might even glimpse a deer, bounding across the road and through the side yard. (Deer, as we suburbanites know, are just big rats, but they're rats with a thrilling, leaping gait that reminds me of a jet ski bouncing over waves.) At moments like this I'm actually pretty happy—even if it means that I have become the kind of guy I used to make fun of.

I'm also lucky. We have worked our way up the real estate food chain to the point where we have a modest version of the complete suburban package: the picket fence, the stone walls, the in-ground pool, the 19th-century house w/wbfpls. We have gardens, thanks to my wife, and thanks to the inevitable, we have a pet cemetery. The residents include Larry, Curly and Moe, the goldfish;

Frisky the hamster, who became feverish and wobbly after eating halfway through E. B. White's "Sub-Treasury of American Humor"; Charlotte the rabbit, buried in a velvet-lined shoe box; and dear, sweet Bailey, our golden retriever, who now rests beneath the bed of primroses that he so irritatingly used to lie on top of. In melancholy moments, I sometimes imagine myself interred right next to him. I'd prefer to be scattered in the nature preserve that's right behind our property, but no doubt that's ecologically unsound. This vestige of presuburbia is the real reason we live where we live: an 80-acre backyard—an expanse of bird-thronged woods and glittering, cattailed marsh—that we don't have to pay taxes on.

The suburbs, it is often said, are neither one thing nor the other—neither country nor city, private nor public. Fair enough, and yet the same is true of most of us. We are neither one kind of person or another, and we have different needs at different times. In an hour— a little less if the traffic cooperates—I can meet you at the Whitney or the Met. In the same amount of time, give or take, I can be crosscountry skiing in the Shawangunks or playing golf in the Poconos. I'm 15 minutes from the rink where I play hockey and the same from a driving range. I don't mind distance (I've got audiobooks and opera CD's in the car), and if I take public transportation, I'll get some work done. Over the years, in fact, commuting has become a necessary escape valve; no matter how rotten my day, I've left it behind by the time I pull into my driveway.

In teaching us to compromise, to savor a little of this, a little of that, suburban life also fosters alertness—to the changes of season, obviously, to the moment when first the forsythia and then the azalea burst electrically into bloom, as if somebody had turned on the juice—but also to the little civic rituals and moments of passage that tend to go unobserved in the city. There's the Saturday in early fall, for example, when the playgrounds suddenly sprout nets and orange marking cones and the pint-size soccer kids, in baggy Umbros and Day-Glo shirts, start racing around; there's high school football season, when if the wind is right you can hear the band at halftime all the way across town; there's Halloween and the thrilling buildup, the giant pumpkin-shaped leaf bags out on the lawn, the stuffed witches and cobweb-draped scarecrows scarily arranged by front doors; there's Christmas, when the decorations go up at our tasteful, blue-awninged strip mall (where, with just one stop, you can find most of life's essentials: pizza, groceries, toys, discount dresses and karate lessons); there's Little League in the spring, of course, bringing with it the welcome ping of aluminum against polymer, or whatever it is they use for horsehide these days; there's the first spring trash pickup, when you get to put all your junk out by the curb and can also look over the old couches and toaster ovens and macrame planters your neighbors are throwing out; and then toward the end of May, just about when the lindens have started to scent the air, there's a Saturday when dozens and dozens of white and powder blue stretch limos whoosh through town, bearing the high school kids off to the prom—and off, eventually, to nests of their own.

Watching the whole suburban pageant—the blooming and fading, the growing up, the winding down, the families moving in, the families moving out—is both sad and reassuring. It makes you feel connected, a part of something. The friends I've made out here are not the ones I would have chosen in advance, and I'm now grateful for that. On my street there live, in addition to the obligatory bankers and lawyers, a philosopher, a man who owns a liquor store, two psychologists, a potter, a car dealer, a nurse practitioner, a furniture maker, a school principal and (this is "Sopranos" territory, after all) at least one family rumored to have ties to the Mob. All these people I would never have got to know had we not all turned up here in search of an agreeable place to raise our families. Initially, of course, it was the kids who brought us together, as we squeezed behind neighboring desks on parent-teacher night, carpooled together, cheered for one another's offspring at band concerts and sporting events. But in many cases the friendships have persisted even into empty-nestdom—one more thing we all have in common. In the city I've noticed, people tend to hang out with their own kind—those in the same profession, the same income bracket. The social circles in the burbs are more arbitrary and less wary. They'll take almost anybody in—just as our little town took me, long before I knew I wanted to be taken.

NOTES

1. David Rusk, *Cities Without Suburbs* (Washington, D.C.: Woodrow Wilson Center Press, 1993); Peter Calthorpe and William Fulton, *The Regional City: Planning for the End of Sprawl* (Washington, D.C.: Island Press, 2001); J. Eric Oliver, *Democracy in Suburbia* (Princeton: Princeton University Press, 2001); for Myron Orfield, see excerpts in chapters 14 and 16.

2. Oliver, *Democracy in Suburbia*; Keith Hampton and Barry Wellman, "Neighboring in Netville: How the Internet Supports Community and Social Capital in a Wired Suburb," *City & Community* 2:4 (December 2003) 277–307.

COPYRIGHT INFORMATION

CHAPTER 1: THE TRANSNATIONAL ORIGINS OF THE ELITE SUBURB

Text

1-1. Ralph Waldo Emerson, *Nature Addresses and Other Lectures*, vol. 1 (New York: William H. Wise and Co.,1923), 7–10, 116–17.

1-3. John Claudius Loudon, *The Suburban Gardener and Villa Companion* (London: The author, 1838), 1–2, 8–10, 32–33.

1-4. Andrew Jackson Downing, *The Architecture of Country Houses* (New York: D. Appleton & Co., 1850), v–vi, 39, 40, 78–79, 257–58, 262, 269–70, 321–22.

1-7. Riverside Improvement Company, "Riverside, Progress Prospectus," 1869, reprinted from the collections of the Riverside Public Library in *Landscape Architecture* 21 (July 1931), 283–86.

Essay 1-1. *Crabgrass Frontier: The Suburbanization of the United States* by Kenneth T. Jackson, copyright © 1985 by Oxford University Press, Inc. Used by permission of Oxford University Press, Inc. Excerpt from pages 20–22, 25–30, 42–50, 54–55, 57–59, 68–72.

Essay 1-2. *Bourgeois Utopias* by Robert Fishman. Copyright © 1987 by Basic Books, Inc. Reprinted by permission of Basic Books, a member of Perseus Books, L.L.C. Excerpt from pages 18–23, 25–29, 31–35, 38, 51–53, 55.

Essay 1-3. John Archer, "Colonial Suburbs in South Asia, 1700–1850, and the Spaces of Modernity," in *Visions of Suburbia*, ed. Roger Silverstone (London: Routledge, 1997), 26–28, 40–46.

Figures (Listed here by figure number)

Fig. 1-1. T. Addison Richards, *American Scenery: Illustrated, with Thirty-two Engravings on Steel* (New York: Leavitt & Allen, 1854), 53.

Fig. 1-2. Andrew Jackson Downing, *The Architecture of Country Houses* (New York: D. Appleton & Co., 1850), 78 facing plate.

Fig. 1-3. Andrew Jackson Downing, *The Architecture of Country Houses* (New York: D. Appleton & Co., 1850), 322 facing plate.

Fig. 1-4. The Metropolitan Museum of Art, Harris Brisbane Dick Fund, 1924 (24.66.1433) Photograph, all rights reserved, The Metropolitan Museum of Art.

Fig. 1-5. Photograph courtesy of John Archer, 1978.

Fig. 1-6. Photograph courtesy of John Archer, 1978.

Fig. 1-7. *Crabgrass Frontier: The Suburbanization of the United States* by Kenneth T. Jackson, copyright © 1985 by Oxford University Press, Inc. Used by permission of Oxford University Press, Inc. Map from page 26.

Fig. 1-8. "View of Clapham Common," anon., circa 1800. Courtesy of Guildhall Library, Corporation of London.

Fig. 1-9. Henry Davidson Love, *Vestiges of Old Madras, 1640-1800* (London: John Murray, Ltd., 1913), 356 facing place.

Fig. 1-10. Photograph courtesy of John Archer, 1988.

Fig. 1-11. Photograph courtesy of John Archer, 1988.

CHAPTER 2: FAMILY AND GENDER IN THE MAKING OF SUBURBIA

Text

Figures

CHAPTER 3: TECHNOLOGY AND DECENTRALIZATION

Text

Figures

Fig. 3-5. Chicago Historical Society, *Chicago Daily News*, Negative # DN-0090258.

Fig. 3-6. *Palliser's New Cottage Homes and Details* (New York, Palliser and Palliser and Co., 1887), plate 45.

Fig. 3-7. H. C. Bunner, *The Suburban Sage: Stray Notes and Comments on His Simple Life* (New York: Keppler and Schwartzman, 1896), 85.

Fig. 3-8. "On the Line at Nine," *House Beautiful* 53 (April 1923), 415.

CHAPTER 4: ECONOMIC AND CLASS DIVERSITY ON THE EARLY SUBURBAN FRINGE

Text

4-1. Ernest Burgess, "Urban Areas," in *Chicago: An Experiment in Social Science Research*, eds. T. V. Smith and Leonard D. White (Chicago: University of Chicago Press, 1929), 113–118.

4-2. William Dean Howells, *Suburban Sketches* (Boston: Houghton, Mifflin, 1882, original copyright, 1872), 60–63, 64–65, 68–69, 70–72, 87–90.

4-4. Graham Taylor, *Satellite Cities: A Study of Industrial Suburbs* (New York & London: D. Appleton, 1915), 1, 2, 6, 26–27, 91–92, 95, 100–101, 125.

4-5. Harlan Paul Douglass, *The Suburban Trend* (New York & London: Century Co., 1925), 1–6, 74, 75, 84–87, 94–98, 121.

4-7. "Department Store Branches in Suburbs Succeed, Multiply," *Business Week,* October 1, 1930, p. 10.

Essay 4-1. "Capitalist Development and the History of American Cities" by David Gordon, from *Marxism and the Metropolis*, Second Edition, edited by William Tabb and Larry Sawers, copyright © 1978, 1984 by Oxford University Press, Inc. Used by permission of Oxford University Press, Inc. Excerpt from pages 25–29, 44–55.

Essay 4-2. Richard Harris and Robert Lewis, "The Geography of North American Cities and Suburbs, 1900–1950: A New Synthesis," *Journal of Urban History* 27 (March 2001), 262–72, 274–78, 280–84. Copyright © 2001 Sage Publications, Inc. Reprinted by permission of Sage Publications, Inc.

Figures

Fig. 4-1. Ernest Burgess, "Urban Areas," in *Chicago: An Experiment in Social Science Research*, eds. T.V. Smith and Leonard D. White (Chicago: University of Chicago Press, 1929), 115.

Fig. 4-2. William Dean Howells, *Suburban Sketches*, (Boston: Houghton, Mifflin,1882, original copyright, 1872), 42.

Fig 4-3. William Dean Howells, *Suburban Sketches*, (Boston: Houghton, Mifflin and Company, 1882, original copyright, 1872), 64.

Fig. 4-4. H. C. Bunner, *Jersey Street and Jersey Lane: Urban and Suburban Sketches*, (New York: Charles Scribner and Sons, 1896), 192.

Fig. 4-5. Everett Chamberlin, *Chicago and Its Suburbs* (Chicago: T.A. Hungerford & Co., 1874), 360.

Fig. 4-6. Courtesy of Library of Congress, Prints and Photographs Division, FSA/OWI Collection, LC-USF 34-051864-D DLC.

Fig. 4-7. Courtesy of Library of Congress, Prints and Photographs Division, Historic American Buildings Survey, HABS, ALA, 37-Birm, 22-2.

Fig. 4-8. Courtesy of the Frances Loeb Library, Harvard Design School, Call # 119278.

Fig. 4-9. Samuel Parsons, Jr., "Small Country Places," in *Homes in City and Country*, ed. Russell Sturgis et. al. (New York: Charles Scribner and Sons, 1893), 149.

Fig. 4-10. Pittsburgh Survey (presumed), photographer and provenance unknown.

Fig. 4-11. Courtesy of Library of Congress, Prints and Photographs Division, FSA-OWI Collection, LC-USF344-000877-ZB DLC (b&w film neg.).

Fig. 4-12. Courtesy of Emil Pocock.

Fig. 4-13. Courtesy of Library of Congress, Prints and Photographs Division, Theodor Horydczak Collection, LC-H814-T01-1049 DLC (b&w film dup. neg.).

Fig. 4-14. Richard Harris and Robert Lewis, "The Geography of North American Cities and Suburbs, 1900-1950: A New Synthesis," *Journal of Urban History* 27 (March 2001), 266. Copyright © 2001 Sage Publications, Inc. Reprinted by permission of Sage Publications, Inc.

Fig. 4-15. Richard Harris and Robert Lewis, "The Geography of North American Cities and

CHAPTER 5: THE POLITICS OF EARLY SUBURBIA

Text

5-1. Adna F. Weber, "Suburban Annexations," *North American Review* 166 (May 1898), 612–17.

5-2. "Highland Park, Very Well Satisfied, Is Deaf to Annexation," *Detroit Saturday Night*, November 25, 1922.

5-3. Thomas H. Reed, "Metropolitan Government," in Roderick McKenzie, *The Metropolitan Community* (New York: McGraw-Hill, 1933), 303–10.

5-4. "The Election," *The Glendale News*, April 8, 1910, p. 2; "Political Announcements," *South Pasadena Record*, March 17, 1910, p. 2.

5-5. "Letter to the Editor," *South Gate Tribune*, July 3, 1925; "Trustees Pass Light Bill," *South Gate Tribune*, July 17, 1925, p. 1.

Essay 5-1. Ann Durkin Keating, *Building Chicago: Suburban Developers and the Creation of a Divided Metropolis* (Columbus: Ohio State University Press, 1988), 79, 80–87, 88–89, 90, 96, 120, 122–24. Used by permission of Ann Durkin Keating.

Essay 5-2. Jon C. Teaford, *Post-Suburbia: Government and Politics in the Edge Cities* (Baltimore: Johns Hopkins University Press, 1997), 9–19, 21–30, 32–33, 38–43. Copyright © 1997 The Johns Hopkins University Press. Reprinted with permission of The Johns Hopkins University Press.

Figures

Fig. 5-1. Map by David Deis, 2005.

CHAPTER 6: IMAGINING SUBURBIA: VISIONS AND PLANS FROM THE TURN OF THE CENTURY

Text

6-1. Ebenezer Howard, *Garden Cities of To-morrow* (Being the 2nd ed. of *Tomorrow, a Peaceful Path to Real Reform, 1898)* (London: Swan Sonnenschein and Co., 1902).

6-2. Carol Aronovici, "Suburban Development," *Annals of the American Academy of Political and Social Science* 51 (January 1914), 234-38.

6-3. H. S. Firestone, "Firestone Park, Akron, Ohio: A Splendidly Conceived Housing Development of the Firestone Tire and Rubber Company," in *Homes for Workmen: A Presentation of Leading Examples of Industrial Community Development* (New Orleans: Southern Pine Association, 1919), 199-202.

6-4. F. E. M. Cole, "Chicago's Most Unique Suburb," *Suburban Life* 5 (November 1907), 282-85.

6-6. Clarence S. Stein, *Toward New Towns for America* (New York: Reinhold Publishing, 1957), 41, 44, 51, 61, 65-66, 67-68, 72.

Essay 6-1. Margaret Crawford, *Building the Workingman's Paradise: The Design of American Company Towns* (New York: Verso, 1995), 80-89, 95-98. Used by permission of Verso Press.

Essay 6-2. Mary Corbin Sies, "'God's Very Kingdom on the Earth': The Design Program for the American Suburban Home, 1877-1917," in *Modern Architecture in America: Visions and Revisions*, eds. Richard G. Wilson and Sidney K. Robinson (Ames, Iowa: Iowa State University Press, 1991). Used by permission of Mary Corbin Sies.

Figures

Fig. 6-1. Ebenezer Howard, *Garden Cities of To-Morrow* (Being the 2nd ed. of *Tomorrow, a Peaceful Path to Real Reform, 1898)* (London: Swan Sonnenschein and Co., 1902).

Fig. 6-2. H. S. Firestone, "Firestone Park, Akron, Ohio: A Splendidly Conceived Housing Development of the Firestone Tire and Rubber Company," in *Homes for Workmen: A Presentation of Leading Examples of Industrial Community Development* (New Orleans: Southern Pine Association, 1919), 200.

Fig. 6-3. F. E. M. Cole, "Chicago's Most Unique Suburb," *Suburban Life* 5 (November 1907), 283.

Fig. 6-4. Sears, Roebuck and Company, *Honor Bilt Modern Homes* (Chicago: Sears, Roebuck and Co., 1926), 1.

Fig. 6-5. Clarence S. Stein, *Toward New Towns for America* (New York: Reinhold Publishing, 1957), 49.

Fig. 6-6. Clarence S. Stein, *Toward New Towns for America* (New York: Reinhold Publishing, 1957), 46.

Fig. 6-7. "View of Civic Center, Broadacre City." Drawings of Frank Lloyd Wright are Copyright © 1958 The Frank Lloyd Wright Foundation, Taliesin West, Scottsdale, AZ.

Fig. 6-8. Margaret Crawford, *Building the Workingman's Paradise: The Design of American Company Towns* (New York: Verso Press, 1995), 97. Used by permission of Verso Press.

CHAPTER 7: THE OTHER SUBURBANITES: CLASS, RACIAL, AND ETHNIC DIVERSITY IN EARLY SUBURBIA

Text

7-1. "European versus American Homes," *Chicago Tribune*, January 19, 1890, p. 10.

7-3. Sophonisba P. Breckenridge and Edith Abbott, *The Delinquent Child and the Home* (New York: Charities Publication Committee, 1912), 74, 81–83.

7-4. Margaret F. Byington, *Homestead: The Households of a Mill Town* (New York: Charities Publication Committee, 1910), 3-5, 46–48, 53, 56–62, 106.

7-5. Los Angeles Chamber of Commerce, Industrial Department, *Facts About Industrial Los Angeles: Nature's Workshop* (Los Angeles: Los Angeles Chamber of Commerce, 1927), 10.

7-6. Mary Helen Ponce, *Hoyt Street: An Autobiography* (Albuquerque: University of New Mexico Press, 1993), 3-8, 11, 12-14.

7-7. Selection from pages 8-11 from *I Had a Hammer* by Hank Aaron and Lonnie Wheeler. Copyright © 1991 by Henry Aaron and Lonnie Wheeler. Reprinted by permission of HarperCollins Publishers.

Essay 7-1. Becky M. Nicolaides, *My Blue Heaven: Life and Politics in the Working-Class Suburbs of Los Angeles, 1920–1965* (Chicago: University of Chicago Press, 2002), 13–14, 22–38. Copyright © 2002 by The University of Chicago.

Essay 7-2. Andrew Wiese, *Places of Their Own: African American Suburbanization in the Twentieth Century* (Chicago: University of Chicago Press, 2004), 67–93. Copyright © 2004 by The University of Chicago.

Figures

Fig. 7-1. Chicago Historical Society, Negative # ICHi-03656.

Fig. 7-2. Margaret F. Byington, *Homestead: The Households of a Mill Town* (Russell Sage Foundation, 1910), 48 facing plate.

Fig. 7-3. Margaret F. Byington, *Homestead: The Households of a Mill Town* (Russell Sage Foundation, 1910) 60 facing plate.

Fig. 7-4. Photograph by Becky Nicolaides, 2005.

Fig. 7-5. Courtesy of Library of Congress, Prints and Photographs Division, FSA-OWI Collection, LC-USF34-063658-D DLC (b&w film neg.).

Fig. 7-6. Courtesy of Library of Congress, Prints and Photographs Division, FSA-OWI Collection, LC-USF34-063665-D DLC (b&w film neg.).

Fig. 7-7. Courtesy of Library of Congress, Prints and Photographs Division, FSA-OWI Collection, LC-USF33-000433-M4.

Fig. 7-8. Photograph courtesy Glenn T. and Helen L. Seaborg.

Fig. 7-9. Copyright © 1929-1940 The Sanborn Map Company, The Sanborn Library, LLC. All rights reserved. Further reproductions prohibited without prior written permission from The Sanborn Library, LLC.

Fig. 7-10. *Cleveland Gazette*, June 14, 1924.

Fig. 7-11. Photograph by Andrew Wiese, 1996.

Fig. 7-12. Courtesy of the Estate of Elizabeth Meade Smith.

CHAPTER 8: THE TOOLS OF EXCLUSION: FROM LOCAL INITIATIVES TO FEDERAL POLICY

Text

8-1. Frederick Lewis Allen, "Suburban Nightmare," *The Independent* 114 (June 13, 1925), 670–71.

8-2. Jesse Clyde Nichols, "When You Buy a Home Site You Make an Investment; Try to Make it a Safe One," *Good Housekeeping* 76 (February 1923), 38–39, 172–76.

8-3. Deed to lots 12 and 13, Fairmount Addition to City Heights, East San Diego, California, Office of the County Recorder, San Diego, California.

Fig. 9-3. Robert Coates & Associates Homes Advertisement, *The Oregonian* (Portland), June 25, 1950, p. **7.

Fig. 9-4. Home Builders & Suppliers Homes Advertisement, *Arizona Daily Star*, June 18, 1950, p. 12A.

Fig. 9-5. "Manor Homes," Lakeview, Long Island, *Amsterdam News*, May 16, 1953, p. 34.

Fig. 9-6. Courtesy of the City of Lakewood Historical Collection.

Fig. 9-7. Aerial View of Lakewood, California, 1954. Pacific Air Industries. 54-2548. Long Beach, California: PAI, 1954. 4"x 5" negative dated December 15, 1954. From the collections of the Map and Imagery Laboratory, Davidson Library, University of California, Santa Barbara. Copyright 2006 The Regents of the University of California. All rights reserved.

Fig. 9-8. Courtesy of Gregory C. Randall.

Fig. 9-9. Courtesy of Gregory C. Randall.

Fig. 9-10. Photograph by Becky Nicolaides, 2005.

Fig. 9-11. Elizabeth Sweeney Herbert, "This is How I Keep House," *McCalls* 76 (April 1949), 41.

Fig. 9-12. Courtesy of Library of Congress, Prints and Photographs Division, Gottscho-Schleisner Collection, LC-G613-73745 DLC (bl and white film neg).

Fig. 9-13. Barbara M. Kelly, *Expanding the American Dream: Building and Rebuilding Levittown* (Albany: State University of New York Press, 1993), 67. Copyright © 1993 by State University of New York. Reprinted by permission of State University of New York Press, Albany.

Fig. 9-14. Barbara M. Kelly, *Expanding the American Dream: Building and Rebuilding Levittown* (Albany: State University of New York Press, 1993), 81. Copyright © 1993 by State University of New York. Reprinted by permission of State University of New York Press, Albany.

CHAPTER 10: CRITIQUES OF POSTWAR SUBURBIA

Text

10-1. From the song, *Little Boxes*. Words and music by Malvina Reynolds. Copyright © 1962 Schroder Music Co. (ASCAP). Renewed 1990. Used by permission. All rights reserved.

10-2. William H.Whyte, Jr., *The Organization Man* (New York: Simon & Schuster, 1956), 6, 7, 267, 280, 281, 283, 284, 286–87, 351–52, 357, 358, 359, 361. Used by permission of Alexandra Whyte.

10-4. Lewis Mumford, *The City in History: Its Origins, Its Transformations, and Its Prospects* (New York: Harcourt, Brace & World, 1961), 485, 486, 494, 495, 512, 513. Copyright © 1961 and renewed 1989 by Lewis Mumford, reprinted by permission of Harcourt, Inc. Published in the British Commonwealth by Secker & Warburg, reprinted by permission of The Random House Group Ltd.

10-5. *The Feminine Mystique* by Betty Friedan. Copyright © 1983, 1974, 1973, 1963 by Betty Friedan. Used by permission of W.W. Norton & Company, Inc. Published in the British Commonwealth and used by permission of Victor Gollancz, an imprint of The Orion Publishig Group. Excerpt from pages 15, 18, 19–21, 32, 243, 245–46, 247, 253–54.

10-7. Jean Pascoe, "Suburban Women's Lib: Turning Mrs. into Ms.," *McCall's* 100 (September 1973), 36.

10-8. *The Stories of John Cheever* by John Cheever, copyright © 1978 by John Cheever. Used by permission of Alfred A. Knopf, a division of Random House, Inc. and the Wylie Agnecy. Excerpt from pages 210–218.

10-9. Peter Blake, *God's Own Junkyard: The Planned Deterioration of America's Landscape* (New York: Holt, Rinehart and Winston, 1964), 7. Reprinted by the permission of Russell & Volkening as agents for the author. Copyright © 1963, 1964 by Peter Blake, renewed in 1991, 1992 by Peter Blake.

10-11. Bennett M. Berger, "The Myth of Suburbia," *Journal of Social Issues* 17 (1961), 38–49. Used by permission of Blackwell Publishing.

10-12. *The Levittowners* by Herbert J. Gans, copyright ©1967 by Herbert J. Gans. Used by permission of Pantheon Books, a division of Random House, Inc.

Figures

Fig. 10-1. Reprinted by Permission of the Estate of Claude Smith Jr.

Fig. 10.2. Photograph by Dan Weiner, January 1, 1953. Courtesy of Time Life Pictures/Getty Images, Image #50603608. All Rights Reserved.

Fig. 10-3. Illustration from "Why Young Mothers Feel Trapped," *Reader's Digest* (January 1961), 99.

Fig. 10-4. First image: Trousdale Estates: Pacific Air Industries, 56-2966, Long Beach, California: PAI, 1956, 4 x 5", negative dated October 8, 1956. From collections of the Map and Imagery Laboratory, Davidson Library, University of California, Santa Barbara. Copyright © 2006 The Regents of the University of California. All rights reserved. Second image: Courtesy of Library of Congress, Prints and Photographs Division, FSA-OWI Collection, LC-UYSF34-073417-D DLC.

Fig. 10-5. From MAD #165 © 1974 E.C. Publications, Inc. All Rights Reserved. Used with Permission.

CHAPTER 11: POSTWAR SUBURBS AND THE CONSTRUCTION OF RACE

Text

11-1. "Let Freedom Ring," *Chicago Defender*, May 15, 1948, p. 18. Used by permission of the Chicago Defender.

11-2. "Real Estate: 'Exclusive...Restricted," *U. S. News & World Report* 24 (May 14, 1948), 22–23. Copyright © U.S. News & World Report, L.P. Reprinted with permission.

11-3. "FHA Asked to Curb Negro Housing Ban," *New York Times*, March 12, 1949, p. 19; "FHA Can't Prevent Housing Ban," *New York Times*, March 19, 1949, p. 12. Copyright © 1949 by The New York Times Co. Reprinted with permission.

11-4. Selection from pages 103-119 from *Forbidden Neighbors* by Charles Abrams. Copyright © 1955 by Harper & Brothers. Reprinted by permission of HarperCollins Publishers.

11-5. U.S. Commission on Civil Rights, *Hearings before the United States Commission on Civil Rights: Housing*, vol. 1, *Hearings Held in New York, February 2–3, 1959* (Washington, D.C.: U.S. Government Printing Office, 1959), 268–70.

11-6. Ralph Guzman, "The Hand of Esau: Words Change, Practices Remain in Racial Covenants," *Frontier* 7 (June, 1956), 13, 16. Reprinted with permission from the June, 1956 issue of *Frontier*.

11-7. Atlanta Housing Council, "Proposed Areas for Expansions of Negro Housing in Atlanta, Georgia," May, 1947, Box 252, file 1, Papers of the Atlanta Urban League, Robert W. Woodruff Library of the Atlanta University Center, Atlanta, Georgia.

11-8. Open Letter, Southwest Citizens Association, Inc., January 28, 1954, and Atlanta Resident to Mayor William Hartsfield, September 28, 1956. Papers of the Atlanta Bureau of Planning, Box 3, files 5 and 6, Kenan Research Center at the Atlanta History Center, Atlanta, Georgia.

11-9. Selwyn James, "'We're Learning to Live Together,'" *Redbook Magazine* 109 (June 1957), 38-39, 106–8. Used by permission of Redbook Magazine.

Essay 11-1. George Lipsitz, "The Possessive Investment in Whiteness: Racialized Social Democracy and the 'White' Problem in American Studies," *American Quarterly* 47:3 (1995), 218–24, 232–33. Copyright © The American Studies Association. Reprinted with permission of The Johns Hopkins University Press.

Essay 11-2. Bruce Haynes, *Red Lines, Black Spaces: The Politics of Race and Space in a Black Middle-Class Suburb* (New Haven, CT: Yale University Press, 2001) xvii–xix, 93–94, 96, 101–13, 150–52. Copyright © 2001 by Bruce D. Haynes. Reprinted by permission of Yale University Press.

Figures

Fig 11-1. Atlanta Housing Council, "Proposed Areas for Expansions of Negro Housing in Atlanta, Georgia," May, 1947, Box 252, file 1, Papers of the Atlanta Urban League, Robert W. Woodruff Library of the Atlanta University Center, Atlanta, Georgia.

Fig 11-2. Robert Norwood – Norwood Manor Billboard, 1955. Atlanta Urban League Papers, Box 326 Folder 7, Robert W. Woodruff Library of the Atlanta University Center.

Fig 11-3. Proposed Subdivision Plan for Urban Villas, 1948. Atlanta Urban League Papers, Box 251 Folder 7, Robert W. Woodruff Library of the Atlanta University Center.

Fig. 11-4. "New Kids in the Neighborhood" by Norman Rockwell. Reprinted by permission of the Norman Rockwell Family Agency. Copyright ©1967 The Norman Rockwell Family Entities.

CHAPTER 12: THE CITY–SUBURB DIVIDE

Text

12-1. William Laas, "'The Suburbs Are Strangling the City,'" *New York Times Magazine*, June 18, 1950, pp. 22, 52–53.

12-2. Lew Phelps, "Model Municipality: San Leandro, Calif., Manages to Surmount Many of the Problems That Plague Cities," *Wall Street Journal*, March 4, 1966, p. 10. Copyright © 1966 by Dow Jones & Co., Inc. Reproduced with permission of Dow Jones & Co, Inc. in the format Other Book via Copyright Clearance Center.

12-3. U.S. Commission on Civil Rights, *Housing: 1961 Commission on Civil Rights Report* (Washington, D.C.: Government Printing Office, 1961), 1–2.

12-4. *Report of the National Advisory Commission on Civil Disorders* (Washington, D.C.: Government Printing Office, 1968), 1–2, 218, 224–25.

12-5. *Savage Inequalities* by Jonathan Kozol, copyright © 1991 by Jonathan Kozol. Used by permission of Crown Publishers, a division of Random House, Inc. and Jonathan Kozol. Excerpt from pages 41–42, 53–58, 63–67.

Essay 12-1. Peter O. Muller, *The Outer City: The Geographical Consequences of the Urbanization of the Suburbs* (Resource Paper No. 75-2) (Washington, D.C.: Association of American Geographers, 1976), 1–3, 29, 30, 33, 34, 35, 37, 38, 40, 42, 43, 44. Copyright © 1976 by the American Association of Geographers. Used by permission of the American Association of Geographers.

Essay 12-2. Robert O. Self, *American Babylon: Race and the Struggle for Postwar Oakland* (Princeton, NJ: Princeton University Press, 2003), 96–111, 129–31. Copyright © 2003 Princeton University Press. Reprinted by permission of Princeton University Press.

Figures

Fig. 12-1. Photograph by Andrew Wiese, 1995.

Fig. 12-2. Photography by Andrew Wiese, 2005.

Fig. 12-3. Suburban Alameda County in the 1960s. Cartography Lab, University of Wisconsin. Courtesy of Robert O. Self.

CHAPTER 13: THE POLITICAL CULTURE OF SUBURBIA

Text

13-1. Letters to the Editor, *Los Angeles Times*, May 15, 1978, part 2, p. 7; June 3, 1978, part 2, p. 5.

13-2. Neil H. Jacoby, "Would Prop. 13 Really Lighten the Load? Yes: Bloated Government Will Be the Only Loser," *Los Angeles Times*, June 4, 1978, part 5, p. 1. Used by permission of Neil H. Jacoby, Jr.

13-3. "The Message from California," *Commonweal* 105 (August 4, 1978), 483–84. Copyright © 1978 Commonweal Foundation, reprinted with permission.

13-4. Stephanie Simon, "20 Years Later, Prop. 13 Still Marks California Life," *Los Angeles Times*, May 26, 1998, part 1, p.1. Copyright © 1998 by Stephanie Simon, *Los Angeles Times*. Reprinted with permission.

13-5. Robert C. Wood, *Suburbia: Its People and Their Politics* (Boston: Houghton Mifflin, 1958), 137–38, 140, 141, 147, 148–49, 153, 194–97. Used by permission of Ayer Company Publishers.

13-6. Kevin P. Phillips, *The Emerging Republican Majority* (New Rochelle, N.Y.: Arlington House, 1969), 175-184. Used by permission of Kevin Phillips.

13-7. William Schneider, "The Suburban Century Begins: The Real Meaning of the 1992 Election," *The Atlantic Monthly*, July 1992, pp. 33–44. Used by permission of William Schneider.

13-8. Ronald Brownstein and Richard Rainey, "GOP Plants Flag on New Voting Frontier," *Los Angeles Times*, November 22, 2004, pp. A1, A14–15. Copyright © 2004 by Ronald Brownstein and Richard Rainey, *Los Angeles Times*. Reprinted with permission.

Essay 13-1. Sylvie Murray, *The Progressive Housewife: Community Activism in Suburban Queens, 1945–1965* (Philadelphia: University of Pennsylvania Press, 2003), 1–7, 9–13. Reprinted by permission of the University of Pennsylvania Press.

Essay 13-2. Lisa McGirr, *Suburban Warriors: The Origins of the New American Right* (Princeton, NJ: Princeton University Press, 2001), 3–4, 5, 8, 10–11, 18, 39–40, 42, 54–57, 58–60, 95, 97, 98,

CHAPTER 14: RECENT SUBURBAN TRANSFORMATIONS, 1970–2000

Text

Figures

CHAPTER 15: OUR TOWN: INCLUSION AND EXCLUSION IN RECENT SUBURBIA

Text

Figures

CHAPTER 16: THE FUTURE OF SUBURBIA

Text

Figures

Index

page numbers in bold denote an excerpt
page numbers in italics denote an illustration